The Grammar of Grace

The Grammar of Grace

Readings from the Christian Tradition

EDITED BY
Kent Eilers,
Ashley Cocksworth,
AND Anna Silvas

FOREWORD BY
Katherine Sonderegger

CASCADE *Books* • Eugene, Oregon

THE GRAMMAR OF GRACE
Readings from the Christian Tradition

Copyright © 2019 Wipf and Stock. All rights reserved. Except for brief quotations in critical publications or reviews, no part of this book may be reproduced in any manner without prior written permission from the publisher. Write: Permissions, Wipf and Stock Publishers, 199 W. 8th Ave., Suite 3, Eugene, OR 97401.

Cascade Books
An Imprint of Wipf and Stock Publishers
199 W. 8th Ave., Suite 3
Eugene, OR 97401

www.wipfandstock.com

PAPERBACK ISBN: 978-1-61097-233-8
HARDCOVER ISBN: 978-1-4982-8576-6
EBOOK ISBN: 978-1-5326-7089-3

Cataloguing-in-Publication data:

Names: Eilers, Kent, editor. | Cocksworth, Ashley, editor. | Silvas, Anna, editor. | Sonderegger, Katherine, foreword.

Title: The grammar of grace : readings from the Christian tradition / Edited by Kent Eilers, Ashley Cocksworth, and Anna Silvas.

Description: Eugene, OR: Cascade Books, 2019 | Includes bibliographical references.

Identifiers: ISBN 978-1-61097-233-8 (paperback) | ISBN 978-1-4982-8576-6 (hardcover) | ISBN 978-1-5326-7089-3 (ebook)

Subjects: LCSH: Christianity. | Christian literature.

Classification: BR53 .G71 2019 (print) | BR53 (ebook)

Manufactured in the U.S.A.   06/07/19

Kent dedicates this book to Tammy, Hannah, and Abigail

Ashley dedicates this book to the students at the
Queen's Foundation for Ecumenical Theological Education,
Birmingham, UK

Anna Silvas dedicates this book to Pauline Allen,
a great mentor and friend

Contents

List of Illustrations | xiii

Permissions | xv

Foreword | xxi

Preface | xxiii

Acknowledgments | xxv

Introduction | xxvii

Section I: Patristic (1st century—7th century)

Introduction | 3

A. Before Nicaea (–325)

1. St. Clement of Rome, *First Letter of Clement* | 7
2. *Shepherd of Hermas* | 11
3. *The Letter to Diognetus* | 15
4. St. Ignatius of Antioch, *Letter to the Romans* | 19
5. St. Polycarp, *Letter to the Philippians & Martyrdom* | 23
6. St. Irenaeus of Lyons, *Against Heresies* | 27
7. St. Clement of Alexandria, *Christ the Educator* | 30
8. Origen, *Commentary on Romans & On First Principles* | 35

B. After Nicaea (325–)

9. St. Athanasius of Alexandria, *On the Incarnation, Against the Arians, & To Adelphius* | 40
10. St. Ephrem the Syrian, *Hymns on Faith: 14, Nisibene Hymns: 50, & Armenian Hymns: 49* | 51

11. St. Cyril of Jerusalem, *Catechetical Lecture 21* | 59

12. The Desert Fathers and Mothers, *Sayings and Lives* | 62

13. St. Gregory of Nazianzus, *On the Soul, On The Two Covenants and the Appearing of Christ, On Providence, & Another Prayer for a Safe Journey* | 67

14. St. Basil of Caesarea, *The Rule of St. Basil* | 70

15. St. Gregory of Nyssa, *The Great Catechism* | 75

16. St. John Chrysostom, *Homily on Hebrews 7* | 81

17. St. Augustine of Hippo, *Confessions* | 85

18. St. Jerome, *Letter 52: To Nepotian* | 89

19. St. Cyril of Alexandria, *Commentary on the Gospel of John & Luke* | 93

20. St. Benedict of Nursia, *Rule* | 98

21. St. Gregory the Great, *Book of Pastoral Rule* | 102

Section II: Medieval (6th century—15th century)

A. Late Patristic—Medieval, Eastern

Introduction | 109

22. Pseudo-Dionysius the Areopagite, *Mystical Theology* | 112

23. St. Maximus the Confessor, *The Ascetic Life* | 117

24. St. John of Damascus, *On the Orthodox Faith & Against Those Who Decry Images* | 121

25. Kassia the Melodist, *Hymn for the Theophany & O Lord, she who in many sins* | 126

26. St. Symeon the New Theologian, *Invocation of the Holy Spirit & Hymns 17, 25, & 21* | 130

27. Gregory of Sinai, *On Commandments and Doctrines, & On the Signs of Grace and Delusion* | 134

28. St. Gregory Palamas, *Triads* | 138

29. St. Nicholas Kabasilas, *On the Life in Christ* | 143

B. Medieval, Western—Mystical and Monastic

Introduction | 151

30. Venerable Bede, *Ecclesiastical History* | 154

31. Hugh of St. Victor, *In Praise of the Bridegroom* | 158

CONTENTS

32. William of St. Thierry, *Meditative Orations* | 162

33. St. Bernard of Clairvaux, *Homilies on the Song of Songs* | 166

34. St. Hildegard of Bingen, *The Life of Hildegard & Scivias* | 170

35. St. Francis of Assisi, *Fioretti* | 175

36. St. Bonaventure, *The Journey of the Mind into God* | 179

37. Johannes "Meister" Eckhart, *Treatise on the Birth of the Eternal Word in the Soul, Homily on the Birth of Jesus, & Treatise on Detachment* | 183

38. St. Julian of Norwich, *The Revelations of Divine Love* | 187

39. *The Cloud of Unknowing* | 191

40. Thomas à Kempis, *The Imitation of Christ* | 194

C. Medieval, Western—Scholastic

Introduction | 201

41. St. Anselm of Canterbury, *Proslogion* | 204

42. Peter Abelard, *Pentecost Hymn* | 208

43. Peter Lombard, *Four Books of Sentences* | 211

44. St. Thomas Aquinas, *Commentary on the Gospel of John & Homily on the Eucharist* | 215

45. Blessed John Duns Scotus, *Ordinatio* | 220

46. St. Catherine of Siena, *The Dialogue* | 224

Section III: Reformation & Post-Reformation (16th century—18th century)

Introduction | 231

A. Lutheran

47. Martin Luther, *The Freedom of a Christian* | 234

48. *Augsburg Confession & The Formula of Concord* | 239

49. Johann Arndt, *True Christianity* | 243

50. Argula von Grumbach, *To the Council of Ingolstadt & An Answer in Verse* | 246

CONTENTS

B. Reformed

51. John Calvin, *Golden Booklet of the True Christian Life* | 253
52. Richard Sibbes, *The Bruised Reed and the Smoking Flax* | 258
53. John Owen, *Communion with God* | 262
54. Jonathan Edwards, *Charity and Its Fruits* & *Apostrophe to Sarah Pierpont* | 266

C. Anabaptist

55. Balthasar Hubmaier, *Eighteen Theses Concerning the Christian Life* & *Summa of the Entire Christian Life* | 271
56. Menno Simons, *The New Birth* & *The True Christian Faith* | 276
57. Anna Jansz, *Martyr's Song* | 281
58. Pilgram Marpeck, *Five Fruits of Repentance* | 286

D. Catholic

59. Juan de Valdés, *The Christian Alphabet* | 291
60. St. Teresa of Ávila, *The Book of Her Life* | 295
61. St. John of the Cross, *En una noche oscura*, *Ascent of Mt. Carmel*, *Sayings of Light and Love*, & *Prayer of a Soul Taken with Love* | 300
62. St. Francis de Sales, *Introduction to the Devout Life* | 305

E. Anglican

63. Thomas Cranmer, *Collect for the First Sunday in Lent* & *The Institution of a Christian Man* | 309
64. Lancelot Andrewes, *The Holy Spirit* & *Points of Meditation Before Prayer* | 314
65. George Herbert, *Grace* & *The Country Parson* | 319
66. Charles Wesley, "Father whose everlasting love" & John Wesley, *The Means of Grace (Sermon 16)* | 323

Section IV: Modern and Postmodern (19th century to present)

Introduction | 331

A. Lutheran

67. Albrecht Ritschl, *The Christian Doctrine of Justification and Reconciliation* | 334
68. Dietrich Bonhoeffer, *Discipleship & Life Together* | 339
69. Wolfhart Pannenberg, *Systematic Theology, Vol. 3* | 345
70. Tuomo Mannermaa, *Christ Present in Faith* | 350

B. Reformed

71. Friedrich Schleiermacher, *The Christian Faith* | 356
72. Karl Barth, *The Christian Life* | 360
73. Reinhold Niebuhr, *The Nature and Destiny of Man* | 364
74. Marilynne Robinson, *Gilead* | 368

C. Catholic

75. Henri de Lubac, *The Mystery of the Supernatural* | 372
76. Adrienne von Speyr, *The Victory of Love* | 377
77. Gustavo Gutiérrez, *The Power of the Poor in History* | 381
78. Janet Soskice, *Trinity and "the Feminine Other"* | 386

D. Orthodox

79. Sergei Bulgakov, *The Comforter* | 391
80. Vladimir Lossky, *The Mystical Theology of the Orthodox Church* | 396
81. John Zizioulas, *Being as Communion* | 401

E. Anabaptist & Baptist

82. James McClendon, *Doctrine: Systematic Theology, Vol. 2* | 405
83. John Howard Yoder, *Body Politics & The Politics of Jesus* | 410
84. Thomas Finger, *A Contemporary Anabaptist Theology* | 414

F. Anglican

85. Michael Ramsey, *The Glory of God and the Transfiguration of Christ* | 419
86. Sarah Coakley, "*Deepening 'Practices'*" | 423
87. John Milbank, *Being Reconciled* | 427
88. Kathryn Tanner, *The Economy of Grace* | 430

G. Evangelical

89. J. Gresham Machen, *Christianity and Culture* | 434
90. John Stott, *Basic Christianity* | 439
91. J. I. Packer, *Rediscovering Holiness* | 443
92. Donald Bloesch, *The Crisis of Piety* | 448

H. Contextual

93. Anne Carr, *Transforming Grace* | 453
94. Delores S. Williams, *Sisters in the Wilderness* | 458
95. François Kabasélé, *Christ as Ancestor and Elder Brother* | 463
96. Andrew Sung Park, *The Wounded Heart of God* | 467

Subject Index | 479

Scripture Index | 497

List of Illustrations

Figure 1. Icon, "Descent into Hell," (1495 – 1504). State Russian Museum, Sankt Petersburg. Public Domain. | xxx

Figure 2. Michelangelo Merisi da Caravaggio, "The Calling of St. Matthew" (1599-1600). San Luigi dei Francesi, Rome. Public Domain. | xxxii

Figure 3. Doctrinal Pressures | xxxvii

Permissions

We gratefully acknowledge permission to republish the following copyrighted material (the bibliography contains material in the public domain).

I.7. Clement of Alexandria. *Christ the Educator*. The Fathers of the Church 23. Translated by Simon P. Wood, 4–5, 49–50, 86–89. New York: Catholic University of America Press, 1954. Reprinted with permission of Catholic University of America Press.

I.8. Origen. *Commentary on the Epistle to the Romans, Books 6–10*. The Fathers of the Church 104. Translated by Thomas P. Scheck, 1–2, 10–12. Washington, DC: Catholic University of America Press, 2002. Reprinted with permission of Catholic University of America Press.

I. 10. Ephrem the Syrian. *Hymns on Faith: 14; Nisibene Hymns: 50;* and *Armenian Hymns: 49*. In *The Harp of the Spirit: Eighteen Poems of Saint Ephrem*. 2nd Enlarged Edition. Studies Supplementary to Sobernost No. 4. Translated and edited by Sebastian Brock, 18–20; 56–58, 77–79. Fellowship of St. Alban and St. Sergius, 1983. Reprinted with permission of Fellowship of St. Alban & St. Sergius and Sebastian Brock.

I. 12. Jerome. *Life of Paul the First Hermit* and Rufinus, *History of the Monks of Egypt*. In *The Desert Fathers*. Translated by Helen Waddell, 39, 56. New York: Random House, 1998. Reprinted with permission of the University of Michigan Press; *The Alphabetical Collection*. In *The Sayings of the Desert Fathers*. Translated by Benedicta Ward, 9, 10, 64, 2, 4, 6, 3–4, 21–22, 229, 230, 230–31, 103, 187, 171, 123, 134, 138, 131, 111. Kalamazoo, MI: Cistercian Studies, 1975. Reprinted with permission of Liturgical Press.

I. 13. Gregory of Nazianzus. *On the Soul; On Two Covenants and the Appearing of Christ; On Providence; Another Prayer for a Safe Journey*. In *On God and Man: The Theological Poetry of St Gregory of Nazianzus*. Translated by Peter Gilbert, 67, 72–75, 76–77, 80, 87. New York: St. Vladimir's Seminary Press, 2001. Reprinted with permission of St. Vladimir's Seminary Press.

I. 14. Basil of Caesarea. *The Rule of St. Basil*. From *The Rule of St. Basil in Latin and English: A Revised Critical Edition*. Translated by Anna M. Silvas, 139–41, 143–44, 145–49. Collegeville, MN: Liturgical Press, 2013. Reprinted with permission of Liturgical Press.

I. 17. Augustine of Hippo. *Confessions*. From *St. Augustine of Hippo, Confessions*. Translated by R. S. Pine-Coffin, 207, 228–29, 231–33, 241–44. London: Penguin Books, 1961. Reprinted with permission of Penguin Books Ltd.

PERMISSIONS

I. 19. Cyril of Alexandria. *Commentary on John*. From *Commentary on John*, Vol. 1. Translated by David R. Maxwell, 60–62. Ancient Christian Texts. Downers Grove, IL: IVP Academic, 2013. Reprinted with permission from InterVarsity Press.

I. 20. Benedict of Nursia. *Rule*. From *RB 1980: The Rule of St. Benedict in Latin and English with Notes*. Translated by Timothy Fry, 157, 159, 161, 163, 165, 167. Collegeville, MN: The Liturgical Press, 1981. Reprinted with permission of Liturgical Press.

I. 21. Gregory the Great. *Book of Pastoral Rule*. From *The Book of Pastoral Rule*. Translated by George E. Demacopoulas, 76–77, 102, 149, 151–52. Crestwood, NY: St. Vladimir's Seminary Press, 2007. Reprinted with permission of St. Vladimir's Seminary Press.

II. 23. Maximus the Confessor. *The Ascetic Life*. From *St. Maximus the Confessor: The Ascetic Life, The Four Centuries on Charity*. Ancient Christian Writers Vol. 21. Edited, annotated, and translated by Polycarp Sherwood, 103–35. Westminster: Paulist Press, 1955. Reprinted with permission of Paulist Press.

II. 26. Symeon the New Theologian. *Invocation of the Holy Spirit, Hymn 17, Hymn 20,* and *Hymn 25*. From Hymns. From *Divine Eros: Hymns of Saint Symeon the New Theologian*. Translated by Daniel K. Griggs, 33–35, 95–96, 100, 194–98, 147. Crestwood, NY: St. Vladimir's Seminary Press, 2010. Reprinted with permission of St. Vladimir's Seminary Press.

II. 27. Gregory of Sinai. *On Commandments and Doctrines* and *On the Signs of Grace and Delusion*. From *The Philokalia: The Complete Text compiled by St Nikodimos of the Holy Mountain and St Makarios of Corinth*. Translated by G. E. H. Palmere, et al., 212, 237, 257–59. London: Faber and Faber, 1995. Reprinted with permission of Faber and Faber.

II. 28. Gregory Palamas. *Triads*. From *Gregory Palamas: The Triads*. Translated by Nicholas Gendle, 28, 41, 50–51, 32–33, 33, 57, 57–58, 74, 83. Mahwah, NJ: Paulist Press, 1983. Reprinted with permission of Paulist Press.

II. 29. Nicholas of Cabasilas. *On the Life in Christ*. From *The Life in Christ*. Translated by Carmino J. deCatanzaro, 161, 129, 193, 212, 217, 228. Crestwood, NY: St. Vladimir's Seminary Press, 1974. Reprinted with permission of St. Vladimir's Seminary Press.

II. 31. Hugh of St. Victor. *In Praise of the Bridegroom*. From *On Love: A Selection of Works of Hugh, Adam, Richard, and Godfrey of St. Victor*. Translated by Hugh Feiss, 125–34. Turnhout: Brepols, 2011. Reprinted with permission of Brepols Publishers.

II. 32. William of Saint-Thierry. *Meditative Orations*. From *On Contemplating God, Prayer, Meditations*. Translated by Penelope Lawson, 125–33. Kalamazoo, MI: Cistercian Publications, 1977. Reprinted with permission of Liturgical Press.

II. 33. Bernard of Clairvaux. Homilies on the Song of Songs 74 and 83. From *Bernard of Clairvaux on the Song of Songs 4*. Cistercian Fathers Series 40. Translated by Irene Edwards, 89–92, 182–83. Kalamazoo, MI: Cistercian Publications, 1980. Reprinted with permission of Liturgical Press.

II. 34. Hildegard of Bingen. *The Life of Hildegard*. From *Jutta and Hildegard: the Biographical Sources*. Translated by Anna Silvas, 139, 159–60, 179. Turnhout: Brepols, 1998. Reprinted with Permission from Brepols Publishers; Hildegard of Bingen. *Scivias*. From *Hildegard of Bingen Scivias*. Translated by Columba Hart, Jane Bishop et al., 358, 361–63. Mahwah, NJ: Paulist Press, 1990. Reprinted with Permission from Paulist Press.

PERMISSIONS

II. 38. Julian of Norwich. *The Revelations of Divine Love*. From *Revelations of Divine Love (Short Text and Long Text)*. Translated by Elizabeth Spearing, 47–49, 79–82, 179. London: Penguin Books, 1998. Reprinted with permission of Penguin Books Ltd.

II. 39. *The Cloud of Unknowing*. From *The Cloud of Unknowing and Other Works*. Translated by A. C. Spearing. 23–28. London: Penguin Books, 2001. Reprinted with permission of Penguin Books Ltd.

II. 40. Thomas à Kempis. *The Imitation of Christ*. From *The Imitation of Christ, A New Translation*. Translated by Leo Shirley-Price, 27–28, 67–68, 89, 97–99. London: Penguin Books, 1952. Reprinted with the permission of Penguin Books Ltd.

II. 41. Anselm of Canterbury. *Proslogion*. From *St. Anselm's Proslogion with a Reply on Behalf of a Fool by Gaunilo and The Author's Reply to Gaunilo*. Translated by M. J. Charlesworth, 145–55. Oxford: Clarendon Press, 1965. Reprinted with permission from Oxford University Press.

II. 42. Peter Abelard. *Pentecost Hymn*. From *The Hymns of Abelard in English Verse*. Translated by Jane Patricia, 84–85. Lanham, MD: University Press of America, 1986. Reprinted with permission of University Press of America.

II. 43. Peter Lombard. *Four Books of Sentences: On Charity*. From *Peter Lombard The Sentences*. Translated by Giulio Silano, 88, 97. Toronto: Pontifical Institute of Mediaeval Studies, 2007. Reprinted with permission of the Pontifical Institute of Mediaeval Studies.

II. 44. Thomas Aquinas. *Commentary on the Gospel of St John*. Translated by James A. Weisheipl. Albany, NY: Magi, 1998. http://dhspriory.org/thomas/SSJohn.htm#02. Reprinted with permission of Catholic University Press of America; Thomas Aquinas. *Homily on the Eucharist*. From *St. Thomas Aquinas Theological Text; Selected and Translated with Notes and an Introduction By Thomas Gilby*. Translated and edited by Thomas Gilby, 365–66. London: Oxford University Press, 1955. Reprinted with permission of Oxford University Press.

II. 45. Duns Scotus. *Ordinatio IV*. From *Duns Scotus Philosophical Writings*. Translated by Allan Wolter, 134–38, 157 162. Edinburgh: Thomas Nelson and Sons, 1962. Reprinted with permission of Hackett Publishing Co., Inc.

III. 49. Johann Arndt. *True Christianity*. Johann Arndt, *True Christianity (Classics of Western Spirituality)*. Translated by Peter Erb, 22–24, 145, 117–18, 129, 212–13, 270–71. Mahwah, NJ: Paulist Press, 1979. Reprinted with permission of Paulist Press.

III. 50. Argula von Grumbach. *To the Council of Ingolstadt* and *An Answer in Verse*. In *Argula Von Grumbach: A Woman's Voice in the Reformation*. Translated and edited by Peter Matheson, 116–22, 174–78, 192–93. London: T&T Clark, 2013. Reprinted with permission of Bloomsbury Publishing Plc.

III. 51. John Calvin. *Golden Booklet of the True Christian Life*. From *Golden Booklet of the True Christian Life: A Modern Translation from the French and the Latin*. Translated by Henry J. Van Andel, 17–18, 47–55. Grand Rapids, MI: Baker, 2004. Reprinted with permission of Baker Books, a division of Baker Publishing Group.

III. 53. John Owen. *Of Communion with God the Father, Son, and Holy Ghost, each person distinctly, in love, grace, and consolation; or, the saints' fellowship with the Father, Son and Holy Ghost unfolded*. From *Communion with God*. Abridged and modernized by R. J. K. Law, 4, 5–6, 7–8, 10–11. Edinburgh: Banner of Truth Trust, 1991. Reprinted with permission of Banner of Truth Trust, https://banneroftruth.org.

III. 54. Jonathan Edwards. *Charity and Its Fruits* and *Apostrophe to Sarah Pierpont*. From *The Works of Jonathan Edwards Online*. Vol. 8 and Vol. 40. Jonathan Edwards Center, 2008–2016. Reprinted with permission of Yale University Press.

III. 55. Balthasar Hubmaier. *Eighteen Theses Concerning the Christian Life* and *Summa of the Entire Christian life*. In *Balthasar Hubmaier: Theologian of Anabaptism*. Edited and translated by H. Wayne Pipkin and John H. Yoder, 33–34, 84–88. Scottdale, PA: Herald Press, 1989. Reprinted with permission of Herald Press.

III. 56. Menno Simons. *The New Birth* and *The True Christian Faith*. In *The Complete Writings of Menno Simons*. Edited by John Christian Wenger. Translated by Leonard Verduin, 92–95, 397–99. Scottdale, PA: Herald Press, 1956, 1984. Reprinted with permission of Herald Press.

III. 57. Anna Jansz. *Martyr's Song, Hymn 18*. In *Songs of the Ausbund Volume I*. Translated by Arnold C. Snyder. Edited by Edward Cline. Millersburg, OH: Ohio Amish Library, 1998. Reprinted with permission of Ohio Amish Library.

III. 58. Pilgram Marpeck. *Five fruits of Repentance*. In *The Writings of Pilgram Marpeck*. Translated and edited by William Klassen and Walter Klassen, 485–97. Scottdale, PA: Herald Press, 1978. Reprinted with permission of Herald Press.

III. 59. Juan de Valdés. *The Christian Alphabet*. In *Spiritual and Anabaptist Writers*. Edited by George H. Williams and Angel M. Mergel. Translated by Angel M. Mergal, 373–376. Philadelphia: Westminster John Knox, 1957. Reprinted with permission of Westminster John Knox Press.

III. 60. Teresa of Avila. *The Book of her Life*. In *The Collected Works of St. Teresa of Avila*, 3 Vol. Translated by Kieran Kavanaugh and Otilio Rodriguez, Vol. 3: 386; Vol. 1: 93–97, 113–14. Washington, DC: Institute of Carmelite Studies Publications, 1985. Reprinted with permission of ICS Publications.

III. 61. St. John of the Cross. *The Ascent of Mount Carmel*, *Sayings of Light and Love*, and *Prayer of a soul taken with love*. In *The Collected Works of St. John of the Cross*. Translated by Kieran Kavanaugh, and Otilio Rodriguez, 179–81, 201, 668–69. Washington, DC: Institute of Carmelite Studies, 1979. Reprinted with Permission of ICS Publications.

III. 63. Thomas Cranmer. "Collect for the First Sunday in Lent." In *The Book of Common Prayer*, 86. Cambridge: Cambridge University Press, 2006. Extracts from *The Book of Common Prayer*, the rights in which are vested in the Crown, are reproduced by permission of the Crown's Patentee, Cambridge University Press.

III. 64. Lancelot Andrewes. *The Holy Spirit* and *Points of Mediation before Prayer*. In *Before the King's Majesty: Lancelot Andrews and His Writings*. Edited by Raymond Chapman, 49–51, 125–26. Norwich: Canterbury Press, 2008. Reprinted with permission of Hymns Ancient and Modern Ltd.

III. 66. Charles Wesley. "Father, whose Everlasting Love." In *Hymns on God's Everlasting Love*. Bristol: Farley, 1741. https://divinity.duke.edu/initiatives/cswt. Reprinted with permission of The Center for Studies in the Wesleyan Tradition, Duke Divinity School; John Wesley. "The Means of Grace" (Sermon 16). Reprinted with permission from the Wesley Center of Applied Theology at Northwest Nazarene University. http://wesley.nnu.edu/john-wesley/the-sermons-of-john-wesley-1872-edition/sermon-16-the-means-of-grace/.

IV. 67. Albrecht Ritschl. *The Christian Doctrine of Justification and Reconciliation: The Positive Development of the Doctrine*. Translated by H. R. Mackintosh and A. B. Macaulay, 30–35. Eugene, OR: Wipf and Stock, 2004. Reprinted with permission of Wipf and Stock Publishers.

IV. 68. Dietrich Bonhoeffer. *The Cost of Discipleship*. Translated by Reginald H. Fuller, 45–48, 54. New York: MacMillan Publishing Company, 1963. Reprinted with permission of Hymns Ancient and Modern Ltd. and Simon and Schuster, Inc.; *Life Together*. Translated by John W. Doberstein, 17, 21–25. New York: HarperCollins, 1954. Reprinted with permission of HarperCollins Publishers.

IV. 69. Wolfhart Pannenberg. *Systematic Theology*, Vol. 3. Translated by Geoffrey Bromiley, 211–17, 234–36. Grand Rapids: Eerdmans, 2001. Reprinted with permission of Wm. B. Eerdmans Publishing Company.

IV. 70. Tuomo Mannermaa. *Christ Present in Faith: Luther's View of Justification*. Translated by Kirsi Stjerna, 1, 3–4, 5, 16–17, 19–22. Minneapolis: Fortress Press, 2005. Reprinted with permission of Augsburg Fortress Press.

IV. 71. Friedrich Daniel Ernst Schleiermacher. *The Christian Faith*. Translated by H. R. Mackintosh and J. S. Stewart, 505–8. London: T&T Clark, 1999. Reprinted with permission of Bloomsbury T&T Clark International, an imprint of Bloomsbury Publishing Plc.

IV. 72. Karl Barth. *The Christian Life: Church Dogmatics IV/4—Lecture Fragments*. Translated by Geoffrey W. Bromiley, 205, 206–7, 211, 212–13, 214–15. Edinburgh: T&T Clark, 1981. Reprinted with permission of Bloomsbury T&T Clark International, an imprint of Bloomsbury Publishing Plc.

IV. 73. Reinhold Niebuhr. *The Nature and Destiny of Man: A Christian Interpretation—Volume 2: Human Destiny*. 102–4, 113–14, 119. Louisville: Westminster John Knox Press, 1996. Reprinted with permission of Westminster John Knox Press.

IV. 74. Marilynne Robinson. *Gilead*. 133–36, 139. New York: Farrar, Straus, and Giroux, 2004. Reprinted with permission of Farrar, Straus, and Giroux.

IV. 75. Henri de Lubac. *The Mystery of the Supernatural*. Translated by Rosemary Sheed, 69–70, 75–76, 80–81, 86–88, 94–96. New York: Crossroads, 1998. Reprinted with permission of The Crossroads Publishing Company.

IV. 76. Adrienne von Speyr. *The Victory of Love: A Meditation on Romans 8*. Translated by Lucia Wiedenhöver, 49–50, 79–79. San Francisco: Ignatius Press, 1990. Reprinted with permission of Ignatius Press.

IV. 77. Gustavo Gutiérrez. *The Power of the Poor in History: Selected Writings*. Translated by Robert R. Barr, 3–22. Eugene, OR: Wipf and Stock, 2004. Reprinted with permission of Wipf and Stock Publishers.

IV. 78. Janet Soskice. "Trinity and 'the Feminine Other.'" In *New Blackfriars* (1994) 2–17. Reprinted with permission of John Wiley & Sons, Inc.

IV. 79. Sergei Bulgakov. *The Comforter*. Translated by Boris Jakim, 298–304. Grand Rapids: Eerdmans, 2004. Reprinted with permission of Wm. B. Eerdmans Publishing Company.

IV. 80. Vladimir Lossky. *The Mystical Theology of the Eastern Church*. Translated by a group of members of the Fellowship of St. Alban and St. Sergius, 196–98, 199, 200–3. Yonkers, NY: St. Vladimir's Seminary Press, 1997. Reprinted with permission of James Clark and Co.

IV. 81. John Zizioulas. *Being as Communion: Studies in Personhood and Church*. 53–56. Crestwood, NY: St. Vladimir's Seminary Press, 1985. Reprinted with permission of St. Vladimir's Seminary Press.

IV. 82. James McClendon. *Doctrine: Systematic Theology, Volume 2*. 135–36, 137, 142–45. Nashville: Abingdon Press, 2003. Reprinted with permission of Abingdon Press.

IV. 83. John Howard Yoder. *Body Politics: Five Practices of the Christian Community Before the Watching World*. 78-79. Waterloo: Herald Press, 1992. Reprinted with permission of Herald Press; *The Politics of Jesus*, Second Edition. 228, 232–33, 237–38. Grand Rapids: Eerdmans, 1972/1994. Reprinted with permission of Wm. B. Eerdmans Publishing Company.

IV. 84. Thomas Finger. *A Contemporary Anabaptist Theology*. 148–51, 563, 564. Downers Grove, IL: InterVarsity Press, 2004. Reprinted with permission of InterVarsity Press.

IV. 85. Michael Ramsey. *The Glory of God and the Transfiguration of Christ*. Eugene, OR: Wipf and Stock, 2009, 144–47, 152. Reprinted with permission of Wipf and Stock Publishers.

IV. 86. Sarah Coakley. "Deepening 'Practices': Perspectives from Ascetical and Mystical Theology." In *Practicing Theology: Beliefs and Practices in Christian Life*, 80–81, 90–91, 92, 93. Grand Rapids: Eerdmans, 2001. Reprinted with permission of Wm. B. Eerdmans Publishing Company.

IV. 87. John Milbank. *Being Reconciled: Ontology and Pardon*, ix, xi, 70, 180–81. London: Routledge, 2003. Reprinted with permission of Taylor & Francis Books UK.

IV. 88. Kathryn Tanner. *Economy of Grace*, 63–64, 75–76, 84–85. Minneapolis: Augsburg Press, 2005. Reprinted with permission of Augsburg Fortress Press.

IV. 90. John Stott. *Basic Christianity*. 136–37, 139–41. Downers Grove, IL: InterVarsity, 1958, 1971, 1976. Reprinted with permission of InterVarsity Press and InterVarsity Press UK through PLSclear.

IV. 91. James Innell Packer. *Rediscovering Holiness: Know the Fullness of Life with God*, 87–88, 90–94. Ann Arbor, MI: Servant, 2000. Reprinted with permission of Baker Publishing Group.

IV. 92. Donald G. Bloesch. *The Crisis of Piety: Essay Toward a Theology of the Christian Life*. Colorado Springs: Helmers and Howard, 1968/1988, 26–27, 33–36. Reprinted with permission of Helmers and Howard.

IV. 93. Anne E. Carr. *Transforming Grace: Christian Tradition and Women's Experience*, 8–9, 145, 147–50. San Francisco: Harper and Row, 1988. Reprinted with permission of HarperCollins Publishers.

IV. 94. Delores S. Williams. *Sisters in the Wilderness: The Challenge of Womanist God-Talk*, 2–3, 5, 51–52, 54–55, 143–44, 145, 147–48. Maryknoll, NY: Orbis Books, 2013. Reprinted with permission of Orbis Books.

IV. 95. François Kabasélé. "Christ as Ancestor and Elder Brother." In *Faces of Jesus in Africa*, edited by Robert J. Schreiter, 117, 119, 121–22. Maryknoll, NY: Orbis Books, 1991. Reprinted with permission of Orbis Books.

IV. 96. Andrew Sung Park. *The Wounded Heart of God: The Asian Concept of Han and the Christian Doctrine of Sin*, 10, 45, 120–21, 138, 170–72, 174. Nashville: Abingdon Press, 1993. Reprinted with permission of Abingdon Press.

Foreword

By Katherine Sonderegger

Jesus said to Simon: Put out into the deep, and let down your nets for a catch (Luke 5:4). A voyage out into the deep: that is the Christian life. There is little to prepare us for such a journey. Like Simon Peter we set our hands to the daily task, mending our nets, casting them out for a catch; or, as for so many of us, casting them out with little hope of reward. The fishermen that day had caught nothing, even after a night spent at sea. Their livelihood was bound up in that catch; their families dependent utterly on the fish snagged in the net that day. Like them, we toil in our lives for the necessities of the everyday, and for those without work, the very elements of a human life—food, shelter, dignity—are put at risk, perhaps exhausted. The great French historian Fernand Braudel taught us to look into the past as "la longue durée," that which endures, and our Gospel text witnesses to just such long-lasting constancy. In our day, across our globe, fishermen put out to sea, trawling for a catch that dwindles, perhaps now even in the deep sea, perhaps everywhere; perhaps that way of life itself endangered, exhausted. And in our cities and small towns, in every reach of the planet, women and men seek work, even children too, and perhaps catch nothing, though they seek the whole night through. Necessity and risk; need and longing; dependence and dignity: these are the perduring elements of a human life, la longue durée, that knits us together with Simon Peter and the sons of Zebedee, that night along the Galilean sea.

But in the midst of that hardship, Jesus tells us to put out into the deep. The great draft of fish, tearing the nets in their weight and bounty, come after a cast into the deep waters, after the exhaustion of a fruitless night, catching nothing. Abundance, after loss; discipleship, after leaving safe shores. But just what are these depths Jesus calls us to? The Christian life is not led in the shallows, nor does it begin in safe harbors. As Lord, Jesus brings us into deep and open water, and there gives us our life's work. It may be that the depths he calls us to are the rich expanses of the spiritual life—of prayer and contemplation and silence. Perhaps he brings us to the edge of the inward journey, the deep mystery of the inner life, a landscape far more demanding and marvelous, St. Augustine said, than any seen with the human eye. Perhaps the deep waters are the world of injustice and cruelty turned upside down by a gospel that feeds the hungry and casts down kings from their thrones. Perhaps the voyage into open water is a season of discipline, of *askesis*, in which the commandments of God are not just known but practiced, taken into our daily life, into our marrow. Perhaps it is the life of love, the depths that reach even to the enemy, the traitor, the lost. And perhaps the Christian life is the abundant life, the overflowing banquet, the overflowing heart. Jesus Christ takes us with Him into the depths, into the depths of His life, His dying and rising. It is a life of grace, the grace of discipleship and of great hope.

The voyage into the deep might begin for you with the book you hold in your hands. Our editors have put together rich fare, of great variety and weight. We can learn the contours of a life of grace by following the pattern of these Christians, their vision of a life lived for God. Here we can listen to Christians whose way of life is ringed about by martyrdom, early in the church's life but also in full stride, in the sixteenth century. We follow the development of monasticism, its flowering in the mystical tradition, and its companion in medieval university theology. The modern world is fully represented, from the churches of the Reformation, to the Catholic and Orthodox, and the living theologians who guide the churches' teaching on the Christian life in the midst of a bewildering world. Saints are here; but sinners, too; mystics and contemplatives, great intellects and great spirits; and ordinary, faithful disciples. The breadth of the Christian search for depth, and the prayers for a heart and ears to hear Christ's call: these are powerfully represented in the excerpts contained here. Our editors exhort us to take these excerpts up with a prayerful and open heart, to read generously and attentively, allowing these Christian voices to serve as *witnesses*, not to a dead past, but to a flowing river of tradition and, upward, to a living God; for all are alive to Him. May this book be a constant travelling companion on this pilgrimage of ours; and may the Christian life, in its startling radicality and grace, grow in depth and daring, and in love for our Good God, who calls us out from death into His marvelous Light.

Rev. Kate Sonderegger, PhD
William Meade Chair in Systematic Theology,
Virginia Theological Seminary

Preface

> I handed on to you as of first importance what I in turn had received.
>
> —1 Corinthians 15:3

This anthology is a collection of readings on *the Christian life*. They were carefully selected from every era of history and from every major Christian tradition. They include letters, sermons, treatises and disputations, poems, songs and hymns, confessions, biblical commentary, and even part of a novel. In each case, the subject is life with God, in God, and for God. Christians have a very long history of making anthologies, and we happily join the tradition.[1] From St. Augustine's *Speculum de scriptura sacra* to John Wesley's *A Christian Library*, Christians have excerpted and gathered readings to make them ready at hand for later study and reflection.

In making selections, we chose men and women whose theology of the Christian life represents the breadth of Christianity in their time or tradition. Of course, each is limited in their own ways, and none offers a total picture. Nonetheless, each portrays the Christian life according to the norms and patterns of their place in the church's long story. Once people were chosen, we then selected writings that best present their vision of life with God. No selection is comprehensive of a person's entire vision or a total picture of their theology of grace. Rather than panoramas, the selections are representative snapshots.

A few remarks about the presentation of readings. Each begins with a brief "verbal icon" that presents the author as an embodied person. Relevant aspects of biography, spirituality, and historical context are introduced. All of this is done with an eye toward helping the reader comprehend and engage. A short preview of the selection concludes the icon. We made every effort to present the readings as they appear in their previously published forms. However, in some selections we updated archaic language to increase readability, and in a few others we revised translations after consulting the original language (amended texts are identifed in footnotes). In a

---

1. See Griffiths, *Religious Reading*, 97–108, 148–81.

handful of selections we added section breaks to help the reader follow the argument, again citing these in footnotes. Several readings in the modern and postmodern section include footnotes from the original text, and these were retained when germane to the author's argument. We did not, however, retain the numbering of the notes from the original. All notes in these selections begin at 1. Finally, the reader will notice the titles "St." (Saint), "Ven." (Venerable), or "Bl." (Blessed) with many authors. These signify the process of sainthood in the Roman Catholic and Eastern Orthodox traditions (and some others). We retained the titles to emphasize the ongoing significance of these people for worshipping communities.

These portraits of life with God are a rich and rewarding resource for ongoing reflection. They are not merely on the Christian life but *for* the Christian life. For individuals and groups wanting to deepen their knowledge of what life with God entails, these readings offer a deep well. "How does one go about living a Christian life?" Lauren Winner asks. "The question of how to live a Christian life isn't answered by a list of dos and don'ts. It's answered by looking at lives that have been lived in response to Jesus."[2] These authors lived in response to Jesus, and their descriptions instruct and encourage just as they may scandalize and surprise. A deep well indeed.

The book can also be a resource for theologians and students of Christian theology. It can be used in classrooms for courses concerning Christology, Sanctification, or the Church, among others. Reading this collection with students is an invitation to join this vast and ongoing conversation. It may also, we hope, resource the work of theological retrieval. "For I handed on to you as of first importance what I in turn had received," Paul said, and he told Timothy to do likewise (1 Cor 15:3; 2 Tim 2:14). When theology is practiced in the mode of retrieval, yesterday's witness to the gospel is a resource for the church today.[3]

Life with God requires testimony. Grace calls for "the poetry *and* the prose of knowing."[4] We hope this anthology fuels and inspires both.

---

2. Winner, "Foreword," 1.

3. See Eilers and Buschart, "An Overtaking of Depth," 1–20; Buschart and Eilers, *Theology as Retrieval*, especially the Introduction; Webster, "Theologies of Retrieval," 583–99.

4. Wyman, *My Bright Abyss*, 4.

Acknowledgments

Collecting, curating, and introducing these readings was a shared editorial labor. It was also, beautifully and even surprisingly, a labor nearing Christian friendship. "The right kind of friendship between us should begin in Christ, be maintained according to Christ, and have its end and value referred to Christ," wrote Aelred of Rievaulx.[1] Something like this began developing over the years of working together, and given our geography—North America, the United Kingdom, and Australia—this was surely God's grace. For that we are delighted and *grateful*.

Many others deserve thanks. The initial vision and shape for this collection came about through conversations with Kyle Strobel. Several others were also helpful as we identified readings: Christopher Hall, Todd Billings, W. David Buschart, Charles Nienkirchen, John Webster, Donald Wood, Steve Duby, Rachel Starr, Jonathan Dean, Judith Rossall, Nicola Slee, and Jane Craske. Rodney Clapp and Wipf & Stock believed in the project and threw their weight behind it, remaining supportive through challenges and delays. The cost of republishing copyrighted material was paid through a generous grant from Huntington University, which also provided a sabbatical leave that enabled Kent to complete large portions of his work. Similarly, colleagues at the Queen's Foundation, Birmingham generously covered Ashley's workload during a period of study leave that enabled him to advance much of his work. Several research assistants were invaluable as well. Editing an anthology in the confusing and tangled thicket of today's copyright environment is a monumental feat. Thank you Alli Dozet, Allie Brown, Hannah Briton, and most of all Don Eilers (Kent's father). Don joyfully gave many, many hours to corresponding with publishers, negotiating contracts, and securing permissions (*Thank you, Dad!*).

Finally, as this book was being completed we were encouraged by family members and friends, colleagues, and church families, sometimes lifting our arms when the work threatened to overwhelm. To all of you, may God make "all grace abound" (2 Cor 9:8).

Kent Eilers, Ashley Cocksworth, and Anna Silvas
Lent, 2018

---

1. Aelred of Rievaulx, *Spiritual Friendship*, 30.

Introduction

> You have died, and your life is hidden with Christ in God.
>
> —Colossians 3:3

> If any want to become my followers, let them deny themselves and take up their cross and follow me.
>
> —Mark 8:34

There is a moment in the life of Moses when the significance of the incarnation becomes apparent. God covers Moses with his hand so he will not be destroyed by the proximity of God's glory. Already God had promised his covenant faithfulness for Moses and his people, but it was not enough for Moses. "My presence will go with you, and I will give you rest," God assured (Exod 33:14). The God of Abraham, Isaac, and Jacob promised to surely go with Moses and his complaining and rebellious Hebrews. Moses desires more: "Show me your glory, I pray" (v. 18). Let me not merely know your promise to be near, Moses desires, but let me see *you*; let me encounter the shining weight of your presence. The request draws God's sharp warning, and then God shields Moses with his hand as he passes by, a merciful concession. "You cannot see my face," God warns, "for no one shall see me and live" (v. 20).

This encounter between God and Moses makes the Apostle John's words about the incarnation all the more incredible. The same God who shields Moses from his glory is the One whose glory is *seen* in the face of Jesus. "The Word became flesh and lived among us," John testifies, "and we have *seen* his glory, the glory as of a father's only son, full of grace and truth" (John 1:14; cf. 1 John 1:1–4). What Moses was denied, we have in the face of Jesus for he is the glory of God in our midst. It is wondrous and astounding all at once: the great King, the infinite Creator, the "God and Father of all, who is above all and through all and in all" goes into the far country to redeem his creation from sin (Eph 4:6; Luke 19:12)! John echoes the close encounter of God and Moses to make the point. "No one has ever seen God," but John's long encounter with Jesus changed everything. The entire calculus of proximity with God changed.

INTRODUCTION

"It is God the only Son, who is close to the Father's heart, who has made him known" (John 1:18). As one who was *with* Jesus, indeed his beloved disciple, John testifies that to look upon the face of Jesus is to *see* the glory of God—the full, shining weight of his presence. The experience of life with God was forever altered.[1]

When Christians turn their attention to the experience of life with God, they are bearing witness to the peculiar shape of *the Christian life*. Jesus—without qualification or restriction—is the glory of God in the midst of God's creation, for he is the Only-Begotten God (John 1:14). Through fellowship with Jesus in the power of his Spirit we are drawn into the very fellowship of the Father and the Son. That is the Christian life. Life with God, life *in* God, life *for* God. The Christian life is the utterly peculiar existence of the one whose place in the cosmos is fundamentally and irreducibly altered by their association with Jesus, the Son of God. The person who allies themselves to Jesus in faith is "in Christ" as the Apostle Paul puts it time and again (e.g. Rom 8:1). Being *in* Jesus is essential. It is the most basic element of the Christian life. The Christian's geographical and temporal location still marks us as creatures in time and space, but the "place" that is most fundamental, most descriptive of our essential nature, is that we are *in* Christ. The embodied existence that unfolds in Christ and yet also within the temporal frame of one's life on earth is *the Christian life*.

Christians have given witness to life with God from the earliest apostles. The New Testament nearly bursts with descriptions. On the lips of Jesus in the Gospels it is friendship, carrying one's cross, abiding in Jesus, accepting his yoke, and most frequently *following* him. In the New Testament letters, the apostles refract Jesus' teaching into reconciliation, justification, redemption, adoption, imitation, participation, abiding, and being hidden in God (to name only a few). And in every era since, Christians follow suit. They bear witness to their lives with God in terms that resonate both with the biblical testimony and the habits of thought and practice that are native to their time and culture, tradition, and personal experience. In this way, Christian theology always has its feet on the ground in time and space; it is always local.

Theology is local but also *normed*. This simply means that Christian thought and speech about God and life with God does not follow its own whimsy. It follows Holy Scripture as it is interpreted in the church under the illumination of the Holy Spirit.[2] The Old and New Testaments, read according to the teaching of the apostles about Jesus the Christ, have guided and directed Christian theology from its earliest. This is certainly true of Christian teaching about life with God. A scriptural antecedent stands in some sense behind every selection in this anthology.

In what follows, a quick glance at the New Testament will sharpen the reader's attention so as to see those scriptural antecedents more readily. This leads us naturally to

---

1. In the Greek Fathers, the flesh of Christ is a veil that both reveals and conceals.

2. The history of Christian doctrine shows that Scripture can function in various ways in different theologies. See Allen, *Theological Method*; Holcomb, ed., *Theologies of Scripture*; Kelsey, *Proving Doctrine*.

reflect on the central thread in every account of Christian life: grace. We then conclude with some suggestions for engaging the readings in this volume. Think of it as a brief theological primer for reading such a diverse collection of Christian writings.

Proximity and Pilgrimage

The Gospels teem with descriptions of life with God, all of them centering on *proximity* and *pilgrimage*. Jesus announces the Kingdom of God and calls people to come *near* him and then to *follow* him. Life with Jesus is a matter of proximity and pilgrimage.

Coming near Jesus first entails repentance and belief. "The time has come . . . Repent and believe the good news!" John the Baptist proclaimed (Mark 1:15). In believing, one's center of gravity shifts to Jesus. Mental assent fails to capture the full weight of it, for believing in Jesus is to keep Jesus' teachings. "Abide in me as I abide in you . . . As the Father has loved me, so I have loved you; abide in my love. If you keep my commandments, you will abide in my love, just as I have kept my Father's commandments and abide in his love" (John 15:4, 10–11). The call Jesus gives to be his disciple (learner) is, however, not only to follow his teachings but to follow the course of his life. "If any want to become my followers, let them deny themselves and take up their cross daily and follow me" (Luke 9:23; Matt 10:38). Repentance and belief are fundamental but only the first steps of active pilgrimage. "The only man who has the right to say that he is justified by grace alone," wrote Dietrich Bonhoeffer, "is the man who has left all to follow Christ."[3]

Proximity to Jesus is indistinguishable from daily, costly *pilgrimage* along the way of his life. The Christian is both united to Jesus by faith (proximity) and progressively drawn closer into Jesus' orbit (pilgrimage). Jesus' priorities become ours, his rule of life our own, and the total commitment to God's kingdom that led to his martyrdom will also be ours. Following Jesus' way entails joining his mission, being drawn into the proclamation of God's kingdom on which Jesus' mission centered. "Go therefore and make disciples of all nations," Jesus commands, "baptizing them in the name of the Father and of the Son and of the Holy Spirit, and teaching them to obey everything that I have commanded you. And remember, I am with you always, to the end of the age" (Matt 28:19–20). Even as Jesus' followers are sent on a missional pilgrimage, they are reminded of his proximity. Jesus will be *with* us in the power of his Holy Spirit.

Jesus' teaching about *proximity* is refracted in a number of ways by the New Testament authors. One of Paul's favorite images is adoption. More than mere association with Jesus, life with God is a change of status so fundamental that it is like a change in one's family of origin. Adopted into God's family, the Christian is elevated beyond less-favored, younger siblings to co-heirs with Christ (Rom 8:15–17; Gal 4:5; Eph 1:5, 2:19). Adoption draws the orphan into a family and with the acquisition of the family's name

---

3. Bonhoeffer, *Cost of Discipleship*, 51.

is *held* there, or hidden. Thus Paul writes that we are "hidden with Christ in God" (Col 3:3). Paul even stretches our scriptural imagination back to Genesis to offer description of the Christian life. Our proximity to Jesus is so entirely transformative that we are made *new creations* (2 Cor 5:17). It seems that the inexplicability and magnitude of being in Christ drives Paul to heap image upon image in trying to portray it. In his Letter to the Colossians, he practically trips over himself as he multiplies metaphors:

> For in [Christ] the whole fullness of deity dwells bodily, and you have come to fullness in him, who is the head of every ruler and authority. In him also you were circumcised with a spiritual circumcision, by putting off the body of the flesh in the circumcision of Christ; when you were buried with him in baptism, you were also raised with him through faith in the power of God, who raised him from the dead. And when you were dead in trespasses and the uncircumcision of your flesh, God made you alive together with him, when he forgave us all our trespasses, erasing the record that stood against us with its legal demands. He set this aside, nailing it to the cross. He disarmed the rulers and authorities and made a public example of them, triumphing over them in it (Col 2:9–15).

Burial and resurrection; death and life. What could more effectively evoke the dramatic proximity of life with God than burial *with* Jesus and sharing *his* resurrection to new life (cf. Rom 6)? Perhaps Peter finds it. Our relation to Jesus is not merely close but *transcendently* close—proximate in the way only God can make possible. We are made so near to Jesus that we become participants "of the divine nature" (2 Pet 1:4).

Life with God as proximity to Jesus is beautifully portrayed in the Anastasis icon (Fig. 1. Descent into Hell).

INTRODUCTION

In one visual space, Christ's defeat of death and sin are presented together with Christ's resurrection. He wears white, representing his resurrection to new life, and his robes float upward, suggesting his descent to Hades. On Hades' broken doors Jesus stands victorious (cf. Ps 107:16). He holds "the keys of Death and of Hades," signified by the keys drifting in the abyss (Rev 1:18). Through his death he defeats and humiliates the Evil One, depicted as the chained skeleton under Jesus' feet (Col 2:15; Heb 2:14).

The icon depicts the consequences of Christ's resurrection. On top of the broken doors of death he stands with Adam and Eve grasped by the wrists. He pulls them out of the tomb as he ascends, signifying the effect of Christ's finished work on the death in us and around us. "There is no crime so atrocious, no shame so abysmal, no failure so profound as to put us beyond the transforming power of the risen Lord Jesus Christ," says Fleming Rutledge.[4] The icon invites us to see ourselves in the face of Adam or Eve: grasped by the wrist and drawn out of our grave! Such proximity to Jesus—yes, even to being *grasped by the Resurrected One*—pivots our relation to sin and death and the Evil One. He leads us by the hand into union with God and each other. "For God so loved the world that he gave his only Son, so that everyone who believes in him may not perish but may have eternal life. Indeed, God did not send the Son into the world to condemn the world, but in order that the world might be saved through him" (John 3:16-17).

Without proximity to Jesus we are image-bearers darkened with sin and without hope of sharing God's life. What God provides and makes possible through Jesus we call "grace." "The world is perfected by being brought into closer relations with the God who perfects it," Kathryn Tanner writes. "In union with God, in being brought near to God, all the trials and sorrows of life—suffering, loss, moral failing, the oppressive stunting of opportunities and vitality, grief, worry, tribulation and strife—are purified, remedied and reworked through the gifts of God's grace."[5]

The *pilgrimage* of following Jesus is also refracted by New Testament authors. Jesus calls the Christian into fellowship, and Paul speaks repeatedly of the life which follows as imitation. "Be imitators of God, as beloved children," Paul writes, "and live in love, as Christ loved us and gave himself up for us, a fragrant offering and sacrifice to God" (Eph 5:1; cf. 1 Cor 11:1; Phil 2:1–11). Imitating Jesus is imitating God. This is the force of the incarnation: Jesus presents the pattern for life as image-bearers with our darkness removed, healed from the deadly sickness of sin, and all those in proximity to him by faith who are indwelt by his Spirit are drawn in his train. The newness of sharing Christ's life may cause us to believe our journey is now complete, but our pilgrimage stretches out *yet* in front of us. Christ has not completed his work but will at his return (Phil 1:4). Adopted into the family of God, creation still groans and we wait "eagerly" for our body's redemption (Rom 8:23). The Christian is thus a unique

4. Rutledge, *The Undoing of Death*, 312.
5. Tanner, *Jesus, Humanity, and the Trinity*, 2.

creature: an elect exile. We are elect of God, chosen, but still journeying toward our true home (1 Pet 1:1-4; cf. John 14:3). Jesus initiates our pilgrimage and brings it to completion, even as we daily seek to conform our lives to the pattern of Jesus' life in worship and service.

Caravaggio's *The Calling of St. Matthew* vividly depicts the Jesus-initiated character of Christian pilgrimage in the church (Fig. 2).

Jesus is presented with arm and finger outstretched to Matthew. There is no question to whom Jesus points. No hesitation from Matthew is recorded in the Gospel, but Caravaggio presents him in the posture that many of the Gospel's readers certainly find themselves. Matthew's eyebrows are raised as he points at himself uncertainly, "Me? Do you know who I am, a tax collector?" Caravaggio invites us to find ourselves in any one of the faces at the table. If not Matthew, in shocked disbelief, then perhaps the boy with his head down and attention focused on coins. Or maybe we sees ourselves in the boy on the near side of the table. He leans in, not the subject of Jesus' gesture, but Caravaggio suggests that he too is caught up in the divine drama of this moment.

Matthew, of course, does follow Jesus, and Caravaggio wants the viewer to see what leads Matthew out of his seat: the call of Jesus is the divine call, the call of God.

INTRODUCTION

There are no halos in Caravaggio's scenes. He employs light another way to indicate divine activity. The light from the window falls across Jesus' face and hand beneath the sign of the cross, and then, following the direction of his pointing finger, onto the face of Matthew. We are meant to see Jesus' calling as God's calling: "Follow me" (Matt 9:9).

The narrative seems incomplete at first glance. Caravaggio leaves Matthew in his moment of decision, but he hints toward its completion in the figure who stands next to Jesus: Peter. Peter points as well, but his posture is slouched and his outstretched arm lacks Jesus' confidence. Peter represents the church that takes up the mission of Jesus in his name, making disciples of men and women like Matthew. Though Matthew still sits, doubtful of Jesus' call, Caravaggio suggests his future place in the person of Peter. Light falls across Peter's shoulder and hand. God is at work through Peter as well who stands in proximity to Jesus. Jesus is "with him" as he makes disciples and baptizes in his name (Matt 28:18–20). What Caravaggio evokes in this scene Paul likens to planting and watering. The efficacy of the church's ministry depends upon the Spirit who brings growth to the seeds that are planted and watered by the church (1 Cor 3:7). Peter may be pointing, but the divine light is where our gaze should rest.

The Grammar of Grace

In the history of Christian thought, proximity and pilgrimage are the scriptural antecedents of portrayals of Christian life. In some portrayals, the attention rests more heavily on proximity than pilgrimage, stressing the stability of one's life in God through participation in Christ. Others more strongly emphasize pilgrimage, stressing the pursuit of virtue and service in the church that springs from obedience to Christ's post-resurrection command. Whichever receives more stress, at the center of both stands *grace*. Having been drawn into proximity to Jesus through the power of the Holy Spirit, the Christian's pilgrimage of love and service is *initiated* and *enabled* by God in Christ. Christian theology, following the New Testament authors, calls this *grace* (*charis* in Greek and later *gratia* in Latin).

When speaking of life with God, no word in the Christian vocabulary is more direct or comprehensive than grace. In the New Testament, grace (*charis* in Greek) appears over 150 times, mostly in Paul's writings. How do we refer to the unique character and accomplishment of what God did through the person of Jesus? Grace, Paul would say. Following Paul, throughout the Christian tradition there has been no thread more central to the tapestry of the whole, nothing more tightly woven into the fabric of what it means to share Jesus' life than *grace*. The Christian life is the result of God's taking a person dead in sin, making them alive through faith in Christ, and then calling them forward into a pilgrimage of worship and mission. It is all grace. *Grace* initiates and accomplishes God's economy of salvation.

> You were dead through the trespasses and sins in which you once lived, following the course of this world, following the ruler of the power of the air, the spirit that is now at work among those who are disobedient. All of us once lived among them in the passions of our flesh, following the desires of flesh and senses, and we were by nature children of wrath, like everyone else. But God, who is rich in mercy, out of the great love with which he loved us even when we were dead through our trespasses, made us alive together with Christ—by grace you have been saved—and raised us up with him and seated us with him in the heavenly places in Christ Jesus, so that in the ages to come he might show the immeasurable riches of his grace in kindness toward us in Christ Jesus. For by grace you have been saved through faith, and this is not your own doing; it is the gift of God—not the result of works, so that no one may boast. For we are what he has made us, created in Christ Jesus for good works, which God prepared beforehand to be our way of life (Eph 2:1–10).

The person once dead is now alive and drawn forward into the works God prepared. The whole sequence of redemption, from its origin in God to its fulfillment in the Christian's glorification at Christ's return, is grace.

From what in the divine life does his grace spring; is it some divine lack, some unrequited need? No. God is "the Holy One in your midst" and not a mortal like us (Hos 11:9). "It is as Father, Son and Spirit that God is of himself," John Webster reminds us, grounding our theology of grace in the doctrine of the Trinity. God is "utterly free and full, in the self-originate and perfect movement of his life; grounded in himself, he gives himself, the self-existent Lord of grace. . . . *God is from himself, and from himself gives himself.*"[6] God does not depend on another but has "life *in himself*" (John 5:26). Thus, the grace of God which meets us in the face of Jesus does not spring from some lack in God but from his utterly complete, full, and beautiful life *as love*: "For God so loved the world that he gave his only Son . . ." (John 3:16). And the love he offers awakens return.

Hans Urs von Balthasar likens God's love in redemptive action to a mother who awakens her child's love with her smile.[7] God "radiates love, which kindles the light of love in the heart of man, and it is precisely this light that allows man to perceive this, the absolute Love: "For it is the God who said, 'Let light shine out of darkness,' who has [shone] in our heart to give the light of the glory of God in the face of Christ" (2 Cor 4:6). In this face, the primal foundation of being smiles at us as a mother and as a father."[8] Before Christ, it is not that we are without relation to

---

6. Webster, *God Without Measure*, Vol. 1, 19. Emphasis in original.

7. "Love in redemptive action" is Torrance's expression (Torrance, *The Doctrine of Grace in the Apostolic Fathers*, 21). Likewise: "Grace is the transcendent Christ in gracious and forgiving and enabling motion" (32).

8. Balthasar, *Love Alone is Credible*, 76.

God, for we are his creatures and made after his image. There is a relation already present, but we can only turn in love toward God when our lives are *interrupted* by grace. "Insofar as we are his creatures, the seed of love lies dormant within us as the image of God (*imago*). But just as no child can be awakened to love without being loved, so too no human heart can come to an understanding of God without the free gift of his grace—in the image of his Son."[9]

The most remarkable feature of these diverse readings is not really their difference but their shared *grammar of grace.* Present in every selection is a common grammar of God's unmerited and transformative favor that comes to us in the person of Jesus Christ and is brought to life in us through the work of the Holy Spirit as a pilgrimage of worship and mission. "Grammar" is a way to describe this commonality amidst difference. In everyday speech and Christian doctrine, grammar makes speech intelligible within a particular community. Language is lively and often spontaneous, but grammar is the agreed-upon rules that make it stable enough for communication.[10] This is true for the readings in this book. The grammar of grace is the *continuity* and *stability* that runs through each portrayal of life with God, and it makes each portrayal intelligible in the church.

The Christian life is incomprehensible apart from God's grace. This fact is present in the New Testament and likewise in the selections of this anthology. The readings offer different vantage points, emphasize different facets of life with God, and follow different styles, but constant throughout is the *grammar of grace.*[11]

The Christian Life in Doctrinal, Historical, and Communal Perspective

The Christian life is the focus of each selection in this book, but the reader quickly realizes that approaches and portrayals of life with God are sometimes remarkably different. This can be disorienting. It can also be disheartening if we suppose that differences signal a lack of essential continuity in the history of Christian thought, the absence of a central thread. We need some way to discern the causes of difference so as not to be so distracted by them that we lose our grip on the common thread: the *grammar of grace.* We suggest approaching the selections from three perspectives: theological, historical, and communal. Taken together, they are a 'lens' for reading the selections which helps clarify the causes of difference. Think of what follows as a brief, theological primer for reading Christian writings.

9. Ibid.

10. Theology is sometimes described as "grammar." See Dalferth, *Crucified and Resurrected*, especially chapter 4; Adams, "Confessing the Faith," 209–21.

11. The subject of this anthology is not actually the doctrine of grace, which has a very long history. Such a collection would need to include a different set of readings. See Whitley, ed., *The Doctrine of Grace*; Oaks, *A Theology of Grace in Six Controversies*; Lubac, *A Brief Catechesis on Nature and Grace*; Oden, *The Transforming Power of Grace*.

First, the *theological* perspective. At its most theologically essential, the term "Christian life" is shorthand for *life with God*. It names the form of human existence that progresses from union with Christ (its beginning) toward glorification (its culmination) through the power of the Holy Spirit (its enablement) in the fellowship of the Church (its context). Said differently, the Christian life names the temporal experience of God's eternal purposes for fellowship as they are realized in human beings according to God's grace. God's gracious purpose to conform fallen people to the image of Christ takes shape and fulfills itself in time and space; this is the Christian life.

As a topic of Christian teaching and belief, what is called "the Christian life" is really a coinherence of doctrines or "teachings." Several doctrines converge on the doctrine of life with God, theologically speaking. This is simply how Christian doctrine works. It is inherently systematic, but not necessarily in the sense of the modern discipline of "systematic theology." Instead, theology is essentially interrelated and interconnected as a consequence of its pursuit of "coherence and comprehensiveness."[12] Theology can be called systematic, in this sense, "when it traces links between discrete theological loci, or when the treatment of a single locus or issue is shaped by the awareness of its potential to interlock with other loci, indeed, in some cases, its dependence on them for its own shape."[13] In other words, theology is like a web in which each doctrine is connected to another and so on. Or, it is like a crystal in which each doctrine is another facet of the central Christian confession, "Jesus is Lord." Looking intently through any one facet, all at once we see the structure of the whole and so gain a renewed perspective of the particular facet through which we look.[14]

It should be said that the metaphors of web and crystal can give the false impression that theology is entirely tidy and fixed.[15] When actually, in practice, theology is always on the move in time and space, within the ebb and flow of actual lives in relation to God and others. Thus Karl Barth described theology as "painting a bird in flight."[16] Theologians constantly find themselves running up against the limits of words and the poverty of our concepts. Hilary of Poitiers beautifully captures this:

> Let your imagination range to what you may suppose is God's utmost limit and you will find him present there. Strain as you will there is always a further horizon towards which to strain. Infinity is His property, just as the power of making such effort is yours. Words will fail you, but His being will not be circumscribed. . . . Gird up your intellect to comprehend Him as a whole; He eludes you. God, as a whole, has left something within your grasp, but this something is inextricably involved in His entirety. . . . Reason, therefore,

---

12. Williams, *The Architecture of Theology*, 1.
13. Ibid.
14. See Eilers and Strobel, "The Christian Life in Dogmatic Key."
15. I am grateful to Ashley Cocksworth for reminding me of this.
16. Barth, *Evangelical Theology*, 7.

cannot cope with Him, since no point of contemplation can be found outside Himself and since eternity is eternally His.[17]

It is not that we have *nothing* to say about God, but that in *everything* we say there remains depth to God's life, a surplus of Godhead, we never fully plumb.

When looking across two millennia of Christian thought, we see the Christian life most closely related to *Christology* (the person and work of Christ), *Pneumatology* (the Spirit's work of Illumination and Sanctification), *Salvation* (Justification and Union with Christ), the *Church* (Sacraments and Mission), and *Eschatology* (Glorification) (Fig. 3).

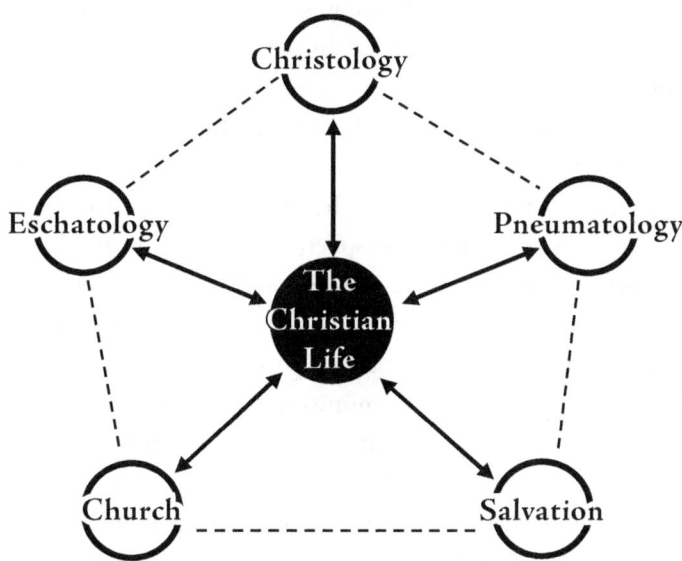

This is the web of doctrines that exerts the most "pressure" on the shape of one's theology of life with God. These five are not the only doctrines that inform teaching on the Christian life. At another level of remove, the doctrines of God, Creation, and Providence are relevant. Thus, for instance, variations between sixteenth-century portrayals of Christian life show different configurations between the doctrines of the Church and Sanctification. Reading with a theological perspective illuminates similarities between Patristic and Reformation accounts. Both heavily rely on the doctrine of Christ's person, even though Patristic visions of life with God were uninvolved with the issues debated in the sixteenth century.

Second, the *historical* perspective. Presentations of life with God should be read with an eye to the historical circumstances of the author. Like the doctrinal cluster around the doctrine of the Christian life, the historical situation of an author "presses" on her portrayal of life with God. It must not be forgotten—though it so often is when reading—that behind words stand an embodied human person. The demands of her

17. Hilary of Poitiers, *On the Trinity*, 2.6.

day, her personality and temperament, and her own life with God are all influences that press her vision of Christian life into a particular shape. For instance, the earliest Christians were under regular and intense persecution from the Romans, and this was not unlike the Anabaptists of the seventeenth century. In both cases persecution influenced their use of Scripture, the images with which they pictured the Christian life, and their use of historical sources. Seventeenth-century Anabaptists remembered early Christian persecution and likened their experience to them, even when their persecutors were Europeans who also claimed membership in the church.

Third, making sense of difference also requires a *communal* perspective. The authors in this anthology are unavoidably enmeshed in various communities. They also have a family in which they are a son or daughter, and perhaps a brother or sister. In the course of life they form various friendships and alliances, and they are mentored and pastored by people they admire. Sometimes the people they esteem in one season of life later become adversaries, and their theology becomes—painfully we are sure—at odds with the heroes of earlier days. Marriage may also be part of an author's life, and perhaps parenthood, the roles of husband or wife, father or mother adding to the storehouse of experiences and perspectives that inform their theology. Or they may live during a time when theologians were predominantly celibate. Their deepest attachments form, therefore, in the context of committed monastic fellowship. They may not know what it means to be a spouse or parent, but they give themselves fully to the gifts of friendship in Christian communities of service, study, and prayer.

None of the authors in the collection drift unmoored from the Christian tradition but are carried along, as in streams, within traditions of faith. And as members of traditions, we are carried along according to the "flow" and "inclination" of those traditions, as Hans Küng puts it. "Flow" and "inclination" is another way of rendering the idea of "pressure." That is, our presentations of Christian life are always given as theological, historical, and communal influences "press" on them. Or, on Küng's metaphor, they are given within a particular tradition that draws them along in certain directions. A tradition is like a flowing stream, he shows, and the image should remind us that all theology is not only pressured into shape by its associations but is *limited* as well.

> Every school of theology has its own particular direction of flow and inclination, different for Greek patristic theology and for the theology of Augustine, different for Thomists and for Scotists. This flow does not in itself imply an overflow into error but it does imply limitation. No particular gradient ought to claim absolute authority; the water can pour into the valley by many different routes. Perhaps one riverbed channels the waters more swiftly and impressively than another—without meanderings or stagnation. Yet its flow will be finite and circumscribed, not comparable to the all-inclusive infinity of the ocean. The direction of flow determines the strengths and weaknesses of any theology. Strength, because in the direction of the incline all flows easily and is swiftly carried along. Seemingly immovable log jams of problems are sped

downstream with the utmost ease. But also weaknesses, because as a result of its fall the current may readily leave its channel, undercut and overrun dams. Any theology, even the best, can in its own way become a victim of its own inclination. Any theology, even the best, has its most dangerous currents precisely at the point of maximum flow. God's word alone is the all-encompassing ocean, alive and yet at rest.[18]

No single portrayal of life with God is complete or comprehensive of the whole. Every depiction of life with God is drawn along within the current of its place within the Christian tradition, the intellectual habits of the day in which it was given, and the practices of the church in which the person who gave it was a participant.

Thus, any person who gives account of the Christian life, any person who seeks to portray life with God, must return again to the "all-encompassing ocean" of Holy Scripture. There we find *again* the antecedents that direct and enliven our teaching about Christian life. And there we also find the stability and continuity amidst all the difference between portrayals of Christian life, the central thread: the grammar of grace.

This brief, theological primer for reading Christian writings would not be complete without some mention of the reader's *disposition*. That is, as we approach these texts what is our posture? What is required *of us*? We recommend receptivity, hospitality, and empathy. Read receptively, turning toward the author as a brother or sister on the pilgrimage of Christian life, a fellow member of Christ's church. Read hospitably. Despite an author's otherness, let their witness "enter your space" rather than turning it away at the door. And read with empathy. Attempt to see as the author sees. Do not merely consider the possibility that someone might see the Christian life that way; attempt to see it that way *yourself*.[19]

* * *

The reader's attention should settle now on this collective witness to life with God. John Wesley's counsel from the fourth volume of his anthology is entirely fitting:

> May we all learn from these worthies, to be not almost only, but altogether Christians! To reckon all things but dung and dross for the excellency of the experimental knowledge of JESUS CHRIST! And not to count our lives dear unto ourselves, so we may finish our course with joy![20]

> *How glorious is that Kingdom, where the saints dwell in light! Clad in white robes, they follow the Lamb wherever he goes.* (Magnificat antiphon, Feast of All Saints)

Kent Eilers

---

18. Küng, *Justification*, 278–79.
19. See Eilers, "Hermeneutical Empathy."
20. Wesley, *A Christian Library*, vol. 2, part 1, para. 5.

Section I: Patristic

I. Patristic

Introduction

The readings in this section are drawn from the Patristic era, so named because the infant church's influential leaders and teachers are called "fathers" (*pater* is "father" in both Greek and Latin).[1] Their writings are best understood when their *historical*, *communal*, and *theological* contexts are kept in view.

Historically, three developments are important. First, early Christians in the Roman Empire were under near constant threat of imperial persecution. The fact that martyrdom was often a real and tangible possibility colored their entire understanding of the Christian life. The second event is the conversion of the Emperor Constantine on or about 312 and the subsequent Edict of Milan in 313 which brought imperial persecution to an end. After the defeat of Licinus in 324 Christianity ascended as *the* religion of the Roman Empire. Up to this time, the call of martyrdom demanded one's highest devotion to Christ, even to death. When persecution ended, many Christians sought to maintain the contest with "the world" by fleeing the cities of the Empire for lives of self-denial and prayer in the desert. For those early "Desert Fathers and Mothers" the Christian life was portrayed through the lens of disciplined, costly obedience to the pilgrimage of faith in the company of like-minded Christians. Third, the Council of Nicaea (325) was a watershed moment. Christianity's ascension to imperial status required the church to clarify and define its beliefs. The true and full divine nature of the *Logos* was the primary focus of the meeting at Nicaea. Several more general councils subsequently met on other topics (for instance, the Council of Chalcedon, 451). For the leaders of the church who remained in the cities as bishops

---

1. Women are glaringly absent from the theology of early Christianity for at least two reasons. First, we have few written sources from women in this era. Second, what constitutes a theological work is often restricted to doctrinal treatises, sermons, or biblical commentary. Of these we have almost no examples from women (Cohick and Hughes, *Christian Women in the Patristic World*, xxvi-xxviii). More generally, the following resources are particularly useful introductions to this era, its people, culture, and habits of thought: Ayres, *Nicaea and its Legacy*; Benedict XVI, *The Fathers of the Church*; Berardino, *Encyclopedia of Ancient Christianity*; Green, *Shapers of Christian Orthodoxy*; Kelly, *Early Christian Doctrines*.

and presbyters, the "enthusiasm of martyrdom" was replaced by "the enthusiasm of orthodoxy."[2] For to live the life in Christ, one must understand accurately and reverently the Christ who addresses and inspires our faith.

Each selection that follows here, therefore, has a *communal* context, that is, the roles and relationships that helped shape the author. The ancient writers in this section were all leaders of *the church* in some capacity. St. Gregory the Great led the Western Church as Pope, and nearly all the rest were bishops. Like Irenaeus, Basil, and Chrysostom, they shepherded their congregations, preaching and giving spiritual guidance, and led the churches of their region. St. Ephrem was a deacon. He played a more local role, writing hymns for his church, and was only recognized more widely after his death. Many Church Fathers were associated with ascetic communities for some portion of their life, such as Basil, Chrysostom, and Augustine. The most familiar abbot from this section is surely St. Benedict, and less well known are the Desert Abbas and Ammas.

Finally, there are also theological contexts for each reading. We might highlight two significant theological tropes here: the doctrine of grace and the concept of *theosis*.

First, portrayals of life with God are intimately tied to particular *doctrines of grace*. Every doctrine of grace is, as it were, a certain "framing" of the relationship between divine and human action. That is, the acts of divine grace that accomplish God's work of salvation have some relation to human acts of faith, repentance, pilgrimage, service of others, and so on. The account of that relation between divine grace and human action differs among doctrines of God. What does not differ for both the Eastern, Greek Church and the Western, Latin Church is this: divine grace is essential and pivotal for the Christian life. The visitation of God's grace initiates the life in Christ, guides its unfolding, and leads to its completion (John 3:3–8; Rom 8:28–30, etc.). The difference, however, between East and West lies in the modulations of *cooperation*. Put simply: Greek theologies of the Christian life have no difficulty affirming human cooperation with God's grace (*synergia*), while Latin theologies following Augustine tend to cast humans as utterly incapable of cooperating with the grace of God due to the effects of original sin. The slightest gesture of human cooperating with God is dependent on a prior visitation of grace.

In the Latin Church, the prevailing doctrine of grace developed along the lines of St. Augustine's theology (fifth century). Augustine understood the "terrible gravity of sin" to be so overwhelming as to obliterate any possibility of the human will's initiative.[3] Inherited sin is so disastrous that it totally destroys one's capacity for cooperation with grace. If "God's grace works with itself alone," as Augustine had it, very little theological space is left to justify cooperation.[4] Augustine's influence on Western theology has been immense, shaping the general trajectories of the doctrine of grace

---

2. Watson, "Grace in the Latin Fathers to St. Augustine," 111.
3. "Terrible gravity of sin" is Nörregaard's phrase (Nörregaard, "Grace in Saint Augustine," 126).
4. Ibid., 124.

into the medieval era and beyond. On this conception, natural *resistance* characterizes the human person as she is met by the grace of God.

In the East, Greek theologians before and after Augustine viewed the person in terms of natural *receptiveness* to grace.[5] The Greek Fathers considered both creation and salvation acts of grace. Because humans are created by God, even despite the fall, we are fitted, by nature, for cooperation with grace. Gregory of Nazianzus thus wrote, without to his mind depleting the importance of divine grace for the Christian life, "Salvation must depend upon us as well as upon God" (Oration 35; cf. Phil 2:12–13).[6] Whatever natural receptivity for grace pertains to the human by virtue of being created by God, the grace of God must still come to them in order to be redeemed and perfected. "As fish cannot live without, or as man cannot walk without feet," Macarius of Egypt wrote, "so without the Lord Jesus and without the activity of the Divine power it is impossible to know God's mysteries and wisdom, or to be a rich and Christian man" (Homily 15.20).[7]

Second, all portrayals of the individual Christian life assume a larger story of redemption. The nearly universal term used among the Patristic writers is known as *theosis* ("divinization" or "deification"). Scripturally, the language of *theosis* came about in the fires of the fourth-century Arian controversy, from putting together those profound texts on the incarnation of God the Logos/Word, the pre-existent Son of God (as in John, Luke, Paul, Peter), and that powerful word about our *partaking in the Divine Nature*, from 2 Peter 1:3-5.

> His divine power has given us everything needed for life and godliness, through the knowledge of him who called us by his own glory and goodness. Thus he has given us, through these things, his precious and very great promises, so that through them you may escape from the corruption that is in the world because of lust, and may become participants of the divine nature. For this very reason, you must make every effort to support your faith with goodness, and goodness with knowledge.

St. Athanasius's statement is the pith of the idea: "God became man so that man might become God." It is startling, paradoxical language, perhaps, and must be understood accurately and with nuance.

In the doctrinal debates and theological expositions of the Fathers, it was hammered out very clearly that what is meant by *theosis* is the antithesis of pagan pantheism. The Christian faith is radically unlike philosophical monism, Advaita Hinduism, and Buddhism in one all-important metaphysical point. God, the ultimate and transcendent reality, the creator of heaven and earth (Gen 1:1), the fountain of life (Ps

---

5. Gloubokowsky, "Grace in the Greek Fathers (To St. John of Damascus) and Inter-Church Union," 61–74.
6. Quoted in ibid., 77.
7. Quoted in ibid., 79.

36:9), says 1 John 4:8, is love. Love means relation, and relation means persons, indeed a communion of persons. A pure cosmic monad, cannot, on its own level, "love," and hence cannot be "love." So, interior to the ineffable mystery of God are love, relation, and person. Our Lord Jesus Christ names the persons in God as the Father, the Son, and the Holy Spirit (cf. Matt 28:19). This is the Holy Trinity of Christian faith. Each of these divine persons shares in the uncreated nature of God.

Theosis in the Christian scheme of things cannot, therefore, mean that our human nature and our unique individuality somehow dissolve and merge indistinguishably with the divine nature. No, no, no. Not only do we retain our proper humanity and each our own personhood, but we genuinely find our redemption and plenitude as they are taken up in Christ. We find our true, sublime, and unimaginable freedom thereby, when through the ministry of Christ, we enter into and are wholly taken up in the God-man, and endowed by him with a participation in his own relation to God. The Christian who participates in Christ is incorporated into his sonship of the ineffable God and Father. And this he can do for us, because his work—his self-emptying, passion, and cross—has infinite and cosmic power before God. What the Son is in his risen and glorified humanity—now entered into the innermost life of the Trinity—is infinitely efficacious through his divine personhood.[8]

As we spiritually mature, this gradual assimilation to Christ progressively floods and pervades our whole being, body, mind, and soul, or begins to do so, even in this life. It is like a journey of return to our original nature, created in the image and according to the likeness of God, only more so, because our Lord Jesus Christ, the incarnate Only-Begotten of the Father, is so incomparably more than the original unfallen nature of Adam and Eve. What we gain in him far surpasses even the beauty of Adam and Eve's unfallen state. In the dramatic paradoxical expression of the Easter *Exsultet*: "O happy fault, O necessary sin of Adam, that gained for us such and so great a Redeemer!"

Kent Eilers and Anna Silvas

---

8. That is, through the "hypostatic union" of his humanity with the Divine Logos, in Chalcedonian terms.

I. Patristic

A. Before Nicaea (–325)

1. St. Clement of Rome (d. ca. 99) | *First Letter of Clement*

Clement was the third successor to Peter the apostle as bishop in Rome and considered the first of the church's so-called Apostolic Fathers. To be clear, the title, "Apostolic Father," does not mark Clement as an apostle of Jesus himself. Clement, and others like him included in the following selections, lived at the critical hinge between the apostles of Jesus and everyone after. The Apostolic Fathers are so named because they lived at that critical hinge.

Clement's connection to the apostles solidified his authority as a leader in the church. In Philippians 4:3 Paul identifies Clement as his co-worker, a connection universally acknowledged in the early church. Irenaeus, another Apostolic Father, notes the connection: Clement "had seen the blessed Apostles" and "been conversant with them"; indeed, he "might be said to have the preaching of the apostles still echoing [in his ears], and their traditions before his eyes."[1] It was the connection between the apostles and Clement that gave his *First Letter* to the church in Corinth its unique authority. For nearly a hundred years the letter was read in the Corinthian church as a part of its liturgy.

In the *First Letter of Clement* (ca. 96), Clement writes from his position as leader of the Roman church to the church in Corinth. Like Paul before him, Clement writes about divisions in the Corinthian church. Strife had arisen and younger members had deposed a group of elders. The overall thrust of the letter is consistent: those who divided the church should learn humbly, repent, and return to God, and then unity and peace might be restored to the church.

Clement's vision of the Christian life occupies a central place in his argument. Christians are called to obedience, humility, love. Like so many other early Christian writers, Clement shows that the Christian life is grounded in nothing other than God who establishes Christian existence through Christ and his Spirit. "Seeing, therefore, that we are the portion of the Holy One," Clement writes, "let us do all those things

---

1. Irenaeus, *Against Heresies*, 3, 3, 3.

which pertain to holiness." Much like the Apostle Paul, the *imperatives* of the Christian life (moral action) are founded on the *indicatives* of the Christian life (salvation in Christ). What Christians should *do* (imperative) is grounded in what is *already true* of them (indicative). In the following selections, Clement first grounds Christian holiness in God's knowledge, power, and faithfulness to his promises (27–30). Then, drawing on military imagery, he appeals to Christ as the one to whom the Christian "soldier" is devoted (36–38; cf. 2 Tim 2:3–4; 1 Tim 1:18).

First Letter of Clement (c. 96)

Chapter 27—In the hope of the resurrection, let us cleave to the omnipotent and omniscient God.

Having then this hope, let our souls be bound to Him who is faithful in His promises, and just in His judgments. He who has commanded us not to lie, shall much more Himself not lie; for nothing is impossible with God, except to lie (cf. Titus 1:2; Heb 6:18). Let His faith therefore be stirred up again within us, and let us consider that all things are near Him. By the word of His might He established all things, and by His word He can overthrow them. "Who will say to Him, What have you done? or, Who will resist the power of His strength?" (Wis 12:12, 11:22) When and as He pleases He will do all things, and none of the things determined by Him shall pass away (cf. Matt 24:35). All things are open before Him, and nothing can be hidden from His counsel. "The heavens declare the glory of God, and the firmament shows His handiwork. Day unto day utters speech, and night unto night shows knowledge. And there are no words or speeches of which the voices are not heard" (Ps 14:1–3)[2].

Chapter 28—God sees all things: therefore let us avoid transgression.

Since then all things are seen and heard [by God], let us fear Him, and forsake those wicked works which proceed from evil desires; so that, through His mercy, we may be protected from the judgments to come. For where can any of us flee from His mighty hand? Or what world will receive any of those who run away from Him? For the Scripture says in a certain place, "Where shall I go, and where shall I be hid from your presence? If I ascend into heaven, You are there; if I go away even to the uttermost parts of the earth, there is your right hand; if I make my bed in the abyss, there is your Spirit" (Ps 139:7–10). Where, then, shall any one go, or where shall he escape from Him who comprehends all things?

2. Clement's Old Testament references are from the Septuagint.

A. BEFORE NICAEA (–325)

Chapter 29—Let us also draw near to God in purity of heart.

Let us then draw near to Him with holiness of spirit, lifting up pure and undefiled hands to Him, loving our gracious and merciful Father, who has made us partakers in the blessings of His elect. For thus it is written, "When the Most High divided the nations, when He scattered the sons of Adam, He fixed the bounds of the nations according to the number of the angels of God. His people Jacob became the portion of the Lord, and Israel the lot of His inheritance" (Deut 32:8, 9). And in another place [the Scripture] says, "Behold, the Lord takes to Himself a nation out of the midst of the nations, as a man takes the first-fruits of his threshing-floor; and from that nation shall come forth the Most Holy" (Num 28:27 & 2 Chr 31:14).

Chapter 30—Let us do those things that please God,
and flee from those He hates, that we may be blessed.

Seeing, therefore, that we are the portion of the Holy One, let us do all those things which pertain to holiness, avoiding all evil-speaking, all abominable and impure embraces, together with all drunkenness, seeking after change, all abominable lusts, detestable adultery, and execrable pride. "For God," says [the Scripture], "resists the proud, but gives grace to the humble" (Prov 3:34; Jas 4:6; 1 Pet 5:5). Let us cleave, then, to those to whom grace has been given by God. Let us clothe ourselves with concord and humility, ever exercising self-control, standing far off from all whispering and evil-speaking, being justified by our works, and not our words. For [the Scripture] says, "He that speaks much, shall also hear much in answer. And does he that is ready in speech deem himself righteous? Blessed is he that is born of woman, who lives but a short time: be not given to much speaking" (Job 11:2, 3). Let our praise be in God, and not of ourselves; for God hates those that commend themselves. Let testimony to our good deeds be borne by others, as it was in the case of our righteous forefathers. Boldness, and arrogance, and audacity belong to those that are cursed of God; but moderation, humility, and meekness to those who are blessed by Him....

Chapter 36—All blessings are given to us through Christ.

This is the way, beloved, in which we find our Savior, even Jesus Christ, the High Priest of all our offerings, the defender and helper of our infirmity. By Him we look up to the heights of heaven. By Him we behold, as in a glass, His immaculate and most excellent face. By Him are the eyes of our hearts opened. By Him our foolish and darkened understanding blossoms up anew towards His marvelous light. By Him the Lord has willed that we should taste of immortal knowledge, "who, being the brightness of His majesty, is by so much greater than the angels, as He has by inheritance obtained a more excellent name than they" (Heb 1:3, 4). For it is thus written, "Who makes His angels spirits, and His ministers a flame of fire" (Ps 2:7, 8; Heb 1:5). But concerning His Son the Lord spoke thus: "You are my Son, today have I begotten you. Ask of me, and I will give you the heathen for your inheritance, and the uttermost parts of the earth for your possession" (Ps 2:7, 8). And again He says to Him, "Sit at My right hand, until I make your enemies your footstool" (Ps 110:1). But who are His enemies? All the wicked, and those who set themselves to oppose the will of God.

Chapter 37—Christ is our leader, and we His soldiers.

Let us then, men and brethren, with all energy act the part of soldiers, in accordance with His holy commandments. Let us consider those who serve under our generals, with what order, obedience, and submissiveness they perform the things which are commanded them. All are not prefects, nor commanders of a thousand, nor of a hundred, nor of fifty, nor the like, but each one in his own rank performs the things commanded by the king and the generals. The great cannot subsist without the small, nor the small without the great. There is a kind of mixture in all things, and from it arises mutual advantage. Let us take our body for an example (1 Cor 12:12). The head is nothing without the feet, and the feet are nothing without the head; indeed, the very smallest members of our body are necessary and useful to the whole body. But all work harmoniously together, and are under one common rule for the preservation of the whole body.

Chapter 38—Let the members of the Church submit themselves, and no one exalt himself above another.

Let our whole body, then, be preserved in Christ Jesus; and let everyone be subject to his neighbor, according to the special gift bestowed upon him. Let the strong not despise the weak, and let the weak show respect unto the strong. Let the rich man provide for the wants of the poor; and let the poor man bless God, because He has given him one by whom his need may be supplied. Let the wise man display his wisdom, not by [mere] words, but through good deeds. Let the humble not bear testimony to himself, but leave witness to be borne to him by another (cf. Prov 27:2). Let him that is pure in the flesh not grow proud of it, and boast, knowing that it was another who bestowed on him the gift of continence. Let us consider, then, brethren, of what matter we were made,—who and what manner of beings we came into the world, as it were out of a sepulcher, and from utter darkness (cf. Ps 139:15). He who made us and fashioned us, having prepared His bountiful gifts for us before we were born, introduced us into His world. Since, therefore, we receive all these things from Him, we ought for everything to give Him thanks; to whom be glory for ever and ever. Amen.[3]

---

3. Translation revised for readability.

I. Patristic

A. Before Nicaea (–325)

2. *Shepherd of Hermas* (1st or 2nd Century)

Among early Christians the *Shepherd of Hermas* was wildly popular. Composed sometime during the second century, the *Shepherd* was widely cited by well-known figures like Tertullian, Irenaeus, Origen, and Augustine. Some even considered it divinely inspired Scripture, reading it publically as part of the liturgy in many Greek and Latin churches. Its popularity eventually waned, for various reasons, and by the fourth century it was falling from favor. Some still believed the *Shepherd* was beneficial for private reading (like Athanasius and Jerome), but its liturgical use was declining, and it was ultimately rejected as part of the canon of Scripture (see *Muratorian Fragment*, eighth century).

Despite its popularity among early Christians, modern readers may find it a strange text. Parts of it read like autobiography, others like moral instruction, and others record fantastic visions of monsters and crumbling towers. Of course, the imagery is all part of the book's dramatic and memorable allegories.[1] The tower represents the church, built of different people, and the monster portrays the trials facing her. These allegories were influential among Christians who read the text, particularly its portrayal of the Christian life. Not unlike John Bunyan's image-rich allegory *Pilgrim's Progress* (seventeenth century), the *Shepherd of Hermas* dramatically portrays the Christian life in terms of costly obedience, personal sacrifice, and hope for Christ's return.

In the Shepherd, the Christian life is a sharp break from life before baptism. For all who turn to Christ and are baptized, forgiveness awaits, and the pilgrimage toward God in Christ begins. Seen through the character of Hermas, the pilgrimage of the Christian life is fraught with temptation and, tragically, sin and further repentance.

---

1. In various writings throughout history the *Shepherd's* imagery appears time and again: such as, Hildegard of Bingen's (1098–1179) visionary work *Scivias*, some sixteenth-century Bibles, the English mystic Francis Quarles's (1592–1644) poem "Even like Two Little Bank-Conjoined Brooks," and the twentieth-century Carl G. Jung's *Psychological Types* (Osiek, *Shepherd of Hermas*, 7).

SECTION I: PATRISTIC

Post-baptismal sin was evidently on the minds of many early Christians. Are sins after baptism forgiven? Is forgiveness found in Christ *again* and *again*?

As the *Shepherd* presents it, the character of Hermas discovers the mercy of God through his encounter with the angel of repentance. Yes, he learns, God *is* sure to forgive, but the Christian must not tarry in sin. They must not delay for Christ is not long in returning. In this sense, the *Shepherd's* portrait of the Christian life resonates with themes found in the book of James: faith in Christ without works is "dead" (chapter 2). The text invites readers to perceive their sins and their calling under the most serious and realistic light (even as some will question if its vision of divine grace sufficiently resonates with the biblical witness).[2]

The following excerpts are taken from Book 3. In the first selection, Hermas is met by the angel of repentance who stresses the necessity of immediate and sincere repentance. The second selection follows shortly after the first and emphasizes the need to do penance in order to receive genuine repentance. The third selection portrays the church as a tower which is currently under construction. The angel of repentance uses this allegory to emphasize the *certainty* of Hermas's repentance as well as the *urgency* to repent and live in obedience to Christ's commands.

Shepherd of Hermas (1ˢᵗ or 2ⁿᵈ Century)

Book III.6.1[3]

Sitting in my house, and praising the Lord for all that I had seen [in the visions provided by the angel of repentance], and reflecting on the commandments—that they are excellent, and powerful, and glorious, and able to save a man's soul—I said within myself, "I shall be blessed if I walk in these commandments, and everyone who walks in them will be blessed.

Book III.7

[The Angel of Repentance asks Hermas] "Do you think . . . that the sins of those who repent are remitted? Not altogether, but he who repents must torture his soul, and be exceedingly humble in all his conduct, and be afflicted with many kinds of affliction; and if he endure the afflictions that come upon him, then he [Jesus Christ] who created all

---

2. Despite ambiguity in the text itself, the *Shepherd* contributed to a widely held view among many early Christians that forgiveness for sin was given only once after baptism.

3. On the annotation: Book III (Shepherd is divided into three books).10 (second level of division is by "similitude" or "parable").4 (third level of division is by chapter).

things, and endured them with power, will assuredly have compassion . . . and this will He do when He sees a heart of every penitent pure from every evil thing. . . .

Book III.9.31–33

"I, who am the messenger of repentance, deem you happy if you are among those who are innocent as children, because your part is good, and honorable before God. Moreover, I say to you all, who have received the seal of the Son of God, be clothed with simplicity, and be not mindful of offenses, nor remain in wickedness. Lay aside, therefore, the recollection of your offenses and bitternesses, and you will be formed in one spirit. And heal and take away from you those wicked schisms, that if the Lord of the flocks come, He may rejoice concerning you. And He will rejoice, if He finds all things sound, and none of you shall perish. But if He finds any one of these sheep strayed, woe to the shepherds! . . .

Heal yourselves, therefore, while the tower [the Church] is still building. The Lord dwells in men that love peace, because He loves peace; but from the contentious and the utterly wicked He is far distant. Therefore, restore to Him a spirit that is as sound as you received it. For when you have given a fuller a new garment, and desire to receive it back entire at the end, if, then, the fuller return you a torn garment, will you take it from him and not rather by angry, and abuse him saying, "I gave you a garment that was entire: why have you rent it, and made it useless, so that it can be of no use on account of the rent which you have made in it?" . . . If, therefore, you grieve about your garment, and complain because you have not received it entire, what do you think the Lord will do to you, who gave you a sound spirit, which you have rendered altogether useless, so that it can be of no service to its possessor? For its use began to be unprofitable, seeing it was corrupted by you. Will not the Lord, therefore, because of this conduct of yours regarding His Spirit, act in the same way, and deliver you over to death? Assuredly, I say, he will do the same to all those whom He shall find retaining a recollection of offences. Do not trample His mercy under foot, He says, but rather honor Him, because He is so patient with your sins, and is not as you are. Repent, for it is useful to you.

"All these things which are written above, I, the Shepherd, the messenger of repentance, have showed and spoken to the servants of God. If therefore you believe, and listen to my words, and walk in them, and amend your ways, you shall have it in your power to live: but if you remain in wickedness, and in the recollection of offences, no sinner of that class will live unto God. All these words which I had to say have been spoken to you."

The shepherd said to me, "Have you asked me everything?" And I replied, "Yes, sir." "Why do you not ask me about the shape of the stones that were put into the building [which is the Church], that I might explain to you why we filled up the shapes?" And I said, "I forgot sir." "Hear now, then," he said, "about this also. These are they who have now heard my commandments, and repented with their whole hearts. And when the Lord saw that their repentance was good and pure, and that they were able to remain in it, He ordered their former sins to be blotted out. For these shapes were their sins, and they were leveled down, that they might not appear."

Book III.10.4

The angel then said to me, "Conduct yourself manfully in this service, and make known to everyone the great things of God, and you will have favor in this ministry. Whoever, therefore, will walk in these commandments, shall have life, and will be happy in this life; but whosoever will neglect them will not have life, and will be unhappy in this life . . . Do good works, therefore, you who have received good from the Lord; unless, while you delay to do them, the building [the Church] be finished, and you be rejected from the edifice: there is now no other tower being built."[4]

---

4. Translation revised for readability.

I. Patristic

A. Before Nicaea (–325)

3. *The Letter to Diognetus* (late 2nd century)

In every historical and social circumstance, people have a particular way of understanding the composition of the human person (anthropology). Such understandings inevitably come into play when Christians witness to the truth of the gospel in the context of their circumstances. Christians have sought to do this—to contextualize the gospel—in every historical and cultural situation. The *Letter to Diognetus* is a telling example of just this instinct. The author (unknown) likens the Christian's presence in the world to the hidden existence of the soul within the body, a common way of understanding the human person at the time, and then appropriates this conception to address the Christian life. The portrayal goes like this: just as the *soul* dwells in the body but does not belong to it, so *Christians* reside in the world but do not belong to it (sections V–VI). For the person who is in Jesus Christ through the power of the Spirit, their citizenship lies *in heaven* and they sojourn here in the world as foreigners (cf. Phil 3:20; Eph 2:19–22; 1 Pet 2:9–17).

As the *Letter to Diognetus* shows, the Christian life has an unavoidably *pilgrim-like* character: the Christian is always *in* but never *of* the world (cf. 1 Pet 1:1–3). Likewise, life in Christ has an irreducible (though not always readily apparent) direction and telos. Living in this world, the Christian's very existence points forward to the fulfillment of all things in Christ. It is also significant for the author of the *Letter* that this eschatological dimension of the Christian life is not an accidental feature of Christianity's place in history. No, the pilgrimage of Christian life was established by God's "great and unutterable design" accomplished through his Son, "like a king sending his son who is himself a king" (VII).

SECTION I: PATRISTIC

The Letter to Diognetus (late 2ⁿᵈ century)

V.

For Christians cannot be distinguished from the rest of the human race by country or language or customs. [2] They do not live in cities of their own; they do not use a peculiar form of speech; they do not follow an eccentric manner of life. [3] This doctrine of theirs has not been discovered by the ingenuity or deep thought of inquisitive men, nor do they put forward a merely human teaching, as some people do. [4] Yet, although they live in Greek and barbarian cities alike, as each man's lot has been cast, and follow the customs of the country in clothing and food and other matters of daily living, at the same time they give proof of the remarkable and admittedly extraordinary constitution of their own commonwealth. [5] They live in their own countries, but only as aliens. They have a share in everything as citizens, and endure everything as foreigners. Every foreign land is their fatherland, and yet for them every fatherland is a foreign land. [6] They marry, like everyone else, and they beget children, but they do not cast out their offspring. [7] They share their board with each other, but not their marriage bed. [8] It is true that they are "in the flesh," but they do not live "according to the flesh." [9] They busy themselves on earth, but their citizenship is in heaven. [10] They obey the established laws, but in their own lives they go far beyond what the laws require. [11] They love all men, and by all men are persecuted. [12] They are unknown, and still they are condemned; they are put to death, and yet they are brought to life. [13] They are poor, and yet they make many rich; they are completely destitute, and yet they enjoy complete abundance. [14] They are dishonored, and in their very dishonor are glorified; they are defamed, and are vindicated. [15] They are reviled, and yet they bless; when they are affronted, they still pay due respect. [16] When they do good, they are punished as evildoers; undergoing punishment, they rejoice because they are brought to life. [17] They are treated by the Jews as foreigners and enemies, and are hunted down by the Greeks; and all the time those who hate them find it impossible to justify their enmity.

VI.

To put it simply: the manner in which the soul is in the body; that is the same manner in which Christians are in the world. [2] The soul is dispersed through all the members of the body, and Christians are scattered through all the cities of the world. [3] The soul dwells in the body, but does not belong to the body, and Christians dwell in the world, but do not belong to the world. . . . [4] The soul, which is invisible, is kept under guard in the visible body; in the same way, Christians are recognized when they are in the world, but their religion remains unseen. [5] The flesh hates the soul and treats it as an enemy, even though it has suffered no wrong, because it is prevented from enjoying its pleasures; so too the world hates Christians, even though it suffers no wrong at their hands, because they range themselves against its pleasures. ⁶The soul loves the flesh that hates it, and its members; in the same way, Christians love those who hate them. ⁷The soul is shut up in the body, and yet itself holds the body together; while Christians are restrained in the world as in a prison, and yet themselves hold the world together. ⁸The soul, which is immortal, is housed in a mortal dwelling; while Christians are settled among corruptible things, to wait for the incorruptibility that will be theirs in heaven. ⁹The soul, when faring badly as to food and drink, grows better; so too Christians, when punished, day by day increase more and more. ¹⁰It is to no less a post than this that God has ordered them, and they must not try to evade it.

VII.

As I have indicated, it is not an earthly discovery that was committed to them; it is not a mortal thought that they think of as worth guarding with such care, nor have they been entrusted with the stewardship of merely human mysteries. ²On the contrary, it was really the Ruler of all, the Creator of all, the invisible God himself, who from heaven established the truth and the holy, incomprehensible word among men, and fixed it firmly in their hearts. Nor, as one might suppose, did he do this by sending to men some subordinate—an angel, or principality, or one of those who administer earthly affairs, or perhaps one of those to whom the government of things in heaven is entrusted. Rather, he sent the Designer and Maker of the universe himself, by whom he created the heavens and confined the sea within its own bounds—him whose hidden purposes all the elements of the world faithfully carry out, him from whom the sun has received the measure of the daily rounds that it must keep, him whom the moon obeys when he commands her to shine by night, and whom the stars obey as they follow the course of the moon. He sent him by whom all things have been set in order and distinguished and placed in subjection—the heavens and the things that are in the heavens, the earth and the things in the earth, the sea and the things in the sea, fire, air, the unfathomed pit, the things in the heights and in the depths and in the realm between; God sent him to men.

³Now, did he send him, as a human mind might assume, to rule by tyranny, fear, and terror? ⁴Far from it! He sent him out of kindness and gentleness, like a king sending his son who is himself a king. He sent him as God; he sent him as man to men. He willed to save man by persuasion, not by compulsion, for compulsion is not God's way of working. ⁵In sending him, God called men, but did not pursue them; he sent him in love, not in judgment. ⁶Yet he will indeed send him someday as our Judge, and who shall stand when he appears? . . .

VIII.

... No man has ever seen God or made him known, but he has manifested himself. ⁶And he manifested himself through faith, by which alone it has been made possible for us to see God. ⁷For God, the Master and Maker of the universe, who made all things and determined the proper place of each, showed himself to be long-suffering, as well as a true friend of man. ⁸But in fact he always was and is and will be just this—kind and good and slow to anger and true; indeed, he alone is good. ⁹And when he had planned a great and unutterable design, he communicated it to his Child alone. ¹⁰Now, as long as he kept back his own wise counsel as a well-guarded mystery, he seemed to be neglecting us and to take no interest in us; ¹¹but when he revealed it through his beloved Child and made known the things that had been prepared from the beginning, he granted us all things at once. He made us both to share in his blessings and to see and understand things that none of us could ever have looked for.[1]

---

1. Translation revised for readability.

I. Patristic

A. Before Nicaea (–325)

4. St. Ignatius of Antioch (ca. 35–ca. 107) | *Letter to the Romans*

Ignatius was born less than ten years after Jesus' crucifixion. Like Clement, he lived during the critical years after the apostles when the church was taking shape (see previous selection). Central Christian beliefs were being discerned in the context of worship, and the faith was being lived out in the midst of Roman culture. We know nothing about Ignatius's early life or how he became the leader of Antioch's young church, but he left behind seven letters.

In his letters, one of Ignatius's main concerns was the humanity of Christ. The nature of Christ's incarnation lies at the center of Christian faith. How it's understood, Ignatius was aware, directly affects the church's worship and the character of her life in the world. In Ignatius's letter to the church in Smyrna, for example, he connects the incarnation to the church's social ethics and worship. Those who reject Christ's authentic humanity, "have no concern for love, none for the widow, the orphan, the afflicted, the prisoner, the hungry, the thirsty. They stay away from the Eucharist and prayer, because they do not admit that the Eucharist is the flesh of our Savior Jesus Christ which suffered for our sins, which the Father raised up by his goodness" (Smyrn. 6). The reality of Christ's true, authentic humanity matters for worship *and* mission. In the flesh—not the illusion of the flesh—the Incarnate Son cared for the poor and the needy, and it is his life that Christians imitate.

Ignatius thus exhorted Christians to guard the teaching of Christ's humanity *and* to be known for imitating Christ's example. Mere profession of faith is not enough. "For there is not now a demand for mere profession, but that a man be found continuing in the power of faith to the end," Ignatius wrote to the Ephesians (Eph 14). Imitating Christ requires martyrdom, as Ignatius saw it, because the Christian life should echo Christ's life even to death (cf. Paul's Letter to the Colossians 1:24 and Philippians 3:8). He applied the same principle to himself as he looked toward martyrdom. Ignatius was sentenced to death during the reign of Emperor Trajan for reasons unknown to us.

The necessity of martyrdom, as Ignatius saw it, clarifies why he pleaded with Christians in Rome not to inhibit his death: martyrdom was necessary to complete his imitation of Christ. In the following selection from that letter, Ignatius explains that dying on account of Christ would fulfill his life as a disciple. He saw his life in such close continuity to Christ's that he even describes his martyrdom in language echoing Christ's final supper: "I am the wheat of God, and let me be ground by the teeth of the wild beasts, that I may be found the pure bread of Christ" (Rom IV). Simply put: the Christian life imitates Christ's life, *even to death.*

The Epistle to the Romans (early second century)

Ignatius, who is also called Theophorus, to the Church which has obtained mercy, through the majesty of the Most High Father, and Jesus Christ, His only-begotten Son; the Church which is beloved and enlightened by the will of Him that wills all things which are according to the love of Jesus Christ our God, which also presides in the place of the region of the Romans, worthy of God, worthy of honor, worthy of the highest happiness, worthy of praise, worthy of obtaining her every desire, worthy of being deemed holy, and which presides over love, is named from Christ, and from the Father, which I also salute in the name of Jesus Christ, the Son of the Father: to those who are united, both according to the flesh and spirit, to every one of His commandments; who are filled inseparably with the grace of God, and are purified from every strange taint, [I wish] abundance of happiness unblameably, in Jesus Christ our God.

I.

Through prayer to God I have obtained the privilege of seeing your most worthy faces, and have even been granted more than I requested; for I hope as a prisoner in Christ Jesus to salute you, if indeed it be the will of God that I be thought worthy of reaching the goal. For a good beginning has been made, if I may obtain grace to cling to my lot without hindrance to the end. For I am afraid of your love, lest it should injure me. For it is easy for you to accomplish what you please; but it is difficult for me to attain to God, if you spare me. . . .

II.

Pray, then, do not seek to confer any greater favor upon me than that I be sacrificed to God while the altar is still prepared; that, being gathered together in love, you may sing praise to the Father, through Christ Jesus, that God has deemed me, the bishop of

Syria, worthy to be sent for from east to west. It is good to set like the sun and go from the world to God, that I may rise again to Him.

III.

You have never envied any one; you have taught others. Now I desire that those things may be confirmed [by your conduct], which in your instructions you enjoin [on others]. Only request in my behalf both inward and outward strength, that I may not only speak, but [truly] will; and that I may not merely be called a Christian, but really be found to be one. For if I be truly found [a Christian], I may also be called one, and be then deemed faithful, when I shall no longer appear to the world. Nothing visible is eternal. "For the things which are seen are temporal, but the things which are not seen are eternal" (2 Cor 4:18). For our God, Jesus Christ, now that He is with the Father, is all the more revealed [in His glory]. Christianity is not a thing of silence only, but also of [manifest] greatness.

IV.

... I am the wheat of God, and let me be ground by the teeth of the wild beasts, that I may be found the pure bread of Christ. Rather entice the wild beasts, that they may become my tomb, and may leave nothing of my body; so that when I have fallen asleep [in death], I may be no trouble to anyone. Then, when the world shall not see so much as my body, I will truly be a disciple of Christ. Entreat Christ for me, that by these instruments I may be found a sacrifice [to God].

V.

From Syria even unto Rome I fight with beasts, both by land and sea, both by night and day, being bound to ten leopards, I mean a band of soldiers, who, even when they receive benefits, show themselves all the worse. But I am the more instructed by their injuries [to act as a disciple of Christ]; "yet am I not thereby justified." May I enjoy the wild beasts that are prepared for me; and I pray they may be found eager to rush upon me, which also I will entice to devour me speedily, and not deal with me as with some, whom, out of fear, they have not touched. But if they be unwilling to assail me, I will compel them to do so. Pardon me [in this]: I know what is for my benefit.

Now I begin to be a disciple. And let no one, of things visible or invisible, envy me that I should attain to Jesus Christ. Let fire and the cross; let the crowds of wild beasts; let tearings, breakings, and dislocations of bones; let cutting off of members; let shatterings of the whole body; and let all the dreadful torments of the devil come upon me: only let me attain to Jesus Christ.

VI.

All the pleasures of the world, and all the kingdoms of this earth, shall profit me nothing. It is better for me to die in behalf of Jesus Christ, than to reign over all the ends of the earth. "For what shall a man be profited, if he gain the whole world, but lose his own soul?" Him I seek, who died for us: Him I desire, who rose again for our sake. This is the gain which is laid up for me. Pardon me, brethren: do not hinder me from living, do not wish to keep me in a state of death; and while I desire to belong to God, do not ye give me over to the world. Suffer me to obtain pure light: when I have gone thither, I shall indeed be a man of God. Permit me to be an imitator of the passion of my God. If anyone has Him within himself, let him consider what I desire, and let him have sympathy with me, as knowing how I am straitened. . . .

VII.

For though I am alive while I write to you, yet I am eager to die. My love has been crucified, and there is no fire in me desiring to be fed; but there is within me a water that lives and speaks, saying to me inwardly, Come to the Father. I have no delight in corruptible food, nor in the pleasures of this life. I desire the bread of God, the heavenly bread, the bread of life, which is the flesh of Jesus Christ, the Son of God, who became afterwards of the seed of David and Abraham; and I desire the drink of God, namely His blood, which is incorruptible love and eternal life. . . .

IX.

Remember in your prayers the Church in Syria, which now has God for its shepherd, instead of me. Jesus Christ alone will oversee it, and your love [will also regard it]. But as for me, I am ashamed to be counted one of them; for indeed I am not worthy, as being the very last of them, and one born out of due time. But I have obtained mercy to be somebody, if I shall attain to God. My spirit salutes you, and the love of the Churches that have received me in the name of Jesus Christ, and not as a mere passerby. For even those Churches which were not near to me in the way, I mean according to the flesh, have gone before me, city by city, [to meet me].[1]

---

1. Translation revised for readability.

I. Patristic

A. Before Nicaea (–325)

5. St. Polycarp (69–155) | *Letter to the Philippians* & *Martyrdom*

Polycarp was a disciple of the Apostle John (according to Irenaeus and Jerome), born just four years after Paul and Peter's execution. The first generation of Christians after the apostles have a unique place in the Christian story. They had not walked with Jesus, but they carried forward the Christian message from those who had: God was present in Jesus as Lord to redeem his creation (John 3:16). Tradition has it that a group of apostles appointed Polycarp the bishop of Smyrna (Asia Minor). Like Timothy before him, Polycarp sought to fulfill Paul's challenge: "guard what has been entrusted to your care" (1 Tim 6:20).

Of Polycarp's writings we have only one, a pastoral letter to the church in Philippi, part of which is included below. But it is not for his pen that he is typically remembered. Polycarp was among the first Christian martyrs. In fact, The *Martyrdom of Polycarp*, written within a year of his death, was the first ancient document to use the term *martyr* to describe one who dies on account of their Christian faith. Polycarp was martyred by the Romans at the age of eighty-six. History offers little clarity about the causes of Roman interest in Polycarp (opposition to idol worship was probably involved—cf. *Martyrdom*, ch. 11). Although the political circumstances of his death remain hazy, The *Martyrdom of Polycarp* gives a tantalizing glimpse at the character of his faith as death approached. As guards prepared to bind Polycarp to the stake he refused: "Leave me as I am; for He who gives me strength to endure the fire, will also enable me, without your securing me by nails, to remain on the pyre unmoved" (*Martyrdom*, ch. 13).

Our selections are from two sources: *Letter to the Philippians* and *The Martyrdom of Polycarp*. In Polycarp's *Letter to the Philippians* he portrays the Christian life as the *imitation* of Christ. The christological backdrop for that portrayal is Christ's full, authentic humanity. Following the Apostle Paul (e.g., Eph 5, Phil 2), Polycarp shows that confessing Christ's real, authentic, true humanity is not an abstract doctrinal claim—something about which theologians might idly banter. Rather, the imitation of Christ *depends* on the historical reality of Christ's humanity!

One can emulate Christ's hope and patience (chs. 8–9) precisely because he came "in the flesh" (ch. 7), Polycarp writes. Reasoning about ethics through the frame of Christ's incarnation is also found in the first letter of Polycarp's teacher, John, which Polycarp references in chapter 7. We also include a very short excerpt from *The Martyrdom of Polycarp*. There we glimpse Polycarp's attitude about martyrdom, a not uncommon end for many Christians in the patristic era.

Letter to the Philippians (2nd Century)

Polycarp, and the presbyters with him, to the Church of God sojourning at Philippi: Mercy to you, and peace from God Almighty, and from the Lord Jesus Christ, our Savior, be multiplied. . . .

Chapter 7. Avoid the Docetics, and persevere in fasting and prayer

"For whosoever does not confess that Jesus Christ has come in the flesh, is antichrist"; [1 John 4:3] and whosoever does not confess the testimony of the cross, is of the devil; and whosoever perverts the oracles of the Lord to his own lusts, and says that there is neither a resurrection nor a judgment, he is the first-born of Satan. Wherefore, forsaking the vanity of many, and their false doctrines, let us return to the word which has been handed down to us from the beginning; "watching unto prayer," [1 Peter 4:7] and persevering in fasting; beseeching in our supplications the all-seeing God "not to lead us into temptation," [Matt 6:13; 26:41] as the Lord has said: "The spirit truly is willing, but the flesh is weak" [Matt 26:41; Mark 14:38].

Chapter 8. Persevere in hope and patience

Let us then continually persevere in our hope, and the earnest of our righteousness, which is Jesus Christ, "who bore our sins in His own body on the tree," [1 Pet 2:24] "who did no sin, neither was guile found in His mouth," [1 Pet 2:22] but endured all things for us, that we might live in Him. Let us then be imitators of His patience; and if we suffer for His name's sake, let us glorify Him. For He has set us this example in Himself, and we have believed that such is the case.

Chapter 9. Patience inculcated

I exhort you all, therefore, to yield obedience to the word of righteousness, and to exercise all patience, such as you have seen [set] before your eyes, not only in the case of the blessed Ignatius, and Zosimus, and Rufus, but also in others among yourselves, and in Paul himself, and the rest of the apostles. [This do] in the assurance that all these have not run in vain, but in faith and righteousness, and that they are [now] in their due place in the presence of the Lord, with whom also they suffered. For they loved not this present world, but Him who died for us, and for our sakes was raised again by God from the dead.

Chapter 10. Exhortation to the practice of virtue

Stand fast, therefore, in these things, and follow the example of the Lord, being firm and unchangeable in the faith, loving the brotherhood, and being attached to one another, joined together in the truth, exhibiting the meekness of the Lord in your interaction with one another, and despising no one. When you can do good, do not defer it, because "alms delivers from death" [Tobit 4:10, 12:9]. All of you, be subject one to another "having your conduct blameless among the Gentiles" [1 Pet 2:12], that you may both receive praise for your good works, and the Lord may not be blasphemed through you. But woe to him by whom the name of the Lord is blasphemed! Teach, therefore, sobriety to all, and manifest it also in your own conduct....

Chapter 12. Exhortation to various graces

For I trust that you are well versed in the Sacred Scriptures, and that nothing is hid from you; but to me this privilege is not yet granted. It is declared then in these Scriptures, "Be angry, and sin not," and, "Let not the sun go down upon your wrath" [Eph 4:26]. Happy is he who remembers this, which I believe to be the case with you. But may the God and Father of our Lord Jesus Christ, and Jesus Christ Himself, who is the Son of God, and our everlasting High Priest, build you up in faith and truth, and in all meekness, gentleness, patience, long-suffering, forbearance, and purity; and may He bestow on you a lot and portion among His saints, and on us with you, and on all that are under heaven, who shall believe in our Lord Jesus Christ, and in His Father, who "raised Him from the dead" [Gal 1:1]. Pray for all the saints. Pray also for kings, and potentates, and princes, and for those that persecute and hate you, and for the enemies of the cross, that your fruit may be manifest to all, and that you may be perfect in Him....

These things I have written to you by Crescens, whom up to the present time I have recommended unto you, and do now recommend. For he has acted blamelessly among us, and I believe also among you. Moreover, you will hold his sister in esteem when she comes to you. Be safe in the Lord Jesus Christ. Grace be with you all. Amen.

The Encyclical Epistle of the Church at Smyrna Concerning the Martyrdom of the Holy Polycarp (c. 155)

Chapter XIV—The prayer of Polycarp

They did not nail him then, but simply bound him. And he, placing his hands behind him, and being bound like a distinguished ram [taken] out of a great flock for sacrifice, and prepared to be an acceptable burnt-offering to God, looked up to heaven, and said, "O Lord God Almighty, the Father of your beloved and blessed Son Jesus Christ, by whom we have received the knowledge of you, the God of angels and powers, and of every creature, and of the whole race of the righteous who live before you, I thank you for counting me worthy of this day and this hour, that I should have a part in the number of your martyrs, in the cup of your Christ, to the resurrection of eternal life, both of soul and body, through the incorruption [imparted] by the Holy Ghost. Among whom may I be accepted this day before you as a fat and acceptable sacrifice, according as you, the ever-truthful God, has foreordained, has revealed beforehand to me, and now has fulfilled. For this reason I also praise you for all things, I bless you, I glorify you, along with the everlasting and heavenly Jesus Christ, your beloved Son, with whom, to you, and the Holy Ghost, be glory both now and to all coming ages. Amen."[1]

---

1. Translations revised for readability.

I. Patristic

A. Before Nicaea (–325)

6. St. Irenaeus of Lyons (d. ca. 202) | *Against Heresies*

We know little of Irenaeus's early years, except that he was born in Asia Minor and likely raised in the city of Smyrna. There, Irenaeus himself reports, he sat under the teaching of Polycarp, the disciple of John the Apostle (*Against Heresies*, 3.3.4).[1] By 175, Irenaeus had moved westward and ascended to the position of Bishop in Lyons (present-day France). Leading the church from a prominent Western city with a faith and mind-set formed in the East, Irenaeus would be an important link between East and West.[2]

As bishop, Irenaeus was responsible for shepherding his flock, contending for the faith in the presence of his pagan neighbors, and responding to false teachings which swirled during the early years of the church. His lengthy treatise *Against Heresies* centers on that task. He sought to show how the teachings of the Valentinians, among others, were inconsistent, even incompatible, with the gospel. Among early Christians, debates about Jesus were never matters of merely "academic" interest. Theologians like Irenaeus had no interest in maintaining tidy abstractions or policing the borders of the church's conceptual apparatus. The gospel was at stake. What Christians believe about the work of God in Christ to redeem sinners and heal creation, Irenaeus understood, leads directly back to what Christians believe about the *person* of Jesus the Messiah.

The teachings of the Valentinians could not be stomached. Jesus was not truly human but only had the *appearance* of humanity, they taught. Their question was this: could God's chosen Messiah be truly and authentically human, that is, human in every way that we are human? The Valentinians could not accept this. Their Gnostic metaphysics simply prevented them from seeing that such a thing could be fitting for God. God's Messiah could not be truly, fully, and authentically human because, they believed, the physical world is tainted and impure. Various groups came and went with similar

---

1. Eusebius says the same in *Ecclesiastical History*, 5.20.5–6.
2. Shelton, "Irenaeus," 18.

views, like the Eutychians, but the objection was always the same (and remains the same today): Christ couldn't be *really* human, not in the same sense that we are human. Against the denial of God's flesh-taking (literally, "incarnation"), Irenaeus sought to keep the church moored to the apostolic witness: "Since, therefore, the children share flesh and blood, he himself likewise shared the same things" (Heb 2:14).

In our selection from *Against Heresies*, Irenaeus puzzles over the question, How can finite, sinful creatures see an infinite and holy God? The Bible repeatedly uses the language of sight to describe one's encounter with God—either in person, or by faith, in this life, and in the next. But how can it be so, given who and what God is and who and what we are? How Irenaeus answers the question says a great deal about his theology of the Christian life. First, we are led to see God *through* the Son. The Son is integral to seeing God, fundamental both to the Christian's life in time and in eternity (see ch. 5). Second, the Spirit of God makes it possible that we might see God: the Spirit "Spirit truly preparing man in the Son of God."

Irenaeus presents a beautifully Trinitarian portrait of life with God in which divine grace sets the Christian unalterably toward the vision of the living God, made possible through the actions of the Son and the Spirit. One cannot see God "on his own powers." Instead, the Son—not the mirage of a human but the *incarnate* Son, Irenaeus worked hard to ensure we remember—"leads" us to the Father and the Spirit "prepares us *in* the Son" (5).

Against Heresies, Book 4, Chapter 20, sections 5–6 (190)

5. These things did the prophets set forth in a prophetical manner; but they did not, as some allege, [proclaim] that He who was seen by the prophets was a different [God], the Father of all being invisible. Yet this is what those [heretics] declare, who are altogether ignorant of the nature of prophecy. For prophecy is a prediction of things future, that is, a setting forth beforehand of those things which shall be afterwards. The prophets, then, indicated beforehand that God should be seen by men; as the Lord also says, "Blessed are the pure in heart, for they shall see God" (Matt 5:8). But in respect to His greatness, and His wonderful glory, "no man shall see God and live" (Exod 33:20), for the Father is incomprehensible; but in regard to His love, and kindness, and as to His infinite power, even this He grants to those who love Him, that is, to see God, which thing the prophets did also predict. "For those things that are impossible with men, are possible with God" (Luke 18:27).

For man does not see God by his own powers; but when He pleases He is seen by men, by whom He wills, and when He wills, and as He wills. For God is powerful in all things, having been seen at that time indeed, prophetically through the Spirit, and seen, too, adoptively through the Son; and He shall also be seen paternally in the kingdom of heaven, the Spirit truly preparing man in the Son of God, and the Son leading him to the Father, while the Father, too, confers [upon him] incorruption for eternal life, which comes to everyone from the fact of his seeing God. For as those who see the light are within the light, and partake of its brilliancy; even so, those who see God are in God, and receive of His splendor. But [His] splendor vivifies them; those, therefore, who see God, do receive life. And for this reason, He, [although] beyond comprehension, and boundless and invisible, rendered Himself visible, and comprehensible, and within the capacity of those who believe, that He might vivify those who receive and behold Him through faith. For as His greatness is past finding out, so also His goodness is beyond expression; by which having been seen, He bestows life upon those who see Him. It is not possible to live apart from life, and the means of life is found in fellowship with God; but fellowship with God is to know God, and to enjoy His goodness.

6. Men therefore shall see God, that they may live, being made immortal by that sight, and attaining even unto God; which, as I have already said, was declared figuratively by the prophets, that God should be seen by men who bear His Spirit [in them], and do always wait patiently for His coming. As also Moses says in Deuteronomy, "We shall see in that day that God will talk to man, and he shall live"(Deut 5:24). For certain of these men used to see the prophetic Spirit and His active influences poured forth for all kinds of gifts; others, again, [beheld] the advent of the Lord, and that dispensation which obtained from the beginning, by which He accomplished the will of the Father with regard to things both celestial and terrestrial; and others [beheld] paternal glories adapted to the times, and to those who saw and who heard them then, and to all who were subsequently to hear them.

Thus, therefore, was God revealed; for God the Father is shown forth through all these [operations], the Spirit indeed working, and the Son ministering, while the Father was approving, and man's salvation being accomplished. As He also declares through Hosea the prophet: "I," He says, "have multiplied visions, and have used similitudes by the ministry (*in manibus*) of the prophets" (Hos 12:10). But the apostle expounded this very passage, when he said, "Now there are diversities of gifts, but the same Spirit; and there are differences of ministrations, but the same Lord; and there are diversities of operations, but it is the same God which works all in all. But the manifestation of the Spirit is given to every man for the common good" (1 Cor 12: 4–7). But as He who works all things in all is God, [as to the points] of what nature and how great He is, [God] is invisible and indescribable to all things which have been made by Him, but He is by no means unknown: for all things learn through His Word that there is one God the Father, who contains all things, and who grants existence to all, as is written in the Gospel: "No man has seen God at any time, except the only-begotten Son, who is in the bosom of the Father; He has declared [Him]."[3]

3. Translation revised for readability and paragraph breaks inserted.

I. Patristic

A. Before Nicaea (–325)

7. St. Clement of Alexandria (ca. 150–ca. 215) | *Christ the Educator*

Clement was born in the middle of Christianity's second century and was an influential missionary to the educated and wealthy classes of Alexandria. It appears Clement was converted as an adult after a long, intentional quest to understand the Christian faith. His search took him from Athens to Sicily, and then from Syria-Palestine to Alexandria, where he finally settled.

In Alexandria Clement began a school for Christian training (or "catechetical school"). Alexandria was a metropolitan city and fertile soil for the Hellenistic philosophies of the day (e.g., Stoicism and Gnosticism). Fittingly, in *Christ the Educator*, Clement likens the Christian life to the teacher/student relationship. As the head of the catechetical school this would have been a natural, familiar way for Clement to render the Christian life. The pedagogical metaphor may also be serving Clement's persistent effort to present Christian truth *through* the philosophical lenses of his day. Stoicism and Gnosticism were the familiar modes of thought for his educated and wealthy audience, and Clement frequently utilizes them.

Like Christians in every place and time, Clement was compelled to contextualize the Christian faith. Efforts at contextualization fall onto a predictable spectrum. On one end, a theology touches down as lightly as possible on the thought-forms of its setting, and on the other end a theology uses them robustly to teach and persuade. The latter was Clement's approach. From the many citations of Greek philosophers in Clement's writings, it is clear that he is not opposed to Greek philosophy; rather, he leverages it to present Christian teaching. Not unlike the Old Testament, Greek philosophy is for Clement a "way to Christ."[1]

Throughout *Christ the Educator* Clement unflinchingly takes up language, concepts, and modes of thought common to his listeners and then uses the Scriptures to reinterpret and recast them. He leverages Stoic ideals of wisdom and Platonic reasoning to persuade. They become tools in his hands that lead the uncommitted

---

1. Mees, "Clement of Alexandria," 548.

to Christ, their greatest teacher. Does Clement compromise Christian truth by making it captive to the philosophies he uses? Or does using them offer accessible entry points for the uncommitted? These are the perennial questions for any contextual theology like Clement's.

In our selection, we see Clement aligning Stoic wisdom with discipleship (ch. 1) and using Christ to reinterpret the Gnostic emphasis on knowledge. Clement recasts the Gnostic vision of *logos* according to Christ, the true *Logos*—"the all-loving Word (*Logos*)." The allusions to Gnostic terminology and thought would not have been lost on Clement's educated and wealthy students in Alexandra. Clement wants them to see that Jesus is *the Logos* and thus their true teacher. Christ is "the Educator of little ones" who leads us to salvation in God and then progressively conforms us to Christ. Like other patristic theologians, Clement used Christian teaching to transform the Greek idea of education as *paideia*. Thus, the peculiar shape of Christ's *paideia* is never merely the formation of a mind but the conforming of an entire life to the image of Christ.[2]

Christ the Educator (early third century)

Book 1, Chapter 1

O you who are children! An indestructible corner stone of knowledge, holy temple of the great God, has been hewn especially for us as a foundation for the truth. This corner stone is noble persuasion, or the desire for eternal life aroused by an intelligent response to it, laid in the ground of our minds.

For, be it noted, there are these three things in man: habits, deeds, and passions. Of these, habits come under the influence of the word of persuasion, the guide to godliness. This is the word that underlies and supports, like the keel of a ship, the whole structure of the faith. Under its spell, we surrender, even cheerfully, our old ideas, become young again to gain salvation, and sing in the inspired words of the psalm: 'How good is God to Israel, to those who are upright of heart.' As for deeds, they are affected by the word of counsel, and passions are healed by that of consolation.

These three words, however, are but one: the self-same Word who forcibly draws men from their natural, worldly way of life and educates them to the only true salvation: faith in God. That is to say, the heavenly Guide, the Word, once He begins to call men to salvation, takes to Himself the name of persuasion (this sort of appeal, although only one type, is properly given the name of the whole, that is, word, since the whole service of God has a persuasive appeal, instilling in a receptive mind the

---

2. See Young, "*Paideia* and the Myth of Static Dogma."

desire for life now and for the life to come); but the Word also heals and counsels, all at the same time. In fact, He follows up His own activity by encouraging the one He has already persuaded, and particularly by offering a cure for his passions.

Let us call Him, then, by the one title: Educator of little ones, an Educator who does not simply follow behind, but who leads the way, for His aim is to improve the soul, not just to instruct it; to guide to a life of virtue, not merely to one of knowledge. Yet, that same Word does teach. It is simply that in this work we are not considering Him in that light. As Teacher, He explains and reveals through instruction, but as Educator He is practical. First He persuades men to form habits of life, then He encourages them to fulfill their duties by laying down clear-cut counsels and by holding up, for us who follow, examples of those who have erred in the past. Both are most useful: the advice, that it may be obeyed; the other, given in the form of example, has a twofold object either that we may choose the good and imitate it or condemn and avoid the bad.

Healing of the passions follows as a consequence. The Educator strengthens souls with the persuasion implied in these examples, and then He gives the nourishing, mild medicine, so to speak, of His loving counsels to the sick man that he may come to a full knowledge of the truth. Health and knowledge are not the same; one is a result of study, the other of healing. In fact, if a person is sick, he cannot master any of the things taught him until he is first completely cured. We give instructions to someone who is sick for an entirely different reason than we do to someone who is learning; the latter, we instruct that he may acquire knowledge, the first, that he may regain health. Just as our body needs a physician when it is sick, so, too, when we are weak, our soul needs the Educator to cure its ills. Only then does it need the Teacher to guide it and develop its capacity to know, once it is made pure and capable of retaining the revelation of the Word.

Therefore, the all-loving Word, anxious to perfect us in a way that leads progressively to salvation, makes effective use of an order well adapted to our development; at first, He persuades, then He educates, and after all this He teaches. . . .

Chapter 7

We have now shown that not only does Scripture call all of us children, but also it figuratively calls us who follow Christ, little ones, and that the only perfect being is the Father of all (in fact, the Son is in Him, and the Father is in the Son). If we would follow right order, we should now speak of the Educator of little ones and explain who He is.

He is called Jesus. On occasion, He speaks of Himself as a Shepherd, as when He says: 'I am the Good Shepherd.' In keeping with this metaphor of shepherds leading their sheep, He leads His children, the Shepherd with the care of His little ones. The little ones, in their simplicity, are given the figurative name of sheep; 'And there shall be one sheep-fold,' He says, 'and one Shepherd.'

Therefore, the Word who leads us His children to salvation is unquestionably an Educator of little ones. . . . The material He educates us in is fear of God, for this fear instructs, us in the service of God, educates to the knowledge of truth, and guides by a path leading straight up to heaven.

Education is a word used in many different senses. There is education in the sense of the one who is being led and instructed; there is, that of the one who leads and gives instruction; and thirdly, there is education in the sense of the guidance itself; and finally, the things that are taught, such as precepts. The education that God gives is the imparting of the truth that will guide us correctly to the contemplation of God, and a description of holy deeds that endure forever. Just as the general directs a line of battle with the safety of his soldiers in mind, and as the helmsman pilots his ship conscious of his responsibility for the lives of his passengers, so the Educator, in his concern for us, leads His children along a way of life that ensures salvation. In brief, all that we could reasonably ask God to do for us is within the reach of those who trust in the Educator of little ones. Again, just as the helmsman does not always sail with the wind, but sometimes when there is a squall, sets his prow head on against it, so, too, the Educator never falls in with the winds sweeping through this world, nor does He suffer His children to be driven like a ship into a wild and unregulated course of life. Rather, assisted only by the favorable breeze of the Spirit of truth, He holds steadfastly to the rudder, that is, the hearing of His children, until He brings them safely to anchor in the port of heaven. . . .

Chapter 12

From the subjects that we have already discussed it must be concluded that Jesus, our Educator, has outlined for us the true life, and that He educates the man who abides in Christ. His character is not excessively fear-inspiring, yet neither is it overindulgent in its kindness. He imposes commands, but at the same time expresses them in such a way that we can fulfill them.

It seems to me that the reason that He formed man from dust with His own hands, gave him a second birth through water, increase through the Spirit, education by the Word, thereby guiding him surely to the adoption of sons and to salvation with holy precepts, was precisely that He might transform an earth-born man into a holy and heavenly creature by His coming, and accomplish the original divine command: 'Let us make mankind in our image and likeness.' It is Christ, in fact, who is, in all its perfection, what God then commanded; other men are so only by a certain Image.

As for us, children of a good Father, flock of a good Educator, let us fulfill the will of the Father, let us obey the Word, and let us be truly molded by the saving life of the Savior. Then, since we shall already be living the life of heaven which makes us divine, let us anoint ourselves with the never-failing oil of gladness, the incorruptible oil of good odor. We possess an unmistakable model of incorruptibility in the life of the Lord and are following in the footsteps of God.

His main concern is to consider the way and the means by which the life of man might be made more conformable to salvation. He does truly make this His concern. He seeks to train us to the condition of a wayfarer, that is, to make us well girded and unimpeded by provisions, that we might be self-sufficient of life and practice a moderate frugality in our journey toward the good life of eternity, telling us that each one of us is to be his own storehouse: 'Do not be anxious about tomorrow.' He means to say that he who has dedicated himself to Christ ought to be self-sufficient and his own servant and, besides, live his life from day to day.

We are educated not for war but for peace. In war, there is need for much equipment, just as self-indulgence craves an abundance. But peace and love, simple and plain blood sisters, do not need arms nor abundant supplies. Their nourishment is the Word, the Word whose leadership enlightens and educates, from whom we learn poverty and humility and all that goes with love of freedom and of mankind and of the good. In a word, through Him we become like God by a likeness of virtue. Labor, then, and do not grow weary; you will become what you dare not hope or cannot imagine.

As there is one sort of training for philosophers, another for orator and another for wrestlers, so, too, there is an excellent disposition imparted by the education of Christ that is proper to the free will loving the good. As for deeds, walking and reclining at table, eating and sleeping, marriage relations and the manner of life, the whole of a man's education all become illustrious as holy deeds under the influence of the Educator. The education He gives is not overstrained, but in harmony [with man's needs]. That is why the Word is called Savior, because He has left men remedies of reason to effect understanding and salvation, and because, awaiting the favorable opportunity, He corrects evil, diagnoses the cause for passion, extracts the roots of unreasonable lusts, advises what we should avoid, and applies all the remedies of salvation to those who are sick.

This is the greatest and most noble of all God's acts: saving mankind. But those who labor under some sickness are dissatisfied if the physician prescribes no remedy to restore their health; how, then, can we withhold our sincerest gratitude from the divine Educator when He corrects the acts of disobedience that sweep us on to ruin and uproots the desires that drag us into sin, refusing to be silent and connive at them, and even offers counsels on the right way to live? Certainly we owe Him the deepest gratitude.

Do we say, then, that the rational animal, I mean man, ought to do anything besides contemplate the divinity? I maintain that he ought to contemplate human nature, also, and live as the truth leads him, admiring the way in which the Educator and His precepts are worthy of one another and adapted one to the other. In keeping with such a model, we ought also to adapt ourselves to our Educator, conform our deeds to the Word, and then we will truly live.

I. Patristic

A. Before Nicaea (–325)

8. Origen (ca. 184–253) | *Commentary on Romans* & *On First Principles*

Origen lived and died during a time in the Roman Empire when Christian persecution broke out frequently and severely. His father Leonides was martyred by the Emperor Severus (202), which left young Origen to support his mother and six brothers. Years later Origen's life ended, broken and battered, after being tortured by the Emperor Decius. It was Origen's denial of the faith the Emperor sought. It would have been a massive blow to the church, but Origen would not relent. His father gave his life for the faith, and Origen did no less.

It should hardly surprise that Origen's approach to theology and biblical interpretation was influenced by the thought-forms of his day. Origen was exceedingly well-educated, and his theology developed in conversation with his culture's philosophical systems. However, describing himself as a "man of the church" (Homily 16), Origen was not purely a philosopher. He tried, like Clement of Alexandria before him and St. Augustine after him, to utilize the best of pagan thought for the sake of Christian teaching and worship. The avenues through which Origen sought to make that confession are astounding. Perhaps the most prolific author of antiquity, Christian or pagan, his works include doctrinal theology, scores of biblical commentaries, hundreds of sermons, and several apologetic works. For example, in response to Jewish and pagan critics of the Christian faith, Origen translated the entire Old Testament in six parallel columns: one in Hebrew and five in various Greek renderings (known as the *Hexapla*). A translation such as this would have been a life's work, but he also composed an eight-volume response to the objections of the philosopher Celsus (*Contra Celsum*).

Like other influential apologists, Origen sought to demonstrate the truth of Christian belief in conversation with his culture's habits of thought and philosophy. Despite the volume of his achievements, he was controversial in his time and remains so even today. He drew criticism from his contemporaries both for the manner in which he closely wedded Christian belief with pagan philosophy and for his interpretations of Scripture. He could not overcome his critics and was condemned as a heretic at the Council of Constantinople (AD 553). His condemnation did not, however, cause Origen to be forgotten. During the Reformation Luther and Erasmus quarrelled over Origin, and today theologians, biblical scholars, and philosophers still gather to discuss his work.

Origen's view of the Christian life is wound around Scripture, conversant with actual Christian experience, and robustly doctrinal. In the selections that follow, all three facets appear. First, in the course of interpreting passages from Romans 6, Origen shows that the Christian life is life inextricably bound to the Holy Spirit. His reading of Scripture is both straightforward and evocative. Second, we also find the spiritual, or practical, dimensions of the Christian life. Life in Christ is a *genuine* battle. The conflict between desires of "the flesh" and the Spirit's desires not an illusion. An actual battle is being waged in which the Christian's real act of the will is required. Contrary to the Stoics, Origen is no fatalist: "everyone has it within his own power" to pay allegiance to the Spirit (notice his reference to the stars). Third, in the excerpt from *On First Principles*, Origen frames the Christian life in doctrinal terms. The Trinity sets the terms for understanding the Christian life: from the Father we have existence, from the Son we have reason, and from the Spirit the grace to be holy.

Commentary on Romans (Book 6) (early 3rd century)

Romans 6:12-14—"Therefore, do not let sin exercise dominion in your mortal body to make you obey its desires. And do not present your members to sin as weapons of wickedness; but present yourselves to God as those who are alive from the dead, and your members to God as weapons of righteousness. For sin will have no dominion over you, since you are not under law but under grace"

(3) For all of those things that we have enumerated above as works of the flesh are like a kind of army [of sin], conducting military operations under their king of sin and subject to its law, which is written in the members of the flesh. For it is certain that, in view of the fact that the flesh offers obedience to the desires of sin, "the flesh desires contrary to the Spirit and the Spirit contrary to the flesh; and these are opposed to each other" [Gal 5:17].

(4) But notice that when the Apostle gives the command, saying, "Do not let sin exercise dominion in your mortal body, to make you obey its desires," he is showing that the matter lies within our power, that sin should not exercise dominion in our body. For unless it were in our power that sin should not exercise dominion in us, he would not have given the command at all. So how is it possible for sin not to exercise dominion in our flesh? If we do what the Apostle himself says, "Put to death your

members that are earthly" [Col 3:5], and if "we always carry around in our body the death of Christ" [2 Cor 4:10]. For it is certain that where the death of Christ is being carried around, it is not possible for sin to exercise dominion. For the power of the cross of Christ is so great that when it is placed before the eyes and when it is faithfully retained in one's mind so that the attentive eye of the mind should be fastened on the death of Christ, no [sinful] desire, no lust, no feeling of rage, no sin of envy will be able to get the upper hand; in its presence the entire army of sin and the flesh, which we enumerated above, is at once put to flight. But in fact sin itself does not exist since its substance could not exist except in works and deeds. So then, there is within us both the desire to sin, which has a kingdom in the flesh, and there is also the Spirit's desire, which has a kingdom in the mind, according to what he have said above, "The flesh desires contrary to the Spirit but the Spirit desires contrary to the flesh" [Gal 5:17]. Consequently, when we desire what is not permissible or what is not befitting or what is not profitable, that is the desire of the flesh. But when our soul desires and faints for the time when it may see the salvation of God, that is the desire of the Spirit. . . .

> *Romans 6:19—"I am speaking in human terms because of the weakness of your flesh. For just as you presented your members as slaves to impurity and iniquity leading to unrighteousness, so now present your members as slaves to righteousness leading to sanctification."*

(2) Through these words the Apostle strikes a certain shame upon his hearers, that they might pay out to righteousness and sanctification at least as much obedience as they had previously bestowed on impurity and iniquity. What then could be put in more human terms? I mean, what could be so light, what could be so free from burden, which absolutely no weakness of the flesh can excuse? He says, "Just as you presented your members as slaves to righteousness for sanctification." It is hardly the cause for boasting that one should be a slave to the virtues as much as one is to the vices. For righteousness ought to be esteemed far more and with much more earnestness. But I am behaving, he says, in human and general terms. I demand the same things, I seek similar things [from you]. A little while ago your feet where running off to the temples of demons; now let them run to the Church of God. Previously they were running off to shed blood; now let them run out to save it. Earlier your hands were stretched forth to plunder the property of others; now stretch them forth to lavish your own goods upon others. Previously your eyes were looking around for a woman or some property to lust after; now let them look around for the poor, the weak, the needy, in order to show them mercy. Your ears were formerly thrilled by listening to worthless talk and derogatory remarks about good men; let them now be converted to hearing the word of God, to the explanation of the law, and to receiving wisdom's instruction. Let the tongue, which was accustomed to abuse, cursing, and obscene speech, now be converted to blessing the Lord at all times. Let it bring forth wholesome and sincere speech to that it might give grace to the hearers

and speak truth with its neighbor. But what need is there to pursue every detail? After all, it is perfectly plain to you as well that in each of the members the service a person presented to the vices, should apply to the virtues, and that the impulse that a person presented to uncleanness should now change to chastity and sanctification. It certainly seems that he has named righteousness here for all the virtues together, just as, on the other hand, he set down iniquity for all the vices together. He has of course added, "righteousness [leading to] sanctification," whereby he was plainly commending the part of chastity both in a general way, in conjunction with the other virtues, and, specifically, as a virtue in and of itself. Moreover, observe how everywhere through these matters he notes the freedom of the will and shows that everyone has it within his own power that the services he was previously paying out to iniquity should be paid out to righteousness and sanctification, once one's purpose has been converted to better things. This could not be done at all if one's nature were fighting against this, as some think, or if the course of the stars opposed it.

On First Principles[1] (early 3rd Century)

I.3.8. Having made these declarations regarding the Unity of the Father, and of the Son, and of the Holy Spirit, let us return to the order in which we began the discussion. God the Father bestows upon all, existence; and participation in Christ, in respect of His being the word of reason, renders them rational beings. From which it follows that they are deserving either of praise or blame, because capable of virtue and vice. On this account, therefore, is the grace of the Holy Ghost present, that those beings which are not holy in their essence may be rendered holy by participating in it.

Seeing, then, that firstly, they derive their existence from God the Father; secondly, their rational nature from the Word; thirdly, their holiness from the Holy Spirit,—those who have been previously sanctified by the Holy Spirit are again made capable of receiving Christ, in respect that He is the righteousness of God; and those who have earned advancement to this grade by the sanctification of the Holy Spirit, will nevertheless obtain the gift of wisdom according to the power and working of the Spirit of God. And this I consider is Paul's meaning, when he says that to "some is given the word of wisdom, to others the word of knowledge, according to the same Spirit." And while pointing out the individual distinction of gifts, he refers the whole of them to the source of all things, in the words, "There are diversities of operations, but one God who works all in all" [1 Cor 12:6]. Whence also the working of the Father, which confers existence upon all things, is found to be more glorious and magnificent, while each one, by participation in Christ, as being wisdom, and knowledge, and sanctification, makes progress, and advances to higher degrees of perfection; and seeing it is by partaking of the Holy Spirit that any one is made purer and holier, he

---

1. Paragraph breaks have been inserted for readability.

obtains, when he is made worthy, the grace of wisdom and knowledge, in order that, after all stains of pollution and ignorance are cleansed and taken away, he may make so great an advance in holiness and purity, that the nature which he received from God may become such as is worthy of Him who gave it to be pure and perfect, so that the being which exists may be as worthy as He who called it into existence. For, in this way, he who is such as his Creator wished him to be, will receive from God power always to exist, and to abide forever. That this may be the case, and that those whom He has created may be unceasingly and inseparably present with Him, Who IS, it is the business of wisdom to instruct and train them, and to bring them to perfection by confirmation of His Holy Spirit and unceasing sanctification, by which alone are they capable of receiving God.

In this way, then, by the renewal of the ceaseless working of Father, Son, and Holy Spirit in us, in its various stages of progress, shall we be able at some future time perhaps, although with difficulty, to behold the holy and the blessed life, in which (as it is only after many struggles that we are able to reach it) we ought so to continue, that no satiety of that blessedness should ever seize us; but the more we perceive its blessedness, the more should be increased and intensified within us the longing for the same, while we ever more eagerly and freely receive and hold fast the Father, and the Son, and the Holy Spirit. But if satiety should ever take hold of any one of those who stand on the highest and perfect summit of attainment, I do not think that such an one would suddenly be deposed from his position and fall away, but that he must decline gradually and little by little, so that it may sometimes happen that if a brief lapse take place, and the individual quickly repent and return to himself, he may not utterly fall away, but may retrace his steps, and return to his former place, and again make good that which had been lost by his negligence.

I. Patristic

B. After Nicaea (325–)

9. St. Athanasius of Alexandria (296–373) | *On the Incarnation, Against the Arians, & To Adelphius, Bishop and Confessor*

St. Athanasius of Alexandria was instrumental as the early church sought to articulate its teaching about the divinity of the Incarnate Son. In the third and fourth centuries, the church required greater clarity about its teaching that Jesus was God and thus worthy of worship and devotion. Since the apostles, Christians proclaimed that Jesus was God the Son and had worshipped him as such. Having come face to face with the risen Jesus, the Apostles, like Thomas, declared, "My Lord and my God!" (John 20:28) Jesus was worthy of worship *as God*. It would not be until the fourth century, however, before Christian doctrine caught up with Christian devotion.

What does worshipping Jesus as God entail for the "God-ness" of God the Father to whom Jesus prayed? And what does worshipping Jesus as God require the church to believe regarding his divinity? Is he God in the same way as the Father, or does he share the Father's divinity but remains in some important way still less divine than the Father? This was the interpretation put forward by the bishop Arius, during the second decade of the fourth century. Jesus, according to Arius, was "divine" but not God in the same sense as the Father. Jesus was not, like the Father, uncreated and eternal; and thus not God in the same sense. The questions that occupied Arius and his interlocutors were questions of worship just as much as they were questions about official church teaching: *to whom does the church rightly direct worship and prayer*? They are likewise questions about witness: *to whom does the church point as the source of redemption and reconciliation with God*?

Athanasius's lasting contribution came through his steady and unwavering commitment, despite great hardship, to articulate the authentic presence of God in the person of Jesus. Very little is known of his earliest years. He was raised in Egypt along the banks of the Nile, and he was just a boy during the horrific persecution of the emperor Diocletian. Some accounts of his youth recount stories of him baptizing his playmates along the seashore.[1] Gregory of Nazianzus wrote that he "meditate[d] on every book of the Old and New Testament, with a depth such as none else has applied even to one of them."[2] As a teenager, he prepared for ministry by living in the home of the Bishop of Alexandria who brought young Athanasius as his secretary to the First Council of Nicaea. The bishops joined in Nicaea to address the teaching of Arius (325) and drafted the following confession of Jesus' divinity: "God of God, light from light, true God of true God, begotten not made, of the same substance as the Father, through whom all things were made." Three years after the Council, when Athanasius was around thirty years old, he was ordained bishop of Alexandria.

Athanasius's most well-known work is the treatise *On the Incarnation,* in which he defends the teaching of the apostles that the bishops at Nicaea summarized in the Creed. The date of its composition is not clear. If he penned it before Nicaea, then it served as a guiding document for the Council, and if it was composed after the Council, then it was an articulate expression of their decision.[3] *On the Incarnation* has stood for millennia as a concise and eloquent statement of orthodox Christology. What does it mean that the Son of God enfleshed himself for our sake? As Athanasius phrases it, "God became man so that man might become God" (*Incarnation,* 54:3). Nothing short of Jesus' full and true divinity could affect such an incredible result.

We include three selections from Athanasius, each with a short introduction. In each selection Athanasius portrays the Christian life in direct connection to the Incarnate Son. He does not set out to offer an account of Christian existence, but his theology of the Son naturally leads to it. This is the general pattern we find throughout the Patristic era.[4]

In the first selection, from *On the Incarnation,* Athanasius cites the Christian life as *evidence* for the divinity and power of Christ. Rather than diminish God's power to save, the incarnation *demonstrates* it in the Christian's life. As Peter Leithart puts it, "God is deathless, and the deified believer no longer fears death."[5] Their life is a "monument to [Christ's] Victory over death and its corruption," writes Athanasius. In and through redeemed existence one sees not merely the Christian herself but Jesus' divinity.

---

1. Rufinus of Aquileia, *Church History,* 10.15.

2. Gregory of Nazianzus, *Oration* 21, 6. Cited in Weinandy, *Athanasius,* 1.

3. For those who place the date after Nicaea, see Barnes, *Athanasius and Constantius,* 12–13, and Camplani, "Athanasius of Alexandria," 276. For the earlier, traditional date see Clifford, "St. Athanasius," para 5.

4. See Fairbairn, *Grace and Christology in the Early Church*; Fairbairn, "Introduction"; Maxwell, "Christology and Grace in the Sixth-Century Latin West," 77-93.

5. Leithart, *Athanasius,* 170.

SECTION I: PATRISTIC

On the Incarnation (c. 318 / 328)

Chapter 5—The Resurrection

... (27) A very strong proof of this destruction of death and its conquest by the cross is supplied by a present fact, namely this. All the disciples of Christ despise death; they take the offensive against it and, instead of fearing it, by the sign of the cross and by faith in Christ trample on it as on something dead. Before the divine sojourn of the Savior, even the holiest of men were afraid of death, and mourned the dead as those who perish. But now that the Savior has raised His body, death is no longer terrible, but all those who believe in Christ tread it underfoot as nothing, and prefer to die rather than to deny their faith in Christ, knowing full well that when they die they do not perish, but live indeed, and become incorruptible through the resurrection. But that devil who of old wickedly exulted in death, now that the pains of death are loosed, he alone it is who remains truly dead. There is proof of this too; for men who, before they believe in Christ, think death horrible and are afraid of it, once they are converted despise it so completely that they go eagerly to meet it, and themselves become witnesses of the Savior's resurrection from it. Even children hasten thus to die, and not men only, but women train themselves by bodily discipline to meet it. So weak has death become that even women, who used to be taken in by it, mock at it now as a dead thing robbed of all its strength. Death has become like a tyrant who has been completely conquered by the legitimate monarch; bound hand and foot the passers-by sneer at him, hitting him and abusing him, no longer afraid of his cruelty and rage, because of the king who has conquered him. So has death been conquered and branded for what it is by the Savior on the cross. It is bound hand and foot, all who are in Christ trample it as they pass and as witnesses to Him deride it, scoffing and saying, "O Death, where is thy victory? O Grave, where is thy sting?"

(28) Is this a slender proof of the impotence of death, do you think? Or is it a slight indication of the Savior's victory over it, when boys and young girls who are in Christ look beyond this present life and train themselves to die? Everyone is by nature afraid of death and of bodily dissolution; the marvel of marvels is that he who is enfolded in the faith of the cross despises this natural fear and for the sake of the cross is no longer cowardly in face of it. The natural property of fire is to burn. Suppose, then, that there was a substance such as the Indian asbestos is said to be, which had no fear of being burnt, but rather displayed the impotence of the fire by proving itself unburnable. If anyone doubted the truth of this, all he need do would be to wrap himself up in the substance in question and then touch the fire. Or, again, to revert to our former figure, if anyone wanted to see the tyrant bound and helpless, who used to be such a terror to others, he could do so simply by going into the country of the tyrant's conqueror. Even so, if anyone still doubts the conquest of death, after so many proofs and so many martyrdoms in Christ and such daily scorn of death by His truest servants, he certainly does well to marvel at so great a thing, but he must not be obstinate in

unbelief and disregard of plain facts. No, he must be like the man who wants to prove the property of the asbestos, and like him who enters the conqueror's dominions to see the tyrant bound. He must embrace the faith of Christ, this disbeliever in the conquest of death, and come to His teaching. Then he will see how impotent death is and how completely conquered. Indeed, there have been many former unbelievers and deriders who, after they became believers, so scorned death as even themselves to become martyrs for Christ's sake.

(29) If, then, it is by the sign of the cross and by faith in Christ that death is trampled underfoot, it is clear that it is Christ Himself and none other Who is the Archvictor over death and has robbed it of its power. Death used to be strong and terrible, but now, since the sojourn of the Savior and the death and resurrection of His body, it is despised; and obviously it is by the very Christ Who mounted on the cross that it has been destroyed and vanquished finally. When the sun rises after the night and the whole world is lit up by it, nobody doubts that it is the sun which has thus shed its light everywhere and driven away the dark. Equally clear is it, since this utter scorning and trampling down of death has ensued upon the Savior's manifestation in the body and His death on the cross, that it is He Himself Who brought death to nought and daily raises monuments to His victory in His own disciples. How can you think otherwise, when you see men naturally weak hastening to death, unafraid at the prospect of corruption, fearless of the descent into Hades, even indeed with eager soul provoking it, not shrinking from tortures, but preferring thus to rush on death for Christ's sake, rather than to remain in this present life? If you see with your own eyes men and women and children, even, thus welcoming death for the sake of Christ's religion, how can you be so utterly silly and incredulous and maimed in your mind as not to realize that Christ, to Whom these all bear witness, Himself gives the victory to each, making death completely powerless for those who hold His faith and bear the sign of the cross? No one in his senses doubts that a snake is dead when he sees it trampled underfoot, especially when he knows how savage it used to be; nor, if he sees boys making fun of a lion, does he doubt that the brute is either dead or completely bereft of strength. These things can be seen with our own eyes, and it is the same with the conquest of death. Doubt no longer, then, when you see death mocked and scorned by those who believe in Christ, that by Christ death was destroyed, and the corruption that goes with it resolved and brought to end.

(30) What we have said is, indeed, no small proof of the destruction of death and of the fact that the cross of the Lord is the monument to His victory. But the resurrection of the body to immortality, which results henceforward from the work of Christ, the common Savior and true Life of all, is more effectively proved by facts than by words to those whose mental vision is sound. For, if, as we have shown, death was destroyed and everybody tramples on it because of Christ, how much more did He Himself first trample and destroy it in His own body! Death having been slain by Him, then, what other issue could there be than the resurrection of

His body and its open demonstration as the monument of His victory? How could the destruction of death have been manifested at all, had not the Lord's body been raised? But if anyone finds even this insufficient, let him find proof of what has been said in present facts. Dead men cannot take effective action; their power of influence on others lasts only till the grave. Deeds and actions that energize others belong only to the living. Well, then, look at the facts in this case. The Savior is working mightily among men, every day He is invisibly persuading numbers of people all over the world, both within and beyond the Greek-speaking world, to accept His faith and be obedient to His teaching. Can anyone, in face of this, still doubt that He has risen and lives, or rather that He is Himself the Life? Does a dead man prick the consciences of men, so that they throw all the traditions of their fathers to the winds and bow down before the teaching of Christ? If He is no longer active in the world, as He must needs be if He is dead, how is it that He makes the living to cease from their activities, the adulterer from his adultery, the murderer from murdering, the unjust from avarice, while the profane and godless man becomes religious? If He did not rise, but is still dead, how is it that He routs and persecutes and overthrows the false gods, whom unbelievers think to be alive, and the evil spirits whom they worship? For where Christ is named, idolatry is destroyed and the fraud of evil spirits is exposed; indeed, no such spirit can endure that Name, but takes to flight on sound of it. This is the work of One Who lives, not of one dead; and, more than that, it is the work of God. It would be absurd to say that the evil spirits whom He drives out and the idols which He destroys are alive, but that He Who drives out and destroys, and Whom they themselves acknowledge to be Son of God, is dead.

(31) In a word, then, those who disbelieve in the resurrection have no support in facts, if their gods and evil spirits do not drive away the supposedly dead Christ. Rather, it is He Who convicts them of being dead. We are agreed that a dead person can do nothing: yet the Savior works mightily every day, drawing men to religion, persuading them to virtue, teaching them about immortality, quickening their thirst for heavenly things, revealing the knowledge of the Father, inspiring strength in face of death, manifesting Himself to each, and displacing the irreligion of idols; while the gods and evil spirits of the unbelievers can do none of these things, but rather become dead at Christ's presence, all their ostentation barren and void. By the sign of the cross, on the contrary, all magic is stayed, all sorcery confounded, all the idols are abandoned and deserted, and all senseless pleasure ceases, as the eye of faith looks up from earth to heaven. Whom, then, are we to call dead? Shall we call Christ dead, Who effects all this? But the dead have not the faculty to effect anything. Or shall we call death dead, which effects nothing whatever, but lies as lifeless and ineffective as are the evil spirits and the idols? The Son of God, "living and effective," is active every day and effects the salvation of all; but death is daily proved to be stripped of all its strength, and it is the idols and the evil spirits who are dead, not He. No room for doubt remains, therefore, concerning the resurrection of His body.

Indeed, it would seem that he who disbelieves this bodily rising of the Lord is ignorant of the power of the Word and Wisdom of God. If He took a body to Himself at all, and made it His own in pursuance of His purpose, as we have shown that He did, what was the Lord to do with it, and what was ultimately to become of that body upon which the Word had descended? Mortal and offered to death on behalf of all as it was, it could not but die; indeed, it was for that very purpose that the Savior had prepared it for Himself. But on the other hand it could not remain dead, because it had become the very temple of Life. It therefore died, as mortal, but lived again because of the Life within it; and its resurrection is made known through its works.

(32) It is, indeed, in accordance with the nature of the invisible God that He should be thus known through His works; and those who doubt the Lord's resurrection because they do not now behold Him with their eyes, might as well deny the very laws of nature. They have ground for disbelief when works are lacking; but when the works cry out and prove the fact so clearly, why do they deliberately deny the risen life so manifestly shown? Even if their mental faculties are defective, surely their eyes can give them irrefragable proof of the power and Godhead of Christ. A blind man cannot see the sun, but he knows that it is above the earth from the warmth which it affords; similarly, let those who are still in the blindness of unbelief recognize the Godhead of Christ and the resurrection which He has brought about through His manifested power in others. Obviously He would not be expelling evil spirits and despoiling idols, if He were dead, for the evil spirits would not obey one who was dead. If, on the other hand, the very naming of Him drives them forth, He clearly is not dead; and the more so that the spirits, who perceive things unseen by men, would know if He were so and would refuse to obey Him. But, as a matter of fact, what profane persons doubt, the evil spirits know—namely that He is God; and for that reason they flee from Him and fall at His feet, crying out even as they cried when He was in the body, "We know Thee Who Thou art, the Holy One of God," and, "Ah, what have I in common with Thee, Thou Son of God? I implore Thee, torment me not."

Both from the confession of the evil spirits and from the daily witness of His works, it is manifest, then, and let none presume to doubt it, that the Savior has raised His own body, and that He is very Son of God, having His being from God as from a Father, Whose Word and Wisdom and Whose Power He is. He it is Who in these latter days assumed a body for the salvation of us all, and taught the world concerning the Father. He it is Who has destroyed death and freely graced us all with incorruption through the promise of the resurrection, having raised His own body as its first-fruits, and displayed it by the sign of the cross as the monument to His victory over death and its corruption.

SECTION I: PATRISTIC

Against the Arians (360–365)

The controversy concerning Christ's divinity raged on after the first council of Nicaea (325). In fact, for a long while the tide turned in the favor of Arius and his followers and against Athanasius. Athanasius was exiled five times by four different emperors, spending seventeen of his forty-five years as bishop of Alexandria in exile.

This selection is from Athanasius's treatise, *Four Discourses Against the Arians*, written to refute Arian interpretation of Scripture according to the *regula fidei* (rule of faith). It is important to notice that here again Athanasius's view of the Christian life appears *in the midst of* Christology. Addressing Christ's divinity naturally leads him to portray redeemed existence, rather than treating the Christian life in isolation from other doctrines. Athanasius understands the Christian life as "deification" (or *theosis*), which does not mean the person becomes God—a Christian theologian would never consider the possibility. Rather, through faith and baptism a Christian shares or participates in Christ's relation to the Father. Through their relation to God the Son they "*become partakers of the divine nature*" (2 Pet 1:4). This is why the divinity of God the Son is paramount for Athanasius. The deification of the Christian is understandable only in terms of the deification of Jesus. Athanasius, in a startlingly strong expression, even says that Jesus' deification is so complete, so total, that with him, who is the Word, the Christian herself is made "Word" (*logos*) (III.26.33).[6]

Discourse I, Ch.11

37. But since they allege the divine oracles and force on them a misinterpretation, according to their private sense, it becomes necessary to meet them just so far as to vindicate these passages, and to show that they bear an orthodox sense, and that our opponents are in error.

...

45. But since He Himself is said to be 'exalted,' and God 'gave' Him, and the heretics think this a defect or affection in the essence of the Word, it becomes necessary to explain how these words are used. He is said to be exalted from the lower parts of the earth, because death is ascribed even to Him. Both events are reckoned His, since it was His Body, and none other's, that was exalted from the dead and taken up into heaven. And again, the Body being His, and the Word not being external to it, it is natural that when the Body was exalted, He, as man, should, because of the body, be

---

6. See also Athanasius, *On the Incarnation*: "God became man so that man might become God" (54.3).

spoken of as exalted. If then He did not become man, let this not be said of Him: but if the Word became flesh, of necessity the resurrection and exaltation, as in the case of a man, must be ascribed to Him, that the death which is ascribed to Him may be a redemption of the sin of men and an abolition of death, and that the resurrection and exaltation may for His sake remain secure for us. In both respects he hath said of Him, 'God hath highly exalted Him,' and 'God hath given to Him'; that herein moreover he may show that it is not the Father that hath become flesh, but it is His Word, who has become man, and receives after the manner of men from the Father, and is exalted by Him, as has been said. And it is plain, nor would any one dispute it, that what the Father gives, He gives through the Son. And it is marvelous and overwhelming verily; for the grace which the Son gives from the Father, that the Son Himself is said to receive; and the exaltation, which the Son bestows from the Father, with that the Son is Himself exalted. For He who is the Son of God, became Himself the Son of Man; and, as Word, He gives from the Father, for all things which the Father does and gives, He does and supplies through Him; and as the Son of Man, He Himself is said after the manner of men to receive what proceeds from Him, because His Body is none other than His, and is a natural recipient of grace, as has been said. For He received it as far as His man's nature was exalted; which exaltation was its being deified. But such an exaltation the Word Himself always had according to the Father's Godhead and perfection, which was His.

Discourse II.21

Texts explained; Sixthly, Proverbs viii. 22. Proverbs are of a figurative nature, and must be interpreted as such. We must interpret them, and in particular this passage, by the Regula Fidei. 'He created me' not equivalent to 'I am a creature.' Wisdom a creature so far forth as Its human body. Again, if He is a creature, it is as 'a beginning of ways,' an office which, though not an attribute, is a consequence, of a higher and divine nature. And it is 'for the works,' which implied the works existed, and therefore much more He, before He was created. Also 'the Lord' not the Father 'created' Him, which implies the creation was that of a servant. . . .

70. . . . Whence the truth shows us that the Word is not of things originate, but rather Himself their Framer. For therefore did He assume the body originate and human, that having renewed it as its Framer, He might deify it in Himself, and thus might introduce us all into the kingdom of heaven after His likeness. For man had not been deified if joined to a creature, or unless the Son were very God; nor had man been brought into the Father's presence, unless He had been His natural and true Word who had put on the body. And as we had not been delivered from sin and the curse, unless it had been by nature human flesh, which the Word put on (for we should have had nothing common with what was foreign), so also the man had not been deified, unless the Word who became flesh had been by nature from the Father

and true and proper to Him. For therefore the union was of this kind, that He might unite what is man by nature to Him who is in the nature of the Godhead, and his salvation and deification might be sure. Therefore let those who deny that the Son is from the Father by nature and proper to His Essence, deny also that He took true human flesh of Mary Ever-Virgin; for in neither case had it been of profit to us men, whether the Word were not true and naturally Son of God, or the flesh not true which He assumed. But surely He took true flesh, though Valentinus rave; yea the Word was by nature Very God, though Ario-maniacs rave; and in that flesh has come to pass the beginning of our new creation, He being created man for our sake, and having made for us that new way, as has been said.

Discourse III.26

... We must recur to the Regula Fidei. Our Lord did not come into, but became, man, and therefore had the acts and affections of the flesh. The same works divine and human. Thus the flesh was purified, and men were made immortal. Reference to I Pet. iv. 1. ...

33. Who will not admire this? or who will not agree that such a thing is truly divine? for if the works of the Word's Godhead had not taken place through the body, man had not been deified; and again, had not the properties of the flesh been ascribed to the Word, man had not been thoroughly delivered from them; but though they had ceased for a little while, as I said before, still sin had remained in him and corruption, as was the case with mankind before Him; and for this reason:—Many for instance have been made holy and clean from all sin; nay, Jeremiah was hallowed [Jer 1:5] even from the womb, and John, while yet in the womb, leapt for joy at the voice of Mary Bearer of God; nevertheless 'death reigned from Adam to Moses, even over those that had not sinned after the similitude of Adam's transgression (Rom 5:14)'; and thus man remained mortal and corruptible as before, liable to the affections proper to their nature. But now the Word having become man and having appropriated what pertains to the flesh, no longer do these things touch the body, because of the Word who has come in it, but they are destroyed by Him, and henceforth men no longer remain sinners and dead according to their proper affections, but having risen according to the Word's power, they abide ever immortal and incorruptible. Whence also, whereas the flesh is born of Mary Bearer of God, He Himself is said to have been born, who furnishes to others an origin of being; in order that He may transfer our origin into Himself, and we may no longer, as mere earth, return to earth, but as being knit into the Word from heaven, may be carried to heaven by Him. Therefore in like manner not without reason has He transferred to Himself the other affections of the body also; that we, no longer as being men, but as proper to the Word, may have share in eternal life. For no longer according to our former origin in Adam do we die; but henceforward our origin and all infirmity of flesh being transferred to the Word, we

rise from the earth, the curse from sin being removed, because of Him who is in us, and who has become a curse for us. And with reason; for as we are all from earth and die in Adam, so being regenerated from above of water and Spirit, in the Christ we are all quickened; the flesh being no longer earthly, but being henceforth made Word, by reason of God's Word who for our sake 'became flesh.'

To Adelphius, Bishop and Confessor: against the Arians (370–371)

Following the same pattern as the last selection, Athanasius's portrayal of the Christian life is here knotted together with his defense of Christ's divinity. Referencing 2 Peter 1:4 he describes the Christian life as deification: "He has become Man, that He might deify us in Himself."

We have read what your piety has written to us, and genuinely approve your piety toward Christ. And above all we glorify God, Who has given you such grace as not only to have right opinions, but also, so far as that is possible, not to be ignorant of the devices of the devil. But we marvel at the perversity of the heretics, seeing that they have fallen into such a pit of impiety that they no longer retain even their senses, but have their understanding corrupted on all sides. . . . For formerly, while denying the Godhead of the only-begotten Son of God, they pretended at any rate to acknowledge His coming in the Flesh. But now, gradually going from bad to worse, they have fallen from this opinion of theirs, and become Godless on all hands, so as neither to acknowledge Him as God, nor to believe that He has become man. For if they believed this they would not have uttered such things as your piety has reported against them. . . .

3. We do not worship a creature. Far be the thought. For such an error belongs to heathens and Arians. But we worship the Lord of Creation, Incarnate, the Word of God. For if the flesh also is in itself a part of the created world, yet it has become God's body. And we neither divide the body, being such, from the Word, and worship it by itself, nor when we wish to worship the Word do we set Him far apart from the Flesh, but knowing, as we said above, that 'the Word was made flesh,' we recognize Him as God also, after having come in the flesh. . . .

4. . . . For Creation does not worship a creature. Nor again did she on account of His Flesh refuse to worship her Lord. But she beheld her maker in the Body, and 'in the Name of Jesus every knee' bowed, yea and 'shall bow, of things in heaven and things on earth and things under the earth, and every tongue shall confess,' whether the Arians approve or no, 'that Jesus is Lord, to the Glory of God the Father' (Phil 2:10, 11). For

the Flesh did not diminish the glory of the Word; far be the thought: on the contrary, it was glorified by Him. Nor, because the Son that was in the form of God took upon Him the form of a servant (Phil 2:6, 7) was He deprived of His Godhead. On the contrary, He is thus become the Deliverer of all flesh and of all creation. And if God sent His Son brought forth from a woman, the fact causes us no shame but contrariwise glory and great grace. For He has become Man, that He might deify us in Himself, and He has been born of a woman, and begotten of a Virgin, in order to transfer to Himself our erring generation, and that we may become henceforth a holy race, and 'partakers of the Divine Nature,' as blessed Peter wrote (2 Pet 1:4). And 'what the law could not do in that it was weak through the flesh, God sending His own Son in the likeness of sinful flesh, and for sin, condemned sin in the flesh' (Rom 8:3). . . . [7]

---

[7]. Translation revised for readability.

I. Patristic

B. After Nicaea (325–)

10. St. Ephrem the Syrian (d. 373) | Hymns on Faith: 14, Nisibene Hymns: 50, & Armenian Hymns: 49

Ephrem was a fourth-century deacon who conveyed theological insight primarily through poetry and hymns. Unlike the previous selections in which the media for theology are letters, biblical commentary, and treatises, Ephrem's primary medium was poetry. His poetry was so beautiful and spiritually rich that his contemporaries called him "Harp of the Spirit."

Two features of Ephrem's theology illuminate his poetry. First, Ephrem had a very developed sense of God's utter and unique difference from created reality. God's transcendence was a refrain particularly emphasized among ancient theologians of the East (also found throughout the Bible, e.g. Isa 6). That being said, in both Eastern and Western traditions of Christian theology, God's transcendence is not the final word about God. God's difference from creation is tightly knitted to his absolute likeness in the incarnation of the Son. Ephrem frequently evokes that mystery through vivid juxtapositions, like the final stanza from the first hymn below.

Second, like Athanasius and other theologians in the Greek tradition, Ephrem understood the Christian life as deification (or *theosis*). Athanasius states it succinctly and directly, "God became man that man would become God" (*On the Incarnation*), while Ephrem refracts the same teaching in verse: "He gave us divinity / we gave Him humanity (Hymns on Faith 17).[1] The Christian is enveloped in God's very life—a reality theologians have always struggled to render with human words. Poetry, however, can evoke what lies *beyond* words.

When both features of Ephrem's theology are taken together, his poetry works as a kind of training in *how to see* the world in light of Christ's incarnation.[2] According to Ephrem, spiritual realities are contained within material realities, but we must train

---

1. Brock, *Hymns on Paradise*, 39.
2. Not unlike icons. See Sigurdson, *Heavenly Bodies*, ch. 6.

the eyes of faith to perceive them.³ This helps explain why Ephrem regularly makes interesting and often surprising comparisons between physical things and their hidden, spiritual significance.

Three poems are selected here that accentuate Ephrem's vision of the Christian life, and each also features Ephrem's habit of comparisons. In the first hymn, no. 14, Ephrem emphasizes the origin of worship in God's *grace*. Worship is—like the Christian life itself—*given by grace*. Imaginatively comparing the life of faith to the wedding at Cana in which the host ran out of wine, Ephrem invites God to "fill my mouth with Your praise."

Hymns on Faith: 14 (4th century)

1. I have invited you, Lord, to a wedding feast of song, but the wine—
the utterance of praise—at our feast has failed (John 2:11ff)
You are the guest you filled the jars with good wine,
fill my mouth with Your praise.

Refrain: Praise to You from all who perceive Your truth.

2. The wine that was in the jars was akin and related to
this eloquent wine that gives birth to praise
seeing that that wine too gave birth to praise
from those who drank it and beheld the wonder.

3. You who are so just, if at a wedding-feast not Your own
You filled six jars with good wine (John 2:6),
do You, at this wedding-feast, fill, not the jars,
but the ten thousand ears with its sweetness.

4. Jesus, You were invited to the wedding-feast of others,
here is Your own pure and fair wedding-feast: gladden Your
    rejuvenated people,
for Your guests too, O Lord, need
Your songs; let Your harp utter!

---

3. Brock, *Hymns*, 74.

5   The soul is Your bride, the body too is Your bridal chamber,
    Your guests are the senses and the thoughts.
    And if a single body is a wedding feast for You,
    how great is Your banquet for the whole church!

6   The holy Moses took the synagogue up on Sinai:
    he made her body shine with garments of white, but her heart (Exod 19:14)
        was dark;
    she played the harlot with the calf, she despised the Exalted (Exod 32:1ff)
        one,
    and so he broke the tablets, the book of her covenant (Exod 32:19).

7   Who has ever seen the turmoil and insult
    of a bride who played false in her own bridal chamber, raising
        her voice?
    When she dwelt in Egypt she learnt it from
    the mistress of Joseph, who cried out and played false (Gen 39:15).

8   The light of the pillar of fire and of the cloud (Num 14:14)
    drew into itself its rays
    like the sun that was eclipsed (Matt 27:45)
    on the day that she cried out, demanding the King, a further
        crime (Mark 15:13).

9   How can my harp, o Lord, ever rest from Your praise?
    How could I ever teach my tongue infidelity?
    Your love has given confidence to my shamefacedness,
    —Yet my will is ungrateful.

10 It is right that man should acknowledge Your divinity,
    it is right for heavenly beings to worship Your humanity;
    the heavenly beings were amazed to see how small You became,
    and earthly ones to see how exalted!

Nisibene Hymns: 50

In hymn no. 50, Ephrem again likens the Christian life to worship, dwelling on Christ as the true Light who makes it possible that we might see God. However, even though one "sees" God through Christ, God remains ever and always beyond our full comprehension. God remains unapproachable and hidden even as he is known through Christ's incarnation.

---

1   While I live I will give praise, and not be as if I had no
        existence;
    I will give praise during my lifetime, and will not be a dead
        man among the living.
    For the man who stands idle is doubly dead,
    the earth that fails to produce defrauds him who tills it.

    Refrain: In You, Lord, may my mouth bear the fruit of praise that
        is acceptable to you.

2   In You, Lord, may my mouth give forth praise out of silence.
    Let not our mouths be barren of praise,
    let not our lips be destitute of confession;
    may the praise of You vibrate within us!

3   Those who are themselves fashioned of dust fashion dust, and
        the earthborn labor on the earth.
    We love our bodies, which are akin to us, of the same origin:
    for our roots are dust
    and our branches bear the fruits of our works.

4   "Take no care for today"—yet we are busy caring for years
        ahead.
    He who cloths all reproves those who weave with the example
        of the lilies (Matt 6:38),
    He who sustains all and gives all things to all men
    rebukes the greedy with the greedy crows (1 Kgs 17:6).

5   Our generation is like a leaf whose time, once it falls is over,
    but though the limit of our life is short, praise can lengthen it,
    for, corresponding to the extent of our love,
    we shall acquire, through praise, life that has no measure.

6   For it is in our Lord that the root of our faith is grafted (cf. Rom 11:17);
though far off, He is still close to us in the fusion of love.
Let the roots of our love be bound up in Him,
let the full extent of His compassion be fused in us.

7   O Lord, may the body be a temple (1 Cor 3:16) for Him who built it,
May the soul be a palace full of praise for its architect!
Let not our body become a hollow cavity,
let our souls not be a harbor of loss.

8   And when the light of this temporal breath flickers out
do You relight in the morning the lantern that was extinguished
    in the night.
The sun arrives and with the warmth of its rising
it revives the frozen and relights what has been extinguished.

9   It is right that we should acknowledge that Light which
    illumines all,
for in the morning, when the sun has gone up, lanterns are
    extinguished,
but this new Sun has performed a new deed (cf. Mal 4:2),
relighting in Sheol the lanterns that had been extinguished.

10   In place of death who has breathed the smell of mortality over
    all,
He who gives life to all exhales a life-giving scent in Sheol
(cf. Ecclesiasticus 24:23)
from His life the dead breath in new life,
and death dies within them.

11   The scent of the buried Elisha who gave life to a dead man (2 Kgs 13:21)
    provides a type for this:
a man dead but a day breathed in life from him who was long
    dead;
the life-giving scent wafted from his bones and entered the
    dead corpse
—a symbol of Him who gives life to all.

SECTION I: PATRISTIC

12   Jesus has elucidated for us the symbols that took place at
         Elisha's grave,
    how from an extinguished lantern a lantern can be relit,
    and how, while lying in the grave he could raise up the fallen,
    himself remaining there, but sending forth a witness to Christ's coming.

13   However much, Lord, I would feel You, it is still not You
         yourself I touch,
    for my mind can touch nothing of Your hiddenness:
    it is just a visible, illumined, image
    that I see in the symbol of You; for all investigation into Your being is hidden.

Armenian Hymns: 49

The Christian's participation in the Eucharist is Ephrem's topic in hymn no. 49. The comparisons throughout the hymn reflect Ephrem's theological conviction that Christ's incarnation makes the material world capable of pointing toward and witnessing to God (who is immaterial). Though God's nature and essence always remain beyond human comprehension, God wills to be known through created things. The mystery of our relationship to God is met in the Eucharist where Christ's "holy Body is broken" (2).

---

1   With feeling let us approach, my brethren,
         that Body which the priest offers us;
    let trembling reside on our lips
         as we receive the Medicine of Salvation.

2   At that moment when the holy Body is broken
         we make memory of His sacrifice:
    the body's every limb should tremble
         at the moment when the Only-begotten is sacrificed.

3   Although it is His symbol that is distributed,
         yet it is right that we should gaze on his death:
    greater than all other moments
         is this moment of His sacrifice.

B. AFTER NICAEA (325–)

4   Let us look on with our inner eye,
       beholding Him as he hangs from the tree;
   let our eyes gaze upon that blood
       which flowed from His side.

5   With both awe and love let us draw near in discernment
        to that Medicine of Life;
   let our heart hold in awe His death,
       let our soul yearn for His Mystery.

6   The Israelite People glorified in that manna
       of which even the uncircumcised ate (Exod 16:35 with Josh 5:2–12);
   how much more should we be exalted by this Bread of Life
       to which even the Watchers do not attain.

7   Sampson was exalted, because he drank
       water from the jaw bone of an ass (Judg 15:15–19);
   how much more should he rejoice
       who has been held worthy of Christ's precious Blood.

8   For the People water gushed forth from the rock
       and they drank and were strengthened (Exod 17:6),
   but from the Tree that was on Golgotha
       for the Peoples a fountain gushed forth.

9   With the blade of the sword of the Cherub
       was the path to the Tree of Life shut off (Gen 3:24),
   but to the Peoples has the Lord of that Tree
       given Himself as food.

10 Whereas Eden's other trees were provided
       for that former Adam to eat,
   for us the very Planter of that Garden
       has become the food for our souls.

11 Whereas we had left that Garden
       along with Adam, as he left it behind,
   now that the sword has been removed by the lance (John 19:34)
       we may return there.

12   The People traversed the river and received circumcision (Josh 5:2-12)
> and took pride because they had eaten unleavened bread;
> how much more splendid are the Peoples
> who have been held worthy of the Body of God!

13   The People consumed the lamb at Egypt
> and the symbol it constituted sanctified that People;
> how much more shall the True Lamb
> give sanctification to the Peoples.

14   When the destroyer beheld the blood upon the doors of the People
> he was frightened away (Exod 12:23),
> how much more shall those be put to shame who speak ill
> of the sign of the Beloved Son, the Anointed One.

15   More than all other times should this moment be
> held in honor in your minds,
> for the Son has descended
> to hover (cf. Gen 1:2) over the table of reconciliation.

16   The bones of the dead who are in Sheol
> now drink the dew of life when they are named,
> being remembered before God
> at this moment.

17   And if the dead received benefit at this time,
> how much more shall the living too receive forgiveness.
> Blessed is He who was immolated by one nation
> for the salvation of all nations.

I. Patristic

B. After Nicaea (325–)

11. St. Cyril of Jerusalem (313–386) | *Catechetical Lecture 21*

Little is known of Cyril's early life, but as an adult he was fully embroiled in the Christological controversies that filled the years between the councils of Nicaea (325) and Constantinople (381). Cyril is not generally known for his contribution to those debates, but he made a lasting mark through a series of celebrated lectures to those preparing for baptism. The lectures come to us as the *Catechetical Lectures*.

The first eighteen of these theological lectures were given during Lent to those who were preparing for baptism. Five more were given to the newly baptized during the week of Easter. The five Easter catecheses were called "mystagogical" for they initiate the newly baptized in the mysteries of the Christian faith ("sacraments"). Having experienced baptism, Cyril believed the newly baptized were now ready for the next stage of their initiation to the Christian life. "I waited for the present season," Cyril said, so that "I might lead you by the hand into the brighter and more fragrant meadow of the Paradise before us" (Lecture 19). Being "led by the hand" is an authoritative image and at the same time a gentle one. It speaks of Cyril's role as a theologian tasked to walk the newly initiated into the practices of living the Christian life.

Our selection is taken from Cyril's lecture "On Chrism" (the anointing with oil that follows baptism). Taking 1 John 2 as his text, Cyril claims that baptism makes the Christian "conformable to the Son of God." Then follows chrism, "Christ's gift of grace" through the Holy Spirit. The gift of chrism is integral to the Christian life for it strengthens Christians as they "press forward by good works" toward Jesus Christ. The Christian life thus *begins* in holiness—one's baptism and anointing—and the *unfolding* of redeemed life tends ever and ever more toward holiness and victory. "Stand against the power of the adversary, and vanquish it, saying, I can do all things through Christ which strengthens me (Phil 4:13)," Cyril writes.

SECTION I: PATRISTIC

Catechetical Lectures (c. 348–350)

Lecture 21. On the Mysteries. III: On Chrism.

1 John 2:20-28—But you have an unction from the Holy One, &c.. . . . that, when He shall appear, we may have confidence, and not be ashamed before Him at His coming.

1. Having been baptized into Christ, and put on Christ [Gal 3:27], you have been made conformable to the Son of God; for God having foreordained us to adoption as sons [Eph 1:5], made us to be conformed to the body of Christ's glory [Phil 3:21]. Having therefore become partakers of Christ [Heb 3:14], you are properly called Christ's, and of you God said, Touch not My Christ's [Ps 105:15], or anointed. Now you have been made Christ's, by receiving the antitype of the Holy Ghost; and all things have been worked in you by imitation, because you are images of Christ. He washed in the river Jordan, and having imparted of the fragrance of His Godhead to the waters, He came up from them; and the Holy Ghost in the fullness of His being lighted on Him, like resting upon like. And to you in like manner, after you had come up from the pool of the sacred streams, there was given an Unction, the antitype of that which Christ was anointed; and this is the Holy Ghost; of whom also the blessed Isaiah, in his prophecy respecting Him, said in the person of the Lord, The Spirit of the Lord is upon Me, because He has anointed Me: He has sent Me to preach glad tidings to the poor [Isa 61:1].

2. For Christ was not anointed by men with oil or material ointment, but the Father having before appointed Him to be the Savior of the whole world, anointed Him with the Holy Ghost, as Peter says, Jesus of Nazareth, whom God anointed with the Holy Ghost [Acts 10:38]. David also the Prophet cried, saying, Your throne, O God, is for ever and ever; a scepter of righteousness is the scepter of Your kingdom; You have loved righteousness and hated iniquity; therefore God even Your God has anointed You with the oil of gladness above Your fellows [Ps 45:6, 7]. And as Christ was in reality crucified, and buried, and raised, and you are in Baptism accounted worthy of being crucified, buried, and raised together with Him in a likeness, so is it with the unction also. As He was anointed with an ideal oil of gladness, that is, with the Holy Ghost, called oil of gladness, because He is the author of spiritual gladness, so you were anointed with ointment, having been made partakers and fellows of Christ.

3. But beware of supposing this to be plain ointment. For as the Bread of the Eucharist, after the invocation of the Holy Ghost, is mere bread no longer, but the Body of Christ, so also this holy ointment is no more simple ointment, nor (so to say) common, after invocation, but it is Christ's gift of grace, and, by the advent of the Holy Ghost, is made fit to impart His Divine Nature. Which ointment is symbolically applied to your forehead and your other senses; and while your body is anointed with the visible ointment, your soul is sanctified by the Holy and life-giving Spirit.

4. And you were first anointed on the forehead, that you might be delivered from the shame, which the first man who transgressed bore about with him everywhere; and that with unveiled face you might reflect as a mirror the glory of the Lord [2 Cor 3:18]. Then on your ears; that you might receive the ears which are quick to hear the Divine Mysteries, of which Isaiah said, The Lord gave me also an ear to hear [Isa 1:4]; and the Lord Jesus in the Gospel, He that has ears to hear let him hear [Matt 11:15]. Then on the nostrils; that receiving the sacred ointment you may say, We are to God a sweet savor of Christ, in them that are saved [2 Cor 2:15]. Afterwards on your breast; that having put on the breast-plate of righteousness, you may stand against the wiles of the devil [Eph 6:14, 11]. For as Christ after His Baptism, and the visitation of the Holy Ghost, went forth and vanquished the adversary, so likewise you, after Holy Baptism and the Mystical Chrism, having put on the whole armor of the Holy Ghost, are to stand against the power of the adversary, and vanquish it, saying, I can do all things through Christ which strengthens me [Phil 4:13].

5. Having been counted worthy of this Holy Chrism, you are called Christians, verifying the name also by your new birth. For before you were deemed worthy of this grace, you had properly no right to this title, but were advancing on your way towards being Christians.

6. Moreover, you should know that in the old Scripture there lies the symbol of this Chrism. For what time Moses imparted to his brother the command of God, and made him High-priest, after bathing in water, he anointed him; and Aaron was called Christ or Anointed, evidently from the typical Chrism. So also the High-priest, in advancing Solomon to the kingdom, anointed him after he had bathed in Gihon [1 Kgs 1:39]. To them however these things happened in a figure, but to you not in a figure, but in truth; because you were truly anointed by the Holy Ghost. Christ is the beginning of your salvation; for He is truly the First-fruit, and you the mass [Rom 11:16]; but if the First-fruit be holy, it is manifest that Its holiness will pass to the mass also.

7. Keep This unspotted: for it shall teach you all things, if it abide in you, as you have just heard declared by the blessed John, discoursing much concerning this Unction [1 John 2:20]. For this holy thing is a spiritual safeguard of the body, and salvation of the soul. Of this the blessed Isaiah prophesying of old time said, And on this mountain,—(now he calls the Church a mountain elsewhere also, as when he says, In the last days the mountain of the Lord's house shall be manifest [Isa 2:2];)—on this mountain shall the Lord make for all nations a feast; they shall drink wine, they shall drink gladness, they shall anoint themselves with ointment [Isa 25:6]. And that he may make you sure, hear what he says of this ointment as being mystical; Deliver all these things to the nations, for the counsel of the Lord is for all nations [Isa 5:7]. Having been anointed, therefore, with this holy ointment, keep it unspotted and unblemished in you, pressing forward by good works, and being made well-pleasing to the Captain of your salvation, Christ Jesus, to whom be glory for ever and ever. Amen.[1]

---

1. Translation revised for readability.

I. Patristic

B. After Nicaea (325–)

12. The Desert Fathers and Mothers | *Sayings and Lives*

In the same century that the church, just emerging from public opprobrium, powerlessness, and martyrdom, worked her way to a marriage with the Roman Empire and to social respectability, something extraordinary happened in the deserts of Egypt and Syria: the withdrawal of many men and women from participation in common civic life, in order to seek God in self-denial, prayer, and charity in the wilderness. Louis Bouyer elucidates the significance to the Christian memory of this return to the "desert" themes of Scripture:

> Monasticism and martyrdom—'martyr' let us recall, in Greek, merely signifies 'witness' and nothing more—are but one and the same thing. Monasticism arose in the Church at the very moment, at the end of the Third and beginning of the Fourth century, when martyrdom was disappearing. Monasticism is nothing else than martyrdom reappearing under a new form required by altered circumstances. In the beginning, the Church stood full in open conflict with the world. Then the world seemed to make its peace with her. But could the Church, will she ever be able, to make her peace with it? Certainly not, if with Holy Scripture we understand the 'world' in the sense we were speaking of it just now. But if the world no longer outwardly forces the Church into the contest, it is the Church who, interiorly, must take the contest upon herself. Here on earth, indeed, she could not cease to be militant, that is, combatant. For the Church to compromise with the world, to accept deliverance from conflict with relief, would be to renounce forever the chance of eventual triumph.[1]

An extensive literature documented this movement, bequeathing a nostalgic memory of a lost springtime in later ages in the church, especially in the monastic life. Poignantly the last of these writings, the Spiritual Meadow, records the travelogue of two companions who toured the monastic world of the Near East in the 590s. One of

---

1. Bouyer, *The Meaning of Monastic Life*, 54.

them was the Sophronius who became patriarch of Jerusalem, and had the sorrow of admitting into the city the conqueror Omar in 637. It was the beginning of the historical passion and attrition of Near Eastern Christianity.

Here we select a few "sayings" from this literature. This is a very spare, aphoristic, and gnomic genre, making its spiritual punch with a great concision of words.

Sayings and Lives (4th through 6th centuries)

Life of Paul the First Hermit

... Paul set the door open. And the two embraced each other, and greeted one another by their names, and together they returned thanks to God. After the holy kiss, Paul sat down next to Antony and began to speak, 'Behold him whom you have sought with so much labor, a shaggy white head and limbs worn out with age. Behold, you look upon a man who is soon to be dust. Yet, because *love endures all things* (1 Cor 13:7), tell me, I pray, how fares it with the human race? Are new roofs risen in the ancient cities? Whose empire now holds sway in the world? Are there any that still survive, snared in the error of the demons?' ...

History of the Monks of Egypt

... And after these things, Paphnutius lived one more day in the body. When certain priests came to visit him, he made known to them all that the Lord had revealed to him, saying to them that no-one in the world should be despised, be he a thief, or actor on the stage, or one who tilled the ground and was bound to a wife, or was a merchant or served a trade: for in every condition of life there are souls who please God, who have their hidden deeds in which He delights (cf. Matt 6:4). Whence it is plain that it is not so much profession or habit that is pleasing to God, as the sincerity and affection of the soul, and honesty in deed. And when he had spoken thus about each in turn, he gave up his spirit.

The Alphabetical Collection

While living in the palace, Abba Arsenius prayed to God in these words, 'Lord, lead me in the way of salvation.' And a voice came to him saying, 'Arsenius, flee from men and you will be saved.' Having withdrawn to the solitary life, he made the same prayer again, and he heard a voice saying to him: 'Flee, keep silence, and *pray unceasingly* (1 Thess 5:17), for these are the sources of not sinning.'

One day Abba Arsenius consulted an old Egyptian monk about his thoughts. Someone noticed this and said to him, 'Abba Arsenius, how is it that you, with such a Latin and Greek education, ask this peasant about your thoughts?' He replied, 'I may indeed have learnt Latin and Greek, but I do not yet know the alphabet of this peasant.'

One day at the Cells, there was an assembly about some matter, and Abba Evagrius discoursed at length. Then the priest said to him, 'Abba, we know that if you were living in your own country you would probably be a bishop and a great leader. But now, you sit here as a stranger.' He was filled with compunction and not at all upset, and bowing his head he replied, '*I have spoken once and will not answer; twice but I will proceed no further*' (Job 40:5).

Abba Antony said, 'I saw the snares that the enemy spreads out over the world, and I said groaning, "What can get through such snares?" Then I heard a voice saying to me, "Humility."'

One day some old men came to see Abba Antony. In their midst was Abba Joseph. Wishing to test them, the old man proposed a text from the Scriptures, and, beginning with the youngest, asked them what it meant. Each gave his opinion as he was able. But to each one the old man said, 'You have not understood it'. Last of all he said to Abba Joseph, 'And how would you explain this saying?' He replied, 'I do not know'. Then Abba Antony said, 'Indeed, Abba Joseph has found the say, for he has said, "I do not know."'

Abba Antony said, 'A time is coming when men will go mad, and when they see someone who is not mad, they will attack him, saying, "You are mad! You are not like us."'

A hunter in the desert saw Antony recreating with the brethren, and was shocked. Wishing to show him that it was sometimes necessary to meet the needs of the brethren, the old man said to him, 'Put an arrow in your bow and shoot it.' So he did. The old man said, 'Shoot another,' and he did so. Then the old man said, 'Shoot yet again.' The hunter replied, 'If I bend my bow so much it will break.' Then the old man said to him, 'So it is with the work of God. If we stretch the brethren beyond measure, they will soon break. Sometimes it is necessary to come down to meet their needs.' On hearing these words, the hunter was pierced with compunction. He departed much edified by the old man. As for the brethren, they went home comforted.

The brethren also asked Agathon, 'Of all good works, which requires the most effort?' He answered, 'Forgive me, but I think there is no greater labor than that of prayer to God. For every time a man wishes to pray, his enemies, the demons, try to interrupt him, for they know that it is only by turning him from prayer that they can hinder his journey. Whatever good work a man undertakes, if he perseveres in it, he will attain rest. But prayer is warfare to the last breath.'

It was related of the Amma Sarah that for thirteen years she waged war against the demon of fornication. Never did she pray that the warfare should cease, but only, 'God, give me strength.'

Once the same spirit of fornication attacked her with extra force, reminding her of the vanities of the world. But she gave herself up to the fear of God and to asceticism, and went up on her little terrace to pray. The spirit of fornication appeared to her corporally and said, 'Sarah you have overcome me.' But she replied, 'It is not I who have overcome you, but my master, Christ.'

Amma Syncletica said, 'It is hard toil and struggle for the unrighteous when they turn to God, but afterwards ineffable joy. It is like those lighting a fire who are first assailed by smoke and shed tears, and so they obtain what they seek. For it is written, *Our God is a consuming fire* (Heb 12:29), and we must kindle the divine fire within us with toil and with tears.'

Abba John went to see Abba Joseph and said to him, 'Abba, as far as I can, I recite my little office, I fast a little, I pray and meditate. I live in peace, and as far as I can, I purify my thoughts. What else can I do?' Then the old man stood up and stretched his hands towards heaven, and his fingers became as ten lamps of fire, and he said to him, 'If you will, you can become all flame.'

Abba Joseph related that Abba Isaac said, 'I was sitting with Abba Poemen one day and I saw him in great ecstasy. Being on terms of great freedom of speech with him, I prostrated myself before him and begged him, saying, 'Tell me where you were.' Constrained to answer, he said, 'My thought was with holy Mary, the Mother of God, as she wept by the Cross of the Saviour. O, I wish I could always weep like that.'

Abba Poemen said, 'It is written, *Like the hart that longs for flowing streams, so my soul longs for you my God* (Ps 42:1). For truly harts in the desert encounter many reptiles, and when their venom burns them, they try to come to the springs to drink, in order to assuage the venom's burning. It is the same with monks. Sitting in the desert they are burned by the venom of demons, and they long for Saturday and Sunday to come, that they might go to the springs of water, that is, the Body and Blood of the Lord, to be purified from the bitterness of the evil one.'

Abba Longinus said to Abba Acacius: 'A woman knows she has conceived when she no longer loses blood. So it is with the soul. She knows she has conceived the Holy Spirit when the passions cease coming out of her. But as long as one is held back in the passions, how can one dare to believe that one is sinless? Give your blood and get the Spirit!'

They said of Abba Macarius the Great that he became, as it is written, a god upon earth, because, just as God protects the world, so Macarius covered the faults that he saw, as though he saw them not, and those that he heard, as though he heard them not.

It happened that Abba Moses was struggling with the temptation of fornication. Unable to abide his cell any longer, he went to tell Abba Isidore. The old man exhorted him to return to his cell. But he refused, saying, 'Abba, I cannot.' Then Isidore took him out on the terrace and said to him, 'Look to the west.' He looked and saw a crowd of demons flying about and making a ruckus, about to launch an attack. Then Isidore said to him, 'Look to the east.' He turned about and saw a countless host of holy angels shining with glory. Isidore said, 'See, these are sent by the Lord to the saints to help them, while those in the west fight against them. They who are with us are more in number than those against us.' Then Abba Moses gave thanks to God, plucked up his courage, and returned to his cell.

Abba Macarius was asked, 'How should one pray?' The old man said, 'There is no need to make long speeches. It is enough to stretch out one's hands and say, "Lord, as you will and know how, have mercy!" And if the conflict grows fiercer, add, "Lord, help me!" He knows very well what we need and shows us his mercy.'

The holy fathers were making predictions about the last generation. They said, 'What have we accomplished?' One, the great Abba Ischyrion, replied, 'We have fulfilled the commandments of God.' Others replied, 'And what will those who come after us do?' He said, 'They will struggle to achieve half our works.' They said, 'And what will happen to those who come after them?' He said, 'That generation will not accomplish any works at all, and temptation will be upon them; yet those who are approved in that day shall be greater than either us or our fathers.'

I. Patristic

B. After Nicaea (325–)

13. St. Gregory of Nazianzus (329–390) | *On the Soul, On the Two Covenants and the Appearing of Christ, On Providence, & Another Prayer for a Safe Journey*

Gregory of Nazianzus contributed so significantly to the church's early theology that he is often known simply as "the Theologian." He made his lasting mark contending for the full humanity of Jesus the Christ against the challenges of the Apollinarians, and his pithy axiom is often recounted still today: "What he did not assume, he did not heal" (*Against Apollinarius*). This phrase, so well-remembered, appears in one of Gregory's vast collection of theological poems.

Gregory wrote poetry, in part, so people could easily remember the theological truths they contain. But he also believed poetry should have a place within the church and her theology. Poetry should not only be considered a medium for cultures outside the church. Rather, it should be taken up and employed for the sake of the gospel and for right teaching.

A theme can be discerned in the following poems. When Gregory was a young man he traveled by ship to Athens. A vicious storm arose and his ship was nearly lost (c. 349). The image of a dangerous voyage is the one Gregory often chooses to portray the Christian life in the following theological poems. For Gregory, the Christian life is a hazardous journey, progressing toward our final safe harbor under God's ever-watchful, *ever-capable* care.

On the Soul (late 4th century)

. . . But as in wintry [123]
gales, a seaworthy ship veers round and heads for shore,
while, again, in fairer winds it either spreads its sails out wide,
or sets upon its way by rowers' labors:

so we, being so far fallen from the great God,
cannot make our dear return voyage without a struggle. [128]
So great was the new-sown ruin from which the forefather [Christ] came
to miserable humanity; and out of it has sprung a bumper crop.

On the Two Covenants and the Appearing of Christ

But, seeing as Christ had set in the human body a piece of heaven,
when he saw it blasted with heart-gnawing evil, [35]
and the twisted dragon lorded it over men,
he did not, to raise again his portion, send yet
other aids to treat the disease (for a little cure
is inadequate against great illnesses); but emptying himself
of his glory as the immortal God the Father's motherless Son, [40]
he appeared for me himself, without a father, a strange son;
yet no stranger, since from my own kind came this immortal, being made
man by a virgin mother, so that the whole of him might save the whole of me.
For it was, again, the total Adam who fell, through that illicit taste.
Therefore, humanly, and not after human custom, [45]
in the hallowed womb of a maid inviolate
he took flesh (amazing! To washed-out minds incredible!)
and came, both God and man, two natures gathered into one:
one hidden, the other open to mankind;
of these, the one is God, the latter was created later for us. [50]
He is one God out of both, since the human is mixed with the Godhead,
and, because of the Godhead, exists as Lord and Christ. . . .
But now, since God did not make a god, but fashioned me [85]
inclinable both ways, and slanted, he therefore supports me, along with many others,
who possess one grace of the baptism given to men. For, as once
the Hebrew children escaped destruction by an anointing of blood
which cleansed their doorposts, when in a single night all the firstborn [90]
of the Egyptian people perished: so for me, too, is this washing
a seal of the God who wards off evil—for little children it is
a seal, for grown-ups, again, it is a cure and the finest seal,
divinely flowing from Christ the giver of light: so that, fleeing
the depth of anguish and lifting up the neck lightly from under its burden, [95]
I might turn my two feet back again towards life. For a traveller, too,

Refreshed from toil, rouses his knees again with renewed vigor.
Common to us all is the air, and the earth is common, too.
Common is the heaven so wide, whose circuit revolves the seasons.
Common to humanity is the baptism that saves man.

On Providence

Away with them, those who deny what is divine,
and ascribe no cause to the good, ineffable
composition of the universe,
whether in creation or in the upkeep of all things.
Away with them! who acknowledge a swarm of deities, [5]
or a potency of demons, good and evil.
Away with the deniers of Providence
who, as though afraid of being saved by God,
either assign the universe an erratic "swoosh!"
or else credit it to the movements of the stars. [10] . . .
For us, rather, there's one God who guides the universe,
wisely revolving and forming it, as he wills, [20]
by his own very words and inclinations,
even if it seems not all things turn aright. . . .
It is necessary to accept every turn of the rudder [112]
by which God leads us out from both struggle and storm,
till he has harbored me in a fair haven:
if indeed he did not build the vessel to no purpose,
but towards a good and well-intentioned end.

Another Prayer for a Safe Journey

Not a step is lifted without you,
Christ the Lord, who to your own human kind
Are all good things, and, in everything, have fashioned a right way.
Trusting in you, I too keep to this path; but escort me
uninjured, and ferry all the things my heart has sought,
and, Lord, lead me back again to my humble home
where, night and day, I may supplicate you freely.

I. Patristic

B. After Nicaea (325–)

14. St. Basil of Caesarea (ca. 329–378) | *The Rule of St. Basil* (Small Asketikon)

St. Basil of Caesarea was surnamed "Basil the Great" for good reason. His outstanding leadership left a lasting legacy to the Christian church in several areas. As a theologian he led the "neo-nicene" movement, the last phase of the struggle against Arianism, in which the doctrine of the Trinity was defended on the basis of a clear semantic distinction between *hypostasis* (individual subsistence) and *ousia* (essence, substance). He also discerned that a fractious church needed a renewal of obedience to Christ shown in a serious reform of morals. To that end he evangelized the unruly ascetic movement of his day.[1]

Through the *Asketikon*, both in an earlier edition and a later edition, Basil became the Father of cenobitic (common life) monasticism in both east and west. He instituted the first church-witnessed vow for monks, established the full pattern of the Prayer of the Hours, revised and extended the Eucharistic Anaphora, and through powerful sermons stirred the consciences of wealthy Christians in time of social disaster, such as the great famine of 369. His Basilieiad in Caesarea was a complex "new city" of monastic communities, schools, workshops for the poor, and hospices for the indigent elderly. The early version of the *Asketikon* was translated into Syriac and became a principle source of monastic life in the later "monophysite" churches.[2] It was also translated into Latin, and as "the Rule of Basil" it had a significant influence in the west, especially through incorporation of much of its doctrine into the *Rule of Benedict*, the premier document of Western monasticism.

---

1. "Ascetic" refers to extreme self-discipline for the sake of religious devotion.

2. Such churches held that the incarnate Son had only one divine nature rather than two nature, divine and human (*mono*, one, and *physis*, nature). This view was combated at the Council of Chalcedon in 451 at which the two complete natures of Christ were affirmed: "perfect in Godhead and also perfect in manhood; truly God and truly man . . . one and the same Christ, Son, Lord, Only-begotten, to be acknowledged in two natures, inconfusedly, unchangeably, indivisibly, inseparably . . ."

B. AFTER NICAEA (325–)

The following selection is from Basil's small *Asketikon*, also known as *The Rule of St. Basil* (Questions 2 and 3). *The Rule* took shape as Basil traveled between ascetic communities encouraging and instructing them, and responding to their questions. Some topics were theoretical, but the vast majority were driven by daily concerns of monastics seeking to dedicate every aspect of their shared lives to God. These questions and his replies were written down, collected, and later edited by Basil.

In Questions 2 and 3, Basil unpacks the necessity of monastic life for fulfilling God's two greatest commandments: love God with all your heart and soul and mind and strength, and love your neighbor as yourself (Matt 22:36–39; Mark 12:28–31). These comprise the basic cadence of Christian existence. Living according to that cadence is aided by seclusion but is *fundamentally* and *unavoidably* communal. The images Basil employs are memorable: the noonday sun and the stadium. Loving God is like gazing on the brightness of the noonday sun, a flame without compare. Gazing upon anything else—that is, *loving* anything else—only disappoints (Q2). One could imagine losing themselves in such a sight, but Basil's image of the stadium draws us back to life with others where the pursuit of virtue "shines out more fully and becomes bright" (Q3).

The Rule of St. Basil (c. 366–378)

Question 2

Q: *Since therefore he says that the first commandment concerns love for God, so then, speak to us first of all about this. For we have heard that he ought to be loved; what we want to learn, however, is how this can be fulfilled.*

R: 1. You have taken up the very best introduction to the talk and one most suited to our goal. So, with God's help, let us do as you have said.

It needs to be understood before all else that this commandment seems to be one, yet it embraces and binds together in itself the virtue of all commandments, for the Lord himself says: *On these two commandments hang the law and the prophets* (Matt 22:40) . . .

We have received the commandment to love God: the soul bears the capacity to love implanted within itself by God at its first constitution. Of this we need no proof from without, for each may discover the traces of what we say within himself and from himself. Every human being desires all that is good, and we are drawn by a kind of natural disposition towards all that we think to be good. Indeed, without being taught, we are drawn in love towards blood relatives and those closest to us in the flesh, while we are attached with our whole affection and good services to those from whom we receive benefits.

But what greater good can we have than God? Indeed, *what other good is there but God alone* (cf. Matt 19:17)? What loveliness, what splendor, what beauty which we are naturally moved to love is of such a kind as is in God and more claims our confidence? What grace is so great, what flame of love which sets alight the secret and inward places of the soul is like to that love of God which ought to inflame the hidden places of the mind, especially if it is cleansed of all defilement, if it is a pure soul which with true affection says: *I am wounded by love* (Song 2:5)?

The utterly ineffable love of God—as I at any rate experience it—which can be more easily experienced than spoken of is a certain inexplicable light. Even if speech should cite or compare a lightning flash or a dazzling brilliance, still, the hearing cannot take it in. Invoke if you will the rays of the morning star, the splendors of the moon, or the light of the sun itself—in comparison with that glory they are all more obscure and murkier by far than an ink black night and the gloom of a dense fog compared with the flawlessly clear light of the noon-day sun. . . .

It follows now to explain that commandment which we said is the second in order and power. We have already said above that the law cultivates and nurtures those powers which are implanted in the soul by the Creator. Since we are charged *to love our neighbor as our very self* (Matt 22:39), let us see whether there is also in us the power and the capacity to fulfill this commandment.

Who does not know that man is a domesticated and sociable animal, not one savage and wild? Nothing is more characteristic of our nature than that each has need of the other, and seeks out the other and loves what he seeks. Since the Lord sowed the seeds of these virtues in us, without doubt he also seeks fruit from them, and as the testimony of our love for him, he accepts our love for our neighbors. For *By this*, he says, *all shall know that you are my disciples, if you love one another* (John 13:35). And he has so joined together these two commandments in every way that the works of mercy which are done for our neighbor he refers to himself. For *I was hungry*, he says, *and you gave me to eat* (Matt 25:35). And he says of the other things done for our neighbor that he is the one receiving them, since he says *When you did this to one of the least of these brothers of mine you did it to me* (Matt 25:40).

Therefore by means of the first the second also is completed, but by means of the second there is an ascent and a return to the first, so that if anyone loves the Lord he without doubt also loves his neighbor, for *Whoever loves me,* says the Lord, *keeps my commandments* (John 14:15). But *this*, he says, *is my commandment that you love one another* (John 15:12). Thus whoever loves his neighbor completes his love for God, since it is he who receives to himself whatever is bestowed on the neighbor. . . .

It is of the greatest help in preserving the memory of God to dwell in retirement and seclusion. For to live mixing with those who act without a care for the fear of God and who show contempt towards his commandments is greatly harmful as the word of

Solomon bears witness saying: *Do not dwell with a wrathful man lest you learn his ways and acquire snares for your soul* (Prov 22:24), and again the saying: *Come out from their midst and be separated says the Lord* (2 Cor 6:17) makes the same point.

That we may not therefore admit inducements to sin through the eyes or the ears and so, little by little, through long habit become settled in a most wretched way of life, and again that we might be able to give time to prayer, we ought first of all seek a retired dwelling. For by this means we cut out former habits in which we behaved contrary to the commandment of God. And this is no mean struggle, to reexamine and recall oneself from a former unworthy way of life, because behavior strengthened by length of time acquires, as it were, the force of nature. Therefore we ought before all else to *deny ourselves and take up the cross* of Christ and so *follow him* (Matt 16:24). . . .

Question 3

Q: *Since your discourse has shown us the danger of living among those who hold the commandments of God in contempt, we now want to learn whether it is better for one who has withdrawn from such society to live privately by himself or to associate his life with brothers of the same goal and of the same mind?*

R: I observe that to lead a life in common with those of the same will and purpose is of advantage in many ways.

First, even in regard to bodily needs and the provision of sustenance not one of us suffices for himself alone, and so for those things which are necessary for the provision of our life we need our tasks to be for one another. Just as the foot of a man has use of its own powers, yet has need of others, and without the aid of the other limbs could neither fulfill its own task nor suffice with its own powers, so also this is what happens, it seems to me, in the solitary life, since what it has cannot be of use and what it lacks it cannot obtain. Besides, the very character of love does not allow an individual to seek his own interests, for the Apostle says: *Love seeks not its own* (1 Cor 13:4).

Second, the individual does not easily recognize his own faults and vices since there is no one to reprove him and it can easily happen to such a man as it is written: *Woe to one alone, for if he falls there is none else to raise him up* (Eccl 4:10). Moreover, the commandments are more easily fulfilled by the many, but by someone alone, when one commandment appears to have been fulfilled, another is hindered. For how do you think that one alone shall *visit the sick* or else *welcome the stranger?* (Matt 25:35–36)

But if *we all are the body* of Christ *and each members of the other* (Rom 12:5) then we ought to be fitted and joined together through our harmony into the compact of one body in the Holy Spirit. But if each of us chooses the solitary life, that is, for no cause or principle that is pleasing to God or that pertains to that common dispensation of others, but to satisfy one's own will and passion—how could we, thus split off and divided, fulfill and apply that harmonious relation of the members towards each another? For such a one will neither *rejoice with the joyful* or *weep with those who weep* (cf. Rom 12:15), because he is separated and divided from others, and shall be unable to know the needs of his neighbors.

Then too, one alone cannot suffice to receive all the gifts of the Holy Spirit, since the distribution of the Spirit is given *according to the proportion of each one's faith* (cf. Rom 12:6), so that what is distributed to each in part comes together again and acts together as do limbs to the building up of the one body. For *to one is given the word of wisdom, to another the word of knowledge, to another faith, to another prophecy, to another the gifts of healings* (1 Cor 12:8) and so on, each of which the individual receives from the Spirit of God is brought forth in common. It therefore happens that one who lives secluded and separate may perhaps receive one gift, and this very gift he renders useless unless since he accomplishes nothing with it, but buries it in himself. The one whose danger this was—and how great a danger!—all you were have read the gospel know (cf. Matt 25:18–25). If however he shares his gift with others he both enjoys what he himself has received and it is multiplied in him by sharing it with others, and he is no less advanced by the gift of others.

Besides, the life of the saints in common has many other advantages, which cannot all be enumerated now. For the present, as we have said, it is far more conducive to fostering the gifts of the Holy Spirit than if we spent our life in solitude, and much safer and more helpful for warding off the ambushes of the enemy which are brought in from without. Hence one will be roused more easily from sleep, should it happen that anyone *falls asleep* in that slumber which leads to *death* (cf. Ps 12:4)....

For behold, the Lord too did not deem the mere teaching of the word sufficient, but wished to deliver to us an example of humility in very deed, when he, *having girded himself with a linen cloth, washed the feet of* his *disciples* (John 13:5). Whose feet then will you wash? For whom will you perform the duties of care? In comparison with whom shall you be lower or even the *last* (Mark 9:35), if you live by yourself? Yes, and that saying: *A good and delightful thing it is when brothers dwell in unity,* which the Holy Spirit compares to the high-priestly *anointing flowing down from the head upon the beard* (Ps 132:1–2), how shall this be accomplished by dwelling alone?

For here is a kind of stadium in which progress is made through the exercise of virtue; in which meditation of the divine commandments shines out more fully and becomes *bright-that common dwelling of brothers in unity* among themselves (Ps 132:1), which possesses in itself the likeness and example of the saints which the divine Scripture records in the Acts of the Apostles, where it says: *All the believers were of one mind and held all things in common* (Acts 2:44).[3]

---

3. Section numbers have been removed.

I. Patristic

B. After Nicaea (325–)

15. St. Gregory of Nyssa (335–394) | *The Great Catechism*

Gregory of Nyssa is one of the three great Cappadocian Fathers, so named because of their relation to the city of Cappadocia in present-day Turkey. In early adulthood he resisted the intense spiritual trajectory of his elder sister Macrina and brother Basil. Instead he married and pursued a career as a rhetorician in Caesarea. Gregory was only later won over to service of the church as bishop in 371, following the loss of his wife and through the persuasions of his brother Basil (now metropolitan of the city). As Bishop, Gregory defended Nicene Trinitarianism on various fronts. He continued his brother's combat with extreme Arianism, now expressed by Bishop Eunomius and his followers. The error was the same: Eunomius denied the complete, authentic divinity of the incarnate Son. Gregory also refuted the opposite christological error of Apollinarius of Laodicea who denied Christ's rational human soul. It was the first shot across the bow of the huge Christological controversies that culminated at the Council of Chalcedon (451).

Gregory's purpose in the *Great Catechism*, however, was less to refute false teachers than to build the faith of young initiates to Christianity. The reader still finds hints of the controversies in the *Catechism*, but they only appear as instances of helping the one growing in the faith to discern truth from error. Gregory describes the purpose of the *Catechism* as follows: "We have thought it as well only to say just so much on the subject of faith as is involved in the language of the Gospel, namely, that one who is begotten by the spiritual regeneration may know who it is that begets him, and what sort of creature he becomes" (38). Notice what Gregory includes, because it says so much about his approach to the Christian life: the *source* of the Christian life in the triune God—"who it is that begets him"—and the *character* of the Christian life itself —"what sort of creature he becomes." Gregory follows the pattern of other ancient theologians we have included thus far in this section. Each addresses the Christian life *not on its own* as a topic unto itself, but rather they treat the Christian life through its association with primary matters of theology: God's life in himself (the "immanent Trinity") and his outward actions (the "economic Trinity").

In the *Catechism*, Gregory addresses the Christian life in terms of its three constitutive features: baptism, the Eucharist, and sin's mortification (putting to death). These three constitute the *cadence* and *pattern* of the Christian life. Through them the Christian life is grounded in the saving work of God accomplished in Christ (baptism), nourished through the Spirit (Eucharist), and evidenced in the Christian's death to sin (mortification). The selection includes just his teaching on baptism and mortification.

The Great Catechism (c. 385)

Chapter 35 (Baptism)

But the descent into the water, and the trine immersion of the person in it, involves another mystery. For since the method of our salvation was made effectual not so much by His precepts in the way of teaching as by the deeds of Him Who has realized an actual fellowship with man, and has effected life as a living fact, so that by means of the flesh which He has assumed, and at the same time deified, everything kindred and related may be saved along with it, it was necessary that some means should be devised by which there might be, in the baptismal process, a kind of affinity and likeness between him who follows and Him Who leads the way. Needful, therefore, is it to see what features are to be observed in the Author of our life, in order that the imitation on the part of those that follow may be regulated, as the Apostle says, after the pattern of the Captain of our salvation [Heb 2:10; 12:2].

For, as it is they who are actually drilled into measured and orderly movements in arms by skilled drill-masters, who are advanced to dexterity in handling their weapons by what they see with their eyes, whereas he who does not practice what is shown him remains devoid of such dexterity, in the same way it is imperative on all those who have an equally earnest desire for the Good as He has, to be followers by the path of an exact imitation of Him Who leads the way to salvation, and to carry into action what He has shown them. It is, in fact, impossible for persons to reach the same goal unless they travel by the same ways. For as persons who are at a loss how to thread the turns of mazes, when they happen to fall in with someone who has experience of them, get to the end of those various misleading turnings in the chambers by following him behind, which they could not do, did they not follow him their leader step by step, so too, I pray you mark, the labyrinth of this our life cannot be threaded by the faculties of human nature unless a man pursues that same path as He did Who, though once in it, yet got beyond the difficulties which hemmed Him in. I apply this figure of a labyrinth to that prison of death, which is without an egress and environs the wretched race of mankind.

What, then, have we beheld in the case of the Captain of our salvation? A three days' state of death and then life again. Now some sort of resemblance in us to such things has to be planned. What, then, is the plan by which in us too a resemblance to that which took place in Him is completed? ... Seeing, then, the death of the Author of our life subjected Him to burial in earth and was in accord with our common nature, the imitation which we enact of that death is expressed in the neighboring element. And as He, that Man from above [John 3:31; 1 Cor 15:47], having taken deadness on Himself, after His being deposited in the earth, returned back to life the third day, so every one who is knitted to Him by virtue of his bodily form, looking forward to the same successful issue, I mean this arriving at life by having, instead of earth, water poured on him, and so submitting to that element, has represented for him in the three movements the three-days-delayed grace of the resurrection.

Something like this has been said in what has gone before, namely, that by the Divine providence death has been introduced as a dispensation into the nature of man, so that, sin having flowed away at the dissolution of the union of soul and body, man, through the resurrection, might be refashioned, sound, passionless, stainless, and removed from any touch of evil. In the case however of the Author of our Salvation this dispensation of death reached its fulfillment, having entirely accomplished its special purpose. For in His death, not only were things that once were one put asunder, but also things that had been disunited were again brought together; so that in this dissolution of things that had naturally grown together, I mean, the soul and body, our nature might be purified, and this return to union of these severed elements might secure freedom from the contamination of any foreign admixture. ...

In what, then, does this imitation consist? It consists in the effecting the suppression of that admixture of sin, in the figure of mortification that is given by the water, not certainly a complete effacement, but a kind of break in the continuity of the evil, two things concurring to this removal of sin—the penitence of the transgressor and his imitation of the death. By these two things the man is in a measure freed from his congenital tendency to evil; by his penitence he advances to a hatred of and averseness from sin, and by his death he works out the suppression of the evil. But had it been possible for him in his imitation to undergo a complete dying, the result would be not imitation but identity; and the evil of our nature would so entirely vanish that, as the Apostle says, "he would die unto sin once for all" [Rom 11:10]. But since, as has been said, we only so far imitate the transcendent Power as the poverty of our nature is capable of, by having the water thrice poured on us and ascending again up from the water, we enact that saving burial and resurrection which took place on the third day, with this thought in our mind, that as we have power over the water both to be in it and arise out of it, so He too, Who has the universe at His sovereign disposal, immersed Himself in death, as we in the water, to return [Phil 1:23] to His own blessedness.

If, therefore, one looks to that which is in reason, and judges of the results according to the power inherent in either party, one will discover no disproportion in these results, each in proportion to the measure of his natural power working out the effects that are within his reach. For, as it is in the power of man, if he is so disposed, to touch the water and yet be safe, with infinitely greater ease may death be handled by the Divine Power so as to be in it and yet not to be changed by it injuriously. Observe, then, that it is necessary for us to rehearse beforehand in the water the grace of the resurrection, to the intent that we may understand that, as far as facility goes, it is the same thing for us to be baptized with water and to rise again from death. . . .

Chapter 40 (Mortification of Vice)

But, as far as what has been already said, the instruction of this Catechism does not seem to me to be complete. For we ought, in my opinion, to take into consideration the sequel of this matter; which many of those who come to the grace of baptism overlook, being led astray, and self-deceived, and indeed only seemingly, and not really, regenerate. For that change in our life which takes place through regeneration will not be change, if we continue in the state in which we were. I do not see how it is possible to deem one who is still in the same condition, and in whom there has been no change in the distinguishing features of his nature, to be any other than he was, it being palpable to everyone that it is for a renovation and change of our nature that the saving birth is received. And yet human nature does not of itself admit of any change in baptism; neither the reason, nor the understanding, nor the scientific faculty, nor any other peculiar characteristic of man is a subject for change. Indeed the change would be for the worse if any one of these properties of our nature were exchanged away for something else.

If, then, the birth from above is a definite refashioning of the man, and yet these properties do not admit of change, it is a subject for inquiry what that is in him, by the changing of which the grace of regeneration is perfected. It is evident that when those evil features which mark our nature have been obliterated a change to a better state takes place. If, then, by being "washed," as says the Prophet [Isa 1:16], in that mystic bath we become "clean" in our wills and "put away the evil" of our souls, we thus become better men, and are changed to a better state.

But if, when the bath has been applied to the body, the soul has not cleansed itself from the stains of its passions and affections, but the life after initiation keeps on a level with the uninitiate life, then, though it may be a bold thing to say, yet I will say it and will not shrink; in these cases the water is but water, for the gift of the Holy Ghost in no ways appears in him who is thus baptismally born; whenever, that is, not only the deformity of anger, or the passion of greed, or the unbridled and unseemly thought, with pride, envy, and arrogance, disfigures the Divine image, but the gains, too, of injustice abide with him, and the woman he has procured by adultery still even after that ministers to his pleasures. If these and the like vices, after, as before, surround the life of the baptized, I cannot see in what respects he has been changed; for I observe him the same man as he was before. The man whom he has unjustly treated, the man whom he has falsely accused, the man whom he has forcibly deprived of his property, these, as far as they are concerned, see no change in him though he has been washed in the laver of baptism. They do not hear the cry of Zacchaeus from him as well: "If I have taken anything from any man by false accusation, I restore fourfold"[Luke 14:8]. What they said of him before his baptism, the same they now more fully declare; they call him by the same names, a covetous person, one who is greedy of what belongs to others, one who lives in luxury at the cost of men's calamities.

Let such an one, therefore, who remains in the same moral condition as before, and then babbles to himself of the beneficial change he has received from baptism, listen to what Paul says: "If a man think himself to be something, when he is nothing, he deceives himself" [Gal 6:3]. For what you have not become, that you are not. "As many as received Him," thus speaks the Gospel of those who have been born again, "to them gave He power to become the sons of God"[John 1:12]. Now the child born of any one is entirely of a kindred nature with his parent.

If, then, you have received God, if you have become a child of God, make manifest in your disposition the God that is in you, manifest in yourself Him that begot you. By the same marks whereby we recognize God, this relationship to God of the son so born must be exhibited. "He opens His hand and fills every living thing with His good pleasure." "He passes over transgressions." "He repents Him of the evil." "The Lord is good to all, and brings not on us His anger every day." "God is a righteous Lord, and there is no injustice in Him"[Ps 145:16; 103:12; Joel 2:13; Ps 7:11; Ps 112:15]; and all other sayings of the like kind which are scattered for our instruction throughout the Scripture;—if you live amidst such things as these, you are a child of God indeed; but if you continue with the characteristic marks of vice in you, it is in vain that you babble to yourself of your birth from above. Prophecy will speak against you and say, "You are a 'son of man,' not a son of the Most High. You 'love vanity, and seek after leasing.' Know you not in what way man is 'made admirable' [Ps 4:2, 3]? In no other way than by becoming holy."

It will be necessary to add to what has been said this remaining statement also; viz. that those good things which are held out in the Gospels to those who have led a godly life, are not such as can be precisely described. For how is that possible with things which "you have not seen, neither ear heard, neither have entered into the heart of man"[Isa 64:4; 1 Cor 2:9]? . . . Since, then, these things are set before us as to be expected in the life that follows this, being the natural outgrowth according to the righteous judgment of God, in the life of each, of his particular disposition, it must be the part of the wise not to regard the present, but that which follows after, and to lay down the foundations for that unspeakable blessedness during this short and fleeting life, and by a good choice to wean themselves from all experience of evil, now in their lifetime here, hereafter in their eternal recompense.[1]

---

1. Translation revised for readability and paragraph breaks inserted.

I. Patristic

B. After Nicaea (325–)

16. St. John Chrysostom (349–407) | *Homily on Hebrews 7*

John was born in Syria to wealthy parents who ensured a thorough education. Whatever public career may have stood before him, John's loyalties gradually shifted toward the church and her ministry. In his early twenties he was nominated as lector (reader of Scripture in public worship), but instead he sought a monastic life in seclusion. John lived in the desert for nearly a decade before the harsh lifestyle so adversely affected his health that he returned to the city. He entered Holy Orders as a deacon in 381, five years later was ordained a priest in Antioch, and finally in 398 he took the mantle of bishop of Constantinople.

During the twelve years of John's priesthood in Antioch he preached constantly, and his eloquence made such an impression on those who heard him that he was later nicknamed Chrysostom, literally "golden-mouth." As bishop of Constantinople, John's new public responsibilities were unmistakably colored by his years in the desert. Like a monastic totally dedicated to the Lord's commands, John the bishop called for strict faithfulness to the precepts of the gospel in the church, and he sought to bring the gospel to bear on every facet of society. Perhaps not surprisingly his attempts at reform were met with intense opposition: he was deposed in 403 and a year later exiled by the emperor. After living under guard for three years, he died in 407.

We find in his sermons a "spirituality which corresponds to every state of life."[1] From his experience as an ascetic he preached to those in public service or monastic vows, and to laymen he proclaimed the Word as their priest. To all he appealed for the imitation of Christ.

Our selection is from Chrysostom's sermon on Hebrews 7 in which He exhorts Christians to be *imitators of Christ*. He has seen many in the church whose lives bear no fruit. Preached in Constantinople, perhaps the resistance he faced as bishop was already leaving its mark. Chrysostom shows how the grace of God—which establishes the Christian life apart from human effort—should *lead* to costly, Christ-like behavior.

---

1. Malingrey and Zincone, "John Chrysostom," 432.

"Let us not barter away the salvation of God for an easy life," he says likening salvation to valuable merchandise, "but let us make merchandise of it, and increase it." The Christian life imitates Christ, following his costly, cross-shaped footsteps.

Homily on Hebrews 7 (likely during his term as Bishop of Constantinople, 398–403)

Hebrews 7:28—For the law appoints as high priests those who are subject to weakness, but the word of the oath, which came later than the law, appoints a Son who has been made perfect forever (NRSV).

(9) Since then we have such an High Priest, let us imitate Him: let us walk in His footsteps. There is no other sacrifice: one alone has cleansed us, and after this, fire and hell. For indeed on this account he repeats it over and over, saying, "one Priest," "one Sacrifice," lest anyone supposing that there are many [sacrifices] should sin without fear. Let us then, as many as have been counted worthy of The Seal [baptism], as many as have enjoyed The Sacrifice, as many as have partaken of the immortal Table, continue to guard our noble birth and our dignity for falling away is not without danger.

And as many as have not yet been counted worthy these [privileges], let not these either be confident on that account. For when a person goes on in sin, with the view of receiving holy baptism at the last gasp, oftentimes he will not obtain it. And, believe me, it is not to terrify you that I say what I am going to say. I have myself known many persons, to whom this has happened, who in expectation indeed of the enlightening [baptism] sinned much, and on the day of their death went away empty. For God gave us baptism for this cause, that He might do away our sins, not that He might increase our sins. Whereas if any man have employed it as a security for sinning more, it becomes a cause of negligence. For if there had been no Washing, they would have lived more warily, as not having [the means of] forgiveness. You see that we are the ones who cause it to be said "Let us do evil, that good may come" (Rom 3:8).

Wherefore, I exhort you also who are uninitiated, be sober. Let no man follow after virtue as a hireling, no man as a senseless person, no man as after a heavy and burdensome thing. Let us pursue it then with a ready mind, and with joy. For if there were no reward laid up, ought we not to be good? But however, at least with a reward, let us become good. And how is this anything else than a disgrace and a very great condemnation? Unless you give me a reward (says one), I do not become self-controlled. Then am I bold to say something: you will never be self-controlled, no not even when you live with self-control, if you do it for a reward. You don't esteem virtue at all, if you don't love it. But on account of our great weakness, God was willing that for a time it should be practiced even for reward, yet not even so do we pursue it.

But let us suppose, if you will, that a man dies, after having done innumerable evil things, having also been counted worthy of baptism (which however I think does not readily happen), tell me, how will he depart from here to heaven? Not indeed called to account for the deeds he had done, but yet without confidence; as is reasonable. For when after living a hundred years, he has no good work to show, but only that he has not sinned, or rather not even this, but that he was saved by grace only, and when he sees others crowned, in splendor, and highly approved: even if he fall not into hell, tell me, will he endure his despondency?

(10) But to make the matter clear by an example, Suppose there are two soldiers, and that one of them steals, injures, overreaches, and that the other does none of these things, but acts the part of a brave man, does important things well, sets up trophies in war, stains his right hand with blood; then when the time arrives, suppose that (from the same rank in which the thief also was) he is at once conducted to the imperial throne and the purple; but suppose that the other remains there where he was, and merely of the royal kindness does not pay the penalty of his deeds, let him however be in the last place, and let him be stationed under the King. Tell me, will he be able to endure his despair when he sees him who was [ranked] with himself ascended even to the very highest dignities, and made thus glorious, and master of the world, while he himself still remains below, and has not even been freed from punishment with honor, but through the grace and kindness of the King? For even should the King forgive him, and release him from the charges against him, still he will live in shame; for surely not even will others admire him: since in such forgiveness, we admire not those who receive the gifts, but those who bestow them. And as much as the gifts are greater, so much the more are they ashamed who receive them, when their transgressions are great.

With what eyes then will such an one be able to look on those who are in the King's courts, when they exhibit their sweatings out of number and their wounds, whilst he has nothing to show, but has his salvation itself of the mere loving-kindness of God? For as if one were to beg off a murderer, a thief, an adulterer, when he was going to be arrested, and were to command him to stay at the porch of the King's palace, he will not afterwards be able to look any man in the face, although he has been set free from punishment: so too surely is this man's case.

For do not, I beseech you, suppose that because it is called a palace, therefore all attain the same things. For if here in Kings' courts there is the Prefect, and all who are about the King, and also those who are in very inferior stations, and occupy the place of what are called Decani [those who buried the dead] (though the interval be so great between the Prefect and the Decanus) much more shall this be so in the royal court above.

And this I say not of myself. For Paul lays down another difference greater even than these.[2] For (he says) as many differences as there are between the sun and the moon and the stars and the very smallest star, so many also between those in the kingdom [of Heaven]. And that the difference between the sun and the smallest star is far greater than that between the Decanus (as he is called) and the Prefect, is evident to all. For while the sun shines upon all the world at once, and makes it bright, and hides the moon and the stars, the other often does not appear, not even in the dark. For there are many of the stars which we do not see. When then we see others become suns, and we have the rank of the very smallest stars, which are not even visible, what comfort shall we have?

Let us not, I beseech you, let us not be so slothful, not so inert, let us not barter away the salvation of God for an easy life, but let us make merchandise of it, and increase it. For even if one be a Catechumen, still he knows Christ, still he understands the Faith, still he is a hearer of the divine oracles, still he is not far from the knowledge; he knows the will of his Lord. Why does he procrastinate? Why does he delay and postpone? Nothing is better than a good life whether here or there, whether in case of the Enlightened or of the Catechumens.[3]

---

2. Chrysostom mistakenly believed Paul authored Hebrews.
3. Translation revised for readability.

I. Patristic

B. After Nicaea (325–)

17. St. Augustine of Hippo (354–430) | *Confessions*

St. Augustine was a monumental figure in his day, and for a thousand years after his death his writings largely defined the theology of the Latin Church. "Augustine is the end of one era as well as the beginning of another," writes Justo González. "He is the last of the ancient Christian writers, and the forerunner of medieval theology. The main currents of ancient theology converged in him, and from him flow the rivers, not only of medieval scholasticism, but also of sixteenth century Protestant theology."[1] Beyond the role of Augustine's thought in church doctrine, many have found a spiritual way point or reference marker in his memoir, *Confessions*. Augustine voices the experience of following Christ amidst competing loyalties, writing of the conflict between the desires of life and the desire which God grants to seek after and love him.

Augustine knew of competing loyalties even in his childhood home. His father was a pagan who worshipped the gods of the empire, and his mother Monica was a committed, zealous Christian. She saw in a dream that Augustine would become a Christian and prayed for him relentlessly. Even despite Augustine's youthful dismissal of Monica's faith and his rejection of orthodox Christianity she still prayed. In his twenties, Augustine struggled. He was divided between the popular philosophies of his day (Manichaeism and Neoplatonism), divided between his love for his concubine and his mother's wishes for him to marry, and divided between his sexual desires and his increasing sense of guilt.

As Augustine describes his conversion, he was sitting in a garden with the book of Romans when a child's sing-song voice drifted over the wall, "take up and read." He did, falling upon Romans 13:13–14. "No further would I read," he later wrote, "nor needed I: for instantly at the end of this sentence, by a light as it were of serenity infused into my heart, all the darkness of doubt vanished away" (book 8, ch. 12). Without delay he wrote of his conversation to his bishop, Ambrose. He was baptized a

---

1. González, *A History of Christian Thought*, vol. 2, 15.

year later, shortly thereafter moved to Thagaste to initiate an ascetic community, and within a few years was ordained bishop of Hippo.

Conversion brought peace to Augustine's restless heart but not the end to competing desires, as we see in the following selection from *Confessions*. He acknowledges that bodily life—the life God intended for us as creatures—involves pleasure and the satisfaction of our senses. Good smells gladden us, tastes please us, the experience of being valued brings satisfaction, and new insights delight our minds. Augustine warns, however, that unless our desires are conformed to the love of God, they will us away from him. "Augustine does not say that human desire should be extinguished," as some read Augustine, "but that it should be cultivated."[2] The Christian life is a therapy that orders desire according to its true and ultimate *telos*: the love of God. The pleasures of desire will always disappoint when sought for their own sake rather than how they may lead us to worship and love God. As Augustine confesses, "Happiness is to rejoice in you and for you and because of you" (Book 10, ch. 22).[3]

Confessions, Book 10 (379–400)

O Lord, the depths of man's conscience lie bare before your eyes. Could anything of mine remain hidden from you, even if I refused to confess it? I should only be shielding my eyes from seeing you, not hiding myself from you. But now that I have the evidence of my own misery to prove to me how displeasing I am to myself, you are my light and my joy. It is you whom I love and desire, so that I am ashamed of myself and cast myself aside and choose you instead, and I please neither you nor myself except in you. . . .

I have learnt to love you late, Beauty at once so ancient and so new! I have learnt to love you late! You were within me, and I was in the world outside myself I searched for you outside myself and, disfigured as I was, I fell upon the lovely things of your creation. You were with me, but I was not with you. The beautiful things of this world kept me far from you and yet, if they had not been in you they would have had no being at all. You called me; you cried aloud to me; you broke my barrier of deafness. You shone upon me; your radiance enveloped me; you put my blindness to flight. You shed your fragrance about me; I drew breath and now I gasp for your sweet odor. I tasted you, and now I hunger and thirst for you. You touched me, and I am inflamed with love of your peace. . . .

---

2. Sigurdson, *Heavenly Bodies*, 485.

3. It is also fruitful to trace the relationship between Augustine's Christology and his view of the Christian life. See, *Tractates on John*, Sermon 22.8–10 (John 5:26); *Enchiridion*, ch. 14.53: "Mysteries of Christ's Mediatorial Work and Justification."

B. AFTER NICAEA (325–)

There can be no hope for me except in your great mercy. Give me the grace to do as you command, and command me to do what you will! You command us to control our bodily desires. And, as we are told, when I knew that no man can be master of himself, except of God's bounty, I was wise enough already to know whence the gift came. Truly it is by continence that we are made as one and regain that unity of self which we lost by falling apart in the search for a variety of pleasures. For a man loves you so much the less if, besides you, he also loves something else which he does not love for your sake. O Love ever burning, never quenched! O Charity, my God, set me on fire with your love! You command me to be continent. Give me the grace to do as you command, and command me to do what you will! . . .

I must now speak of a different kind of temptation, more dangerous than these because it is more complicated. For in addition to our bodily appetites, which make us long to gratify all our senses and our pleasures and lead to our ruin if we stay away from you by becoming their slaves, the mind is also subject to a certain propensity to use the sense of the body, not for self-indulgence of a physical kind, but for the satisfaction of its own inquisitiveness. This futile curiosity masquerades under the name of science and learning, and since it derives from our thirst for knowledge and sight is the principal sense by which knowledge is acquired, in the Scriptures it is called gratification of the eye. For although, correctly speaking, to see is the proper function of the eyes, we use the word of the other senses too, when we employ them to acquire knowledge. We do not say 'Hear how it glows,' 'Smell how bright it is,' 'Taste how it shines,' or 'Feel how it glitters,' because these are all things which we say that we see. Yet we not only say 'See how it shines' when we are speaking of some thing which only the eyes can perceive, but we also say 'See how loud it is,' 'See how it smells,' 'See how it tastes,' and 'See how hard it is.' So, as I said, sense-experience in general is called the lust of the eyes because, although the function of sight belongs primarily to the eyes, we apply it to the other organs of sense as well, by analogy, when they are used to discover any item of knowledge.

We can easily distinguish between the motives of pleasure and curiosity. When the senses demand pleasure, they look for objects of visual beauty, harmonious sounds, fragrant perfumes, and things that are pleasant to the taste or soft to the touch. But when their motive is curiosity, they may look for just the reverse of these things, simply to put it to the proof, not for the sake of an unpleasant experience, but from a relish for investigation and discovery. What pleasure can there be in the sight of a mangled corpse, which can only horrify? Yet people will flock to see one lying on the ground, simply for the sensation of sorrow and horror that it gives them. They are even afraid that it may bring them nightmares, as though it were something that they had been forced to look at while they were awake or something to which they had been attracted by rumors of its beauty. The same is true of the other senses, although it would be tedious to give further examples. It is to satisfy this unhealthy curiosity that freaks and prodigies are put on show in the theatre, and for the same reason men are led to investigate the secrets of nature, which are irrelevant to our lives, although such knowledge is of no value to them and they wish to gain it merely for the sake of knowing. It is curiosity, too, which causes men to turn to sorcery in the effort to obtain knowledge for the same perverted purpose. And it even invades our religion, for we put God to the test when we demand signs and wonders from him, not in the hope of salvation, but simply for the love of the experience.

In this immense forest, so full of snares and dangers, I have pared away many sins and thrust them from my heart, for you have given me the grace to do this, O God, my Savior. But as long as my daily life is passed in the midst of the clamor raised by so many temptations of this sort, when can I presume to say that nothing of this kind can hold my attention or tempt me into idle speculation? It is true that the theatres no longer attract me; the study of astrology does not interest me; I have never dealt in necromancy; and I detest all sacrilegious rites. But how often has not the enemy used his wiles upon me to suggest that I should ask for some sign from you, O Lord my God, to whom I owe my humble, undivided service? I beseech you, by Christ our King and by Jerusalem the chaste, our only homeland, that just as I now withhold my consent from these suggestions, I may always continue to ward them off and keep them still farther from me. But when I pray to you for the salvation of another, the purpose and intention of my prayer is far different. For you do what you will and you grant me, as you always will, the grace to follow you gladly.

Yet who can tell how many times each day our curiosity is tempted by the most trivial and insignificant matters? Who can tell how often we give way? So often it happens that, when others tell foolish tales, at first we bear with them for fear of offending the weak, and then little by little we begin to listen willingly. I no longer go to watch a dog chasing a hare at the games in the circus. But if I should happen to see the same thing in the country as I pass by, the chase might easily hold my attention and distract me from whatever serious thoughts occupied my mind. It might not actually compel me to turn my horse from the path, but such would be the inclination of my heart; and unless you made me realize my weakness and quickly reminded me, either to turn my eyes from the sight and raise my thoughts to you in contemplation, or to despise it utterly and continue on my way, I should simply stop and gloat. What excuse can I make for myself when often, as I sit at home, I cannot turn my eyes from the sight of a lizard catching flies or a spider entangling them as they fly into her web? Does it make any difference that these are only small animals? It is true that the sight of them inspires me to praise you for the wonders of your creation and the order in which you have disposed all things, but I am not intent upon your praises when I first begin to watch. It is one thing to rise quickly from a fall, another not to fall at all.

My life is full of such faults, and my only hope is in your boundless mercy. For when our hearts become repositories piled high with such worthless stock as this; it is the cause of interruption and distraction from our prayers. And, although, in your presence, the voices of our hearts are raised to your ear, all kinds of trivial thoughts break in and cut us off from the great act of prayer.

I. Patristic

B. After Nicaea (325–)

18. St. Jerome (374–420) | *Letter 52: To Nepotian*

Eusebius Hieronymus, known as Jerome, is best known for his Latin translation of the Bible, the "Vulgate." He began the work in 382, under the support of the Roman Emperor Damasus, and he completed it after twenty-three years of immersion in Scripture. "Make knowledge of the Scripture your love," Jerome once wrote. "Live with them, meditate on them, make them the sole object of your knowledge and inquiries" ("Letter to Paulinus"). Jerome surely did, and the Vulgate remained the standard Latin translation of the Bible for more than 1,000 years. Jerome's Latin made its way into the liturgy of the Western church, making it—*literally*—the language of faith and worship.

Jerome's immersion in the Bible was matched by his commitment to the monastic ideal (asceticism). He was baptized in Rome at nineteen, then traveled extensively in the eastern parts of the Empire where he joined several ascetic communities. Jerome was drawn to the monastic life particularly when it was pursued in community, seen in this letter to a young monk.

> I should like you to have the society of holy men so as not to be thrown altogether on your resources. For if you set out upon a road that is new to you without a guide, you are sure to turn aside immediately either to the right or to the left, to lay yourself open to the assaults of error, to go too far or else not far enough, to weary yourself with running too fast or to loiter by the way and to fall asleep. (*Letter to Rusticus*)

The ascetic life was hard on so many levels, and Jerome knew it from his own experience. Again to Rusticus, "In my youth when the desert walled me in with its solitude I was still unable to endure the promptings of sin and the natural heat of my blood; and, although I tried by frequent fasts to break the force of both, my mind still surged with [evil] thoughts." When Jerome returned to Rome he was hard-pressed to find monastic dedication in the bustling city.

As the secretary to the emperor, Jerome frequently criticized church elites for falling short of ascetic ideals. In a biting remark, he takes words from Acts 3:6 and mocks,

"Many, while they do not say it in words, by their deeds declare: I have not faith and mercy, but such as I have, silver and gold—that I don't give to you either" (*Letter to Eustochium*). Few measured up to Jerome's ideal (including himself).

Our selection is from Jerome's letter to Nepotian, formerly a soldier and now a young presbyter. "Do not look to your military experience," Jerome warns, knowing he will find a standard there which differs sharply from Jesus' teaching. Instead, "be what you are called" (5). Nepotian's entire way of thinking about his place in the world and the cadence of his life has to change to fulfill his new vocation in the church. No less is true for every Christian. Regardless of one's role in society or the church, the Christian life entails a radical reframing of one's place in the world: "be what you are called."

Letter 52: To Nepotian (394)

1. Again and again you ask me, my dear Nepotian, in your letters from over the sea, to draw for you a few rules of life, showing how one who has renounced the service of the world to become a monk or a clergyman may keep the straight path of Christ, and not be drawn aside into the haunts of vice. . . .

5. A clergyman, then, as he serves Christ's church, must first understand what his name means; and then, when he realizes this, must endeavor to be what he is called. For since the Greek word κλῆρος means "lot," or "inheritance," the clergy are so called either because they are the lot of the Lord, or else because the Lord Himself is their lot and portion.[1] Now, he who in his own person is the Lord's portion, or has the Lord for his portion, must so bear himself as to possess the Lord and to be possessed by Him. He who possesses the Lord, and who says with the prophet, "The Lord is my portion," can hold to nothing beside the Lord. For if he hold to something beside the Lord, the Lord will not be his portion. Suppose, for instance, that he holds to gold or silver, or possessions or inlaid furniture; with such portions as these the Lord will not deign to be his portion. I, if I am the portion of the Lord, and the line of His heritage, receive no portion among the remaining tribes; but, like the Priest and the Levite, I live on the tithe (Num 18:24), and serving the altar, am supported by its offerings (1 Cor 9:13). Having food and raiment, I shall be content with these (1 Tim 6:8) and as a disciple of the Cross shall share its poverty.

I beseech you, therefore, and again and yet again admonish you; do not look to your military experience for a standard of clerical obligation. Under Christ's banner

---

1. The political context is helpful for understanding Jerome's emphasis on amassing wealth (one's "lot" as he calls it). Roman law prevented men in church vocations from receiving a financial inheritance. As he says below, "clergymen and monks alone lie under a legal disability, a disability enacted not by persecutors but by Christian emperors." This added temptation to those in priestly orders to amass wealth for themselves.

seek for no worldly gain, lest having more than when you first became a clergyman, you hear men say, to your shame, "Their portion shall not profit them." Welcome poor men and strangers to your homely board, that with them Christ may be your guest. A clergyman who engages in business, and who rises from poverty to wealth, and from obscurity to a high position, avoid as you would the plague. For "evil communications corrupt good manners" (1 Cor 15:33). You despise gold; he loves it. You spurn wealth; he eagerly pursues it. You love silence, meekness, privacy; he takes delight in talking and effrontery, in squares, and streets, and apothecaries' shops. What unity of feeling can there be where there is so wide a divergency of manners? . . .

6. Shameful to say, idol-priests, play-actors, jockeys, and prostitutes can inherit property: clergymen and monks alone lie under a legal disability, a disability enacted not by persecutors but by Christian emperors.[2] I do not complain of the law, but I grieve that we have deserved a statute so harsh. Cauterizing is a good thing, no doubt; but how is it that I have a wound which makes me need it? The law is strict and far-seeing, yet even so rapacity goes on unchecked. By a fiction of trusteeship we set the statute at defiance; and, as if imperial decrees outweigh the mandates of Christ, we fear the laws and despise the Gospels. If heir there must be, the mother has first claim upon her children, the Church upon her flock—the members of which she has borne and reared and nourished. Why do we thrust ourselves in between mother and children?

It is the glory of a bishop to make provision for the wants of the poor; but it is the shame of all priests to amass private fortunes. I who was born (suppose) in a poor man's house, in a country cottage, and who could scarcely get of common millet and household bread enough to fill an empty stomach, am now come to disdain the finest wheat flour and honey. I know the several kinds of fish by name. I can tell unerringly on what coast a mussel has been picked. I can distinguish by the flavor the province from which a bird comes. Dainty dishes delight me because their ingredients are scarce and I end by finding pleasure in their ruinous cost.

I hear also of servile attention shown by some towards old men and women when these are childless. They fetch the basin, beset the bed and perform with their own hands the most revolting offices. They anxiously await the advent of the doctor and with trembling lips they ask whether the patient is better. If for a little while the old fellow shows signs of returning vigor, they are in agonies. They pretend to be delighted, but their covetous hearts undergo secret torture. For they are afraid that their labors may go for nothing and compare an old man with a clinging to life to the patriarch Methuselah. How great a reward might they have with God if their hearts were not set on a temporal prize! With what great exertions do they pursue an empty heritage! Less labor might have purchased for them the pearl of Christ.

10. Many build churches nowadays; their walls and pillars of glowing marble, their ceilings glittering with gold, their altars studded with jewels. Yet to the choice of Christ's ministers no heed is paid. And let no one allege against me the wealth of the

2. See note 1.

temple in Judaea, its table, its lamps, its censers, its dishes, its cups, its spoons, and the rest of its golden vessels. If these were approved by the Lord it was at a time when the priests had to offer victims and when the blood of sheep was the redemption of sins. They were figures typifying things still future and were "written for our admonition upon whom the ends of the world have come" (1 Cor 10:11). But now our Lord by His poverty has consecrated the poverty of His house. Let us, therefore, think of His cross and count riches to be but dirt. . . .

16. Let us never seek for presents and rarely accept them when we are asked to do so. For "it is more blessed to give than to receive" (Acts 20:35). Somehow or other the very man who begs leave to offer you a gift holds you the cheaper for your acceptance of it; while, if you refuse it, it is wonderful how much more he will come to respect you. The preacher of continence must not be a maker of marriages. Why does he who reads the apostle's words "it remains that they that have wives be as though they had none" (1 Cor 7:29)—why does he press a virgin to marry? Why does a priest, who must be a monogamist (1 Tim 3:2) urge a widow to marry again? How can the clergy be managers and stewards of other men's households, when they are bidden to disregard even their own interests? To wrest a thing from a friend is theft but to cheat the Church is sacrilege. When you have received money to be doled out to the poor, to be cautious or to hesitate while crowds are starving is to be worse than a robber; and to subtract a portion for yourself is to commit a crime of the deepest dye. I am tortured with hunger and are you to judge what will satisfy my cravings? Either divide immediately what you have received, or, if you are a timid almoner, send the donor to distribute his own gifts. Your purse ought not to remain full while I am in need. No one can look after what is mine better than I can. He is the best almoner who keeps nothing for himself.

17. You have compelled me, my dear Nepotian, in spite of the castigation which my treatise on Virginity has had to endure—the one which I wrote for the saintly Eustochium at Rome—you have compelled me after ten years have passed once more to open my mouth at Bethlehem and to expose myself to the stabs of every tongue. For I could only escape from criticism by writing nothing—a course made impossible by your request; and I knew when I took up my pen that the shafts of all gainsayers would be launched against me. I beg such to hold their peace and to desist from gainsaying: for I have written to them not as to opponents but as to friends. I have not inveighed against those who sin: I have but warned them to sin no more. My judgment of myself has been as strict as my judgment of them. When I have wished to remove the mote from my neighbor's eye, I have first cast out the beam in my own (Matt 7:3–5). I have calumniated no one. Not a name has been hinted at. My words have not been aimed at individuals and my criticism of shortcomings has been quite general. If any one wishes to be angry with me he will have first to own that he himself suits my description.[3]

---

3. Paragraph breaks inserted.

I. Patristic

B. After Nicaea (325–)

19. St. Cyril of Alexandria (376–444) | *Commentary on the Gospel of John & Luke*

Cyril was born in the influential city of Alexandria nearly half a century after the Council of Nicaea. The Creed of Nicaea offered grammar for the mystery of the incarnation, but debates continued for centuries over the nature of Christ's person. Cyril was in the thick of those wranglings throughout his session as the patriarch of Alexandria. Like his uncle Theophilus who preceded him, Cyril engaged his adversaries, often violently.

It was probably Nestorius, patriarch of Constantinople, who received the full force of Cyril's energies. Or at least it is Cyril's combat with Nestorius that most remember (his ire against the Novatians or the Jews of Alexandria was no less harsh). At the heart of Cyril's opposition to Nestorius was Cyril's position that Nestorius's teaching depleted the saving power of Christ. Specifically, Nestorius taught that "Mother of God" (*Theotokos*) should not be applied to Mary, the mother of Jesus. "Mother of Christ" is more appropriate, he argued. As Cyril interpreted this, it appeared Nestorius taught only an external association between the Son of God and our human flesh. Mary, argued Cyril, was properly the Mother of God because the Son of God truly took humanity to himself in her womb while no less remaining divine (in every sense that the Father is divine). "God of God, light of light, very God of very God" as it was worded at Nicaea. But if one follows Nestorius, Cyril tried to show, then Jesus is merely a man and not able to save (as Athanasius argued). The debate over Mary's appropriate title was the same debate about the saving significance of the incarnation—all over again, but from a slightly different angle. "If one follows Nestorius," William Anderson nicely summarizes, then "the suffering and saving acts of Jesus the Christ were, presumably, not those of God incarnate but those of one who was *merely man*."[1] Simply put, who Jesus *is* (Christology) critically matters for what God accomplishes through him *for us* (soteriology).

---

1. Anderson, ed., *A Journey Through Christian Theology*, 104.

We should keep in mind Cyril's concerns when reading the following selections from his commentaries on the Gospels of John and Luke. His method is characteristic of so many theologians during this era. The Christian life is rarely an isolated focus, as we might find it in contemporary systems of doctrine. Instead, in the course of addressing the person of Christ, it naturally occurs to address life *in Christ*. Christ's divine nature is essential for the Christian life. Christ saves by divinizing us—that is, bringing the divine image in us to its fruition by making us divine through union with Christ. (This was, and remains, the dominant conception for salvation among Eastern theologians.) Through the Spirit the Christian "partakes" of the divine nature offered to them in Christ (2 Pet 1:4). If not divine himself by nature, then Christ cannot give what our salvation requires. Thus Cyril writes, the Son "gives what belongs to him alone by nature" and thereby we become "participants in him through the Spirit."

Commentary on the Gospel of John (c. 425)

John 1:12—But to all who received him, who believed in his name, he gave power to become children of God.

This judgment is truly just and worthy of God. The firstborn Israel is cast out because it did not want to remain God's own, nor did it receive God's Son when he dwelt among his own. It rejected the bestower of nobility and drove away the giver of grace. But the Gentiles received him by faith. Therefore, it is reasonable that Israel will receive the wages of its senselessness. It will grieve over the loss of good things and receive the bitter fruit of its own foolishness, being stripped of sonship. But the Gentiles will revel in the blessings that come from faith. They will find the bright rewards of obedience, and they will be transplanted into Israel's place. They will be cut off from their natural wild olive tree and be grafted contrary to nature into the good olive tree [Rom 11:24]. Israel will hear, "Woe to you, sinful nation, people full of sin, wicked seed, lawless children. You forsook the Lord and provoked the Holy One of Israel" [Isa 1:4]. But one of Christ's disciples will say to the Gentiles, "You are a chosen race, a royal priesthood, a holy nation, God's own people, in order that you may proclaim the mighty acts of him who calls you out of darkness into his marvelous light" [1 Pet 2:9]. When they received the Son through faith, they received the power to be ranked among the children of God.

The Son, by his authority, gives what belongs to him alone by nature and sets it forth as a common possession, making this a sort of image of the love he has for humanity and for the world. We who bore the image of the earthly man could not escape corruption unless the call to sonship placed in us the splendor of the image of the heavenly man [1 Cor 15:49]. We became participants in him through the Spirit. We were sealed into his likeness, and we ascend to the archetypal form of the image according to which Holy Scripture says we were also made. Once we recover the ancient beauty of our nature in this way and are refashioned in relation to the divine nature, we will be superior to the evils that befell us because of transgression. Therefore, we rise up to an honor above our nature because of Christ.

However, we will not be sons of God unchangeably like he is, but we will be sons of God in relation to him by the grace of imitation. He is the true Son existing from the Father, but we are adopted because of his love for humanity, and we receive as a share in grace the words "I said, 'You are gods, and you are all sons of the Most High'" [Ps 82:6]. The created and servile creation is called to glories above its nature by the mere nod and will of the Father. But the Son and God and Lord will not acquire being God and Son by the will of God the Father or only because the Father wants it that way, but he shines forth from the very substance of the Father, and he possesses the good of that substance by nature. The Son is recognized to be the true Son, and he is proven so by comparison with us. Being something by nature is different from being something by adoption, and being something truly is different from being something by imitation. We are called sons by adoption and by imitation. Therefore, he is Son by nature and in truth. We who are made sons too are compared with him. We enjoy the good that comes by grace rather than the honors that come by nature.

John 1:13—Those who were born not from blood, nor from the will of the flesh, nor from the will of a husband, but born of God.

Those who are called by faith in Christ to God's sonship, he says, have put off the poverty of their own nature. The one who honors them glorifies them by grace, as by a bright robe, and they ascend to an honor beyond their nature. They are no longer called children of the flesh, but rather offspring of God by adoption. Notice what care the blessed Evangelist took in his discussion. Since he was about to say that believers are born of God, he has to devise a safeguard for us. Otherwise, someone might think that believers spring from the nature of God the Father in truth and reach an unchangeable likeness with the Only Begotten. Or they might think that the words "from the womb before the dawn I begat you" [Ps 110:3] apply in a looser sense also to him. That would drag him [the Son] down to the nature of created beings since he too is said to be begotten of God. First he says that the natural Son gave them power to become children of God, thereby introducing the idea of adoption and grace. Then he goes on without danger to say, "They were born of God." This is to show the magnitude of his grace toward them since he gathers, as it were, what is alien to God the Father into a natural kinship and raises what is servile to lordly nobility because of his fervent love toward it.

Perhaps someone might say, "What then do believers in Christ have that is greater or more special compared with Israel since it too is said to be born of God according to the statement, 'I begat and raised sons, but they rejected me'" [Isa 1:2]? I think one must reply to this by saying first that "the law has a shadow of the good things to come, not the image itself of the realities" [Heb 10:1]. He did not give this to the Israelites to possess in truth, but it was written for them in the form of a type and a sketch "until the time of restoration" [Heb 9:10], as it is written. At that time, he will reveal those who call on God the Father with more fitting and truer worship because the Spirit of the Only Begotten dwells in them. The former had the "Spirit of slavery to fear," the latter "the Spirit of sonship" for freedom "in whom we cry, 'Abba, Father'" [Rom 8:15]. Therefore, the people who were going to ascend to sonship through faith in Christ were described ahead of time in Israel in shadows, just as we of course understand circumcision in the Spirit to be typified ahead of time in ancient days in Israel's flesh. In sum, everything that we have, they had in type.

In addition, we say that Israel was called to sonship in type through the mediator Moses. Therefore, they were also baptized into him, as Paul says, "in the cloud and in the sea" [1 Cor 10:2]. They were taken from idolatry to the law of slavery when the angel administered the commandment to them in writing [Gal 3:19]. But those who rise to divine sonship through faith in Christ are baptized not into anything originate but into the holy Trinity itself through the Word who is the mediator. He joins what is human to himself through the flesh that was united to him, and he is joined by nature to the Father since he is by nature God. In this way, the slaves ascend to sonship through participation in the true Son since they are called and so to speak raised to the honor that is in the Son by nature. Therefore, we who received the new birth through the Spirit by faith are called born of God, and that is what we are.

Since some recklessly dare to lie about the Holy Spirit just as they lie about the Only Begotten, saying that he is an originate creature and completely removing him from consubstantiality with God the Father, come let us marshal once again the discourse on the right faith against their unbridled tongues and beget the material for aiding ourselves and our readers. My friends, if God's own Spirit—who, because he is God's own, exists essentially in God—is neither God by nature nor from God but is another besides him and is of the same nature as created beings, how are we who are born through him called "born of God"? Either we will say that the Evangelist is certainly lying or, if he is telling the truth and it is so and not otherwise, the Spirit will be God and from God by nature. When we are considered worthy to participate in him through faith in Christ, we are made sharers in the divine nature [2 Pet 1:4] and are called "born of God." Therefore, we are called gods not only because we fly up to glory beyond ourselves by grace but also because we have God now dwelling and abiding in us, according to the statement in the prophet, "I will dwell in them and walk in them" [2 Cor 6:16; Lev 26:12].

Let those who are so full of ignorance tell us how we who have the Spirit dwelling in us are the temple of God, as Paul says [1 Cor 3:16], if he is not God by nature? If he is an originate creature, why then, when we defile the body in which the

Spirit dwells—the Spirit who possesses the entire natural property of God the Father and likewise of the Only Begotten—does God destroy us on the grounds that we are destroying the temple of God? How will the Savior be telling the truth when he says, "Those who love me will keep my word, and my Father will love them, and we will come to them and make our home with them" [John 14:23] and dwell in them? Though the Spirit is the one who dwells in us, we believe that through him, we also have the Father and the Son at the same time, just as John himself said again somewhere in his epistles: "By this we know that we abide in him and he in us, because he has given us of his Spirit" [1 John 4:13].

Commentary on the Gospel of Luke (likely before the Council of Chalcedon, 451)

The same vision of the Christian life is found in Cyril's commentary on Luke but in tighter, shorter form. From God the Son the Christian has life—life that is the Son's because he shares life with the Father. In other words, that he shares life with God the Father (John 5:26) means that the Son comes to us overflowing with life to give, life to offer of himself.

Luke 22:17–22— . . . And He took bread, and gave thanks, and broke it, and gave to them, saying, This is My body, which is given for you: do this in remembrance of Me . . . .

To be made partakers of Christ, both intellectually and by our senses, fills us with every blessing. For he dwells in us, first, by the Holy Spirit, and we are his abode, according to that which was said of old by one of the holy prophets. "For I will dwell in them", he says, "and lead them: and I will be to them a God, and they shall be to Me a people" [Ezek 37:27; Heb 8:10]. . . .

God the Father is by His own nature Life; and as alone being so, he caused the Son to shine forth who also himself is Life: for it could not be otherwise with him who is the Word that proceeded substantially from the Life: for he must, I say must, also himself be Life, as being One who sprang forth from Life, from him who begat him.

God the Father therefore gives life to all things through the Son in the Holy Spirit: and everything that exists and breathes in heaven and on earth, its existence and life is from God the Father by the Son in the Holy Spirit. Therefore neither the nature of angels, nor anything else whatsoever that was made, nor aught that from non-existence was brought into being, possesses life as the fruit of its own nature: but, on the contrary, life proceeds, as I said, from the substance which transcends all: and to it only it [Life] belongs, and is possible that it can give life, because it is by nature Life.

I. Patristic

B. After Nicaea (325–)

20. St. Benedict of Nursia (ca. 480–547) | *Rule*

Benedict was born as the Roman Empire was coming apart. As a young man he moved from his home in Nursia to the bustling city of Rome, but he was disillusioned by its immorality and paganism. Leaving the city behind, he sought the mountains east of Rome to pursue an extreme form of asceticism, living as a hermit high in a lonely cave in the wild country. After years in isolation, he agreed to serve as abbot (spiritual leader) for the monks of a nearby monastery. They got more than they bargained for. Gregory writes in his biography of Benedict that his discipline was so strict that they tried to poison him. Benedict returned to his solitary life.

Life in seclusion, Benedict knew, was an incomplete Christian life. He later established the monastery at Cassino, where he composed his *Rule*. As with Benedict's *Rule*, other ascetic communities composed and then lived according to shared norms of life. Monastic rules "created ordered environments so that the monks and nuns inhabiting these well-ordered monasteries could focus on what was most important—love of God and neighbor."[1] Benedict's *Rule* shows his awareness of monasticism in the East and the West, and he draws heavily from others already in use.[2]

Benedict's *Rule* is clearly strict but not without reason. He views the Christian life as a battle. "This message of mine is for you," he writes in the opening portions of his *Rule*, "if you are ready to give up your own will, once and for all, and armed with the strong and noble weapons of obedience to do battle for the true King, Christ the Lord." Like soldiers preparing for battle, the Christian cannot expect to perform on the field of battle without strict preparation: "The labor of obedience will bring you back to him [God] from whom you had drifted through the sloth of disobedience." Obedience creates attentive, wide-awake readiness for God. "Let us open our eyes," Benedict writes, "to the light that comes from God, and our ears to the voice from

---

1. Peters, *The Story of Monasticism*, 66.
2. See Fry, ed., *RB 1980*, 65–112.

heaven that every day calls out this charge: 'If you hear his voice today, do not harden your hearts' (Ps 94:8)."

In the following selection from Benedict's *Rule*, keep in mind that grace and works are never in the kind of tension that some (particularly Protestants) might detect. Benedict says in the same breath that all good works are in the Lord's power and by his grace, and then goes on to say, "Never swerving from his instructions, then, but faithfully observing his teaching in the monastery until death, we shall through patience share in the sufferings of Christ that we may *deserve* also to share in his kingdom" (emphasis added). For Benedict, good works *prove* grace rather than earn it. Thus, on one hand he says, "If we wish to dwell in the tent of this kingdom, we will never arrive unless we run there by doing good deeds." But at the same time it is *all grace*, for the good deeds one performs are done according to Christ's power. Thus, on the other hand, he writes, "What is not possible to us by nature, let us ask the Lord to supply by the help of his grace." The tension Benedict portrays is not grace in competition with works or works in competition with grace. Rather, the tension is inherent to the Christian life as a *battle of obedience* in which Christians strive to conform their will to the will of their king, Christ the Lord.

Rule (c. 529)

Prologue

Listen carefully, my son, to the master's instructions, and attend to them with the ear of your heart. This is advice from a father who loves you; welcome it, and faithfully put it into practice. The labor of obedience will bring you back to him from whom you had drifted through the sloth of disobedience. This message of mine is for you, then, if you are ready to give up your own will, once and for all, and armed with strong and noble weapons of obedience do battle for the true King, Christ the Lord.

First of all, every time you begin a good work, you must pray to him most earnestly to bring it to perfection. In his goodness, he has already counted us as his sons, and therefore we should never grieve him by our evil actions. With his good gifts which are in us, we must obey him at all times that he may never become the angry father who disinherits his sons, nor the dread lord, enraged by our sins, who punishes us forever as worthless servants for refusing to follow him to glory.

Let us get up then, at long last, for the Scriptures rouse us when they say: *It is high time for us to arise from sleep* (Rom 13:11). Let us open our eyes to the light that comes from God, and our ears to the voice from heaven that every day calls out to this charge: *If you hear his voice today, do not harden your hearts* (Ps 94[95]:8). And again:

You that have hearts to hear, listen to what the Spirit says to the churches (Rev 2:7). And what does he say? *Come and listen to me, sons; I will you teach you the fear of the Lord* (Ps 33[34]:12). *Run while you have the light* of life *that the darkness* of death *may not overtake you* (John 12:35).

Seeking his workman in a multitude of people, the Lord calls out to him and lifts his voice again: *Is there anyone here who years for life and desires to see good days?* (Ps 33[34]:13). If you hear this and your answer is "I do," God then directs these words to you: If you desire true and eternal life, *keep your tongue free from vicious talk and your lips from deceit; turn away from evil and do good; let peace be your quest and aim* (Ps 33[34]:14-15). Once you have done this, *my eyes will be upon* you *and my ears will listen* for your *prayers; and even before you ask me, I will say* to you: *Here I am* (Isa 58:9). What, dear brothers, is more delightful than this voice of the Lord calling to us? See how the Lord in his love shows us the way of life. Clothed then with faith and the performance of good works, let us set out on this way, with the Gospel for our guide, that we may deserve to see him *who has called* us *to his kingdom* (1 Thess 2:12).

If we wish to dwell in the tent of this kingdom, we will never arrive unless we run there by doing good deeds. But let us ask the Lord with the Prophet: *Who will dwell in your tent, Lord; who will find rest upon your holy mountain?* (Ps 14[15]:1). After this question, brothers, let us listen well to what the Lord says in reply, for he shows us the way to his tent. *One who walks without blemish*, he says, *and is just in all his dealings; who speaks the truth from his heart and has not practiced deceit with his tongue; who has not wronged his fellowman in any way, nor listened to slanders against his neighbor* (Ps 14[15]:2–3). He has *foiled* the *evil one*, the devil, at every turn, flinging both him and his promptings far *from the sight* of his heart. While these temptations were still *young, he caught hold of them and dashed them against* Christ (Ps 14[15]:4; 136[137]:9). These people *fear the Lord*, and do not become elated over their good deeds; they judge it is the Lord's power, not their own, that brings about the good in them. *They praise* (Ps 14[15]:4) the Lord working in them, and say with the Prophet: *Not to us, Lord, not to us give the glory, but to your name alone* (Ps 113:9[115:1]). In just this way Paul the Apostle refused to take credit for the power of his preaching. He declared: *By God's grace I am what I am* (1 Cor 15:10). And again he said: *He who boasts should make his boast in the Lord* (2 Cor 10:17). That is why the Lord says in the Gospel: *Whoever hears these words of mine and does them is like a wise man who built his house upon a rock; the floods came and the winds blew and beat against the house, but it did not fall: it was founded on rock* (Matt 7:24–25).

With this conclusion, the Lord waits for us daily to translate into action, as we should, his holy teachings. Therefore our life span has been lengthened by way of a truce, that we may amend our misdeeds. As the Apostle says: *Do you not know that the patience of God is leading you to repent* (Rom 2:4)? And indeed the Lord assures us in his love: *I do not wish the death of the sinner, but that he turn back to me and live* (Ezek 33:11).

B. AFTER NICAEA (325–)

Brothers, now that we have asked the Lord who will dwell in his tent, we have heard the instruction for dwelling in it, but only if we fulfill the obligations of those who live there. We must, then, prepare our hearts and bodies for the battle of holy obedience to his instructions. What is not possible to us by nature, let us ask the Lord to supply by the help of his grace. If we wish to reach eternal life, even as we avoid the torments of Hell, then—while there is still time, while we are in this body and have time to accomplish all these things by the light of life—we must run and do now what will profit us forever.

Therefore we intend to establish a school for the Lord's service. In drawing up its regulations, we hope to set down nothing harsh, nothing burdensome. The good of all concerned, however, may prompt us to a little strictness in order to amend faults and to safeguard love. Do not be daunted immediately by fear and run away from the road that leads to salvation. It is bound to be narrow at the outset. But as we progress in this way of life and in faith, we shall run on the path of God's commandments, our hearts overflowing with the inexpressible delight of love. Never swerving from his instructions, then, but faithfully observing his teaching in the monastery until death, we shall through patience share in the sufferings of Christ that we may deserve also to share in his kingdom. Amen.

I. Patristic

B. After Nicaea (325–)

21. St. Gregory the Great (540–604) | *Book of Pastoral Rule*

St. Gregory, known simply as "the Great" or "the Theologian," lived while the church refined its understanding of spiritual guidance. Gregory played an important role, partly because of his influence as Pope (590–604), and partly because his experience of ascetic life and spiritual direction lent authority and authenticity to his work *The Book of Pastoral Rule*.

Born to a wealthy and intensely religious family—two of Gregory's family members had been Pope—he was well-educated and soon given civic responsibility. As an administrator, he showed himself highly competent but, preferring the ascetic life, he stepped away from public duties and turned his home into a monastery. His administrative skills were not forgotten, however, and he was later drawn back into public life, against his wishes. Gregory's preference for simplicity and his heart for spiritual guidance reappeared as he served the Pope in Constantinople. There he became the abbot (spiritual leader) for the community of Italian monks. Gregory assumed the same role of St. Andrews after returning to Rome in 585. In 590, he was elected Pope, the same year he published *The Book of Pastoral Rule*.

The Book of Pastoral Rule was informed by years of spiritual leadership and met the unique needs of the Church in the sixth century. New converts had been flooding into the church ever since the conversion of Constantine (early fourth century), which raised questions about the sincerity of their conversion and commitment. In search of the devotion to life in Christ that was previously demanded of those who weathered imperial persecution, many fled to the desert and to monasteries. Two models of spiritual care thus developed: one for ascetic communities in the deserts and another for lay communities in the cities. It was not long, however, until the two models merged as desert ascetics returned to the city in various leadership positions (many at Gregory's appointment). Not surprisingly, the demands of pastoral ministry and the ideals of ascetic life soon found themselves in tension. As Gregory shows in *Pastoral Rule*, a priest must run a parish *and* care for souls.

B. AFTER NICAEA (325–)

Pastoral Rule might at first appear relevant only to those in positions of church leadership, but, actually, we find a nuanced picture of the Christian life relevant to any Christian. For Gregory, the Christian (and thus the spiritual director) must vigilantly attend to their inner life in order to discern the heart's tendencies toward virtue or vice. The real challenge is that vice often masquerades as virtue. This is where the wisdom and sensitivity of Gregory's *Pastoral Rule* is found: discerning the difference between virtue and vice for the sake of conforming one's life to Christ and offering spiritual care in his name.

Book of Pastoral Rule (590)

Part II, § 9 That the spiritual director should attentively consider that many vices appear as virtues

The spiritual director ought to know that there are many vices that appear as virtues. For example, greed disguises itself as frugality and wastefulness is thought to be generosity. Often laziness is accounted kindness and wrath appears to be spiritual zeal. And excessive haste is confused with the efficiency of promptness, while tardiness is taken for serious deliberation. It is necessary, therefore, that the director of souls carefully discern the difference between the virtues and vices so that, on the one hand, he does not allow greed to take hold of the heart of [the sinner] who appears frugal or, on the other hand, so that he does not allow another to boast of his generosity, when, in effect, he is simply being wasteful. Moreover, the director must be careful that he not pass over what he should punish, and thereby drag the laity with him to an eternal punishment. Reciprocally, he must not punish so forcefully that he sins more grievously himself. He must not spoil his opportunity for good and serious work with immature anticipation, nor should he postpone good works because they might transform into something evil. . . .

Part III, §9 The impatient and the patient

The impatient and the patient should be advised differently. The impatient should be told that when they fail to curb their spirit, they are carried into many types of iniquity that they do not desire, because clearly impetuousness drives the mind where it does not want to go. In such a state, the mind does not know what it does and then later is full of regret when it learns what it has done. The impatient should also be told that when they act hastily as a result of their emotions, they sometimes act as though they were someone else, and afterwards they rarely are aware of what they have done. . . .

On the other hand, the patient should be advised that they not pity themselves on the inside for what they appear to tolerate on the outside. Otherwise, they will corrupt by internal malice the great virtue of sacrifice that they outwardly offer. Moreover, their sin of self-pity, which humans do not recognize but which is identified as a sin by divine examination, will become worse in proportion to the fraudulent show of virtue before others.

Therefore, the patient should be told to study how to tolerate those whom it is necessary for them to love. For if love does not follow patience, the virtue on display will transform itself into the greater sin of wrath. Thus, when Paul says: "Love is patient," he immediately adds: "it is kind" (1 Cor 13:4). Clearly, those who are tolerated in patience are also loved with unceasing kindness. And so, the same great teacher when he was persuading his disciples of the virtue of patience, was saying: "Let all bitterness, and wrath, and indignation, and clamor, and blasphemy be put away from you" (Eph 4:31). And having put all outward matters in good order, [Paul] turned to the internal life when he added: "with all malice:" . . .

It often comes to pass for the patient that when they suffer adversity or hear insults, they are not afflicted by vexation but display patience so that they do not lose the innocence of their heart. But afterwards, when they recall to their memory the things that they endured, they become inflamed by the fire of aggravation, begin to look for revenge, and by retracting the meekness they had in their tolerance, transform it into malice. These persons are more quickly aided by the preacher if the reason for their change is disclosed. For the cunning adversary wages war against two persons: that is by inflaming the first one to offer insults and then to provoke the other to return those insults because of the injury. But it often happens that while [the devil] is victorious in persuading the first to inflict the injury, he can himself be conquered if the recipient bears the insult with equanimity. But because [the devil] was victorious over the first by incensing him, he then turns all his energy to the second and is angered by this one's strength and initial success. Wherefore, because [the devil] was not able to move the latter by the slinging of insults, he temporarily ceases his open assault and seeks a more appropriate time for deception by provoking the patient man with secret suggestions. And having lost his public campaign, he burns to lay hidden snares. Then, in a moment of stillness, [the devil] returns to the soul of the victor and reminds him of the temporal harm or the darts of insult that he endured, and by grossly exaggerating the harm that was suffered, he makes it appear that it was an intolerable injustice. And so [the devil] leads the mind into great sorrow to the point where a man who is typically patient, becoming a captive despite his victory, is embarrassed to have endured that evil with, such equanimity and despairs that he did not return the insults. Such a man then looks for the occasion to repay the injustice.

Part III, §22 Those who live in discord and those who are peaceful

Those who live in discord and those who are peaceful should be advised differently. Those who live in discord should be advised that, they know with certainty that whatever virtues they may possess, they will not become spiritual if they are unable to be united with their neighbor. For it is written: "The fruit of the Spirit is charity, joy, and peace" (Gal 5:22). Therefore, the one who does not care to keep the peace refuses to bear the fruit of the Spirit. Thus, Paul says: "When there is envy and contention among you, are you not carnal?"(1 Cor 3:3) And again, he says: "Follow peace with all men and in all holiness, for without, it, no one will see God" (Heb 12:14). And again, he admonishes them, saying: "Strive to keep the unity of the Spirit in the bond of peace: one body and one spirit, even as you are called in one hope of your calling" (Eph 4:3–4). The "one hope of your calling," therefore, is not achieved if we do not strive for it with a mind in unity with our neighbor. . . .

On the other hand, those who are peaceful should be advised that they if they love the peace that they have too excessively, they might lose that peace that is everlasting. Generally, tranquility tempts the serious intent of the mind so that there is a relationship between the easiness of what might occupy the mind and its willingness to engage in something more difficult, just as there is a relationship between being satisfied with the present and not concerning oneself with the eternal. Thus the Truth, speaking himself, when he distinguished between supernal and earthly peace so that he might coax his disciples away from the present, said: "My peace I leave to you; my peace I give to you" (John 14:27). In other words, "I leave a transitory peace; I give a lasting one." For if the heart is fixed on that which is left, it will never attain what is given. Therefore, the present peace should be loved, but it should not be our focus. For if it is loved immoderately, the soul that loves it can easily fall into sin.

Therefore, those who are peaceful should be advised that if they desire human peace too greatly, they might fail to reprove the evil conduct of others. And by condoning that behavior, they will, sever themselves from the peace of the Creator for by avoiding external quarrels, they will be punished for breaking their internal alliance [with God]. For what is transitory peace if not a footprint of eternal peace? Therefore, what could be more demented than to love a footprint, pressed in dust, but not love the one who made the impression? Thus David, when he would bind himself to the internal, footprints of peace, testifies that he did not hold any concord with, evil persons, saying: "Did I not hate them who hated you, God, and waste away because of your enemies? I hated them with a perfect hate because they have become my enemies" (Ps 138:21). For to hate God's enemies with a perfect hatred is to love what they were made to be but to reprove what they do; in other words, to reprove the action of the wicked but to remain of assistance to them.

Therefore, we must well consider what a great sin it is if we silence our criticism of the wicked and hold peace with them, when such, a great prophet offered as a sacrifice to God that he would provoke he wicked against himself on account of the Lord.

Section II: A.
Late Patristic—Medieval, Eastern

II. Medieval

Introduction: Late Patristic—Medieval, Eastern

The later Eastern Christian tradition we may take to last from the reign of Emperor Justinian, 527–565, up to the Turkish conquest of Constantinople in 1453. Such a demarcation, however, is more for our historical convenience than reflective of any epochal shift in the thinking and practice of the Christian faith by Easterners. Just as politically and culturally, a certain continuity was the keynote—the Eastern Roman Empire survived the Western by a thousand years—so the piety of the Constantinopolitan Church and its daughters continued the mind-set (*phronema*) of the Fathers of the Church, with some shifts, developments, and losses.

The beginning of this period saw the Eastern Christian world disturbed by the christological aftershocks of the Council of Chalcedon (451), the struggle to settle a doctrinally accurate account of the Divine "dispensation" or "economy" (*oikonomia*), i.e., of the incarnation of the Divine Logos for the redemption and salvation of the human race. The issue of icons in the eighth and ninth centuries was also christological: how far does the "enfleshment" of God the Word affect the material and visible cosmos? Answer: totally. If so, are these elements now capable of serving as an image of the enfleshed Image? Answer: yes. Under the impact of Islam, and of rationalist ideas, the emperors tried to enforce the removal of all figurative sacred art in the liturgy and piety of the church. In this great convulsion it was above all monks and women who were the champions of Orthodoxy, as we shall hear below in the case of Kassia and her spiritual father, St. Theodore of Stoudion.

This episode also illustrates the deleterious impact on the polity of the Eastern church of the dominance of a sacralized emperor. In the fourth century the apparent marriage of empire and church had seemed to many Christians an event to celebrate. In reality it was something of a poisoned chalice, bequeathing to churches of Constantinopolitan lineage (i.e., Greek, Romanian, and the various Slavic Orthodox) a permanent fault-line of susceptibility to the prevailing ethnic, national, or political ascendency.

The spiritual inscape of this Christian tradition is from first to last *liturgical*, both in the outward sacred rites of the church, and in her innermost spiritual aspects: for

SECTION II: A. LATE PATRISTIC—MEDIEVAL, EASTERN

Trinitarian doxology in the communion of the Ecclesia is the *telos* (end) of man, his ultimate vocation. The journey of our reclamation and transformation in Christ is the work of the Mystery of Christ communicated in the Holy Liturgy. Our participation in "the Mysteries" (= Eucharistic liturgy) shapes our progress in prayer toward *theoria* (contemplation) and *teleiosis* (perfection or "reaching the end"), which is *theosis*, a term that means our "deification" by participation in and through God the Incarnate Word, Christ our Lord (see Section I Introduction). To pass with Christ the High Priest through the veil into the Holy of Holies (cf. Heb 9) is the pattern of our passing into the divine darkness of contemplation, in Christ, of the ineffable and incomprehensible Father. So we have a complete coinherence of the earthly altar, the heavenly altar, and the altar of the human heart in prayer.

Sadly, this period saw not only the widening gap between the Greek speaking and Latin speaking spheres of Christianity, but also the final estrangement of both spheres from the churches of the Christian homeland: the Near East. But this did not happen without many enrichments from the Semitic Christian world. Syrian contributions to the Catholic ("universal") mix include the Pseudo-Macarian Homilies, with their emphasis on experiential spirituality (later recapitulated in Symeon the New Theologian), Pseudo-Dionysius, whose exposition of the Negative or Apophatic Way, in which the human soul moves beyond all created analogies to union with the Unknowable God in the "bright darkness," the "learned ignorance," and all the other startling paradoxes that he uses, would have a huge influence in both East and West; Romanus the Melodist, who elevated the lyrical character of the liturgy; and St. John Damascene, who recapitulated the state Catholic doctrine in the early eighth century.

The doctrinal high-water mark of this period is the figure of St. Maximus the Confessor. In him, all the fraught tensions of the christological debates reach their most searching negotiations. He elucidated the soteriological imperative of a distinct human will in the incarnate Christ (reprising somewhat the debates earlier in the West between Augustine and the Pelagians): i.e., why Christ's possession of a will in his humanity, distinct from a divine will was necessary for our salvation. The understanding of the Christian East of the human free will/divine grace polarity is encapsulated in the word *synergeia* (cf. 1 Thess 3:2), i.e., the "co-working" of the believer with God. Seemingly irreducible opposites are thereby held in poise: the freedom and responsibility of the human person, even if toiling under the effects of the fall, and the sublimely gratuitous gift of salvation on the initiative of God, the lover of man. Perhaps we can take the following passage in Maximus's Letter to the Presbyter George as representative:

> Of that which is hidden, as far as possible, he made manifestation, and of that which admits of no limit he bestowed such comprehension as was enough for the grasp of the mind and the apprehension of the Holy Spirit, for he accomplished the one and the other through that philanthropic ('loving to man') condescension, of what was beyond man, which made it manifest, *deifying*

through grace those who willingly ascend together with it (synanabainontas), and who through the kenosis of the Word receive of his fullness in the completion of the work of the commandments.

Just as in the West there was a flowering of mysticism amid the political and social distresses of the waning Middle Ages, so also in the inexorable diminishment of the Eastern Roman Empire by the conquests of the Arabs and the Turks, the mystical theology of the Eastern church underwent a new, and initially controversial development in *Hesychasm* (from *hesychia*, "quiet" or "tranquility"). Its leading apologist, Gregory Palamas, monk of Mt. Athos and later Archbishop of Thessaloniki, negotiated the tension between the incomprehensibility of the divine nature to the human intellect, and the experiential knowledge of God in contemplative prayer, by positing a distinction between God's essence (unknowable) and his uncreated energies (knowable), as exemplified in the vision of the "uncreated light" of the transfigured Christ on Mt. Tabor.

Thus the Greek theological and spiritual tradition attains its loftiest account of the Christian interior life, just as its this-worldly *oikoumene,* or the Christian civilizational settlement under a Christian emperor, was passing away.

Anna Silvas

II. Medieval

A. Late Patristic—Medieval, Eastern

22. Pseudo-Dionysius the Areopagite (520s) | *Mystical Theology*

It is fitting that we begin our survey of Medieval Eastern Christian writers with Pseudo-Dionysius, because of the three-pronged influence his writings were to have in the medieval period, in the Christian Near East, the Greek and Slavic East, and the Latin West. He is a seminal figure in the history of Christian mystical and liturgical theology.

The herald of "unknowing knowing" would be pleased to have stayed a great unknown. He hides himself beneath the immensity of the mysteries he serves with surpassing eloquence and insight. He also hides himself under the name of Dionysius ("Denys"), Paul's convert on the Areopagus in Athens (Acts 17:34), first bishop of Athens. His *Ecclesiastical Hierarchy* (in which he imports the term "hierarchy" to Christian discourse) reflects details of the Syrian Liturgy. It appears, then, that he was a priest-monk from Syria, bilingual in Syriac and Greek, steeped in the Greek Fathers, especially the Alexandrians, Clement and Origen, and the Cappadocian Fathers, and in the Neo-Platonist philosophers Plotinus and Proclus. He wrote in the early sixth century, as late as the 520s. His surviving works (called the Corpus Areopagiticum) are *The Divine Names*, *Mystical Theology*, *The Celestial Hierarchy*, *Ecclesiastical Hierarchy,* and ten *Letters*. His writings first found acceptance among the earliest "Monophysite" Fathers and then in a wider Chalcedonian/dyophysite audience, beginning with St. Maximus the Confessor.

Our selection consists of nearly the whole of *Mystical Theology*, a short work which sums up Denys's theology of the higher end of the Christian's journey toward sublime union with God. It is translated anew from the Greek, with acknowledgements to Parker's literal translation, and occasionally to the insights of Luibhead's more liberal translation. We here translate the many "hyper" prefixes as "transcendent(ly)."

For Denys the mystery at the heart of Christianity is Christ, and the access given in him to the Father, and so to the Trinity. This mystery is in the first place communicated in the church's Holy Liturgy, which becomes in turn the "launch pad," so to speak, for the liturgy of the heart, the interior progress in prayer as we gradually enter more deeply into the experiential knowledge of God, a progress full of paradoxes, because of the incomprehensibility of the divine nature. Denys's *Mystical Theology* above all bears witness to St Paul's: *Great indeed is the mystery of piety* (1 Tim 3:16).

Mystical Theology (520s)

I.1

O Trinity, transcendent being and divinity and goodness, guardian of the godly wisdom of Christians, direct us to the transcendently unknowable and transcendently luminous and highest pinnacle of the mystic sayings,[1] where the simple and absolute and changeless mysteries of theology are veiled in the transcendently bright obscurity[2] of the silence disclosing hidden realities, an obscurity that shines in the deepest darkness above the most transcendently bright, which, through the wholly intangible and invisible, fills eyeless intellects to overflowing with the glories of transcendent beauties.

So then do I pray. But do you, dear Timothy, by your assiduous practice in the mystic visions,[3] leave behind both the senses and intellectual operations, and everything sensible and intelligible, and all that is not, and all that is, and be raised without knowing toward union, as far as attainable, with the One who transcends all being and knowledge, for by unimpeded and absolute ecstasy, in purity, from yourself and all things, you will be raised on high, to that ray of the divine darkness, transcending all being, when you have cast away all things, and are released from all things.

I.2

But see that none of the uninitiated[4] listen to these things—those I mean who are caught up in existences[5], and cannot imagine that there is anything beyond these

---

1. The sacred words of the Scriptures and the Liturgy.

2. Following the Septuagint vocabulary (itself following distinct Hebrew terms), mystical theology distinguishes between *skoteinos*, generic darkness of any kind, and *gnophos* = deep/thick/impenetrable darkness, or thick cloud. It is difficult to consistently maintain the distinction in English. "Gloom" has been used to translate *gnophos*, but has an unhelpfully depressive connotation. "Obscurity" is chosen here.

3. The prolonging of the all-significant acts and words of the liturgy in contemplative prayer.

4. Those Christians who have not yet begun to journey more deeply into the Mystery through contemplative prayer.

5. I.e., individual, ostensible existences.

existences, but think, by their own knowledge, that they know him *who has made the darkness his hiding place* (Ps 18:11).

But if the Divine mystagogies[6] are beyond such as these, what is one to say of those even more uninitiated, those who depict the transcendent Cause of all from the lowest of existences, and say that it in no way surpasses the godless and multitudinous forms fashioned by themselves?

One must both ascribe and affirm the characteristics of all existing things to that Cause, since it is the Cause of all, and even more fittingly deny them all to it, since it surpasses all. Yet must not one think that the negations are opposed to the affirmations, but far rather, that what is above every paring away and attribution, is above all deprivations.

I.3

So the divine Bartholomew[7] said at any rate: that theology is both ample and scanty, and that the Gospel is broad and great, and yet cut short. This is what he seems to me to have understood supernaturally: that the good Cause of all is both rich in words, and at the same time of few words, and even wordless, that is, having neither word nor conception, because it exists above all this transcendently, and is manifested unveiled and in truth only to those who pass through things wholly polluted and things pure, and ascend above every ascent of all the holy summits, leaving behind all divine lights and sounds, and heavenly words, and advancing *into the obscurity where he* really *is* (Exod 20:21), who, as the Oracles say, is beyond all things.

Not for nothing was the divine Moses himself first bidden to be purified, and then to be separated from those who were not so.[8] After every purification he hears the many-voiced trumpets, and sees many lights flashing many-streaming rays; then he is separated from the many, and with chosen priests he attains to the summit of the divine ascents.

Nevertheless, he does not meet with God himself, for he contemplates not him who is unseen, but the place *where he is*. Now this I think signifies that the most divine and sublime of all that is seen and intuited are but suggestive sketches of what is on a level below him who transcends all. Through them the presence of him who is above all conception is indicated, surmounting the highest intelligible ["noetic"] summits of his most holy places. Then Moses is released from what is seen and sees, and advances into the obscurity of the Unknowing which is the truly

---

6. "Mystagogy" is "guidance into the Mysteries," i.e., explanation of the inner sense of the liturgy, and by organic extension, "mystical" as we might think of it.

7. The reference is possibly to the *Gospel of Bartholomew*, no longer extant, one of several apocryphal works which passed under the Apostle's name.

8. A description of Moses's ascent in Exodus 19 and 20 begins. It was treated in great detail by St. Gregory of Nyssa's *Life of Moses*, which is definitely an influence here.

mystical,[9] wherein he dismisses all cognitive apprehensions and enters within the wholly intangible and unseen, belonging completely to him who is beyond all and from none. Thus, belonging neither to himself nor to another, he is united entirely to the Unknown by the inactivity of all knowledge in his better part, and in knowing nothing, he knows in a way transcending intellect.

II.

We pray that we may come to that transcendently bright obscurity, and by not seeing and not knowing, to see and to know him who is above sight and knowledge in our very not seeing and not knowing. For this is really to see and to know and to hymn the Transcendent transcendently, through the paring away[10] from all existent realities. It is like those who are making a freestanding statue. They pare away every obstacle that impedes the clear view of what is concealed. Simply by this cutting away only, they bring to light the beauty that lies hidden.

But it is necessary I think to hymn the parings away in a different way to the affirmations. For we made the affirmations by beginning from the first things and then descended through the middle terms to the lowest, but now, as we make the ascents from the lowest to the highest, we pare away all things, so that we may know that Unknowing unveiled, enshrouded under all that can be known in existent realities, and may see that transcendent obscurity, which is hidden by all the light in existing things.

III.

In the *Theological Outlines*,[11] then, we hymned the most authoritative expressions of affirmative theology[12]—how the divine and good nature is spoken of now as unitary, now as threefold; what in it is spoken of as Fatherhood and Sonship; what the theology of the Spirit is intended to disclose; how the Lights in the heart of Goodness sprang forth from the immaterial and indivisible Good, and remained, in their branching forth, without departing from the coeternal abiding in himself[13] and in themselves and in each other; how the transcendently existent Jesus takes substance in truly human natural qualities[14]—and whatever other truths made known by the Oracles, are hymned throughout the *Theological Outlines*.

---

9. In the liturgical register of the work, "mystical" means one who has penetrated into the innermost sanctuary where the divine secrets are revealed/communicated.

10. The sense is pruning, cutting away, removing; abstracting, "disaffirming," negation.

11. An otherwise unknown work of the author.

12. I.e. *kataphatic* theology.

13. I.e., the Father, as the *arche* of the Trinity.

14. On the cusp of what is acceptable to both "Monophysites" and "Dyophysites." "Human nature" is a phrase Monophysites would never use. But here we have plural adjectives involving "nature," which

Now in the *On the Divine Names*: how He is named Good, how Being, how Life and Wisdom and Power—and whatever else is understood of divine naming. In the *Symbolic Theology*: what are the names transferred from the senses to things divine? What are the divine forms, what the divine appearances and parts and instruments, what the divine places and adornments, what the angers, what the griefs and the rages, what the inebriations and the after-effects, what the oaths and what the curses, what the fallings asleep and what the awakenings—and all the other sacredly fashioned similitudes, pertaining symbolically to the divine typology?

And I think that you will have noted how the last are wordier than the first. For it was necessary that the *Theological Outlines* and the unfolding of the *Divine Names* should be of fewer words than the *Symbolic Theology*; since the more we look to things above, the more words shrink before the overall views of intelligible ["noetic"] realities. For that matter, when we presently pass into the obscurity above intellect, we shall find, not fewness of words, but an entire lack of words and an absence of intellection.

Formerly, verbal discourse, in descending from the above to the lowest, widened in proportion to the measure of descent; but now, in rising from the below to the transcendent, it is constricted in proportion to the ascent, and following upon every ascent, it will be utterly voiceless and united wholly to the unutterable.

You ask, of course, why we who affirmed the divine attributes by beginning from the highest level, now begin the divine paring away from the lowest levels? Because when we attribute to that which is above every attribute, we must make our proposed affirmation from that which is more akin to it, whereas when we pare away from that which is above all paring away, we pare away that which is furthest removed from it. Are not life and goodness more apt than air and stone, and not being given to inebriation and rage, more apt than not being spoken of or conceived of?

IV.

We say therefore that the Cause of all things and of being, that is above all things, is neither non-existent, nor non-living, nor unreasoning, nor without mind; neither is it a body, nor a shape, nor a species, nor a quality, nor a quantity, nor a weight; neither is it in a place, nor is it seen, nor tangible to the senses, nor does it sense,[15] nor is sensed; it has no disorder or disturbance, not being oppressed by material passions, nor is it powerless, as being subject to the chances of sense, nor in need of light; it neither is nor has alteration, or decay, or division, or privation, or fluctuation, or anything else perceptible to the senses.[16]

---

they would use, so most literally: "in humanly natural realities."

15. I.e., obtain partial knowledge by the operation of material senses.

16. Original translation by Anna Silvas of Pseudo-Dionysius, *Mystical Theology I–IV*. In *Patrologia Graeca* 3.997A–1040D.

II. Medieval

A. Late Patristic—Medieval, Eastern

23. St. Maximus the Confessor (580–662) | *The Ascetic Life*

Maximus was born, according to Maronite sources, in the Holy Land, in what is now the Golan Heights. His family however were probably upper class, since Maximus received a high-level secular education and entered the imperial service in Constantinople. He was already head secretary to Emperor Heraclius (r. 610–641), when he entered a monastery in Chrysopolis, on the Anatolian shore of the Bosporus. The Avar/Slav invasions in the late 620s forced him to flee to North Africa, via Crete, Cyprus, and Alexandria. It would be hard to overstate the internal strife of the church in Maximus's lifetime, and the numerous assaults on Christendom from without, culminating in the spectacular irruption of Islam. Forged in the midst of this relentless turmoil, Maximus's peculiar emphasis on charity and the love of enemies gains its special significance and authority.

Maximus found a friend and mentor in the great advocate of Chalcedonian Christology, St. Sophronius (of Jerusalem), who alerted him to the perils of monoenergistic doctrine. From him Maximus imbibed firm dyophysite (Christ has two natures) and dyothelite (Christ has both a divine will and a human will) principles, going on to expound magisterially the distinction between "person" and "nature," concluding centuries of christological debate. Still in Africa, in 645 Maximus debated publicly with Pyrrhus, monothelite ex-Patriarch of Constantinople. Admitting his error, Pyrrhus travelled with Maximus to Rome in 645/6. Here Maximus lived for some eight years, being present for the election of Pope St. Martin I, and taking part in the Lateran Council of 649. Its Canons 10 & 11 condemning Monothelitism clearly bear Maximus's stamp. It is a marvelous moment: the collaboration of the Roman papacy and of Greek speaking Eastern Monks in a common doctrinal, spiritual, and ecclesial purpose.

Emperor Constans II, however, was a determined Monothelite, and asserted his imperial prerogatives over the church. In 653 he arrested Pope Martin and Maximus. They were taken to Constantinople to endure years of judicial persecution for "heresy." Maximus was subjected to a final terrible trial in 362, which sentenced him to be scourged, have his tongue and right hand cut off, and be exiled to the eastern shore of the Black Sea. These acts being carried out, he died shortly after his arrival in Lazika, Georgia, on August 13, 662.

The following is a catena of passages from the *Liber Asceticus*. It is an introductory dialogue with a novice on the Christian ascetic life, yet it touches on themes later discussed more fully, e.g. in 19 the role of the "mind" (really the "nous") in our human and Christian vocation. The "nous" is not the world of man's subjective ideas, feelings, reasonings, but the highest part of the soul capable under grace of contact with the living, transcendent, and ineffable God. Chapter 43 foreshadows the importance in Maximus' Christology of our salvation—the same thing as our deification—in understanding why there are two energies and two wills in God the Word incarnate who saves us.

The Ascetic Life (c. 630s)

19. And the brother said, "And what should one do, Father, to be able to devote oneself continuously to God?"

And the old man answered, "It is impossible for the intellect ('nous') to devote itself perfectly to God, except that it possess these three virtues: love, self-mastery and prayer. Love tames anger; self-mastery quenches concupiscence; prayer withdraws the intellect and presents it, stripped, to God himself. These three virtues comprise all virtues; without these the mind cannot devote itself to God." . . .

24. "Thoughts are the conceptions of things. Now, some things are sense-perceptible [αἰσθητά], some intelligible ('noetic'). The intellect ('nous'), therefore, as it tarries with these things, carries the thoughts of them about with itself. But the grace of prayer joins the intellect to God, and drawing to God, withdraws it from all thoughts. Then the intellect, being naked to him, and associating with him, becomes God-like. And being such, it asks of him what is proper, and at no time fails of its petition. Hence the Apostle bids us to *pray unceasingly* (1 Thess 5:17), in order that by joining the intellect unremittingly to God, we break off little by little our passionate attachment to material things. 25. . . . unceasing prayer is to maintain the intellect in great reverence and attachment to God by yearning, and to cling always to hope in him, to be of good courage in him in all things, as much in our activities as in what befalls us.

26. "With such dispositions, therefore, the Apostle *prayed without ceasing* (1 Thess 5:17). For in every activity and in all that befell him, he clung to hope in God. For this reason the saints always rejoiced in their tribulations, that they might come

to the habit of divine love. . . . But woe to us wretches who have abandoned the way of the holy Fathers, and for that reason are destitute of every spiritual work!'

27. Then the brother said, "Father, why do I have no compunction?"

And the old man answered: "Because *there is no fear of God before our eyes* (Ps 36:1); because we have become *the haunt of all evils* (cf. Rev 18:2), and for that reason we scorn as a mere thought the fearful punishment of God. For who does not experience compunction at hearing Moses speaking of sinners in God's person: *A fire is kindled in my heart. It shall burn to the lowest hell. . . . I will heap evils upon them, and will spend my arrows upon them* (Deut 32:22) . . . and at hearing Jeremiah say: *O give glory to the Lord your God, before it grows dark, and your feet stumble upon the dark mountains!* (Jer 13:16) . . . and again: *Your own apostasy shall chastise you, and your own wickedness shall rebuke you! Know and see that it is a bitter thing for you that you have left me, says the Lord. I planted you a fruitful vineyard, entirely genuine. How have you changed into bitterness, O alien vineyard?* (Jer 2:19, 21) . . .

33. "How then can we be called Christians, who have nothing at all of Christ in us? . . . 37. . . . what our Lord said of the unhappy Pharisees, I hear also of ourselves— *we* are the modern hypocrites, who have received such abundant grace and are yet worse disposed than they.

34. "Now perhaps someone will say: I have faith, and faith is enough for me for salvation. But James contradicts him, saying: *the devils also believe and tremble* (Jas 2:19), and again, *faith without works is dead* (Jas 2:17, 26)—as also works without faith. How then do we believe in him? Is it that we believe him about future events, but about transient, present realities we do not believe him, and so we immerse ourselves in material things and *live in the flesh* (cf. Rom 8:5, 12) and battle *against the Spirit* (Gal 5:17)? . . .

40. "After having heard all this, and being deeply struck with compunction, the brother, in tears, said to the old man: 'From what I see, Father, there is no hope of salvation left me. *For my iniquities have gone over my head* (Ps 38:4). Yet I beg you, tell me what I must do.'"

Then the old man answered and said, *with men, salvation is possible, but with God, all things are possible* (Matt 19:26), as the Lord himself has said. Therefore *let us come before his presence in contrition and thanksgiving. Let us adore and fall down and weep before the Lord who made us, for he is our God* (Ps 95:6–7) . . .

41. "We then, who have knowledge of the fear of the Lord, and yes, from both the Old and New Testaments, knowledge of his gentleness and loving-kindness, *let us turn back to him with all our heart* (cf. Joel 2:12). And why should we perish, brothers? Sinners are we? Let us cleanse our hands. Twofaced? Let us purify our hearts. Let us bewail, let us mourn, let us weep because of our sins. Let us quit our vices; let us trust the mercies of the Lord. Let us fear his threats; let us keep his commandments. Let us love one another with our whole heart. Let us say 'brothers' even of those who hate us and revile us, that the Lord's name may be glorified and manifest in its joyfulness.

Let us, when one is harassed by another, grant pardon to one another, since we are all warred upon by a common enemy...

"Let us rid ourselves of negligence and sloth, and stand valiantly against the spirits of wickedness. *And we have an advocate with the Father, Jesus Christ the Just One, and he is the propitiation for our sins* (1 John 2:1–2). Let us beseech him with a pure heart, and with our whole soul, and he will forgive our sins. [Citations of Ps 145:18, 50:14–15, Isa 58:6–10 follow.] You see how when we loosen every tie of wickedness from our hearts, and undo all the knots of contracts exacted for grudges, and hasten to do good for our neighbor with our whole soul—you see how we are illumined with the light of knowledge, and freed from the disgrace of passions, and filled with every virtue, and are illumined by God's glory and freed of all ignorance, and as we pray for all things in accord with the mind of Christ (cf. Phil 2:5), we are heard, and shall have God with us continually and be filled with godly desire?

42. "Let us then love one another, and be loved by God; let us be patient with one another, and he will be patient with our sins. Let us not *render evil for evil* (Rom 12:17), and we shall not receive the due for our sins. For we find the forgiveness of our trespasses in forgiving our brothers. The mercy of God is hidden in mercifulness to our neighbor. Therefore the Lord said: *Forgive, and you shall be forgiven* (Luke 6:37), and, *If you will forgive men their offences, your heavenly Father will also forgive your offences* (Matt 6:14), and again, *Blessed are the merciful, for they shall obtain mercy* (Matt 5:7), and *With the measure you mete out, it shall be measured to you in turn* (Matt 7:2). See, the Lord has bestowed on us the method of salvation, and *given us power to become sons of God* (John 1:12). So in the end, therefore, our salvation is in the grasp of our will.

43. "Let us therefore give ourselves entirely to our Lord, that we may receive him in turn entire. Let us become gods through him, for that is why he who by nature is God and Master, became man. Let us obey him, and he will without ado vindicate us against our enemies...

45. "Let us flee the world, and *the world's ruler* (cf. Eph 6:12); let us leave the flesh and carnal things; let us run on towards *heaven*, there let us have *our citizenship* (cf. Phil 3:20). Let us imitate the divine Apostle. Let us lay hold of *the author of life* (Acts 3:15); let us rejoice in *the fountain of life* (Ps 36:9). With the angels let us make chorus; with the archangels hymn our Lord Jesus Christ, to whom be glory and power, together with the Father and the Holy Spirit, now and ever and for endless ages. Amen."[1]

---

1. Translation revised from Maximus the Confessor, *The Ascetic Life*, in *Patrologia Graeca* 90.912–56.

II. Medieval

A. Late Patristic—Medieval, Eastern

24. St. John of Damascus (676–749) | *On the Orthodox Faith* & *Against Those Who Decry Images*

A Syrian priest-monk, John was born in the early years of the Arab conquest of the Christian Near East. His father was Sarjun Mansur, a chief financial officer of Caliph Malik. Discovering Cosmas, a Sicilian monk, in the slave market, Sarjun purchased and freed him and made him tutor to his sons. From Cosmas John acquired a high level of theological and spiritual education in the tradition. The onset of the Iconoclastic controversy was the first stimulus to John's theological activity. Ironically under the Caliph's protection, he wrote against the iconoclastic policies of Emperor Leo the Isaurian, beginning in 726. His three public letters stiffened popular resistance to the imperial coercions. The legitimacy of icon-veneration, he explained, is sourced squarely in the incarnation of God the Word, when the invisible and ineffable God was rendered visible, bridging matter and spirit.

John embraced the monastic life at Mar Saba in the Judean wilderness, and was eventually ordained a priest by the Patriarch of Jerusalem. He became a magisterial synthesizer of the tradition, so much so that some have called him a proto-scholastic. His "summa theologica" is the *Fountain of Wisdom*, which comprises three books in which John, steeped in the Scriptures and shot with phrases from the Fathers, sums up the defined orthodox faith of the Catholic Church in the mid-eighth century. In the second book he adds some twenty new heresies to Epiphanius's *Panarion*. His last entry is a sustained refutation of Muhammad and Islam.

We read below from the third book, called "An Exposition of the Orthodox Faith." Translated into Latin in 1150, this became a prized resource for the high medieval writers of the West. John records the traditional Patristic account of the procession of the Spirit, before it became a fraught issue in the Filioque controversy, the ancient Eastern tradition of the translation of Mary's body to heaven (the Assumption), a high Eucharistic doctrine of both the Real Presence and Sacrifice, and, as examples of unwritten Apostolic tradition, triple baptismal immersion, and facing the east for prayer. We finish with a few phrases from John's early work *Against Those who Decry Images*.

John also contributed richly to liturgical hymnody. Some of these theological poems have reached English, as in the Easter hymn, from the third ode of the "Golden Canon," in which John recycles the words of his much beloved St. Gregory the Theologian: "Yesterday with You in burial lying; now with You in triumph I arise. Yesterday the partner of your dying; raise me with you far beyond the skies."

On the Orthodox Faith (c. 730s)

II.30. Through his incorruption the devil, when he had fallen as the result of his own free choice, was firmly established in wickedness, so that there was no room for repentance and no hope of change: just as the angels also, when they had made free choice of virtue became through grace immovably rooted in goodness.

It was therefore necessary that man should first be put to the test—for man untried and unproven would be worth nothing—and, being perfected by trial through the observance of the command, thus receive incorruption as the prize of his virtue. For being intermediate between God and matter he was destined, if he kept the command, to be delivered from his natural relation to existing things and to be made one with God's estate, and to be immovably established in goodness, whereas, if he transgressed and inclined instead to what was material, and tore his mind from the Author of his being, I mean God, his fate was to be corruption, and he would become subject to passion instead of passionless, and mortal instead of immortal, and dependent on connection and unsettled generation. And in his desire for life he would cling to pleasures as though they were necessary to maintain it, and would fearlessly abhor those who sought to deprive him of these, and transfer his desire from God to matter, and his anger from the real enemy of his salvation to his own brethren. The *devil's envy* (cf. Wis 2:24) then was the reason for man's fall. For that same demon, so full of envy and with such hatred of the good, would not suffer us to enjoy the delights of heaven while he himself was kept below on account of his arrogance. Hence the false one tempts miserable man with the hope of Godhead, and leading him up to as great a height of arrogance as himself, hurls him down into a pit of destruction just as deep.

III.1. Man, therefore, was snared by the assault of the arch-enemy, and broke his Creator's command, was stripped of grace, put off his confidence with God, covered himself with the asperities of a toilsome life—for this is the meaning of the fig-leaves—and was clothed about with death, that is, with mortality and the grossness of flesh—for this is what the garment of skins signifies—and was banished from Paradise by God's just judgment, and condemned to death, and made subject to corruption. Yet, notwithstanding all this, God, in His pity, Who gave him his being, and Who in His graciousness had bestowed on him a life of happiness, did not disregard man, but first trained him in many ways and called him back, by groans and trembling, by the deluge of water, and the utter destruction of almost the whole race, by confusion and diversity of tongues, by the rule of angels, by the burning of cities, by figurative manifestations of God, by wars and victories and defeats, by signs and wonders, by manifold faculties, by the law and the prophets: for by all these means God earnestly strove to emancipate man from the wide-spread and enslaving bonds of sin which had made life such a mass of iniquity, and to effect man's return to a life of happiness. For it was sin that brought death like a wild and savage beast into the world to the ruin of the human life.

Now it behooved the Redeemer to be without sin, and not rendered liable through sin to death, and further, that His nature be strengthened and renewed and trained by labour and taught the way of virtue which leads away from corruption to the life eternal and, in the end, reveal the mighty ocean of love for man that envelops Him. For the very Creator and Lord Himself undertakes a struggle in behalf of the work of His own hands, and learns by toil to become Master. And since the enemy snares man by the hope of Godhead, he himself is snared in turn by the veil of the flesh, and so at once the goodness and wisdom, the justice and might of God are disclosed. God's goodness is revealed in that He did not disregard the frailty of His own handiwork, but was moved with compassion for him in his fall, and stretched forth His hand to him; and His justice in that when man was overcome He did not make another victorious over the tyrant, nor did He snatch man from death by might, but in His goodness and justice He made him who had become the slave of death through his sins, himself once more a conqueror, and so rescued like by like, most difficult though it seemed; and His wisdom is seen in His devising the most fitting solution of the difficulty. For by the good pleasure of our God and Father, the Only-begotten Son and Word of God and God, *Who is in the bosom of the God and Father* (John 1:18), consubstantial (*homoousios*) with the Father and the Holy Spirit, Who was before the ages, is without beginning and Who *in the beginning was with God* and Father *and was God* (John 1:1), and exists *in the form of God* (Phil 2:6), *bowed the heavens and came down* to earth (Ps 18:9): that is to say, He, without humiliation humbled His lofty station which was not to be humbled, and condescended to His servants, with a condescension ineffable and incomprehensible—for that is what the *coming down* signifies. And God being perfect becomes perfect man, and brings to perfection the newest of all new things, the only new thing under the Sun, through which the boundless might of God is manifested. For what is greater, than that God should become Man? And *the Word became flesh* (John 1:14) without being changed, of the Holy Spirit and Mary the holy and ever-virgin *Theotokos*. And the only lover of man acts as mediator between God and man, being conceived in the Virgin's chaste womb without will or desire, or conjunction of a man or pleasurable generation, but through the Holy Spirit and the first offspring of Adam. And He becomes obedient to the Father as one of us, and finds a remedy for our disobedience in what He had assumed from us, and became a pattern of obedience to us without which there is no attaining of salvation.

III.6. . . . For God the Word omitted none of the things which He implanted in our nature when He formed us in the beginning, but took them all upon Himself, body and soul both intelligent and rational, and all their properties. For the creature that is devoid of one of these is not man. But He in His fullness took upon Himself me in my fullness, and was united whole to whole that He might in His grace bestow salvation on the whole man. For what has not been assumed cannot be healed.

III.14. And once again, the Gospel tells us that, *He, having come into the place, said "I thirst": and they gave Him some vinegar mixed with gall, and when He had tasted it He would not drink* (Matt 27:33–34 + John 19:28–29). If, then, on the one hand it was as God that He suffered thirst and when He had tasted would not drink, surely He must be subject to passion also as God, for thirst and taste are passions. But if it was not as God but altogether as man that He was thirsty, likewise as man He must be endowed with volition.

Moreover, the blessed Paul the Apostle says, *He became obedient unto death, even the death of the cross* (Phil 2:8). But obedience is subjection of the real will, not of the unreal will. For that which is irrational is not said to be obedient or disobedient. But the Lord having become obedient to the Father, became so, not as God but as man. For as God He is not said to be obedient or disobedient. For these are of the things that are under one's hand, as the inspired Gregory said. Wherefore Christ, then, is endowed with volition as man.

III.26. The Word of God then itself endured all in the flesh, while His divine nature which alone was passionless remained void of passion. For since the one Christ, Who is a compound of divinity and humanity, and exists in divinity and humanity, truly suffered, that part which is capable of passion suffered as it was natural that it should, but that part which was void of passion did not share in the suffering. For the soul, indeed, since it is capable of passion shares in the pain and suffering of a bodily cut, though it is not cut itself but only the body: but the divine part which is void of passion does not share in the suffering of the body.

IV.4. Hail, O Christ, Word and Wisdom and Power of God, and God omnipotent! What can we the helpless give You in return for all these good gifts? For all are Yours, and You ask nothing of us save our salvation, You who are Yourself the bestower of this, and yet are grateful to those who receive it, through your unspeakable goodness. Thanks be to You who gave us life, and granted us the grace of a happy life, and restored us to that when we had gone astray, through Your unspeakable condescension.

Against those who decry images (c. 710–20)

III.112-115 And may Christ fill you with the joy of His resurrection most holy flock of Christ, Christian people, chosen race, body of the Church, and make you worthy to walk in the footsteps of the saints, of the shepherds and teachers of the Church, leading you to enjoy His glory in the brightness of the saints. May you gain His glory for eternity, with the Uncreated Father, to whom be praise for ever. Amen.[1]

---

1. Translations revised.

II. Medieval

A. Late Patristic—Medieval, Eastern

25. Kassia the Melodist (c. 810–c. 865) | *Hymn for the Theophany* & *O Lord, she who in many sins*

Born to an aristocratic family of Constantinople, and as highly educated in the Hellenic and Patristic classics and in music as women of that class could be, Kassia's character was forged as a girl in the last convulsions of the Iconoclastic Controversy. She joined the women and monks who staunchly resisted the imperial campaign, being beaten on one occasion by soldiers for aiding imprisoned monks. The contours of her life we infer from a range of sources, which include three letters to her from the spiritual father of her youth, the great Theodore the Studite, staunch opponent of divorce and remarriage, last of the Greek Fathers to advocate collaboration with the Pope of Rome, reformer of Greek monastic communities, and both confessor-champion and theologian of icon-veneration.

There is a famous story that Kassia appeared in a "bride-show" for the young Emperor Theophilos, the tenth-century Chronicler's text of which is included here. Historically true or not, the story accurately conveys Kassia's forthright speech and quick wit, known otherwise from her writings, and her typological reading of the Scriptures. In this story she implicitly portrays Mary, "the woman" of the Gospel (John 2:4, 19:25–27), as the new Eve, a topos extending the Adam/Christ typology of Romans 5:14 and 1 Corinthians 15:22, 45, going back almost to sub-apostolic times (Justin Martyr). Her troparion to St. Barbara, evincing the same "theology of woman," so to speak, follows.

Kassia, anyway, had no wish to marry, but to pursue the monastic calling instead. She eventually headed a monastery of nuns in the west of Constantinople, not far from the men's monastery of Stoudion, so hugely influential in the Medieval Greek church. She became renowned for both as a social commentator and as a spiritual teacher, testified in her many epigrams, poems, and sacred chants which survive. The monks did not memorialize their friendship with her by writing her life, but by including some of her chants in the liturgical books that they were editing. She is the only female poet to be accorded this privilege.

Included below is a stanza from her hymn for the Theophany (Epiphany) in which she enters into the dispositions of John the Baptist when he receives Jesus' request to be baptized by him. She elaborates these dispositions dramatically and theologically. This jewel of a hymn shows how utterly penetrated she was by the patristic, theological, and liturgical way of meditating on the Scriptures.

Finally we post Kassia's most famous work, her troparion for Orthros, or Lauds of Holy Week, "O Lord, she who in many sins," in which she enters with deepest empathy into the plight of the sinful woman of Luke 7:36–50, mingled with the anointing at Bethany of Mark 14:3–9, John 12:1–8. As with her other hymns, Kassia also set this hymn to music, so that she is properly called "Melodos" and is truly a theologian who sings.

Chronicle of Symeon the Logothete (10th cent.)

In the year of the world 6323, and of the divine Incarnation 823, the Emperor of the Romans Theophilos, son of Michael the Stammerer, 12 years. His mother Euphrosyne, being resolved to give him a wife, assembled various maidens of peerless beauty, of whom there was a certain maiden, the fairest bloom among them, called Kassia, and another named Theodora. Giving him a golden apple, Euphrosyne told him to give it to the one who pleased him the most. Astonished by the Kassia's beauty, Emperor Theophilos said: "Ach, what deplorable things gushed forth through woman!" She answered, not without a certain modesty: "Ah yes, but also through woman the better things spring." Struck to the heart by this word, Theophilos passed her by and gave the golden apple to Theodora who came from Paphlagonia.

The malign Enemy,
who once gained the Foremother
as an instrument for sin,
has been put to shame,
worsted by a woman,
for he who was incarnate of a Virgin,
the Word of the Father,
simple and immutable,
as he alone is known,
has undone the curse of Eve and Adam.

Hymn for the Theophany (c. 850s)

When you, O Christ, appeared,
the Master among the servants,
and came to the streams of the Jordan,
and had hands laid on you by your servant the Forerunner (cf. Luke 1:17, Mal 3:1),
and were baptized in the water,
the ranks of the angels were astonished to see
the greatness of your condescension, O Benefactor,
who accepted the flesh
to be baptized for us
and wipe away the filth of mortals.
Glory to you, O Lord!

Jesus, the Christ,
enlightener of those in darkness (Luke 1:79)
accomplisher of our refashioning,
came as a petitioner to John,
calling out to be baptized by him:
"Be willing to wash me in these waters!
In them I shall make new the nature of men,
grown old in corruption (Dan 13:52 Septuagint, cf. Eph 4:22)
and wholly enslaved
by the craft of the Serpent."
Glory to you, O Lord!

"O my Maker, how shall I who am *grass*, (cf. Ps 90:5, 103:15)
lay hands upon you who are *fire*? (cf. Heb 12:29 et al.)
How shall the streams of the *river* receive you,
who are a great *sea* (cf. Sir 24:31) of *divinity* (cf. Col 2:9)
and the inexhaustible *fountain of life*? (Ps 36:9)
How shall I baptize you who, having no defilement
remove the filth of men? (cf. Ezek 22:15, et al.)
For which, for our sake, you were born of the Pure One,"
said he who was born of the Barren One (cf. Luke 1:36):
"*It is I who have need of baptism from you!*" (Matt 3:14)
Glory to you O Lord!

A. LATE PATRISTIC—MEDIEVAL, EASTERN

O Lord, she who in many sins (c. 850s)

O Lord, she who had fallen into many sins (cf. Luke 7:37),
discerning your divinity,
takes up the rank of a myrrh-bearer (cf. Luke 23:55–24:1),
and mourning, brings you myrrh,
before your *burial* (Mark 14:8).
Alas for me! she says,
for the night smothers me—
a goading of passion
murky and moonless,
a craving for sin!
Accept *the fountains of my tears* (Jer 9:1),
You who disperse from clouds
the waters of the sea (cf. Sir 40:11, Amos 9:6, Ps 77:17).
Stoop down to me,
to the groaning of my heart,
You who *bowed down the heavens* (Ps 18:9)
in your ineffable self-emptying (*kenosis*, Phil 2:7)!
I shall fervently kiss your undefiled feet,
and then I shall wipe them
with the hairs of my head (cf. Luke 7:38),
at whose sound in Paradise,
breaking upon her ears
in the cool of the evening,
Eve hid in fear (cf. Gen 3:8).
O who can fully trace out
the multitude of my sins
and the depths of your mercies,
O Saviour of souls, my Saviour?
Do not turn not aside from me your handmaid,
O bearer of great and unmeasured mercy![1]

---

1. Translation by Anna Silvas from the tenth-century Chronicle of Symeon the Logothete at *Patrologia Graeca* 109, col 685C, and from the Greek text in Antonía Tripolitis, *Kassia: the legend, the woman, and her work* (New York: Garland, 1992), 12, 30–32 and 76–78.

II. Medieval

A. Late Patristic—Medieval, Eastern

26. St. Symeon the New Theologian (949–1022) | *Invocation of the Holy Spirit* & *Hymns 17, 25, & 21*

Born to a devout aristocratic family of Basileion in Galatia, Symeon completed his middle schooling in Constantinople and was set for higher studies, when at fourteen years of age he met a monk, not a priest, of the famed monastery of Stoudion, Symeon the Pious, in whom he found a spiritual father. He forsook the higher secular curriculum and studied monastic writers under the elder Symeon's direction. On his advice Symeon did not yet enter a monastery. For years he served an aristocratic family in a "worldly" way of life by day, and in prayer and reading by night. Finally, Symeon the elder sent him, at age twenty-seven, to join the run-down monastery of St. Mammas, whose reforming hegoumen he was soon to become.

Symeon was heir to the charismatic, experiential, even enthusiast elements of the Pseudo-Macarian stream of monastic tradition. He was also well aware of the Evagrian tradition, Pseudo-Dionysius, and recent Fathers and theologians. These influences he wove into a synthesis all his own. A man of living impatience with a minimalist, nominal Christianity, with the Church as mere institution, with bishops as hollow men of mere facades, with theology as anemic ratiocination, he became a thorn in the side of the less overtly zealous, whether monks resentful of the greater austerities, prayer, and simplicity he promoted in his own monastery, or with the doctrinal authorities of the Patriarchate, especially, Stephen, ex-Metropolitan of Nicomedia, who targeted the "novelties" of his ideas. The Patriarch banished him across the Bosporus in 1009. He camped out in the ruined monastery of St. Marina, revived it, and here wrote most of his hymns.

One of his doctrines that got him into trouble with the official and theological church concerned his total emphasis on the need of a spiritual father. Somewhat like ideas about Confessors in the second century as intercessors for people's sins, and the old Donatist idea that a priest's personal holiness was material to the valid administration of the sacraments: Symeon taught that deep personal experience of God qualified to absolve another's sins, and that the lack of it annulled the communication of any real spiritual help. He is the great champion of the necessity of the lived experience of the Holy Spirit for a true Christian life, as we see here in his splendid Hymn to the Holy Spirit. Our selection ends with a severe questioning by Symeon why anyone who is without this experience would dare to speak of God.

Invocation of the Holy Spirit (c. 1010–20)

Come, *true light* (John 1:9). Come, *life eternal* (1 John 5:20). Come, *hidden mystery* (Eph 3:9). Come, treasure without name. Come, reality ineffable. Come, O Face incomprehensible. Come, exultation without end. Come, unfading Light. Come, unfailing expectation of all who are being saved. Come, Awakener of those who sleep. Come, *Resurrection* of the dead (John 11:25). Come, *Mighty One* (Luke 1:49, et al), ever creating, refashioning and transforming all things by your will alone. Come, Invisible One (cf. John 14:17) whom none may touch and handle. Come, you who abide unmoved, yet who at every hour are entirely in movement; who draw near to us who lie in hell, yet who are above the heavens (Eph 4:10).

Come, most beloved name repeated over and over again; yet who You are and what your nature is, it is not permitted us to say or know. Come *Eternal Joy* (Isa 35:10). Come *Imperishable Crown* (1 Pet 5:4). Come Royal Purple of our great God and King. Come crystalline cincture set with gems (cf. Dan 10:5, Rev 22:1). Come, Unapproachable Sandal (cf. John 1:27). Come Robe of Royal Purple and truly Right Hand that effects all things. Come, You whom my wretched soul has desired and does desire.

Come, you, the Alone, to the alone, for I am alone, as you see. Come You who separated me from everyone and made be alone upon the Earth. Come, You have become desire itself in me and Who made me to desire You, the utterly Unapproachable. Come, my breath and my life (Acts 17:25). Come, consolation of my dejected soul. Come, my joy, and glory, and endless delight.

I thank You because You have become *one spirit with me* (1 Cor 6:17), not mingling, unmoved, immutable God over all things; because You have become *all in all* for me (Rom 3:5), nourishment utterly indescribable and utterly without expense, endlessly overflowing the lips of my soul and gushing forth in the fountain of my heart (John 4:14), raiment flashing forth and burning up the demons, purification through incorrupt and holy tears that wash me through and through, tears that You give freely to those whom you visit. I thank you because you have become an unfading Light and unsetting Sun to me, You who have nowhere to hide, Who *fill the whole world with your glory* (Isa 66:1). You have never hidden Yourself from anyone. It is we who always hide ourselves from You, not wishing to come to You. For where would you hide, You who nowhere have a place of repose, and why? You never turn anyone away at all, and do not turn from any of them.

So now Master, dwell in me and inhabit me, and remain constantly and inseparably in your servant, until my death, O Good One, that I also may be found in You, both in my departure and after my departure (cf. Phil 3:9), O Good One, and reign with You (2 Tim 2:12), God over all things (Rom 9:5). *Stay with me*, Master (Luke 24:29), and let me not be alone, so that when my enemies come, *always seeking to devour* my soul (cf. 1 Pet 5:8), and find You abiding in me, they shall flee entirely, and shall have no strength against me, when they see You Who are mightier than all things, seated in the home of my humbled soul (Mark 3:27).

Truly Master, You remembered me while I was in the world of ignorance. You picked me out, and separated me from the world, and *set me before the Face of your glory* (Jude 24). So now keep me always within, standing always upright and immovable in your dwelling within me, so that watching You continually, I the corpse, may live; and possessing You, I the poor hireling, may become rich, richer than all kings (cf. Luke 15:25), and that eating and drinking You (cf. John 6:54), and every hour being vested with You, I shall revel in the unspeakably Holy. For You are every good, and every glory, and every fruition, and to You glory is fitting, You the holy, consubstantial, and life-giving Trinity, Trinity in Father, Son and Holy Spirit venerated and proclaimed and worshipped by all the faithful, both now, and always and unto ages of ages. Amen.

Hymn 17 (c. 1010–1020)

... I know O Saviour, that no other has failed you as I have, nor done the deeds I have done, wretch that I am, and that I have also been a cause of ruin for others. But again I know this, indeed I am persuaded of this my God, that neither the magnitude of failures, nor the multitude of sins, nor the shame of deeds shall succeed in surpassing your great benevolence; that You abundantly pour out your mercy, beyond all telling and transcending the mind, upon those who fall (cf. Titus 3:6) and who fervently repent. You both purify them and illumine them, making them participants of light and *partakers of* your *divinity* (2 Pet 1:4). You both consort and converse with them as your lawful friends (cf. Exod 33:11).

O infinite kindness! O inexpressible love! Wherefore I prostrate and call fervently to You. Just as you received the prodigal (cf. Luke 15:20) and the prostitute at their approach (cf. Luke 7:38), so You received me, O Merciful, who repent from my soul. And you have considered the drops of my tears as a fountain ever gushing forth, O my Christ. In them wash my soul; wash also my body of the defilement of the passions, and wash my heart of every wickedness, for that is the root and fount of all sin (cf. Mark 7:21). Wickedness is the seed of the wicked sower, and where it is sown, it sprouts and rears up high, and produces a great many young shoots of wickedness and evil (cf. Matt 13:24-30). Tear out their roots from the depths, O my Christ, and purify my soul and implant fear in the furrows of my heart. O Merciful, deign that your fear take root in the furrows and sprout up well, that it may grow high as a safeguard of your commandments . . .

Now the flower and fruit which fear begets is outside the world; these know how to snatch away the mind, and to take up the soul along with it, and throw them out of the world. "How, tell me, does love throw them out of the world? I would like to know this clearly." These things are inexpressible, as I said. Nevertheless, attend and I shall tell. Love is the divine Spirit (1 John 4:16), the light that works and illumines all things; but it is not from the world, nor in any way something of the world, nor a creature, for it is uncreated, and outside all creatures, uncreated among creatures. Understand what I say to you my child!

Hymn 25 (c. 1010–1020)

How shall I describe, Master, the vision of your Face, how shall I tell of the unutterable contemplation of your Beauty? How shall the utterance of the tongue compass what the world does not contain, how could anyone express your benevolence? For I was sitting with the light of a lamp shining on me, illuminating the gloom and darkness of the night, seemingly occupied with reading by the light, as if examining the sayings and considering the syntax. I had thus began, O Master, meditating on these things, when suddenly You appeared from above, far greater than the sun, and You shone from the heavens as far as my heart . . .

But O what intoxication of light, O what movements of fire, O what swirling of flame worked in me, wretch that I am, by You and Your glory! That glory I understand and I say it, is your Spirit, the Holy, of the same nature and the same honor, O Word; the same race, the same glory, of the same substance, alone with the Father and with you O Christ, God of all things (Eph 4:6)! Prostrate in worship I give thanks that You have deigned me worthy to know something of the power of Your divinity.

Hymn 21 (c. 1010–1020)

But if you do not know that the eye of your intellect ('nous') has been opened and is seeing the light, if you have nothing of the sweetness of the Divine, if you have not been illumined by the divine Spirit, if you have not wept tears painlessly, if you have not seen your mind cleansed, if you have not known your heart purified (cf. Matt 5:8) and shining bright reflections, and if you have not found Christ within you, even surpassing all hope, and you were never astounded at seeing the divine Beauty, and you did not forget human nature, seeing yourself entirely transformed: tell me then, how do you not tremble to speak about God? How dare you, who are all flesh, and have not *become spirit* like Paul (cf. Rom 8:9), speak or philosophize about the Spirit?[1]

---

1. Translation slightly revised.

II. Medieval

A. Late Patristic—Medieval, Eastern

27. Gregory of Sinai (c. 1265–1346) | *On Commandments and Doctrines* & *On the Signs of Grace and Delusion*

The long and much traveled life of this apostle of stillness and tranquility ("hesychia"), began with his birth in the village of Clazomene near Smyrna, where he led a conventional life until his abduction by Turks in the year 1290. On being ransomed, he entered a monastery in Cyprus, but soon departed for St. Catherine's Monastery, Mt. Sinai, where he steeped himself in the tradition of the great Sinaite Father, St. John Climacus. After years of humble service he took on the "great schema," the habit of monks with the highest commitment to ascesis and prayer. Leaving Sinai, he went first to Jerusalem, and then to Crete, where he learned from the monk Arsenios of recent developments in hesychast spirituality and the practice of the Jesus Prayer. From there, around the year 1300 he moved to Mt Athos, to the Magoula skete (a skete is an aggregation of hermits unlike the larger, more formal cenobitic monastery), an adjunct of Philotheou monastery. He settled down to the assiduous practice of hesychasm. Turkish raids on Athos in the 1320s, however, drove him to resettle in the Strandzkha Mountains in southeastern Bulgaria.

Gregory promoted a moderate form of hesychast practice. Together with his younger contemporary, Gregory Palamas, he is most known for drawing Athonite monasticism deep into the orbit of the hesychast tradition, which expresses the mature longing of Greek theological spirituality for theosis, that assimilation of the human to the divine only made possible in Jesus, the incarnate Divine Logos. The ultimate spiritual goal is the vision of the "divine light" or "uncreated energies" as disclosed in the Gospel accounts of the Transfiguration of Christ (Matt 17, Mark 9, Luke 9).

The classic anthology of monastic and hesychast writings, the Philokalia, preserves five generous selections from Gregory's written works, from two of which we draw here. Of particular interest is Gregory's correlation of the eucharistic liturgy with the liturgy of the heart, his doctrine of the call of all Christians to consummate holiness, his exposé of the spiritual malaise of stagnant and casual Christians, his warnings against our entertaining the counterfeits presented to our imagination, and against reasoning powers that hinder our true advance in Christ.

On Commandments and Doctrines (c. 1310–20)

43. The kingdom of heaven is like the tabernacle built by God, which He disclosed as a pattern to Moses (cf. Exod 25:40); for it has also an outer and an inner sanctuary. Into the first will enter all who are priests of grace. But into the second—which is noetic—only they will enter who in this life have attained the divine darkness of theological wisdom, and there as true hierarchs have celebrated the triadic liturgy, entering into the tabernacle that Jesus Himself has set up, where He acts as their consecrator and chief Hierarch before the Trinity, and illumines them ever more richly with His own splendor . . .

112. Before the fruition of the blessings which transcend the intellect, and as a foretaste of that enjoyment, the noetic activity of the intellect mystically offers up the Lamb of God upon the altar of the soul and partakes of Him in communion. To eat the Lamb of God upon the soul's noetic altar is not simply to apprehend Him spiritually or to participate in Him; it is also to become an image of the Lamb as He is in the age to come. Now we experience the manifest expression of the Mysteries; hereafter we hope to enjoy their very substance.[1]

113. For beginners, prayer is like a joyous fire kindled in the heart; for the perfect it is like a strong sweet-scented light. Or again, prayer is in the preaching of the Apostles, an action of faith or, rather, faith itself, *that makes real for us the things for which we hope* (Heb 11:1): active love, angelic impulse, the power of the bodiless spirits, their work and delight, the Gospel of God, the heart's assurance, hope of salvation, a sign of purity, a token of holiness, knowledge of God, baptism made manifest, purification in the water of regeneration, a pledge of the Holy Spirit, the exultation of Jesus, the soul's delight, God's mercy, a sign of reconciliation, the seal of Christ, a ray of the noetic sun, the heart's dawn-star, the confirmation of the Christian faith, the disclosure of reconciliation with God, God's grace, God's wisdom or, rather, the origin of true and absolute Wisdom; the revelation of God, the work of monks, the life of hesychasts, the source of stillness and expression of the angelic state. Why say more? Prayer is God, who accomplishes everything in everyone (cf. 1 Cor 12:6), for there is a single action of Father, Son and Holy Spirit, activating all things through Christ Jesus.

---

1. The eucharistic liturgy here is intended for consummation in the liturgy of heaven via the liturgy of the heart offered "on the altar of the soul."

SECTION II: A. LATE PATRISTIC—MEDIEVAL, EASTERN

On the Signs of Grace and Delusion (c. 1310-20)

1. As the great teacher St. John Chrysostom states, we should be able to say that we need no help from the Scriptures, no assistance from others, but are instructed by God; for *all will be taught by God* (Isa 54:13; John 6:45) in such a way that we learn what we ought to know from Him and through Him. And this applies not only to those of us who are monks but to each and every one of the faithful: we are all called to bear *the law of the Spirit written on the tablets of our hearts* (2 Cor 3:3), and to attain, like the Cherubim, the supreme privilege of conversing directly, through pure prayer in the heart, with Jesus.

But because we are infants at the time of our renewal through Baptism we do not understand the grace and the new life bestowed upon us. Unaware of the surpassing grandeur of the honor and glory in which we share, we fail to realize that we ought to grow in soul and spirit through the keeping of the commandments and so perceive noetically what we have received. Because of this most of us succumb through indifference and servitude to the passions in a state of benighted obduracy. We do not know whether God exists, or who we are, or what we have become, although through Baptism we were made sons of God, sons of light, and children and members of Christ. If baptized when grown up, we feel that we have been baptized only in water and not by the Spirit. And even though we have been renewed in the Spirit, we "believe" only in a formal, lifeless and ineffectual sense, and say that we are full of doubts.

Because we are in fact unspiritual, we live and behave unspiritually. If we repent, we understand and practice the commandments only extrinsically and not spiritually. And if after many labors a revelation of grace is by God's compassion granted to us, we take it for a delusion. Or if we hear from others how grace acts, we are persuaded by envy to regard that too as a delusion. So we remain corpses until we die, failing to live in Christ or to be inspired by Him. According to Scripture, at the time of our death or our judgment, even that which we possess will be taken away from us because of our lack of faith and our despair (cf. Matt 25:29). We do not understand that the children must be like the father, that is to say, we are to be made gods by God and spiritual by the Holy Spirit; for *that which is born of the Spirit is spirit* (John 3:6). But we are unregenerate, even though we have become members of the faith and heavenly, and so the Spirit of God does not dwell within us (cf. Gen 6:3). Because of this the Lord has handed us over to strange harassments and to captivity, and slaughter flourishes, perhaps because He wishes to correct evil, or cut it off, or heal it by more potent remedies.

2. With the help of God, therefore, who inspires those who announce good tidings (cf. Ps 68:11 Septuagint), we must first enquire how one finds Christ—or, rather, how one is found *by* Him, since we already possess and have received Him through Baptism in the Spirit, as St. Paul says, *Do you not realize that Jesus Christ dwells within you?* (2 Cor 13:5) We must then ask how to advance or, simply, how to retain what we have discovered.

The best and shortest course is to give a brief summary of the whole spiritual journey from start to finish, long though it is. Many, indeed, have been so exhausted by their efforts to discover what they were seeking, that on finding the starting-point, they have remained content with this, and not tried to advance farther. Encountering obstacles and turning aside unawares from the true path, they think that they are on the right track—when actually they are veering futilely off course. Others, on reaching the halfway point of illumination, then slacken, wilting before reaching the end; or they revert through a slipshod way of life and become beginners again. Yet others, on the point of attaining perfection, grow inattentive and self-conceited, relapsing to the state of those in the middle way or even of beginners. Beginners, those in the middle way and the perfect have each their distinctive characteristic: for the first it is activity, for the second illumination, for the third purification and resurrection of the soul.

3. The energy of the Holy Spirit, which we have already mystically received in Baptism, is realized in two ways. First—to generalize—this gift is revealed, St. Mark tells us, through arduous and protracted practice of the commandments. To the degree that we effectively practice the commandments the radiance of the gift is increasingly manifested in us. Secondly, it is manifested to those under spiritual guidance through the continuous invocation of the Lord Jesus, repeated with conscious awareness, that is, through mindfulness of God. In the first way it is revealed more slowly, in the second more rapidly, if one diligently and persistently learns to dig the ground and locate the gold. Thus if we wish to realize and know the truth and not be led astray, let us seek to possess only the heart-engrafted energy in a way that is entirely without shape or form, not trying to contemplate in our imagination what we take to be the figure or similitude of things holy or to see any colors or lights. For in the nature of things the spirit of delusion deceives the intellect through such specious fantasies, especially in the early stages, in those who are still inexperienced. On the contrary, let our aim be to keep only the energy of prayer active in our hearts, for it brings warmth and joy to the intellect, and sets the heart alight with an ineffable love for God and man. It is on account of this that humility and contrition flow richly from prayer. For prayer in beginners is the unceasing noetic activity of the Holy Spirit. To begin with it rises like a fire of joy from the heart; in the end it is like light made fragrant by divine energy.[2]

---

2. Translation slightly revised.

II. Medieval

A. Late Patristic—Medieval, Eastern

28. St. Gregory Palamas (1296–1359) | *Triads*

Gregory was born in 1296 in Constantinople. His father, an officer in Emperor Andronikos II Palaiologos's administration, died when his son was only seven. The Emperor took the education of the fatherless lad in hand, intending him for imperial service. Gregory however retired to Mt. Athos at age twenty, committing himself to the Christian ascetic struggle, first at Vatopedi monastery, then the Great Lavra, and finally in a skete where he gave himself to the practice of hesychasm or the prayer of the heart. In 1326, he took refuge in Thessaloniki from Turkish raids, being ordained a priest there at the canonical age of thirty. He returned to Mt. Athos in 1331.

The turning point of Gregory's life came during the 1330s when Barlaam of Calabria began attacking the Athonite monks, sceptical of hesychastic practices. Gregory's fellow monks asked him to step up to their defense. Thus our quiet monk, whose whole study was retirement, ascesis, and interior prayer, was drawn into a cauldron of theological controversy and political havoc that lasted for the rest of his life.

At issue was the nature of theological method: is the experience of the love of God, and noetic assimilation to God in ascesis and prayer integral to true theology, or does using a reason abstracted from the *nous*, as apparently trending in the contemporary West, compromise true theology? At issue too was the tension between the access given us in Christ to a direct, sanctifying and deifying knowledge of God on the one hand, and on the other, the utter transcendence and incomprehensibility of God's nature and being to our finite capacities. It was Gregory's gift and task to show how these two poles of the Christian doctrine of salvation could be sustained together, by exploring the distinction, already adumbrated by the Cappadocian Fathers, between the knowability of the uncreated "energies" or activities or operations of God, on the one hand, exemplified in the apostles' vision of "the Taboric Light" of Christ transfigured, and, on the other hand, the unknowability of the essence, substance, or transcendent being of God in itself.

The controversy raged to and fro in the 1340s, and this devotee of tranquility underwent many strange vicissitudes, even to spending a year as a captive of the Turks. He was appointed Archbishop of Thessaloniki in 1347. A council in 1351 conclusively exonerated him and confirmed his doctrine as the doctrine of the Orthodox Church.

The following is a chain of texts from Gregory's *Triads*, early in Gregory's contention with Barlaam. We begin with his insistence on the integral role of our bodies in the life in Christ, and end with the character of the "uncreated light" of Taboric vision.

Triads (late 1330s)

I.i.20. A life which hope in God has liberated from every care (cf. Matt 6:25–34) naturally impels the soul towards the contemplation of God's creatures.[1] Then it is struck with amazement, deepens its understanding, continues to glorify the Creator, and through this sense of wonder is led forward to what is greater. According to St. Isaac, "It comes upon treasures which cannot be expressed in words,"[2] and using prayer as a key, it penetrates thereby into the mysteries which *no eye has seen, nor ear heard, nor have they entered into the heart of man* (1 Cor 2:9), mysteries manifested by the Spirit alone to those who are worthy, as St. Paul teaches.

I.ii.1. My brother, do you not hear the words of the Apostle: *our bodies are the temple of the Holy Spirit who is in us* (1 Cor 6:19), and again: *we are the house of God* (Heb 3:6)? For God Himself says: *I will dwell in them and walk with them and I shall be their God* (2 Cor 6:16). So why should anyone who possesses mind ("nous") be indignant at the thought that our mind dwells in that whose nature it is to become the dwelling place of God? How can it be that God at the beginning caused the mind to inhabit the body? Did even He do ill thereby? No, brother, such views befit the heretics, who claim that the body is an evil thing, a fabrication of the wicked one.

II.ii.7. Was not this man Barlaam the first to . . . criticize those who have real knowledge because they feel bodily pain? Indeed, some of the Fathers have declared that fasting is of the essence of prayer: "Hunger is the stuff of prayer," they say. Others say it is its "quality," for they know that prayer without compunction has no quality.

And what will you reply when you are told, "Thirst and vigils afflicted the heart, and when the heart was afflicted, tears flowed"? And again, "Prayer is the mother of tears, and also their daughter." Are these not naturally wretched, bitter and wounding for those who have scarcely tasted "the blessed affliction," but become sweet and

---

1. I.e., intuitive "seeing" (*theoria*) the cosmos and all its elements as transparent to and leading to the threshold of the Creator.

2. Homily 72 of Isaac, a seventh-century bishop of the Church of the East; the Greek translation of his works entered into the mainstream of the Hesychast tradition.

inoffensive for those who possess the fullness of joy? . . . Do you see that this bodily distress not only causes no obstacle to prayer, but largely contributes to it? Why does God bestow them as a grace, according to him who says: "If in your prayer, you have obtained tears, then God has touched the eyes of your heart, and you have recovered intellectual sight?" . . .

I.iii.4. The human mind too, and not only the angelic, transcends itself, and by victory over the passions acquires an angelic form. It too will attain to that light and will become worthy of a supernatural vision of God, seeing not the divine essence, but seeing God by a revelation appropriate and analogous to Him. One sees, not in a negative way—for one does see something—but in a manner transcending negation ("apophasis"). For God is not only beyond knowledge, but also beyond unknowing. His revelation itself is also truly a mystery of a most divine and extraordinary kind, since the divine manifestations, even if symbolic, remain unknowable by reason of their transcendence. They appear, in fact, according to a law which is not appropriate to either human or divine nature—being as it were *for* us, but yet *beyond* us—so that no name can properly describe them. And this God indicated in reply to Manoah's question: *What is your name? He replied "It is marvelous"* (Judg 13:17–18); for that vision, being not only incomprehensible but also unnamable, is nonetheless *wonderful*. However, although this vision be beyond negation, yet the words used to explain it are inferior to the negative way. Such explanations proceed by use of examples or analogies, and that is why the word "like," denoting a simile, appears so often in theological discourse; for the vision itself is ineffable and surpasses all expression.

I.iii.5. Therefore when the saints contemplate this divine light within themselves, seeing it by the deifying communion of the Spirit, through the mysterious visitation of perfecting illuminations—then they behold the garment of their deification, their mind being glorified and filled by the grace of the Word, beautiful beyond measure in His splendor; just as on the mountain the divinity of the Word glorified with divine light the body conjoined to it. For *the glory which the Father gave him* (John 17:22), he himself gives to those who are obedient to Him, as the Gospel says: *He willed that they should be with Him and contemplate His glory* (John 17:24).

II.iii.8. The monks know that the essence of God transcends the fact that it is inaccessible to the senses, since God is not only above all created things, but is even beyond Godhead.[3] The excellence of Him Who surpasses all things is not only beyond all affirmation, but also beyond all negation; it exceeds every excellence attainable by the mind. This hypostatic[4] light, seen spiritually by the saints, they know

---

3. We are in the paradoxical language of Pseudo-Dionysius here. This means that what God actually is surpasses (but does not abrogate) the best articulations given us to use of his substance and essence. Moreover, ultimately he is "personal," in the *arche* that is the Father.

4. Or "objective" as we might say. It has real existence, and is not a figment of subjective perceptions. Gregory also may be referring to that divine light communicated through the humanity of Christ from the divine nature to which it was united "hypostatically." The individual subject ("hypostasis") in the compound of two natures that is Christ, is the divine person of the Logos, the Son, the

by experience does exist, as they tell us, and that it exists not only symbolically, as do manifestations produced by fortuitous events, but it is an illumination immaterial and divine, a grace invisibly seen and ignorantly known. *What* it is, they do not pretend to know.

II.iii.9. This light is not the essence of God, for that is inaccessible and incommunicable; it is not an angel, for it bears the marks of the Master. It sometimes makes a man go out of the body, or, without separating him from the body, elevates him to an ineffable height. At other times it transforms the body and communicates its own splendor to it, when, miraculously, the light which deifies the body becomes accessible to the eyes. Thus indeed did the great Arsenius appear when engaged in hesychastic combat; similarly Stephen, whilst being stoned (cf. Acts 6:17), and Moses, when he descended from the mountain (cf. Exod 34:9). Sometimes the light "speaks" clearly, as it were, with ineffable words to one who contemplates it. Such was the case with Paul (cf. 2 Cor 12:4). According to Gregory the Theologian, "It descends from the elevated places where it dwells, so that He who in His own nature from eternity is neither visible to nor containable by any being may in a certain measure be contained by a created nature." He who has received this light, but concentrating upon himself, constantly perceives in his mind that same reality which the children of the Jews call *manna,* the bread that came down from on high . . .

III.i.12. Again, Basil the Great, having shown that the God Who is adored in three Persons is a unique Light, speaks of the "God *Who dwells in light unapproachable*" (1 Tim 6:16). This is why the apostles fell to the ground, unable to rest their gaze on the glory of the light of the Son, because it was a *Light unapproachable.* The Spirit too is Light, as we read: *He who has shone in our hearts by the Holy Spirit* (2 Cor 4:6). If then *the unapproachable light* is true and this light was unapproachable, the light was not some simulacrum of divinity, but truly the light of true divinity, not only the divinity of the Son, but that of the Father and the Spirit too. This is why we sing together to the Lord as we celebrate the annual Feast of the Transfiguration: "In your light which appeared today on Thabor, we have seen the Father as Light and also the Spirit as Light" . . .

III.i.27. The grace of deification thus transcends nature, virtue and knowledge, and, as St. Maximus says, "all these things are inferior to it." Every virtue and imitation of God on our part indeed prepares those who practise them for divine union, but the mysterious union itself is effected by grace. It is through grace that "the entire Divinity comes to dwell in fullness in those deemed worthy", and all the saints dwell in God with their entire being, receiving God in His wholeness, and gaining no other reward for the ascent to Him than God Himself. "He is conjoined to them as a soul is to its body, to its own limbs";[5] judging it right to dwell in believers by authentic adoption,

---

only-begotten of the Father.

5. These passages are cited from one of Maximus's *Ambigua,* unidentified, in the vicinity of *Patrologia Graeca* xci 1000–1300.

according to the gift and grace of the Holy Spirit. So when you hear that God dwells in us through the virtues, or that by means of the memory He comes to be established in us, do not imagine that deification is simply the possession of the virtues, but rather that it resides in the radiance and grace of God, which really come to us through the virtues. As St. Basil the Great says, "A soul which has curbed its natural impulses by personal *ascesis* and the help of the Holy Spirit, becomes worthy, according to the just judgment of God, of the splendor imparted to the saints."[6]

---

6. Basil, Letter 2.4. Translation slightly revised.

II. Medieval

A. Late Patristic—Medieval, Eastern

29. St. Nicholas Kabasilas (1323–1392) | *On the Life in Christ*

Nicholas took the surname of his maternal uncle, Neilos Kabasilas, successor of Palamas as archbishop of Thessaloniki. Hence uncle's and nephew's biographies have sometimes been confused in popular accounts.

Born in the city of Thessaloniki to an aristocratic family, Nicholas received a high level of education. He spent his younger adult life much involved in political and civil affairs, being entrusted by his friend, Emperor John VI Kantakouzenos, with several important missions. After John's abdication in 1354, amidst military and political failure, Nicholas followed him into retirement, becoming a priest monk of the Mangana monastery, and a poet and writer of introductory theological works and mystagogy.

Bilingual in Greek and Latin, Nicholas had a nuanced attitude to the Latins. Though he was a friend of Cydones who opposed the mystical doctrine of St. Gregory Palamas, Nicholas accepted the Council of 1351 that vindicated Gregory's doctrine for the Orthodox Church. He was sufficiently acquainted with Latin theology and even liturgy, both to critique it, and to comment on it sympathetically when he judged it fitting: e.g., he deemed the prayer before the Consecration in the Roman Canon, "Supplices te rogamus," the equivalent of the epiclesis in the eastern anaphoras.

His two best known works are *On the Life in Christ* and *Commentary on the Divine Liturgy*. They are characterized by an intensely christocentric sacramental realism. To Nicholas the ground of the Christian life is without doubt prayerful participation in the church's liturgy, ordered to the realization in us of what Christ communicates to us there. Translator Carmino J. deCatanzaro encapsulates his synthesis of interior liturgy of the heart and participation in the sacred liturgy of the church: "At the heart of his teaching on mental [noetic, contemplative] prayer Cabasilas would unite that interior

Eucharist which is the uninterrupted invocation of the Name, with the frequent partaking of the heavenly Bread which is the sacramental root of the presence of Christ in the believer's heart."[1] We follow him below in a catena of texts from his *On the Life in Christ* that show how baptism, chrismation, and the Eucharist draw us on the path to union with Christ. Impressive, too, is Nicholas's profound sense of the heart of Christ, and that we are all called to abide in that heart.

On the Life in Christ (c. 1370s)

VI.2. Anyone who has chosen to live in Christ should cleave to that Heart and Head, for we obtain life from no other source. But this is impossible for those who do not will what He wills. It is necessary to train one's purpose, as far as humanly possible, to conform to Christ's will and to prepare oneself to desire what He desires and to enjoy it, for it is impossible that contrary desires persist in one and the same heart. As he says: *the evil man out of the evil treasure of his heart knows how to produce* nothing else *but evil* (cf. Luke 6:45), and the good man that which is good.

Since the faithful in Palestine desired the same things, they *were*, it says, *of one heart and soul* (Acts 4:32). Similarly, if someone does not share in Christ's purpose but goes contrary to his command, he does not order his life according to Heart of Christ but plainly leans to a different heart. In contrast, *God found David to be according to his Heart* (Acts 13:22), because he said: *I have not forgotten Your commands* (Ps 119:16). Since it is impossible to live in Christ unless we depend on His Heart, and one cannot depend on Him without willing what He wills, let us study to love the same that He loves, and rejoice in the same that he does, that we may live. . . . Accordingly we must strive above all to avert the eye of the soul from vanities by maintaining the heart always in good thoughts, so that it never yields to evil thoughts through idleness.

While there is much that can fittingly supply matter for contemplation, work for the soul, and delight and employment for the mind, it would appear that consideration of the Mysteries[2] and the riches we gain from them would be most pleasing and profitable both for speech and reflection. Let us reflect on what we were before we were initiated[3] and what we have become by being initiated, on our former servitude and our present freedom and royal state, on the benefits already bestowed on us and on those which yet await us. Above all let us think on Him who is the Giver

---

1. Cabasilas, *The Life in Christ*, 33.
2. The sacraments.
3. I.e., received holy baptism, chrismation, and participation in the Eucharist.

of all these gifts: how great His beauty, what His kindness, how He has loved man, and how great is His love.

When such beauties and attractions take hold in the mind and gain possession of the soul, it is not easy to contemplate anything else or transfer desire to a different object. His benefits overwhelm us by their number and greatness, and the affection which moves him to bestow them is greater than the thoughts of man can conceive.

Just as human affection, when it abounds, overpowers those who love, and causes them to be beside themselves, so God's love for man *emptied* God (cf. Phil 2:7). He does not remain in His own place and summon the slave; He seeks him out by coming down to him in person. He who is rich attains the pauper's hovel, and displays his love by approaching in person. Though He seeks a return of love, he does not withdraw when he is treated with disdain. He is not angry when ill-treated. Even when repulsed he *waits at the door* (Rev 3:20), and does everything to show us that he loves us, even to enduring suffering and death to prove it. . . .

IV.10. If the name of kinship signifies some kind of sharing and, as I think, indicates those who share in common blood, then the only sharing of blood, the only kinship and sonship, is that which we share with Christ. Accordingly, when men have received this kind of birth it occludes even their natural generation, for it says: *as many as received Him, he gave power to become children of God* (John 1:13). Even though they were already begotten, and those who begat them were flesh, and natural generation preceded the spiritual, yet the second birth so greatly prevails over the first that neither trace nor name of it remains. Thus, just as the Holy Bread brings in the new man, it uproots and casts out the old. This too is an effect of the Holy Table,[4] for it says that *those who received Him were not born of blood* (John 1:13). Whenever we receive him, we realize this word *Receive* (Matt 26:26), and the Mystery of which it speaks. It is clear that we are called to the Banquet in which we truly take Christ into our hands and receive him with our mouth, are mingled with him in soul and united with him in body and commingled in blood. And rightly so; for those who receive the Savior and hold fast to him to the end, He himself is the Head who governs, and they the members fit for Him . . .

So great is the abundance of benefits from the Holy Table that it delivers us from judgment, wipes out the disgrace which comes from sin, renews our youth, and binds us closer to Christ himself than any physical bonds. In short, among all the sacred rites, it is the Eucharist that eminently perfects us in true Christianity. . . . In this way the saints are holy and blessed because of the Blessed One who is with them. Through Him they become alive instead of dead, wise instead of unwise, holy, righteous, and sons of God instead of defiled, wicked, and servile. From themselves and from human nature and effort there is nothing whatever which enables them to be justly so called. Rather, they are holy because of the Holy One, righteous and wise because of the Righteous and Wise One who abides with them. In short, if men

---

4. Cabasilas is speaking of participation in the Eucharist.

are really worthy of being called by these great and august names, their appellation derives from Him, especially because their own efforts and powers are so far from capable of making them righteous and wise, that their righteousness is mere wickedness and their wisdom sheer folly.

VI.14. Now the true *Bread*[5] *which strengthens the heart of man* (Ps 104:15), and *came down from heaven to bring* us *life* (cf. John 6:32) will suffice for all things. He will intensify our eagerness and remove the inborn sluggishness of the soul. We must seek Him in every way, so that we feed on Him and ward off hunger by constantly attending this banquet. Nor should we abstain unnecessarily from the Holy Table and thus greatly weaken our souls, on the pretext that we are not really worthy of the Mysteries. Instead, we must resort to the priests [for Confession] on account of our sins in order that we may drink of the cleansing Blood. But if we know these things we should by no means incur guilt from great offences so that we are excluded from the Holy Table. It is the ungodly who approach the sacred gifts after committing *a sin unto death* (1 John 5:16).[6] Those who are not afflicted by such diseases may not rightly flee from that Bread. For those who in their wills are still fighting its embers, it is right to beware of the Fire and not receive Christ to dwell in them until they have been reconciled to him. Those whose wills are rightly disposed but who are sickly in other respects, need the strengthening medicine, and should betake themselves to him who bestows spiritual health and *has borne our infirmities and carried our offences* (Isa 53:4), rather than shun him who will heal them, on the pretext of their ailments.[7]

The Blood of Christ, then, closes the doors of our senses and allows nothing to pass through them which can harm us. Nay more! By sealing the doors, it wards off the Destroyer (cf. Exod 12:13) and makes the heart into which it has been poured a temple of God . . . It strengthens the mind *with a governing spirit* (Ps 51:12 Septuagint), as David says, and subdues *the mind of the flesh* (Rom 8:6), that we may enjoy a profound calm.

VII.15. Thus the life in Christ is concealed and thus manifested by the light of good works, which is love. The brightness of all virtue consists in love, and, as far as human effort is concerned, this constitutes the life in Christ. So one would not err in calling it life, for it is union with God. This union is life, just as we know that death is separation from God. For this reason Christ says: *His commandment is eternal life* (John 12:50). Speaking of love the Saviour also says, *the words I speak to you are spirit and life* (John 6:63), of which love is the sum, and *he who abides in love abides in God*

---

5. Cabasilas exhorts the salutary effects of frequent eucharistic communion. In so doing, he was going against the popular liturgical sensibilities of the time.

6. Otherwise called mortal sin, which is grave sin committed after holy baptism.

7. Gregory teaches that those in mortal sin must never approach the Eucharist without reconciliation in confession, while those of lesser moral and spiritual sicknesses, strugglers whose will is still at least partly upright, should not fail to approach the divine medicine of the Eucharist.

and God in him (1 John 4:16), which is the same as abiding in life and life in him, for he says: *I am the life* (John 11:25) . . .

What then may life be more fittingly called than love? For that which alone survives and does not allow the living to die when all things have been taken away is life—and such is love. When *all things have passed away in the age to come,* as Paul says (1 Cor 13:8,10), love remains, and this alone suffices for life in Christ Jesus our Lord, to whom is due all glory forever. Amen.

Section II. B. Medieval, Western | Mystical and Monastic

II. Medieval

Introduction: Medieval, Western | Mystical and Monastic

The early medieval period in the West we may take to follow the death of Pope St. Gregory (604) up to the death of St. Bernard of Clairvaux (1153), followed by the High Middle Ages (late twelfth through thirteenth centuries) and the Late Middle Ages (fourteenth through fifteenth centuries). Writers and representatives of the higher end of the Christian spiritual life in the early medieval period include Bede, Hincmar of Reims, Paschasius Radbertus, John Scotus Eriugena, Anselm, the great Cluniac abbots, the Cistercian Fathers, and many others.

This era saw the widening political and cultural gap between: 1. the Eastern Roman empire, once it had lost its Western territories, now addressing the evangelization of the Slavs; 2. the West, now addressing itself to the Christianization of barbarian tribes in north and central Europe; and 3. the Christian Near East, whose evangelizing mission was to reach the Pacific coast of China, but soon to enter its long historical passion beneath the Islamic ascendancy. Constantinople almost forgot how to speak Latin, the West almost forgot how to speak Greek, while the great Syriac-speaking Christian civilization, and the Coptic, Armenian, Georgian, and Ethiopian churches, were cut off from both the Latin and Greek worlds (both were "the Romans" and "Westerners" to them).

The church of the early medieval West continued the tradition of the Latin Fathers, inheriting especially St. Augustine's theology of the holy Trinity and his account of St. Paul on grace and salvation, Pope Leo on the office of Peter in the Church, and Pope Gregory the Great's scriptural hermeneutic and his teaching on the contemplative end of prayer. Other writers of seminal influence were Cassian, who conveyed the Egyptian Evagrian tradition, and the Rule of St. Benedict, which incorporated much of St. Basil. A patrimony of Greek Fathers translated into Latin from the time of Rufinus and Jerome continued as a leaven, augmented by further translation work culminating in Eriugena's magnificent contribution, especially of Pseudo-Dionysius.

St. Ephrem "the Syrian," deemed a Doctor of the Church, was the flag-bearer of Near Eastern and Semitic Christianity.

The best intuitions of Christian spiritual life at this period were guarded by the monks. Up to the Carolingian era (800+), Western monasticism looked to its Eastern antecedents and to a variety of homegrown spiritual fathers in the West. Under Charlemagne's successors the Rule of Benedict (sixth century) became normative for Western monks—so much so that the ninth to twelfth centuries have been called the "Benedictine Centuries."

The Patristic/early Medieval hermeneutic of Scripture interpreted the sacred page in what one might call a range of "keys," in continuity with the Alexandrian tradition. In ascending order they are: 1. the literal (the immediate narrative context, with great reverence for the actual words); 2. the moral (the lesson for our conduct taught by this text); 3. the typological (how this text fits into salvation history); and 3. the anagogical (how this word leads us onward and upward to ultimate glory).

The *deep speaking unto deep* of the Christian Mystery meant that the whole of creation was potentially full of sacred "signs" for good or for ill; it was part of a deeply liturgical approach to life, well integrated into the color of the local community, and the agricultural and seasonal round of the year. The ultimate criterion of life was the glory of God, not usefulness to man. Monasteries, as we can see from Bede below, were a pastoral leaven among the local communities, who flocked to them to join in the mass, the liturgy of the hours, for the education of children, and to give and receive all sorts of practical aid besides, such as helping in hostels for the sick, the elderly, and travelers.

The spiritual approach of this period has been called "monastic theology," i.e., theology worked out in the milieu of sacred liturgy, interior desire for God, and contemplative prayer. One might sum up its best insights by looking at three influential teachings on the dynamic of prayer and the life in Christ. One is the term *lectio divina* ("divine reading") from the Rule of Benedict 48:1, meaning a way of reading Scripture, whether privately or in the public liturgy, implicitly disposed to contemplative union with God. A second is Augustine's famous tag, "verbo crescente verba deficiunt" ("as the Word increases, the words fall away" [*Sermo* 288, 5: PL 38, 1307; *Sermo* 120, 2: PL 38, 677]), meaning that that the more we mature in prayer, the more the medium of "words" fades before interior intimacy with "the Word," that is, Jesus Christ. Thirdly, we have the Ladder of Monks by Guigo the Carthusian at the end of this period, who imagined progress in prayer as a Ladder of four steps:

> *Lectio* (reading of sacred texts, including mastering its literal aspects).
>
> *Meditatio* (pausing and repeating especially pregnant words; a favorite image of the early medievals for this was a cow's rumination, or "chewing the cud").
>
> *Oratio* (the prayer of the heart kindled from meditation).

Contemplatio (wordless intimacy with the Word, in the communion of the Father and the Spirit).

Later-day Western commentators like to add a practical or "useful" note with a fifth rung, say, "missio" or "evangelizatio." But Christians of the era would hardly think of justifying prayer by instrumentalizing it. Trinitarian doxology is the end of man, i.e., assimilation to Christ, and in him to communion in the life of the Trinity. The glow of witness and love for others would spread of its own accord from this holy fire.

By the eleventh and twelfth centuries, the times were changing. The conversion of the Vikings concluded the Christianization of the pagan tribes of the North and West. The church's achievement included, not the least, communicating the Christian understanding of marriage. The onset of the Medieval Warm Period led to milder weather in the north and more fruitful crops. Urbanization and commerce were on the rise. The tenth-century Cluniac monastic reform had perhaps succeeded too well and succumbed to the effects of institutionalization. Like an Indian summer of the old monastic theology, the Victorines and the Cistercians came, bringing their own kind of "warming" of Christian hearts with a sense of devotion to the person of Christ the Word and to his blessed Mother, and expounding a mystical theology warmed by the glowing ardors of the Song of Songs.

Anna Silvas

II. Medieval

B. Medieval, Western: Mystical and Monastic

30. Venerable Bede (c. 672–735) | *Ecclesiastical History*

To introduce Bede, what better than his own modest account of himself at the end of his *Ecclesiastical History of the English People*, book 5, chapter 24? Bede lived his life immersed in the Scriptures, sung and enacted in the round of the holy liturgy, pondered in Lectio Divina, and shared in a life of ecclesial fellowship, exposition, and teaching. He concludes his great work with a prayer expressive of the spirit of Lectio Divina, then follows with a brief "bio":

> And now I pray You, O good Jesus, that as You have graciously given me to drink in with delight the words of Your knowledge, so You would mercifully grant me to attain one day to You, the fountain of all wisdom and appear forever before Your Face.

> Thus much concerning the ecclesiastical history of Britain, and especially of the race of the English, I, Baeda, a servant of Christ and a priest of the monastery of the blessed apostles St. Peter and St. Paul, which is at Wearmouth and at Jarrow, have with the Lord's help composed so far as I could gather it, either from ancient documents or from the traditions of the elders or from my own knowledge. I was born in the territory of the said monastery, and at the age of seven I was, by the care of my relations, given to the most reverend Abbot Benedict (St. Benedict Biscop), and afterwards to (Abbot) Ceolfrid, to be educated. From that time I have spent the whole of my life within that monastery, devoting all my pains to the study of the Scriptures. Amidst the observance of monastic discipline and the daily charge of singing in the Church, it has ever been my delight to learn or teach or write. In my nineteenth year I was admitted to the diaconate, in my thirtieth to the priesthood, both by the hands of the most reverend Bishop John (St. John of Beverley), at the bidding of Abbot Ceolfrid. From the time of my admission to the priesthood to my present fifty-ninth year, I have endeavored for my own use and that of my brethren, to

B. MEDIEVAL, WESTERN: MYSTICAL AND MONASTIC

make brief notes upon the holy Scripture, either from the works of the venerable Fathers or in conformity with their meaning and interpretation.[1]

The following passage is from *Ecclesiastical History,* book 2, chapters 12 and 13. We must imagine a scene very like Theoden's golden hall of Meduseld in The Lord of the Rings. Paulinus is St. Paulinus of York, one of the missionaries sent to the Anglo-Saxons by Pope Gregory I. Edwin is King of Northumbria. Bede paints a picture of a world of honest pagans slowly summoning the courage to name as "nothing" ("nihil") the spiritual place they have inhabited until now, and to feel their way towards the dawn of a new hope in Christ.

Ecclesiastical History (finished c. 731)

... When his predecessor Aethelfrith, was persecuting him, Edwin wandered for years as an exile, hiding in various places and kingdoms, till at last he came to Raedwald, begging him to give him protection against the snares of his powerful persecutor. Raedwald received him willingly, and promised to perform what was asked of him.

But Aethelfrith . . . sent messengers to bribe that king with a great sum of money to murder him, but without effect. He sent a second and a third time, offering a greater bribe each time, and, moreover, threatening to make war on him if his offer should be rejected. Raedwald, whether terrified by his threats, or won over by his gifts, complied with this request, and promised either to kill Edwin or to deliver him up to the envoys.

A faithful friend of his, on hearing this, went into Edwin's chamber, where he was going to bed, for it was the first hour of the night, and calling him out, told him what the king had promised to do to him, adding, "If, therefore, you are willing, I will this very hour conduct you out of this province, and lead you to a place where neither Raedwald nor Aethelfrith shall ever find you." He answered, "I thank you for your good will, yet I cannot do what you propose . . . For whither now shall I fly, who have for so many long years been a vagabond through all the provinces of Britain, to escape the snares of my enemies?" His friend left and Edwin remained alone outside. Sitting with a heavy heart before the palace, he began to be overwhelmed with many thoughts, not knowing what to do, or which way to turn . . .

On a sudden in the stillness of the dead of night he saw a person approaching, whose face and habit were strange to him, at sight of whom, seeing that he was unknown and unlooked for, he was not a little startled. The stranger drew near, greeted him, and asked why he sat there in solitude on a stone troubled and awake at that

---

1. Translation revised from Thurston, "The Venerable Bede," para. 2 and 4.

time, when all others were taking their rest and fast asleep. Edwin in his turn asked, what it was to him, whether he spent the night within doors or abroad. The stranger in reply said, "Do not think that I am ignorant of the cause of your grief, your sleeplessness and sitting alone outside. For I certainly know who you are, and why you grieve, and the evils that you fear will soon fall upon you. But tell me, what reward would you give the man who should deliver you out of these troubles, and persuade Raedwald neither to do you any harm himself, nor to deliver you up to be murdered by your enemies?" Edwin replied, that he would give such a one all that he could in return for so great a benefit . . . Then the other spoke a third time and said, "But if he who should truly foretell that all these great blessings are about to befall you, could also give you better and more profitable counsel for your life and salvation than any of your fathers or kindred heard before, would you consent to submit to him, and to follow his wholesome guidance?" Edwin at once promised that he would in all things follow the teaching of that man who should deliver him from so many great calamities, and raise him to a throne . . .

While the royal youth still sat there alone, glad of the comfort he had received, but still troubled and earnestly pondering who he was and whence he came who had spoken to him so, his above mentioned friend returned to him and greeted him with a smiling face. "Rise," said he, "go in. Calm yourself and put away your anxious cares, and compose yourself in body and mind to sleep, for the king's resolve is changed, and he intends you no harm, but rather to keep his pledged faith; for when he had privately made known to the queen his intention of doing what I told you before, she dissuaded him from it, reminding him that it was altogether unworthy of so great a king to sell his good friend in such distress for gold, and to sacrifice his own honour, which is more valuable than all other adornments, for the love of money." In short, the king did as she said, and not only refused to deliver up the banished man to his enemy's messengers, but helped him to recover his kingdom. . . . Thus Edwin, in accordance with the prophecy he had received, not only escaped the danger from his enemy, but, after the king's death, succeeded him on the throne.

Yet he delayed to receive the Word of God preached by Paulinus. Being accustomed, as has been said, to sit many hours alone, and to ponder seriously with himself what he was to do, and what religion he was to follow, the man of God came to him one day, laid his right hand on his head, and asked whether he knew that sign. The king, trembling, was ready to fall down at his feet, but Paulinus raised him up, and speaking to him with the voice of a friend, said, "Consider, by the gift of God you have escaped the hands of the enemies whom you feared. Consider, you have obtained from His bounty the kingdom that you desired. Take heed not to delay to perform your third promise. Accept the faith, and keep the precepts of Him Who has delivered you from temporal adversity, and raised you to the honour of a temporal kingdom; and if, from this time forward, you shall be obedient to His will, which through me He signifies to you, He will also deliver you from the everlasting torments of the wicked, and make you partaker with Him of His eternal kingdom in heaven."

On hearing these words, King Edwin answered that he was both willing and obliged to receive the faith which Paulinus taught, but that he would still confer about it with his chief friends and counselors, so that if they too were of his opinion, they might all together be consecrated to Christ in *the font of life* [Ps 35:9, here = baptism].

Paulinus consented and the king did as he said. He held a council with the wise men, and asked of all of them one by one what he thought of this teaching unknown to them until now, and the new worship of divinity that was being preached. The chief of his own priests, Coifi, immediately answered him, "Consider O King what it is that is now preached to us, for I truly declare to you what I have learnt beyond doubt, that the religion which we have hitherto professed has nothing ["nihil"] of virtue or profit in it . . . Whence it remains, that if you examine these new teachings which are now being preached to us, and find them better and of more power, we should hasten to receive them without any delay."

Another of the king's chief men, approving of his wise and persuasive words, added: "The present life of men on the earth, O King, in comparison with that time which is unknown to us, seems to me like the swift flight of a sparrow through the house in which you sit at supper in the wintertime with your ealdormen and thanes, with the fire blazing in the midst warming the hall, while the wintry storms of rain or snow are raging outside. The sparrow, flying in at one door and immediately out of another, while it is within, is safe from the wintry tempest; but after a very short space of calm lasting only a moment, it soon passes from winter into winter, vanishing from your eyes. So this life of man appears for a brief while, but of what follows or what went before we know nothing at all. If, therefore, this new teaching tells us something more certain, it seems worthy of being followed."

The other elders and king's counsellors, thus divinely admonished, spoke likewise. However Coifi added that he wished to hear more attentively Paulinus himself speaking of the God Whom he preached. When at the king's command Paulinus had done so, Coifi, on hearing his words, cried out, "Already I have long perceived that what we worshipped was nothing ["nihil"]; because the more diligently I sought after truth in that worship, the less I found it. But now I freely confess that such truth evidently appears in this preaching as can bestow on us the gifts of life, of salvation, and of eternal happiness . . ."

What more is there to say? The king openly assented to the preaching of the Gospel by blessed Paulinus. Then, renouncing idolatry, he declared that he received the faith of Christ.

II. Medieval

B. Medieval, Western: Mystical and Monastic

31. Hugh of St. Victor (1096–1141) | *In Praise of the Bridegroom*

Born of a noble family in Saxony, Hugh joined the Canons Regular of St. Augustine at Hamerleve, near Halberstadt. His uncle Reinhard, Bishop of Blankenburg, advised that he transfer to the school he had attended at the Abbey of St. Victor in Paris. Here Hugh spent the rest of his life, becoming head of the school and preceptor of the Victorine tradition, which was later to include such well-known names as Richard of St. Victor.

Several cross-currents of the time converge in Hugh: early scholasticism, i.e., the use of the dialectical method in theology, and empirical observation of nature on the one hand; a strict traditional orthodoxy, and a sensibility for liturgical symbolism and mystical theology on the other. Hugh of St. Victor and Bernard of Clairvaux between them enriched the Western tradition with the spousal mysticism of Origen, Ambrose, Gregory of Nyssa, and Gregory the Great, spun of course from the scriptural use of marriage as an analogy for the relationship of God and Israel (cf. Hos 2:14–20), and of Christ and the Church (cf. Mark 2:19, Eph 5:33). Hugh did not set out to teach a spirituality of marriage, but he assumed it existed. To him, *affectio maritalis*, the disposition of husband and wife towards each other, illuminated the relationship between Christ and his church, God and the Christian soul. Indirectly through his mystical theology, and directly through his exploration of the sacramentality of marriage, Hugh opened up a greater awareness of the spiritual potency of the vocation to Christian marriage.

Hugh's contributions to mystical theology went further. Through his *Commentary on the Celestial Hierarchy*, he rekindled in the West an interest in the mystagogical works of the sixth-century Syrian theologian, Pseudo-Dionysius (in Scotus Eriugena's translation). In the following texts from Hugh's *In Praise of the Bridegroom* we see him interpreting the Song of Songs in the key of a nuptial mystery between the Lord and the individual Christian soul.

B. MEDIEVAL, WESTERN: MYSTICAL AND MONASTIC

In Praise of the Bridegroom (early 1130s)

1. *I will go for myself to the mountain of Myrrh and to the hills of Lebanon,* and I will speak to my bride: *"You are utterly beautiful my nearest and there is no blemish in you. Come to Lebanon my bride, come to Lebanon. You will come and cross to Mount Seir and Hermon from the dens of lions, from the mountains of leopards."* (Song 4:6b–8)

2. *I will go for myself,* he says. He goes *for himself,* because a unique love admits no one to share its secret. He goes for himself, because he who allows no one to share his love does not want a companion on the journey. But, you ask, who is this and who is his bride? The bridegroom is God; the bride is the soul. The bridegroom is home when he fills the mind with interior joy; he goes away when he takes away the sweetness of contemplation. By what likeness is the soul called the bride of God? She is a bride because she is dowered with gifts of graces. She is a bride because she is united ("sociata") with him in a chaste love. She is a bride, because through the inspiration[1] ("aspirationem") of the Holy Spirit she shall be made fruitful with the virtues, her offspring.

3. There is no soul who has not received a betrothal-gift ("arram") from this bridegroom. One kind of betrothal gift, however, is common, another kind is special. It is a common betrothal-gift that we have been born, that we have sensation, that we know, and that we discriminate. It is a special betrothal-gift that we are *reborn* (cf. 1 Pet 1:23), that we have obtained remission of sins, that we have received gifts ("carismata") of virtues. What each one has is his betrothal gift.... And so the loving Creator, in accord with his goodness, dispenses whatever human weakness bears in this life, in order either to correct evil or to promote virtue. For this reason we ought to *give thanks in all things* (1 Thess 5:18), so that, as we *acknowledge his mercy* everywhere (cf. Isa 63:7), we may always advance in love for him.

4. *I will go for myself,* he says, *to the mountain of Myrrh.* Myrrh, which is bitter to the taste and keeps the bodies of the dead from rotting, signifies the mortification of the flesh. Lebanon, which is interpreted as "brightening," signifies purity of heart. This then is the way that the bridegroom comes to the bride. He comes by way of *the mountain of Myrrh* and *the hills of Lebanon,* because first *he puts to death the craving* ("concupiscentia") *of the flesh* (cf. Rom 8:13) through abstinence, and then wipes away the ignorance of the mind through purity of heart. After that, as though *on the third day* (cf. Matt 17:23 et al., John 20:16), he comes to converse with the bride and enflames her soul with desire for him. Hence it is fitting that he says *mountain of Myrrh* and not *hill of Myrrh,* and *hills of Lebanon* and not *mountain of Lebanon,* because we must be steadfast in affliction, and humble when we succeed in virtue. The height of the mountain signifies the preeminence of magnanimity, and the moderate height of the hill stands for the restraint of humility. We interpret *on the mountain of Myrrh* as strength against the craving of the flesh; *on the hills of Lebanon* as the illumination of

---

1. Perhaps more literally, the "being breathed upon" of the Holy Spirit.

the mind against ignorance; the conversation of the bridegroom as charity opposing malevolence and hardness of heart.

5. Power pertains to the Father, wisdom to the Son, and charity to the Holy Spirit. In another context this is said in reference to sinning against the Father and the Son and the Holy Spirit respectively. For when we sin through weakness, we sin against the Father as though against power. When we sin through ignorance, we sin against the Son as though against wisdom. However, when we sin through malice, we *sin against the Holy Spirit* (cf. Mark 3:29) as though against love. Therefore sinning against the Father and the Son is forgiven here or in the future. Since one who sins from weakness or ignorance has some excuse in his fault, he ought also to have some remission of punishment—either in this life, or in the next world, so that if he persists in evil he undergoes a more bearable punishment. However, those who sin from wickedness have no excuse for their crimes, and therefore they should have no remission of punishment. If they repent in this world, they must be punished until they give full satisfaction, or, if they do not repent, they must be punished with full damnation in the world to come. And so, such as these find no remission here or in the world to come, not because pardon (*venia*) is denied to penitents, but because full satisfaction is owed for full-blown sin.

6. "I will speak," he says, "to my bride." God speaks in two ways to a soul: in one way to the prostitute, in another to the bride; in one way to the sordid, in another to the beautiful; in one way to the sinner, in another to the justified. He rebukes the foulness of the former; he praises the beauty of the latter. By his rebuke he strikes fear into the former; by his praise he enkindles the latter to love ("amorem"). He speaks to the former when he shows her blemishes to her; he speaks to the latter when he reminds her of the gifts which he has granted to her. He *illumines the darkness* (2 Sam 2:29) of the former, so that she may recognize what she is and deplore what she has done; he touches the latter with a sense of interior sweetness, so that she may recall what she has received and not forget him who gave it.

7. "I will speak," he says, "to my bride." "If I am that bridegroom, if I am going to speak to the bride, know that I can speak of nothing but love ('amorem')." Therefore, after the bridegroom had said this to himself, he immediately undertook a journey; and, coming and seeing the bride, then—as though struck with wonder at her beauty ("specie")—burst forth in these words: *You are utterly beautiful, my nearest*. Alternatively, this phrase is joined with the preceding "I will speak to my bride," namely in this way: *You are utterly beautiful, my nearest*. But the former reading is more elegant: *You are utterly beautiful, my nearest*. And so, you are utterly beautiful because you are nearest; if you were not nearest, you would not be utterly beautiful.

8. Notice what he said: *You are utterly beautiful, my nearest*. Each soul is either turned away from God or turned toward God. Of those turned away, one is distant, another is most distant. Of those turned toward God, one is near, another is nearest. She who is distant is dirty now, but not utterly; she who is most distant is utterly dirty.

Likewise, she who is near is beautiful, but still not totally so; she who is nearest is utterly beautiful: *You are utterly beautiful my dearest.*

9. *And there is no blemish in you.* He is wholly beautiful ("totus speciosus") in whom no beauty is lacking. He is wholly beautiful in whom there is nothing sordid. "I am entirely beautiful because everything beautiful is in me. You are utterly beautiful because there is nothing sordid in you. *There is no blemish in you.*"

10. *Come to Lebanon, my bride.* Up to now, we have heard by what road the bridegroom came to the bride and what he said when he came to her. Next let us hear by what road the bride should come to the bridegroom. He says, *Come to Lebanon.* He invites and he calls her, because he has come to her not to stay with her, but to draw her to himself.

11. *Come to Lebanon, come to Lebanon. You will come.* Twice he invites her saying, *Come.* The third time he adds firmly: *You will come.* But what is this affirmation, if not a congratulation, by which he rejoices over our good resolution? It is as if he said: "I praise your obedience; I see your resolution; I am not unaware of your devotion. I call and you answer; I invite and you are ready." Therefore, *You will come.* But why does he say *come* twice? He does it so that whoever is outside of him may first *return to himself* (Luke 15:17), and whoever is within him may ascend above himself. First, he is in us and warns wrongdoers to return to their heart; then he is above us to invite those justified to himself. "*Come,*" he says, "*come.* From outside come within yourself. Then, within, come from above yourself to me."[2]

---

2. Translation slightly revised.

II. Medieval

B. Medieval, Western: Mystical and Monastic

32. William of St. Thierry (c. 1075–1148) | *Meditative Orations*

Born into a noble family at Liège, William studied at the Cathedral school of either Reims or Saône, and in the year 1111 joined the Benedictine monastery of St. Nicaise in Reims. He was chosen as abbot of the nearby monastery of St. Thierry in 1119. His meeting with Bernard of Clairvaux in 1118 led to a lifelong friendship between the two, and a keen desire on William's part to join the Cistercian reform. Bernard, however, insisted he keep to his post as Abbot of St. Thierry. William in his turn promoted a number of monastic reforms in the Benedictine communities of the Reims diocese. He resigned his abbacy in 1135 and retired to the Cistercian monastery of Signy. Alert to the rationalist tendency in contemporary theology, he warned Bernard of aspects of the logician Abelard's teachings.

In the history of mystical theology in the Western church, William is notable for his use of the Greek Fathers, i.e., Origen, Gregory of Nyssa, Evagrius, and Pseudo-Dionysius, in Scotus Eriugena's translation and as recently revived in the West by his contemporary, Hugh of St. Victor. This is evident in his mature *Golden Epistle*, an instruction and encouragement to contemplative life he wrote near the end of his life, for the Carthusian novices at Mont-Dieu, in which he sketches the journey of the soul to true freedom, from the state of the animal soul ("anima"), through the intellect ("mens"), to the spirit ("spiritus"). He also wrote a lengthy *Exposition of the Epistle to the Romans*, in which he takes a thoroughly monastic and contemplative approach, celebrating the centrality of the grace of God in the Christian spiritual life.

In the following selection from *Meditativae Orationes*, or *Meditative Prayers* (1128–1135), patterned on Augustine's prayer soliloquies in the *Confessions*, William weaves a wonderful *lectio divina* of scriptural texts around the theme of Christ as the door. Note too, the sense of the heart of Christ, into which, William says, we enter through the "door" of his pierced side.

B. MEDIEVAL, WESTERN: MYSTICAL AND MONASTIC

Meditative Orations (c. 1135)

1. *I saw a door opened in heaven,* says blessed John, *and the first voice which I heard was as it were of a trumpet speaking to me, which said: "Come up hither"* (Rev 4:1) . . .

4. That Beloved Disciple of yours was not the only one to find the way to heaven, nor was *the open door* revealed to him alone (Rev 4:1). Not by a herald, or by any prophet, but out of your own mouth to all you openly proclaimed: *I am the door; If anyone enters by me, he shall be saved* (John 10:9). You are *the door*, then, Lord; and when you say: *if anyone enters by me,* you open, manifestly, to all who will.

But what use is it for us who are upon the earth to see the door in heaven standing open, if we cannot ascend there? Paul answers thus: *He who ascends is the same also as he who descended* (cf. Eph 4:10). Who then is he? He is Love. For it is love in us that mounts up to you, O Lord, because it is the love in you that comes down to us. You who loved us, came down to us; by loving you we shall mount up to you. You who declared: *I am the door,* by your own self I pray you: *open yourself to us* (Matt 25:11), that you may show more clearly what is the house that you open, and when you open, and to whom. The house of which you are *the door* is heaven, as we said before; and heaven is where the Father dwells, of whom we read: *The Lord's throne is in heaven* (Ps 11:4). And truly, no one comes to the Father except through You who are *the door* . . .

6. Then answer us who seek and yearn for you, I beg you: *Where do you dwell?* (John 1:38). You answer promptly, saying: *I am in the Father and the Father is in me* (John 14:10), and in another place: *On that day, you shall know that I am in the Father, and you in me, and I in you* (John 14:20), and yet again: *I in them, and you in me, that they may be made perfect in oneness* (John 17:23). Therefore your place ("locus") is the Father, and you (are) the Father's place ("locus"), and not only that, but we also are your place, and you ours. Since, Lord Jesus, you are in the Father and the Father is in you, then, O most high and undivided Trinity, you are yourself the place of your abode, you are yourself your heaven. Just as your Being has no fount outside yourself, so you need no place in which to dwell, save of and in yourself.

7. When you dwell in us, then, we are your heaven, most assuredly. Yet you are not yourself sustained by dwelling in us; no, it is your sustaining that makes us a dwelling for you. And you are our heaven, to which we may ascend, and in which we may dwell. As I see it, then, our dwelling in you or yours in us is heaven for us. But for you *the heaven of heavens* (cf. Deut 10:14) is your eternity, where you are what you are in your own self. The Father is in the Son, and the Son is in the Father, and the bond that unites Father and Son is the Holy Spirit, who comes not as it were from somewhere else to be the link between you, but who exists as such by virtue of his unity of being with you both.

It is the Holy Spirit too, who creates and sets in order the unity that makes us one among ourselves and in you. He makes us, who were by nature *sons of wrath* (Eph 2:3), to be sons of God by grace, as the Apostle says *Behold what manner of love the Father has bestowed on us, that we should be called, and be, the sons of God* (1 John 3:1). We are indeed sons by a *Gift* (John 14:26), who is the Holy Spirit. And a little further we read: *Beloved, now we are the sons of God, and it has not yet appeared what we shall be. But we know that, when he shall appear, we shall be like him, for we shall see him as he is* (1 John 3:2).

8. Whereas the birth of the Son from the Father belongs to the eternal divine nature, our birth as sons of God is an adoption of grace. The former birth is not something that comes into being, nor does it effect a unity; it is itself a oneness in the Holy Spirit. The latter birth, however, has no existence of itself, but comes into being through the Holy Spirit, insofar as it is stamped with the likeness of God. This unity of course transcends the limits of our human nature, but fall short of the unity that belongs to the being of God. The Holy Spirit is called the seed of this birth, for the Apostle says of him: *Whoever is born of God does not commit sin, for his seed remains in him, and therefore he cannot sin* (1 John 3:9).

Moreover, the *likeness* of God (cf. Gen 1:27) will be conferred on us by the sight of God, when we not only see that he exists, but *see him as he is* (1 John 3:2); that is the likeness that will make us like to him, since for the Father to see the Son is to be what the Son is, and vice versa. For us, however, to see God is to be like God. This unity, this likeness is itself the heaven where God dwells in us, and we in him . . .

11. These blessings, that were hidden in your secret heaven through the ages, you at the end of the ages unveiled to the world's longing eyes, when you opened in heaven *the door* that is yourself. You opened that door when your grace appeared to all men, teaching them *when* your *kindness and love appeared* (Titus 3:4), saving us not by works of righteousness that we have done, but according to your mercy. The heavens being thus opened, all the good and delight and glory of heaven poured itself out upon the earth. And then, O God, you who *did not spare your own Son, but delivered him up for us all* (Rom 8:32), the greatness of your kindness in our regard was declared openly to all. You made known your salvation to the world, and *in the sight of all the nations you revealed your righteousness* (Ps 98:2), which you had made over to us in the blood of your only-begotten Son. And he himself rendered to you for our salvation the pure obedience that proceeds from love, and gave to us the love that sprang from obedience. And then you *blessed our earth* (Ps 85:1); thenceforth she began *to yield her fruit* (Ps 85:12). Thenceforth the high road to heaven lay open to all men, a high road trodden by martyrs and apostles, and all the saints who, by the example of the charity and grace received from you, set themselves at naught for you, and were not afraid to give their lives for you.

The *unsearchable riches* of your glory Lord (cf. Eph 3:8), were hidden in your secret place in heaven until the soldier's spear opened the side of your Son our Lord and Savior on the cross, and there flowed from it the mysteries of our redemption (cf. John 19:34). Now we may not only thrust our finger or hand into his side, like Thomas (cf. John 20:27), but through that open door may enter whole, O Jesus, even into your heart, the sure *seat* of your *mercy* (cf. Exod 25:30), even into your holy soul that *is filled with the fullness of God* (Col 2:19), *full of grace and truth* (John 1:14), full of our salvation and consolation.

12. Open O Lord the ark-door of your side (cf. Gen 6:16), that all your own who shall be saved may enter in, before this flood that is overwhelming the earth. Open to us your body's side, that those who long to see the secrets of the Son may enter in, and may receive the sacraments that flow therefrom, even the price of their redemption. Open the door of your heaven, that your redeemed may *see the good things of God in the land of the living* (Ps 27:13), even if they still labor in the land of the dying. Let them see and long, and yearn and run; for you have become *the way* by which they go, *the truth* to which they go, *the life* for which they go (John 14:16). The *way* is the example of your lowliness, the *truth* is the pattern of your purity, the *life* is life eternal.

All these, *the way, the truth and the life* you have become for us, merciful Father, sweet Lord, loving Brother.

II. Medieval

B. Medieval, Western: Mystical and Monastic

33. St. Bernard of Clairvaux (1090–1153) | *Homilies on the Song of Songs*

Born into a devout and loving family of the highest Burgundian nobility, Bernard excelled at school in Latin literature and rhetoric. His mother's death when he was eighteen precipitated something of a crisis as to the direction of his life. Three years later, at twenty-one years of age, he entered the struggling monastery of newly reformed Benedictine monks at Citeaux, with thirty followers—with his own father to follow later. Such were his precocious piety and capacity for dynamic leadership, he was sent only three years later in 1115 to lead a new foundation at what became known as Clairvaux, "Bright Valley." The forty foundations made in turn from Clairvaux led to the explosion of the Cistercian Order in Europe.

As the champion of a new Christianized code of chivalry, Bernard supervised the writing of the Rule of the Knights Templar in 1128. This same Christian chivalrous spirit is seen in his devotion to the Mother of God, for whom he popularized the title "Our Lady." When one of his monks became Pope Eugene III, he wrote for him *de Consideratione*, a bracing admonition to truthful Christian living for the prelates of the church: prayer and meditation were to be the spring of action. He preached the Second Crusade in 1144, and energetically quelled outbreaks of anti-Judaism. The failure of the Second Crusade clouded his last years.

In monastic spirituality Bernard and the Cistercians recalled the intensely liturgical Christianity of the "Benedictine Centuries" to a renewed austerity and poverty, warmed by a new, more personal note of devotion to Christ and to the Virgin Mary. He reasserted the capital importance for monks of *lectio divina*—the "divine reading" of the Scriptures as a vademecum of maturing in contemplative prayer in the Holy Spirit. In his *85 Homilies on the Song of Songs*, he articulates a mystical theology using the spousal analogy in a tradition that goes all the way back to the Alexandrians.

On the eight-hundredth anniversary of his death Pope Pius XII aptly called him "the Last of the Fathers," for although Bernard won the theological battle against Abelard at the Council of Sens (1141), Abelard, in a sense, won the war, since his reliance upon strict dialectical method in theology became the norm in the Western church in the following century. In the following homily, we hear a modest disclosure of Bernard's own intimate experience of the Bridegroom, the Word, proposed that it might be an incentive to all the disciples and lovers of the Word.

Homilies on the Song of Songs (begun 1135, never finished)

74:5. Now *bear with my foolishness a little* (2 Cor 11:1). I want to tell you of my own experience, as I promised. Not that it is of any importance . . . I admit that the Word has also come to me—*I speak as a fool* (2 Cor 12:1)—and has come many times. But although he has come to me, I have never been conscious of the moment of his coming. I perceived his presence, I remembered afterwards that he had been with me; sometimes I had a presentiment that he would come, but I was never conscious of his coming or his going. And where he comes from when he visits my soul, and where he goes, and by what means he enters and goes out, I admit that I do not know even now; as John says: *You do not know where he comes from or where he goes* (John 3:8). There is nothing strange in this, for of him it was said, *Your footsteps will not be known* (Ps 77:19). The coming of the Word was not perceptible to my eyes, for he has no color; nor to the ears, for there was no sound; nor yet to my nostrils, for he mingles with the mind, not the air; he has not acted upon the air, but created it. His coming was not tasted by the mouth, for there was not eating or drinking, nor could he be known by the sense of touch, for he is not tangible. How then did he enter? Perhaps he did not enter because he does not come from outside? He is not one of the things which exist outside us. Yet he does not come from within me, *for he is good* (Ps 106:1), and *I know there is no good in me* (cf. Rom 7:18). I have ascended to the highest in me, and look! the Word towers above that. In my curiosity I have descended to explore my lowest depths, yet I found him even deeper. If I look outside myself, I saw him stretching beyond the furthest I could see; and if I looked within, he was still further within. Then I knew the truth of what I had read, *in him we live and move and have our being* (Acts 17:28). And blessed is the man in whom He has his being, who lives for Him and is moved by Him.

6. You ask then how I knew he was present, when his ways can in no way be traced (cf. Rom 11:33)? He is *life and power* (Heb 4:12), and as soon as he enters in, he awakens my slumbering soul; he stirs and soothes and pierces my heart (cf. Song 4:9), for before it was hard as stone (cf. Sir 3:27), and diseased. Thus he began to pluck out and destroy, to build up and to plant, to water dry places and to illumine the dark (cf. Jer 1:10); to open what was closed and to warm what was cold; *to make the crooked*

straight and the rough places smooth (Isa 40:4), so that *my soul may bless the Lord, and all that is within me may praise his holy name* (Ps 103:1).

So when the Bridegroom, the Word, came to me, he never made known his coming by any signs, not by sight, not by sound, not by touch. It was not by any movement of his that I recognized his coming; it was not by any of my senses that I perceived he had penetrated to the depth of my being. Only by the movement of my heart, as I have told did I perceive his presence; and I knew *the power of his might* (Eph 1:13), because my faults were put to flight and my human yearnings brought into subjection. I have marveled at *the depths of his wisdom* (Eccl 7:25) when *my secret faults* (Ps 19:13) have been revealed and made visible; at the very slightest amendment of my way of life I have experienced his goodness and mercy; in *the renewal and remaking of the spirit of my mind* (Eph 4:23), that is of my inmost being, I have perceived the excellence of his glorious beauty (cf. Ps 49:2), and when I contemplate all these things I am filled with awe and wonder at his manifold greatness (cf. Ps 150:2).

7. But when the Word has left me, all these spiritual powers weaken and become faint and begin to grow cold, as though you had removed the fire from under the boiling pot, and this is a sign of his going. Then my soul *must needs be sorrowful* (Matt 26:38) until he returns, and *my heart again is stricken within me* (Ps 108:22)—the sign of his returning.

When I have had such experience of the Word, is it any wonder that I take to myself the words of the Bride, calling him back when he has withdrawn (cf. Song 5:6)? For although my fervor is not as strong as hers, yet I am transported by a desire like hers. For as long as I live the word "return!" the word for the recall of the Word, will be on my lips. As often as he slips away from me, so often shall I call him back. From the burning desire of my heart I will not cease to call out him, begging him to return, as if after someone who is departing, and I implore him to *restore to me the joy of his salvation* (Ps 51:14), yes, to restore to me himself.

83:1. During the last three days I have spent the time allotted me in showing the affinity between the Word and the soul. What was the value of all that labor? Surely this: we have seen how every soul—even if *burdened with sin* (cf. 2 Tim 3:6), enmeshed in vice, ensnared by the allurements of pleasure, a captive in exile, imprisoned by the body, *caught in the mud* (Ps 68:3), fixed in the mire, bound to its members, a slave to care, distracted by business, afflicted with sorrows, wandering and straying, filled with anxious forebodings and uneasy suspicions, *a stranger in a hostile land* (Exod 2:22), and, according to the prophet, sharing the defilement of the dead and *counted with those who go down into hell* (Bar 3:11)—every soul, I say, so standing under condemnation and without a hope, has the power to turn and find that it may not only breathe the fresh air of the hope of pardon and mercy, but dare also to aspire to the nuptials of the Word, not fearing to enter into covenant with God or to bear the sweet yoke of love (cf. Matt 11:30) with the King of the angels . . .

2. Why then does it not set to work? There is a great natural gift[1] in us, and if it is not allowed full play the rest of our nature will go to ruin, as if eaten away by the rust of decay... It strays—as is the nature of spiritual substances, in its affections, or rather in its defections, and it degenerates and become unlike itself when it becomes unlike him in its depravity of life and manners; but this unlikeness is not the destruction of its nature, but a defect, for natural goodness is increased as much by comparison with itself as it is spoiled by communication with evil. So the soul returns and is converted (cf. Song 7:10) to the Word, to be reformed by him and conformed to Him. In what way? In charity—for he says: *Be imitators of God, like dear children, and walk in love, as Christ also has loved you* (Eph 5:1).

3. Such conformation weds the soul to the Word, for one who is like the Word by nature shows himself like him too in the exercise of his will, loving as she is loved. When she loves perfectly, the soul is wedded to the Word. What is lovelier than this conformation? What more desirable than charity, by whose operation, O soul, not content with a human master, you approach the Word with confidence, cleave to him with constancy, speak to him as to a familiar friend, and refer to him in every matter with an intellectual grasp proportionate to the boldness of your desire? Truly this is a spiritual compact, a holy marriage. It is more than a compact, it is an embrace: an embrace where identity of will *makes of the two one spirit* (1 Cor 6:17)....

It is from loving, not fearing, that love receives its name. Let someone filled with horror or stupor or fear or wonder be content with reverence; where there is love all these are unimportant. Love is sufficient for itself; when love is present it absorbs and conquers all other affections. Therefore it loves what it loves, and it knows nothing else. He who is justly honored, held in awe, and admired, prefers to be loved. He and the soul are Bridegroom and Bride. What other bond or constraint do you look for between those who are betrothed, except to love and be loved?[2]

---

1. Bernard plays on the traditional distinction between the "image" and "likeness" of Genesis 1:26. His "natural gift" is the original human constitution *in the image of God,* our fundamental ordination to God as the "end" of our human existence. *Likeness,* however, refers to whether there is an actual correspondence to God, a genuine assimilation to God in moral and spiritual terms. It is the task of redemption and salvation, of ascesis and prayer, to recover that likeness and to mature in it.

2. Translation revised.

II. Medieval

B. Medieval, Western: Mystical and Monastic

34. St. Hildegard of Bingen (1098–1179) | *The Life of Hildegard* and *Scivias*

Born the tenth child in a family of the lower nobility in mid-Rhineland, and early showing signs of paranormal experiences, Hildegard was offered by her parents as a "tithe" to God in the year 1106, i.e., she was a child "oblate." Such commitments were not reckoned entirely binding until personal profession was made at a valid age. On November 1, 1112 Hildegard was enclosed as an anchoress with her spiritual mother, Bl. Jutta von Sponheim (a cousin of Emperor Lothair II) and another companion, at the monks' monastery of Disibodenberg. Her formative culture then was anti-Salian, pro-papal, and pro-monastic. Largely educated and formed by the liturgy, she had mastered Latin by her later life.

The reformed monastic milieu in which her vocation matured was a last flowering of the older pre-scholastic, patristic, and monastic culture that was already on the way out in the West by the time she died in 1179. This tradition was qualified in her case by her extraordinary visionary gifts, her keen intellect, her highly symbolic and imaginative approach to interpreting Scripture, her strongly prophetic persona, her musical compositions, and her many writings. Hildegard was the precursor of many women prophets and saints to come in the Western High and Late Middle Ages.

On Jutta's death in 1136, Hildegard was elected prioress of the now expanded and cramped women's community. She battled severe opposition to establish a separate cenobitic monastery for the women at Rupertsberg (near Eibingen) on the Rhine. Warmly supported by her archbishop Henry, endorsed by St. Bernard, and approved by Pope Eugene III, she flourished as a visionary prophet who promoted church reform. She undertook preaching tours up and down the Rhine, when she gave the moral and spiritual condition of the clergy a thorough going-over. She was much sought after as a healer and as a spiritual diagnostician with a special gift for mental illnesses. In one extraordinary episode of her life, she was the successful impresario of the exorcism of a notorious recidivist demoniac, Sigewize.

B. MEDIEVAL, WESTERN: MYSTICAL AND MONASTIC

In 2012 the German Pope, Benedict XVI, enrolled Hildegard as a Doctor of the Church. In his monumental *Life of Hildegard* the monk Theodoric of Echternach incorporated many autobiographical passages from Hildegard, otherwise lost. In the following excerpts from the *Life*, she recounts pivotal visionary experiences. We see the spiritual interpretation, instinct with faith and Catholic and monastic tradition, to which she subjected them. We end with a passage from her most famous work, the *Scivias* ("*Know the ways of the Lord*"), in which she interprets one of her visions to show the dissemination of the saving Word of God in history.

The Life of Hildegard (1181–87)

When I was forty-two years and seven months old, the heaven opened, and a fiery light of the greatest brilliance came forth and suffused my whole brain and my whole heart and breast with a flame, yet enkindling not so as to burn but to warm, just as the sun does when it warms anything on which it pours out its rays. And suddenly I savoured the meaning and interpretation of books, that is, the Psalter, the Gospel, and other Catholic books of both the Old and New Testament. All this came about even though I did not know how to analyse the syntax of the words, or to divide their syllables or had any knowledge of their cases or tenses . . .

Then in this same vision I was constrained by the great pressure of my pains to reveal openly what I had seen and heard. But I was very afraid, and blushed at the thought of proclaiming what I had kept silent about for so long. Nevertheless, from then on my veins and my marrow were filled with the strength which I had lacked from my infancy and youth. I told these things to a certain monk, my *magister*, who was of a worthy way of life and a loving disposition, and like a stranger to the prying ways of many people, so that he listened generously to these strange tales. He marveled at them, and ordered me to discreetly write them out, until he could see what they were and where they came from. But as soon as he concluded that they were from God, he made them known to his Abbot, and from then on was very keen to work with me in these things . . .

In this vision I understood without any human instruction the writings of the prophets, of the Gospels and of other saints and of certain philosophers, and I expounded a number of their texts, although I had scarcely any knowledge of literature, since the woman who taught me was not a scholar. Then I also composed and sung chant with melody, to the praise of God and his saints, without being taught by anyone, since I had never studied neumes or any chant at all.

When these things had been brought to the hearing of the church of Mainz and discussed, they all declared that they were from God and from the prophecy which the prophets of old had prophesied. Then my writings were taken to Pope Eugene while he was staying in Trier. He was pleased to have them read publicly before many, and read them out himself. Putting great trust in God's grace, he sent his blessing along with a letter, and ordered me to carefully commit to writing whatever I saw or heard in vision . . .

Some time later I saw an extraordinary mystical vision, at which all my inward parts trembled, and my body lost all capacity of feeling—for my knowing was changed into another mode in which, as it were, I did not know myself. It was as if the inspiration of God were sprinkling drops of sweet rain into my soul's knowing, the very same with which the Spirit instructed John the Evangelist when he drank in from the breast of Jesus the most profound of revelations. His senses at that time were so touched by the sacred Divinity that he revealed hidden mysteries and works, saying *In the beginning was the Word . . .* (John 1:1) etc.

For it was the Word, which before all created things had no beginning, and after them shall have no end, which summoned all created things into being. He brought his work into being like a smith causing his work to shower sparks. In this way, what was predestined by him before ever the world was, appeared in visible form. Therefore man is the work of God along with every creature. But man is also said to be the worker of the Divinity and a shadow of his mysteries, and should in all things reveal the Holy Trinity, for *God made him in his image and likeness* (Gen 1:26). So, just as Lucifer for all his malice could not bring God to naught, so too, he shall not succeed in destroying the human race, however much he tried to with the first man.

And thus the vision mentioned above taught me and allowed me to expound the words of this Gospel and everything it speaks of, which from the beginning is the work of God. And I saw that this same explanation would have to be the beginning of another writing which had not yet been revealed, in which many questions about the creations of the divine mystery would need to be considered . . .

The Word of God, by Whom all things were made, was Himself begotten before time in the heart of the Father; but afterward, near the end of time, as the Old Testament saints had predicted, He became incarnate of the Virgin; and in assuming humanity he did not forsake Deity, but being one and true God with the Father and the Holy Spirit, he sweetened the world with his sweetness and illumined it with the brilliance of his glory. Hence, *the pillar you see beyond the tower of anticipation of God's will* designates the ineffable mystery of the Word of God; for in that true Word, the Son of God, all the justice of the New and Old Testaments is fulfilled. This justice was opened up to believers for their salvation by divine inspiration, when the Son of the Supreme Father deigned to become incarnate of the sweet Virgin. And the virtues showed themselves to powerful in the anticipation of God's will which was the beginning of the circumcision. Then the mystery of the Word of God was also declared in strict justice by the voice of the patriarchs and prophets, who foretold that He would be manifest in justice and godly deeds and great severity, doing the justice of God and leaving no injustice free to evade the commands of the Law . . .

Scivias (1142–51)

III.3.1. . . . *And from the second edge, facing the North, there goes forth a marvelously bright radiance, which shines and reflects as far as the edge that faces the South.* That is to say that from the second edge, which is the New Testament and stands opposed to the devil, there issue the words of My Son, which come forth from Me and return to Me. For when the sun, which is My Son, stands forth in the flesh, the light of the holy Gospel shines in His preaching, and pours itself out from Him and His disciples as fruits of blessing, and then returns into the fountain of salvation, where it reaches the guides, those who profoundly search into the words of the Old and New Testaments. And they show how wisdom is raised up in that Sun who enlightens the world and burns like the noonday in his elect.

III.4.10. . . . *And in the* radiance *which is so widely diffused, you see apostles, martyrs, confessors and virgins and many other saints, walking in great joy.* For in the clear light in which My Son preached and spread the truth there have grown up apostles who announce that true light, and martyrs who faithfully shed their blood like soldiers, and confessors who act after my Son, and virgins who follow the Supernal Branch, and all My other elect, who rejoice in the fountain of happiness and font of salvation, baptized in the Spirit and going ardently from virtue to virtue.

III.4.11. *And the third edge, facing the South, is broad and wide in the middle, but thinner and narrower at the bottom and top, like a bow drawn and read to shoot arrows.* That is to say, as the Gospel was spread, the wisdom of the saints was broadened. They burned in the Holy Spirit, seeking the Spirit in depth so as to find through Him the deepening of their understanding of the word of God, strengthened by the faith of the Christian people. And so, the sense of the Scriptures that went forth from the mouth of the holy Doctors broadened too. They searched the depths of the Scriptures' astringency, and made it known to the many who learned from them, and thus they too enlarged their senses through knowing more of the wisdom and knowledge of the divine Scriptures. At the beginning of the Church's institution—as it were, at the bottom of the edge—this knowledge was narrower and less studied, for the people did not yet embrace with the love they gave it afterwards. And at the end of time—as it were, at the edge's summit—divine wisdom will not be lovable to them as deeds are lovable, but they will hide their knowledge and keep it for themselves, as if they had no obligation to do good works, for they will know divine wisdom only on the outside, as in a dream . . .

III.4.12. *And in this light appears a dove, with a gold ray coming out of its mouth which sheds brilliant light on the pillar;* for in the heart of the radiant Father, in the brilliance of the light of the Son of God burns the Holy Spirit, Who comes from on high and declares the mysteries of the Son of the Most High, to redeem the people seduced by the ancient serpent. And thus the Holy Spirit inspires all the commandments and all the new testimonies, giving before the Incarnation of the Lord the law of His glorious mysteries, and then showing the same glory in the Incarnation itself. And the Spirit's inspiration is a golden splendor and a high and excellent illumination, and by this outpouring He make known, as was said, the mystical secrets of God's Only-Begotten to the ancient heralds who showed the Son of God through types and marveled at His coming from the Father and his miraculous arising in the dawn of the Virgin. And thus the Spirit in his power fused the Old Testament and the Gospels into one spiritual seed, from which grew all justice.

And thus you cannot contemplate the divine glory because of the immense power of Divinity; no mortal can see it except those to whom I will foreshadow it. Therefore take care not to presume rashly to look upon what is divine, as the trembling that seizes you teaches.

II. Medieval

B. Medieval, Western: Mystical and Monastic

35. St. Francis of Assisi (1181–1226) | *Fioretti*

What can we say of the Poverello ("little poor man"), Francis of Assisi, bright jewel of sanctity in the High Middle Ages, a great saint of the universal church in any age, whose appeal reaches even now far beyond Christians? Born of a French (Provençal) mother and an Italian merchant father in sunny, verdant Umbria, Francis grew up in moneyed ease and privilege. At first aspiring to the life of chivalry as a knight, a year's incarceration as a prisoner led him to sober thoughts about his life; he began losing his taste for the wordly life.

Through the grace of a kiss given to a disfigured leper, his heart melted with love for the cross of our Lord Jesus Christ. He became a changed man. Praying before an image of the Crucified in the abandoned church of San Damiano he heard a command: "Francis, go and repair my house, which as you see, is falling into ruin." At first, he thought it meant repair the building, but really, the Lord's purpose with him was much larger. As he felt and prayed his way into a radically evangelical way of life, he turned chivalry upside down by "wedding" Lady Poverty. The tone of Francis's courtesy owed more to the vernacular culture of the troubadours than to the Latin culture of the Schools and the old monastic orders, and even less to the new intellectual mood of Bologna and Paris, the first universities beginning at that time. Francis's Canticle of the Creatures is the earliest surviving poem in Italian.

The band of brothers that gathered around him grew into the Order of Friars Minor ("lesser brothers"): the "Franciscans." Of the various evangelical groups appearing in that period, this one was known for maintaining a sense of insertion in the wider Catholic Church, and indeed sought and received the endorsement of Pope Innocent III. Many are the episodes told of Francis, perhaps most charmingly in the classic fourteenth century anthology of folk, oral, and written sources, the Fioretti ("little flowers"): the receiving of Lady Clare, the reconciliation of hardened enemies, his mission to Sultan Al Khalil in the Holy Land, the preaching to the birds when the humans would not listen, the taming of the ravaging wolf of Gubbio, the invention of the first Christmas crib scene, etc.

In the following additions to the Fioretti, we read of the culminating event of Francis's life on Monte La Verna in Tuscany, in September 1224, two years before he died, when, as Dante put it: "on that crag between Tiber and Arno he received from Christ the final seal" (*Paradiso* 11.106–7). St. Paul had once declared: *I bear on my body the marks* [Greek: *stigmata*] *of the Lord Jesus Christ* (Gal 6:17). Now the marks of the Lord's passion appeared in Francis's body, an outward sign of his entire inward and outward assimilation to Christ.

Fioretti (early 14th century)

With a good and holy intention, Brother Leo crossed the bridge and quietly entered the Saint's cell. By the bright moonlight shining through the door he saw that he was not in the cell. Not finding him, he thought that he might be praying somewhere outside in the woods. So he came out and silently walked among the trees looking for him by the light of the moon. And at last he heard St. Francis' voice speaking, and went closer to hear what he was saying. In the moonlight he saw St. Francis on his knees with his face raised to the sky and his hands held out to God, saying these words in fervor of spirit: "Who are you my dearest Lord, and what am I, your vilest worm and unprofitable servant?" And these words he repeated over and over again, and said nothing else . . . .

As he turned, St. Francis heard the rustling of the leaves under his feet, and commanded him not to stir, but to await his coming. . . . When St. Francis, then, came up to him, he said: "Who are you?" and Brother Leo, in fear and trembling, answered: "Father, I am Brother Leo." And St. Francis said to him: "Why have you come here, little brother Lamb? Did I not forbid you to observe me? Now tell me, by holy obedience, whether you have seen or heard anything?" And Brother Leo replied: "Father, I heard you speak and say many times, 'Who are you, my dearest Lord? and who am I, your most vile worm and your most unprofitable servant?'" And then, kneeling before St. Francis, Brother Leo accused himself of disobedience to his command, and begged him to explain to him the meaning of the words which he had heard, and to tell him also those which he had not heard. Then St. Francis, seeing that, for his simplicity and purity, God had revealed so much to Brother Leo, consented to reveal and also explain that which he desired to know further; and spoke to him thus:

"Know, little brother Lamb of Jesus Christ, that when I said those words which you heard, two great lights were before my soul. One was the knowledge of myself, the other the knowledge of the Creator. When I said: 'Who are you, my dearest

Lord?' I was in a light of contemplation in which I beheld the abyss of the infinite goodness and wisdom and power of God. When I said: 'Who am I?' I was in a light of contemplation in which I saw the grievous abyss of my own vileness and misery. This is why I said: 'Who are you, the Lord of infinite wisdom and goodness, who deign to visit me, a most vile and abominable and contemptible worm?' And in that flame which you beheld was God, who spoke under that appearance to me, as he spoke of old to Moses . . ."

The day before the Feast of the most Holy Cross, as St. Francis was praying secretly in his cell, an angel of God appeared to him, and spoke to him thus from God: "I have come to admonish and encourage you to prepare yourself to receive in all patience and humility that which God will give and do to you." St. Francis replied: *"I am ready to bear patiently whatever my Lord shall be pleased to do to me."* And so the angel departed.

On the following day—being the Feast of the Holy Cross—St. Francis was praying before daybreak at the entrance of his cell. Turning his face towards the east, he prayed in these words: "O Lord Jesus Christ, two graces I ask of you before I die; the first, that in my lifetime I may feel, as far as possible, both in my soul and body, that pain which you, sweet Lord, endured in the hour of your most bitter Passion; the second, that I may feel in my heart as much as possible of that excess of love by which you, O Son of God, were inflamed to suffer so cruel a Passion for us sinners." And continuing a long time in that prayer, he understood that God had heard him, and that, so far as is possible for a mere creature, he should be permitted to feel these things.

Having then received this promise, St. Francis began to contemplate most devoutly the Passion of Jesus Christ and his infinite charity; and so greatly did the fervour of devotion increase within him that he was all transformed into Jesus by love and compassion.

Then the whole of Mount La Verna appeared enwrapped in an intense fire which illumined all the mountains and valleys around, as if the sun were shining in strength upon the earth, for which reason the shepherds who were watching their flocks in that country were filled with fear, as they themselves afterwards told the brethren, declaring that this light had been visible on Mount La Verna for upwards of an hour. And because of the brightness of that light, which shone through the windows of the inn where they were tarrying, some muleteers who were travelling in Romagna arose quickly, supposing that the sun had risen, and saddled and loaded their beasts; but as they began their journey, they saw that light disappear, and the visible sun arise . . .

Being thus inflamed in that contemplation, on that same morning he beheld a Seraph descending from heaven with six fiery and resplendent wings. This seraph drew nigh with rapid flight to St. Francis, so that he could plainly discern him and perceive that he bore the image of one crucified. The wings were so disposed that two were spread over the head, two were outstretched in flight, and the other two covered the whole body. And when St. Francis beheld it, he was much afraid, and filled simultaneously with joy and grief and wonder. He felt great joy at the gracious presence of Christ, who appeared to him so familiarly and looked upon him so lovingly, but, on the other hand, beholding him thus crucified, he felt exceeding grief and compassion. He marvelled much at so astounding and singular a vision, knowing well that the infirmity of suffering accorded ill with the immortality of a seraphic spirit. And in that perplexity of mind it was revealed to him by him who thus appeared, that this vision had been thus shown to him by divine providence, so that he might understand that, not by martyrdom of the body, but by a consuming fire of the soul, he was to be transformed into the express image of Christ crucified in that wonderful apparition.

Then, after long and secret conference together, that marvellous vision disappeared, leaving in the heart of St. Francis an exceeding fire and ardour of divine love, and on his flesh a wonderful trace and image of the Passion of Christ. For upon his hands and feet began immediately to appear the figures of the nails, as he had seen them on the body of Christ crucified, who had appeared to him in the likeness of a Seraph. And thus the hands and feet appeared pierced through the centre by the nails, the heads of which were seen outside the flesh in the palms of the hands and the soles of the feet, and the points of the nails stood out at the back of the hands, and the feet in such a manner that they appeared to be twisted and bent back upon themselves . . . Likewise, on the right side there appeared the image of an unhealed wound, as if made by a lance, and still red and bleeding, from which drops of blood often flowed from the holy breast of St. Francis, staining his tunic and his drawers . . .

Now although these very holy wounds—inasmuch as they were imprinted on him by Christ, gave very great joy to his heart, nevertheless they gave unbearable pain to his flesh and bodily senses . . .

Lastly, in regard to this Third Consideration, when St. Francis had finished the fast of St. Michael the Archangel, by divine revelation he made ready to return to St. Mary of the Angels. He called Brother Masseo and Brother Angelo, and after many holy words and instructions, commended to them as strongly as he could that holy mountain, saying that he had to go back to St. Mary of the Angels with Brother Leo. And after this he bade farewell to them and blessed them in the name of Jesus Crucified. And he granted their request, and held out to them his very holy hands adorned with those glorious stigmata, to see and touch and kiss. And leaving them thus consoled, he departed and went down the holy mountain.

II. Medieval

B. Medieval, Western: Mystical and Monastic

36. St. Bonaventure (1221–1274) | *The Journey of the Mind into God*

Giovanni Fidanza was born in 1221 in the Umbrian town of Bagnoregio and died at the Second Council of Lyons in 1274. He joined the Order of Friars Minor in 1243, taking the name Bonaventure ("happy chance"/ "good fortune"), and studied at Paris under Alexander of Hales. He took the chair in Theology in 1253 at the Friar's Studium in Paris at about the same time as Thomas Aquinas, his counterpart as a theologian among the Dominicans.

Elected four years later as Minister General, Bonaventure left his academic career for the duties of pastoral and spiritual service to an Order rocked by the controversies of the *Zelanti* faction. They followed the Millenarian views of the Calabrian abbot, Joachim of Fiore, who had predicted a new Age of the Spirit to commence in 1260. Two years later, in 1259, Bonaventure retreated from this turmoil to pray on Monte La Verna, where he pondered deeply Francis's experience on this very spot of the six-winged seraph in the form of Christ crucified. The seraph's six wings (cf. Isa 6:2) suggested to Bonaventure a spiritual ascent through six progressive illuminations, from the first conversion of the mind through to the mystical heights of contemplating the mystery of God as Trinity. So inspired, he penned there on the mountain a brief work, *Itinerarium mentis in Deum*, "The Journey of the Mind into God," a précis of his entire theological outlook. "Mens" in medieval Latin usage was richer than "mind" in modern English. It could even supply for "intellectus" (= the Greek *noos*), the "fine point of the spirit," the "reins and the heart" of the Hebrew Scriptures. In Bonaventure it meant the will informed by the intellect, as the "faculty" by which love expresses itself. The theology of the "Seraphic Doctor," as he is called, was a prolonged dredging of Scripture, maintaining in the West the mystical and "platonic" hermeneutic of patristic theology, providing something of an alternative to the prevailing Thomism of later centuries.

There is a delightful story that Thomas Aquinas once went to consult his friend, Bonaventure, who was writing his *Life of Francis*. Finding him rapt in prayer, Thomas retired, commenting, "It is better to leave a saint to write about a saint."

In the following we read from the Introduction and the final chapter of the *Itinerarium*, where Bonaventure, familiar as he was with Hugh of St. Victor, calls on the apophatic theology of Pseudo-Dionysius, especially the theme of the paradoxical "bright darkness" encountered by prayer as it matures in contemplation.

The Journey of the Mind Into God, Prologue (1259)

1. To begin I invoke the eternal Father, the first Principle[1] from Whom all illumination *descends as from the Father of Light, by Whom are given all the best and perfect gifts* (Jas 1:17), through His Son our Lord Jesus Christ, that at the intercession of the most holy Virgin Mary, mother of our very God and Lord (cf. John 20:28) Jesus Christ, and of blessed Francis, our father and leader, He may *illumine the eyes of our mind* (Eph 1:18) *to guide our feet into the way of that peace* (Luke 1:79) *which surpasses all understanding* (Phil 4:7), the *peace* which our Lord Jesus Christ announced and *gave* to us (cf. John 14:27), which lesson our father Francis always taught, who at the beginning and at the end of all his preaching announced peace, who wished for peace in every greeting, and yearned for ecstatic peace in every moment of contemplation, as a citizen of that Jerusalem of which that man of peace said who was peaceable with those that hated peace (cf. Ps 119:6–7): *Pray for the things that are for the peace of Jerusalem* (Ps 122:6), knowing that the throne of Solomon was nothing except in peace, since it is written: *His dwelling place is in peace and His abode in Sion* (Ps 75:2).

2. Since . . . I, exhausted, sought this peace—I, a sinner, who have succeeded to the place of that most blessed father after his death, the seventh Minister General of the brothers, although in every way unworthy—it happened that by the divine will in the thirty-third year after the death of that blessed man I ascended to Mount La Verna as to a quiet place, in the desire of seeking spiritual peace; while staying there I meditated on the ascent of the mind into God, where, among other things there occurred that miracle which happened in the same place to the blessed Francis himself, namely the vision of the winged Seraph in the likeness of the Crucified. While considering this vision, I saw immediately that it signified the suspension of our father himself in contemplation and the way by which he came to it.

3. For by those six wings are rightly to be understood six stages of illumination by which the soul, as by steps or progressive movements, is disposed to pass into peace by the ecstatic elevations of Christian wisdom. The way, however, is only through the most burning love of the Crucified Who so transformed Paul, *caught up into the third heaven* (2 Cor 12:2), into Christ, that he said, *With Christ I am nailed to the cross, yet I live, now not I, but Christ lives in me* (Gal 2:19). The same therefore so absorbed the mind

---

1. Bonaventure articulates the doctrine of "mon-arché": the Father as the "principle" of the Trinity.

of Francis that his soul was manifested in his flesh and he bore the most holy stigmata of the Passion in his body for two years before his death. The symbol of the six-winged Seraph, therefore, signifies six stages of illumination, which begin with God's creations and lead up to God, into Whom no one can enter properly save through the Crucified . . . Accordingly John says in his Apocalypse: *Blessed are they who wash their robes in the blood of the Lamb, that they may have a right to the Tree of Life and may enter by the gates into the City* (Rev 22:14); as if to say that one cannot enter into the heavenly Jerusalem through contemplation unless one enters through the blood of the Lamb as through a gate. For one is not disposed to contemplation which leads to the elevation of the mind unless one becomes like Daniel *a man of desires* (Dan 9:23). But desires are kindled in us in two ways: by the cry of prayer, which makes one groan with the murmuring of the heart, and by a flash of apprehension by which the mind turns most directly and intensely to the rays of light [cf. Ps 34:5, 36:9].

4. It is therefore to the cry of prayer through Christ crucified, by Whose blood we are purged of the filth of vice, that I first invite the reader . . .

Chapter Seven . . .

1. Now that these six considerations have been studied as the six steps of the true *throne of Solomon* (cf. 1 Kgs 1:46) by which one ascends to peace, where one who is truly peaceful reposes in peace of mind as if in the inner Jerusalem; . . . during the first six days in which the mind must be exercised until it finally arrives at the Sabbath of rest, having beheld God outside itself through His traces and in His traces, within itself by His image and in His image (cf. Gen 1:27), and above itself by the likeness of the divine light shining down upon us and *in that light* (Ps 36:9), as far as possible in this life and the exercise of our mind—until, finally, on the sixth level we reach the point of beholding in the first and highest Principle and in *the Mediator of God and men, Jesus Christ* (1 Tim 2:5), such realities of which no likeness can be found at all in created things and which surpass all the insight of the human intellect. It remains that by looking upon these things that the mind rises on high and passes beyond not only this sensible world but also itself. In this passing over, Christ is *the way* (John 14:6) and *the door* (John 10:7), the ladder (Gen 28:12, cf. John 2:51) and the vehicle like *the mercy-seat*[2] over the ark of God (Exod 25:20), and *the Mystery which has been hidden from all eternity* (Eph 3:9).

2. He who with full face looks to this mercy-seat through looking upon Him suspended on the Cross, in faith, hope, and charity, through devotion, wonder, exultation, appreciation, praise, and jubilation, makes a Pasch—that is, a 'passing over' (Exod 12:11) with Him, that by the staff of the Cross he may pass over the Red Sea from Egypt into the Desert, where he may taste the *hidden manna* (Rev 2:17), and may rest with Christ in the tomb as if outwardly dead, yet knowing, as far as possible in our

---

2. Or "propitiatory," or "throne of mercy."

earthly condition, what was said on the Cross to the thief cleaving to Christ: *Today you shall be with me in Paradise* (Luke 23:43).

3. This was shown to the blessed Francis when, in the transport of contemplation on the high mountain—where I thought out these things which I have written—there appeared to him the six-winged Seraph nailed to the Cross, as I and several others have heard from the companion who was with him[3] when he passed over into God through transports of contemplation and became an example of perfect contemplation, even as previously he had been of action. Like another Jacob he was changed into Israel (cf. Gen 32:28),[4] so through him all the truly spiritual are invited by God by example rather than word to such a passing over and transport of the mind.

4. If this passing over is to be perfect, all intellectual operations must be abandoned, and the whole summit of our affection be transferred and transformed into God. This, however, is mystical and most secret, *which no man knows but he who has received it* (Rev. 2:17)—nor does he receive it unless he desires it; nor does he desire it unless *the fire* of the Holy Spirit, Whom Christ *sent to earth* (cf. Luke 12:49), has inflamed his marrow. And therefore the Apostle says that this mystic wisdom is revealed through the Holy Spirit (cf. 1 Cor 2:10).

5. Since, then, nature is powerless in this matter and industry only slightly able, little should be given to inquiry but much to unction, little to the tongue but much to inner joy, little to words and to writings and all to the Gift of God, that is, to the Holy Spirit, little or nothing to creation and all to the creative essence, the Father, the Son, and the Holy Spirit, saying with Dionysius to God the Trinity: (Citations follow of Pseudo-Dionysius, *De Mystica Theologia* I.1).

6. If you should ask how these things come about, question grace, not instruction; desire, not intellect; the cry of prayer, not the pursuit of study; the spouse, not the schoolteacher; God, not man; darkness, not clarity; not light, but the wholly flaming fire which will bear you aloft to God with fullest unction and burning affection. This *fire is God* (cf. Heb 12:29, Exod 24:17), the *furnace* whose *fire* leads to *Jerusalem* (Isa 31:9); and Christ the man kindles it in the fervor of His burning Passion (cf. Luke 12:49–50), which he alone truly perceives who can say: *My soul rather chooses hanging and my bones death* (Job 7:15). He who chooses this death can see God because this is undoubtedly true: *Man shall not see me and live* (Exod 33:20). Let us then die and pass over into the darkness; let us impose silence on cares, concupiscence, and imaginings; let us *pass over* with the crucified Christ *from this world to the Father* (John 13:1).

---

3. This was Brother Leo, a priest and Francis's dearest companion. He lived a long life, dying in 1270. He became a special friend and defender of St. Clare and was present at her death. Leo was a preceptor of the "Spiritual" element in the Order.

4. A traditional etymology of "Is-ra-el" was 'a man (*ish*) who sees (*ra*) God (*El*)'.

II. Medieval

B. Medieval, Western: Mystical and Monastic

37. Johannes "Meister" Eckhart (c. 1260–1327/8) | *Treatise on the Birth of the Eternal Word, Homily on the Birth of Jesus,* & *Treatise on Detachment*

Eckhart von Hochheim was born in the village of Tambach, in Thuringia, of obscure family background. He joined the Order of Preachers in Erfurt at eighteen years of age, studied in Cologne, attained twice the post of *Magister* ("*Meister*") in the University of Paris (a rare attainment), held the Dominican chair of theology, and taught in Strassbourg and Cologne. For years he was prior in Erfurt and sometime Dominican provincial in Saxony, acquitting himself as a competent administrator and reformer of his Order. In the midst of this busy life he wrote works in both Middle High German and Latin, was much sought after as a preacher (in German), a guide in the spiritual life to many, specially to the Beguines and the emergent Flemish/Rhineland mystical tradition, and notably to its greatest representative, Ruysbroeck. His best known disciples among the Dominicans were Tauler and Suso, who were more circumspect than he in their discourse. In the fifteenth century, Nicholas of Cusa studied him.

Towards the end of his life Archbishop Henry of Cologne launched a campaign to have Eckhart investigated for heresy, targeting neo-platonizing and supposedly pantheistic tendencies, his dichotomization of the unmanifest and the manifest Absolute or Godhead, and certain ideas about the birth of Christ in the soul. Henry's chief worry seems to have been the danger of low-end popular heresy in the vernacular being bred from high-end mystical language in Latin. Eckhart was vindicated, but Henry persisted till he secured an adverse judgment. Eckhart was outraged, since he intended to be nothing but a loyal son of the church. He appealed to Pope John XXII, and travelled to Avignon to defend himself. The result was a qualified papal judgment in 1329 which reduced Henry's 150+ propositions to twenty-eight. But by then Eckhart had already departed this earth.

Since his rediscovery in the mid-nineteenth century, a wide variety of ideologues has tried to coopt Eckhart to the cause, which perhaps demonstrates that Archbishop Henry's concerns were not entirely misplaced. "While serious scholars reject such extreme interpretations, these exaggerated views do serve to indicate that Meister Eckhart was and is a daring and difficult thinker, a man who escapes any easy categorization, and frequently a scandal to the timid and conventional."[1]

In the following homily, we can see the Eckhart's manner of interpreting Scripture in a consistently interiorizing and personalizing way.

Treatise on the Birth of the Eternal Word (1310s)

Now we will speak of the coming of our Lord Jesus Christ as he is born today at this holy season from his blessed mother the Virgin Mary, and again, as he is born from grace in the perfect soul, for that is the whole end of Christ's work upon earth. And we shall ask nine questions from which any pious man may tell whether the eternal Word is born in him or not.

The first question is, how to prepare for the interior speaking of the eternal Word? Several things are needed. First, purity of life and mind. Next, the peace and freedom of a still and silent heart which is speaking to no creature and is spoken to by none, whether of the senses or the spirit. And now for a hard saying that few will understand. While the soul is speaking her own word and her noble word, the Father cannot speak his Word in her; while the soul is begetting her own "son," i.e. the noblest work of her understanding, the Father is not able to beget his Son in her to her best advantage. Thirdly, the soul must forsake herself in order to conceive the eternal Word like St. Paul and Mary, the Mother of God, in whom the eternal Word was uttered perfectly. The mind must die to itself, disowning itself and becoming God's own. Fourthly, the mind must lift up its intellect and see, for seeing is the most vigorous work and noblest of which the soul is capable. Mark how eagerly he comes. He says: *Behold I stand at the door and knock!* (Rev 3:20) Fifthly, it behooves us greatly to desire this birth, for desire is the root of all virtue and goodness.

The second question is, what is God's birth in the soul? Nothing less than a special divine motion in a special heavenly mode whereby God wrests the spirit from the tumult of creaturely unrest into his motionless unity where God can communicate himself to the soul in his divinity. There man enjoys his Word, in the Father in its first discriminate emanation, and together with the Father as an essential Person, and in the Holy Spirit as the limit set to their eternal bliss, and it is in the soul as the reflection of her intellectual prototype, and in all creatures as the preserver of their being. For God speaks his Word in every creature, but no creature is aware of it save rational creatures only. The soul is reborn into God when she turns to God and pursues his eternal Word right into the Paternal heart where God makes naked revelation of his birth to the soul. The soul falls upon this birth which is revealed to

---

1. From "Foreword" in *Meister Eckhart*, 5.

her, with love and knowledge. As the Father comes into the soul in his Word, so in the Word the soul is returned into the Father. That we may eternally play this game in God, God help us....

Homily on the Birth of Jesus (c. 1310s)

For this nativity God wants, and must have, a vacant, free and unencumbered soul where there is nothing but himself alone, which waits for nothing and for no one but God. As Christ says: "*Whoever loves anything else but me*, whoever clings *to father, mother*, or many other things, *is not worthy of me. I came upon earth, not to bring peace, but a sword*—to cut away all things, to part you from brother, child, mother, and friend, who are really your foes" (cf. Matt 10:34–37). For truly, your comforts are your foes. Does your eye look at everything, your ear listen to everything, and your heart remember everything? Then in these your soul is destroyed....

We must sink into oblivion and ignorance. In this silence, this quiet, the Word is heard. There is no better method of approaching this Word than in silence, in quiet: we hear it, and we know it aright, in unknowing. To one who knows nothing it is clearly revealed.

But you may object: "Sir, you place our salvation in ignorance. That seems mistaken. God made man to know, as the prophet says: *Lord, make them know* (Ps 83:18). Where ignorance remains, there is defect and illusion. One remains brutish, an ape, a fool, as long as one is ignorant."

But I speak of transformed knowledge, not ignorance that comes from lack of knowing. It is by knowing that we arrive at this unknowing. Then we know with divine knowing, then our ignorance is ennobled and adorned with supernatural knowledge. Then we are more perfect in suffering than in action.

According to one authority, the sense of hearing is far nobler than the sense of sight. For we learn wisdom more through the ear than through the eye, and live this life more wisely ... Hearing draws in more, seeing leads out more. In eternal life we are far happier in our ability to hear than in our capacity to see, because the act of hearing the eternal Word is *inside* me, whereas the act of seeing goes *out* from me. Hearing, I am receptive, seeing, I am active.

Now our bliss does not consist in being active, but in being receptive to God. As God surpasses his creatures, so God's work surpasses mine. It was out of love that God set our happiness in suffering, for we undergo much more than we do,[2] and receive in return incomparably more than we give. Every divine gift is the preparation for some new and richer gift, each gift enlarging our capacity and desire to receive one that is greater still. Some theologians say that the soul is symmetrical to God in this respect, so that the soul is infinite in receiving or conceiving. The soul can suffer profoundly, as God can act omnipotently, and so the soul is transformed into God. God must act,

---

2. I.e., what we undergo, have done unto us, befall us, is much more than what we actively do.

and the soul must suffer, if he is to know and love himself in her, and she is to know with his knowledge, and love with his love. . . .

Treatise on Detachment (c. 1320s)

I have read many writings of heathen philosophers and sages, and of the Old Covenant and the New, and have sought earnestly and with greatest diligence to find the best and highest virtue, the virtue which will enable someone to knit himself most closely to God, and in which he is most like his exemplar, Christ, as he was when he was in God, before God ever created creatures. And having studied all these writings to the best of my ability, I find that this virtue is none other than absolute detachment from all creatures. Our Lord said to Martha: *Only one thing is needful* (Luke 10:42), which is as good as saying that anyone who wishes to be serene and pure needs only one thing: detachment. . . .

I rank detachment above love, because love constrains me to suffer all things for God's sake, whereas detachment constrains me to receive nothing but God. Now it is far better to accept nothing but God, than to suffer all things for God's sake. For in suffering one is concerned with creatures, from whom the suffering comes, whereas detachment is free from creatures. I can demonstrate that detachment accepts no one but God in this way: anything that is received must be received *in* something. But detachment is so nearly nothing that there is nothing rarified enough to stay *in* this detachment, except God. He is so simple, so ethereal that he can live in the solitary heart. Detachment, then, accepts God alone. Anything which is received, is received and grasped by its receiver in accordance with the constitution of the receiver. And so anything conceived is known and understood according the mind of him who understands, and not according to its own conceivability . . .

Then again I ask: What is the prayer of the solitary man? My answer is that detachment and emptiness cannot pray at all, for whoever prays, desires something from God—something to be added to him, or something to be taken away. But the heart that is detached has no desire for anything, nor has it anything to be delivered from. So it has no prayers at all; its only prayer consists in being one with God. This what St Dionysius is referring to when he comments on St. Paul's words: *In a race, all the runners run, but only one gains the prize* (1 Cor 9:24). All the powers of the soul are competing for the crown, which falls to the essence alone. According to Dionysius, this race is none other than the flight from creation to union with uncreated nature. Gaining this the soul loses her name. God absorbs her in himself so that as herself she comes to nothing, just as the sunlight swallows up the dawn and reduces it to nothing. Only absolute detachment brings the soul to this place.

St. Augustine has an apt word here: "the soul has a private door into the divine nature at the point where for her, all things come to nothing."[3]

---

3. Translation revised.

II. Medieval

B. Medieval, Western: Mystical and Monastic
38. St. Julian of Norwich (1342–ca. 1416) | *The Revelations of Divine Love*

The little that is known of Julian's background is drawn from her writings. From the homely images she uses to convey her sense of God's goodness, it appears that she was nurtured in a loving family. Thereafter she appears to have spent her whole life in Norwich in Norfolk, England. It is unclear whether she was a single person, a widow, or a Benedictine nun before she was enclosed as an anchoress, i.e., a special kind of hermit, a female "anchorite" consecrated to prayer in a cell or "anchorhold" with a garden, attached to a church, where the liturgy might be attended and the sacraments received through a window in the church wall. Anchoresses might have extensive social ministry, for folk would come up to their little grilled window to tell of their temporal and spiritual struggles, and obtain consolation and guidance from those whom they esteemed as spiritual mothers.

The governing event of Julian's life occurred in May 1373 during a near-death illness, when she experienced a series of "shewings" or revelations of Jesus Christ. On recovering her health, she penned an account of them in what is now known as the Short Text of her *Revelations of Divine Love*. The first surviving woman writer in English, she wrote in the Norwich dialect of Middle English, which was only then reasserting its ascendency over French among the upper classes. She continued pondering the meaning of these revelations, until some twenty years later she wrote out a more theologically interpreted version, known as the Long Text. Even so, she re-edited it many times. As "Mary kept all these things and pondered them in her heart" (Luke 2:19, 51), so Julian's pondering of the "shewings" appear to have been a lifelong "work in progress," which no doubt continued into eternity.

Julian was rediscovered in the twentieth century through new editions of her work, and is now regarded as a preeminent representative of the late medieval English mystics. In the following passage we see Julian's prevailing sense of metaphysical goodness—the entire world is created by a good God, loving to man—and at the same time, the clear distinction she owns between the created and the uncreated, between

God the Trinity and the human being, who nevertheless is inalienably ordained to God. Several times we hear her most famous saying, a great consolation to many, as she struggles unequally with the mystery of iniquity, that is, the sin that we know all too well from its hindering effects within us, as compared with the overwhelming goodness of God shown forth in our Lord Jesus. That sin is "necessary" ("behovely" is her original word, here "must needs be") is hyperbolic, as in the famous exclamation of the *Exsultet* of the Paschal Liturgy: "O happy fault, O necessary sin of Adam, that gained for us such and so great a Redeemer!"

Revelations of Divine Love (c. 1390s)

5. It was at this time that our Lord showed me a spiritual vision of his familiar love. I saw that for us he is everything good and strengthening to our help. He clothes us, enwrapping us for love, enfolding us and embracing us for tender love, never to leave us, being himself all that is good for us, as I saw it.

In this vision he showed me a little thing, the size of a hazelnut in the palm of my hand, and it was round like a ball. Looking at it with the eye of my understanding I thought, "What can this be?" And the answer came to me, "It is all that is made." I marveled that it could last, for I thought it might have fallen suddenly into nothingness, it was so small. And I was answered in my understanding, "It lasts, and ever shall, because God loves it. And so do all things have being by the love of God."

In this "little thing" I saw three properties. The first is that God made it; the second is that God loves it; and the third is that God sustains it. But what he is who is in truth Maker, Sustainer and Lover I cannot tell, for until I am substantially united to him I can never have full rest or true bliss—until, in other words, I have so cleaved to him that there is nothing at all that is made between my God and me. This little thing that is made, I thought it might have fallen into nothingness for littleness. We need to know this, and set at naught all that is made, if we are to love and possess God who is not made.

This is the reason why we have no ease in heart or soul, for we seek our rest here in matters so trivial where no rest is to be had, while we ignore our God, who is almighty, all wise and all-good, who is true rest. God wills to be known, and is pleased that we should rest in him, for nothing that is less than he is, can satisfy us. This is why, until all that is made is set at naught, no soul is at rest. When she is deliberately so detached for love of him who is all, only then can she experience spiritual rest.

God also showed me that it pleases him very greatly when a simple soul comes to him, nakedly, openly, and familiarly. For, as I understand this revelation, it is the natural yearning of the soul touched by the Holy Spirit, to say: "O God, of your goodness, give to me yourself, for you are enough for me, and to pay you full worship I may ask nothing less. Were I to ask anything less, I should always be in want. But in you alone I have all." . . .

6. . . . For the goodness of God is the highest prayer and reaches down to our lowest need. It quickens our soul and gives it life, and causes it to grow in grace and virtue . . . For as the body is clad with clothing, and the flesh with skin, and the bones with flesh, and the heart with the chest, so are we, soul and body, clad and enclosed in the goodness of God. Yes, and even more closely than that, since all these things fade and waste away, whereas the goodness of God is forever whole, and nearer to us beyond compare. For truly our Lover desires that our soul cleave to him with all her might, and ever cleave to his goodness. For beyond our heart's imagining, this most pleases God, and sooner speeds the soul . . .

27. After this, our Lord reminded me of the longing I had for him; and I saw that nothing hindered me but sin, and I saw that this was true of all of us. And I thought that if sin had never existed, we should all have been as pure and like him as God made us (cf. Gen 1:27, Col 3:15). And so in my folly I had often wondered why in his great foreseeing wisdom God could not have prevented the beginning of sin, for then, thought I, all would have been well. I ought surely to have abandoned these thoughts, but nonetheless I grieved and sorrowed over this question without reason or judgment. But Jesus, who in this vision informed me of all I needed, answered with this assurance: "*Sin must needs be* (cf. Matt 18:7)—but all shall be well, and all shall be well, and all manner of thing shall be well."

With this naked word "sin" our Lord brought to my mind in sum all that is not good, and the shameful scorn and the uttermost humiliation that he bore for us in this life, and his dying, and all the pains of his creatures, whether in body or spirit—for we are all to some extent brought to nothing and shall be brought to nothing following our Lord Jesus until we are purged, that is, till our mortal flesh is brought to nothing, and all our inward affections that are not good. He gave me insight into these things, along with all pains that ever were and ever shall be. Compared with these I understood that Christ's Passion was the greatest pain and surpassed them all. And all this was shown in a flash, and quickly changed into comfort; for our good Lord did not want the soul to be afraid of this ugly sight.

But I did not see *sin,* for I believe it has no substance or portion of being, nor could it be known, were it not for the suffering that it causes. And this suffering it seems to me to be something transient, for it purges us and makes us know ourselves and so ask for mercy. For the Passion of our Lord sustains us against all this, and such is his blessed will. And because of the tender love which our Lord feels for all who shall be saved, he sustains us willingly and sweetly, meaning thus: "It is true that sin is the cause of all this suffering, but all shall be well, and all shall be well, and all manner of things shall be well." . . .

28. Thus I saw how Christ has compassion on us on account of sin. And as I was earlier filled with suffering and compassion at Christ's Passion, so now I was filled with compassion for all my fellow Christians, for those well-beloved who shall *be* saved, that is, God's servants, for Holy Church, which shall be shaken with sorrows and anguish and tribulation in this world, just as men shake a cloth in the wind. And to this God made answer: "I shall make some great thing out of this in heaven, something eternally worthy and everlastingly joyful."

And I saw as far as this: that our Lord rejoices with pity and compassion in the tribulations of his servants. To bring every person whom he loves to his bliss, he lays on each one something that is no lack in his sight, but by which they are lowered and put to shame in this world, scorned and mocked, and even cast out. And he does this to prevent the harm that would be done to them by the pomp and vainglory of this wretched life, and to prepare their way to heaven, to his bliss that has no end, for he says: "I shall break you from your vain passions and your vicious pride, and after that I shall gather you, and render you humble and meek, clean and holy, through making you one with me." And then I saw that whenever a man has compassion on his fellow-Christian—it is Christ in him . . .

He wants us to know that all shall turn us to glory and profit through his Passion; to know, moreover, that we do not suffer alone; to see him as our ground . . . To see this shall save us from groaning and despair in the midst of our pains, if we see that our sin well deserves it, but that his love excuses us.

29. . . . while I understood all this I was still troubled and grieved. . . . Our blessed Lord answered most humbly and cheerfully, showing me that Adam's sin was the greatest harm that was ever done, or ever shall be till the world's end, and he showed that this is openly known through all the Holy Church upon earth. Furthermore he taught that I should consider the glorious atonement; since this atonement is incomparably more pleasing to God and more glorious in saving mankind than Adam's sin was ever harmful. What our blessed Lord's teaching means is that we should take heed of this: "Since the greatest possible harm I have turned to the good, I wish you to know thereby that I shall turn to the good all harms of lesser degree."

86. And from the time that this was shown, I often longed to know what our Lord meant. And fifteen years and more later my spiritual understanding received an answer: "Do you want to know what our Lord meant? Know well that Love was his meaning. Who showed you this? Love. What did he show? Love. Why did he show it to you? For Love. Hold fast to this, and you will know and understand more of the same, but you will never understand or know from it anything else for all eternity."[4]

---

4. Translation revised.

II. Medieval

B. Medieval, Western: Mystical and Monastic

39. *The Cloud of Unknowing* (late 14th century)

The Cloud of Unknowing is another jewel of that mysterious flourishing of Catholic mysticism that took place in late fourteenth century England—precisely in the midst of innumerable political, social, and ecclesial dislocations and distresses. It is written in a northern East midlands dialect of Middle English. There is no consensus as to its author—Walter Hilton was once suggested, but that is discounted now. More likely it was written by a Carthusian priest-monk whose Order forbade its writers to sign their name to their works. So its purpose may be compared with William of St. Thierry's *Golden Epistle.* Everything about the content suggests a well-read person of great spiritual experience, long dedicated to the contemplative life.

The *Cloud* is intended for those who are truly committed to seeking the perfection of the life in Christ in contemplative prayer. Its tone is that of an elder guiding novices. The mystical theology of the *Cloud* inherits from the Cappadocian Fathers the doctrine of the incomprehensibility of the divine nature to the human intellect, and understands that this is the chief reason (though not the only one) why we are liable to encounter darkness as we progress in genuine contemplative prayer. It breathes in a more simplified form the theological apophaticism of the Cappadocians' interpreter, Pseudo-Dionysius. The author seems to call on St. Gregory of Nyssa and his *Life of Moses,* in which Gregory expounds Moses's progress from light (the visible fire) through cloud and finally into deep darkness; certainly he knows the world of the Desert Fathers and their insistence on spiritual guidance, and also Sts. Augustine and Gregory the Great, and the more recent authors, St. Bernard and Richard of St. Victor. His apophatic mystical theology points forward to that of St. John of the Cross.

The Cloud of Unknowing (late 14th century)

Only see: all rational beings, angels and men, have in them, each individually, two principal active faculties, one a faculty of knowledge, and the second a faculty of love; and God their maker is forever beyond the reach of the first of these, the intellectual faculty, but by means of the second, the loving faculty, he can be fully grasped by each individual being, insofar as each single loving soul, by virtue of love, embraces within itself him who is fully sufficient—and incomparably more than fully—to fill the all the souls and angels that can ever exist. And this is the unending marvelous miracle of love, which can never be concluded; for God will always do it, and will never cease from doing it. Let anyone who has the grace to see this, see it, for to experience this is unending bliss, and to lack it is unending pain . . .

You did well to say "for the love of Jesus," for in the love of Jesus shall be your help. Love is so great a power that it makes all possessions common. Love Jesus, therefore, and all that he has is yours. As God he is the maker and giver of time; as Man he is the true governor of time; and as God and Man together he is the truest judge and auditor of the spending of time. So bind yourself to him in love and faith, and then, by means of that bond, you will be an equal partner with him and with all who are thus bound to him by love, that is, with our Lady, Holy Mary, who was full of all grace in the keeping of time, with all the angels of heaven who may never waste time, and with all the saints in heaven and upon earth who, by the grace of Jesus, keep exact account of time by means of love . . .

And so attend to this work of contemplation and the marvelous way it operates within your soul. For, truly understood, it is just a sudden and, as it were, unforeseen stirring, springing swiftly to God like a spark from a coal. And it is marvelous how many stirrings can occur in an hour in a soul that is given to this work. And yet, in just a single one of all these stirrings, it can happen that you forget the whole world, suddenly and completely. But straight after such stirring, because of the flesh's corruption, the soul falls back down into some thought or action, done or not done. But what of that? For straight afterwards it rises again as suddenly as it did before . . .

And so, for the love of God take care in this work, and do not struggle in your intellect or imagination in any way. For I tell you truly, it cannot be achieved by that kind of struggle; so give it up and do not attempt it.

Do not suppose, because I call it a darkness or a cloud, that it is a cloud condensed out of the vapors that fill the air, or a darkness like that in your house at night when your candle is out. By intellectual ingenuity you can imagine such a darkness or cloud brought before your eyes on the brightest day of summer, just as, on the other hand, you can imagine, in the darkest night of winter, a clear shining light. Give up such errors; that is not what I mean. For when I say "darkness," I mean an absence of knowing, in the sense that everything you do not know, or have forgotten, is dark to you, because you cannot see it with your mind's eye. And for this reason it is not called a cloud in the air, but a cloud of unknowing that is between you and your God . . .

For he can well be loved, but he cannot be thought. By love he can be grasped and held, but by thought, neither grasped nor held. And therefore, though it may be good at times to think specifically of the kindness and excellence of God, and though this may be a light and a part of contemplation, all the same, in the work of contemplation itself, it must be cast down and covered with a cloud of forgetting. And you must step above it steadfastly but deftly, with a devoted and delightful stirring of love, and struggle to pierce that darkness above you; and beat on that thick cloud of unknowing with a sharp dart of longing love, and do not give up, whatever happens.[1]

---

1. Translation slightly revised.

II. Medieval

B. Medieval, Western: Mystical and Monastic

40. Thomas à Kempis (ca. 1380–1471) | *The Imitation of Christ*

The *Imitation* is a literary monument to that fourteenth-century movement in the Low Countries called the Devotio Moderna, promoted by the "Brethren of the Common Life," founded by Gerard Groote in 1375. This was a community unsatisfied by contemporary monastic/religious life, and suspicious of the speculations of late medieval theology and even of mystical theology. It seems, then, that they were not so much "modern" as archaizing, being more at home with the ascetical and moral aspects of the old-time Latin patristic and monastic theology.

The *Imitation* began with notes taken down from the oral teachings of two or three of these Brethren. Thomas Hemerken of Kempen, or Thomas À Kempis in Latin, was the end redactor or final author of these notes, which he augmented with his own reflections and suffused with his own long matured interior spirit. He translated the final work from the original Netherlandish into Latin. The *Imitation* was destined to be one of the most widely read books on the Christian spiritual life for centuries.

Born to a tradesman's family about 1380 in the little Rhineland town of Hämerken near Düsseldorf, Thomas was educated by the Brethren of the Common Life, joined their community, and was ordained priest in 1413. He devoted the rest of his long life to quietly living the round of the community life, ministering in the liturgy, educating novices, and both copying and composing books for the Brethren's schools. In a way, he almost reminds us of Bede, and if a valid thought, we have come a long round circle in the history of Western spirituality.

Ronald Knox's summary is apt: "The whole work was meant to be, surely, what it is: a sustained irritant that will preserve us, if it is read faithfully, from sinking back into relaxation; from self-conceit, self-pity, self-love. It offers consolation here and there, but always at the price of fresh exertion, of keeping your head pointing upstream. Heaven help us if we find easy reading in the *Imitation of Christ*."[1]

---

1. Thomas à Kempis, *The Imitation of Christ*, 8.

B. MEDIEVAL, WESTERN: MYSTICAL AND MONASTIC

The Imitation of Christ (1418–27)

1.1. *He that follows Me, shall not walk in darkness* (John 8:12), says the Lord. These are the words of Christ, whereby we are urged to imitate his life and manner, if we would be truly illumined and freed from all blindness of heart. Let it therefore be our chief study to meditate on the life of Jesus Christ.

The teaching of Christ surpasses all the teachings of the Saints, and whoever has his Spirit he shall find therein *the hidden manna* (Rev 2:17). But it happens that many, from hearing the Gospel often, are little affected, because *they have not the Spirit of Christ* (cf. Rom 8:9). But if you would understand Christ's words and truly taste them, you must strive to conform your whole life after his pattern.

What good will it do you to dispute learnedly about the Trinity, if you are lacking in humility, and thus are displeasing to the Trinity? Truly, sublime words do not make a man holy and just; it is a virtuous life that makes him dear to God. I should rather feel compunction than know how to define it. If you knew the whole Bible outwardly, and the sayings of all the philosophers, what would all that profit you without charity and the grace of God? *Vanity of vanities, and all is vanity* (Eccl 1:2) but to love God *and serve Him alone* (Luke 4:8). This is the highest wisdom: to despise the world and to aim for the Kingdom of Heaven.

It is vanity, therefore, to seek perishable riches and to trust in them. It is vanity also to pursue honors and to raise oneself to a high dignity. It is vanity to follow *the desires of the flesh* (Gal 5:16), and to desire that which hereafter must bring a heavy penalty. It is vanity to wish for a long life, and to care little for a good life. It is vanity to attend only to the present life, and not to look to the things that are to come. It is vanity to love that which quickly passes away, and not to be hastening to the place where everlasting joy abides.

Often call to mind the proverb: *The eye is not sated with seeing, nor is the ear filled with hearing* (Eccl 1:8). Strive, therefore, to wean your heart from the love of things visible, and to concern yourself with things invisible; for they who indulge the pleasures of their senses sully their conscience and lose the grace of God...

2.1. *The Kingdom of God is within you* (Luke 17:21), says our Lord. Turn then with all your heart to the Lord, and forsake this wretched world, and your soul shall find rest. Learn to despise outward things and give yourself to inward things, and you shall see the Kingdom of God coming within your soul. *The Kingdom of God is peace and joy in the Holy Spirit* (Rom 14:17) which is not given to the wicked. Christ will come to you and will disclose to you his consolations, if you will prepare for him a dwelling place within you. *All his glory and beauty is within* (Ps 45:13), and there it is his pleasure to be. Many are His visits to the man of interior life. With such a one He holds delightful converse, granting him sweet comfort, much peace, and a wondrous and exceeding intimacy.

Come then, faithful soul, prepare your heart for this your Bridegroom, that he may deign to come to you and dwell in you, for He himself says: *Whoever loves me, keeps my word, and we will come to him and make our abode in him* (cf. John 14:23).

3.1. *I will hear what the Lord God shall speak in me* (Ps 85:8)

Happy is that soul who hears the Lord speaking within her, and receives from His mouth the word of comfort. Happy the ears which hearken to the strains of the divine whisper (cf 1 Kgs 19:3), and give no heed to the mutterings of the world (cf. Jer 46:22). Happy the ears indeed which listen to truth itself teaching within, and not to the voice sounding without. Happy the eyes which are shut to outward things and attentive to inward things. Happy are they who penetrate to internal things, and strive to prepare themselves more and more by daily exercises for the attainment of heavenly secrets. Happy they who long to give themselves wholly to God and free themselves from earthly impediments. Consider these things, O my soul, and shut fast your doors to the importunities of the senses, that you may hear what the Lord your God shall speak within you. And this is what your Beloved says: "*I am your salvation* (Ps 35:3), your *Peace* (cf. John 16:33), and your *Life* (cf. John 1:4). *Abide in me* (John 15:4), and you shall find peace." . . .

Never repose your whole trust and reliance in a weak and mortal human being, however helpful and dear to you he may be. Nor should you be too grieved if sometimes he opposes you and contradicts you. Those who take your part today may oppose you tomorrow, for human beings are as changeable as the weather. *Put your whole trust in God* (Prov 3:5, 1 Pet 5:7); direct your worship and love to Him alone. He will defend you, and dispose all things to the best. *Here* you *have no abiding city* (Heb 13:14), so that wherever you may be, you are a stranger and a pilgrim (1 Chr 29:15). You will never enjoy peace until you become inwardly united to Christ.

3.6. "Son, you are not yet a courageous and purposeful lover."

"Why is this Lord?"

"Because as soon as you encounter a little adversity, you abandon your undertaking and seek too eagerly for solace. A courageous lover stands firm in temptation, and gives no consent to the cunning persuasions of the enemy. As I please him in prosperity, so I do not displease him in adversity.

"A wise lover does not value so much the gift of the beloved, as the love of the giver. He esteems the affection above the gift, and sets all gifts far below the beloved. The noble lover rests not in the gift, but in me above every gift. Hence, all is not lost if sometimes you feel less devotion for me and for my saints than you would. That full and sweet affection which you sometimes know is the effect of a moment's grace, and a foretaste of the heavenly country. Yet do not rely on it too much, for it comes and goes. But to strive against evil impulses of the mind, and to spurn the promptings of the devil, is a sure sign of power and great merit.

"Let no strange fantasies disturb you, from whatever source they come, but hold fast an upright intent towards God. It is no illusion if at times you are suddenly rapt to the heights, and as swiftly return to the usual wanderings of the heart. For these you endure rather than do, and as long as they do not please you, and you resist them, will bring you gain and not loss.

"Know it well that the ancient Enemy is working in every way to thwart your longing for the good, and to keep you from every devout exercise, from veneration of the saints, and especially from reverent remembrance of my Passion, from the benefit of recollecting your sins, from keeping watch over your own heart, and from any firm resolve to advance in the good. He insinuates many evil thoughts to discourage you and cause you to fear, and hold you back from prayer and holy reading. Humble confession is abhorrent to him, and if he could, he would make you cease from Communion. Give him no credence; pay him no heed, however often he lays out his cunning snares to entrap you. Say to him: *Begone, unclean spirit* (Matt 4:10), shame on you wretch! How foul you are to mutter such thoughts in my ears. Depart from me, you most wicked deceiver! You *shall have no part in me!* (John 14:30) Jesus will *be with me as my strong champion, and* you *will stand confounded* (cf. Jer 20:11). I would rather die and bear any kind of torture than consent to you. *Hold your peace and be still!* (Mark 4:39). However much you plague me, I will not hearken to you ever again. *The Lord is my light and my salvation; whom shall I fear?* (Ps 27:1) *Though a host encamp against me, my heart shall not be daunted* (Ps 40:21), *The Lord is my helper and my redeemer* (Ps 27:3).

"Give battle, as a good soldier, and if sometimes you fall through weakness, recover your strength even more than before, trusting in my still more abundant grace. Moreover, be on your guard against vain complacency and conceit, for these lead many into error, and some fall into almost incurable blindness of heart. Let the downfall of the proud who presumed upon their own strength, be a warning to you, and keep you always humble."[2]

---

2. Translation revised.

Section II. C.
Medieval, Western | Scholastic

II. Medieval

Introduction: Medieval, Western | Scholastic

From the time of the Gregorian reforms of the eleventh century, the Western church began asserting her freedom from being dominated in her own sphere by civil rulers. At first, the highest levels of church governance were one with the prophetic element of the church, the monastic reform movement. But gradually the vital link between the papacy and the spirit of reform dissolved, especially after the death of St. Bernard of Clairvaux.

A substantial shift of theological mentality took place in the Western church between the late twelfth century and the mid-thirteenth century. Beginning with the intellectual and ecclesiastical "elites," this shift gradually rippled through the fabric of the church. The reconfiguration of theology to the scholastic method, the incorporation of the first universities, and the assimilation of a "baptized" and corrected Aristotelian worldview in the thirteenth century, confirmed a tendency—one might prefer to say a temptation—in the West toward rationalism and analysis. Reason, in *practice*, instead of being the humble but valued handmaid of *noos*/intellect in its highest function of contemplation/adoration, began to lose "sapience," forget witness, allow love to grow cold. Canon law became a science, which contributed to an ever more juridical conception of the church as institution. The spirit of Bologna (the first university, focused on law) and of Paris (the second university, focused on scholastic philosophy and theology) quickly colonized much of the Latin church. Rationalism even began to touch the liturgy. The holy liturgy, in which the whole of creation, of human beings and angels are gathered in Trinitarian doxology, lost ground in the West as *theologia prima* (primary theology), the mainspring and touchstone of Christian piety, "God-language," and the Christian life.

Not that this was the case in the early and great souls among the Scholastics. For it is clear that some of these masters of dialectic were also mystics. Still drawing on a living earlier tradition, intentionally orthodox, imbued with the liturgy, they inwardly matured to the great integration of all things in Christ. Of no one was this truer than Thomas Aquinas, whose spiritual trajectory took a very Augustinian, if not to say "Platonic" turn in the end. For him, in the end, the encounter with Christ the Word eclipsed all words and discursive reasoning, and reduced him to silence. Intriguingly, his order of friars, the Dominicans, straddled a wide variety of contrary spiritual currents through the later middle ages, from the qualified Aristotelian realism of Thomist scholasticism, to the paradoxical and provocative language of the German mystics of the fourteenth century, to the very different ecstatic and prophetic style of the Italian Catherine of Siena, and even to the intensely anti-Aristotelian Nominalism of Durandus of St. Pourçain.

The Western or Latin church, as remarked earlier, was but one of the three major breakups (or breakdowns) of ancient Christianity during the early Middle Ages. Sadly, despite all attempts at reunion, and fearful scandals of Christian-on-Christian hostility, such as the Greek massacre of the Latins in 1182, and the Latin sack of Constantinople in 1204, the estrangement of the Western church and the churches of the Eastern Roman orbit was consummated in the fall of "the great City" to the Turks in 1453. In the West, the "Catholic" Church had fairly narrowed down to the *Latin* church, in its late medieval instantiation.

Yet even in the West, something of the older, patristic way of theology and spiritual life continued with the heirs of St. Francis of Assisi. So, for example, the "subtle doctor," the Franciscan Duns Scotus, was a master of discursive reasoning, but quite the Augustinian in his premises about God and salvation, human nature, grace, and the possibility of knowing God. For even though the Franciscans participated in the new university-based theological world very competently, they were by no means wedded to an Aristotelian worldview, even in a corrected, Christianized form. Continuing the tradition of Augustine and the Victorines, they were the champions of love over knowledge as the end of our life in Christ, and more likely to allow play to emotion and experience along with reason in the spiritual life, although admittedly they lost liturgical sensibility. Nevertheless, the words that the great Franciscan Bonaventure had carved in the choir stalls at Fonte Columbo: "Si cor non orat, in vanum lingua laborat" (If the heart does not pray, then the tongue labors in vain) were a perennial warning against the succumbing of the liturgy to extrinsicism and formalism. They match perfectly the exhortation centuries earlier in the Rule of Benedict 19:7: "sic stemus ad psallendum ut mens nostra concordat voci nostrae" (let us so stand to the psalmody that our mind accords with our voice).

The church in the turbulent, restless West, drew to the end of the Middle Ages in a tired, compromised and febrile condition. Instead of reform, the popes of the time were more interested in promoting the worldly pomp and neo-paganism of the Italian Renaissance. Paradoxically, the new age of modernity that was emerging owed not a little to the triumph of dialectical reason in philosophy and theology during the thirteenth century, and to the rationalist and naturalist tendencies unleashed thereby. It could be argued that the very changes and shifts in the Western church herself, were, in some sense, the seeds of modernity, and even, ultimately, of secularism.

Still, the church, the Bride of Christ, was ever much more than an institution of mere human policy. The triumph of the sanctifying Spirit in a host of saints and "little ones" in this era sustained her and kept her from withering on the vine. Indeed, it is striking how in the high and later Middle Ages a long line of mystics and mystical theologians, women saints and prophets, with the sap of Christ the true vine in their veins, arose to bear witness to the light in dark and troubled times.

Anna Silvas

II. Medieval

C. Medieval, Western: Scholastic

41. St. Anselm of Canterbury (ca. 1033–1109) | *Proslogion*

Anselm was born in the shadow of Mont Blanc and the Matterhorn, in the Vale of Aosta. His mother was his first preceptor in piety and guardian of the best lessons of childhood. After her death, Anselm had a falling-out with his father, and set out wandering, until he came upon the abbey of Bec in Normandy. He stopped at its famous school, where the Prior Lanfranc had lately revived the traditional Latin curriculum of the quadrivium and trivium. He entered there as a monk in the year 1060, contending with an attraction to the eremitic life and to contemplative prayer, proclivities that always stayed with him. Three years later he himself was prior. Formed to the Scriptures, the Western Church Fathers and the culture of monastic Lectio Divina, he began writing out his prayerful theological reasonings. In 1078 he was elected abbot. The (Norman) English came to know him through his visits to Lanfranc, by then the Archbishop of Canterbury. Acceding to the tentative but eventually firm invitation of King William II, he became Archbishop of Canterbury in 1093. Holding firmly to the primacy of the See of Peter, and insisting on the freedom of the church from royal (i.e., lay) investiture of bishops and abbots, his troubles with William and his son Henry I were a trial run for those of Beckett with Henry II a century later.

Anselm was an early exemplar of the scholastic method in Latin theology, i.e., demonstration according to strict rules of dialectical argument. In his *Cur Deus Homo* on the incarnation he articulated the "satisfaction" or "restitution" understanding of Christ's atonement. In philosophy he is famous for the ontological argument in his *Proslogion* for the existence of God. All this was the work of a profoundly prayerful, theologically minded monk. We can learn Anselm's understanding of the Christian spiritual life from the great prayers into which even his treatises regularly revert. In the following concluding passages of his *Proslogion*, he ponders God as one Good, and in what consists eternal joy.

Proslogion (1077–78)

Ch 23. You are this *Good* (Mark 10:18), O God the Father; and this is Your Word, that is, Your Son. For there cannot be anything else than what You are, or anything greater or less than You, in the Word by which you utter Yourself. For your Word is true even as You are truthful, and is therefore the very truth that You are that is not other than You. And you are so simple that there cannot be born of You anything other than what You are. This itself is the Love, one and common to You and to Your Son, which is the Holy Spirit proceeding from both. For this same Love is not unequal to You or to Your Son since Your love for Yourself and Him, and His love for You and Himself, are as great as You and He are. Nor is that which is not different from You and Him alien to You and Him; nor can there proceed from Your supreme simplicity what is other than that from which it proceeds. Thus, whatever each is singly, that the whole Trinity is altogether: Father, Son and Holy Spirit; since each is singly not other than the supremely simple unity and the supremely unified simplicity which can be neither multiplied nor differentiated.

Moreover, one thing is necessary (Luke 10:42). This is, moreover, that one thing necessary in which is every good, or rather, which is wholly and *uniquely* and completely and *solely Good* (cf. Mark 10:18, Matt 19:17, Luke 18:19)...

Ch 24. Now, my soul, rouse and lift up your whole understanding and think as much as you can on what kind and how great this Good is. For if particular goods are enjoyable, consider carefully how enjoyable is that Good which contains the joyfulness of all goods—not such as we have experienced in created things, but as different from this as the Creator differs from the creature. For if life that is created is *good* (cf. Gen 1:25), how good is the Life that creates? If the salvation that has been brought about is joyful, how joyful is the Salvation that brings about all salvation? If wisdom in the knowledge of things which have been brought into being is lovable, how lovable is the Wisdom which has brought all into being out of nothing? Finally if there are many great delights in delightful things, of what kind and how great is the delight in Him who made these same delightful things?

Ch 25. Whoever enjoys this *Good*, what shall be his and what shall not be his? Whatever he wishes shall certainly be his and whatever he does not wish shall not be his. In fact, all the goods of body and soul will be there such that *no eye has seen, nor ear heard, nor the heart of man conceived* (1 Cor 2:9).

Why then, O insignificant man, do you wander about so much, seeking the goods of your soul and body? Love the *one Good* (Mark 10:18) in which all goods things are, and that is sufficient. Desire the simple Good which contains every good, and that is enough. For what do you love, O my flesh, what do you desire, O my soul? It is there, it is there, whatever you love, whatever you desire. If beauty delights you, *The just will shine like the Sun* (Matt 13:43). If swiftness or strength or freedom of the body which nothing can withstand, *they will be like the angels of God* (Matt 22:30); for it is *sown as a natural body and shall rise as a spiritual body* (1 Cor 15:44) by a supernatural power. If it is a long and healthy life, a healthy eternity and an eternal health is there, since *the just shall live forever* (Wis 5:16), and *the salvation of the just is from the Lord* (Ps 36:39). If it is satisfaction, they will be satisfied *when the glory of the Lord shall appear* (Ps 16:15). If it is quenching of thirst, *they will be inebriated with the abundance of the house of God* (Ps 35:9). If it is melody, there the choirs of angels play unceasingly to God. If it is pleasure of any kind, not impure but pure, God *will make them drink from the torrent of His pleasure* (Ps 36:8). If it is Wisdom, the very Wisdom of God will show itself to them (cf. Wis 9:17). If it is friendship, they will love God more than themselves and one another as themselves, and God will love them more than they love themselves because it is through Him that they love Him and themselves and one another, and He loves Himself and them through Himself....

What joy there is indeed and how great it is where there exists so great a *Good!* O human heart, O needy heart, O heart experienced in suffering, indeed overwhelmed by suffering, how greatly you would rejoice if you abounded in all these things! Ask your heart whether it could comprehend its joy in a blessedness so great?...

Indeed, to the degree that one loves another, so he will rejoice in the good of that other; therefore, just as each one in that perfect happiness will love God incomparably more than himself and all others with him, so he will rejoice immeasurably more over the happiness of God than over his own happiness and that of all the others with him. But if they *love God with all their heart, their whole mind, their whole soul* (cf. Matt 22:37), while their whole heart, their whole mind, their whole soul are not equal to the grandeur of this love, they will assuredly so rejoice with their whole heart, their whole mind, and their whole soul, that their whole heart, their whole mind, their whole soul will not be equal to the fullness of their joy.

Ch 26. My God and my Lord, my hope and the joy of my heart, tell my soul if this is the joy of which You speak through Your Son: *Ask and you shall receive, that your joy may be complete* (John 16:24). For I have discovered a joy that is complete and more than complete. Indeed, when the heart is filled with that joy, the mind is filled with it, the soul is filled with it, the whole man is filled with it, yet joy beyond measure will remain. The whole of that joy, then, will not enter into those who rejoice, but those who rejoice will enter *into the joy of the Lord* (Matt 25:21). But surely that joy in which Your chosen ones will rejoice is that which *neither eye has seen, nor ear heard, nor has it entered into the heart of man* (1 Cor 2:9). I have not yet said or thought, then, Lord, how greatly your blessed will rejoice. They will, no doubt, rejoice as much as they love, and they will love as much as they know. How much will they know You then, and how much will they love You? In all truth, *neither eye has seen, nor ear heard, nor has it entered into the heart of man* in this life how much they shall know You and love You in that life.

I pray O God, that I may know You and love You, so that I may rejoice in You. And if I cannot do so fully in this life, may I advance gradually until it comes to fullness. Let the knowledge of You grow in me here, and there be made complete; let Your love grow in me here, and there be made complete, so that here my joy may be great in hope, and there be complete in reality. Lord, by your Son You command, or rather, counsel us to ask and you promise that we shall receive so that our *joy may be complete* (John 16:24). I ask you Lord according to your counsel through our admirable counselor, that I may receive what You promise through Your truth so that my *joy may be complete*. God of truth, I ask that I may receive that my *joy may be complete*.

Until then, let my mind meditate on it, my tongue speak of it, my heart love it, my mouth preach it. Let my soul hunger for it, my flesh thirst for it, my whole being desire it, until I *enter into the joy of the Lord* (Matt 25:21), *who is God*, Three in One, *blessed forever. Amen* (Rom 1:25).[1]

---

1. Translation revised.

II. Medieval

C. Medieval, Western: Scholastic

42. Peter Abelard (1079–1142) | *Pentecost Hymn*

Pierre le Pallet was the first-born in a family of the minor nobility in Brittany. He showed an early attraction to dialectic and Aristotelian logic. Indeed, he studied under the proto-nominalist Roscelin of Compiegne. A charismatic teacher but a restless spirit, Abelard, as he now named himself, set up schools in various places, attracting much enthusiasm from students. An early work, *Theologia*, was suspect for its rationalistic account of the Trinity and for Sabellianism. His *Commentary on the Epistle to the Romans*, written in the mid-1130s toward the end of his life while teaching in Paris, led to his being accused of subjectivism and for teaching that Christ's atonement was merely that of a moral exemplar.

His affair with his student, Heloise of Argenteuil (ending in clandestine marriage), was followed by her uncle Fulbert's drastic retribution (Abelard was forcibly castrated). Abelard then entered the Benedictine monastery of St. Denis near Paris. His restlessness, however, continued as he searched out other monastic and scholarly venues, until finally he met his nemesis in Bernard at the Council of Sens in 1141. Bernard targeted him for rationalism in theology, i.e., for his scholastic method and the erroneous doctrinal conclusions it brought him to. Abelard appealed to Pope Innocent II, but attracted an excommunication instead. He spent his last months under the benign supervision of the Cluniac monks.

In the late 1120s Abelard come again into contact with Heloise, by then the superior of a monastery of nuns called the Paraclete. He shared with her sisters a number of hymns for which he had written both the words and the music. One of these is his Pentecost Hymn below, in which Abelard lauds the traditional seven gifts of the Holy Spirit (cf. Isa 11:1–2 Septuagint and Vulgate), opposing them to the "seven demons of wickedness," possibly signifying the traditional Latin "seven deadly sins" as listed by Gregory the Great.

C. MEDIEVAL, WESTERN: SCHOLASTIC
Pentecost Hymn (1129)

The Holy Spirit comes to share
His burning altar in our heart.
Accept, O God, your temples there;
With virtues dedicate their art.
These are the sevenfold gifts you as God possess,
Binding seven demons of wickedness.
These your gifts are goodness and holiness.

The *fear* of God can set us free,
But wickedness must first abate.
The poor on earth with such a key
May enter rich in heaven's gate.
Yea, master, give us this; give to us graciously.
Give the guilty less than their penalty.
Yours the glory, yours be the victory.

And give us force of *holiness* (= *piety*);
Let not temptation overwhelm.
The mild and merciful possess
This grace and all the earthly realm.
Yea, Master, give us this.

Let *knowledge* fall on us as well,
Through which we know the grace of tears.
Your pardon casts its holy spell
When we have paid up all arrears.
Yea, Master, give us this.

With holy *might* (= *fortitude*) your strength is shed
On those who thirst for righteousness.
The fullness of the very Bread:
Its vigor pilgrim souls express.
Yea, Master, give us this.

And give us highest *counsel*, Lord;
For which your mercy will suffice.
So then you may allow reward;
For this you ask, not sacrifice.
Yea, Master, give us this.

In *understanding* you are known
As God within the Trinity
The pure in heart can see alone
The Kingdom's high sublimity.
Yea, Master, give us this.

You give us *wisdom* finally,
In which the sons of God take rest.
The name of Father makes them free
To sanctify what there is blest.
Yea, Master, give us this.

By force of the apostle's prayers
Whom you made new at Pentecost,
Give us the grace such as theirs,
And strengthen us, lest we be lost.
These are the sevenfold gifts that you as God possess,
Binding seven demons of wickedness.
These your gifts are goodness and holiness.

II. Medieval

C. Medieval, Western: Scholastic

43. Peter Lombard (c. 1100–1160) | *Four Books of Sentences*

Born to a poor family in Piedmont at the end of the eleventh century, Peter Lombard's piety and potential were noted by Odo, bishop of Lucca, who commended him to St. Bernard's patronage. Thanks to this, Peter was able to pursue higher studies at the Cathedral school of Reims, and then at the school of St. Victor in Paris, where Hugh of St. Victor was one of his masters. He reached his theological maturity at the Cathedral School of Notre Dame, one of the constituent schools soon to be incorporated as the University of Paris. He wrote his *Four Books of Sentences* between 1150 to 1152 as a compilation of scriptural and Patristic sources under systematic doctrinal headings. It was a hugely successful work, becoming the standard theology textbook of the Western church in the High Middle Ages. All theological students whetted their skills on it.

Of seminal importance was Peter's discussion of "sacrament" in its book 4, distinction 26; although there may be many "signs" of sacred realities, he said, all of them "sacramental" in a broad sense, a "sacrament" of Christ, properly speaking, is a sign of an invisible divine grace which effectively bestows what it signifies. Lombard discerned seven sacraments proper among all the sacred rites of the church, and Christian marriage was one of them. All the ancient churches, in or out of communion with Rome, recognized the great tradition in these seven sacraments. Lombard endorsed Hugh's view that the determinative cause of marriage was the exchange of free mutual consent, not the act of consummation. This was the view that prevailed among the theologians, although not the canonists. Lombard became Archbishop of Paris in 1159, but died in the following year. In the following passage from his Distinction 17, we hear his exposition from Scripture and from St. Augustine that charity *is* the Holy Spirit.

Four Books of Sentences, Bk I, Distinction 17: On Charity (1150–52)

1.2. A certain premise is made which is necessary to this consideration, namely that the Holy Spirit is the love by which we love God and neighbor. In order that this may be taught more intelligibly and perceived more fully, a certain premise must be made which is very necessary to this end. It has been said above [Distinction 10], and it has been shown by sacred authorities, that the Holy Spirit is the love of the Father and the Son by which they love each other and us. It must be added to this that the very same Holy Spirit is the love or charity by which we love God and neighbor. When this charity is in us, so that it makes us love God and neighbor, then the Holy Spirit is said to be sent or given to us; and whoever loves the very love by which he loves his neighbor, in that very thing loves God, because that very love is God, that is, the Holy Spirit.

1.3. By authoritative texts he confirms this to be the case. Lest in such a great matter we should appear to interject anything of our own, let us confirm by sacred authorities what has been said above. Concerning this, Augustine, in *On the Trinity*, book 8, says: "He who loves his neighbor must necessarily love that love itself above all else, for *God is love* (1 John 4:8, 4:16); it follows that he should love God above all else." Also, in the same place, "*God is love* as the Apostle John says. To what end, then, do we go running to the heights of heaven and the depths of the earth, seeking him who is with us, if we wish to be with him? Let no one say: I do not know what to love. Let him love his brother, and love love itself. For he knows the love by which he loves more than [he knows] the brother whom he loves. And so he can already know God more than his brother; know him more because he is more present, more deeply within himself, more certain. Embrace God who is love, and embrace God in love. Love is the very thing which conjoins all the good angels and all the servants of God in the bond of holiness. For the more holy we are and the more emptied of the swelling of pride, the more we are filled with love; and with what is he filled who is full of love, if not with God?" By these words, Augustine sufficiently shows that the very love by which we love God and neighbor is love. . . .

2.1. . . . But although fraternal love is God, it is not the Father or the Son, but only the Holy Spirit, who is properly and specifically called love or charity in the holy Trinity. Hence Augustine, in *On the Trinity*, book 15: "If among God's gifts there is none greater than love, and if no gift of God is greater than the Holy Spirit, what follows more compellingly than that he himself is the love which is called both God, and of God. For John says: *Love is from God* (1 John 4:7), and shortly: *God is love* (1 John 4:8). Here he makes it clear that he called the same love *God* which he said to be *from God*. Therefore, God from God is love." (Augustine, *De Trinitate* Bk 15, c17, n 31) . . .

4.2. Here it is noted how the Holy Spirit is given. In the same book, Augustine commends this Gift and explains more plainly how it is given. He says: "As the Apostle says: *The love of God is poured into our heart through the Holy Spirit who is given to us* (Rom 5:5). There is nothing more excellent than this Gift of God! It is this alone which distinguishes the children of the Kingdom from those of Perdition. Other gifts are also given by the Holy Spirit, but they profit nothing without charity. Therefore, unless the Holy Spirit is given to each so as to make him a lover of God and his neighbor, he is not transferred from the left hand to the right hand (cf. Matt 25.31–33). Nor is the Holy Spirit properly called a Gift unless in regard to love. Whoever does not have this, even *if he speak all tongues, and have prophecy and all knowledge and all faith, and have shared out all his wealth and given his body to be burned, it shall profit him nothing* (1 Cor 13:1–3). What a great *Good* is this, then, without which even such goods as these cannot bring someone to eternal life! For it is this love or charity—for both are the same thing—that leads to the Kingdom.

Therefore the love which is from God and is God, is properly, the Holy Spirit, through whom God who is charity is poured into our hearts, and through which charity the whole Trinity dwells in us. Therefore most rightly the Holy Spirit, although he is God, is also called *the Gift of God* (Acts 8:2). And what are we rightly to understand by this Gift except that charity which leads to God and without which any other gift of God does not lead to God." [Augustine, *De Trinitate* Bk 15, cc 17–18, nn 31–32] Also, in the same work, "John, wishing to speak more plainly of this matter, said: *By this we know that we abide in him, and he in us, that he has given us of his Holy Spirit* (1 John 4:13). Therefore the Holy Spirit, of whom he has given us, causes us to abide in God and God in us. This is what love does. And so he is God who is love, and so he is the one signified when we read *God is love* (1 John 4:8, 16). From this it is manifest that the Holy Spirit is charity."

6.7. . . . Just as it is said that God is *our hope and our patience* (Ps 70:5), because it is he who makes us hope and be patient, so charity is said to be an affection of the spirit, because by it our spirit is drawn to loving God. And you will not be surprised if charity, although it is the Holy Spirit, is called a movement of the mind, since even in the Book of Wisdom it is said of *the Spirit of Wisdom*, which *reaches from end to end*, that he is an act which is *mobile, certain, unstained* (Wis 8:1, 7:22). But this is said not because Wisdom is something mobile or some act, but because it reaches all things in its immobility, not by local motion, but in such a way that it is always everywhere, and is never confined. Likewise, then, charity is called a movement of the spirit: not because it is itself an emotion of affection or a power of the spirit, but because through it, as if it were a power, the mind is drawn and moved.

6.8. But if charity is the Holy Spirit, *who works in each as he wills* (1 Cor 12:11), since through him the human mind is drawn and moved to believing or hoping and the like, as it is to loving, why is charity also not called a movement or affection of the mind towards believing or hoping, as towards loving?—To which it may well be answered that charity, namely the Holy Spirit, works the other acts and movements of the virtues by means of the virtues whose acts they are: thus, the act of faith, that is, to believe, by means of faith; and the act of hope, that is, to hope, by means of hope, for charity works the said acts by faith and hope. But it works the act of loving, that is, to love, by itself alone and not by means of any other virtue. And so it works this act otherwise than the other acts of virtue; and so Scripture speaks differently of this act than the others because it attributes this one especially to charity.

6.9. And so charity is truly the Holy Spirit. Hence Augustine, treating the above mentioned sentence of the Apostle in the same book, says that charity is that good than which there is none better, and by this he signifies that it is God, saying, "If nothing separates us from his love, what can not only be better, but also more certain than this good?" [Augustine, *de moribus Ecclesiae catholicae* I.II.18] See how he says that nothing is better than charity? And so charity is the Holy Spirit, who is God and the Gift or grant of God. He shares out the gifts to each of the faithful, while he himself is not divided, but is given undivided to each. Hence Augustine, commenting on John's statement that the Spirit is given to Christ *not by measure* (John 3:34), says: "To others there is a sharing out, not of the Spirit himself, but of his gifts" . . . [1]

---

1. Translation revised.

II. Medieval

C. Medieval, Western: Scholastic

44. St. Thomas Aquinas (1225–1274) | *Commentary on the Gospel of John & Homily on the Eucharist*

"Nothing but you, Lord! ('Non nisi te Domine')." So the friar and mystic Thomas Aquinas answered the Lord when asked what spiritual gift he would have. That was towards the end of 1273, by which time he had spent nearly thirty years in the Order of Preachers (the "Dominicans"), studying, teaching, and writing sacred doctrine.

Born at Roccasecca in the Kingdom of Sicily, Thomas eschewed his noble birth, the family castle, and the proffered abbacy of Monte Cassino. Family obstruction delayed his entering the Dominicans for a year, which he spent in prayer, reading the Scriptures, and studying Lombard's *Sentences*. Most of his life as a friar was spent in Paris, Cologne, and various priories in Italy. From his immersion in a wide range of authors, especially Augustine and the Latin transmission of Pseudo-Dionysius, Plato, Aristotle, and the scriptural commentaries of the Fathers, both East and West, his many creative syntheses emerged, notably his *Summa Contra Gentiles*, which rescued Aristotle for Christians from the pantheist and skeptical wrappings of his Muslim commentators, and from Aristotle's own ideas of eternal matter, and the *Summa Theologiae*, his theological magnum opus—which he abandoned unfinished, because the Lord, it seems, answered his prayer above in the affirmative. In the last half year of his life Thomas was visited with so overwhelming a noetic experience of God that all his toil in the medium of words and discursive reason seemed to him, he said, like straw, and he could not write another word.

Aquinas's legacy of a Christianized Aristotelianism and Scholastic method instinct with the Catholic tradition, "Thomism," was to acquire in time an almost canonical status in the Latin church, which designated him "Angelic Doctor" both for the purity of his inspired wisdom and his practical chastity.

In the following we first read from Thomas's *Commentary on the Gospel of John*, which gives us insight into the mystical heart and contemplative mind of Thomas.

For him the example of the Evangelist invites the disciple to move from the natural philosophy of the ancients to divine wisdom in Christ.

In his *Homily on the Eucharist*, Thomas begins with the patristic doctrine of *theosis* or deification, a constant theme of the Christian East that continued also in the West. Secondly, we see here a hint of Thomas's use of classical ontology to analyze the consecrated eucharistic species, an approach which was to profoundly affect the liturgical and devotional sensibility of the Latin church. "Substance" here is the same as *ousia* in the *homo-ousios* of the Niceno-Constantinpolitan Creed, denoting the kind of thing that something *is*. Just as the Son *is* the same kind of reality that the Father is, so the bread and wine, once "eucharistized" by the Divine Word (St. Justin Martyr), *are* his body and his blood—and soul and divinity; indeed, his divine person.

Commentary on John (1269–72)

I saw the Lord seated on a high and lofty throne, and the whole house was full of his majesty, and the things that were under him filled the temple (Isa 6:1).

1. These are the words of a contemplative, and if we regard them as spoken by John the Evangelist they apply quite well to showing the nature of this Gospel. For as Augustine says in his work, *On the Agreement of the Evangelists*: "The other Evangelists instruct us in their Gospels on the active life; but John in his Gospel instructs us also on the contemplative life." The contemplation of John is described above in three ways, in keeping with the threefold manner in which he contemplated the Lord Jesus. It is described as high, full, and perfect. It was high: *I saw the Lord seated on a high and lofty throne*; it was full: *and the whole house was full of his majesty*; and it was perfect: *and the things that were under him filled the temple*.

2. As to the first, we must understand that the height and sublimity of contemplation consists most of all in the contemplation and knowledge of God. *Lift up your eyes on high, and see who has created these things* (Isa 40:26). A man lifts up his eyes on high when he sees and contemplates the Creator of all things. Now since John rose above whatever had been created—mountains, heavens, angels—and reached the Creator of all, as Augustine says, it is clear that his contemplation was most high. Thus: *I saw the Lord*. And because, as John himself says below (John 12:41), "Isaiah said this because he had seen his glory," that is, the glory of Christ, "and spoke of him," the Lord *seated on a high and lofty throne* is Christ.

Now a fourfold height is indicated in this contemplation of John. A height of authority; hence he says: *I saw the Lord*. A height of eternity; when he says, *seated*. One of dignity, or nobility of nature; so he says, *on a high throne*. And a height of incomprehensible truth; when he says, *lofty*. It is in these four ways that the early philosophers arrived at the knowledge of God.

3. Some attained to a knowledge of God through his authority, and this is the most efficacious way. For we see the things in nature acting for an end, and attaining to ends which are both useful and certain. And since they lack intelligence, they are unable to direct themselves, but must be directed and moved by one directing them, one who possesses an intellect. Thus it is that the movement of the things of nature toward a certain end indicates the existence of something higher by which the things of nature are directed to an end and governed. And so, since the whole course of nature advances to an end in an orderly way and is directed, we have to posit something higher which directs and governs them as Lord; and this is God. This authority in governing is shown to be in the Word of God when it says, *Lord*. Thus the Psalm says: *You rule the power of the sea, and you still the swelling of its waves* (Ps 89:9), as though saying: "You are the Lord and govern all things." John shows that he knows this of the Word when he says below: *He came unto his own* (John 1:11), i.e., to the world, since the whole universe is his own.

4. Others came to a knowledge of God from his eternity. They saw that whatever was in things was changeable, and that the more noble something is in the grades of being, so much the less it has of mutability. For example, the lower bodies are mutable both as to their substance and to place, while the heavenly bodies, which are more noble, are immutable in substance and change only with respect to place. We can clearly conclude from this that the first principle of all things, which is supreme and more noble, is changeless and eternal. The prophet suggests this eternity of the Word when he says *seated*, i.e., presiding without any change and eternally. *Your throne, O God, is forever and ever* (Ps 45:6); *Jesus Christ, the same yesterday, today, and forever* (Heb 13:8). John points to this eternity when he says below: *In the beginning was the Word* (John 1:1).

5. Still others came to a knowledge of God from the dignity of God; and these were the Platonists. They noted that everything which is something by participation is reduced to what is the same thing by essence, as to the first and highest. Thus, all things which are fiery by participation are reduced to fire, which is such by its essence. And so, since all things which exist participate in existence and are beings by participation, there must necessarily be at the summit of all things something which is existence by its essence, i.e., whose essence is its existence. And this is God, who is the most sufficient, the most eminent, and the most perfect cause of the whole of existence, from whom all things that are participate in existence. This dignity is shown in the words, *on a high throne*, which, according to Denis, refer to the divine nature. *The Lord is high above all nations* (Ps 113:4). John shows us this dignity when he says below: *the Word was God* (John 1:1), with "the Word" as subject and "God" as predicate.

6. Yet others arrived at a knowledge of God from the incomprehensibility of truth. All the truth which our intellect is able to grasp is finite, since according to Augustine,

"everything that is known is bounded by the comprehension of the one knowing"; and if it is bounded, it is determined and particularised. Therefore, the first and supreme Truth, which surpasses every intellect, must necessarily be incomprehensible and infinite; and this is God. Hence the Psalm says: *Your greatness is above the heavens* (Ps 8:1), i.e., above every created intellect, angelic and human. The Apostle says this in the words: *He dwells in unapproachable light* (1 Tim 6:16). This incomprehensibility of Truth is shown to us in the word *lofty*, i.e., above all the knowledge of the created intellect. John implies this incomprehensibility to us when he says below, *No one has ever seen God* (Jn 1:18).

Thus, the contemplation of John was high as regards authority, eternity, dignity, and the incomprehensibility of the Word. And John has passed on this contemplation to us in his Gospel . . .

Homily on the Eucharist (1264)

The only-begotten Son of God, intending to make us *partakers of his divine nature* (2 Pet 1:4), took our nature on himself, becoming man that he might make men gods. Everything of ours that he adopted he turned to our salvation. His body he offered to God the Father on the altar of the Cross as a sacrifice in order that we might be reconciled. His blood he shed both as a price to redeem us from our wretched bondage and as a cleansing from all sin.

He has left to his faithful his very Body for food and his very Blood for drink (cf. John 6:55), nourishment for them under the appearance of bread and wine, and an abiding memorial (Luke 22:19, 1 Cor 11:24) of his noble purpose. How precious then, how marvelous, how health-giving, how well appointed his banquet! Nothing is more precious, for in the Lord's Supper the food put before us is not *the flesh of bulls and goats* (Ps 50:13), as in olden times, but Christ himself, our very God.

Nothing is more marvelous, for there it comes to pass that the substance of bread and wine is changed into the Body and Blood of Christ. He is there, perfect God and perfect man, under the show of a morsel of bread and a sip of wine. He is eaten by his faithful, but not mangled. Nay, when this sacrament is broken, he remains entire in each piece. The appearance of bread and wine remains, but it is not bread or wine. Here is faith's opportunity, faith which takes what is unseen or disguised, and keeps the senses from misjudging about the common appearances.

Nothing is more health-giving, for in this Sacrament sins are purged away, the strength renewed, and the mind fortified with generous spiritual gifts. Offered in the Church for the living and the dead, it is meant for all, and all obtain its benefits. Nothing is better appointed, for the sweetness of this Sacrament none can express. There, comfort is drawn as from the fountainhead of the Spirit (cf. John 14:14); there is found the memorial of Christ's exceeding love for us in his sufferings.

In order to bring his boundless love home to the hearts of his faithful, he founded this Sacrament after he had celebrated the Passover with his disciples, as the Last Supper was ending: *Jesus, knowing that his hour was come that he should depart out of this world unto the Father, having loved his own who were in the world, he loved them to the end* (John 13:1). This is the Sacrament of the everlasting *showing forth of his death until he come again* (1 Cor 11:26), the embodied fulfillment of all the ancient types and figures, the mighty joy of those who sorrow until he shall come again: *Then their hearts shall rejoice, and their joy no man shall take from them* (John 16:22).

II. Medieval

C. Medieval, Western: Scholastic

45. Blessed John Duns Scotus (ca. 1265–1308) | *Ordinatio*

Here we have a phenomenon: an Augustinian Scholastic, Blessed John Duns Scotus. His double surname indicates that he was a Scot from the village of Duns, near the English border. His father, Ninian, had a brother who was a Franciscan friar and priest, Fra Elias. John followed his uncle into the Friars Minor at Dumfries. He studied philosophy and theology at Oxford in the 1280s. In those days it took about thirteen years' study to gain a baccalaureate in theology. On March 17, 1291 he was ordained priest at St. Andrew's Priory in Northampton, England by Oliver Sutton, Bishop of Lincoln, which diocese then included Oxford.

In the academic year 1298–1299 Scotus publicly lectured on the first two books of Lombard's Sentences. He left Oxford for Paris in 1302, and began lecturing on the Sentences again. The Dominican Meister Eckhart was there at the time, and Scotus assisted the Franciscan Master Gonsalvus in his famous disputation with Eckhart.[1] In June 1303 Scotus was expelled from France with eighty other friars for refusing to side with King Philip IV against Pope Boniface VIII. He returned late in 1304 to resume his lectures on the Sentences. He became Doctor of Theology in 1305, and Franciscan Regent Master at Paris in 1306–1307, the pinnacle of theological acclaim. In this period he disputed and determined his *Quodlibetal Questions*. In October 1307 he transferred to the Franciscan studium at Cologne, where he began as lector, but died a year later on November 8, 1308, at only forty-three years of age.

The following passages are from Scotus's *Ordinatio*, a revised and edited form of his lectures on the Sentences at Oxford that gained him his baccalaureate. Here we sample some of his finely pondered assessment whether it is possible to conclude by reason to the immortality of the human soul and the resurrection of the body. He surveys some of the philosophers and Church Fathers at length, but in the end affirms that what none of the philosophers could attain, the gift of faith does attain.

---

1. *Duns Scotus*, xxiii.

Ordinatio IV.43.q.2: On the Immortality of the Soul and the Resurrection (originally delivered 1298–99; revised and edited 1303–08)

Question: Can it be known by natural reason that there will be a general resurrection of mankind?

A natural desire cannot be in vain. Man, however, has a natural desire to live forever, and it can be known by natural reason that such a desire exists . . . Where a natural aversion of something exists, it is only because of a natural desire or love for something else. But man has a natural aversion for death. This is evident both from experience and from what the Apostle says to the Corinthians: *We do not wish to be unclothed, but rather to be clothed over* (2 Cor 5:4).

Also, it is known that we seek happiness by our very nature. This is clear from *Nicomachaean Ethics,* Bk I [ch. 7] in regard to beatitude in general and from *Nicomachaen Ethics* Bk X [ch. 7–8]. But from natural reason it is known that beatitude must be eternal. Hence, it is known from natural reason that man is ordained to some eternal perfection. Proof of the minor: Augustine proves it thus: "And if life quits him by his dying, how can the blessed life remain with him? And when it quits him, no doubt it ether quits him unwillingly, or willingly or neither. If unwillingly, how is the life blessed which is so within his will as not to be within his power? . . . how much less is he blessed who is quitted against his will, not by honor, nor by possessions, nor by any other thing, but by the blessed life itself, since he will have not life at all . . ." [*de Trin.* xiii, ch. 8]

. . . Now it is naturally known that beatitude is the end of the human species. Therefore, it is naturally known that at least some individual can attain it. But he cannot attain it in this life because of the many attendant miseries, such as the vicissitudes of fortune, bodily infirmity, imperfect knowledge and virtue, instability and fatigue in the exercise of even the most perfect acts, since no activity, however delightful it may be at the beginning, can continue to be delightful. Moreover, when such an activity causes what is delightful to become distasteful, it will no longer be performed. Now it is known by natural reason that beatific vision is not something distasteful. Neither is it something that the soul can possess alone in separation from the body, for in this way *man* would not attain his goal. Accordingly, this end will be attained in another life by the whole man, body and soul together. It seems then, that natural reason can reach this conclusion at least in regard to those ways by which man will attain his end.

To the contrary:

Augustine, speaking of the life that is eternal and immortal in *de Trinitate* Bk xiii, ch. 10, says: "Whether human nature can receive this . . . is no small question . . . Assuredly, of those who endeavor to discover it from human reasonings, scarcely a few, and they endowed with great abilities and abounding in leisure, and learned with the most subtle learning, have been able to attain to the investigation of the immortality of the soul alone."

Furthermore, in *Acts* xvii [18] it is related that certain Athenians listening to Paul said: "*He seems to be a herald of strange gods,*" *because he proclaimed to them Jesus and the Resurrection.* Nevertheless, these Athenians were philosophers whose *forte* was the use of natural reason, as is clear from the case of the convert Dionysius, who was one of them. But it does not seem that what appeared to them to be so far from the truth is known adequately by natural reason. Hence it is evident here that what Paul adduces in this connection is meant to be nothing more than a kind of persuasive form of argument . . .

This much is clear, that if any argument proves the resurrection, it must be one based on something that is proper to man and does not belong to other perishable things. But such a thing would not be matter, not even incorruptible matter. Neither is it some form that can be destroyed. For even if such a form exists in man, even more excellent than any brute form, still this would not provide an adequate argument for the resurrection of man as a whole. Hence the argument must be based upon that form which is specific to man, or upon some operation that man enjoys by reason of this form.

The method used to establish the thesis is to proceed from three propositions. If all these three can be known by natural reason, the proposed conclusion will follow. The three propositions are:

1. *The intellective soul is the specific form of man;*

2. *The intellective soul is incorruptible.* From which two it follows that the specific form of man is incorruptible. To these a third is added:

3. *The specific form of man will not remain forever outside the composite.*

Hence it follows that at some time the same composite will be restored. This second return [John] Damascene calls the resurrection [*de fide orthodoxa* iv, ch. 26]: "The resurrection is the second rising of what has been dissolved." Let us consider these three positions in order and see to what extent they are evident . . .

As to the first . . . no philosopher of any note has been found to deny this except that accursed Averroes in his commentary on *de Anima*, Bk iii, where his fantastic conception, intelligible neither to himself nor to others, assumes that the intellective part of man is a sort of separate substance united to man through the medium of sense images. But neither he nor his followers to this day have been able to explain this union.

. . . The second way to prove the resurrection is by *a posteriori* arguments.[2] Some probable arguments of this kind were mentioned in the initial arguments, for instance, those concerning the happiness of man. To the latter, the following argument based on the justice of a rewarding God is added. In the present life the virtuous suffer more punishments than those who are wicked. It is this line of argument that the Apostle seems to

---

2. Tracing back to a probable cause from empirical observations.

have in mind in the first Letter to the Corinthians [15:19]: *If we have had hope in Christ with this life only in view, we are of all men the most to be pitied,* etc.

These *a posteriori* arguments, however, are even less conclusive than the *a priori* proof[3] based on the proper form of man, since it is not clear from natural reason that there is one ruler who governs all men according to the laws of retributive and punitive justice. It could even be said that the good act is itself sufficient reward for anyone, as Augustine says in the *Confessions,* Bk I: "For it is even as you have appointed, that every inordinate desire should bring its own punishment," so that sin itself is the first punishment of sin.

It is clear then that when the saints argued *a posteriori* for the proposed conclusion, they did not intend to give anything more than probable persuasive proofs. Gregory, for instance, having laid down certain proofs says: "Whoever does not wish to believe because of these reasons, let him believe because of faith" [*Moralia in Job* xiv. cap. xl, *PL* 32 col. 1077]. The same is true of Paul's teachings in *Acts* [17:31, 26:23], and in the first epistle to the Corinthians [15], where he uses the example *of the grain that falls into the earth*, or where he argues from the resurrection of Christ that if Christ be risen, the dead will rise again, or where he appeals to the notion of a just reward. Such arguments are nothing else than probable persuasive proofs, or they are reasons derived from premises that are matters of belief, as is evident if we examine them individually.

. . . From all this it is apparent how much thanks must be given to our Creator, who through faith has made us most certain of those things which pertain to our end and to eternal life—things about which the most learned and ingenious men can know almost nothing according to Augustine's statement in *De Trinitate,* BK XIII, c. ix: "Scarcely a few, etc." "But if faith be there—that faith which is to be found in all those to whom [Jesus] has given the power to become sons of God—there is no question about it," for of this he has made those who believe in him most certain.

---

3. Deducing from a premise, in this case a revealed truth, that precedes sense observation.

II. Medieval

C. Medieval, Western: Scholastic

46. St. Catherine of Siena (1347–1380) | *The Dialogue*

One of the most remarkable prophetic figures of the middle ages, Caterina di Benincasa, or "La Populana" ("woman of the people"), as she was called, was born a twin prematurely from the twenty-third pregnancy of her mother, Lapa, who outlived her daughter. Her father, Jacopo, owned and ran a busy cloth-dying workshop in Siena. A merry child who was nicknamed "Euphrosyne" (cheerful, mirthful), Catherine came to the early crisis of her life in her sixteenth year when pressured to accept the destiny of marriage. While she resolutely kept to virginity for the Lord, she nevertheless declined the life of a nun, carving herself a religious niche of sorts in the Dominican Third Order for the devout faithful living in the world. Set at liberty by her father, she pursued austere asceticism in her family home and progressed rapidly in contemplative prayer; by age twenty-one she was a mystic.

Urged by the Lord in prayer, she left her seclusion for public life, serving the sick and indigent, preaching a renewed turning to Christ in the church, and striving mightily as a peacemaker between the Guelph and Ghibelline factions then tearing the Italian city-states apart. To her it was imperative that the French captivity of the Roman papacy be ended. Her first meeting with the papal court in Avignon is a study in prophetic boldness, as when she told the Pope: "I smelt the stench of the sins here [in the papal court] while I was still at home in my town." She convinced Pope Gregory XI to return to Rome, only to witness the beginning of the great Western Schism under his successor, Urban VI, which well-nigh crushed her with a sense of failure. After three months of intense suffering offered for the church she died at only thirty-three years of age. Pope Paul VI designated her a Doctor of the Church. There is something unique in Catherine, who integrates in herself the best of the monastic and mystical tradition of the West, with the practical, realist, and firmly intellectual tradition of the Dominicans.

Catherine dispatched many a flaming letter in her career, nearly 400 of them. She was quite capable of keeping three secretaries busy simultaneously on three different documents. In 1377–1378, after experiences in prayer of heaven, hell, and purgatory, she composed her great theological work, the *Dialogue of Divine Providence*, a series of exchanges between the Eternal Father and the human soul represented by Catherine herself. We read here from its concluding chapter 167, which is a long meditation on Light, above all on the light of faith, in which light alone we see the light of God.

The Dialogue (1378)

How this most devout soul, thanking and praising God, makes prayer for the whole world and for the Holy Church, and commending the virtue of faith, brings this work to an end:

Then that soul, having seen with the eye of the intellect, and having known by the light of holy faith the truth and excellence of obedience, hearing and tasting it with love and ecstatic desire, gazed upon the divine majesty and gave thanks to Him, saying:

"Thanks, thanks be to You, Eternal Father, for You have not despised me, the work of Your hands, nor turned Your face from me, nor despised my desires; You, the Light, have not disregarded my darkness; You, the true Life, have not considered my living death; You, the Physician, have not been repelled by my grave infirmities; You, the eternal Purity, have not considered the many miseries of which I am full; You, the Infinite, have overlooked that I am finite; You, who are Wisdom, have overlooked my folly.

Your wisdom, Your goodness, Your kindness, Your infinite good, have not despised me for these endless evils and sins, and the many others which are in me. No, *in your light you have given me light* (cf. Ps 36:9). Through Your wisdom I came to know the truth, and in your mercy I have found Your charity, and the love of my neighbor. What has constrained You? Not my virtues, but only Your charity.

May that same charity constrain You to illumine the eye of my intellect with the light of faith, that I may know and understand the truth which You have revealed to me. Grant that my memory may be capable of retaining Your benefits, that my will be kindled with the fire of Your charity, and that fire so work in me that I give my body even to blood, and that by that blood given for love of the Blood, together with the key of obedience, I may unlock the door of Heaven.

I ask this of You with all my heart, for every rational creature, both in general and in particular, in the mystical body of holy Church. I confess and do not deny that You loved me before I existed, and that You love me unspeakably much, as one mad with love for Your creature.

O eternal Trinity! O Godhead! which Godhead gave to the Blood of Your Son its worth, You are a deep sea, Eternal Trinity, a deep sea (cf. Ps 36:6, Job 38:16, Mic 7:19), in which the deeper I enter the more I find, and the more I find the more I seek. The soul cannot be sated with Your *abyss* (Ps 42:7), for she continually hungers after You, Eternal Trinity, desiring *to see* You, *the Light, in Your light* (Ps 36:9). *As the hart that yearns for the fountain of living water, so my soul yearns* (Ps 42:1) to escape the prison of this dark body and to see You in truth.

How long, O Eternal Trinity, O fire and abyss of love, shall Your face be hidden from my eyes? Melt at once the cloud of my body. The knowledge which You have given me of Yourself in Your truth, constrains me to long to abandon the heaviness of my body, and to give my life for the glory and praise of Your Name, for I have tasted and seen with the light of the intellect *in Your light*, your *abyss*, eternal Trinity, and the beauty of Your creature, for, looking at myself in You, I saw that I am *Your image* (Gen 1:27), and that you have endowed me with power from yourself, eternal Father, and with Your wisdom, which belongs to Your only-begotten Son, shining in my intellect and my will, and with Your Holy Spirit who proceeds from You and Your Son, by whom I am able to love You. You, Eternal Trinity, are my Creator, and I am the work of Your hands, and I know through the new creation which You have given me in the Blood of Your Son, that You are enamored of the beauty of Your workmanship.

O Abyss, O eternal Godhead, O deep sea! What more could you have given me than the gift of your very self? You are the fire *ever burning but not consumed* (Exod 3:2), you are *a fire consuming* (Heb 12:29) in your heat all the soul's self-love. You are a fire warming all chill and giving light. *In your light* you have made known to me your truth: You are that light beyond all light that illumines the eye of the intellect supernaturally, clarifying the light of faith so abundantly and so perfectly, that I see that my soul is alive (cf. John 8:12), and *in this light* receives You—*the true light* (John 1:9). By the Light of faith I have acquired wisdom in the wisdom of the Word—Your only-begotten Son. In the light of faith I am strong, constant, and persevering. In the light of faith I hope: do not allow me to *faint along the way* (Mark 8:3). This light, without which I should still *walk in darkness* (John 8:12), teaches me the road, and for this I said, O Eternal Father, that You have illumined me with the light of holy faith.

Of a truth this light is a sea, for the soul revels in You, Eternal Trinity, peaceful Sea. The water of this sea is not turbid, and causes the soul no fear, for she knows the truth; it is a deep which manifests sweet secrets, so that where the light of Your faith abounds, the soul is certain of what she believes. This water is an enchanted *mirror* (2 Cor 3:18) into which You, Eternal Trinity, bid me to gaze, holding it with the hand of love, that I may see myself, who am Your creature, there represented in You, and Yourself in me through the union which You made of Your Godhead with our humanity. For this light I know represents to myself You—the Supreme and Infinite Good, Good Blessed and Incomprehensible, Good Inestimable. Beauty above all beauty; Wisdom above all wisdom—for You are Wisdom itself.

You, *the food of angels* (Ps 78:25), have given Yourself in a fire of love to men (cf. Luke 12:49); You, the garment which covers all our nakedness, feed the hungry with Your sweetness. O Sweetness without any bitterness, O Eternal Trinity, I have known *in Your light* which You gave me with the light of holy faith, the many and wonderful things You have declared to me, explaining to me *the path of* supreme *perfection* (Ps 101:2), so that I may no longer serve You in darkness, but in the light, and that I may become the mirror of a good and holy life, and rise up from my miserable sins, for through them I have served You till now in darkness. I have not known Your truth and have not loved it. Why did I not know You? Because I did not see You with the glorious light of the holy faith; because the cloud of self-love darkened the eye of my intellect, but You, the Eternal Trinity, have dissipated the darkness with Your light.

Who can attain to Your Greatness, and give You thanks for such immeasurable gifts and benefits as You have given me in this doctrine of truth, which has been a special grace over and above the ordinary graces which You also give to Your other creatures? You have been willing to condescend to my need and to that of Your creatures—the need of looking within. Having first given the grace to ask the question, You reply to it, and You satisfy Your servant, penetrating me with the ray of grace, so that *in that light* I may give You thanks.

Clothe me, clothe me with Yourself, O Eternal Truth, that I may run my mortal course with true obedience and the light of holy faith, with which light I feel that my soul is once again to become inebriated."

Section III. Reformation and Post-Reformation

III. Reformation and Post-Reformation

Introduction

The era from which these selections are drawn is known as the Reformation.[1] The name misleads by giving the impression of a single reform, when actually Western European Christianity during the sixteenth century saw many *different* reformations. The once unified Roman Church was splintered into new traditions by some reformers, soon known as "Protestant" (after the Diet of Speyer, 1529). Martin Luther, John Calvin, Balthasar Hubmaier, and Thomas Cranmer stand at the headwaters of those traditions. From them new forms of Protestant Christianity took shape: Reformed, Lutheran, Anabaptist, and Anglican. The name "Post-Reformation" names the subsequent era in which the contributions of Luther, Calvin, and the others were developed and hammered out by Protestants. Under the Catholic heading in this section, readings from Juan de Valdes, Teresa of Avila, John of the Cross, and Francis de Sales portray the Christian life as it was presented by those who remained in the Church of Rome.

Historical perspective. For many hundreds of years prior to the sixteenth century, the Church of Rome had undergone many reforms of varying degrees of success. Some reforms centered on renewing the spirituality of the Church (such as the *devotio moderna* of Erasmus), others on reforming monastic orders, while others focused on the Church's ecclesiastical structures (like the conciliar movement of the fifteenth century). Second, in the centuries preceding the Reformation the political structures of Europe were rapidly changing. Once-unified Christendom declined as European nation-states exercised authority in distinction from and sometimes in opposition to the Church (often through taxation). It would have been unthinkable to question to the Pope's authority some centuries earlier, yet by the sixteenth century the intellectual

---

1. Among the very many available resources, the following are especially useful: Hillerbrand, *The Oxford Encyclopedia of the Reformation*; McGrath, *Reformation Thought*; Kolb et al., eds., *The Oxford Handbook of Martin Luther's Theology*; Lehner et al., eds., *The Oxford Handbook of Early Modern Theology, 1600–1800*; Rublack, *The Oxford Handbook of the Protestant Reformations*.

and political climate was greatly changing. The cultural and intellectual climate fostered an environment in which sixteenth-century reformations rapidly bloomed.[2]

Communal perspective. These authors were embodied men and women, living within the fellowship of the church during a time of great upheaval. Church allegiance during the sixteenth century was frequently a matter of life and death and always a matter of intense personal importance. People, *everyday* people, were for the first time in Western European history having to decide how they identified themselves as Christian. Would they remain in the Church of Rome, which held out the means of grace through the sacraments, or would they join the Protestants? The stakes were incredibly high, a fact that Christians in the modern West can hardly fathom.

One's affiliation with Rome or with the Protestants could lead to painful death, for oneself or one's entire family! Anna Jansz died for her Protestant convictions, and we include a portion of the letter she wrote to her son while imprisoned. Many others lived, but their communities were torn apart. John Calvin and Menno Simons, both reformers, were forced to move across Europe. Frances de Sales, a Catholic priest, went door to door in his parish gently persuading anyone who would listen to return to their Roman home.

Theological perspective. At least two doctrines should be kept in view: the doctrine of grace and the Christian's vocation. Both underwent significant changes as Reformers brought them within the scope of their interpretation of Scripture. We consider each in turn.

First, the *doctrine of grace* concerns the nature of God's grace, the need of sinful persons for that grace, the manner in which persons receive God's grace, and the effects of grace upon those who receive it. During the medieval era, the doctrine of grace was grounded on St. Augustine's theology and remained relatively stable. As Augustine had it, "what else are the justified but those who had been made righteous, namely, by him [God] who justifies the ungodly so that the ungodly becomes a righteous person."[3] The generally held view by the Church of Rome in the centuries between Augustine and the sixteenth century was this: the Church mediates the grace of God to persons in original sin which justifies them over the course of their pilgrimage of faith. No sinful person can be justified before God except by grace, and because the church mediates grace by administering the sacraments, the Church is essential for the full process of justification.

Reformation doctrines of grace differed in two fundamental ways. First, they grounded justification in faith *alone*. Article 4 of the Augsburg Confession summarizes nicely: By faith alone we obtain the remission of sins for Christ's sake, and that by faith alone we are justified, i.e., of unrighteous men made righteous, or regenerated (Article IV). Sinful persons are declared righteous before God on account of faith and nothing else besides faith. This teaching was rejected by the Church of Rome at the

---

2. See Taylor, *A Secular Age*, Part I.
3. St. Augustine, *De spiritu et litera.* Quoted in Ocker, "Evil and Grace," 27.

Council of Trent (1545–1563). They maintained that faith alone, without the sacraments, is insufficient for justification (chapters 8 and 9).

Sixteenth-century doctrines of grace differed in another important way. The Reformers understood the Christian life in terms of justification—*God's work of declaring a person righteous*—and sanctification—*the process of being made holy*. Medieval theology largely held them together, seeing justification as a process of being made righteous and holy. The Reformers, however, separated the event of justification and the process of sanctification in order to stress that sinful persons bring nothing to their salvation and only contribute to their sanctification by the gift of the Holy Spirit.

Second, the understanding of Christian *vocation* underwent massive changes at the hands of the reformers. Something broader than "job" or "career" is meant by the term as it was generally used in Medieval and Reformation theology. One's vocation in the Christian sense was the all-encompassing pilgrimage of faith. Every Christian was faced with the question: who can enter the *full* pilgrimage of faith? To whom is that vocation open? The answer in medieval theology, on one level, was anyone who receives justifying grace. On another level, however, the full pilgrimage of life with God is *not* open to everyone in the same way. Monastics and priests devote themselves totally to lives of prayer and devotion, and can therefore expect higher degrees of Christian perfection.

The Reformers rejected entirely the medieval theology of vocation, instead extending the invitation of pilgrimage to all Christians. "Whoever crawls out of baptism," Luther wrote, "can boast that he has already been consecrated a priest, bishop and pope . . . It follows from this argument that there is truly no essential difference among laity, priest, bishop, as they say, in terms of responsibility or assignment, and in terms of their place in society."[4]

Opening the *full* vocation of Christian pilgrimage to every Christian was also a feature of some Catholic contemporaries. Juan de Valdes, included in this section, counseled a woman to see herself just as much drawn into the pilgrimage of faith as nuns and monks. She should expect no less perfection than her monastic brothers and sisters. "I marvel at what you say," she wrote to Valdes, "because I have all my life been told that friars and nuns are in the rule of perfection by the, vows that they make, if they observe them." Valdes responded, "Let them say so, *signora*, and give credit to me that, whether friars or nonfriars, they possess so much of Christian perfection as they have of faith and love of God, and not a grain more" (*The Christian Alphabet*). What matters, Valdes stressed in very close conformity with Protestant Reformers, was not one's station in life but one's commitment to love God and neighbor.

Kent Eilers

---

4. Luther, *Luther's Works*, 44.128. Quoted in Leppin, "Luther's Transformation of Medieval Thought," 119.

III. Reformation and Post-Reformation

A. Lutheran

47. Martin Luther (1483–1546) | *The Freedom of a Christian*

Each person in this anthology wove threads into the tapestry of the Christian tradition. Some go unnoticed, but Luther's threads stand out in bold relief for many. To some he is a hero of the faith, recalling the church to the heart of the gospel of grace; and to others he is a contentious villain, dividing the church from within. Luther is a study in extremes, a bull of a man whose struggle to experience God's grace was woven into his efforts to reform the church.

Martin was the first of seven children in the Luther family, and though his parents were not wealthy they educated him according to the standards of the time. At five he trained in Latin, and at fourteen he left for boarding school. Four years later he entered the University of Erfurt, distinguishing himself as an avid student. Luther's academic dedication typified him; his way was all or nothing. Not surprisingly, at twenty-three when he entered monastic life in Erfurt he chose the strictest: the Augustinian Order. Dedication to ascetic life, however, did nothing to assuage the acute sense of inadequacy before God that increasingly marked every feature of Luther's life. "Though I lived as a monk without reproach," he later wrote of his early years in the order, "I felt that I was a sinner before God with an extremely disturbed conscience." Reflecting on his first mass, "Who am I," he questioned, "that I should lift up my eyes or raise my hands to the divine Majesty?"

While studying Romans in 1515, however, Luther fell upon an understanding of God's unconditional acceptance on account of faith alone. It was these words in particular: "For in the gospel the righteousness of God is revealed—a righteousness that is by faith from first to last, just as it is written: 'The righteous will live by faith'" (Rom 8:1). Upon reading this, Luther wrote, "Here I felt that I was altogether born again and had entered paradise itself through open gates." Two years later, Luther was so convinced of God's justification by faith alone, and likewise troubled by developments in the Church's practice of selling indulgences, that he initiated a discussion among the university faculty at Wittenberg, where he was teaching (the now famous nailing of ninety-five theses to the door of Wittenberg). A firestorm ensued, too complicated and lengthy to recount here. Luther was eventually excommunicated from the Church, but not before a wave of reform movements rippled outward from Wittenberg. Those ripples joined some already in motion and initiated many others, ultimately forming several new traditions of Christianity (Lutheranism, Calvinism, and Anabaptism).

In this selection from *The Freedom of a Christian* Luther addresses an obvious question raised by his interpretation of justification by faith: what of works? How does God's unconditional acceptance of the sinner by faith relate to the clear calling of God to obey his commands, to conform one's life to the pattern of Jesus the Messiah? Pay special attention to the way Luther repeatedly alludes to Jesus Christ. For Luther, the person of Jesus—fully and truly God and likewise fully and truly human—is the ultimate *warrant* for his portrait of the Christian life. Jesus was "at once free and a servant," thus the Christian is free on account of faith and called to serve their neighbors in joy and love.

The Freedom of a Christian (1520)

Introduction

Christian faith has appeared to many an easy thing; nay, not a few even reckon it among the social virtues, as it were; and this they do, because they have not made proof of it experimentally, and have never tasted of what efficacy it is. For it is not possible for any man to write well about it, or to understand well what is rightly written, who has not at some time tasted of its spirit, under the pressure of tribulation. While he who has tasted of it, even to a very small extent, can never write, speak, think, or hear about it sufficiently. For it is a living fountain, springing up unto eternal life, as Christ calls it in the 4th chapter of St. John.

Now, though I cannot boast of my abundance, and though I know how poorly I am furnished, yet I hope that, after having been vexed by various temptations, I have attained some little drop of faith, and that I can speak of this matter, if not with more elegance, certainly with more solidity than those literal and too subtle disputants who have hitherto discoursed upon it, without understanding their own words. That I may open, then, an easier way for the ignorant—for these alone I am trying to serve—I first lay down these two propositions, concerning spiritual liberty and servitude.

A Christian man is the most free lord of all, and subject to none; a Christian man is the most dutiful servant of all, and subject to every one.

Although these statements appear contradictory, yet, when they are found to agree together, they will be highly serviceable to my purpose. They are both the statements of Paul himself, who says: "Though I be free from all men, yet have I made myself servant unto all" (1 Cor 4:19), and: "Owe no man anything, but to love one another" (Rom 8:8.) Now love is by its own nature dutiful and obedient to the beloved object. Thus even Christ, though Lord of all things, was yet made of a woman; made under the law; at once free and a servant; at once in the form of God and in the form of a servant.

The Threefold Power of Faith

A. Faith Frees from the Law. Now since these promises of God are words of holiness, truth, righteousness, liberty, and peace, and are full of universal goodness; the soul, which cleaves to them with a firm faith, is so united to them, nay, thoroughly absorbed by them, that it not only partakes in, but is penetrated and saturated by, all their virtue. For if the touch of Christ was healing, how much more does that most tender spiritual touch, nay, absorption of the word, communicate to the soul all that belongs to the word. In this way, therefore, the soul, through faith alone, without works, is from the word of God justified, sanctified, endued with truth, peace, and liberty, and filled full with every good thing, and is truly made the child of God; as it is said: "To them gave he power to become the sons of God, even to them that believe on his name" (John 1:12.)

From all this it is easy to understand why faith has such great power, and why no good works, nor even all good works put together, can compare with it; since no work can cleave to the word of God, or be in the soul. Faith alone and the word reign in it; and such as is the word, such is the soul made by it; just as iron exposed to fire glows like fire, on account of its union with the fire. . . .

B. Faith Honors God. Let us consider this as the first virtue of faith; and let us look also to the second. This also is an office of faith, that it honors with the utmost veneration and the highest reputation him in whom it believes, inasmuch as it holds him to be truthful and worthy of belief. For there is no honor like that reputation of truth and righteousness, with which we honor him, in whom we believe. What higher credit can we attribute to any one than truth and righteousness, and absolute goodness? On the other hand, it is the greatest insult to brand any one with the reputation of falsehood and unrighteousness, or to suspect him of these, as we do when we disbelieve him.

Thus the soul, in firmly believing the promises of God, holds Him to be true and righteous; and it can attribute to God no higher glory than the credit of being so. The highest worship of God is to ascribe to Him truth, righteousness, and whatever qualities we must ascribe to one in whom we believe. In doing this the soul shows itself prepared to do His whole will; in doing this it hallows His, name, and gives itself up to be dealt with as it may please God. For it cleaves to His promises, and never doubts that He is true, just, and wise, and will do, dispose, and provide for all things in the best way. . . .

C. Faith Unites the Soul to God. The third incomparable grace of faith is this, that it unites the soul to Christ, as the wife to the husband; by which mystery, as the Apostle teaches, Christ and the soul are made one flesh. Now if they are one flesh, and if a true marriage—nay, by far the most perfect of all marriages—is accomplished between them (for human marriages are but feeble types of this one great marriage), then it follows that all they have becomes theirs in common, as well good things as evil things; so that whatsoever Christ possesses, that the believing soul may take to itself and boast of as its own, and whatever belongs to the soul, that Christ claims as his. . . .

In this is displayed the delightful sight, not only of communion, but of a prosperous warfare, of victory, salvation, and redemption. For since Christ is God and man, and is such a person as neither has sinned, nor dies, nor is condemned,—nay, cannot sin, die, or be condemned; and since his righteousness, life, and salvation are invincible, eternal, and almighty; when, I say, such a person, by the wedding-ring of faith, takes a share in the sins, death, and hell of his wife, nay, makes them his own, and deals with them no otherwise than as if they were his, and as if he himself had sinned; and when he suffers, dies, and descends to hell, that he may overcome all things, since sin, death, and hell cannot swallow him up, they must needs be swallowed up by him in stupendous conflict. For his righteousness rises above the sins of all men; his life is more powerful than all death; his salvation is more unconquerable than all hell.

Thus the believing soul, by the pledge of its faith in Christ, becomes free from all sin, fearless of death, safe from hell, and endowed with the eternal righteousness, life, and salvation of its husband Christ. Thus he presents to himself a glorious bride, without spot or wrinkle, cleansing her with the washing of water by the word; that is, by faith in the word of life, righteousness, and salvation. Thus he betrothes her unto himself "in faithfulness, in righteousness, and in judgment, and in lovingkindness, and in mercies" (Hos 2:19, 20.) . . .

Service to the Neighbor

Lastly, we will speak also of those works which he performs towards his neighbor. For man does not live for himself alone in this mortal body, in order to work on its account, but also for all men on earth; nay, he lives only for others and not for himself. For it is to this end that he brings his own body into subjection, that lie may be able to serve others more sincerely and more freely; as Paul says: "None of us liveth to himself, and no man dieth to himself. For whether we live, we live unto the Lord; and whether we die, we die unto the Lord" (Rom 14:7, 8.) Thus it is impossible that he should take his ease in this life, and not work for the good of his neighbors; since he must needs speak, act, and converse among men; just as Christ was made in the likeness of men, and found in fashion as a man, and had His conversation among men.

Yet a Christian has need of none of these things for justification and salvation, but in all his works he ought to entertain this view, and look only to this object, that he may serve and be useful to others in all that he does; having nothing before his eyes but the necessities and the advantage of his neighbor. Thus the Apostle commands us to work with our own hands, that we may have to give to those that need. He might have said, that we may support ourselves; but he tells us to give to those that need. It is the part of a Christian to take care of his own body for the very purpose that, by its soundness and wellbeing, he may be enabled to labor, and to acquire and preserve property, for the aid of those who are in want; that thus the stronger member may serve the weaker member, and we may be children of God, thoughtful and busy one for another, bearing one another's burdens, and so fulfilling the law of Christ.

Here is the truly Christian life; here is faith really working by love; when a man applies himself with joy and love to the works of that freest servitude, in which he serves others voluntarily and for nought; himself abundantly satisfied in the fullness and riches of his own faith....

Thus a Christian, like Christ his head, being full and in abundance through his faith, ought to be content with this form of God, obtained by faith; except that, as I have said, he ought to increase this faith, till it be perfected. For this faith is his life, justification, and salvation, preserving his person itself and making it pleasing to God, and bestowing on him all that Christ has; as I have said above, and as Paul affirms: "The life which I now live in the flesh I live by the faith of the Son of God" (Gal 2:20.) Though he is thus free from all works, yet he ought to empty himself of this liberty, take on him the form of a servant, be made in the likeness of men, be found in fashion as a man, serve, help, and in every way act towards his neighbor as be sees that God through Christ has acted and is acting towards him. All this he should do freely, and with regard to nothing but the good pleasure of God, and he should reason thus:

Lo! my God, without merit on my part, of His pure and free mercy, has given to me, an unworthy, condemned, and contemptible creature, all the riches of justification and salvation in Christ, so that I no longer am in want of anything, except of faith to believe that this is so. For such a Father then, who has overwhelmed me with these inestimable riches of His, why should I not freely, cheerfully, and with my whole heart and from voluntary zeal, do all that I know will be pleasing to Him, and acceptable in His sight? I will therefore give myself, as a sort of Christ, to my neighbor, as Christ has given Himself to me; and will do nothing in this life, except what I see will be needful, advantageous, and wholesome for my neighbor, since by faith I abound in all good things in Christ....

We conclude therefore that a Christian man does not live in himself, but in Christ, and in his neighbor, or else is no Christian; in Christ by faith, in his neighbor by love. By faith he is carried upwards above himself to God, and by love he sinks back below himself to his neighbor, still always abiding in God and His love, as Christ says: "verily I say unto you, hereafter ye shall see heaven open, and the angels of God ascending and descending upon the Son of man" (John 1:51).[1]

1. Subheadings added for readability.

III. Reformation and Post-Reformation

A. Lutheran

48. *Augsburg Confession* (1530) & *The Formula of Concord* (1578)

Martin Luther initiated the reform movement that later took his name (Lutheranism), but it was left to others, like Philip Melanchthon (1497–1560), to more coherently and systematically give an account of this emerging tradition of faith. Such an account was needed for at least two reasons. First, because some teachings of Luther and his followers markedly diverged from accepted tradition, the Roman Church demanded a clear account. And second, men and women were struggling to make sense of worship and practice on the level of village and city life. It was for them not a matter of preference (as it is for many today), but of life and death as shifting church allegiances would put them afoul of princes and rulers.

The Augsburg Confession was offered to representatives of the Roman Church at the Diet of Augsburg (1530). The Emperor Charles the V convened the meeting to "display diligence in hearing, understanding, and considering with love and kindness the opinions and views of everybody, in order to reduce them to one single Christian truth and agreement." The Confession offered by Lutheran representatives at the Diet was meant to clearly state the Lutheran understanding of faith to which representatives from the Roman Church could offer a response. Martin Luther was involved in the initial stages of drafting the Confession, but it was Melanchthon who attended the Diet and presented it. The selection below has two parts centering on the doctrine of justification. The first part, "Confession of the Lutherans," is the concise statement of faith concerning justification that was offered to Church officials on June 25, 1530. On August 3, Roman theologians offered a response (not included here). In the second part, "Lutheran Defense," we have Melanchthon's rebuttal to the Roman response. When taken together the two parts nicely portray the Lutheran understanding of justification and how it was understood to be different from the accepted tradition in the Church of the time.

Like the Augsburg Confession, the Formula of Concord is also a statement of Lutheran faith, but the context of its development was different. Conflict with the Roman Church generated the need for the Augsburg document, whereas the Formula of Concord was published more to unify and hold together the Lutheran tradition as it had developed since Augsburg. The selections included here again center on the topic of justification.

Augsburg Confession (1530)

Confession of the Lutherans: Article IV—Of Justification (presented June 25, 1530)

Also [our churches] teach that men cannot be justified before God by their own strength, merits, or works, but are freely justified for Christ's sake, through faith, when they believe that they are received into favor, and that their sins are forgiven for Christ's sake, who, by His death, has made satisfaction for our sins. This faith God imputes for righteousness in His sight (Rom 3 and 4).

Lutheran Defense: response to the Roman confutation of Article IV, prepared by Philip Melanchthon (presented September 22, 1530)

In the Fourth, Fifth, Sixth, and, below, in the Twentieth Article, they condemn us, for teaching that men obtain remission of sins not because of their own merits, but freely for Christ's sake, through faith in Christ. (They reject quite stubbornly both these statements.) For they condemn us both for denying that men obtain remission of sins because of their own merits, and for affirming that, through faith, men obtain remission of sins, and through faith in Christ are justified. . . .

Here the scholastics, having followed the philosophers, teach only a righteousness of reason, namely, civil works, and fabricate besides that without the Holy Ghost reason can love God above all things. For, as long as the human mind is at ease, and does not feel the wrath or judgment of God, it can imagine that it wishes to love God, that it wishes to do good for God's sake. (But it is sheer hypocrisy.) In this manner they teach that men merit the remission of sins by doing what is in them, i.e., if reason, grieving over sin, elicit an act of love to God, or for God's sake be active in that which is good. And because this opinion naturally flatters men, it has brought forth and multiplied in the Church many services, monastic vows, abuses of the mass; and, with this opinion the one has, in the course of time, devised this act of worship and observances, the other that. And in order that they might nourish and increase confidence in such works, they have affirmed that God necessarily gives grace to one thus working, by the necessity not of constraint but of immutability (not that He is constrained, but that this is the order which God will not transgress or alter).

In this opinion there are many great and pernicious errors, which it would be tedious to enumerate. Let the discreet reader think only of this: If this be Christian righteousness, what difference is there between philosophy and the doctrine of Christ? If we merit the remission of sins by these elicit acts (that spring from our mind), of what benefit is Christ? If we can be justified by reason and the works of reason, wherefore is there need of Christ or regeneration (as Peter declares, 1 Pet 1:18ff)? . . .

Thus the adversaries teach nothing but the righteousness of reason, or certainly of the Law, upon which they look just as the Jews upon the veiled face of Moses; and, in secure hypocrites who think that they satisfy the Law, they excite presumption and empty confidence in works (they place men on a sand foundation, their own works) and contempt of the grace of Christ. On the contrary, they drive timid consciences to despair, which laboring with doubt, never can experience what faith is, and how efficacious it is; thus, at last they utterly despair. . . .

Now we will show that faith (and nothing else) justifies. Here, in the first place, readers must be admonished of this, that just as it is necessary to maintain this sentence: Christ is Mediator, so is it necessary to defend that faith justifies, (without works). For how will Christ be Mediator if in justification we do not use Him as Mediator; if we do not hold that for His sake we are accounted righteous? But to believe is to trust in the merits of Christ, that for His sake God certainly wishes to be reconciled with us. Likewise, just as we ought to maintain that, apart from the Law, the promise of Christ is necessary, so also is it needful to maintain that faith justifies. (For the Law does not preach the forgiveness of sin by grace.) For the Law cannot be performed unless the Holy Ghost be first received. It is, therefore, needful to maintain that the promise of Christ is necessary. But this cannot be received except by faith. Therefore, those who deny that faith justifies, teach nothing but the Law, both Christ and the Gospel being set aside. . . .

Thus far, in order that the subject might be made quite clear, we have shown with sufficient fullness, both from testimonies of Scripture, and arguments derived from Scripture, that by faith alone we obtain the remission of sins for Christ's sake, and that by faith alone we are justified, i.e., of unrighteous men made righteous, or regenerated. . . .

Formula of Concord, III. The Righteousness of Faith (1578)

. . . Concerning the righteousness of faith before God we believe, teach, and confess unanimously, in accordance with the comprehensive summary of our faith and confession presented above, that poor sinful man is justified before God, that is, absolved and declared free and exempt from all his sins, and from the sentence of well-deserved condemnation, and adopted into sonship and heirship of eternal life, without any merit or worth of our own, also without any preceding, present, or any subsequent works, out of pure grace, because of the sole merit, complete obedience, bitter suffering, death, and resurrection of our Lord Christ alone, whose obedience is reckoned to us for righteousness.

These treasures are offered us by the Holy Ghost in the promise of the holy Gospel; and faith alone is the only means by which we lay hold upon, accept, and apply, and appropriate them to ourselves. This faith is a gift of God, by which we truly learn to know Christ, our Redeemer, in the Word of the Gospel, and trust in Him, that for the sake of His obedience alone we have the forgiveness of sins by grace, are regarded as godly and righteous by God the father, and are eternally saved. Therefore it is considered and understood to be the same thing when Paul says that we are justified by faith, Rom 3:28, or that faith is counted to us for righteousness, Rom 4:5, and when he says that we are made righteous by the obedience of One, Rom 5:19, or that by the righteousness of One justification of faith came to all men, Rom 5:18. For faith justifies, not for this cause and reason that it is so good a work and so fair a virtue, but because it lays hold of and accepts the merit of Christ in the promise of the holy Gospel; for this must be applied and appropriated to us by faith, if we are to be justified thereby. Therefore the righteousness which is imputed to faith or to the believer out of pure grace is the obedience, suffering, and resurrection of Christ, since He has made satisfaction for us to the Law, and paid for (expiated) our sins. For since Christ is not man alone, but God and man in one undivided person, He was as little subject to the Law, because He is the Lord of the Law, as He had to suffer and die as far as His person is concerned. For this reason, then, His obedience, not only in suffering and dying, but also in this, that He in our stead was voluntarily made under the Law, and fulfilled it by this obedience, is imputed to us for righteousness, so that, on account of this complete obedience, which He rendered His heavenly Father for us, by doing and suffering, in living and dying, God forgives our sins, regards us as godly and righteous, and eternally saves us. This righteousness is offered us by the Holy Ghost through the Gospel and in the Sacraments, and is applied, appropriated, and received through faith, whence believers have reconciliation with God, forgiveness of sins, the grace of God, sonship, and heirship of eternal life. . . .

Likewise also the disputation concerning the indwelling in us of the essential righteousness of God must be correctly explained. For although in the elect, who are justified by Christ and reconciled with God, God the Father, Son, and Holy Ghost, who is the eternal and essential righteousness, dwells by faith (for all Christians are temples of God the Father, Son, and Holy Ghost, who also impels them to do right), yet this indwelling of God is not the righteousness of faith of which St. Paul treats and which he calls *iustitiam Dei*, that is, the righteousness of God, for the sake of which we are declared righteous before God; but it follows the preceding righteousness of faith, which is nothing else than the forgiveness of sins and the gracious adoption of the poor sinner, for the sake of Christ's obedience and merit alone.[1]

---

1. Bookofconcord.org includes citation numbers throughout both documents that hyperlink to various parts of the document. These have been removed.

III. Reformation and Post-Reformation

A. Lutheran

49. Johann Arndt (1555–1621) | *True Christianity*

Published in 1605, revised in 1606, and expanded into its present four-book form a few years later, *True Christianity* is a classic articulation of Lutheran spirituality. Running into multiple editions, it was once reputed that the book could be found in every German home. Its influence reached further still. References to *True Christianity* scatter the pages of John Wesley's diaries, and, some years later, the journals of the nineteenth-century Danish philosopher Søren Kierkegaard. All this helped to elevate its author, Johann Arndt, to the highest acclaim. Arndt has been heralded as the "Father of German Pietism" and even the "second Luther." Christocentric, mystical, concerned with interiority, introspection, and sanctification, *True Christianity* anticipated many aspects of the later German pietistic tradition undertaken in deep dialogue with Lutheran doctrinal sensibilities.

The title of the book says something about the theological task to which Arndt was committed. He sought to define Christianity in its "truest" form against two perceived falsifications. The first concerned the growing distinction he saw between piety and practice: he wanted to find a way to an authentically inward Christianity that did not negate the call to active, practical Christian service (in imitation of Christ). And the second concerned the distinction that was emerging between the theological scholasticism of the day and the practical piety that Arndt considered to be at the core of true Christianity. Indeed, to much appeal, *True Christianity* cut through the dry "scholastic" method that was dominating and dividing the theological scene at the time. Arndt can be seen to draw imaginatively and liberally from the Bible, nature, everyday experience, the medieval mystical traditions, and whatever else he saw around him to draw the reader into a rich and vibrant "union" with the grace of God. Arndt's *True Christianity*, then, aimed at a fully integrated account of Christianity: practical and pious, spiritual and dogmatic—and in this sense, has an enduring value to the living out of the Christian faith in discipleship and prayer today.

True Christianity (1610)

Many think that theology is a mere science, or rhetoric, whereas it is a living experience and practice. Everyone now endeavours to be eminent and distinguished in the world, but no one is willing to learn to be pious. Everyone now seeks men of great learning, from whom one may learn the arts, languages, and wisdom, but no one is willing to learn, from our only teacher, Jesus Christ, meekness and sincere humility, although his holy, living example is the proper rule and directive for our life. . . . He who loves Christ will also love the example of his holy life, his humility, meekness, patience, suffering, shame, and contempt, even if the flesh suffers pain. . . . No one can love Christ who does not follow the example of his holy life. . . . Christians now desire an imposing, magnificent, rich Christ, conformed to the world, but no one wishes to receive or to confess and to follow the poor, meek, humble, and despised Christ. He will, therefore, say: *I never knew you; you were not willing to know me in my humility, and therefore I do now know you in your pride* (Matt 7:23). . . . Now, to this end, dear Christian, this book will serve as a guide, [showing you] not only how you may, through faith in Christ, obtain forgiveness of your sins, but also how you may properly use the grace of God to lead a holy life. True Christianity consists, not in words or in external show, but in living faith, from which arises righteous fruits, and all manner of Christian virtues, as from Christ himself. . . .

Faith is a deep assent and unhesitating trust in God's grace promised in Christ and in the forgiveness of sins and eternal life. It is ignited by the Word of God and the Holy Spirit. Through this faith we receive forgiveness of sins, in no other way than through pure grace without any of our own merits (Eph 2:8) but only by the merits of Christ. For this reason, our faith has a certain ground and is not unsteady. This forgiveness of sins is our righteousness, which is true, continual, and eternal before God. . . .

A true Christian is known by a Christian life and not by the name Christian. He who wishes to be a true Christian must endeavour to let one see Christ in him, in his love, humility, and graciousness, for no one can be a Christian in whom Christ does not live. Such a life must be given internally in the heart and by the spirit as an apple gains its strength of growth from the inner power of the tree. The spirit of Christ must rule a Christian's life and make him conformed to Christ, as Paul says in Romans 8:14. . . . The kind of spirit that motivates and moves a man inwardly lives in him externally. Therefore the Holy Spirit is highly necessary for true Christian life. . . . Out of every growing, living spirit of God the Christian virtues must blossom so that the righteous may blossom as a palm tree and as a cedar in Lebanon that the Lord has planted. . . . Therefore, man must first be renewed inwardly in the spirit of his mind after God's image and his inner desires and affections must be conformed to Christ, which Saint Paul says is done according to God's image (Eph 4:23) so that his external life develops from the ground of his heart and that he is internally the same as he is externally before men. . . .

There is no more difficult and burdensome a service than for a man to serve the sinful affectations and particular enmity. . . . We are to treat our fellowman as God treats us. God himself gave nature as an example, that we are to be of the same mind to all men and not to love anyone more or less than another. As he is minded towards us, so we are to be minded toward our neighbors, and as we act toward our neighbours, he will act toward us. He testifies in our hearts to convince us how he is minded towards us. We are to be minded toward our neighbour. . . .

Prayer is the characteristic of a Christian since he is sanctified by the Holy Spirit, is the dwelling place and temple of the Holy Spirit. The Holy Spirit is the teacher and comforter of the contrite heart. For this reason, suffering is useful since the soul is poor and miserable in it and the Holy Spirit is able to pray through it. The basis of our prayer is God's grace in Jesus Christ. This grace makes us alive. Without prayer there is no consolation, no grace, no blessing in our occupation. Prayer protects us against the persecutors who are far from God. Prayer makes us heavenly, ignites us in the love of God, and protects us against sins and misfortune. The second basis for prayer is God's gracious presence. This ought to stir us up at all times and places to speak to God. A third basis of prayer is God's truth. Moses and David were heard in prayer. God has promised to heal all those who suffer. A fourth basis of prayer is God's eternal Word. It is a great consolation to know that faith and prayer have an eternal foundation over which the gates of hell cannot conquer. The power and fruits of prayer are uncountable. . . .

If we are to experience only a small beginning of this blessedness in this life, our union with the highest Good is a good indication of it. Spiritual joy and the taste of divine sweetness are witnesses to it and is discussed throughout the Psalms and the prophets.

Truly, meditative hearts that have given themselves to God taste nothing except God. Everything except God is to them tasteless, bitter, and dead. Therefore, holy souls have a desire for the living fountain that flows forth into eternal life to green meadows that can be found in no place outside of Christ. This is an image, indeed, a beginning of eternal life, in which God will be All in all (1 Cor 15:28), he will be our dwelling place, our food, our satisfaction, our clothing, our love, our delight, our loveliness, our rest, our wisdom, our praise, our life. . . . Therefore, dear soul, prepare yourself, that your heart may be God's dwelling place. Unite yourself with God in this life (Ps 132:4–5). He who is united with God through true conversion in this mortal life before the soul leaves [the body] will remain united with God in the immortal life in all eternity, for God chooses to dwell in the elect and the saints and to fill them with eternal blessedness and indivisible light and glory. In a word, the soul that breaks off from the body, if it is united with God, will remain united with God in all eternity.

III. Reformation and Post-Reformation

A. Lutheran

50. Argula von Grumbach (1492–1554/7) | *To the Council of Ingolstadt* & *An Answer in Verse*

Born a noble woman to the wealthy and influential von Stuaff family (later taking the married name von Grumbach), Argula was just ten years old when she received a Bible from her father. He insisted she read it, and she continued to do so all her life. As a young woman, she related her sympathies for the teachings of Martin Luther and other Protestant Reformers with her father's gift.[1] "What a joy it is when the spirit of God teaches us and gives us understanding" in Scripture, she wrote. "I don't intend to bury my talent, if the Lord gives me grace."

Von Grumbach hardly buried her talent. She publically promoted Protestant teachings, writing many letters and publishing numerous pamphlets. At one time nearly 30,000 of Von Grumbach's pamphlets were in circulation. This was not a role expected from a woman, but she so fully embraced the Protestant teachings of the priesthood of all believers and the principle of Scripture's ultimate authority that she broke from the gender expectations of her day. As Stjema puts it, Von Grumbach found a "Scripture-based emancipation."[2]

The two selections here are among only six of Argula's writings that have survived, and all of them from the years 1523 to 1524. They concern an eighteen-year-old student at the University of Ingolstadt who was imprisoned and sentenced to death for Lutheran associations. Under threat of death the young man recanted and his execution was canceled. Von Grumbach was horrified by his treatment and leapt to his defense. Though she lacked any formal training in theology and spoke no Latin she challenged the University theologians to a public disputation. Her initial appeal to the University,

---

1. We include her here because it seems that Luther's teachings exerted the earliest and most lasting impact on her (see Stjema, *Women and the Reformation*).
2. Stjema, *Women and the Reformation*, 75.

however, only earned her vehement and public ridicule. In sermons from one professor she was called a "female desperado," "wretched and pathetic daughter of Eve," "arrogant devil," "arrogant fool," "heretical bitch," and "shameless whore."[3] Making no progress with the University, von Grumbach wrote to the City Council of Ingolstadt (1523). Excerpts from that letter are included in the first selection below.

The second selection is a poem that Von Grumbach composed in response to a satirical one published earlier that year by a University professor (1524). The anti-Argula poem was crass and grotesque in every sense, even suggesting a sexual basis for her association with Luther. Taken together, in these readings we glimpse a vision of the Christian life in which every man *and* woman is responsible to interpret Scripture (a central tenet of the Reformation) and one's response to their accusers speaks volumes about the character of their life in God's grace.

To the honorable, prudent and wise Magistrates and Council of the town of Ingostadt, my good friends (1523)

I wish you grace and peace in God and add my own cordial greetings as particularly dear brothers in Christ. Recently I have had occasion to write to the university here concerning its actions in relation to Arsacius Seehofer. I was compelled to do so by my Christian duty. I would have thought that they would have kept the matter to themselves, and would have explained to me any errors I had made, though I am not aware of any. Now I hear that the whole affair has become common knowledge. As a result many people have tackled me about it, and my action and my intentions have been grossly misinterpreted.

This is what leads me now to send to you a copy of the same writings, not out of any desire to vindicate myself personally, but simply for the sake of those who might be scandalized by my writing. I would ask you to read it. Have no doubt that the Spirit of God will act as our schoolmaster and pronounce the right judgment on it. So I will await this, for it says in Isaiah 30: "God is a Lord of judgment; blessed are all those who wait on him" [30:18b]. I make my request and exhortation to you as members of Christ, who alone is the head of us all, as Paul writes to the Ephesians in the fourth chapter: "Christ is the head from which the whole body is knitted together" [4:15]. Now we are all incorporated into God through baptism, as it says at the beginning of this chapter: "one body, one Spirit, one hope, one Lord, one faith, one baptism, one God, one Father who is above us all, and through all things in us all . . . " [Eph 4:4–16].

---

3. Ibid., 79.

Therefore call to mind the vow which you made to God at baptism, which states: "I believe, and renounce all the pomp and illusions of the Devil." If we believe and trust in God as best we can, that is, if we confess him (and he will empower us to do this), then he will also confess us, as he says in Matthew 10 [10:32–33]. Therefore to be a Christian means to resist as best we can those who would condemn the word of God; not with weapons, though, but rather with the word of God. For Paul says in Ephesians 4: "Above all else maintain peace and love between each other . . . " [4:3]. What doctor [of theology] could be so learned that his vow is worth more than mine? The Spirit of God is promised to me as much as to him. As God says in Joel 2: "I will pour out of my Spirit on all flesh, and your sons and daughters will prophesy" [2:28].

I hear that some are so angry with me that they do not know how best to speed my passage from life into death. But I know for sure that they cannot harm me unless the power to do so has been given them by God. He will keep me safe, for His name's sake.[4] . . .

In John 9 we read: "The Jews had already conferred, and agreed that whoever confesses Christ should be excommunicated and thrown out of the churches" [John 9:22]. Sadly this is just what your Sophists have done, as the wording of Seehofer's oath demonstrates, replacing the holy Christian Church with the Roman Church, so comprehensively has God blinded and humiliated them. It was, I believe, their insistence and importunity which forced our Princes to use such violence, if they were to get any peace at all from their pressures. They speak the same language as the Jews who said to Pilate: "We have a law according to which he must die" [John 19:7]. . . .

In the name of God, then, if Christians are to be martyred in this town, just as they were in Jerusalem, may God's will be done as far as I am concerned. But pray that God will not impose the same punishment on you, who have been schooled by them. For we have to forsake everything, as it says in Matthew 10: father, mother, brother, sister, children, worldly goods, life and limb . . . Whoever does not forsake these is not worthy of me, says the Lord [10:37]. Even if I were dead already, the word of God would not be wiped out; for it abides forever [1 Pet 1:25].

I am persuaded, too, that if I am given grace to suffer death for his name, many hearts would be awakened. Yes, and whereas I have written on my own, a hundred women would emerge to write against them. For there are many who are abler and better read than I am; as a result they [the university authorities] might well come to be called "a school for women"—already I have no doubt that many among them are secret disciples of the Lord, who, like Nicodemus, are afraid to confess Christ. Yet that is not enough. We have to confess publicly, as it says in Matthew 10 [10:32]; just thinking of Christ does not mean we have confessed him before others. May God grant them a courageous spirit.

Do not let what is said about me scandalize you; as far as my own person is concerned, I pay no head to their persecution. It is a joy to me to be reviled for the sake

---

4. She proceeds by quoting 2 Cor 4:8–11; Ps 3:6; Isa 30:17; 43:5; 51:12.

of the holy gospel [Matt 5:11]. God forgive them, they know not what they do [Luke 23:34]. I pray with all my heart that God may enlighten them, and beg you also to pray for them and for all whose hearts are hardened. Hear the Lord, Isaiah 30: "This people moves God to anger, for they shut their ears to the word of God, and say to the seers: 'see not'" [30:9b-10a].[5] . . .

In Matthew 7 and 13 Christ warns us to beware of the teaching of the Pharisees, which he calls sour dough, and he remarks that a little yeast can sour a lot of dough [Matt 16:6]. In the same way a little false teaching can be harmful and cause much evil. Therefore, my dear friends and brothers in Christ, take good care that you do not perish along with them. May the grace of God preserve you, to which I commend you, your bodies and souls, your good name and worldly goods. Pray to God for me as I pray to God for you.

An Answer in Verse (1524)

In God's name I'll now begin
My reply to that intrepid man
Who says Johannes is his name;
From Landshut, that his claim,
So his identity I can trace. . . .
Choose any day which you prefer
Explain to me if I have erred.
If you produce the word of God
I'll follow, an obedient child, your nod.
Show me my error honestly
As a Christian man should do. . . .
Quite cheerfully with you I'll meet
It's God, my Lord, of whom we'll treat.
For Christ gives me assurance clear (Matthew 10[6])
I never need have any fear.
For even if summoned straight away.
His Father tells us what to say.
He puts his Spirit in our mouths
And speaks for us in such an hour
"You're not the ones who have to speak";

---

5. The paragraph concludes with quotations from Jeremiah 10:22, 23:36b, 40, the last of which she conflates with Matthew 23:4.

6. The Scripture references in the poem were penned in the margins by von Grumbach.

SECTION III. REFORMATION AND POST-REFORMATION

This promise makes my heart to leap.
Although book learning I have not
I'm not afraid—no, not one jot!
I'll come to you without complaint
To praise and honor God's great name
Whom now so coarsely you defile
Making idols, that's your style.
In my weakness God will be
My spirit's strength, to his glory.
As Christ commands me, Matthew Ten, (Matthew 10)
Do no fear at all those men
Who take your body, naught else harm
Fear rather God, of him I warn
With power over body and soul
To drag them both down to hell (Matt 10:28).
Our flesh cannot accomplish this
Unless God's Spirit dwells within;
That this is promised to us all
Is seen in Chapter Two of Joel: (Joel 2)
Neither man, nor womankind
Is excluded there, you'll find.
For God would let his Spirit flow
Upon all flesh—and will not stow
His Spirit in some narrow stall
Which only a tonsured monk can call
His own; and understand alone.
No, God strikes up a different tone:
Your sons and daughters, servants, maids
Will prophesy (Joel 2:28–31); read Scripture straight,
And learn from God what this could mean:
That old folk dream new dreams,
Heaven and earth tell wonders abroad
Before the dread day of the Lord (Joel 1:30).
Look up and read the Gospel of John (John 7)
In Chapter Seven the lesson's drawn (John 7:37–39):
Loudly Christ, our Lord, cries out:

A. LUTHERAN

"Come to me now, whoever thirsts!
From those who follow my decrees,
Living waters will flow free."
Tidings of the Spirit he did preach
Who each of us will truly teach.
Explain all this, please, if you may,
God's word stands here, as plain as day.
Are peasants or women excluded here?
Show me where that's said, good sir!
Who were the apostles—after all
What Universities did they study in?[7]
So listen, as all Christians should,
The Spirit leads us to the truth.
In First Corinthians you will see—(1 Corinthians 2)
That's once you've read it properly (1 Cor 2:9–13).
In Chapter Two declares Saint Paul
That God's good Spirit drives us all
To knowledge, and all things tests,
Plumbing God's being in its depths.
No one knows what in us lurks
But the Spirit which within us works.
Nor to a mortal is ever revealed
The things that are in God concealed.
Only God's Spirit, extolled by Paul,
In these words instructs us all:
The Holy Spirit we received
Out of this world did not proceed;
Rather the Spirit God has sent
That we might not stay ignorant;
Clearly the Spirit to us explains
What by God's gift we have acclaimed, (1 Corinthians 3)
The temple of the Lord we're named.
God's Spirit is within you, read.
Is woman shut out, there, indeed?[8] . . .

    7. Matheson includes the above translation of this line in the footnote as the literal rendering. His translation reads, "What higher learning could they recall."
    8. Lit: "Where is the woman excluded from the man?"

As I find in Matthew written (Matthew 10)
You can read it in Chapter Ten: (Luke 14)
We must turn at once our back
On children, home, and all we have; (Mark 10)
Who loves these more than him
It calls unworthy of the Son,
If God's own word I'd betray,
Yes, gladly give up life and limb.
My Lord and God I love more dear
Than saving my life in craven fear. (Matthew 25)

III. Reformation and Post-Reformation

B. Reformed

51. John Calvin (1509–1564) | *Golden Booklet of the True Christian Life*

Born and raised in France and trained as a lawyer, John Calvin was unexpectedly caught up in the reform movements of the sixteenth century. Calvin encountered the teaching of Luther sometime in the early 1530s and converted to Protestantism. Unlike Luther, who vividly recounts his spiritual development, Calvin rarely wrote of it and never at length. "God subdued my heart to docility," he simply wrote, "which had become hardened against the truth of the gospel" (preface to his commentary on the Psalms).

After becoming "Protestant," as followers of Luther came to be known (literally "protesters"), Calvin was not altogether safe in France and moved to Switzerland. Calvin was a remarkably talented biblical interpreter and systematic thinker, and over the course of his life he preached thousands of sermons, produced scores of biblical commentaries, and wrote numerous editions of the work for which he is best known: *The Institutes of the Christian Religion* (1536). Like Thomas Aquinas before him, Calvin had a knack for seeing across the range of Christian belief, and in *The Institutes* he offers an account of its breadth and depth. It was so widely read across Europe that it led the initially reticent Calvin into a significant leadership role in the Protestant city of Geneva.

The selection here is taken from the little book *The Golden Booklet of the True Christian Life*, originally a chapter of *The Institutes* (1539 edition). Calvin wanted the material widely read by laypeople, so he wrote accessibly and focused on the various dimensions of daily Christian life. "Calvin directs himself to mind, heart, and hand" and is at once "intellectual, mystical, and practical."[1] The material runs right along the

---

1. Henry J. Van Andel, "Preface" in *The Golden Booklet of the True Christian Life*, 10.

ground of the Christian's understanding of themselves as a person redeemed by Christ and living in the Spirit.

Notice the refrain to which Calvin returns again and again: bearing the cross. For Calvin, the Christian should not trust in her own capacities, for reliance upon her own strength only leads away from the grace of God. Thus, bearing the cross of Christ functions to reveal the weakness inherent to being creaturely and sinful, thereby pushing the Christian back onto God in greater and greater dependence. Calvin tries to show that dependence is not an arbitrary point around which to center a portrayal of the Christian life. Instead, bearing the cross was the pattern of Christ's life: "Our Lord was not compelled to bear the cross except to show and prove his obedience to his Father." Whatever difficulty may befall the Christian on account of sharing in Christ's suffering, it leads the Christian into greater conformity to Christ. Like so many before Calvin, the gravitational center that gives his doctrine of the Christian life its basic shape is the incarnation of God the Son.

Golden Booklet of the True Christian Life (1539)

Holiness is the key principle

The plan of Scripture for a Christian walk is twofold: first, that we be instructed in the law to love righteousness, because by nature we are not inclined to do so; second, that we be shown a simple rule that we may not waver in our race.

Of the many excellent recommendations, is there any better than the key principle: Be thou holy, for I am holy?

When we were dispersed like scattered sheep, and lost in the labyrinth of the world, Christ gathered us together again, that he might bring us back to himself.

When we hear any mention of our mystical union with Christ, we should remember that holiness is the channel to it.

Holiness is not a merit by which we can attain communion with God, but a gift of Christ, which enables us to cling to him, and to follow him.

It is God's own glory that we cannot have anything to do with iniquity and uncleanness; therefore, we must keep this in mind if we desire to pay attention to his invitation.

For why where we delivered from the quagmire of iniquity and pollution of this world, if we want to wallow in it as long as we live?

God's holiness admonishes that we must inhabit the holy city of Jerusalem if we wish to belong to the people of God.

Jerusalem is hallowed ground, therefore it cannot be profaned by impure inhabitants.

The Psalmist says, "This one shall abide in the tabernacle of the Lord who walks uprightly and works righteousness."

The sanctuary of the Holy One must be kept immaculate (Lev 19:2; 1 Pet 1:16; Isa 35:10; Ps 15:1–2; 24:3–4). . . .

Crossbearing is more difficult than self-denial

For all whom the Lord has chosen and received into the society of his saints ought to prepare themselves for a life that is hard, difficult, laborious, and full of countless griefs.

It is the will of their heavenly Father to try them in this manner that he may test them.

He began with Christ, his firstborn Son, and he pursues this manner with all his children. . . .

For the apostle teaches that it is the destiny of all God's children "to be conformed to him."

And it is a real comfort to us when we endure many miseries, which are called adversities and calamities, that we partake of the sufferings of Christ, in order that we may pass through our different tribulations as he escaped from an abyss of all evils to the glory of heaven. . . .

For the more we are afflicted by adversities, the more surely our fellowship with Christ is confirmed!

By this fellowship the adversities themselves not only become blessings to us, but they are also aids to greatly promote our happiness and salvation (Matt 16:24, 3:17, 17:5; Heb 5:8; Rom 8:29; Acts 14:22; Phil 3:10).

The cross makes us humble

Our Lord was not compelled to bear the cross except to show and prove his obedience to his Father. But there are many reasons why we should live under a continual cross.

First, whereas we are naturally prone to attribute everything to our human flesh unless we have, as it were, object lessons of our stupidity, we easily form an exaggerated notion of our strength, and we take for granted that, whatever hardships may happen, we will remain invincible.

And we so become puffed up with a foolish, vain, and carnal confidence which arouses us to become haughty and proud toward God, as if our own power would be sufficient without his grace.

This vanity he cannot better repress than by proving to us from experience not only our folly, but also our extreme frailty. Therefore he afflicts us with humiliation, or poverty, or loss of relatives, or disease, or calamities.

Then, because we are unable to bear them, we soon are buried under them.

And so, being humbled, we learn to call upon his strength which alone makes us stand up under such a load of afflictions.

Even the greatest saints, though realizing that they can only be strong in the grace of God and not in themselves, are nevertheless more sure than they ought to be of their own bravery and persistence, unless he leads them by the trials of life into a deeper knowledge of themselves. . . .

Though in prosperity many saints have flattered themselves with perseverance and patience, yet they learned that they had deceived themselves and adversity broke down their resistance.

Warned by such evidences of their spiritual illness, believers profit by their humiliations.

Robbed of their foolish confidence in the flesh, they take refuge in the grace of God.

And when they have done so, they experience the nearness of the divine protection which is to them a strong fortress (Ps 30:6–7).

The cross makes us hopeful

This is what Paul teaches, that "tribulation worketh patience, and patience, experience."

For God's promise to believers that he will help them in their trials, they experience to be true when they persist in their patience supported by his strength and not by their own.

Patience, therefore, affords a proof to the saints that God will actually give them the help he has promised whenever there is need.

And this also confirms their hope, for they certainly would be ungrateful if they did not rely for the future on the truth of God, which they have found to be sure and unchangeable.

Now we see what a stream of benefits flows from the cross. For if we discard the false opinions of our own virtue and discover our hypocrisy which leads us astray with its flatteries, our natural and pernicious pride tumbles down.

When we are thus humbled, we are taught to rely on God alone, and we shall not stumble or sink down in despair.

From this victory we shall gather new hope, for when the Lord fulfills his promises, he confirms his truth for the future. . . .

For it is no small profit to be robbed of our blind self-love so that we become fully aware of our weakness; to have such an understanding of our weakness that we distrust ourselves; to distrust ourselves to such an extent that we put all our trust in

God; to depend with such boundless confidence on God that we rely entirely on his help, so that we may victoriously persevere to the end; to continue in his grace that we may know he is true and faithful in his promises; and to experience the certainty of his promises so that our hope may become firmer (Rom 5:3–4).

The cross teaches obedience

The Lord has still another reason for afflicting his children: to try their patience and teach them obedience.

Indeed, they cannot show any other obedience to him than the one he has given them; but he is pleased in this manner to exhibit and to test the graces which he has conferred on his saints, that they may not remain hidden and become useless.

When God's servants openly manifest his gifts of strength and firmness in their suffering, Scripture says that he is trying their patience.

Hence such expressions as "God tempted Abraham," who proved his devotion from the fact that he did not refuse to sacrifice his only son.

Therefore Peter states that our faith is tried by tribulations, just as gold is tried by fire in a furnace.

Who can deny that it is necessary that this most excellent gift of patience, which a believer has received from God, be developed by practice, so that he becomes sure and convinced of it?

For otherwise men would never esteem it as it deserves.

But if God himself acts justly when he prevents such virtues from becoming obscure and useless by offering us an occasion to exercise them, then this must be the best of reasons for trying the saints, for without affliction they would have not patience.

By the cross they are also instructed, I repeat, to obedience, because in this way they are taught to follow God's desire and not their own.

If everything proceeded according to their wishes, they would not understand what it means to follow God. . . .

Therefore, that we may not become haughty when we acquire wealth; that we may not become proud when we receive honors; that we may not become insolent when we are blessed with prosperity and health, the Lord himself, as he deems fit, uses the cross to oppose, restrain, and subdue the arrogance of our flesh. And he does this by various means which are useful and wholesome for each of us. For we are not all equally afflicted with the same disease or all in need of the same severe cure.

This is the reason why different persons are disciplined with different crosses. The heavenly Physician takes care of the well-being of all his patience; he gives some a milder medicine and purifies others by more shocking treatments, but he omits no one; for the whole world, without exception, is ill (Deut 32:15).

III. Reformation and Post-Reformation

B. Reformed

52. Richard Sibbes (1577–1635) | *The Bruised Reed and the Smoking Flax*

"Of this blest man, let this just praise be given: heaven was in him, before he was in heaven." So said Izaak Walton of Richard Sibbes. Of humble origins, Sibbes soon shot to ecclesiastical fame. Born in Suffolk in 1577 to a wheelwright, he went on to hold several prestigious appointments, including: lecturer at Holy Trinity Church, Cambridge; preacher at Gray's Inn, London; and Master of Catherine Hall, Cambridge, where he remained until his death in 1635. Alongside his Elizabethan Cambridge colleague William Perkins, Sibbes was a prominent leader of the Puritan movement that was gaining traction in the Church of England—though he remains not as well known as some of his puritan comrades.

He lived in unsettled times. Some of his theological allies were leaving the Church of England for congregationalism, others were leaving England altogether to pursue the Puritan ideal in the free lands of America. More generally, bitter disputes raged over church polity, practices, doctrine, and discipline. Despite his theological sympathies for Puritanism and classical Calvinist doctrine, his dissatisfaction with aspects of established church polity (which probably contributed to his dismissal from his lecturing post at Holy Trinity) and his desire for the purification of the Church of England of what he perceived to be its more "catholic piety," Sibbes remained throughout his life a moderate in his churchmanship and therefore assented to the articles of episcopal oversight.

A prolific writer of sermons, among his most famous is a long meditation on Matthew 12:20: *The Bruised Reed and the Smoking Flax*. Preached in English (not Latin), this is a sermon about grace, and how the sinner is "bruised" or "touched" by the loving grace of God. We are never the same after being touched by God's grace— "we must be new creatures," he writes. Published in 1630, while Sibbes was Master of

Catherine Hall, the sermon captures the Puritan zeal that lies at the heart of Sibbes's theology. Expect references to the absolute priority of grace, a radical christocentrism, the importance of personal piety, the bleak reality of sin, confidence in the Bible as "the Book of God," and the assurance in personal salvation. But above all expect a vision of the Christian life as shot through with the comforting grace of God. "When we feel ourselves cold in affection and duty," Sibbes says, "the best way to recover is to warm ourselves at this fire of his love and mercy in giving himself for us."

The Bruised Reed and the Smoking Flax (1630)

"His voice shall not be heard." His voice indeed was heard, but what voice? "Come to me, all you who labor and are heavy-laden" (Matt 11:28). He cried, but how? "Hear, everyone who thirsts, come to the waters" (Isa 55:1). And just as his coming was modest, so it was mild, which is set down in these words: "A bruised reed, he shall not break, and smoking flax, he shall not quench."

We see, therefore, that the condition of those with whom he was to deal was that they were bruised reeds and smoking flax; not trees, but reeds; and not whole, but bruised reeds. . . .

God's children are bruised reeds before their conversion and oftentimes after. Before conversion all (except those who, being brought up in the church, God has delighted to show himself gracious to from their childhood) are bruised reeds, yet in different degrees, as God sees fit. And as there are differences with regard to temperament, gifts and manner of life, so there are in God's intention to use men in the time to come; for usually he empties them of themselves, and makes them nothing, before he will use them in any great services. . . .

This bruising is required before conversion so that the Spirit may make way for himself into the heart by levelling all proud, high thoughts, and so that we may understand ourselves to be what indeed we are by nature. We love to wander from ourselves and to be strangers at home, till God bruises us by one cross or other, and then we "begin to think," and come home to ourselves with the prodigal son (Luke 15:17). It is a very hard thing to bring a dull and evasive heart to cry with feeling for mercy. Our hearts, like criminals, never cry for the mercy of the judge until they are beaten from all evasions. . . .

Let this support us when we feel ourselves bruised. Christ's way is first to wound, and then to heal. No sound, whole soul will ever enter into heaven. When in temptation, think "Christ was tempted for me; my graces and comforts will be according to my trials. If Christ is so merciful as not to break me, then I will not break myself by despair, nor will I yield myself to the roaring lion, Satan, to break me in pieces." . . .

But grace is not only little, but mingled with corruption; therefore a Christian is said to be smoking flax. So we see that grace does not do away with corruption all at once, but some is left for believers to fight with. The purest actions of the purest men need Christ to perfume them; and this is his office. When we pray, we need to pray again for Christ to pardon the defects of our prayers. . . .

This also shows that those who only take Christ as our righteousness but not our sanctification (except by imputation) are misled. To the contrary, it is a great part of our happiness to be under such a Lord. He was not only born for us, and given to us, but our government is likewise upon his shoulder (Isa 9:6, 7). He is our Sanctifier as well as our Savior: he is our Savior by the effectual power of his Spirit from the power of sin, as well as by the merit of his death from the guilt of sin; provided these things are remembered:

1. The first and main ground of our comfort is that Christ as a priest offered himself as a sacrifice to his Father for us. The guilty soul flies first to Christ crucified, who was made a curse for us. From there Christ has the right to govern us; from there he gives us his Spirit as our guide to lead us home.

2. In the course of our life, after we are in a state of grace, if we are overtaken with any sin, we must remember to take recourse first to Christ's mercy to pardon us, and then to the promise of his Spirit to govern us.

3. And when we feel ourselves cold in affection and duty, the best way to recover is to warm ourselves at this fire of his love and mercy in giving himself for us.

4. Again, remember this: that Christ rules us by a spirit of love, from a sense of his love, for which reason his commandments are easy for us. He leads us by his free Spirit, a Spirit of liberty.

As his subjects, we serve him voluntarily. The constraint that he lays upon his subjects is that of love. He draws us sweetly with the cords of love. Yet remember also that he draws us strongly by a Spirit of power. It is not enough that we have motives and encouragements to love and obey Christ from that love of his by which he gave himself for us to justify us; but Christ's Spirit must likewise subdue our hearts, and sanctify them to love him, without which all other motives will be ineffectual.

Our disposition must be changed. We must be new creatures. Those who seek for spiritual love in an unchanged heart, seek for heaven in hell. When a child obeys his father, it is done from reasons which persuade him to obey; and likewise, a child-like nature gives strength to these reasons. It is natural for a child of God to love Christ so far as he is renewed; this is not only from an inducement of reason so to do, but it is likewise from an inward principle and work of grace that those reasons gain their main force. First we are made partakers of the divine nature, and then we are easily induced and led by Christ's Spirit to our spiritual duties. . . .

This power is conveyed to us by faith, after union with Christ in his estates both of humiliation and of exaltation. By faith, we see ourselves not only dead with Christ, but risen and sitting together with him in heavenly places (Eph 2:6). Now, understanding ourselves to be dead and risen, and therefore victorious over all our enemies in our Head, and understanding that his aim in all this is to conform us to himself, we are by this faith changed into his likeness (2 Cor 3:18). And so we become conquerors over all our spiritual enemies, just as he is, by that power which we derive from him who is the storehouse of all spiritual strength for all his people. Christ at length will fulfill his purpose in us, and faith rests assured of it; and this assurance is very operative, stirring us up to join with Christ in his purposes. . . .

Those who are under Christ's government have the spirit of revelation by which they see and feel a divine power sweetly and strongly enabling them to preserve their faith when they feel the contrary; and to hope in a state which is hopeless; and to extend love towards God under signs of his displeasure; and to be heavenly-minded in the midst of worldly affairs and allurements which draw us a contrary way. They feel a power preserving their patience, no, their joy in the midst of causes for mourning, and preserving their inward peace in the midst of assaults. Why else do we stand firm when we are assaulted with temptation and encompassed with troubles, unless it is from a secret strength that upholds us? To make so little grace so victorious over so great a mass of corruption, requires a spirit that is more than human. This is like preserving fire in the sea, and a part of heaven, as it were, even in hell. Here we know where to obtain this power, and to whom to return the praise of it. And it is our happiness that it is so safely hidden in Christ, in one who is so near to God and to us. Since the Fall, God will not trust us with our own salvation. Instead, it is both purchased and kept for us by Christ, and we are purchased and kept for it through faith, worked by the power of God which we lay hold of. This power is gloriously set forth by Paul: it is (1) a great power; (2) an exceeding power; (3) a working and a mighty power; and (4) the same power that raised Christ from the dead (Eph 1:19–20). Grace which is only a persuasive offer, and which is in our power to receive or refuse, is not the grace which brings us to heaven. Rather than this, God's people feel a powerful work of the Spirit, not only revealing to us our misery and our deliverance through Christ, but emptying us of ourselves, as if being redeemed from ourselves; and infusing new life into us, and afterwards strengthening us, and invigorating us when we droop and hang the wing, never leaving us until the conquest is perfect.

III. Reformation and Post-Reformation

B. Reformed

53. John Owen (1616–1683) | *Communion with God*

John Owen was a Puritan pastor and theologian. Born to a Puritan vicar, Owen was surrounded by the spirit of Puritanism from his earliest youth and at twenty-one entered the ministry. For Puritans, the sum and total of Christian life is expressed by the term "communion with God." Communion includes a Christian's outward expression of grace in worship and obedience, and it also names the work of God in Christ from which grace is received through the Holy Spirit. We might say that "communion with God" is the Christian life in Puritan key. J. I. Packer beautifully explains the significance of this for Owen:

> Puritanism first emerged as a quest for the reform of England's public worship, and the substance, mode, and practice of corporate as well as individual worship remains a central Puritan concern throughout the movement's history. Of no one was this truer than of Owen himself, as his works bear witness: over and above his frequent treatments of worship in its various aspects as a distinct topic, he relates just about every theological theme to the worship of God somewhere in his writings. Why this sustained focus on worship? Not only because worship's primary aim it so give God the glory and praise that is his due, but also because worship's secondary end and purpose, inseparably bound up with the first, is to lead worshippers into the sunshine of communion with God—a true foretaste of heaven, in which all spiritual souls find their highest delight.
>
> Thus, to the Puritans, communion between God and man is the end to which both creation and redemption are the means; it is the goal to which both theology and preaching must ever point; it is the essence of true religion; it is, indeed, the definition of Christianity.[1]

---

1. Packer, *A Quest for Godliness*, 12.

For Owen and his Puritan comrades in the Church of England, "communion" names that which is most *basic* about the Christian life: harmonious fellowship with God and man.

In this selection from *Communion with God*, Owen shows how our understanding of communion with God must be grounded and sourced in God's triune nature. In other words, the texture and dynamics of communion with God must be understood in terms of God's particular nature as revealed by Jesus Christ, and not in terms of some general, abstract concept of deity. Communion with God is communion with the particular *triune* God revealed through the incarnation of Jesus Christ. Any account of communion that claims to be Christian must, therefore, be essentially and irreducibly Trinitarian: the triune God is the One revealed through the incarnation of the Son and known by the Holy Spirit. As Owen shows here, the uniquely Trinitarian shape of communion with God includes fellowship with *each* of the divine persons.

Communion with God (1657)

The Apostle John tells us, "There are three that bear witness in heaven, the Father, the Word and the Holy Spirit" (1 John 5:7). And to what do they bear witness? They bear witness to the Sonship of Christ and the salvation of believers in his blood. John is writing of that salvation by blood and water, symbolizing justification and sanctification. Now how do these three persons bear witness to this salvation? They bear witness as three individual, separate witnesses. When God witnesses to our salvation, surely it is incumbent upon us to receive his testimony. The Father bears witness, the Son bears witness and the Holy Spirit bears witness for they are three separate, individual witnesses. So we are to receive each of their testimonies, and as we do so, we have communion with each person of the Godhead severally. In this giving and receiving of this testimony lies a great part of our fellowship with God....

Faith, love, and trust, joy and all other spiritual graces are the means by which the soul has communion with God. These graces are drawn from the soul by prayers and praises which God has appointed for his worship. The Bible clearly shows that by these graces the saints have communion with each person of the Godhead.

Communion with the Father. Faith, love, trust, joy and obedience are the saints' responses to the Father's loving acts shown to them. The Father testifies to and bears witness of his Son (1 John 5:9). In his bearing witness, the Father is to be believed and trusted. When the Father testifies to his Son, his testimony is to be received by faith. "He that believes on the Son of God has the witness in himself" (1 John 5:10). To believe on the Son of God is to receive the Lord Christ as the Son, the Son given to us to fulfill in us the purposes of the Father's love. And we receive the Lord Christ as the Son given to us on the truthfulness of the Father's witness. So when we receive this testimony, we put our faith specially in the Father. So John warns, "He that believes not God," that is, the Father who bears witness to the Son, "has made him a liar." "You believe in God," says our Savior (John 14:1). Here he is referring to the Father, for he adds, "Believe also in me." God is the first truth upon whose authority all truth is based, and on whose authority all divine faith ultimately rests. In this sense, God is not to be thought of as any one person, but as the whole deity, Father, Son and Holy Spirit. So the triune God is the chief object of faith. But in John 14:1 it is the testimony and authority of the Father which concerns us and on which faith is specially fixed. If our faith was not there directed to the Father, the Son could not add, "Believe also in me."

The same is also said of love. John writes, "If any man love the world, the love of the Father is not in him" (1 John 2:15). The love of the Father is our love for the Father and not his love for us. In this instance, the Father is put as the object of love, and is not the cause of our love. And this love given to God as Father is that which he calls his 'honor' (Mal 1:6). . . .

Communion with the Son. Jesus said, "You believe in God, believe also in me" (John 14:1). "Believe" also includes putting faith in Christ personally as the Son, that same divine supernatural faith with which we believe in God, that is, the Father. There must be a believing about Christ, namely, that he is the Son of God, the Savior of the world. Jesus threatened the Pharisees for not believing this fact (John 8:24). In this sense, faith is not directly fixed on the Son because this "believing" is only recognizing the truth that he is Christ, the Son of God, on the testimony of the Father concerning Jesus. But there is also a believing "in" Jesus, called "believing in the name of the Son of God" (1 John 5:13; John 9:36). This "believing" is a putting our trust and confidence in the Lord Jesus Christ, the Son of God, as the Son of God (John 3:16). The Son, whom the Father gave, is to be trusted as the one that gives us everlasting life and who will keep us from perishing. . . . The sum of all this is, "that all men should honor the Son, even as they honor the Father. He that does not honor the Son, does not honor the Father who sent him."

Love for the Lord Jesus Christ is love for him as God and it therefore includes love for him in religious worship. Only where there is such love does the apostolic benediction belong: "Grace be with all those that love our Lord Jesus Christ in sincerity" (Eph 6:24). . . .

Communion with the Holy Spirit. All worship is due also to the Holy Spirit, as he is God and as he is the Spirit of grace. The great sin of unbelief is still described as opposition to, and resisting of, the Holy Spirit. So the Spirit is entitled to all instituted worship, as we see from the appointment of the administration of baptism in his name (Matt 28:19).

So we see that there is no exercise of grace towards God, no act of diving worship given to him, no duty or obedience done for him, but they are distinctly directed to the Father, Son and Spirit. Now in these and in ways similar to these, we have communion or fellowship with God. Therefore we have communion also with each person of the Godhead individually....

There is a communication of grace to us from each of the persons of the Godhead. This being so, the saints must then have communion with each person of the Godhead distinctly.

But there is this difference with each of the persons of the Godhead. The Father communicates with us on the basis of his being the origin of all authority. The Son communicates with us out of a purchased treasury. The Holy Spirit communicates with us by direct personal working in us.

The Father communicates all grace to us by his own authoritative will (John 5:21; Jas 1:18). Life-giving power is vested in the Father. Therefore in sending the Spirit to give us life, Christ is said to do it from the Father (John 14:26; 15:26). But Christ also sends the Spirit himself (John 16:7).

The Son communicates to us out of a purchased treasury. "Of his fullness have all we received" (John 1:16). And from where has Christ god this fullness? "It pleased the Father that in him all fullness should dwell" (Col 1:9). And Paul tells us why that fullness was committed to Christ (Phil 2:8–11). Christ also has authority to communicate his fullness to us (John 5:25–27; Matt 28:18).

The Spirit communicates to us by directly working in us by his power. Romans 8:11: "but if the Spirit of him who raised Jesus from the dead dwells in you, he who raised Christ from the dead will also give life to your mortal bodies through his Spirit who dwells in you."

In this text, we see all the persons of the Godhead agreeing to raise us from death to life.

Here we see the Father's authoritative raising of Jesus from the dead and giving life to our mortal bodies.

Here we see the Son's mediatory work. It is through his death that our bodies shall be raised from death.

Here we see the Spirit's direct work, for by his dwelling in us, the Father will give life to our mortal bodies.

III. Reformation and Post-Reformation

B. Reformed

54. Jonathan Edwards (1703–1758) | *Charity and Its Fruits* & *Apostrophe to Sarah Pierpont*

Jonathan Edwards was an American theologian and pastor from the Puritan tradition. He is best known for his role in the Great Awakening of the eighteenth century, a revival of Christian faith and piety in America and Great Britain. Perhaps his intimate involvement with the Awakening fueled his intense reflection on the Christian life, or maybe it was his natural inclinations toward piety. Whatever the cause, Edwards reflected on the Christian life at great length.

The striking feature of Edwards's portrayal of Christian existence is the degree to which it is Trinitarian from start to finish. Edwards argues, leaning heavily on 2 Peter 1:4, that Christians partake of the divine nature because they partake of the Holy Spirit through union with Christ. The Spirit simply *is* the joy, delight, and grace of God; therefore, the one who partakes of the Spirit partakes of God's own life, which is his love, joy, and beauty.[1]

God's grace is received in the Spirit—not just through the Spirit but actually *in* the Spirit. For Edwards, the Holy Spirit is not something other than God's grace but is God's grace who resides in Christians as their "vital principle." The Spirit unites the Christian to Christ, enlivens them, and turns them toward God in "religious affection" (the affective dimension of faith). A Christian's religious affection is the Spirit's "breathing and acting," and the Spirit who returns God's love draws the Christian into his work (Rom 5:5; 2 Cor 6:6; Col 1:8; Phil 2:1).[2] To experience the grace of God is simply to have the Spirit and thereby to be drawn into the Spirit's activity.

Edwards sees the whole Trinitarian nature of the Christian life in Jesus' prayer of John 17. Jesus prays that Christians would share the love he has for the Father, and

---

1. Jonathan Edwards, *Discourse on the Trinity*, Works of Jonathan Edwards, Vol. 21, 124.
2. Jonathan Edwards, *Treatise on Grace*, Works of Jonathan Edwards, Vol. 21, 185.

Edwards sees the fulfillment of that in the reception of the Spirit. The Spirit *is* the love shared between the Father and the Son, and by receiving the Spirit one experiences that love. The Christian is drawn into the love of the divine life because the Spirit is *its very love*. Christians "possess and enjoy the love and grace of the Father and the Son: for the Holy Ghost is that love and grace."[3]

The first selection, *Charity and Its Fruits*, is the first sermon from a series Edwards preached on 1 Corinthians 13. The sermon concerns love. "The labor of love is the main business of the Christian life," Edwards preached. It flows out of them as they are drawn *into* the love between the Father and the Son through the Spirit. The second selection is a personal note Edwards sketched on the inside cover of his Greek grammar, *Apostrophe to Sarah Pierpoint*. It is a wonderfully personal glimpse into Edwards's love-struck vision of the Christian life at its highest ideal.

Charity and Its Fruits: Sermon One—Love the Sum of All Virtue (1738)

Though I speak with the tongues of men and of angels, and have not charity, I am become as sounding brass, or a tinkling cymbal. And though I have the gift of prophecy, and understand all mysteries, and all knowledge; and though I have all faith, so that I could remove mountains, and have not charity, I am nothing. And though I bestow all my goods to feed the poor, and though I give my body to be burned, and have not charity, it profiteth me nothing. 1 Corinthians 13:1–3. . . .

Doctrine

All that virtue which is saving, and distinguishing of true Christians from others, is summed up in Christian or divine love.

This appears from the words of the text [1 Cor 13:1–3], because so many other things are mentioned which natural men may have. And the things which are mentioned are of the highest kind which it is possible natural men should have, both of privileges and performances. And it is said they avail nothing without this. If any of them were saving, they would avail something without it. And by the Apostle's mentioning so many and so great things, and then saying of them all that they profit nothing without charity, we may understand that there is nothing which avails anything without it. Let a man have what he will, and let him do what he will, it signifies nothing without charity. Which surely implies that charity is the great thing, and that everything which has not this some way or other contained or implied in it is nothing;

---

3. Edwards, *Discourse on the Trinity*, 130.

signifying as much as that this is the life and soul of all religion, without which other things that bear the name of motives are empty and vain. . . .

2. Christian love to both God and men is wrought in the heart by the same work of the Spirit. There are not two works of the Spirit of God, one to infuse a spirit of love to God and another a spirit of love to men. But in doing one he doth the other. The Spirit of God in the work of conversion renews the heart by giving it a divine temper. Ephesians 4:23, "And be renewed in the spirit of your mind." And it is the same divine temper which is wrought in the heart that flows out in love both to God and men.

3. When God and men are loved with a truly Christian love, they are both loved from the same motives. When God is loved aright he is loved for his excellency, the beauty of his nature, especially the holiness of his nature. And it is from the same motive that the saints are loved; they are loved for holiness' sake. And all things which are loved with a truly holy love are loved from some respect to God. Love to God is the foundation of a gracious love to men. Men are loved either because they are in some respect like God, either they have the nature or spiritual image of God; or because of their relation to God as his children, as his creatures, as those who are beloved of God, or those to whom divine mercy is offered, or in some other way from regard to God.

To show the truth of the doctrine . . .

. . . Love is no ingredient in a merely speculative faith; but it is the life and soul of a practical faith. A truly practical and saving faith is light and heat together, or light and love. That which is only a speculative, is only light without heat. But in that it wants spiritual heat or divine love, it is vain and good for nothing. A speculative faith consists only in assent; but in a saving faith are assent and consent together. That faith which has only the assent of the understanding is no better faith than the devils have, for the devils have faith so far as it can be without love. The devils believe and tremble. Now the true spiritual consent of the heart cannot be distinguished from the love of the heart. He whose heart consents to Christ as a Savior loves Christ under that notion, viz. of a Savior. For the heart sincerely to consent to the way of salvation by Christ cannot be distinguished from loving the way of salvation by Christ. There is an act of choice or election in true and saving faith, whereby the soul chooses Christ for its Savior, and accepts and embraces him as such. But as was observed before, election whereby it chooses God and Christ is one act of love. It is a love of choice. In the soul's embracing Christ as a Savior there is love. . . .

Application . . .

. . . The gospel brings to light the love between the Father and the Son, and declares how that love has been manifested in mercy; how that Christ is God's beloved Son in whom he is well pleased. And there we have the effects of God's love to his Son set before us in appointing him to the honor of a mediatorial kingdom, in appointing him to be the [Lord and Judge] of the world, in appointing that all men should honor the Son even as they honor the Father. There is revealed the love which Christ has to the Father, and the wonderful fruits of that love, as particularly his doing such great things, and suffering such great things in obedience to the Father, and for the honor of the Father's justice, authority and law.

There it is revealed how the Father and the Son are one in love, that we might be induced in like manner to be one with them, and with one another, agreeable to Christ's prayer, John 17:21–23, "That they all may be one; as thou Father art in me and I in thee, that they also may be one in us; that the world may believe that thou hast sent me. And the glory which thou gavest me I have given them; that they may be one, even as we are one; I in them, and thou in me, that they may be made perfect in one; and that the world may know that thou hast sent me, and hast loved them, as thou hast loved me." The gospel teaches us the doctrine of the eternal electing love of God, and reveals how God loved those that are redeemed by Christ before the foundation of the world; and how he then gave them to the Son, and the Son loved them as his own. . . .

III. Our subject exhorts us to seek a spirit of love, to grow in it more and more, and very much to abound in the works of love. If love is so great a thing in Christianity, so essential and distinguishing, yea, the very sum of all Christian virtue, then surely those that profess themselves Christians should live in love, and abound in the works of love; for no works are so becoming as those of love. If you call yourself a Christian, where are your works of love? Have you abounded, and do you abound in them? If this divine and holy principle is in you, and reigns in you, will it not appear in your life, in works of love? Consider what deeds of love have you done? Do you love God? What have you done for him, for his glory, for the advancement of his kingdom in the world? And how much have you denied yourself to promote the Redeemer's interest among men? Do you love your fellowmen? What have you done for them? Consider your former defects in these respects, and how becoming it is in you as a Christian hereafter to abound more in deeds of love. Do not make excuse that you have not opportunities to do anything for the glory of the God, for the interest of the Redeemer's kingdom, and for the spiritual benefit of your neighbors. If your heart is full of love, it will find vent; you will find or make ways enough to express your love in deeds. When a fountain abounds in water, it will send forth streams. Consider that as a principle of love is the main principle in the heart of a real Christian, so the labor of love is the main business of the Christian life. Let every Christian consider these things; and may the Lord give you understanding in all things, and make you sensible what spirit it becomes you to be of, and dispose you to such an excellent, amiable, and benevolent life, as is answerable to such a spirit, that you may not love only in word and tongue, but in deed and truth.

SECTION III. REFORMATION AND POST-REFORMATION

Apostrophe to Sarah Pierpont (Edwards's future wife) (1723)

They say there is a young lady in (New Haven) who is beloved of that almighty Being, who made and rules the world, and that there are certain seasons in which this great Being, in some way or other invisible, comes to her and fills her mind with exceeding sweet delight, and that she hardly cares for anything, except to meditate on him—that she expects after a while to be received up where he is, to be raised out of the world and caught up into heaven; being assured that he loves her too well to let her remain at a distance from him always. There she is to dwell with him, and to be ravished with his love, favor, and delight forever. Therefore, if you present all the world before her, with the richest of its treasures, she disregards it and cares not for it, and is unmindful of any pain or affliction. She has a strange sweetness in her mind, and sweetness of temper, uncommon purity in her affections; is most just and praiseworthy in all her actions; and you could not persuade her to do anything thought wrong or sinful, if you would give her all the world, lest she should offend this great Being. She is of a wonderful sweetness, calmness and universal benevolence of mind; especially after those times in which this great God has manifested himself to her mind. She will sometimes go about, singing sweetly, from place to [place]; and seems to be always full of joy and pleasure; and no one knows for what. She loves to be alone, and to wander in the fields and on the mountains, and seems to have someone invisible always conversing with her.

III. Reformation and Post-Reformation

C. Anabaptist

55. Balthasar Hubmaier (c. 1480–1528) | *Eighteen Theses Concerning the Christian Life & Summa of the Entire Christian Life*

Balthasar Hubmaier contributed to the Anabaptist wing of the Reformation for only three years before his death at the stake, but he immediately established himself as its principal theologian. Born in Frieburg, Hubmaier later studied in the university there before earning his doctorate in theology in 1512 at the University of Ingolstadt under John Eck (the theologian principally responsible for refuting Lutheran teachings at the Diet of Augsburg). He taught theology at Ingolstadt for only a year before accepting a call as cathedral preacher in Regensburg and then later at the cathedral in Waldshut. Hubmaier preached and ministered for over a decade, but his allegiances were shifting. It is not at all clear when or how, but by 1523 Hubmaier had aligned himself with the Reformer Ulrich Zwingli and in 1525 was baptized as an adult.

Zwingli was a transitional figure between Lutherans and Anabaptists. He led the reformation movement in Zurich. Working with city officials, he was content to move slowly and without generating conflict that would hurt the public order. Many were less patient. Dissatisfaction grew around Zwingli during the early years of the 1520s in Zurich, leading eventually to a series of re-baptisms in the city during 1525 (Anabaptism literally means "re-baptism"). Hubmaier's connection to Zwingli and eventual re-baptism places him at the genesis of the Anabaptist tradition.

Hubmaier soon became a significant figure in the Anabaptist movement. The vast majority of early Anabaptists were not formally trained as theologians, and many had only minimal education. Hubmaier's training, however, prepared him for point-by-point debate on topics like free will, original sin, and infant baptism. His contribution to the movement at its inception was foundational.

Two selections are included here. *Eighteen Theses Concerning the Christian Life* was published the year before Hubmaeir's baptism (1524). It is a handy summary of his early theology. Nothing is distinctly Anabaptist (early Anabaptists followed Zwingli on nearly every point). Hubmaeir's emphasis on the role of Scripture, however, marked Anabaptist thought from its beginning: simple, straightforward interpretation of the Bible (following Luther). Hubmaier wrote the second selection, *Summa of the Entire Christian Life*, not long after his baptism in 1525. The tract offers a telling portrait of the Christian life as understood by the radical reformers.

Eighteen Theses Concerning the Christian Life (1524)

Beloved Lords and brethren: According to an ancient usage coming from the age of the apostles, when weighty matters arise concerning the faith, some of those to whom preaching God's Word has been commanded gather in a Christian attitude to confer and to weight the Scriptures in order to continue unitedly to feed the Christian sheep according to the content of God's Word. . . .

In order that we not waste much time on human teachings, on our own opinions and fancies, would you bring your Bibles or, if you have none, at least your missals, so that we may Christianly instruct one another on the grounds of the written divine Word. After which I shall provide all of you as well as I can a fraternal meal at my expense, that you not leave without food and drink. . . .

1. Faith alone makes us righteous before God.

2. This faith is the knowledge of God's mercy, which he has shown us by offering his only begotten Son. Here fail those who are Christian in appearance [only], who have only an historical faith in God.

3. Such faith cannot be idle, but must break forth in gratitude toward God and in all sorts of words of brotherly love toward others. This casts down all artifice such as candles, palm branches, and holy water.

4. Only those works are good which God has commanded, and only those are evil which he has forbidden us. Here fall away fish and flesh, cowl and tonsure.

5. The mass is not a sacrifice, but a memorial of the death of Christ, for which reason it cannot be offered either for the dead or for the living. Hereby requiem masses and memorial masses of the seventh day, the thirteenth day, and of the anniversary collapse.

6. As often as such commemoration is held, the death of the Lord shall be proclaimed in the tongue of every land. Here all dumb masses fall on one heap.

7. Images are good for nothing. Henceforth such expenditures shall be devoted not to wood and stone, but to the living needy images of God.

8. Since every Christian believes and is baptized for himself every one should see and should judge Scripture, whether he is being rightly fed and watered by his shepherd.

9. Since Christ alone died for our sin, in whose name alone we are baptized, so shall only he be appealed to as our sole Intercessor and Mediator. Here all pilgrimages fall away.

10. It is far better to translate a single verse of a psalm into each land's language for the people, than to sing five whole psalms in a strange language not understood by the church. Here matins, prime, terce, sext, nones, vespers, compline, and vigils disappear.

11. All teachings, which God himself did not plant, are in vain, interdicted, and shall be uprooted. Hereby fall to the earth Aristotle, scholastics like Thomas, Scotus, Bonaventure, and Occam, and all teaching that does not spring forth from the Word of God.

12. The hour is coming and is now when no one will be counted a priest, except he preach the Word of God. Here fall away early masses, votive, requiem, and middle masses.

13. The fellows of a congregation are obligated to maintain with appropriate food and clothing and to protect those who exposit to them the pure, clear, and unmixed Word of God. This destroys courtisans [i.e.,] pensioners, members of collegia [i.e.,] absentees, and babblers of lies and dreams.

14. Whoever would look for purgatory, on which those who God is their belly have been building for years, is seeking Moses' grave, which he shall never find.

15. To forbid marriage to priests and then tolerate their carnal immorality is to free Barabbas and to kill Christ.

16. To promise chastity in human strength is nothing other than to promise to fly over the sea without wings.

17. He who denies or silences the Word of God for temporal gain trades God's blessing with Red Esau for a lentil stew, and Christ will also deny him.

18. He who does not seek his bread in the sweat of his brow is banned and unworthy of the food he eats. Hereby are cursed all loafers, whoever they be.

Summa of the Entire Christian Life (1525)

First: When Christ teaches the Christian life, he says, "Repent or change your lives, and believe the gospel" (Mark 1:15). Now, it belongs to a change of life that we look into our hearts, and that we remember our deeds and our omissions. Thus, we find that we do that which God has forbidden us and we leave undone what he has commanded us to do. Yes, there is no health in us but rather poison, wounds, and all impurity, which cling to us from the beginning because we are conceived and born in sin. Thus did Job, David, Jeremiah, John, and other God-fearing people lament. Furthermore, a person finds in himself neither help, comfort, nor medicine with which he could help himself. Therefore he must despair of himself and lost heart like the man who had fallen among the killers. Such a miserable little thing is the person who ponders and recognizes himself.

Second: Then the Samaritan must come, that is, Christ Jesus. He brings along medicine, namely, wine and oil, which he pours into the wounds of the sinner. Wine: he leads the person to repentance so that he is sorry for his sins. He brings oil, by which he softens his pain and drives it away, and says, "Believe the gospel that clearly shows that I am your physician who has come into this world to make the sinner just and righteous. The gospel teaches also that I am the only giver of mercy, reconciler, intercessor, mediator, and peacemaker toward God, our father, so that whoever believes in me will not be damned but have eternal life." Through such words of comfort the sinner is enlivened again, comes to himself, becomes joyful, and henceforth surrenders himself entirely to the physician. All his sicknesses he commits, submits, and entrusts to him. As much as it is possible for a wounded person he will also surrender to the will of the physician. He calls upon him for healing so that what the wounded is not able to do out of his capacity, the physician counsels, helps, and promotes him so that he can follow his Word and commandment.... Now this person surrenders himself inwardly in the heart and intention unto a new life according to the rule and teaching of Christ, the physician who has made him whole, from who he received life. Thus Paul confesses publicly that he does not live but Christ lives in him, is life in him, and outside of Christ he confesses that he and his words are empty, worthless, and that he is a lost sinner.

Third: After the person has now committed himself inwardly and in faith to a new life, he then professes this also outwardly and publicly before the Christian church, into whose communion he lets himself be registered and counted according to the order and institution of Christ. Therefore he professes to the Christian church, that in his heart he has been thus inwardly instructed in the Word of Christ and so minded that he has surrendered himself already to live henceforth according to the Word, will, and rule of Christ, to arrange and direct his doing and leaving undone according to him and also to fight and strive under his banner until death. Then he lets himself be baptized with outward water in which he professes publicly his faith and his intention, namely, that he believes he has a gracious, kind, and merciful God and Father in heaven through Jesus Christ, with whom he is well pleased and satisfied. He also has expressed his intention to him and committed himself already in his heart henceforth to change and amend his life.... If he henceforth blackens or shames the faith and name of Christ with public or offensive sins, he herewith submits and surrenders to brotherly discipline according to the order of Christ, Matt 18:15ff.

Fourth: Since, therefore, the person knows and confesses that he is by nature an evil, worm-eaten, and poisoned tree, and neither can nor wants to bring good fruit of himself, this pledge, promise, and public testimony does not happen out of human powers or capacities, for that would be presumptuousness or human arrogance. It rather takes place in the name of God, the Father, and the Son, and the Holy Spirit, or in the name of Lord Jesus Christ, that is, in the grace and power of God. For it is a power. From all this follows that the outward baptism of Christ is nothing else than a public testimony of the inner commitments with which the person confesses and accuses himself before everybody that he is a sinner and confesses himself to be guilty of the same. But at the same time he fully believes that Christ through his death has forgiven him his sins and through his resurrection has made him righteous before God, our heavenly Father. . . . Now the person bursts into word and deed, proclaims and magnifies the name and praise of Christ, so that also through us others may be healed and saved . . .

Here follow persecution, the cross, and all tribulation because of the gospel in the world which hates light and life and loves darkness. . . . It establishes for itself laws, and rules by which it thinks it can be saved and despises the unattractive, plain, and simple rule of Christ. . . .

Fifth: After we have now recognized in faith the inestimable and inexpressible goodness of God clearly and plainly in the Word of God, then we should be thankful to God our heavenly Father . . . So that we do not forget him, Christ Jesus himself, our Savior, has ordained and instituted beautiful memorial in his Last Supper. For when he and his disciples ate together, he took bread, blessed it, and said, "Take, eat, this is my body which is given for you. Do this in remembrance of me." Likewise he took the cup and gave it to them to drink and said, "Take and drink. This is my blood which is shed for you for the forgiveness of sins. Do this in my memory." . . .

From this it follows and is seen clearly that the Supper is nothing other than a memorial of the suffering of Christ who offered his body for our sake and shed his crimson blood on the cross to wash away our sins. But up to the present we have turned this Supper into a bear's mass with mumbling and growling [i.e., words unintelligible to the laity]. . . . The person who practices the Supper of Christ in this way and contemplates the suffering of Christ in a firm faith will also give thanks to God for this grace and goodness. He will surrender himself to the will of Christ, which then is that we also should do to our neighbor as he has done to us and give our body, life, property, and blood for his sake. This is the will of Christ, and since this is once more impossible for us, we should call upon God diligently for grace and strength, so that he might give them to us to make us able to fulfill his will. For if he does not give us grace, we are already lost.

III. Reformation and Post-Reformation

C. Anabaptist

56. Menno Simons (1496–1561) | *The New Birth* & *The True Christian Faith*

Almost nothing is known of Menno Simons before his ordination in 1524 when he was twenty-eight, but he became the founder of the sixteenth-century reform movement known today as the Mennonites.

After his ordination as priest, Simons's tenure in the Church lasted just over a decade before joining the Anabaptists (1536). His decision was not, however, an impulse. Simons recounted that it was initially the Church's teaching about the Eucharist, specifically "transubstantiation," that caused him to struggle with the theology of the Roman Church. He also wrestled with himself about the sacrament of infant baptism, for he found no evidence of it in Scripture.

As Simons wrestled with his growing theological discomfort with Church teachings, many Anabaptists were being persecuted and killed (by Roman authorities and Reformers). One particularly bloody incident involved some people from his own parish, and it seems to have settled his mind about joining the Anabaptists. He wrote, "The blood of these people, although misled, fell so hot upon my heart that I could not stand it, nor find rest in my soul. . . . I saw that these zealous children, although in error, willingly gave their lives . . . for their doctrine and their faith. . . . Pondering these things my conscience tormented me so that I could no longer endure it."[1] After joining a group of Anabaptists who opposed violence and taught pacifism, Simons began traveling throughout the Netherlands and Germany under constant threat of death. The Emperor Charles V even put a price on his head, though he was never caught.

Pacifism is a well-known feature of the tradition founded by Menno Simons. A less well-known facet of his portrait of Christian life is seen in the first selection, *The New Birth*. Simons speaks of *penitence* as a defining mark of Christian existence,

---

1. Krahn and Dyck, "Menno Simons (1496–1561)," para 9.

a mark whose origin lies in the incarnate person of Christ. "For Simons," Sjouke Voolstra explains,

> incarnation is the residence of Christ in the hearts of believers and the transformation of individuals who were not obedient to God into a people subject to God in obedience. The divine presence should not be sought in the host (as in Roman Catholic doctrine), nor in the written symbols of Scripture or the impenetrable heavenly spheres to which these letters refer (as in Erasmus), but rather in the congregation of true penitents. The sanctified life of this congregation constitutes living and visible proof of the real presence of Christ. Grace which fails to bring about moral improvement is no grace . . . Only the belief in Christ's freedom from sin can produce believers who aspire to freedom from sin."[2]

In the second selection, *The True Christian Faith*, Simons accentuates the cost of following Christ.

The New Birth (1537)

My dearly beloved reader, take heed to the Word of the Lord and learn to know the true God. I warn you faithfully to take it, if you please. He will not save you nor forgive your sins nor show you His mercy and grace except according to His Word; namely, if you repent and if you believe, if you are born of Him, if you do what He has commanded and walk as He walks. For if He could save an unrighteous carnal man without regeneration, faith, and repentance, then He did not teach us the truth. But He is the truth, and there is no falsehood in Him. Therefore, I tell you again that you cannot be reconciled by means of all the masses, matins, vespers, ceremonies, sacraments, councils, statutes, and commandments under the whole heavens, which the popes and their colleges have made from the beginning. For they are abominations and not reconciliations, I warn you. In vain, says Christ, do they honor me, teaching commandments of men. . . .

The first birth of man is out of the first and earthly Adam, and therefore its nature is earthly and Adam-like, that is, carnally minded, unbelieving, disobedient, and blind to divine things; deaf and foolish; whose end, if not renewed by the Word, will be damnation and eternal death. If now you desire to have your wicked nature cleared up, and desire to be free from eternal death and damnation so that you may obtain with all true Christians that which is promised them, then you must be born again. For the regenerate are in grace and have the promise as you have heard.

---

2. Voolstra, *Menno Simons*, 66.

The regenerate, therefore, lead a penitent and new life, for they are renewed in Christ and have received a new heart and spirit. Once they were earthly-minded, now heavenly; once they were carnal, now spiritual; once they were unrighteous, now righteous; once they were evil, now good, and they live no longer after the old corrupted nature of the first earthly Adam, but after the new upright nature of the new and heavenly Adam, Christ Jesus, even as Paul says: Nevertheless, I live; yet not I, but Christ liveth in me. Their poor, weak life they daily renew more and more, and that after the image of Him who created them. Their minds are like the mind of Christ, they gladly walk as He walked; they crucify and take their flesh with all its evil lusts. . . .

These regenerated people have a spiritual king over them who rules them by the unbroken sceptre of His mouth, namely, with His Holy Spirit and Word. He clothes them with the garment of righteousness, of pure white silk. He refreshes them with the living water of His Holy Spirit and feeds them with the Bread of Life. His name is Christ Jesus.

They are the children of peace who have beaten their swords into plowshares and their spears into pruning hooks, and know war no more. They give to Caesar the things that are Caesar's and to God the things that are God's.

Their sword is the sword of the Spirit, which they wield in a good conscience through the Holy Ghost.

Their marriage is that of one man and one woman, according to God's own ordinance.

Their kingdom is the kingdom of grace, here in hope and after this in eternal life.

Their citizenship is in heaven, and they use the lower creations such as eating, drinking, clothing, and shelter, with thanksgiving and to the necessary support of their own lives, and to the free service of their neighbor, according to the Word of the Lord.

Their doctrine is the unadulterated Word of God, testified through Moses and the prophets, through Christ and the apostles, upon which they build their faith, which saves our souls. Everything that is contrary thereto, they consider accursed.

Their baptism they administer to the believing according to the commandment of the Lord, in the doctrines and usages of the apostles.

Their Lord's Supper they celebrate as a memorial of the favors and death of their Lord, and an incitement to brotherly love.

Their ban or excommunication descends on all the proud scorners—great and small, rich and poor, without any respect of persons, who once passed under the Word but have now fallen back, those living or teaching offensively in the house of the Lord—until they repent.

They daily sigh and lament over their poor, unsatisfactory evil flesh, over the manifest errors and faults of their weak lives. Their inward and outward war is without ceasing. Their sighing and calling is to the most High. Their fight and struggle is against the devil, world, and flesh all their days, pressing in toward the prize of the high calling that they may obtain it. So they prove by their actions that they believe the Word of the Lord, that they know and possess Christ in power, that they are born of God and have Him as their Father.

The True Christian Faith (1556)

Yes, good reader, the genuine Christian faith required by the Scriptures is so active, effective, and powerful in all those who have rightly grasped it through the grace of the Lord, that they do not fear to forsake father, mother, wife, children, money, and possessions for the Word and testimony of the Lord, to suffer all manner of scorn and disgrace, hardship and prison, distress and anguish, burned at the stake, as may be seen daily in the pious children and faithful witnesses of Jesus, especially in these our Netherlands.

Ah, how many have I known, and know many still at this moment, both men and women, servants and maids (would to God they be increased to the praise and salvation of all to many hundred thousands), who from the inmost of their souls seek Christ and his Word. In all meekness albeit, sincere and holy in doctrine, full of the fear and love of God, ready to help others, merciful, compassionate, meek, sober, chaste, not refractory nor seditious, but quiet and peaceable, obedient to the magistracy in all things not contrary to God. They have, nevertheless, for a number of years not slept in their own beds, and do not now; for they are so much hated by the world that they have been persecuted, betrayed, arrested, exiled, and slain like highwaymen, thieves, and murderers, and that without mercy. And it is for no other reason than that they out of true fear of God do not dare to take part in the abominable, carnal life and the accursed, disgraceful idolatry of this blind world. They neither hear nor acknowledge the unchaste, drunken, harloting priests, and deceiving blind preachers as true apostles and teachers sent from God, nor dare to receive the idolatrous bread with the avaricious, envious, proud, drunkards, harlots, and scamps from their hands. They do not carry their children to the anti-Christian bath and baptism. But they seek such preachers and teachers, also such a baptism, Supper, church, and life, as are in accordance with the Scriptures, and as many stand according to the Word of the Lord.

Behold, before God, it is the truth that I write. Indeed they are such a people, if I know them rightly, who, hypocrites excepted, weep more than they laugh, mourn more than they rejoice after the flesh; who would rather give than receive, and who are ready not only to sacrifice possessions and their all, but also life and death and body for the praise of the Lord, and to the necessary service of their neighbors, according to the command of the Scripture, as much as in them is. No matter how much the poor children are tormented they are still so much strengthened in God that they can neither be moved nor affrighted. They possess their souls with patience, waiting for the joy which is promised. Christ says truly, Ye will be hated of all men for my name's sake, Matt 24:9. . . .

Since then faith so firmly acknowledges that God cannot break His promise, but must keep it, seeing He is the truth and cannot lie, therefore does it make His children free, joyful, and glad in spirit, even if they are confined in prisons and bonds, and if they have to suffer by water and fire, in chains, and at the stake. For they are assured in the Spirit, through faith, that God will not withdraw His promise, but will fulfill it in His own time. For they believe in Christ in whom the promises are sealed, and through Him also acknowledge His grace, Word, and will, notwithstanding that they in former times walked so wickedly and carnally.

III. Reformation and Post-Reformation

C. Anabaptist

57. Anna Jansz (ca. 1509–1539) | *Martyr's Song*

Religious persecution is a *defining* feature in the development of the Anabaptist tradition. Their vision of the Christian life is unalterably refracted through their experience of religious persecution. The hymn of Anna Jansz is a beautiful example of this "martyr piety."

Anabaptists made theological sense of their persecution in various ways, not unlike how Christians in the first centuries interpreted Roman persecution. Some interpreted persecution as verification of their righteousness. Jesus said, "Blessed are you when people insult you, persecute you and falsely say all kinds of evil against you because of me" (Matt 5:11), and this prediction validated suffering for many Anabaptists. It was a sign of their faithfulness to the truth. Others saw religious persecution as a sign of Christ's imminent return, confirmation that Christ's Second Advent was nearly on their doorstep (Matt 24; Mark 13; Luke 21). Jesus said, "They will lay hands on you and persecute you . . . By standing firm you will gain life" (Luke 21:12, 17). Many sixteenth-century Anabaptists read their suffering through these words, and it bolstered their commitment to remain faithful to Christ even to death.

Jansz's initial association with Anabaptism appears to be colored by the end-times fervor around with the city of Münster in 1534 to 1535 (though she lived in Holland). Anabaptists had taken control of the city in order to form a New Jerusalem in preparation for Christ's imminent return. When a leader of the Münsterites visited Holland to proclaim the imminent return of Christ, Anna and her husband were baptized (1534). That leader, Maynaart von Emden, was forcibly driven from the city, and the Münster revolution devolved into infighting, betrayal, and awful bloodshed. Anna renounced the violent political ideals of the Münsterites, favoring instead a pacifist and more spiritually oriented vision of Anabaptism that was growing in her native Holland.

Eventually Anna's commitment to Anabaptism was discovered, and she was sentenced to death by drowning on January 23, 1539. The selection here is called "Martyr's Song," a letter to her infant son Isaiah, written from prison. Anna draws similarities between herself and martyrs from previous ages, finding timeless connection to the apostles and prophets: "Behold, I go today the way of the prophets, apostles and martyrs, and drink of the cup of which they all have drank." The way of martyrdom is the way of Christ himself—*he establishes the pattern for Christian life.* Anna wanted her son to interpret her death according to the example of Christ. To imitate Christ's path to the cross, quite literally to her death, was to follow his calling: "He calls His sheep, and His sheep hear his voice, and follow Him wherever he goes; for this is the way of the true fountain."

Martyr's Song (Ausbund, the 18th Hymn)(1539)

... 3. I am going on the path of the prophets,
The martyrs' and apostles' way;
There is none better.
They all have drunk from the cup,
Even as did Christ himself,
As I have heard it read.
4. All the priests of the King
Traveled on this path alone.
From the beginning they came
To stand upon this road,
As God's true sons and children.
This I have truly understood.
5. These same children under the altar,
Who are a great multitude,
Are described in the Apocalypse:
How they were killed and murdered
And executed with the sword,
Persecuted and banished.
6. They cried out to God: O Lord!
Righteous and Truthful One,
How long until you bring order to the earth

Among people everywhere?
And take revenge on only those
Who with great insolence
7. Have shed blood everywhere,
Murdering innocent people?
Are you willing to punish them
So they no longer cause dishonor,
Driving your own out of the land,
Continuing in their sin?
8. God gives to all [His children] a white robe,
And consoles them with the answer:
To them must still be added
Those who will also be judged
Until the last number of the pious
Is filled and completed.
9. The twenty-four great elders
Come before God's throne
And lay down their crowns,
Honoring the Lamb of God,
Together with all the heavenly hosts
Who live under the sun.
10. All of the pious children of God
Who received the baptism
Sealed upon the their brow
Also came this way,
Following the Lamb wherever it went,
Serving [the Lamb] with desire.
11. Such people must enter this valley,
And all drink from the bitter cup
Until the number is fulfilled.
Zion, the worthy bride of God,
To whom the Lamb itself is betrothed,
Who has calmed the wrath of God.
12. Therefore my dearly beloved son,[1]
May you wish to do my will,

---

1. The hymn is addressed to Anna's son, Isaiah. Stanza 2: "Isaiah hear my testament, My last will before my death / Now comes from my mouth").

And follow my teaching.

If you know a people who spurn every luxury

And pleasure of this world,

May you wish to join them.

13. They are despised and rejected

By this wretched world.

They must carry Christ's cross,

And have no secure place

Because they keep God's word.

They often are hunted down.

14. God lives with such people,

Who are mocked by the world.

Keep company with them.

They will show you the true way,

Lead you away from the path of evil,

Guide you away from hell.

15. Fear no one; set your life

Completely on the pure teaching.

Set aside your body and earthly goods.

Christ bought you at a dear price,

Delivered you from the eternal fire

With his worthy blood.

16. May the Lord sanctify you, my son,

Sanctify your conduct.

May you live in the fear of God

Wherever you are in this entire land.

In all the work you may do,

Do not resist God.

17. Share your bread with the hungry,

Leave no person in need

Who professes Christ.

Also clothe the naked,

Have pity on the sick.

Do not distance yourself from them.

18. If you cannot always be with them,

Show your good will.

Comfort the imprisoned,
Welcome guests cheerfully into your home,
And don't let anyone drive them out.
Then your reward will be greatest.
19. Both your hands should be ready
To do the works of mercy,
To give twofold offerings;
This is spiritual and worldly work:
To set the prisoners free, strengthen the weak;
Then you will truly live.
20. For the rest of what God gives you
You will be taught by the sweat of your brow
By God and the prophets,
To give always to God's people.
May they be happy with you;
Give to them what they ask of you.
21. Do not let falseness come from you,
Then you may have good hope.
God also will reward you
In His Kingdom in the other world.
He will bestow it twofold;
There should be no doubt of this.
22. On the one thousand five hundredth
And thirty-first year
Annelein paid with her life,
Which in virtue soft and mild
Was for Christians a beautiful model,
Given in death as well as in life.
Laus Deo

III. Reformation and Post-Reformation

C. Anabaptist

58. Pilgram Marpeck (d. 1556) | *Five Fruits of Repentance*

Born in Germany during the last decade of the fifteenth century, Pilgram Marbeck shaped early Anabaptist thought by retrieving earlier traditions to offer a mediating position between extremes.[1] On one extreme of early Anabaptism, a group known as the "Spiritualists" focused entirely on the inward realties of Christian life (inner attitudes and feelings). All external ceremonies of the faith were meaningless for Christian life. It was an attractive position for Anabaptists being persecuted over their practices of baptism and the Eucharist. "After all, if true baptism is spiritual and inner, perhaps it wasn't worth losing one's life over an outer ceremony."[2] On the other extreme a group known as the Hutterites were highly legalistic, emphasizing coercive practices to compel Christian holiness.

Marpeck offers a vision of the Christian life that emphasizes both the grace of God which brings about love and freedom, and the pursuit of holiness. "Christ erases the handwriting of the devil," Marpeck writes, "in so that it is no longer the law that reigns, but grace and freedom in Jesus Christ, according to the nature of the true love of God and neighbor. This love in God is the real freedom."[3] Seen here is the often debated relation between law and gospel which was a central issue throughout the entire Reformation era. Marpeck tries to account for both the inner and outer realities of Christian existence: love of God (inner) expressed as love of neighbor (outer).

Marpeck's effort to represent the inner and outer dimensions of Christian life is found in this selection, *Five Fruits of Repentance*. He presents sorrow over sin as a sign of genuine repentance (inner reality) which should produce *visible effects*, or "fruits" (outer reality). Marpeck refracts the very long tradition of Christian penance into

---

1. Southall, "Pilgrim Marpeck: An Ecumenical Anabaptist?," para 14.
2. Ibid., para 9.
3. Marpeck, *The Writings of Pilgram Marpeck*, 315.

a Reformation register. Like other Protestant Reformers, he rejects the sacramental, grace-mediating character of penance while retaining the *role* of sorrow for sin within Christian life. As Marpeck presents it, sorrow for sin drives the Christian *inward*—"ashamed and completely battered and broken in his own eyes"—but also *onto* the grace of God in Christ which leads to love-inspired obedience.[4]

In the selection, note how the direction of Marpeck's writing constantly shifts between his readers and God. Like St. Augustine or Catherine of Siena, Marpeck's theology is wound together with prayer.

Five Fruits of Repentance (1550)

The grace of our Lord Jesus Christ and His compassion be with you and all who are poor in spirit. Amen.

We have reason to thank God our heavenly Father when someone grieves because of his sins, when there are men who come to true repentance through grace, and appear before Christ, the throne of grace, with remorse and regret, confess their sins to Him, recognizing them, through the law of grace, by which they receive grace and more grace....

I write this to you so that we may take careful note of the witness within our hearts so that when we sin we may perform and complete the true fruit of repentance, in order that the wrath of God and the curse of Christ may not come over us to our destruction, as they will certainly come upon all the enemies of God so that the last evil is worse than the first (Luke 11:26).[5]

The First Fruit of True Repentance

This is the first fruit: that the sinner confesses himself guilty of eternal death under the stern, serious righteousness and wrathful vengeance of God; that he becomes ashamed and completely battered and broken in his own eyes, and with fear and trembling appears before the face of God helpless, without comfort, and completely forsaken of all creatures in heaven and on earth; that he has and knows, seeks and recognizes no help in himself or in anything else. He recognizes only his sin and guilt which condemns him with the devil and his followers to hell.... Yes, prior to all other fruit a true penitent must taste what he himself (through the deceit of sin) has done and sown....

---

4. What we find in Marpeck is akin to what Ralph Del Colle terms "evangelical repentance." Evangelical repentance is "sorrow for sin (including the resolution to not continue sinning) [that] presupposes the theological virtue of faith, which is itself a gift of grace" ("Penance," 379).

5. Marpeck goes on to quote from Ps 68, Matt 22:22; Luke 14:16ff; Ps 109:7.

Whoever does not find Christ in this depth (that is, in this true baptism for the remission of sin) will not find Him in the height and joy of glory eternally. For He who descended is the one who has ascended (Eph 4, 10). Whoever desires to eat this paschal Lamb must eat bitter herbs with it (Exod 12 [8]). Nevertheless, it still depends on God's free grace, even when man has tried the innocent bitterness, whether or not He will grant him to partake of the Lamb of God which takes away the sin of the world. Even if we drink the cup of the suffering of guilt, we are not for that reason given the kingdom of God.

We are not to boast of suffering but of grace, since all suffering proceeds from sin and guilt. . . . Whoever therefore would contemplate the goodness of God must first contemplate the severity of sin (Rom 11:22). Thus far briefly concerning the first fruit of repentance.

The Second Fruit of Repentance

The second fruit is that God allows a small light of the hope of His grace to shine along with His condemnation in order that the sinner may anticipate that grace with patience and become aware that he cannot rob God of His grace or seize it. In the meantime he regards the divine hesitation and withholding of grace of the comfort and peace in the Holy Spirit as his blessedness, until the light—the day of grace at the pool of the water of grace—appears in brightness and [the water] be moved for the hope of recovery—or else until Christ, in such hope and patience, finds him in the Portico of Solomon after thirty-eight years of illness in order to take pity on him. Then He bids him rise, takes the agony of sin, the anxiety and distress of conscience, as well as sin itself away, and freely gives him peace and joy in the Holy Spirit. Oh, God, how utterly impatient we are to await your comfort! We like to assume that You would prostrate Yourself at our feet with Your comfort and mercy, and that all we need to do is to confess our sin and devise a sorry and fictitious remorse, in order to be received into the fellowship of Christ, and then the whole matter is made right. Whoever thinks thus will go far off the mark, and be a victim of self-deceit.

The Third Fruit of Repentance

The third fruit of repentance is that the sinner is more in sorrow about what he has done against God than about what he must suffer in consequence. Thus he desires from God (in the hope of His grace) that he not be delivered from cross and suffering until God's will has been satisfied in him and until (like the evildoer on the cross) he desires to be remembered by God. For the thief on the cross had no thought of being delivered from his cross of death. Rather it was the unrepentant evildoer on the left (whom the other admonished for not fearing God, while he committed his own guilt to the care of the innocence of Christ) who said: "If you are the Son of God deliver us and yourself from the cross" (Luke 23:39f.). Thus the viperish penitents still do today who are only sorry that they must suffer because of sin but have no sorrow for the sin itself which is the cause of their suffering. True penitents, however, do not desire to be rid of their deserved suffering but of the sin. . . .

The Fourth Fruit of Repentance

Although sin is lodged within us (according to the first Adamic birth of the flesh), a true penitent does not allow it to rule since he is still suffering on the cross with the innocence of Christ because of sin. For what evildoer still desires or does the evil deed when he is imprisoned and suffers tortures because of his evil deed, unless indeed he be in blasphemous despair? Even less do these sinners allow sin to rule because they are true prisoners of God and suffer agony of conscience because of sin and still have no certain comfort, but merely hope to be rid of sin. It would needs be a monstrous wickedness and impertinence against God to commit sin while one repents, is captive to conscience, and has hope for deliverance. For this reason a true penitent does not allow sin to rule, but along with his repentance, insofar as it is true persevering repentance, accepts the commands of Christ, that he should no longer commit sin, lest the latter evil be worse than the first (Luke 11 [24–26]). . . . Without this all repentance is in vain and the Son of God is crucified and trodden under foot (Heb 6:6; 10:26).

The Fifth Fruit of Repentance

The fifth fruit is that I do not blame any creature in heaven or on earth for my sin or point to it as the cause of my sin, somewhat as follows: If this or that had not been so, I would have been pious enough not to have done it. For original wickedness has its source only in itself. It takes its beginning in and through itself as though it were eternal as a lying false god who himself creates an eternity out of identical, true divine honors; a thief and a murderer, who robs the true God of all honor, and murders those who yield all honor to the true God. . . . Whoever therefore points to any creature in heaven and on earth as the cause of his sin, deceptiveness, and wickedness in order to excuse himself, he accuses his own God, Creator and Maker of all creatures, even though these creatures have been created for all good.

That is the same as blaspheming God, and as though I said: if it were not for God I would not have sinned. . . . "Lord, I, I, I myself am the transgressor. Therefore, my God, do not accuse or punish any other work of your hands because of my sins." All the guilt with its torment and penalty comes justly upon me, me, me. For I have constantly followed that monarch, namely the god of all wickedness and given consent to him by my own impertinence. For You are always my God, Lord, and Deliverer. You have reconquered the power and capability to withstand all wickedness for me and all men, and freely bestowed and given it to us. But I have again wantonly surrendered this power, this judgment, and this righteousness which you achieved, and with which you have judged, fettered, and overcome the rulers of this world; of my own free will I returned to the enemy of my salvation, and have permitted him to rule over my salvation, and have permitted him to rule over me with his wickedness and perversity.... Carelessly I slept until the enemy, thief, and murderer dug into my house, and through deceit of sin sowed weeds in my heart, so that the fall of my house was very great (Matt 24:43; 13:25). Nor will it be built up again, and my heart and soul will not recover. But then, Lord Jesus Christ, You stand surety for the fall and the breach. This I hope for from Your mercy and grace, that you will again save and deliver me from the hand of my enemy, rebuild my house, root out once again the weeds of sin, that You will have compassion on my distress and great poverty, and be merciful to me a poor sinner....

God our heavenly Father grant us grace, and the Lord Jesus Christ, that we be truly humble before the great majesty and goodness of our Father and that we present and reveal ourselves and confess honestly and truly without any falseness of spirit.... Without this eternal regret, pain, and agony of conscious remain together with eternal torment and wherever man forsakes the right and the good and again commits the lie, sin, wickedness together with all unrighteousness remain.

Receive this admonition and reminder therefore together with other Holy Scripture, which directs us, not against the discipline and obedience of the Word of truth, but leads us into it and shows us what serves the praise of God and the salvation of our souls....

The grace of our Lord Jesus Christ be your comfort and that of all of us. In Him we can rejoice in the truth with you, and be comforted and brought joy in our sorrows. Amen.

III. Reformation and Post-Reformation

D. Catholic

59. Juan de Valdes (1509–1541) | *The Christian Alphabet*

Juan de Valdes is a significant voice in the Italian Reformation of the sixteenth century. While still a young man, employed by a Spanish nobleman, Valdes met the Franciscan Reformer, Pedro Ruiz de Alcaraz, who was serving as the nobleman's lay-chaplain. Alcaraz was later imprisoned by the Spanish Inquisition for his involvement with the *alumbrado* movement (a form of mystical Christianity). Living in close proximity, it appears Alcaraz had a long-lasting influence on Valdes. Through Alcaraz, Valdes was introduced to Erasmus, the *alumbrado* emphasis on mystical perception, the Bible, and the writings of Martin Luther and other early Reformers.

The next season of Valdes's life was filled with persecution, powerful spiritual experiences, and growing clarity about the need for church reform. Valdes's association with Alcaraz raised the suspicions of Spanish Inquisitors. He was not convicted, and afterward fled Spain to settle in Italy. Soon after he published his first work, *Dialogue on Christian Doctrine* (1529), which was controversial enough for the Inquisition to ban. By 1531 Valdes feared for his safety, fleeing to Rome and later Naples. There are hints of Valdes's sympathies with Reformation teachings in *Dialogue*, but it was not until his time in Naples that Valdes moved confidently into the public eye as a voice for reform.

Valdes sought reform but it is difficult to classify him as either Protestant or Catholic, though many after his death viewed his work as Protestant. Sometime between 1535 and 1536 Valdes had a profound religious experience and began meeting with a group of like-minded people in Naples, later known as the "Valdesian Circle." He wrote several commentaries on Scripture and, in the company of his discussion partners, he composed *The Spiritual Alphabet*. In this piece the difficulty of classifying Valdes is on display. On one hand, with the Reformers, the doctrine of justification by faith is central. But on the other hand, following the *alumbrado* movement and in contrast to the Reformers, Valdes refused to ground the knowledge of the truth of

Christianity in either Scripture or religious authority. Christianity's truth is known through "inner illumination of the Spirit."[1] Valdes also fits uncomfortably with the Catholic thought of his day. In *Spiritual Alphabet* he avoids the main features of Catholic spirituality that one would expect from a thinker promoting the medieval Christian vision: church hierarchy, priesthood, ceremonies other than the Lord's Supper and Baptism, and devotion to the Virgin or the saints. Though his thought sat at odds with the dominant Catholic theology of his day, Valdes was a voice for reform from *within* the Church.

Our selection is from Valdes's *The Christian Alphabet*. Valdes composed it as a dialogue with his close friend, the widow Giulia Gonzaga. In the text, "V" is Valdes, and "G" is Gonzaga. Composed this way, the text comes to us—hundreds of years later—as practical, spiritual direction in the form of letters. Valdes counsels Gonzaga to pursue Christian perfection, which he likens to leaping into a rushing river with one's eyes fixed on the crucified and risen Christ. Do not fear the river, and do not "set your eyes upon the things of the world," but instead "enamor yourself with Christ, regulating all your works, all your words, all your thoughts by that divine command" to love God and neighbor with all your heart, mind, and strength. Though Gonzaga is concerned that she cannot attain Christian perfection, because she is not a nun, Valdes counsels her otherwise: "Christian perfection consists in loving God above all things and neighbor as yourself."

The Christian Alphabet (c. 1535)

V. [T]ell me whether you have ever crossed any stream by a ford.

G. Yes, I have, many times....

V. And have you seen how by keeping always for your object the view of the land that lies on the other side, you have not felt the swimming of the head, and so have suffered no danger of drowning?

G. I have noticed this too.

V. Then, if you, *signora*, wish to cross the running flood of things of this world, do so in the same manner. Look not upon them with your affections, so that such danger may not happen to you as befalls them who, gazing on the stream, fall into it and are drowned. And endeavor to keep the view of your soul fixed and nailed with Christ, on the cross. And if at any time through want of care, you set your eyes upon the things of the world, in such a manner that you feel your heart incline to them, turn back upon yourself, and return to fix your view upon Christ crucified, and in this way your

---

1. Firpo, *Juan de Valdes and the Italian Reformation*, 40.

course will go on well. And, therefore, I wish you, *signora*, to take above all things, for your principal purpose, to enamor yourself with Christ, regulating all your works, all your words, all your thoughts by that divine command which says: "Thou shalt love the Lord thy God with all thy heart, with all thy mind, and with all thy strength, and thy neighbor as thyself" (Mark, 12:30–31). And I say, hold fast this command as your principal rule, for Christian perfection consists in loving God above all things and your neighbor as yourself.

Christian Perfection

G: I marvel at what you say, because I have all my life been told that friars and nuns are in the rule of perfection by the vows that they make, if they observe them.

V: Let them say so, *signora*, and give credit to me that, whether friars or nonfriars, they possess so much of Christian perfection as they have of faith and love of God, and not a grain more.

G: It would much please me if you could enable me to understand this.

Self-love and Love of God

V: I will do it very willingly. You must know, *signora*, that the human heart is naturally inclined to love; in such a way, it must either love God and all things for God, or it must love itself and all things for itself. That which loves itself does all things for itself. I mean to say that it is so far moved to them as its own self-interest invites it, and thus if it love anything beyond itself, it loves it for itself and for its own interest, and if it have any love toward God, it has it for its own interest and in no other respect. Such a one, friar or nonfriar, because he has his affection in a state of disorder, having placed it in himself, never knows how, or in what manner, he ought to love created things. Rather when he desires to dispose himself to love God, because he does not conceive how to go out of himself, he never discovers the way, and therefore goes continually wandering in mere appearances, and thus being always confused and variable in his affections, bad or good, he lives far away from the life of Christian perfection; and so much the more will he live farther from it as the more he becomes enamored of himself, although he may be very perfect in outward observances; because God requires the heart.

He who loves God performs everything he does for him. I would say that he is moved to this by the love he bears to God, and this he does with as much warmth and earnestness as the degree of affection moves or incites him. And thus if he love anything besides God, he loves it for the sake of God, and because God wills it so, and he likewise loves himself, because he knows that God wills that he be loved. Such a one, friar or nonfriar, because he has his love ordered in God, takes hence the mode and manner how he should love all created things and is most regulated and ordered in his love, and loves nothing inordinately. And now his good works please and are grateful before God, because he is moved to work by the impulse of love, because as God is love, so no work is grateful to him that is not done by love. Agreeable to this is what Saint Augustine says: "Good works follow them who are already justified, and do not go before in him who has to be justified." I mean to say that works are good when done by a person already justified, and none can be justified unless he stand in love and charity with God and his neighbor. In such a manner a person will be more perfect, the more he continues fervent in this love: You can confirm this truth yourself by considering how you estimate what a person does in your affairs when you know that he is not moved to do it by the affection he bears toward you, but by some other design of his own. But since you wish one not born under the obligation to love you, to serve you for love, as all of us are born to love God, think whether God would at least require from us the same that you wish; how much more from those persons who are regenerate and born again in Christ, by the new, spiritual regeneration through faith and baptism; because such of us have a fresh obligation to love God. Speak I of one obligation? Rather should I say infinite obligations, since we see that he loved us infinitely, and Christ loves us, and by infinite modes and ways he sought, and still seeks to bring us to himself and to unite us with himself through grace and love. Reflecting on this, I am sure you will make yourself capable of this truth, that Christian perfection consists in loving God, and that each one will be so much more perfect as he shall so much the more love God, whether he make monastic vows, or whether he make them not, provided only that he keep the vow that he made in baptism by which we are Christians.

G: I rest satisfied now with what you have said of perfection, in such a degree that I already know from your argument what I had not known until now. And since you wish me to take for my chief purpose the love of God and of my neighbor in order to become a perfect Christian, and I determine to do so, it will be well, if you please, to mention some rules by which I may know and understand what it is I ought to do, and how I must conduct myself not to swerve from the love of God and of my neighbor; because I wish absolutely to give myself up to be enamored with God, so much so as may deprive of God's favor, not only you, but a hundred others like you.

V. Be deprived of favor! No! Learn rather, *signora*, that in this divine love then: is no jealousy because it is communicable from itself. And it is thus, that so much the more you love God, so much more you will rejoice that God loves others of us, and that God should be loved by others of us. But leaving this, until you learn it in time by experience, I say, *signora*, that there are no better rules for this that you ask than those God has given to us in his most perfect law, which we understand not like the Jews, but as Christians, in the form and manner in which Christ declared it. It teaches us what we ought to do in order not to swerve from the love of God and of our neighbor.

III. Reformation and Post-Reformation

D. Catholic

60. Teresa of Ávila (1515–1582) | *The Book of Her Life*

Teresa de Cepeda y Ahumada was the granddaughter of a marrano, a Jewish convert. Only with his son, her father, Alonso, was integration with the new Christian polity achieved. The recently reunited Spain was colonizing the Americas (her brother was once Mayor of Quito): it was an age of strong class distinctions and economic depression affecting the poor; early Modernity, the Protestant Revolt in the north, the Council of Trent, the new order of the Jesuits, the spirit of the "Counter Reformation."

After her mother Beatrice died when Teresa was fourteen years of age, she was sent to be educated by the Augustinian nuns. Deliberately tearing herself away from the temptations of worldliness she entered the Carmelite Monastery of the Incarnation in 1535. Acutely intelligent, spirited, and forthright, she began a spiritual and intellectual quest in adverse circumstances, especially for a woman. Life in the Incarnation was slack, even chaotic, the Spanish Church had lost its medieval moorings and a living liturgical sensibility. Amid many struggles she committed herself to interior ("mental") prayer, preoccupied with states of consciousness. She became an expert in discerning these inner movements. In 1555 the Jesuit (later general), Francis Borgia confirmed the genuineness of her spiritual path.

Once she had matured in prayer herself, her next call was do something about the spiritual malaise of her order, and perhaps to contribute something to the church in dire times. Thus began her astonishing career as institutor of a Carmelite Reform, and as foundress of some seventeen new houses of reformed ("discalced" = "unshod") monasteries. She also launched a reform of the male branch, beginning with the young John of the Cross as one of her first two friars.

Teresa began writing at the urging of her (mostly male) spiritual guides and clients. Even bishops sought her spiritual counsel, and one, in Seville, publicly knelt down and asked her blessing. Her magnum opus is *The Interior Castle*, in which she envisages progress in the Christian spiritual life under the image of a castle with seven mansions. First of all you have get out of the noxious swamp of mortal sins and gain admittance through the gate (baptism/penance), then by prayer and perseverance to press on through seven mansions to the luminous jewel in the center which is his majesty, Christ Jesus, and to participation in the life of the Trinity that he shares. It is noteworthy that once she had reached this seventh mansion herself, all the pyrotechnical phenomena (visions, levitations, ecstasies, and the like) for which she was notorious, faded away. She deemed them signs of immaturity.

Having long before been awarded a doctorate posthumously by the University of Salamanca, Teresa in 1970 became the first woman designated a Doctor of the Church.

In the following we begin with the most famous of her many poems, followed by passages from her *Life*, considered by some the greatest Christian autobiography after Augustine's *Confessions*. Here she details her early struggles to make the journey of deep prayer, her sources of reading, and those she sought for spiritual counsel. She brilliantly expounds the shifting patterns of human/divine "synergeia" in prayer through the analogy of watering a garden, from the hard labor of using a bucket, accessing grace in small doses, to the inundation of soaking rain, when grace is doing it all.

The Book of her Life (1554–1565)

Let nothing disturb you,
let nothing affright you.
All things are passing;
God never changes.
Patience obtains all things.
Whoever has God
wants for nothing:
God alone suffices. . . .

7.22. . . . There is so much sluggishness in matters having to do with the service of God, it is necessary that those who serve him become shields for one another, if they are to advance. . . . If some begin to give themselves to God, there are so many to criticize them that they need to seek companionship to defend themselves, until they are strong enough not to be burdened by this criticism. If they do not seek this companionship, they will find themselves in many difficulties.

It seems to me that this is why some saints used to go into the deserts. And it is a kind of humility not to trust in oneself, but to believe that through those with whom one converses, God will help and increase charity as it is shared. There are a thousand graces I would not dare speak of, unless I had the powerful experience of the benefit that comes from this sharing... For in falling I had many friends to help me, but in rising I found myself so alone I am amazed I did not remain forever fallen. I praise the great mercy of God, for it was He alone who gave me His hand. May he be blessed for ever and ever. Amen.

8.2. I voyaged on this tempestuous sea for almost twenty years with these fallings and risings and this evil—since I fell again—and in a life so short of perfection that I paid almost no heed to venial sins. As for mortal sins, though I feared them, I did not fear them as I should have, for I did not avoid the dangers. I would say it is one of the most painful lives, I think, for I neither enjoyed God nor found happiness in the world. When experiencing the enjoyments of the world, I felt sorrow when I recalled what I owed to God; when I was with God, my attachments to the world disturbed me. This is a war so vexatious I do not know how I was able to endure it for a month, let alone for many years.

However I see the great mercy the Lord bestowed upon me, for though I continued to associate with the world, I had the courage to practice prayer. I say courage, for I do not know what would require greater courage... than to betray the King and know that He knows it, and yet never leave His presence. Though we are always in the presence of God, it seems to me that it is different with those who practice prayer, for they are aware that He is looking at them...

4. I have recounted all this at length, as I already mentioned, so that the mercy of God and my ingratitude may be seen; also in order that one might understand the great good God does for a soul that willingly disposes itself for the practice of prayer, even though it is not as disposed as is necessary. I recount this also that one may understand how, if a soul perseveres in prayer in the midst of the sins, temptations and failures of a thousand kinds that the devil places in its path, in the end, I hold it as certain, that the Lord will draw it forth to the harbor of salvation, just as—it now appears—he did for me. May it please His Majesty that I do not get lost again.

5. The good that one who practices prayer obtains has been written about by many saints and holy persons; I mean mental prayer—glory be to God for this great good! If it were not for this good, even though I have little humility, I should not be so proud as to speak of mental prayer...

Whoever has not begun the practice of prayer, I beg for the love of God not to go without so great a good. There is nothing here to fear but only something to desire. Even if there has been no great progress, or much effort to reach such perfection as to deserve the favors and mercies God bestows on the more generous, at least a person will come to understand the way leading to heaven. And if one perseveres, I trust then in the mercy of God, who never fails to repay anyone who has taken Him for a friend. For mental prayer in my opinion is nothing else than an intimate sharing between friends; it means taking time frequently to be alone with Him who we know loves us. In order that love be true and friendship endure, the wills of the friends must be in accord. The Lord's will, as is already known, cannot be at fault; our will is vicious, sensual and ungrateful. If you do not yet love Him as He loves you, because you have not reached the degree of conformity with His will, you will endure this pain of spending a long time with One who is so different from you, when you see how much it benefits you to possess His friendship and how much He loves you.

6. O infinite goodness of my God, for it seems to me I see that such is the way You are and the way I am! O delight of the angels! When I see this, I desire to be completely consumed in loving you! How you certainly do suffer the one who suffers to be with You! O what a good friend You make, my Lord! How you proceed by favoring and enduring. You wait for others to adapt to Your nature, and in the meantime, You put up with theirs! You take into account, my Lord, the times when they love You, and in one instant of repentance, You forget their offenses. . . .

11.6. Beginners must realize that in order to give delight to the Lord they are beginning to cultivate a garden on very barren soil, full of abominable weeds. His Majesty pulls up the weeds and *sows good seed* (Matt 13:37). Now keep in mind that this is already done by the time a soul is determined to practice prayer and has begun to make use of it. With the help of God we must strive like good gardeners to get these plants to grow and take pains to water them so that they do not wither but come to bud and flower, and give forth a most pleasing fragrance to provide refreshment for this Lord of ours (cf. Song 4:16). Then He will often come to take delight in this garden and find His joy among these virtues.

7. But let us see how it must be watered, so that we may understand what we have to do, the labor it will cost us, whether the labor is greater than the gain, and how long it must last. It seems to me that the garden can be watered in four ways. You may draw from a well, which for us is a lot of work. Or you may get it by means of a water wheel and aqueducts in such a way that it is obtained by turning the crank of a water wheel. I have drawn it this way sometimes—the method involves less work than the other, and you get more water. Or it may flow from a river or stream. The garden is watered much better this way because the ground is more fully soaked, and there is no need to water it so frequently—and much less work for the gardener. Or the water may be provided by a great deal of rain. For the Lord waters the garden without any work on our part. This way is incomparably better than all the others mentioned.

8. Now then, these four ways of drawing water to maintain the garden . . . seem applicable to explaining the four degrees of prayer in which the Lord in his goodness has sometimes placed my soul. May it please His goodness that I manage to speak of them in a way beneficial to one of the persons who ordered me to write this, because within four months the Lord has brought him further than I reached in seventeen years. He has prepared himself better, and so without any labor of his own, the flower garden is watered by all these four waters, although the last is still not given except in drops. But he is advancing in such a way that soon he will be immersed in it with

the help of the Lord. And I shall be pleased if you laugh, should this way of way of explaining the matter appear foolish.[1]

---

1. Translated slightly revised.

III. Reformation and Post-Reformation

D. Catholic

61. St. John of the Cross (1542–1591) | *En una noche oscura, The Ascent of Mount Carmel, Sayings of Light and Love,* & *Prayer of a Soul Taken with Love*

In 1529 the nobleman Gonzalo de Yepes gave up his inheritance and rank to marry a poor girl, Catalina Alvarez, of devout and beautiful character. Gonzalo died early from the privations of poverty. The "nuptial mystery" lived so deeply and at such cost by this holy couple passed into the soul of their son, Juan (John), whose deepest intuitions about the Christian mystical life were attuned to the Song of Songs.

Having spent a few years of theological study at Salamanca, and thinking of going over to the Carthusians, John was persuaded by Madre Teresa de Jesus to became one of the first two friars of her Reform of the Carmelite Order. His imprisonment and harsh treatment in the early years of the Reform, which lent such force to his expositions of the "Night of the Soul" and the "Night of the Spirit," are well known. But relegation and suffering attended John afterwards too, keeping this soul of burning intensity largely ignored in his lifetime (except among the women of his Order). His doctrine of the Dark Nights has points of affinity with Eastern Christian apophaticism, textually most of all through Pseudo-Dionysius, whose oxymoron "bright darkness" John replays and then crafts his own, such as "silent music." He was designated "Mystical Doctor" by Pope Pius XI.

John began his writing on mystical themes in lyrical mode, and we begin here with one of his most famous poems. Asked by the nuns to expound his poetry, we read in sober prose of the austere cost of a commitment to true spiritual discipleship. In the final passage below he targets the follies of contemporary illuminism and the subjectivist tendencies of early modernity (I am justified by the strength of my own inner feelings). He even corrects, or at least complements, Teresa, suggesting that it does not matter so much to discern whether private revelations are from God, self, or the devil, since those that are from God are not to be seized upon and become an object of attachment. God is to be loved absolutely for his own sake, on his terms, not instrumentalized for our own agenda. Addiction to private revelations, cocooning ourselves in gratifying psychological experiences, stunts all possibility of spiritual progress.

En una noche oscura (Dark Night of the Soul) (c. 1577–1579)

Upon a gloomy night,
With all my cares to loving ardours flushed,
(O venture of delight!)
With nobody in sight
I went abroad when all my house was hushed.

In safety, in disguise,
In darkness up the secret stair I crept,
(O happy enterprise!)
Concealed from other eyes
When all my house at length in silence slept.

Upon that lucky night
In secrecy, inscrutable to sight,
I went without discerning
And with no other light
Except for that which in my heart was burning.

It lit and led me through
More certain than the noonday clear
To where One waited near
Whose presence well I knew,
There where no other presence might appear.

Oh night that was my guide!
Oh darkness dearer than the morning's pride,
Oh night that joined the lover
To the beloved bride
Transfiguring them each into the other.

Within my flowering breast
Which only for himself entire I save
He sank into his rest
And all my gifts I gave
Lulled by the airs with which the cedars wave.

Over the ramparts fanned
While the fresh wind was fluttering his tresses,
With his serenest hand
My neck he wounded, and
Suspended every sense with his caresses.

Lost to myself I strayed,
My face upon my lover having laid,
From all endeavor ceasing,
And all my cares releasing
Strew them among the lilies there to fade.

The Ascent of Mount Carmel (c. 1578–1579)

22.3. . . . The chief reason why in the Old Law the inquiries made of God were licit, and the prophets and priests appropriately desired visions and revelations from Him, was that at that time faith was not yet perfectly established, nor was the Gospel law inaugurated. It was necessary for them to question God, and that He respond, sometimes by words, sometimes through visions and revelations, now in figures and types, now through many other kinds of signs. All His answers, locutions and revelations concerned mysteries of faith, or matters touching upon or leading up to them. Since the truths of faith are not derived from man but from the mouth of God . . . it was required of them to seek an answer from the mouth of God (cf. Deut 8:3). He therefore reproved them because in their affairs they did not seek counsel from his mouth, that he might answer and direct them to the unknown and the as yet unfounded faith.

But now that the faith is established through Christ, and the Gospel law made manifest in this era of grace, there is no reason for inquiring of him in this way or expecting him to answer as before. In giving us his Son, his only Word (for he possesses no other), He spoke everything to us at once in this sole Word—and He has no more to say.

4. This is the meaning of that passage where St. Paul tries to persuade the Hebrews to turn from communion with God through the old ways of the Mosaic Law, and to fix their eyes instead upon Christ: *That which God formerly spoke to our fathers*

through the prophets in many ways and manners, now, finally in these days He has spoken to us all at once in His Son (Heb 1:1–2). The Apostle indicates that God is, as it were, mute, with no more to say, because what He spoke before to the prophets in parts, he has now spoken all at once by giving us the All, Who is His Son.

5. Any person questioning God or desiring some vision or revelation would not only be guilty of foolish behavior but also of offending him, by not fixing his eyes entirely upon Christ and by living with the desire for some other novelty.

God would respond as follows: If I have already told you all things in My Word, My Son, and if I have no other word, what answer or revelation can I now make that could surpass this? Fasten your eyes upon Him alone (cf. Ps 16:8, Matt 17:8), because in Him I have spoken and revealed all, and in Him you shall discover even more than you ask for and desire. You are making an appeal for visions and locutions that are incomplete, but if you turn your eyes to Him you will find them complete. For He is my entire locution and response, vision, and revelation, which I have already spoken, answered, manifested and revealed to you, by giving Him to you as a brother, companion, master, ransom, and reward. Since that day I descended upon Him with my Spirit on Mount Tabor, proclaiming: *This is my beloved Son in whom I am well pleased. Hear Him!* (Matt 17:5), I have relinquished these methods of answering and teaching, and presented them to Him. *Hear Him,* because I have no more faith to reveal or truths to manifest . . .

7. When Christ dying on the Cross exclaimed: *It is consummated* (John 19:30), He consummated not only these ways, but all the other ceremonies and rites of the Old Law. We must be guided humanly and visibly in all by the law of Christ the man and that of His Church and of His ministers. This is the method of remedying our spiritual ignorances and weaknesses; here we shall find abundant medicine for them all. Any departure from this road is not only curiosity, but extraordinary boldness. One should disbelieve anything coming in a supernatural way, and believe only the teaching of Christ, the man, as I say, and of His ministers who are men. So true is this that St. Paul insists: *If an angel from heaven should preach to you any gospel other than that which we men have preached, let him be anathema* (Gal 1:8) . . .

Sayings of Light and Love (likely composed after 1578)

It makes little difference whether a bird is tied by a thin thread or a cord. For even if tied by thread, the bird will be prevented from taking off just as surely as if tied by cord . . . True, the thread is easier to rend, but however easily this might be done, the bird will not fly free until this is first done (cf. Ps 123:7).

. . .

Reflect that the most delicate flower loses its fragrance and withers the quickest. Guard yourself therefore from seeking to walk in a spirit of delight, for you will not remain constant. Choose rather for yourself a robust spirit, detached from everything, and you will discover abundant peace and sweetness, for savory and durable fruit is garnered in a cold and dry climate.

. . .

God is more pleased by one work, however small, done secretly (cf. Matt 6:4), without desire that it be known, than by a thousand done with desire that others know of them. The person who works for God with purest love not only cares nothing whether others see him, but does not even seek that God should know of them. Such a person would not cease to render God the same services, with the same joy and purity of love, even if God were never to know of them.

Prayer of a Soul Taken with Love (c. after 1578)

But if you are not waiting for my works, what is it that makes You wait, my most clement Lord? Why do you delay? For if, after all, I am to receive the grace and mercy which I entreat of you in your Son, take my mite (cf. Mark 12:42), since you desire it, and grant me this blessing, since you also desire that.

Who can free himself from lowly manners and limitations, if You do not lift him to Yourself, my God, in purity of love? How shall a man begotten and nurtured in lowliness rise up to You, O Lord, if You do not raise him with your hand which made him?

You will not take from me, my God, what you once gave me in Your only Son, Jesus Christ, in Whom You gave me all that I desire. Hence I rejoice that if I *wait* for You, You *will not delay* (Hab 2:3).

Why procrastinate any longer, my soul, since from this very moment you can love God in your heart?

Mine are the heavens and mine is the earth. Mine are the nations; the just are mine, and mine the sinners. The angels of God are mine, and the Mother of God, and all things are mine; and God Himself is mine and for me, because Christ is mine and all for me.

What do you ask then, and what do you seek, my soul? Yours is all of this, and all is for you. Do not engage yourself in anything less, nor pay heed to the crumbs that fall from your Father's table. Go forth and exult in your Glory! Hide yourself in Him, and rejoice, and you will obtain the supplications of your heart.

III. Reformation and Post-Reformation

D. Catholic

62. St. Francis de Sales (1567–1622) | *Introduction to the Devout Life*

Francis de Sales was born to a wealthy, aristocratic family. He initially followed his father's footsteps, taking a degree in law, but abruptly changed direction after a course in theology. Thereafter he dedicated himself to the Church, and, after eventually persuading his father, was ordained in 1593.

For his first leadership post, the Church did not send him to a quiet backwoods but to the heart of the Reformation controversy in Geneva, Switzerland. Geneva was home to the Reformer John Calvin, and the influence of the Roman church in the area was rapidly waning. Francis was just twenty-seven years old when he began as the provost of Geneva, but he volunteered to travel the area evangelizing the Calvinists. He preached, wrote many letters, went door to door distributing pamphlets, and to anyone who would open their door Francis would engage in gentle conversation. Pamphlets were common during the Reformation era, but they were often highly polemical and could rarely be called "gentle." Francis, however, came to be known for a distinctly different approach, one majoring in patience, conversation, and civility.

Francis became bishop of Geneva in 1594, and he continuing his work of spiritual direction. In fact, *Introduction to the Devout Life* originated as a series of letters exchanged with his cousin, Marie de Charmoisy, who sought spiritual counsel for how she might pursue God *wholly* in the midst of court life. As John Ryan explains, "The direction of souls was always a principal activity in the life of St. Francis de Sales as a priest and bishop. He was ready at all times to spend himself in hearing confessions, giving personal instructions, preaching sermons, and writing letters, and it was out of such concern for the advancement and perfection of individual souls that the *Introduction* grew."[1]

---

1. Ryan, "Translator's Introduction," 3.

Francis's portrayal of the Christian life is noteworthy because the pursuit of God is open to all Christians, not only those committed to ecclesiastical service or monastic dedication. Medieval society functioned according to what Charles Taylor calls "hierarchical complementarity," which means that people saw their roles in Christendom in terms of mutual dependence and benefit.[2] The monk prays, for instance, but he prays *for*, or *in the place of*, all. Likewise the peasant labors *for all*, or the lord defends *for all*, etc. Francis, however, envisions that full devotion to God and the pursuit of piety isn't determined by one's earthly vocation. In the Preface to *Introduction* he writes,

> My object is to teach those who are living in towns, at court, in their own households, and whose calling obliges them to a social life, so far as externals are concerned . . . It is an error, or rather a heresy, to wish to banish the devout life from the regiment of soldiers, the mechanic's shop, the court of princes, or the home of married people. . . . Wherever we may be, we can and should aspire to the perfect life.

Introduction to the Devout Life (1609)

PART I. Counsels and Practices Suitable for the Soul's Guidance from the First Aspiration after a Devout Life to the Point when it attains a Confirmed Resolution to Follow the Same

Chapter I. What true Devotion is

You aim at a devout life, dear child, because as a Christian you know that such devotion is most acceptable to God's Divine Majesty. But seeing that the small errors people are wont to commit in the beginning of any under taking are apt to wax greater as they advance, and to become irreparable at last, it is most important that you should thoroughly understand wherein lies the grace of true devotion;—and that because while there undoubtedly is such a true devotion, there are also many spurious and idle semblances thereof; and unless you know which is real, you may mistake, and waste your energy in pursuing an empty, profitless shadow. Arelius was wont to paint all his pictures with the features and expression of the women he loved, and even so we all color devotion according to our own likings and dispositions. One man sets great value on fasting, and believes himself to be leading a very devout life, so long as he fasts rigorously, although the while his heart is full of bitterness;—and while he will not moisten his lips with wine, perhaps not even with water, in his great abstinence, he does not scruple to steep them in his neighbor's blood, through slander and detraction. Another man reckons himself as devout because he repeats many prayers daily, although at the same time he does

---

2. Taylor, *A Secular Age*, 45, 80–81.

not refrain from all manner of angry, irritating, conceited or insulting speeches among his family and neighbors. This man freely opens his purse in almsgiving, but closes his heart to all gentle and forgiving feelings towards those who are opposed to him; while that one is ready enough to forgive his enemies, but will never pay his rightful debts save under pressure. Meanwhile all these people are conventionally called religious, but nevertheless they are in no true sense really devout. When Saul's servants sought to take David, Michal induced them to suppose that the lifeless figure lying in his bed, and covered with his garments, was the man they sought; and in like manner many people dress up an exterior with the visible acts expressive of earnest devotion, and the world supposes them to be really devout and spiritual-minded, while all the time they are mere lay figures, mere phantasms of devotion.

But, in fact, all true and living devotion presupposes the love of God;—and indeed it is neither more nor less than a very real love of God, though not always of the same kind; for that Love one while shining on the soul we call grace, which makes us acceptable to His Divine Majesty;—when it strengthens us to do well, it is called Charity;—but when it attains its fullest perfection, in which it not only leads us to do well, but to act carefully, diligently, and promptly, then it is called Devotion. The ostrich never flies,—the hen rises with difficulty, and achieves but a brief and rare flight, but the eagle, the dove, and the swallow, are continually on the wing, and soar high;—even so sinners do not rise towards God, for all their movements are earthly and earthbound. Well-meaning people, who have not as yet attained a true devotion, attempt a manner of flight by means of their good actions, but rarely, slowly and heavily; while really devout men rise up to God frequently, and with a swift and soaring wing. In short, devotion is simply a spiritual activity and liveliness by means of which Divine Love works in us, and causes us to work briskly and lovingly; and just as charity leads us to a general practice of all God's Commandments, so devotion leads us to practice them readily and diligently. . . .

Chapter 2: *The Nature and Excellence of Devotion*

Those who sought to discourage the Israelites from going up to the Promised Land, told them that it was "a land which eats up the inhabitants thereof" [Num 13:32]; that is, that the climate was so unhealthy that the inhabitants could not live long, and that the people thereof were "men of a great stature," who looked upon the new-comers as mere locusts to be devoured. It is just so, my daughter, that the world runs down true devotion, painting devout people with gloomy, melancholy aspect, and affirming that religion makes them dismal and unpleasant. But even as Joshua and Caleb protested that not only was the Promised Land a fair and pleasant country, but that the Israelites would take an easy and peaceful possession thereof, so the Holy Spirit tells us through His Saints, and our Lord has told us with His Own Lips, that a devout life is very sweet, very happy and very loveable.

SECTION III. REFORMATION AND POST-REFORMATION

The world, looking on, sees that devout persons fast, watch and pray, endure injury patiently, minister to the sick and poor, restrain their temper, check and subdue their passions, deny themselves in all sensual indulgence, and do many other things which in themselves are hard and difficult. But the world sees nothing of that inward, heartfelt devotion which makes all these actions pleasant and easy. Watch a bee hovering over the mountain thyme;—the juices it gathers are bitter, but the bee turns them all to honey,—and so tells the worldling, that though the devout soul finds bitter herbs along its path of devotion, they are all turned to sweetness and pleasantness as it treads;—and the martyrs have counted fire, sword, and rack but as perfumed flowers by reason of their devotion. And if devotion can sweeten such cruel torments, and even death itself, how much more will it give a charm to ordinary good deeds? We sweeten unripe fruit with sugar, and it is useful in correcting the crudity even of that which is good. So devotion is the real spiritual sweetness which takes away all bitterness from mortifications; and prevents consolations from disagreeing with the soul: it cures the poor of sadness, and the rich of presumption; it keeps the oppressed from feeling desolate, and the prosperous from insolence; it averts sadness from the lonely, and dissipation from social life; it is as warmth in winter and refreshing dew in summer; it knows how to abound and how to suffer want; how to profit alike by honor and contempt; it accepts gladness and sadness with an even mind, and fills men's hearts with a wondrous sweetness.

Ponder Jacob's ladder:—it is a true picture of the devout life; the two poles which support the steps are types of prayer which seeks the love of God, and the Sacraments which confer that love; while the steps themselves are simply the degrees of love by which we go on from virtue to virtue, either descending by good deeds on behalf of our neighbor or ascending by contemplation to a loving union with God. Consider, too, who they are who trod this ladder; men with angels' hearts, or angels with human forms. They are not youthful, but they seem to be so by reason of their vigor and spiritual activity. They have wings wherewith to fly, and attain to God in holy prayer, but they have likewise feet wherewith to tread in human paths by a holy gracious intercourse with men; their faces are bright and beautiful, inasmuch as they accept all things gently and sweetly; their heads and limbs are uncovered, because their thoughts, affections and actions have no motive or object save that of pleasing God; the rest of their bodies is covered with a light shining garment, because while they use the world and the things of this life, they use all such purely and honestly, and no further than is needful for their condition—such are the truly devout. Believe me, dear child, devotion is the sweetest of sweets, the queen of virtues, the perfection of love. If love is the milk of life, devotion is the cream thereof; if it is a fruitful plant, devotion is the blossom; if it is a precious stone, devotion is its brightness; if it is a precious balm, devotion is its perfume, even that sweet odor which delights men and causes the angels to rejoice.[3]

---

3. Translation amended at points by Kent Eilers, based on John K. Ryan, *Introduction to the Devout Life*.

III. Reformation and Post-Reformation

E. Anglican

63. Thomas Cranmer (1489–1556) | *Collect for the First Sunday of Lent* & *The Institution of a Christian Man*

Born in 1489, the Cambridge don Thomas Cranmer was plucked from relative obscurity and thrown onto the public stage as one of the scholars chosen to compile the arguments for Henry VIII's divorce from Catherine of Aragon. His reward: the highest office in the land, the archiepiscopacy of Canterbury. Henry's divorce from Catherine of Aragon marked the shift from an English church loyal to Rome to a national church answerable only to the Crown. Cranmer's greatest fame, however, would come from his role in the formation of the defining documents of Henry's Church of England—including the *Book of Common Prayer* and the Articles of Religion. The Articles would later be contained within the Prayer Book, published as one complete theological vision. This is suggestive of Cranmer's insistence on the centrality of the liturgy to Anglican identity. It is in the liturgy that the doctrinal beliefs of the Church of England are classically held. Because of this guiding theological methodology, one of the collects from the *Book of Common Prayer* has been included below alongside *The Institution of a Christian Man* of 1537.

The Collect for the First Sunday of Lent was composed for the 1549 *Book of Common Prayer* (although we will draw from the definitive 1662 edition). It replaced an older version, from the Sarum Missal, that was addressed to "O God" and stressed the Lenten practice of fasting as a work of "merit." Notice how the new collect has been christologically rearticulated (addressed directly to Christ "O Lord") and, in good Reformation fashion, identifies true holiness as a work not of merit but grace. *The Institution of a Christian Man* is a collection of texts that include expositions of the key building blocks of the new Church of England, such as: the creeds, sacraments, commandments, the Lord's Prayer, the Ave Maria, and the doctrines of justification and merit. It was written during Cranmer's tenure in Canterbury. Known sometimes as the "Bishops' Book," *The Institution of a Christian Man* is a significant theological achievement. It draws liberally on continental Reformation thought (Luther and Zwingli in particular) in dialogue with patristic texts to carve out a distinctively Anglican set of doctrinal commitments for the purposes of teaching and preaching. The "Bishops' Book" was evangelical in flavor and aimed to establish some doctrinal ground between the newly reformed Church of England and its Roman roots. The extract below is from its exposition of the Ave Maria and provides a great example of Cranmer reworking the tradition according to these new doctrinal commitments. Notice how—again, betraying the classic marks of Reformation theology—Cranmer spends a good chunk of the exposition simply retelling the story of Mary from *Scripture*. In so doing, he finds in Scripture that the Ave Maria is not a prayer itself but an act of praise: Mary is "the message of praise," he says. But what Cranmer omits to say is as suggestive as what he includes: there is nothing about Mary's intercessory activity. Instead, for Cranmer, stripped from the devotion that had surrounded Mary in late medieval piety, the Anglican Mary is celebrated as "full of grace" for her willingness to say "yes" to God's call.

Cranmer died a heretic and a martyr for the cause of the English Reformation in 1556 under the daughter of the broken marriage of Henry VIII and Catherine of Aragon and committed Catholic Mary I. His collect, said in Anglican churches on the day of his death (March 21), remembers him as the servant who "renewed the worship of your Church and through his death revealed your strength in human weakness." Like Mary, Cranmer lived a life "full of grace" and together they provide a model for the living of the Christian life. Let us then be given the grace to say, as they did, "yes" to God's redeeming love.

Collect for the First Sunday in Lent (1662)

O Lord, who for our sake didst fast forty days and forty nights: Give us grace to use such abstinence, that, our flesh being subdued to the Spirit, we may ever obey thy godly motions in righteousness and true holiness, to thy honour and glory, who livest and reignest with the Father and the Holy Ghost, one God, world without end. *Amen.*

"The Ave Maria" from *The Institution of a Christian Man* (1537)

Hail, Mary, full of grace, the Lord is with thee.
    Blessed art thou amongst women; and blessed is the fruit of thy womb.

For the better understanding of this Ave, or salutation of the angel, we think it convenient, that all bishops and preachers shall instruct and teach the people committed unto their spiritual charge, first, how that it was decreed in the high consistory of the whole Trinity, that after the fall of our first father Adam, by which mankind was so long in the great indignation of God, and exiled out of heaven, the second Person, the everlasting Son of the Father everlasting, should take upon him the nature of man, to redeem mankind from the power of the Devil, and to reconcile the same again to his Lord God; and that he should be so perfect God, and also perfect man. And for this purpose, as St. Luke in his Gospel reporteth: in the sixth month after St. Elisabeth was conceived with St. John the Baptist, the angel Gabriel was sent from God into a city of Galilee named Nazareth, to a virgin, which was despoused or ensured to a man, whose name was Joseph, of the house of David, and the virgin's name was Mary. And when this angel came unto this said virgin, he said these words: *Hail, full of grace, the Lord is with thee: blessed art thou among women.*

And when the virgin hearing these words was much troubled with them, and mused with herself what manner of salutation it should be, the angel said to her: Fear not, Mary, be not abashed: for thou hast found favour and grace in the sight of God. Lo, thou shalt conceive in thy womb, and shalt bring forth a son, and thou shalt call his name Jesus. He shall be great, and shall be called the Son of the Highest: and the Lord God shall give to him the seat of David his father: and he shall reign over the house of Jacob for ever; and his kingdom shall have no end. Then said Mary to the angel. How can this be done, for I know no man? And the angel answering said unto her. The Holy Ghost shall come from above into thee, and the power of the Highest shall overshadow thee: and therefore that holy thing which shall be born of thee shall be called the Son of God. And, lo, thy cousin Elisabeth hath also conceived a son in her old age: and this is the sixth month sith she conceived, which was called the barren woman. For there is nothing impossible to God. To this Mary answered, Lo, I am the handmaid of our Lord; be it done unto me as thou hast spoken. And then forthwith, upon the departure of the angel, and being newly conceived with the most blessed child Jesus, Mary went up into the mountains with speed into a city of Judah; and came to the house of Zachary, and saluted Elisabeth. . . .

Second, that the angel Gabriel, which spake to the virgin, was an high angel, and an high messenger. And truly it was convenient that he should be so. For he came with the highest message that ever was sent, which was the treaty and league of peace between God and man.

And therefore the first word of his salutation (that is to say Hail, or Be joyful) was marvelous convenient for the same: for he came with the message of joy. And so said the other angel, which at the birth of our Savior appeared to the shepherds. I shew to you (said he) great joy, that shall be to all the people. And surely, considering the effects that ensued upon this high message, all mankind had great cause to joy. For man being in the indignation and the displeasure of God, was hereby reconciled; man being in the bonds of the Devil, was hereby delivered; man being exiled and banished out of heaven, was hereby restored thither again. These be such matters of joy and comfort to us, that there never was or shall be, nor can be any like. But not only for this purpose he began with this high word of comfort, but also for that he perceived that the virgin, being alone, would be much abashed and astonished at his marvelous and sudden coming unto her.

And therefore he thought it expedient first of all to utter the word of joy and comfort, which might comfort and put away all fear from the blessed virgin. And he calleth not her by her proper name, but giveth her a new name, calling her *full of grace*. This is now her new name; and this is the highest name that can be in any creature. For her son, the Son of God, was content with this name, where he is by the holy evangelist St. John called also full of grace. And yet she is not in this behalf equal with him. For that she is *full of grace*, she hath it of him. And how could it be otherwise but that she must needs be *full of grace*, that should conceive and bear him that was the very plenitude and fullness of grace, the Lord of grace, by whom is all grace, and without whom is no grace. Holy scripture calleth also St. Stephen full of grace; but he may not be compared with the blessed virgin, ne have communion in this name, *full of grace*, equal with her; for she conceived and bare him that is the author of all grace: and this is the singular grace by which she is called, not only the mother of man, but also the mother of God.

Thirdly, that by these words, *the Lord is with thee*, is declared the name which the angel gave to her, calling her *full of grace*: and they signify, that she was full of God's favor, and full of his grace. For surely our Lord is not with them that be not in grace: he cannot tarry with them that be void of grace, and be in sin. For there is a separation and divorce between the sinful soul and our Lord, as the Wise Man saith. Perverse thoughts make a separation and divorce from God; much more perverse deeds.

Fourthly, that these words, *Blessed art thou among women*, was meant, that there was never woman so blessed. And truly she may well be called so, most blessed amongst all women: for she had great and high prerogatives, which none other woman ever had, hath, or shall have. Is not this an high prerogative, that of all women she was chosen to be mother to the Son of God? . . . Wherefore we may worthily say that she is the most blessed of all other women. And to the intent that all good Christian men should repute and take her so, behold the providence of God, that would by another witness confirm the same. For even the same words that the angel spake, the blessed matron St. Elisabeth spake also: and where the angel made an end, there she began. The angel made an end of his salutation with these words. *Blessed art thou among women*. The blessed matron began her salutation with the same words, declaring that she was inspired with the same Spirit that sent the angel and that they were both ministers of the whole Trinity, the one from heaven, the other in earth. And afterward she added these words, and said, *And blessed is the fruit of thy womb*. These be not the words of the angel, but of St. Elisabeth. For when the virgin Mary came to salute her, the said Elisabeth being inspired with the

Holy Ghost, and knowing that the virgin Mary was conceived, spake these words of the fruit that the virgin should bring forth. . . .

Fifthly, we think it convenient, that all bishops and preachers shall instruct and teach the people committed unto their spiritual charge, that this Ave Maria is not properly a prayer, as the Paternoster is. For a prayer properly hath words of petition, supplication, request, and suit; but this Ave Maria hath no such. Nevertheless the church hath used to adjoin it to the end of the Paternoster, as an hymn, laud, and praise, partly of our Lord and Saviour Jesu Christ for our redemption, and partly of the blessed virgin for her humble consent given and expressed to the angel at this salutation. Lauds, praises, and thanks be in this Ave Maria principally given and yielded to our Lord, as to the author of our said redemption: but herewith also the virgin lacketh not her lauds, praise, and thanks for her excellent and singular virtues, and chiefly for that she humbly consented, according to the saying of the holy matron St. Elisabeth, when she said unto this virgin. Blessed art thou that diddest give trust and credence to the angel's words; for all things that have been spoken to thee shall be performed.

III. Reformation and Post-Reformation

E. Anglican

64. Lancelot Andrewes (1555–1626) | *The Holy Spirit* & *Points of Meditation Before Prayer*

Lancelot Andrewes was one of the Church of England's high-flyers in the late sixteenth and early seventeenth century. After his theological training in Cambridge, and ecclesial appointments in London, under the reign of James I Andrewes occupied the episcopal seats of Chichester, Ely, and then Winchester. During these episcopal tenures he played an instrumental role in the realization of the Authorized Version (the King James Version) of the Bible and was one of the foremost Anglican apologists of his day, conducting his theology largely through his famous sermons. T. S. Eliot once said of his homilies that when Andrewes speaks "from begin to end you are sure that he is wholly in his subject, unaware of anything else, that his emotion grows as he penetrates more deeply into his subject, that he is finally 'alone with the Alone' with the mystery which he is trying to grasp more fully and more firmly."[1]

One of the distinguishing marks of Andrewes's sermons is his engagement with patristic theology. Many of his sermons on the incarnation betray the hallmarks of an Anglican theology of *theosis* shaped in conversation with the theologians of the early church. With the early church he also shares strong interest in the third article of the creed. The Holy Spirit is the subject of the sermon below, in which we find Andrewes appealing to Basil's classic treatise *On the Holy Spirit*. We catch him mid-sermon after he has already provided a firm defense of the *filioque* clause in the Nicene Creed, given an eloquent rendition of his doctrine of *theosis*, and now declares our need for the Holy Spirit in the Christian life to strengthen our "hearing" of the Word of God. The Christian life, for Andrewes, is a holy life inspired and confirmed by the Holy Spirit who makes us by grace into nothing less "partakers of the Divine nature."

---

1. Eliot, *For Lancelot Andrewes*, 28.

In addition to his sermons, Andrewes is remembered for the piety of his prayers, many of which are collated in his *Private Prayers* first published in 1896. He was a devout person of prayer and (in good Anglican fashion) sought to fuse prayer with doctrine. It would be amiss, then, to neglect the theological contribution of his devotional life. To that end, Andrewes's *Points of Meditation Before Prayer*, a short, penetrating set of instructions on the nature of prayer, is included alongside his famous sermon on the Holy Spirit. For it is in prayer, according to Andrewes, that the grace of God is most profoundly experienced: "prayer is colloquy with God," he says channeling the early church.

The Holy Spirit (1612)

Before James I at Whitehall, Whitsunday, 31 May 1612. . . .

Receive? What need we receive any spirit, or receive at all? May we not, out of ourselves, work that will serve our turns? No; for holy we must be, if ever we shall rest in His holy Hill, for "without holiness none shall ever see God." But holy we cannot be by any habit, moral or acquisite. There is none such in all moral philosophy. As we have our faith by illumination, so have we our holiness by inspiration; receive both, both from without.

To a habit the philosophers came, and so Christians may. But that will not serve, they are to go farther. Our habits acquisite will lift us no further than they did the heathen men; no further than the place where they grow, that is, earth and nature. They cannot work beyond their kind—nothing can; nor rise higher than their spring. It is not therefore, "If you have received the habit," but "If you have received the Spirit," we must go by.

But then, why "you have received the Holy Ghost"? No receiving will serve, but of Him? The reason is, it is nothing here below that we seek, but to heaven we aspire. Then, if to heaven we shall, something from heaven must thither exalt us. If "partakers of the Divine nature" we hope to be, as great and precious promises we have that we shall be, that can be no otherwise than by receiving One in whom the Divine nature is. He being received imparts it to us, and so makes us "partakers of the divine nature" and that is the Holy Ghost.

For as an absolute necessity there is that we receive the Spirit, else can we not live the life of nature, so no less absolute that we receive the Holy Spirit, else can we not live the life of grace, and so consequently never come to the life of glory. . . .

Look how the breath and the voice in the way of nature go together; even so do the Spirit and the word in the practice of religion. The Holy Ghost is "Christ's Spirit," and Christ is "the Word." And of that Word, "the word that is preached" to us is an abstract. There must then needs be a nearness and alliance between the one and the other. And indeed, but by our default, "the word and the Spirit," said Esay, shall never fail or ever part, but one be received when the other is. We have a plain example of it this day, in St. Peter's auditory, and another in Cornelius and his family; even in the sermon-time, "the Holy Ghost fell upon them" and they so received Him.

Yes, we may see it by this, that in the hearing of the word where He is not received yet He worketh somewhat onward. Upon Felix, took him with a shaking, and further would have gone, but that he put it over to "a convenient time" which convenient time never came. And upon Agrippa likewise, somewhat it did move him, and more it would, but that he was content to be "almost a Christian" to take his religion by a little, as it were upon a knife's point, and was afraid to be "too much" a Christian.

That we see not this effect, that with the word the Spirit is not received as it would be, the reason is it is no sooner gotten than it is lost. We should find this effect, if after we had heard the word, we could get us a little out of the noise about us, and withdraw ourselves some whither, where we might be by ourselves, that when we have heard Him speak to us, we might hear what He would speak in us. When we have heard the voice before us, we might hear the other behind us, "This is the way." When the voice that sounded, the other of Job, "I heard a voice in silence"—there hear Him reprove, teach, comfort us, within. Upon which texts are grounded the soliloquies, the communing with our own spirit, which are much praised by the ancients, to this purpose; for "by a little musing or meditation the fire would kindle" and be kept alive, which otherwise will die. And certain it is that many sparks kindled, for want of this, go out again straight, for as fast as it is written in our hearts, it is wiped out again; as fast as the seed is sown, it is picked up by the fowls again, and so our receiving is in vain, the word and the Spirit are severed, which else would keep together.

Lastly, as the word and the Spirit, so the flesh and the Spirit go together. Not all flesh, but this flesh, the flesh that was conceived by the Holy Ghost, this is never without the Holy Ghost by Whom it was conceived; so that, receive one, and receive both. Ever with this blood there runs still an artery, with plenty of Spirit in it, which makes what we eat there "a spiritual meat," and that in that cup we be "made drink of the Spirit." There is not only "putting on of the hands," but after it, "putting it into our hands." "Putting on of hands," in "receive the bread and the cup"; and "putting it into our hands," in "take, eat, drink." And so, we in case to receive body, blood, Spirit and all, if ourselves be not in fault.

Now then, if we will invite the Spirit indeed, and if each of these, by itself in several, be thus effectual to procure it, put them all, and bind them all together. "Take to you words," Osee's words, words of earnest invocation. "Receive" or take to you "the word," St James' word, "grafted into you" by the office of preaching. "Take the holy mysteries of His body and blood"; and the same, the holy arteries of His blessed Spirit. Take all these in one—the attractive of prayer; the word which is "spirit and life"; the bread of life, and the cup of salvation; and is there not great hope we shall answer St.

Paul's question as he would have it answered, affirmative? "Have you received?" Yes; we have received Him. Yes sure. Then, if ever; thus, if by any way. For on earth there is no surer way than to join all these; and He so to be received, if at all.

So, we began with hearing outward, and we end with receiving inward. We began with one Sacrament, Baptism; we end with the other, the Eucharist. We began with that, where we heard of Him; and we end with this other, where we may and shall, I trust, receive Him. And Almighty God grant we so may receive Him at this good time, as in His good time we may be received by Him thither, whence He this day came of purpose to bring us, even to the holy places made without hands, which is His Heavenly kingdom, with God the Father Who prepared it, and God the Son Who purchased it for us!

Points of Meditation Before Prayer (posthumously published in *The Private Prayers of Lancelot Andrewes, 1675*)

Thou art careful about many things: but one thing is needful.

But we will give ourselves continually to prayer and to the ministry of the word.

Watch ye and pray always, that ye may be accounted worthy to escape the things that shall come to pass.

Love the Lord all thy life and call upon Him for thy salvation. Humble thy soul greatly: for the vengeance of the ungodly is fire and worms.

A man can receive nothing except it be given.

If He prayed that was without sin, how much more ought a smile pray:

> but God is a hearer, not of the voice, but of the heart.

More is done by groanings than by words:

> to this end Christ groaned, for to give us an ensample of groaning.

It is not that God desireth us to be suppliant or loveth that we lie prostrate: the profit thereof is ours and it hath regard to our advantage.

Prayer goeth up, pity cometh down.

God's grace is richer than prayer: God always giveth more than He is asked.

God commandeth that thou ask, and teacheth what to ask, and promiseth what thou dost ask, and it displeaseth Him if thou ask not: and dost thou not ask notwithstanding?

Prayer is a summary of faith, an interpreter of hope.

It is not by paces but by prayers that God is come at.

Faith poureth out prayer and is grounded in prayer.

Therefore go on to labour fervently in prayers,

> always to pray and not to faint,
>
> in spirit and in truth.

Faith is the foundation and basis of prayer:

> the foundation of faith is the promise of God.

Lift up your hearts.

He that made us to live, the same taught us withal to pray. The prayer of the humble pierceth the clouds.

Prayer is colloquy with God.[2]

---

2. Original revised for readability.

III. Reformation and Post-Reformation

E. Anglican

65. George Herbert (1593–1633) | *Grace* & *The Country Parson*

Born into an aristocratic Welsh family, Cambridge trained, Member of Parliament for Monmouth, ordained to the deaconate in 1624, country priest in the south of England, George Herbert is widely considered to be one of the finest poets the seventeenth century produced. Choosing neither ecclesiastical nor parliamentary high office, Herbert spent his days of priestly ministry in a small, country church on the outskirts of Salisbury where much of his time was passed on his knees, in prayer. There he would finish his magnum opus, *The Temple*, which is a collection of poems structured (in a distinctively Anglican way) around an extended reference to the life of the church, and a manual known as *The Country Parson*, which provides instruction on Herbert's vision for parish life.

Fittingly for a poet-priest, many of the poems that form *The Temple* are devotional in tone. They are works of theology that seek not simply to explain but to lead the reader into an encounter with God. The poems are designed to inspire growth in the Christian life. Running through Herbert's poetry is the theme of personal relationship with God. Yet his relationship to God was characterized by struggle. We catch sight of this below in his famous poem on grace of that title. Here we find Herbert putting to verse those feelings of struggle that, if we are honest, are probably familiar to us all. The poem drifts in and out prayer: prayer for grace to "Drop from above!" as a gift to refresh him and renew him, to brighten his world when the "sunne should hide his face." The central repetition of the petition for grace to "Drop from above!" is Herbert's enunciation of the Protestant theology of gift: grace is not achieved but comes to us as gift, from above, and is received with an open, thankful heart. So dependent on the gift of grace is Herbert that should grace not be given he prays to be removed from the world.

His commitment to the Christian life of practicing grace is made clear in his prose as well as his poetry, and especially in his practical manual *The Country Parson*. This treatise is Herbert's vision of what it means to be a priest. Being a priest is a calling to a way of life that practices the grace of God. The extract we will read below is taken from the thirty-third chapter of *The Country Parson*, which is curiously titled "The Parson's Library." Curiously, that is, because in the library of the parson not one book is to be found. The parson is resourced intellectually not by books alone but by, as he says, "a holy Life." In fact, in every room of the parson's house, in every nook and cranny of their existence, is to be found one thing: holiness. Why? Because holiness, by the grace of God, is infectious. It spreads. Holiness begets holiness. Although Herbert is clearly concerned with "the Form and Character of the true pastor," there can be no doubt that these are virtues that also lie at the center of the Christian life more generally. The more we read of *The Country Parson* the more we realize that Herbert is not simply describing the ideal Anglican priest but also speaking of the ideal Christian community—one of grace-filled holiness.

Grace (1633)

My stock lies dead, and no increase
Doth my dull husbandrie improve:
O let thy graces without cease
    Drop from above!

If still the sunne should hide his face,
Thy house would but a dungeon prove,
Thy works nights captives: O let grace
    Drop from above!

The dew doth ev'ry morning fall;
And shall the dew out-strip thy Dove?
The dew, for which grasse cannot call,
    Drop from above.

Death is still working like a mole,
And digs my grave at each remove:
Let grace work too, and on my soul
    Drop from above.

Sinne is still hammering my heart
Unto a hardnesse, void of love:

Let suppling grace, to crosse his art,
   Drop from above.
O come! for thou dost know the way:
Or if to me thou wilt not move,
Remove me, where I need not say,
   Drop from above.

The Parson's Library from *The Country Parson* (1652)

The Country Parson's Library is a holy Life: for besides the blessing that that brings upon it, there being a promise, that if the Kingdom of God be first sought, all other things shall be added, even itself is a Sermon. For the temptations with which a good man is beset, and the ways which he used to overcome them, being told to another, whether in private conference, or in the Church, are a Sermon. He that hath considered how to carry himself at table about his appetite, if he tells this to another, preaches; and much more feelingly, and judiciously, then he writes his rules of temperance out of books. So that the Parson having studied, and mastered all his lusts and affections within, and the whole Army of Temptations without, hath ever so many sermons ready penned, as he hath victories.

And it fares in this as it doth in Physic: He that hath been sick of a Consumption, and knows what recovered him, is a Physician so far as he meets with the same disease, and temper; and can much better, and particularly do it, then he that is generally learned, and was never sick. And if the same person had been sick of all diseases, and were recovered of all by things that he knew; there were no such Physician as he, both for skill and tenderness. Just so it is in Divinity, and that not without manifest reason: for though the temptations may be diverse in diverse Christians, yet the victory is alike in all, being by the self-same Spirit. Neither is this true only in the military state of a Christian life, but even in the peaceable also; when the servant of God, freed for a while from temptation, in a quiet sweetness seeks how to please his God. Thus the Parson considering that repentance is the great virtue of the Gospel, and one of the first steps of pleasing God, having for his own use examined the nature of it, is able to explain it after to others. And particularly, having doubted sometimes, whether his repentance were true, or at least in that degree it ought to be, since he found himself sometimes to weep more for the loss of some temporal things, than for offending God, he came at length to this resolution, that repentance is an act of the mind, not of the Body, even as the Original signifies; and that the chief thing, which God in Scriptures requires, is the heart, and the spirit, and to worship him in truth, and spirit. Wherefore in case a Christian endeavor to weep, and cannot, since we are not Masters of our bodies, this suffices. And consequently he found, that the essence of repentance, that it may be alike in all God's children (which as concerning weeping it cannot be, some being of a more melting temper then others) consists in a true detestation of the soul, abhorring, and renouncing sin, and turning unto God in truth of heart, and newness of life: Which acts of repentance are and must be found in all Gods servants: Not that weeping is not useful, where it can be, that so the body may join in the grief, as it did in the sin; but that, so the other acts be, that is not necessary: so that he as truly repents, who performs the other acts of repentance, when he cannot more, as he that weeps a flood of tears. This Instruction and comfort the Parson getting for himself, when he tells it to others, becomes a Sermon. The like he does in other Christian virtues, as of Faith, and Love, and the Cases of Conscience belonging thereto, wherein (as Saint Paul implies that he ought, Romans 2:21) he first preached to himself, and then to others.[1]

---

1. Original revised for readability.

III. Reformation and Post-Reformation

E. Anglican

66. Charles Wesley (1707–1788) | *"Father whose everlasting love"*
& John Wesley (1703–1791) | *The Means of Grace (Sermon 16)*

Born in Epworth, Lincolnshire, the Wesley brothers were instrumental in the formation of the evangelical revival movement known as Methodism that was spreading within the Church of England in the eighteenth century. Together the Wesley brothers were a formidable team: John for his gifts in organizing the Methodist societies, his letter writing, his countless sermons, treatises, and commitment to spreading the Methodist message to the farthest corners of England and beyond (often on horseback!); Charles for his incomparable genius for hymn-writing that put to song many of the core Methodist theological sensibilities, not least concerning the theme of grace. Although both Wesleys would self-identify as Anglicans, the Methodist movement began to separate from the Church of England after John's death in 1791. A series of controversies then led to several different Methodist Connexions, of which the largest were the Wesleyans and the Primitives, which united in 1932 to form the Methodist Church as we know it today.

John Wesley's entire theology revolved around his understanding of God's grace and the importance of the active pursuit of holiness. He was brought up as an eighteenth century High Church Arminian, which taught him, in particular, to abhor any form of predestination and to value the disciplined living that seeks holiness of life. In 1738, both brothers experienced an evangelical conversion (John most famously at Aldersgate) leading to a profound sense that grace can be personally and vividly experienced. This was the grace that famously warmed John's heart and the grace that he wanted to share with others. Many of his writings, and in particular his choice genre of theological writing, the sermon, are deep theological explorations of what this grace means in the day-to-day life of the Christian. John's printed sermons were notoriously long, and so the selection below is an extract of a longer sermon on what he called the "means of grace." These are the outward signs through which God's grace is received in the Christian life: prayer, reading the Scriptures, and the Lord's Supper—the key ingredients to any Christian life of grace.

Several other leaders and supporters of the Evangelical Revival were moderate Calvinists who argued that salvation is so dependent on God's grace that we could not contribute to it in any meaningful way. Against them, Wesley constantly emphasized what he called "preventing" grace, which is now normally called "prevenient" grace. Wesley used "preventing" in the eighteenth-century sense of "going before." This is the idea that when it comes to grace, God takes the initiative: grace precedes anything we do and has no bounds. For Wesley, it is grace that provides the means to respond to grace in the first place. Equally, however, the Christian (and those who seek faith) have a responsibility to respond actively to God's grace and to seek holiness of heart and life, including by using the means of grace. Thus salvation is freely available to everyone, but still dependent on the grace of God working within us and cannot be earned.

Methodism, it is often said, was "born in song," and hymns have remained a prominent strand in the theological identity of the tradition to this day. Charles Wesley bequeathed to the church some of the finest congregational hymns in the English language. These hymns are astute works of theology in and of themselves. The brilliance of Charles was to capture in song the distinctive hallmarks of evangelical theology: not least, as we will read in the hymn below, a carefully and christologically orientated account of God's "sufficient, sovereign, saving grace." After all, when it boils down to it, God's grace is not something to be read about in books but is something to be lived, something to praised with "all our bones," and something to be proclaimed "from one generation to another."

Charles Wesley: *Father whose everlasting love* (1741)[1]

Father, whose everlasting love
Thy only Son for sinners gave,
Whose grace to all did freely move,
And sent Him down the world to save;

Help us Thy mercy to extol,
Immense, unfathomed, unconfined;

---

1. Original amended for readability. Like John's sermons, Charles's hymns were also long: just six of the original twenty-seven verses have been reproduced below.

To praise the Lamb who died for all,
The general Savior of mankind.

Thy undistinguishing regard
Was cast on Adam's fallen race;
For all Thou hast in Christ prepared
Sufficient, sovereign, saving grace.

The world He suffered to redeem;
For all He hath the atonement made;
For those that will not come to Him
The ransom of His life was paid.

Why then, Thou universal Love,
Should any of Thy grace despair?
To all, to all, Thy bowels move,
But straitened in our own we are.

Arise, O God, maintain Thy cause!
The fullness of the Gentiles call;
Lift up the standard of Thy cross,
And all shall own Thou diedst for all.

John Wesley: *Sermon 16: The Means of Grace* (1746)

In the following discourse, I propose to examine at large whether there are any means of grace.

By "means of grace" I understand outward signs, words, or actions, ordained of God, and appointed for this end, to be the ordinary channels whereby he might convey to men, preventing, justifying, or sanctifying grace.

I use this expression, "means of grace," because I know none better; and because it has been generally used in the Christian church for many ages, in particular by our own church, which directs us to bless God both for the means of grace and hope of glory; and teaches us, that a sacrament is "an outward sign of inward grace, and a means whereby we receive the same."

The chief of these means are: prayer (whether in secret or with the great congregation); searching the scriptures (which implies reading, hearing, and meditating on them); and receiving the Lord's Supper (eating bread and drinking wine in remembrance of him). And these we believe to be ordained of God, as the ordinary channels of conveying his grace to the souls of men....

According to this, according to the decision of Holy Writ, all who desire the grace of God are to wait for it in the means which he hath ordained; in using, not in laying them aside.

And first, all who desire the grace of God are to wait for it in the way of prayer. This is the express direction of our Lord himself. In his Sermon upon the Mount, after explaining at large wherein religion consists, and describing the main branches of it, he adds: "Ask, and it will be given you; search, and you will find; knock, and the door will be opened for you. For everyone who asks receives, and everyone who searches finds, and for everyone who knocks, the door will be opened" (Matt 7:7–8). Here we are in the plainest manner directed to ask, in order to or as a means of receiving; to seek, in order to find the grace of God, the pearl of great price; and to knock, to continue asking and seeking, if we would enter into his kingdom....

Secondly, all who desire the grace of God are to wait for it in "searching the scriptures." Our Lord's direction with regard to the use of this means is likewise plain and clear. "You search the scriptures," he says to the unbelieving Jews, because it is they that testify on my behalf (John 5:39). And for this very end did he direct them to search the Scriptures, that they might believe in him....

Thirdly, all who desire an increase of the grace of God are to wait for it in partaking of the Lord's Supper. For this also is a direction himself has given.... You openly exhibit the same by these visible signs before God, angels, and men; you manifest your solemn remembrance of his death till he comes in the clouds of heaven....

As to the manner of using them, indeed it wholly depends on whether they should convey any grace at all to the user. It behoves us, first, always to retain a lively sense, that God is above all means. Have a care, therefore, of limiting the Almighty. He does whatever and whenever it pleases him. He can convey his grace, either in or out of any of the means which he hath appointed. Perhaps he will. "For who has known the mind of the Lord? Or who has been his counselor?" (Rom 11:34). Look then every moment for his appearing! Be it at the hour you are employed in his ordinances, or before, or after that hour or when you are hindered from there—he is not hindered. He is always ready, always able, always willing to save. "It is the Lord; let him do what seems good to him" (1 Sam 3:18)....

Secondly, before you use any means let it be deeply impressed on your soul: There is no power in this. It is in itself a poor, dead, empty thing. Separate from God, it is a dry leaf, a shadow. Neither is there any merit in my using this; nothing intrinsically pleasing to God; nothing whereby I deserve any favour at his hands. No, not a drop of water to cool my tongue. But because God bids therefore I do; because he directs me to wait in this way, therefore here I wait for his free mercy, from which comes my salvation.

Settle this in your heart: that the *opus operatum*, the mere work done, profits nothing; that there is no power to save but in the Spirit of God; that there is no merit, but in the blood of Christ; and that, consequently, even what God ordains conveys no grace to the soul if you do not trust in him alone. On the other hand, he that does truly trust in him cannot fall short of the grace of God, even though he were cut off from every outward ordinance, though he were shut up in the centre of the earth.

Thirdly, in using all means, seek God alone. In and through every outward thing, look singly to the power of his Spirit and the merits of his Son. Beware you do not stick in the work itself; if you do, it is all lost labour. Nothing short of God can satisfy your soul. Therefore, eye him in all, through all, and above all.

Remember also, to use all means, as means; not for their own sake, but in order to the renewal of your soul in righteousness and true holiness. If, therefore, they actually tend to this, well; but if not, they are dung and dross.

Lastly, after you have used any of these, take care how you value yourself and how you congratulate yourself as having done some great thing. This is turning all into poison. Think, "If God was not there, what does this avail? Have I not been adding sin to sin? How long, O Lord! Save, or I perish! O lay not this sin to my charge!" If God was there, if his love flowed into your heart, you have forgot, as it were, the outward work. You see, you know, you feel, God is all in all. Be abased. Sink down before him. Give him all the praise. "So that God may be glorified in all things through Jesus Christ" (1 Pet 4:11). Let all your bones cry out, "I will sing of your steadfast love, O Lord, for ever; with my mouth I will proclaim your faithfulness to all generations" (Ps 89.1).[2]

---

2. Original revised for readability.

Section IV. Modern and Postmodern

IV. Modern and Postmodern

Introduction

The readings in this section begin in the modern period and lead us into the present day, which is sometimes termed the "postmodern" age. The term *modern* is notoriously slippery, and *postmodern* slipperier still. Discourse on the origins of both is bewildering.[1] Neither term allows for a clear-cut definition. And nor is there a watertight distinction between the two: they overlap in a messy, complicated way. While for some these terms represent an attempt to organize what is a vast and tumultuous history into more manageable historical periods (though there is disagreement as to when one begins and the other ends), for others they have come to represent different ways of thinking about and relating to God, the self, and the world. Amid these disagreements, what is undisputed is that this period, however understood, saw several complex transformations of the intellectual, social, cultural, and political landscape. No stone would be left unturned once the modern period took hold. All periods in the history of Christianity have been tumultuous of course. That said, no other period of the church's history quite had to face the challenges that emerged here.

The very term *modern* suggests a judgement on the past. Through modern eyes, the received orthodoxies of the past came to look outmoded, antiquated, and obsolete. One such tradition that was rendered newly suspicious by modernity's underlying hermeneutics was the Christian tradition itself. The claims of Christianity were attacked on both philosophical and historical grounds. For many in the modern age, Christianity had simply lost its relevancy and fell behind in the insatiable march of progress. Philosophers such as Friedrich Nietzsche (1844–1900) proclaimed the "death of God." Historians raised doubts about the received history of the Bible. The world had, as the martyr Dietrich Bonhoeffer (1906–1945) would later say, "come of age," finally maturing into an adulthood that could think and act without recourse to traditional authority.

---

1. For some helpful guides through the period, see Ford and Muers, eds., *The Modern Theologians*; Higton and Muers, *Modern Theology*; Jones, ed., *The Blackwell Companion to Modern Theology*; Kapic and McCormack, eds., *Mapping Modern Theology*.

SECTION IV. MODERN AND POSTMODERN

The gauntlet thrown down by modernity is this: in this rapidly changing context how is a doctrine so "traditional" and foundational as that of grace understood in such a way that avoids either simply repeating the past or breaking from it entirely? Perhaps the metaphor of "improvisation" is a useful one in getting to grips with the task in hand. Improvisation is neither identical repetition nor rejection of what has come before.[2] It presents something new but also recognizably familiar. In many of the readings we will encounter in this section we find their authors doing exactly this. They improvise on their respective traditions, and the priorities and concerns inherent to those very traditions, in a non-repetitive way and in a way that keeps deep dialogue with the world around them. In this process of improvisation, new depths to the theology of grace are discovered. Particularly under the conditions of postmodernity, the modern project of improvising on the theme of grace in double dialogue with the past and present led to an explosion of new interpretations. That plurality of understanding could in itself be seen as one of the markers of the transition from modernity to postmodernity and its ideological resistance to one "total" (or "meta") way of seeing the world.

One of the watchwords of this historical period is *freedom*. The modern doctrine of freedom is often characterized by the themes of unbounded independence, absolute autonomy, limitless self-determination, and the rejection of external authority. In what would become that most quintessential of modern utterances, René Descartes (1596–1650) summed up the overwhelming emphasis now placed on the individual: "I think, therefore I am." But "freedom" is also integral to Christianity, and to the theme of grace. Much of modern theology, as well as dialoguing with these new habits of thought and action, also offered some critiques of its own of the culture in which it found itself. Despite the diversity of interpretation the word *grace* produced in this period, there is general agreement among the readings in this section that true human freedom is to be found in the grace of God. This is the paradox of grace: true human freedom is worked out in complete dependency on God and on others.

The aim in what follows is not to resolve the knotty questions thrown up by modernity and perpetuated by postmodernity. Though you might catch sight of some of them and get a sense of some of the challenges theology has faced in this period. Its primary aim is to see how the theme of grace arrived at new interpretations within the course of this period of history. And its hope is that these readings might guide each of us through our own improvisations on grace in double dialogue with the past and the present as we live the Christian life today.

A brief explanation of the term *contextual* is required before we begin. All theology is contextual. It cannot be otherwise. The theological ideas covered throughout this section, as we have said, emerge in constant dialogue with their surroundings (even if the influence of context might sometimes go unnamed). To label, as we have done, only those theologies that fall into the final section of this book as "contextual,"

2. For more on "improvisation," see Ford, *The Shape of Living*.

is misleading. We are using the term for want of a better one. The readings in this final section, diverse as they are, share a way of doing theology that sees issues of gender, race, political liberation, and local context as the most significant starting point for theological investigation.

Ashley Cocksworth

IV. Modern and Postmodern

A. Lutheran

67. Albrecht Ritschl (1822–1889) | *The Christian Doctrine of Justification and Reconciliation*

Alongside Adolf von Harnack, Albrecht Ritschl was one of the great pioneers of the liberal theology which dominated the intellectual horizon of Christian theology towards the end of the "long nineteenth century." Standing in the tradition of Schleiermacher and teaching at the universities of Bonn and later Göttingen, Ritschl was committed to reconstructing theology in light of the Enlightenment critiques of religion and the limits they imposed on the possibility of religious belief.

Sometimes this meant breaking with the beliefs of the past, such as classical two-natures Christology. But as a Lutheran, there was one doctrine Ritschl simply could not reject: the doctrine of justification. For Ritschl, as for Luther, this was the doctrine on which the church would stand or fall. If he could not reject it, he could add his own modern twist to this most traditional of Lutheran doctrines. This twist unfolds systematically in his monumental work *The Christian Doctrine of Justification and Reconciliation* published in three volumes between 1870 and 1874.

On Ritschl's reading of the doctrine, justification is not about deliverance from "guilt," forgiveness of sin, or the reconciliation of the individual Christian to God as it had been for Luther and his heirs. Instead, it is inherently a moral and ethical doctrine rooted in the love of God. Justification is about—in other words—the Christian life. To be more specific, it is about seeing reconciliation as the program of extending the kingdom of God, which for Ritschl is the highest and greatest good around which society would be progressively transformed.

In furnishing his account of the Christian life, Ritschl drew from the life of Jesus of Nazareth. The life, teaching, and death of Jesus presents an account of the Christian life *par excellence*. Living the Christian life means living like Jesus: loving one's neighbor, sharing table fellowship with society's outcast and downtrodden, caring for the sick and for the lonely. In another significant volume, Ritschl developed these ideas around the theme of "Christian perfection," which, although given freely by grace, requires an ethical response in kind to establish on earth the "highest good" that is the kingdom of God. Just as God through Jesus has forgiven our sins, we must forgive the sins of others.

Although the Ritschlian school of theology would come under significant critique in the events that brought the long nineteenth century to a devastating end, his understanding of the "essence of Christianity" as inherently ethical laid the theological foundations for the social gospel movement in the United States, most closely associated with the work of Walter Rauschenbusch. There is still much to learn from Ritschl's approach to theology: to be confident about the continued relevancy of Christianity in a society that might speak otherwise, to be clear that salvation is not simply about heaven but about establishing the kingdom of God on earth, and to be reminded that above all grace is inherently a practical matter.

The Christian Doctrine of Justification and Reconciliation (1870–1874)

The *Kingdom of God* . . . is a directly *religious conception*. This is clear when we consider the phrase as it stood originally—Sovereignty of God. For this combination of words distinctly expresses an operation of God directed towards men. The conception contains two different things. The Kingdom of God is the *summum bonum* which God realises in men; and at the same time it is their common task, for it is only through the rendering of obedience on man's part that God's sovereignty possesses continuous existence. These two meanings are interdependent. Here, however, we have the reason why the conception of the Kingdom of God has the appearance of being a religious conception of a different order from justification and reconciliation. In these operations of God upon sinners, so far as they have already been elucidated, no room is left for a corresponding self-determined activity on the part of man. On the other hand, the moral action demanded by the Kingdom of God or the Sovereignty of God, and therefore itself a part of the latter conception, is committed to men as God's independent and responsible subjects. The range and the character of the separate tasks, which make up the total task of the Kingdom of God, are of such a kind that we have to devote definite attention and continuous purpose to their separate fulfilment, and to the ties which bind them together. In this respect the conception of the Kingdom of God differs in a peculiar way from those other operations of Divine grace. The question remains whether this diversity in nature amongst the chief ideas of Christianity does not put an obstacle in the way of our vindicating the general Christian view, and whether the definition I have given of this religion can surmount the difficulty.

In our desire to get rid of the appearance of contradiction, it is possible some may revert to the fact that the two sets of ideas occupy different planes, inasmuch as justification and reconciliation concern men as sinners, while the Kingdom of God concerns them as reconciled. Such a statement, however, is not quite exact. For it would imply that at the moment of justification, which logically precedes the call to the Kingdom of God, the predication of sin loses its validity altogether. But this is not the case, for the meaning of justification is that it encompasses the whole life of the Christian, and in this constitutive sense forms likewise a continual reminder of sin and guilt, and thus emphasises the necessity for its own continued existence. If what this means is that, as a direct result of justification, the presence of sin is felt so long as a Christian lives, then the call to participate independently in the Kingdom of God arises simultaneously. But in that case the proposed solution of the difficulty is inadequate.

Two lines of thought have been employed to establish the homogeneity of these two sets of ideas. In the first place, human activity, conceived as independent—be its aim salvation or good works—is subordinated to the grace of God, or included in God's operation upon men. Certain apostolic expressions point in this direction. Paul (Phil 2:12, 13) summons every man to work out his own salvation with fear and trembling: because He who works in believers, both to will and to do, is God. The author of the Epistle to the Hebrews (13:21) expresses the wish that God would make his readers perfect in every good work to do His will, while He Himself works in them that which is well-pleasing to Him through Jesus Christ. John (1 John 2:5, 4:12) sees in the exercise of love on the part of Christians the real consummation of the love of God to us, i.e. its complete revelation. This consummation, therefore, would not take place if God's action extended only so far as to give believers the mere potentiality of exercising love. Later teaching also has adhered to this religious estimate of moral action in Christianity. In Catholic theology the validity of the conception of the merits of believers, which depends on their being voluntary, is ultimately counterbalanced by the proposition that all merit is but an effect of grace, understood in its full significance. In the same way in Lutheran theology the moral activity of believers is included, as an effect of *regeneratio*, under the gracious operation of God; and the same thought is still further emphasised by Calvin by his conception of *perseverantia gratiae*. Now, the leading statements of the apostles have never been interpreted in these systems of theology as giving a mechanical explanation of the process in question, and as thus requiring us to abandon the idea of human self-determination formerly admitted. The theology of Calvinism itself stipulates for the reality of human freedom, in contradistinction from nature as such, under the operations of Divine grace. That is to say, the psychological fact is kept in view throughout, that even the operations of Divine grace merely stimulate man to appropriate them in the way which is peculiar to himself. We may ask, consequently, what cognitive interest is satisfied by the thought that one who is working out his own salvation by his own effort, regards God as the author of his purpose and his self-activity? What suggests this twofold way of looking at the matter? I think it is suggested by the claims both of the individual case and of the moral order of the world as a whole. The occupation of the individual in his life's task, his performance of duty, and his formation of character, demand the form of independence and responsibility. This always stands out in the forefront, however definitely he leans on Divine grace. But if, in his own estimation of himself, he merges himself in the whole which his activity serves, if he spends his life upon a service which can only be understood in the light of that whole, and which he has come by without being able to urge the existence of previous purpose due to himself, then the judgment expressed by Paul is the true standard of the humility which befits a Christian.

On the other hand, a closer examination of the conception of justification reveals the fact that this Divine operation does not imply the occurrence of any mechanical process in man. For part of the significance of its relation to faith is, that this self-active faculty in man, without regard to which justification cannot be fully understood, is included under this Divine operation; part, that justification, as calling forth the reaction of faith in man, is in this sense a property of the believer, and continues to be the motive of the religious demeanour which it behoves him to adopt. In both relations, therefore, the conceptions of the Kingdom of God and justification are homogeneous. This holds true in so far as, for one thing, both notions express operations of Divine grace; and, for another, the results of these operations manifest themselves solely in activities which exhibit the form of personal independence. They offer, therefore, really no obstacle to their being linked together in a complete view of Christianity. But in Dogmatics this alternating use of the two principles cannot be avoided. Dogmatics comprehends all religious processes in man under the category of Divine grace, that is, it looks at them from the standpoint of God. But it is, of course, impossible so thoroughly to maintain this standpoint in our experience, as thereby to obtain complete knowledge of the operations of grace. For the standpoint of our knowledge lies in formal opposition to God. Only for an instant can we transfer ourselves to the Divine standpoint. A theology, therefore, which consisted of nothing but propositions of this stamp could never be understood, and would be composed of words which really did not express knowledge on our part. If what is wanted is to write theology on the plan not merely of a narrative of the great deeds done by God, but of a system representing the salvation He has wrought out, then we must exhibit the operations of God—justification, regeneration, the communication of the Holy Spirit, the bestowal of blessedness in the *summum bonum*—in such a way as shall involve an analysis of the corresponding voluntary activities in which man appropriates the operations of God. This method has been already adopted by Schleiermacher. Now those who are strangers to the work of theology urge against this method, that what they are concerned about is the objective bearing of theological doctrines and not the interpretation of them as reflected in the subject, and that this method renders the whole matter uncertain. Such a view is at variance with the right theory of knowledge for in knowledge we observe and explain even the objects of sense-perception, not as they are in themselves, but as we perceive them. If what is intended in Dogmatics is merely to describe objectively Divine operations, that means the abandonment of the attempt to understand their practical bearing. For apart from voluntary activity, through which we receive and utilise for our own blessedness the operations of God, we have no means of understanding objective dogmas as religious truths.

Objective knowledge in this region is disinterested knowledge. Such knowledge, it is true, is quite in place in natural science; but in theology, however coolly we may sketch out its formal relations, we have to do with spiritual processes of such a kind that our salvation depends on them. Merely objective delineation, therefore, far from exhausting theological cognition, does the work in a most inadequate fashion. Whoever thinks that the method to be followed in this book is such as to evaporate the truths of Christianity and expose them to the perils of doubt, betrays in the last resort the paucity of his religious experience, and especially his ignorance of the fact that the more objectively the truths of Christianity are handed down in narrative form, the closer at hand will doubt be found.

Justification, reconciliation, the promise and the task of the Kingdom of God, dominate any view of Christianity that is complete. The outstanding ethical character of this religion comes out in the fact that the *summum bonum*—the Kingdom of God—is promised only as the ground of blessedness, while at the same time it is the task to which Christians are called.

IV. Modern and Postmodern

A. Lutheran

68. Dietrich Bonhoeffer (1906–1945) | *Discipleship* & *Life Together*

Dietrich Bonhoeffer was a Lutheran pastor and theologian. When the Nazi regime assumed power in Germany, he was just twenty-one. He wrote, worked, and eventually died to resist them.

Bonhoeffer was born in a family of academics with theologians in his family tree. As a fourteen-year-old he set himself toward a career in theology. Studying at the Universities of Berlin and Tübingen, he took degrees in theology, and by twenty-four he was back in Berlin as lecturer in systematic theology. Bonhoeffer could have secured a long and profitable teaching career, but he chose instead to resist the Nazis. His eventual involvement in the plot against Hitler's life easily gives a false impression of Bonhoeffer, because it doesn't tell the whole story. Before the plot, he tirelessly supported the Confessing Church and participated in Europe's ecumenical movements to cultivate a church capable of withstanding the Nazi tide. He pastored churches, formed a school to train ministers, spoke publically about the failure of German Christianity to retain its identity in the face of power, and was principally involved in drafting the Barmen Declaration (1934). The Declaration was a public manifesto of allegiance to Jesus Christ over and above all else. One clause reads, "*We repudiate the false teaching that the church can and must recognize yet other happenings and powers, personalities and truths as divine revelation alongside this one Word of God.*" In 1939, as Nazi pressure mounted, some of his friends helped him escape Germany, putting him out of harm's way. He would not remain in safe exile, however, and returned on his own, later explaining his reasons in a letter to Reinhold Niebuhr:

> I shall have no right to participate in the reconstruction of Christian life in Germany after the war if I do not share the trials of this time with my people . . . Christians in Germany will face the terrible alternative of either willing the defeat of their nation in order that Christian civilization may survive, or willing the victory of their nation and thereby destroying our civilization.

I know which of these alternative I must choose, but I cannot make this choice in security.[1]

Bonhoeffer wrote the letter from prison. We have it today, and many others, because Bonhoeffer's impact on his guards was so profound that after his execution they gathered his letters and papers and secretly smuggled them out.

We take our selections from Bonhoeffer's most popular works: *Discipleship* (in German, simply *Nachfolge*, or "following") and *Life Together*. In *Discipleship* (1937), Bonhoeffer develops the distinction between "cheap grace" and "costly grace." As Bonhoeffer saw it, the German church sacrificed the costliness of the gospel for the sake of mere forgiveness of sins. Bonhoeffer credits Luther for bringing the wonder of God's grace—salvation by faith alone—back to the church, but he cautions that when forgiveness is torn away from Jesus' costly obedience, then what remains is merely *cheap* grace. Forgiveness without cost. That is what Bonhoeffer saw when he looked at the state of German Christianity as the Nazi regime steadily rose to power.

The second selection is from *Life Together* (1939) in which Bonhoeffer describes the monastic-like fellowship at the seminary he founded in Finkenwalde. *Life Together* portrays costly grace in action as the form of community life for those who together follow the way of Jesus. The Christian life, for Bonhoeffer, centers on the free gift of God's grace received by faith alone (he was Lutheran to the core), and the shape that one's life takes in the company of grace will be costly. Bonhoeffer's death testifies to that cost.

Discipleship (1937)

Cheap grace is the deadly enemy of our Church. We are fighting today for costly grace.

Cheap grace means grace sold on the market like cheapjacks' wares. The sacraments, the forgiveness of sin, and the consolations of religion are thrown away at cut prices. Grace is represented as the Church's inexhaustible treasury, from which she showers blessings with generous hands, without asking questions or fixing limits. Grace without price; grace without cost! The essence of grace, we suppose, is that the account has been paid in advance; and, because it has been paid, everything can be had for nothing. Since the cost was infinite, the possibilities of using and spending it are infinite. What would grace be if it were not cheap?

Cheap grace means grace as a doctrine, a principle, a system. It means forgiveness of sins proclaimed as a general truth, the love of God taught as the Christian "conception" of God. An intellectual assent to that idea is held to be of itself sufficient

---

1. Bonhoeffer, *Letters and Papers from Prison*, 573.

to secure remission of sins. The Church which holds the correct doctrine of grace has, it is supposed, *ispo facto* a part in that grace. In such a Church the world finds a cheap covering for its sins; no contrition is required, still less any real desire to be delivered from sin. Cheap grace therefore amounts to a denial of the living Word of God, in fact, a denial of the Incarnation of the Word of God.

Cheap grace means the justification of sin without the justification of the sinner. Grace alone does everything, they say, and so everything can remain as it was before. "All for sin could not atone." The world goes on in the same old way, and we are still sinner "even in the best life" as Luther said. Well, then, let the Christian live like the rest of the world, let him model himself on the world's standards in every sphere of life, and not presumptuously aspire to live a different life under grace from his old life under sin. That was the heresy of the enthusiasts, the Anabaptists and their kind. . . . Let the Christian rest content with his worldliness and with this renunciation of any higher standard than that world. He is doing it for the sake of the world rather than for the sake of grace. Let him be comforted and rest assured in his possession of this grace—for grace alone does everything. Instead of following Christ, let the Christian enjoy the consolations of his grace! That is what we mean by cheap grace, the grace which amounts to the justification of sin without the justification of the repentant sinner who departs from sin and from whom sin departs. Cheap grace is not the kind of forgiveness of sin which frees us from the toils of sin. Cheap grace is the grace we bestow on ourselves.

Cheap grace is the preaching of forgiveness without requiring repentance, baptism without church discipline, Communion without confession, absolution without personal confession. Cheap grace is grace without discipleship, grace without the cross, grace without Jesus Christ, living and incarnate.

Costly grace is the treasure hidden in the field; for the sake of it a man will gladly go and sell all that he has. It is the pearl of great price to buy which the merchant will sell all his goods. It is the kingly rule of Christ, for whose sake a man will pluck out the eye which causes him to stumble, it is the call of Jesus Christ at which the disciple leaves his nets and follows him.

Costly grace is the gospel which must be *sought* again and again, the gift of which must be *asked* for, the door at which a man must *knock*.

Such grace is costly because it asks us to follow, and it is *grace* because it calls us to follow *Jesus Christ*. . . . If grace is God's answer, the gift of Christian life, then we cannot for a moment dispense with following Christ. But if grace is the data [i.e. bare facts] for my Christian life, it means that I set out to live the Christian life in the world with all my sins justified beforehand. I can go and sin as much as I like, and rely on this grace to forgive me, for after all the world is justified in principle by grace. I can therefore cling to my bourgeois secular existence, and remain as I was before, but with the added assurance that the grace of God will cover me. It is under the influence of this kind of "grace" that the world has been made "Christian," but at the cost of secularizing the Christian religion as never before. The antithesis between Christian life and the life of bourgeois respectability is at an end.

Life Together (1939)

It is not simply to be taken for granted that the Christian has the privilege of living among other Christians. Jesus Christ lived in the midst of his enemies. At the end all his disciples deserted him. On the Cross he was utterly alone, surrounded by evildoers and mockers. For this cause he had come, to bring peace to the enemies of God. So the Christian, too, belongs not in the seclusion of a cloistered life but in the thick of his foes. There is his commission, his work. "The Kingdom is to be in the midst of your enemies. And he who will not suffer this does not want to be of the Kingdom of Christ; he wants to be among friends, to sit among roses and lilies, not with the bad people but the devout people. O you blasphemous and betrayers of Christ! If Christ had done what you are doing who would ever have been spared?" (Luther). . . .

Christianity means community through Jesus Christ and in Jesus Christ. No Christian community is more or less than this. Whether it be a brief, single encounter or the daily fellowship of years, Christian community is only this. We belong to one another only through and in Jesus Christ.

What does this mean? It means, first, that a Christian needs others because of Jesus Christ. In means, second, that a Christian comes to others only through Jesus Christ. It means, third, that in Jesus Christ we have been chosen from eternity, accepted in time, and united for eternity.

First, the Christian is the man who no longer seeks his salvation, his deliverance, his justification in himself, but in Jesus Christ alone. He knows that God's word in Jesus Christ pronounces him guilty, even when he does not feel his guilt, and God's Word in Jesus Christ pronounces him not guilty and righteous, even when he does not feel that he is righteous at all. The Christian no longer lives of himself, by his own claims and justification, but by God's claims and justification. He lives wholly by God's Word pronounced upon him, whether that Word declares him guilt or innocent.

The death and the life of the Christian is not determined by his own resources; rather he finds both only in the Word that comes to him from the outside, in God's Word to him. The Reformers expressed it this way: our righteousness is an "alien righteousness," a righteousness that comes from outside of us (*extra nos*). They were saying that the Christian is dependent on the Word of God spoken to him. He is pointed outward, to the Word that comes to him. The Christian lives wholly by the truth of God's Word in Jesus Christ. If somebody asks him, Where is your salvation, your righteousness? he can never point to himself. He points to the Word of God in Jesus Christ, which assures him salvation and righteousness. He is as alert as possible to this Word. Because he daily hungers and thirsts for righteousness, he daily desires the redeeming Word. And it can come only from the outside. In himself he is destitute and dead. Help must come from the outside, and it has come and comes daily and anew in the Word of Jesus Christ, bringing redemption, righteousness, innocence, and blessedness.

But God has put this Word into the mouth of men in order that it may be communicated to other men. When one person is struck by the Word, he speaks it to others. God has willed that we should seek and find His living Word in the witness of a brother, in the mouth of man. Therefore, the Christian needs another Christian who speaks God's Word to him. He needs him again and again when he becomes uncertain and discouraged, for by himself he cannot help himself without belying the truth. He needs his brother man as a bearer and proclaimer of the divine word of salvation. He needs his brother solely because of Jesus Christ. The Christ in his own heart is weaker than the Christ in the word of his brother; his own heart is uncertain, his brother's is sure.

And that also clarifies the goal of all Christian community: they meet one another as bringers of the message of salvation. As such, God permits them to meet together and gives them community. Their fellowship is founded solely upon Jesus Christ and this "alien righteousness." All we can say, therefore, is: the community of Christians springs solely from the Biblical and Reformation message of the justification of man through grace alone; this alone is the basis of the longing of Christians for one another.

Second, a Christian comes to others only through Jesus Christ. Among men there is strife. "He is our peace," says Paul of Jesus Christ (Eph 2:14). Without Christ there is discord between God and man and between man and man. Christ became the Mediator and made peace with God and among men. Without Christ we should not know God, we could not call upon Him, nor come to Him. But without Christ we also would not know our brother, nor could we come to him. The way is blocked by our own ego. Christ opened up the way to God and to our brother. Now Christians can live with one another in peace; they can love and serve one another; they can become one. But they can continue to do so only by way of Jesus Christ. Only in Jesus Christ are we one, only through him are we bound together. To eternity he remains the one Mediator.

Third, when God's Son took on flesh, he truly and bodily took on, out of pure grace, our being, our nature, ourselves. This was the eternal counsel of the triune God. Now we are in him. Where he is, there we are too, in the incarnation, on the Cross, and in his resurrection. We belong to him because we are in him. That is why the Scriptures call us the Body of Christ. But if, before we could know and wish it, we have been chosen and accepted with the whole Church in Jesus Christ, then we also belong to him in eternity *with* one another. We who live here in fellowship with him will one day be with him in eternal fellowship. He who looks upon his brother should know that he will be eternally united with him in Jesus Christ. Christian community means community through and in Jesus Christ. On this presupposition rests everything that the Scriptures provide in the way of directions and precepts for the communal life of Christians.

"But as touching brotherly love ye need not that I write unto you: for ye yourselves are taught of God to love one another . . . but we beseech you, brethren, that ye increase more and more" (1 Thess 4:9, 10). God himself has undertaken to teach brotherly love; all that men can and to it is to remember this divine instruction and the admonition to excel in it more and more. . . . One is a brother to another only through Jesus Christ. I am a brother to another person through what Jesus Christ did for me and to me; the other person has become a brother to me through what Jesus Christ did for him. This fact that we are brethren only through Jesus Christ is of immeasurable significance. Not only the other person who is earnest and devout, who comes to me seeking brotherhood, must I deal with in fellowship. My brother is rather that other person who has been redeemed in Christ, delivered from his sin, and called to faith and eternal life. Now what a man is in himself as a Christian, his spirituality and piety, constitutes the basis of our community. What determines our brotherhood is what that man is by reason of Christ. Our community with one another consists solely in what Christ has done to both of us. . . .

IV: Modern and Postmodern

A. Lutheran

69. Wolfhart Pannenberg (1928–2014) | *Systematic Theology*, Vol. 3

Wolfhart Pannenberg was one of the most accomplished and influential Protestant theologians of the twentieth century. Yet growing up reading Nietzsche during the Nazi regime, Pannenberg was an atheist in his early adulthood (so taken with Nietzsche that he read all his writings in a year). Pannenberg later wrote that his movement toward faith was through a series of experiences, the most important of which occurred on a lonely stretch of railroad tracks. "Seeing an otherwise ordinary sunset," he wrote,

> I was suddenly flooded by light and absorbed in a sea of light which, although it did not extinguish the humble awareness of my finite existence, overflowed the barriers that normally separate us from the surrounding world. I did not know at the time that January 6 was the day of Epiphany, nor did I realize that in that moment Jesus Christ had claimed my life as a witness to the transfiguration of this world in the illuminating power and judgment of his glory. But there began a period of craving to understand the meaning of life, and since philosophy did not seem to offer the ultimate answers to such a quest, I finally decided to probe the Christian tradition more seriously than I had considered worthwhile before.[1]

Pannenberg went on to study theology in Berlin, Göttingen, Heidelberg, and Basel (where he studied under Karl Barth for a short time), and he held several professorships, including a twenty-five-year career at the University of Munich.

Pannenberg was a Lutheran, and his portrayal of the Christian life leans heavily on Luther. His account of the Christian life draws out the mystical dimensions of Luther's theology, specifically the Christian's real participation in Christ. Pannenberg presents salvation as our *transformational participation* in the relation of the Son to the Father: "caught up both in the Son's fellowship of love with the Father

---

1. Pannenberg, "God's Presence in History," 160.

and in the obedience of the Son of God on his path to the world."² The Spirit lifts Christians outside themselves into participation in the relation of the Father and the Son and thereby transforms *what* they are. A mystical union takes place through the Spirit's activity in which the believer is, in a *real* way, ontologically transformed (in their very essence).³

This is not the general pattern for Lutheran theologians. Rather than center the Christian life on God's declaration of forgiveness—as post-Reformation Lutherans typically do—Pannenberg develops his account of Christian life by orienting it around *adoption*. Being forgiven by God is indeed a reality of Christian existence, but Pannenberg believes that being adopted by God more effectively contextualizes what happens to Christians when God justifies them. The doctrine of justification, which Luther called the center of Christian theology, doesn't fall away in Pannenberg's theology of the Christian life; he decenters it in such a way that one's *real* transformation is more readily perceived and better represented theologically. Pannenberg believes this is more faithful to the biblical witness than much post-Reformation Protestant theology and returns us to Luther's *mystical* understanding of the Christian's participation in Christ.⁴

Systematic Theology, Vol. 3 (1993)

Adoption as God's Children and Justification

Faith links believers as they rely on him and on the promise of salvation that is given in his message and history. But fellowship with Jesus Christ includes participation in his relation as Son to the Father. This is the "divine sonship" that grants believers assurance of the future "inheritance," the new life manifested already in Jesus Christ. For Paul our being God's children comes to expression in calling on God as Father. We may see here an expression of trust in God and also of love for him in response to his love for us. But in keeping with the sonship of Jesus (cf. Phil 2:5) believers do not receive the Father's love for themselves alone. They can abide in the love of God, and hence in fellowship with God, only as they pass it on to others (Luke 11:4 [cf. 6:36]; Matt 5:44-45). As the children of God, then, believers are caught up both in the Son's fellowship of love with the Father and in the obedience of the Son of God on his path to the world. In other words, those whom the Spirit of God impels are God's children (Rom 8:14). Being God's children is thus of the essence of the Christian life. We see

---

2. Pannenberg, *Systematic Theology*, Vol. 3, 211-12.
3. Ibid., 216, n. 368.
4. Ibid., 215-19.

this point not merely in Paul. We find at least a starting point for the thought in Jesus himself, not merely in the blessing that is promised to peacemakers, that they will be God's children (Matt 5:9), or in the corresponding promise to those who follow God's example and love their enemies (Luke 6:35), but also in the paradigmatic significance that Jesus ascribes to childlike trust in God's fatherly care in respect of our relation to the rule of God. Those who do not receive God's kingdom as little children will not attain to it (Luke 18:17 = Mark 10:15). . . .

What is the relation between adoption and justification? The express formulation of the doctrine of justification as distinct from adoption is a specific theme only in Pauline theology. The related stress on the decisive importance of faith as we stand before God, and our being referred to the grace of God, may be found, however, in all the NT testimonies. Paul's doctrine of justification gave this thought its sharpest formulation, but this way of speaking is not the only one by which primitive Christianity described the salvation of God that is given in Christ. We need only recall the way John speaks of the life and light of divine truth that are manifested in Jesus Christ. God's saving work in Jesus Christ is the central theme of all the NT writings. The doctrine of justification is just one of many ways of expounding the theme. Even for Paul himself it is not the only center of his theology that controls all else. For Paul this center is Jesus Christ, in whose death and resurrection God acted to save all people. . . .

Surveying Justification in the Christian Tradition[5]

For the most part the Greek Fathers interpreted the salvation that Christ has opened up for us along the lines of the Johannine thinking, especially in relation to the incarnation of the Logos and the following with God that is thereby established. This way of looking at things is still today the predominant one in the Orthodox churches. The Pauline doctrine of justification took on central importance for an understanding of salvation only in Western Christianity. But it did so here only by way of the study of Paul by Augustine and his mentor Ambrose and on account of its critical function in the Pelagian controversy. Nevertheless, even in Augustine the effect of Paul's doctrine of justification was limited to its subordination to the idea of the transforming efficacy of the grace or *caritas* that flows out from God. In this way Augustine decisively influenced not merely the understanding of salvation but the doctrine of grace in the Latin Middle Ages.[6] The Reformation, in spite of the breakthrough to a deeper understanding of the true Pauline significance of the doctrine of justification, could not fully free itself from the thrust of relating of the ideas of justification and renewal that went back to Augustine. Luther came closest to doing so with his relating of what is said about justification to the fellowship with Christ that is achieved in the act of faith, whereas the "forensic" [i.e.

---

5. The following subheadings are added to make Pannenberg's argument more transparent.

6. Text corrected. Bromiley's translation incorrectly reads, "*and* the doctrine of grace in the Latin Middle Ages."

legal] concept of justification in Melanchthon and his school along the lines of a divine verdict based on the merits of Christ—a concept that the Formula of Concord stated even more sharply in *SD* 3:11ff—inclines constantly toward supplementary moral renewal in spite of all the distinction it tries to make. . . .

Luther's View: Life Outside Ourselves in Christ

Ecstatic fellowship with Christ, to whom believers entrust themselves, forms the basis of Luther's understanding of justification. He starts here with his view of the act of faith that takes believers out of themselves and sets them in Christ. . . . It is everywhere presupposed [in Luther's lectures on Romans, Galatians, and Hebrews] that faith sets us ecstatically in Christ, who is outside us, and later, too, Luther stressed that the basis of our salvation is outside us. But precisely by the fact that faith in Christ is outside us, Christ is also in us. . . . We see here the Augustinian thought of an exchange between human sins and Christ's righteousness. But unlike Augustine in his commentary on the Psalms, Luther does not base the thought [of the exchange of the Christian's sins with Christ's righteousness] on Christ's intercession but on the union of believers with Christ by faith, which he liked to describe in the language of bride mysticism. For him, then, the righteousness of believers rests on the participation in Christ and his righteousness that is effected by faith. . . . The whole life of Christians in faith might be described as a being in Christ.

Baptized to Share in the Fellowship of the Triune God

Today the theology of the Reformation churches as well as Roman Catholic theology needs to be aware of the limitations of the traditional handing of the theme of justification on both sides of the confessional divide. Each of the two types of confessional teaching has serious defects when compared with the Pauline witness to the righteousness of faith. The Tridentine decree [i.e., the Catholic decree from the Council of Trent] did not pay adequate attention to the decisive significance of faith for the relation of those born again by baptism to God. The Reformation side, Luther apart, does not give due attention to the relation between justification and baptism but attempts, contrary to Paul, to ground the righteousness of faith in the act of pronouncing righteous. Face with these theological shortcomings the churches have little reasons to condemn, for the sake of the gospel, the views on the opposite side that diverge from their own doctrinal model as though their own teaching were perfectly and completely identical with that of the gospel, or even simply with the theology of the apostle Paul. A modern view is that the differences in teaching about justification are the antitheses of two theological schools, both of which are trying to describe fellowship with Jesus Christ as decisive for partaking of salvation, and that in their attempts to do this both stand in need of correction by the witness of scripture.

The same applies in the question of the theological ranking of Paul's vocabulary of justification side by side with other NT accounts of believers' participation in salvation, especially as regards regeneration and adoption into the filial relation of Jesus to the Father. There is no reason to *subordinate* these other descriptions to the idea of justification, particularly as Paul himself already presupposed faith fellowship with Christ in the verdict of justification and then developed this theme in terms of adoption into the filial relation to the Father. We must certainly make an effort to relate to one another the different descriptions of the way believers partake of salvation. We might do this best if we remember that each of them has a relation to baptism. In baptism there takes place our regeneration by the Holy Spirit. Baptism is the basis of the adoption of believers as God's children (Gal 3:26–27; cf. John 1:12–13). Baptism relates to hope of the inheritance of eternal life (1 Pet 1:3–4), which for Paul, too, is part of belonging to God's family (Gal 4:7; Rom 8:17). The word of the righteousness of faith also relates to baptism (Gal 3:24–26; cf. Titus 3:7). Baptism is thus the common reference point for all these theological interpretations

The declaring righteous of those who are linked to Jesus Christ by faith has only a partial function in descriptions of the event, or its result, that is elsewhere called regeneration. Paul could also call this being reconciled to God, or peace with God (Rom 5:1). Defining this state as adoption takes us deeper. Declaring righteous is just one element, the establishing of the reconciliation without which we could not speak of believers sharing in this filial relation to the Father. Being in this relation, however, is the true content of the new relation to God as a result of regeneration. The same applies to faith's fellowship with Christ. This is certainly primarily a fellowship with Christ on his destined way to crucifixion and resurrection. But its core lies in participation in the filial relation of Jesus to the Father and therefore in the intratrinitarian life of God. On this there rests finally the hope of the inheritance of eternal life by resurrection from the dead. Jesus could claim the authority to assure believers and those who confessed him of this hope only because he is the eternal Son of the Father and draws believers into his eternal fellowship with the Father. In this connection we are to understand our acceptance into the filial relation of Jesus to the Father as also the fulfilling of God's purpose for humanity at creation (Col 3:9–10). For with this adoption we are the new humanity that God had in mind at the first, in righteousness and true purity (Eph 4:24).

IV: Modern and Postmodern

A. Lutheran

70. Tuomo Mannermaa (1937–2015) | *Christ Present in Faith: Luther's View of Justification*

The Finnish Lutheran theologian Tuomo Mannermaa was a leader in ecumenical dialogue between the Finnish Lutheran Church and the Russian Orthodox Church. In the 1970s and 1980s, Finnish Lutherans actively engaged with their Russian Orthodox neighbors on themes related to salvation, and from those discussions Mannermaa initiated a fresh and controversial interpretation of Martin Luther's theology. One scholar wrote of him,

> my respect for his quiet faith in Christ and his burning concern for the unity of his church and for the cultivation of a strong faith and life of new obedience in Christ's footsteps deepened at that time and in later encounters. It was clear that the love of the Lord Jesus had shaped this gracious, kindly, pious man.[1]

A group of like-minded scholars gathered around Mannermaa, called the Finnish School or sometimes just the Mannermaa School.

Mannermaa's reading of Luther arose from a close examination of Luther's interpretation of St. Paul's letters, particularly Luther's commentary on Galatians. In 1989, after years of dialogue with Russian Orthodox partners, Mannermaa published *Christ Present in Faith* (originally, *In inpsa fide Christus adest*). Mannermaa argues that the strict distinction between justification and sanctification—that has come to characterize post-Reformation Lutheran theology—is not at all a central or constitutive distinction in the theology of Luther himself. "The doctrine of justification and the idea of sanctification constitute one whole in Luther's theology," Mannermaa contends.[2] Luther's view of justification has *deification* at its center because justification is a divine act of *divinization* that changes a person's relationship with God ontologically (one's

---

1. Kolb, "In Memoriam," para 3.
2. Mannermaa, *Christ Present in Faith*, 46.

essence). This shifts the theological register from *declared* righteousness/forgiveness to being *made* righteous/holy.

Convinced that Luther's concept of faith denotes a "real" union with the person of Christ, Mannermaa argues that believers participate in the very essence of God. Justification is not primarily about forensic declaration but about the real "ontic" presence of Christ in the believer and their participation in the person and work of Christ. The forensic, legal aspect of justification is absorbed, on Mannermaa's reading of Luther, into a theology of *ontic participation*: justification-as-deification not justification-as-declaration.

Controversy broiled around Mannermaa's interpretation and continues to do so today, because it rejects—or at least significantly reworks—the mainstream Lutheran view of justification as forensic and transactional (known as "imputation"). Despite the controversy, however, it is significant given Mannermaa's long pursuit of church unity that his ecumenical spirit carried over into the perception of at least one scholar who disagreed with him. The two never settled their disagreement but, the scholar wrote, "My respect for his quiet faith in Christ and his burning concern for the unity of his church and for the cultivation of a strong faith and life of new obedience in Christ's footsteps deepened at that time and in later encounters. It was clear that the love of the Lord Jesus had shaped this gracious, kindly, pious man."[3]

The following selections from *Christ Present in Faith* show Mannermmaa's argument and the reasons why he believes Luther's view of salvation is based on the Christology of the early church.

Christ Present in Faith (1989)

Introduction

Late-nineteenth and early-twentieth century Protestant scholarship has considered it difficult, if not impossible, to find a mutual point of contact between the Orthodox and Lutheran understandings of Christian faith. Particularly the patristic-Orthodox "doctrine of divinization"[4] and the Lutheran "doctrine of justification" have been considered mutually contradictory....

---

3. Kolb, "In Memoriam."

4. Mannermaa defines the Orthodox doctrine of divinization as follows: "the divine life has been revealed in Christ. In the communion of the church, which is the body of Christ, human beings become participants in this life. In this way, the become partakers of the 'divine nature' (2 Peter 1:4). This "nature," that is, this divine life, permeates their essence like leaven, restoring it to its original state" (*Christ Present in Faith*, 4).

... Instead, the aim of this study is to look for a theological motif in the Lutheran concept of Christian faith which would be analogous to the notion of divinization and could thus serve as a point of contact with Orthodox theology. ...

When one looks for the motifs in Lutheran theology analogous to the concept of divinization, one's attention is drawn to the fact that Lutheran theology and tradition is undoubtedly familiar with the notion of God's essential indwelling in the believer (*inhabitatio Dei*). The class quotation on this *inhabitatio* is found in the *Formula of Concord* (FC), which is one of the Lutheran confessional texts (1577). According to this passage, God, in the very fullness of God's essence, is present in those who believe in God. It is important to recognize that the text explicitly rejects notions that God in godself would not "dwell" in Christians and that only God's "gifts" would be present in them. However, from the point of view of Lutheran self-understanding, the FC gives rise to a problem, namely, that the FC's definition concerning the relation between "justification" and "divine indwelling" is different from that found in Luther's theology, at least as far as terminology is concerned. Thus, in the FC, "justification by faith" merely denotes the forgiveness of sins that is "imputed" to Christians on the basis of the perfect obedience and complete merit of Christ. At the same time the *inhabitatio Dei* is made a separate phenomenon, logically *subsequent to justification*. ...

... At least on the level of terminology, justification and the real presence of God in faith are in danger of being separated by the one-sidedly forensic [i.e. legal] doctrine of justification adopted by the FC and most of subsequent Lutheranism. In Luther's theology, however, both these motifs are completely united in the person of Christ. Christ is both the *favor* and the *donum,* without separation or confusion ... Thus, the notion that Christ is present in the Christian occupies a much more central place in the theology of Luther than in the Lutheran theologies that came after him. Thus, it is easier to find a point of contact with the patristic concept of divinization in Luther's theology that in later Lutheran theologies. The idea of the divine life in Christ that is present in faith lies at the very center of the theology of the Reformer. ...

Chapter 1: The Basis for Justifying Faith ...

Faith as Participation in the person of Christ

It is a central idea of Luther's theology that in faith human beings *really* participate in the person of Christ, and in the divine life and victory that come with him. Or, to say it the other way round: Christ gives his person to us through faith. "Faith" means participation in Christ, in whom there is no sin, death, or curse.

> To the extent that Christ rules by His grace in the hearts of the faithful, there is no sin or death or curse. But where Christ is not known, these things remain.

And so all who do not believe lack this blessing and this victory. "For this" as John says, "is our victory, faith."[5]

In Luther's view, faith is a victory precisely because it unites the believer with the person of Christ, who, in himself, *is* the victory.

According to the Reformer, justifying faith does not merely signify a reception of the forgiveness imputed to a human being for the sake of the merit of Christ, which is the aspect emphasized by the *Formula of Concord*. Faith as real participation is Christ means participation in the institution of "blessing, righteousness, and life" which has taken place in Christ. Christ himself *is* life, righteousness, and blessing, because God is all this "by nature and in substance" (*naturaliter et substantialiter*) (Luther, *Lectures on Galatians*). Therefore, justifying faith means participation in God's essence in Christ. . . .

Hence, because faith means a real union with Christ, and because in Christ the Logos is of the same essence as God the Father, therefore the believer's participation in the essence of God is also real. This is what Luther means when he speaks of Christ as a "gift." Christ is not only the favor (*favor*) of God, that is, forgiveness, but also, in a real manner, a "gift" (*donum*).

Christ as a "gift" (donum)

The idea that Christ is both God's favor (*favor*) and God's gift (*donum*) permeates the entire theology of Luther. "Favor" signifies God's forgiveness and the removal of his wrath. In other words, "favor" is the attitude toward the human being in the "subject" of God. Christ as a "gift," in turn, denotes the real self-giving of God to the human being. The presence of Christ in faith is real, and he is present in it with all his essential attributes, such as righteousness, blessing, life, power, peace, and so forth. Thus, the notion of Christ as a "gift" means that the believing subject becomes a participant in the "divine nature." Indeed, the Reformer often refers to the same passages in the Second Letter of Peter on which also the patristic doctrine of *theopoiesis* is based.[6] . . .

. . . In the following extract, which is taken from a sermon in the so-called *Church Postil*, Luther expresses his thoughts concerning "favor," "gift," and "participation in the divine nature" with particular clarity:

> This is one of those apposite, beautiful (as St. Peter says in 2 Pet 1) precious and very great promises given to us, poor miserable sinners: that we are to become participants in the divine nature and be exalted so highly in nobility that we are not only to become loved by God through Christ, and have His favor and grace as the highest and most previous shrine, but also to have Him, the Lord Himself, dwelling in us in His fullness. Namely (he wants to say), His

---

5. *Lectures on Galatians* (1535), *Luther's Works* 26:282.
6. See, e.g., *Lectures on Galatians* (1535), *Luther's Works* 26:100.

love is not to be limited only to the removal of His wrath from upon us, and to having the fatherly heart which is merciful to us, but we are also to enjoy this love (otherwise it would be wasted and lost love, as it is said: "to love and not to enjoy . . . "), and gain great benefit and riches from it.[7]

Thus, in addition to being the "favor" (forgiveness), Christ is also the "gift." In other words, the presences of Christ means that the believer participates in forgiveness of sins and in the "divine nature." And when participating in God's essence, the Christian also becomes a partaker of the attributes of this essence.

Faith and the communication of attributes (communicatio idiomatum)

The notion that Christians are partakers of the "divine nature" means that they are "filled with all the fullness of God." God's righteousness makes Christians righteous; God's "life lives in them"; God's love makes them love, and so forth. Luther calls this event by various names, one of which "happy exchange." As regards the content of this event, however, the most accurate expression might be the "communication of attributes" (*communicatio idiomatum*), which the Reformer admittedly uses less frequently but which expresses the underlying idea well. The communication is not to be identified with the Christological *communicatio idiomatum*, but it must be understood in an analogical way. The idea of the communication of attributes as well as its relationship with the notion of *inhabitation Christi* is presented clearly, for example, in the following quote:

> And so we are filled with "all the fullness of God." This phrase, which follows a Hebrew manner of speaking, means that we are filled in all the ways in which He fills [a person]. We are filled with God, and he pours into us all His gifts and grace and fills us with His Spirit, who makes us courageous. He enlightens us with His light, His life lives in us, His beatitude makes us blessed, and His love causes love to arise in us. Put briefly, He fills us in order that everything that He is and everything He can do might be in us in all its fullness, and work powerfully.[8]

Faith communicates the divine attributes to the human being, because Christ himself, who is a divine person, is present in faith. Therefore, the believer is given all the "goods" (*bona*) of God in faith. It is easy to see that in Luther's theology the concept of justifying faith and the idea of the indwelling of Christ in faith cannot be separated, as we have already preliminarily stated. Justification does not merely denote the imputation of Christ's merit to the sinner, which would then be followed by the *inhabitatio Dei* as a separate phenomenon. In Luther's theology, justification in the meaning of the FC and the communication of attributes are both expressions and

---

7. *Crucigers Sommerpostille* (1544), WA 21:458, 11–22.
8. *Predict* (1525), WA 17/1:438, 14–28.

different sides of one and the same event. Especially in connection with the doctrine of the communication of attributes, this can be seen very clearly. It is precisely the Christ present in justifying faith who communicates God's saving attributes to the believer in the "happy exchange." God *is* righteousness, and in faith the human being participates in righteousness; God *is* joy, and in faith the human being participates in joy; God *is* life, and in faith the human being participates in life; God *is* power, and in faith the human being participates in power, and so forth.

The notion of the believer's real participation in the "divine nature" in Christ, and the doctrine of the communication of attributes related to it, reveals how essentially and inseparably the Reformer's theology of faith is based on the Christology of the early church and its emphasis on the real and ontological communication of attributes and the twofold nature of Christ. In Luther's theology, however, the patristic concept of redemption with its notion of *theopoiesis* is interpreted with the help of the doctrine of justification.

IV: Modern and Postmodern

B. Reformed

71. Friedrich Schleiermacher (1768–1834) | *The Christian Faith*

Friedrich Schleiermacher is remembered in the church as the "father of modern theology." What this means is that Schleiermacher was one of the first to rethink the essence of Christianity in light of the (potentially devastating) critiques of Christianity raised by the Enlightenment of the seventeenth and eighteenth centuries. To the "cultural despisers" of Christianity, as he called them, he proposed a way of doing theology that attempted to hold together the core teachings of the church, as displayed in the Bible and the Protestant confessions, in the context of the newly minted set of epistemological commitments that defined the shape of modernity. In short: he was amongst the first to exhibit a way of being both fully modern and genuinely Christian. It was a project of retrieval and reinterpretation.

Schleiermacher's theological project gained clarity in the text we read below: *The Christian Faith* published in the early 1830s, which is one of the most important works in the modern theological canon. The extract describes what grace looks like for Schleiermacher in this revisionist form. As with other doctrines, Schleiermacher is less interested in what grace "is" and more interested in describing the "experience" of that grace in the lives of Christians. What kind of experience does grace bring about in the Christian? Well, Schleiermacher finds his answer in the theme of sanctification. Sanctification is the process through which Christians develop in their "God-consciousness," which is a technical term for Schleiermacher's description of what lies at the heart of modern Christianity: a feeling of absolute dependency on the grace of God.

Despite the critiques Schleiermacher's methodological innovation has attracted (most notoriously by Karl Barth), there are at least two things of significance to be learnt as children of the father of modern theology—one methodological, the other theological. (1) Theology, if it is to be truly theological, never stands still. Theology, if it is to remain relevant, must be reinterpreted ever afresh in double dialogue with the world in which we live and with the teachings of the church—notice how Schleiermacher is interacting with sixteenth century ideas as much as nineteenth century thinking in our reading. (2) Sanctification doesn't happen all at once: the Christian life of grace is a long, slow, and sometimes difficult process—a "striving for holiness" that is worked out in fellowship with others and in absolute dependency on grace.

The Christian Faith (1830–1831)

§ 110. In living fellowship with Christ the natural powers of the regenerate are put at His disposal, whereby there is produced a life akin to His perfection and blessedness; and this is the state of Sanctification.

1. The retention of the term "sanctification" is justified because it is scriptural. But as it depends on a rather indefinite concept of the holy, a concept which divergent interpretations and usages have made yet more intricate, a still further exposition is necessary if it is to be used in Dogmatics. The first etymological consideration that has to be taken into account is the Old Testament use of the word for everything separated from ordinary social life and devoted to some use relating to God. This relation to God, however, makes no difference in any activity due to an impulse proceeding from Christ; for since it is produced by the absolutely powerful God-consciousness of Christ, it of itself includes severance from participation in the common sinful life. And fellowship being essential to human nature, this of itself supplies a basis for an active tendency to a new common life; just as, owing to its Old Testament use noted above, the expression carries with it the priestly dignity of all Christians and represents the new common life as a spiritual temple. So that the state of sanctification too may be regarded as service in this temple. This close connexion with characteristically Christian ideas makes the retention of the old term in the vocabulary of Dogmatics all the more desirable in view of the temptation at this point to snatch at expressions which tend to obscure what is peculiarly Christian in the spirit of the new life, and make it harder to distinguish the Christian development from a gradual attainment of perfection along purely natural lines.

The second consideration is the connexion of the term with holiness as a Divine attribute; for of course we hold by the interpretation of this given above. It is, however, also clear that the regenerate man, through the manner of life that we are now going to describe in more detail, develops a conscience also in others, in proportion as all his activities diverge from what happens in the common sinful life.

In both its aspects, however, we cannot call this condition holiness—that is, being holy—but sanctification, which means becoming holy, sanctifying oneself; which we call sanctification, because it is a striving for holiness. If the meaning were being holy, it would imply that a complete transformation had occurred at the moment of regeneration, every link with the sinful common life entirely ceasing, and the whole nature being completely and instantaneously penetrated by the life of Christ and brought under His sway. This change would then be all a part of regeneration, and out of it, there would be no doctrine to state about what later develops out of it.

Sanctification, then, being understood to be progressive—so that the content of time-experience becomes from the turning-point of regeneration ever further removed from what preceded that crisis, and ever approximates more to pure harmony with the impulse issuing from Christ, and therefore to indistinguishability from Christ Himself—we have the two points of view from which sanctification has to be considered.

2. First then, if we compare the state of one who is in process of being sanctified with what existed before regeneration, it is preferable to dwell not on points of difference from the moments in which the mastery of sinfulness was earlier manifested, but rather on the difference from those moments which previously came under preparatory grace. These preparatory workings we cannot limit to approximations to repentance and faith in thought and emotion; they are also to be seen in action; for it is contrary to nature that lively thoughts and strong feelings should have no influence on concurrent actions—stronger or weaker, of course, in proportion to their affinity. Indeed, it is possible that with the frequent repetition of similar influences, the active effects occur more and more easily and become habits. In each separate case, however, the impulse to the alteration of action comes from without and remains effective only for so long as the momentary emotion endures; it is not in a position to reproduce itself from within, as witness the common feeling of having under external compulsion done something quite foreign to one's nature. Such actions are not the doer's own; they belong to an external life that is showing its power within him. Deeds therefore which resemble those of the state of sanctification, but are not rooted in the regeneration of the doer, are properly deeds of the Christian common life exercising its power over the individual. It is thus also with habits formed in the same way, as best seen by reference to the illustration used in Scripture about strangers and fellow-citizens. The latter out of the inner power of their common indwelling characteristic spirit establish law and custom among themselves, and thus their acts are wholly in character. Strangers have no part in the formation of either; they have no formative power in themselves and merely accommodate themselves to custom, acting in many ways according to it even when no demand has been made on them. But if they return to their own country where these foreign influences no longer surround them, they divest themselves with the utmost ease of every adopted habit. It is therefore not the form, and still less the numerical value of separate actions or series of actions that differentiates the state of sanctification from the condition before regeneration. It is the fact that unwillingness to remain in the common life in which sin is ever being propagated has become a power of repulsion, constantly at work in the form of an essential tendency of being, while in itself this is but the consequence of having surrendered to the receptive influence of Christ; a

surrender which throughout the entire sphere of spontaneous activity has consolidated itself as a steadfast willingness to be controlled by Him.

This is still the only tenable distinction if, conversely, we look back on the old life from the standpoint of the new. That strength of the God-consciousness is not original; it is a gift which becomes ours only after sin has developed its power; and what has emerged in time can be removed in time only by its opposite. Hence not merely is approximation to the goal delayed by the fact that what have become habitual and therefore often and easily provoked sins have to be countered by the aforesaid power of repulsion, but inasmuch as the sinfulness of each has a ground in existence prior to him and external to him, his sin cannot be perfectly blotted out, but remains always something in process of disappearance. In so far as it has not yet disappeared, it may make itself visible, and acts will occur within the state of sanctification similar to those common before regeneration, where what emerges is the power of the sinful common life, whereas the traces of preparatory grace lie deeply hidden. Nay more; since even in sanctification growth does not take place without a preliminary struggle between the old man and the new, this struggle cannot at any point in its whole course be viewed as an even advance to increase in the power of the one and decrease in the power of the other. By the influence of the sinful common life around us our own sinfulness is constantly being stirred up again. In itself it might be steadily limited by the growth of the new man, but this cannot equally be said of the reinforcements it receives from without. At least in view of the variegated changes in this sphere, where in the most irregular and unforeseen ways the individual life is held in grip, more firmly or more slackly, by the common sinful life, it could only be explained by a special miracle, and not by the ordinary course of divine grace among men, if in that struggle there were not special moments when the power of sin came out more strongly than in the earlier moments. Even after regeneration, then, many and varied conditions appear, among others repentance, and this by no means always merely in the form of slight compunction for trifles. But this repentance is distinguished from every previous repentance by the fixed inward resolution to be no longer under the power of sin, and is to be conceived as a vanishing quantity in the same way as the repentance which, so long as even in obedience some opposition to the impulses proceeding from Christ makes itself felt, accompanies all actions which appear as fruits of this obedience, yet also show traces of opposition. Even if these intermittent evidences of the continued presence of sin make particular instants, as compared with others, seem relapses, none the less a settled consciousness remains that the longer the series of such fluctuations [are] observed, the greater is the advance seen to be on the whole, and that the certainty of faith as an understanding of what union with Christ means and as a delight in that union is always increasing, so that in the powers put at Christ's disposal sin can never win fresh ground, while all the time it is being dislodged from its former positions. It is chiefly by this fact, that sin can win no new ground, that the state of sanctification is most definitely distinguished from all that went before.

IV: Modern and Postmodern

B. Reformed

72. Karl Barth (1886–1968) | *The Christian Life*

Karl Barth is one of the giants of twentieth century theology. Born in Basel in 1886, he studied at the centers of liberal theology and entered the pastorate as planned in 1909. His theological world came crashing down, however, in 1914 when the signatures of his theological teachers appeared on the so-called "Manifesto of the Intellectuals" written in support of Wilhelm II's policy of militaristic aggression. Thereafter, he devoted his life to charting new trajectories in modern theology that took with uncompromising seriousness the revelation of God in Jesus Christ—a revelation that refused to be tied to war aims.

After losing his teaching position at the University of Bonn for refusing to swear allegiance to Hitler, he was forced in 1935 to take exile in his hometown of Basel where he would remain until his death in 1968. Over the course of his career, he published a massive, thirteen-part volume yet unfinished systematic theology: the *Church Dogmatics*. Spanning some six million words, he wrote at least that much again in other writings.

Selecting a text from this massive corpus on the theme of grace is difficult. Not only because of the sheer quantity but also because Barth was a "theologian of grace" through and through. His *Church Dogmatics* is one long meditation on the theme of grace as revealed in the Word of God. The extract below comes from the very final lectures that would have been revised by Barth and published as the ethical part-volume to his famed doctrine of reconciliation, had he not died before its completion. Published posthumously as *The Christian Life*, this treatise forms Barth's most mature thinking on what it means to live a life full of grace. The part-volume is arranged around the petitions of the Lord's Prayer. The reading below is taken from Barth's meditation on the second petition, which he organizes around the theme of "revolt." It makes for powerful reading. Shot through with political import, the point Barth makes is that grace is a costly kind of grace that calls the Christian (nay, places us "under a binding requirement") to engage in "revolt" against what he calls the "lordless powers": the forces of destruction, oppression, and chaos that work against the "renewal, the deepening and extending" of God's grace in the world.

The Christian Life (1976)

Christians pray to God that he will cause his righteousness to appear and dwell on a new earth under a new heaven. Meanwhile they act in accordance with their prayer as people who are responsible for the rule of human righteousness, that is, for the preservation and renewal, the deepening and extending, of the divinely ordained human safeguards of human rights, human freedom, and human peace on earth. . . .

Christians are summoned by God's command not only to zeal for God's honor but also to a simultaneous and related revolt, and therefore to entry into a conflict. Revolt or rebellion is more than the rejection of a particular possibility. Rejection can undoubtedly mean non-participation in actualizing the possibility. But it does not have to do so. One can obviously reject a possibility, that is, judge it negatively, and then for various reasons take part in its actualization. Furthermore, even the sharpest rejection does not in itself include within it one thing, namely, entry into the struggle for the actualization of a very different possibility opposed to the first one. In the thought, speech, and action demanded of Christians, the issue is not just that of rejecting what they see to be a bad possibility but that of rising up and revolting against its actualization: a revolt that has positive meaning and inner necessity because another possibility stands with such splendor before the eyes of the rebels that they cannot refrain from affirming and grasping it and entering into battle for its actualization. Their revolt against the first possibility is thus only the complement or the reverse side of their commanded struggle for this one. Because of this one it is unavoidable. In word and deed they say No here because they may and will say Yes there.

Christians thus exist under a binding requirement to engage in a specific uprising. The specific nature of the possibility for whose actualization they have to fight against the other is what makes the commanded revolt a specific one and differentiates it from other revolts. Like all others, they are, of course, acquainted with other revolts. Christians too can simply live and stand in some form of conflict for their free being. They can be in revolt against everything that would take their freedom away or restrict it: against painful conditions of life to which they are subject; against destinies which have led them or are about to lead them where they do not want to go [cf. John 21:18]; primarily and supremely against tyrants, those by whom they find themselves browbeaten, defrauded, and oppressed, who encroach upon them, who intentionally or unintentionally hurt them and threaten to make life impossible for them. They may resist in matters such as this as well. Nevertheless, they are not just people; they are

Christians, or at least they are seeking to be such. To the extent that they are Christians, or are engaged in becoming Christians, their life and its preservation, the possibility of their life and its actualization, cannot be strictly and seriously and primarily the thing for which they stand and rise up and fight. That against which they rebel as Christians cannot properly be that which threatens and imperils them in this regard. It cannot be this or that condition of life, however burdensome. It cannot be a blow of fate or a disposition of fate. It cannot be the persons who are so hostile, no matter how these oppress them. If revolts in such directions are not unfamiliar to them, if they have to admit that secretly or even very openly they often find themselves in revolts of this kind, they still see clearly that these are not their true revolt and that as Christians they can and may refrain from revolts of this kind, and in some circumstances will have to do so. The battles in which they entangle themselves and find themselves entangled along these lines are very different from the good fight of faith which is set before them [1 Tim 6:12]. At any rate, in the fight of faith they may sometimes at least have to accept the renunciation of such revolts or struggles or to see that incipient revolts of this kind are postponed or minimized. . . .

The general plight against which Christians are commanded to revolt and fight is the disorder which both inwardly and outwardly controls and penetrates and poisons and disrupts all human relations and interconnections. Disorder arises and consists in deviation from order. The human race exists in such deviation. The order from which it deviates is the form of an obedient life of people in fellowship with God which includes as such the corresponding form—the guarantee of human right, freedom, and peace—of a life of people in fellowship with one another. The former includes the latter because God is not an egoistic supreme being remote and alien from man and ruling over him as fate. He is the God of man, his Creator, Lord, Helper, and Judge. Furthermore, man for his part does not belong to anybody or to any powers. He belongs to God and is the man of God as God is the God of man. In the revelation of this order, in the declaration of its divine righteousness as the basis and guarantee of human righteousness, God is the One he is, the God who is gracious to man as such, who affirms all men, and who in so doing works all things together for their good. The disorder, which is the great plight under whose pressure people have to suffer, arises and consists—and this is the guilt of mankind as it is also his plight—in the ignoring and transgressing of this order.

The decisive action of their revolt against disorder, which, correctly understood, includes within itself all others, is their calling upon God in the second petition of the Lord's Prayer: "Thy kingdom come." . . . Thus to pray the prayer does not excuse them from provisionally rebelling and battling the disorder in their own human thoughts and words and works. On the contrary, they cannot pray the prayer aright without in so doing being projected into this corresponding action of their own which is provisional but nonetheless serious in this particular sphere.

B. REFORMED

When man, alienated from God, tries to live a lordless life, in no case does this result in his becoming the lord and master of the possibilities of his own life. . . . In the foolish and hopeless attempt to escape from the sphere of God's lordship, it is not so simple for man to become and be even a little God and Lord with the implied approximation to God's supremacy and controlling power in the fashioning of human existence. Even a partially free control has always been everywhere the myth, but only the myth and illusion, of the person who thinks and claims that he has come of age and is now sovereign and autonomous. In thinking this—and the more self-consciously and emphatically he does so, the more—he is overtaken by the opposite. He ceases to be the free lord and master he could and should have been in the sphere of God's lordship if, instead of fleeing from God, he had oriented himself to him. Parallel to the history of his emancipation from God there runs that of the emancipation of his own possibilities of life from himself: the history of the overpowering of his desires, aspirations, and will by the power, the superpower, of his ability. His capacities when he uses them, as Goethe describes so vividly and with such frightening profundity in his poem *The Sorcerer's Apprentice*, become spirits with a life and activity of their own, lordless indwelling forces. To be sure, he thinks he can take them in hand, control them, and direct them as he pleases, for they are undoubtedly the forces of his own possibilities and capacities, of his own ability. In reality, however, they escape from him, they have already escaped from him. They are entities with their own right and dignity. They are long since alienated from him. They act at their own pleasure, as absolutes, without him, behind him, over him, and against him, according to the law by which they arose, in exact correspondence to the law by which man himself thought that he should flee from God. As he did to God, so the different forms of his own capacity now do to him. In reality, he does not control them but they him. They do not serve him but he must serve them. He is the more their football and prisoner the less he is aware of the reversal that has long since taken place between him and them, and the more he still rocks himself in the illusion of his lordship and mastery over them. If we are to see the disorder and unrighteousness which corrupt human life and fellowship, we must not only not deny, but consider very seriously, not merely man's rebellion against God, but also the rebellion unleashed by it, that of human abilities, exalting themselves as lordless forces, against man himself.

IV: Modern and Postmodern

B. Reformed

73. Reinhold Niebuhr (1892–1971) | The Nature and Destiny of Man

The twenty-fifth anniversary issue of *Time* magazine, that great barometer of American culture, featured a cover image of the theologian, ethicist, minister, social critic, and public intellectual, Reinhold Niebuhr. An accolade of this stature says something of the huge impact of Niebuhr on American life and thought. Indeed, his agenda-setting books have been said to influence generations of theologians and public figures—including Martin Luther King, Jr. and Barack Obama. Niebuhr spent much of his working life at Union Theological Seminary in New York, where he would indeed pen some of the most influential books in twentieth-century American theology. Topping that list is the two-volume work based on his 1939 Gifford Lectures, *The Nature and Destiny of Man,* from which we'll draw below.

    As a minister in Detroit in the 1920s, where he was touched by the harsh reality of rapidly industrializing urban life, he preached what was known at the time as the "social gospel." And he practiced what he preached by working towards alleviating the social problems he encountered. Later, however, Niebuhr would become increasingly skeptical of the human predicament. He would replace his commitment to the social gospel with what he termed "Christian realism" that was more "realistic" about the possibility of social holiness. The social order, Niebuhr had now decided, is broken. It seeks self-elevation, self-deception, and inordinate self-assertion that can be summed up in one word: pride—the denial of our true nature and destiny. To counter the human condition of pride, and its gravitational pull inwards, requires more than proclamations of the social gospel, however well intended. It required grace—"the power of God in man," through the work of the Holy Spirit.

B. REFORMED

These ideas were developed more systematically in *The Nature and Destiny of Man*. The book is not without its controversy. In fact, Niebuhr's category of pride inspired Valarie Saiving's hugely influential essay of 1960 on the "human condition," which set about uncovering the gendered nature of theological reflection about sin and salvation. Niebuhr's diagnosis of the human condition as full of pride, Saiving concluded, reflects more the experience of men than women. This important critique notwithstanding, there are two interrelated themes of Niebuhr's worth holding in mind as we meditate on the particularities of our own human condition. (1) Against the stream of modern Western thought, there is no such thing as unqualified autonomy—the *nature* of the Christian life is destined to be relation with God and others and (2) despite the profundity of the sin (however explicated), the Christian life is *destined* for grace.

The Nature and Destiny of Man (1943)

Every facet of the Christian revelation, whether of the relation of God to history, or of the relation of man to the eternal, points to the impossibility of man fulfilling the true meaning of his life and reveals sin to be primarily derived from his abortive efforts to do so. The Christian gospel nevertheless enters the world with the proclamation that in Christ both "wisdom" and "power" are available to man; which is to say that not only has the true meaning of life been disclosed but also that resources have been made available to fulfil that meaning. In Him the faithful find not only "truth" but "grace."

The whole of Christian history is filled with various efforts to relate these two propositions of the Christian faith to each other, in such a way that the one will not contradict the other. These efforts are never purely academic; for the two sides of the gospel correspond to two aspects of historic reality. The two emphases are contained in the double connotation of the word "grace" in the New Testament. Grace represents on the one hand the mercy and forgiveness of God by which He completes what man cannot complete and overcomes the sinful elements in all of man's achievements. Grace is the power of God over man. Grace is on the other hand the power of God in man; it represents an accession of resources, which man does not have of himself, enabling him to become what he truly ought to be. It is synonymous with the gift of the "Holy Spirit". The Spirit is not merely, as in idealistic and mystical thought, the highest development of the human spirit. He is not identical with the most universal and transcendent levels of the human mind and consciousness. The Holy Spirit is the spirit of God indwelling in man. But this indwelling Spirit never means a destruction of human self-hood. There is therefore a degree of compatibility and continuity between human self-hood and the Holy Spirit. Yet the Holy Spirit is never a mere extension of man's spirits or identical with its purity and unity in the deepest or highest levels of consciousness. In that sense all Christian doctrines of "grace" and "Spirit" contradict mystical and idealistic theories of fulfilment.

The conception in Christian thought of a fulfilment and completion of life by resources which are not man's own, prevents Christian ideas of fulfilment by grace from standing in contradiction to the more fundamental conviction that human life and history cannot complete themselves; and that sin is synonymous with abortive efforts to complete them. It is furthermore in consistent relation with the proposition that man perceives the completeness beyond his incompleteness and the holiness beyond his sin only by faith. For if it is possible to become aware of the limits of human possibilities by a faith which apprehends the revelation of God from beyond those limits, it must be possible to lay hold of the resources of God, beyond human limits, by faith. And this certainly is reinforced by the character of the Christian revelation, according to which God is not a supernal perfection to which man aspires, but has resources of love, wisdom and power, which come down to man. The very apprehension of the "wisdom of God," the completion of the structure of meaning by faith, must have connotations of "power" in it. For if we understand the possibilities and limits of life from beyond ourselves, this understanding has some potentialities of fulfilling the meaning of life. It breaks the egoistic and self-centred forms of fulfilment, by which the wholesome development of man is always arrested and corrupted. For this reason it is not possible to give a fully logical or exactly chronological account of the relation of faith to repentance, of the apprehension of truth which is beyond our comprehension to the shattering of the self by a power from beyond ourself. If a man does not know the truth about God, who is more than an extension of his self (a truth to be known only by faith), he cannot repent of the premature and self-centred completion of his life around a partial and inadequate centre. But it can be, and has been, argued with equal cogency, that without repentance, that is, without the shattering of the self-centred self, man is too much his own god to feel the need of, or to have the capacity for, knowing the true God. The invasion of the self from beyond the self is therefore an invasion of both "wisdom" and "power," of both "truth" and "grace." The relation of insight to will, of wisdom to power, in this experience is too intricate to be subject to precise analysis. . . .

The self in this state of preoccupation with itself must be "broken" and "shattered" or, in the Pauline phrase, "crucified." It cannot be saved merely by being enlightened. It is a unity and therefore cannot be drawn out of itself merely by extending its perspective upon interests beyond itself. If it remains self-centred, it merely uses its wider perspective to bring more lives and interests under the dominion of its will-to-power. The necessity of its being shattered at the very centre of its being gives perennial validity to the strategy of evangelistic sects, which seek to induce the crisis of conversion. The self is shattered whenever it is confronted by the power and holiness of God and becomes genuinely conscious of the real source and centre of all life. In Christian faith Christ mediates the confrontation of the self by God; for it is in Christ that the vague sense of the divine, which human life never loses, is crystallized into a revelation of a divine mercy and judgment. In that revelation fear of judgment and hope of mercy are so mingled that despair induces repentance and repentance hope.

The Christian experience of the new life is an experience of a new selfhood. The new self is more truly a real self because the vicious circle of self-centredness has been broken. The self lives in and for others, in the general orientation of loyalty to, and love of, God; who alone can do justice to the freedom of the self ever all partial interests and values. This new self is the real self; for the self is infinitely self transcendent; and any premature centering of itself around its own interests, individually or collectively, destroys and corrupts its freedom. . . .

Whenever the power of sinful self-love is taken seriously there is a concomitant sense of gratitude in the experience of release from self. It is felt: that this is a miracle which the self could not have accomplished. The self was too completely its own prisoner by the "vain imagination" of sins to be able to deliver itself. Just as the truth of God which breaks the vicious circle of false truth, apprehended from the self as the false centre, can never be other than "foolishness" to the self-centred self until it has been imparted by "grace" and received by faith; so also the power which breaks the self-centred will must be perceived as power from beyond the self; and even when it has become incorporated into the new will, its source is recognized in the confession "I, yet not I".

IV: Modern and Postmodern

B. Reformed

74. Marilynne Robinson (1943–) | *Gilead*

Marilynne Robinson is an American novelist and theologian (though not in the formal academic or ecclesial sense). In 2005 she won the Pulitzer Prize for her novel, *Gilead*. Her other novels, *Housekeeping, Home,* and *Lila*, and her collections of non-fiction essays, have all received critical acclaim. All of Robinson's writing is informed by her Christianity, which is nowhere more apparent than in this selection from *Gilead*.

Robinson sensed God as a very young girl long before she ever had words for it. "I felt God as a presence before I had a name for him and long before I knew words like 'faith' or 'belief.' I was aware to the point of alarm of a vast energy of intention, all around me, barely restrained, and I thought everyone must be aware of it."[1] Robinson marvels over our capacity to be "awake and alert" to the world and to ourselves, and she refracts it through her characters.[2]

Robinson never draws her reader's gaze away from the world but *toward* it. God's presence is always *this-worldly*.[3] "I like Calvin's metaphor," she concedes, "nature is a shining garment in which God is revealed and concealed."[4] Calvin saw creation as a beautiful, glorious, and magnificent theater, and in Robinson's fiction, the world is luminous with God.[5] God loves his creation with such "pained and rapturous love" that all of it has worth, especially human persons.[6] We are worthy for we are loved by God, and

1. Robinson, *The Death of Adam*, 228–29.
2. Robinson, quoted in Isaacs, "Marylinne Robinson reflects on grace, the value of life," para. 7.
3. See Eilers, "The Beauty and Strangeness of Being."
4. Robinson, *When I Was a Child I Read Books*, 9.
5. Calvin, *Institutes*, 1.14.20; 1.58; 2.6.1.
6. Robinson, *When I Was a Child I Read Books*, 128.

through attentiveness to the worth of another person we are led toward God. In Robinson's fiction, the pilgrimage of faith entails loving attentiveness to each other, through which we discover our worth in God's great and persisting love for us.

This is all glimpsed in the selection from *Gilead*. The novel centers on an elderly pastor, John Ames, and his letters to his very young son. In this excerpt, John reflects on the importance of the Fifth Commandment: "Honor your Father and Mother." He explains that honoring parents originates in *perceiving* them rightly as gifts from God, sacred icons of God's great love for us. "The great kindness and providence of the Lord has given most of us someone to honor—the child his parent, the parent his child." God gives us to each other, and by attending to others as sacred gifts we are led to Him (the logic is remarkably like Calvin's opening move in the *Institutes*). Honor you mother, Ames tells his son, and the rewards will be great: "at the root of real honor is always the sense of the sacredness of the person who is its object."

Through John Ames and his young son, Robinson wants us to see that perception of God is grounded in *this-worldly* relations. We discover our worth as beings extravagantly loved by God through loving those unique and sacred persons who God gives us to love.

Gilead (2004)

Sometimes I almost forget my purpose in writing this, which is to tell you things I would have told you if you had grown up with me, things I believe it becomes me as a father to teach you. There are the Ten Commandments, of course, and I know you will have been particularly aware of the Fifth Commandment, Honor your father and your mother. I draw attention to it because Six, Seven, Eight, and Nine are enforced by the criminal and civil laws and by social custom. The Tenth Commandment is unenforceable, even by oneself, even with the best will in the world, and it is violated constantly. I have been candid with you about my suffering a good deal at the spectacle of all the marriages, all the households overflowing with children, especially Boughton's—not because I wanted them—but because I wanted my own. I believe the sin of covetise is that pang of resentment you may feel when even the people you love best have what you want and don't have. From the point of view of loving your neighbor as yourself (Leviticus 19:18), there is nothing that makes a person's fallenness more undeniable than covetise—you feel it right in your heart, in your bones. In that way it is instructive. I have never really succeeded in obeying that Commandment, Thou shalt not covet. I avoided the experience of disobeying by keeping to myself a good deal, as I have said. I am sure I would have labored in my vocation more effectively if I had simply accepted covetise in myself as something inevitable, as Paul seems to do, as the thorn in my side, so to speak. "Rejoice with those who rejoice." I have found that difficult too often. I was much better at weeping with those who weep. I don't mean that as a joke, but, it is kind of funny, when I think about it.

If I had lived, you'd have learned from my example, bad as well as good. So I want to tell you where I have failed, if the failures were important enough to have had real consequences, as this one certainly was.

But to return to the matter of honoring your mother. I think it is significant that the Fifth Commandment falls between those that have to do with proper worship of God and those that have to do with right conduct toward other people. I have always wondered if the Commandments should be read as occurring in order of importance. If that is correct, honoring your mother is more important than not committing murder. That seems remarkable, though I am open to the idea.

Or they may be thought of as different kinds of law, not comparable in terms of their importance, and honoring your mother might be the last in the sequence relating to right worship rather than the first in the series relating to right conduct. I believe this is a very defensible view.

The apostle says, "Outdo one another in showing honor," and also "Honor everyone." The Commandment is much narrower. The old commentators usually say "your father and mother" means anyone in authority over you, but that is the way people thought for a long time and a lot of harm came from it—slavery was "patriarchal," and so on. Anyone who happens to have authority over you is your parent! Then there have been some vicious, brutal parents in this world. "What do you mean, grinding the faces of the poor!" Does the text anywhere say, "Children will be given good things and *parents* will be sent empty away"? No, because parents are not equated with the rich or those in authority. Nowhere in Scripture is there father who behaves wickedly toward his child, but the rich and powerful in Scripture are wicked much more often than not. And if honoring authority means only that you don't go out of your way to defy it, that really cheapens the notion of honoring as it would apply to an actual mother. It would not be anything beautiful or important enough to be placed right at the center of the Ten Commandments, for goodness' sake.

I believe the Fifth Commandment belongs in the first tablet, among the laws that describe right worship, because right worship is right perception (see especially Romans 1), and here the Scripture commands right perception of people you have a real and deep knowledge of. How you would honor someone differs with circumstances, so you can only truly fulfill a general obligation to show honor in specific cases of mutual intimacy and understanding. If all this seems lopsided in favor of parents, I would point out again that it is the consistent example of parents in the Bible that they honor their children. I think it is notable in this connection that it is not Adam but the Lord who rebukes Cain. Eli never rebukes his sons, Old Samuel his. David never rebukes Absalom. At the very end, poor old Jacob rebukes his sons as he blesses them. A remarkable thing to consider.

There's a sermon here. The Prodigal Son as the Gospel text. I should ask Boughton if he has noticed this. But of course he has, of course he has. I must give that more thought.

My point here is that the great kindness and providence of the Lord has given most of us someone to honor—the child his parent, the parent his child. I have great respect for the uprightness of your character and the goodness of your heart, and your mother could not love you more or take greater pride in you. She has watched every moment of your life, almost, and she loves you as God does, to the marrow of your bones. So that is the honoring of the child. You see how it is godlike to love the *being* of someone. Your *existence* is a delight to us. I hope you never have to long for a child as I did, but oh, what a splendid thing it has been that you came finally, and what a blessing to enjoy you now for almost seven years. . . .

What the reading yields is the idea of father and mother as the Universal Father and Mother, the Lord's dear Adam and His beloved Eve; that is, essential humankind as it came from His hand. There's a pattern in these Commandments of setting things apart so that their holiness will be perceived. Every day is holy, but the Sabbath is set apart so that the holiness of time can be experienced. Every human being is worthy of honor, but the conscious discipline of honor is learned from this setting apart of the mother and father, who usually labor and are heavy-laden, and may be cranky or stingy or ignorant or overbearing. Believe me, I know this can be a hard Commandment to keep. But I believe also that the rewards of obedience are great, because at the root of real honor is always the sense of the sacredness of the person who is its object. In the particular instance of your mother, I know that if you are attentive to her in this way, you will find a very great loveliness in her. When you love someone to the degree you love her, you see her as God sees her, and that is an instruction in the nature of God and humankind and of Being itself. That is why the Fifth Commandment belongs on the first tablet. I have persuaded myself of it.

IV: Modern and Postmodern

C. Catholic

75. Henri de Lubac (1896–1991) | *The Mystery of the Supernatural*

Born to an ancient noble family in the south of France, in 1913 Henri de Lubac renounced his aristocratic background and entered the Society of Jesus. During his theological formation, which because of the Great War took place as much in exile (in England) as it did in his homeland, de Lubac was drafted into the French army to fight in the resistance. His experience of war had a lasting effect—both physically and theologically. When war would return to Europe a few decades later de Lubac's resistance would take place not on the battlefield but through a movement of "spiritual resistance," which included his involvement in the anti-Nazi journal *Témoignage chrétien* ("Christian Testimony"). His resistance against Nazism forced de Lubac into hiding. It was in this context of war and resistance that the theological seeds were sown for the reading below.

De Lubac was also one of the driving forces behind the *ressourcement* movement that contributed to the significant changes in the Catholic Church brought about by Vatican II. The *ressourcement* movement advocated a return to the original sources of Christianity, especially the writings of the early church. De Lubac was himself a fine historian who made significant contributions in the area of historical theology not least by making available a vast quantity of patristic texts in their original language and in translation. Recovering and engaging these sources, for de Lubac, was not simply a matter of historical interest. It was an urgent theological imperative which aimed at nothing less than the renewal of the church. On his return to the actual sources of Thomas Aquinas, for example, de Lubac felt that some of the dominant strands of modern Catholic theology had misunderstood what Thomas meant by the relation between nature and grace—between, that is, the natural and the supernatural. The strand of Thomistic theology du Lubac set out to critique focused, we will see below, on the concept of "pure nature." While much of modern Catholic theology spoke of a separation of the natural (that is, "pure nature") from the supernatural, de Lubac wanted to recover a more integrated account of their relationship. This new way of looking at grace would be explored systematically in his seminal text *Surnaturel* of 1946.

The implications of de Lubac's reconnecting of nature with grace for the Christian life were as vast as they were controversial. His rejection of "pure nature" meant that nothing is totally natural or fully independent of grace. All of nature is open to God. Culture is thus seen in a new, graced light—God gives grace to the whole of creation, infusing it and making it sacred. Most significantly, perhaps, is the implication that there is a natural desire for the supernatural in the Christian life. Human beings are naturally (rather than supernaturally) motivated to seek relationship with God. Grace, in this sense, perfects and works within nature rather than externally "upon" it. This strand of de Lubac's theology of grace proved particularly controversial since it could seem to bypass the traditional teaching that belief in God is defined by the Church in its responsibility as the "dispenser of grace." So controversial were de Lubac's views that he would once again find himself in "hiding." He was removed from his professorial duties at the Catholic University of Lyons and many of his books, including *Surnaturel*, were silenced by the Vatican. The extract below is taken from his 1965 book *Le Mystere du surnaturel*, published nearly twenty years after the publication of *Surnaturel* and around a decade after his being allowed to return to Lyons. In the book de Lubac returns to the theme of "pure nature" and seeks to clarify some of the controversy *Surnaturel* caused. Despite the turbulent relationship de Lubac had with ecclesial authority during the first half his life, the second half proved more stable. As we have said, he was hugely influential at Vatican II and the implementation of its theological reforms, and in 1983, at the age of eighty-two, he was made a cardinal by Pope John Paul II.

The Mystery of the Supernatural (1965)

It is said that a universe might have existed in which man, though without necessarily excluding any other desire, would have his rational ambitions limited to some lower, purely human, beatitude. Certainly I do not deny it. But having said that, one is obliged to admit—indeed one is automatically affirming—that in our world as it is this is not the case: in fact the "ambitions" of man as he is cannot be limited in this way. Further, the word "ambitions" is no longer the right one, nor, as one must see even more clearly, is the word "limits." In me, a real and personal human being, in my concrete nature—that nature I have in common with all real men, to judge by what my faith teaches me, and regardless of what is or is not revealed to me either by reflective analysis or by reasoning—the "desire to see God" cannot be permanently frustrated without an essential suffering. To deny this is to undermine my entire

Credo. For is not this, in effect, the definition of the "pain of the damned"? And consequently—at least in appearance—a good and just God could hardly frustrate me, unless I, through my own fault, turn away from him by choice. The infinite importance of the desire implanted in me by my Creator is what constitutes the infinite importance of the drama of human existence. It matters little that, in the actual circumstances of that existence, immersed as I am in material things, and unaware of myself, this desire is not objectively recognized in its full reality and force: it will inevitably be so the day I at last see my nature as what it fundamentally is—if it is ever to appear to me in this way. . . . For this desire is not some "accident" in me. It does not result from some peculiarity, possibly alterable, of my individual being, or from some historical contingency whose effects are more or less transitory. *A fortiori* it does not in any sense depend upon my deliberate will. It is in me as a result of my belonging to humanity as it is, that humanity which is, as we say, "called." For God's call is constitutive. My finality, which is expressed by this desire, is inscribed upon my very being as it has been put into this universe by God. And, by God's will, I now have no other genuine end, no end really assigned to my nature or presented for my free acceptance under any guise, except that of "seeing God." . . .

Such a being, then, has more than simply a "natural desire" to see God, *desiderium naturale*, a desire which might be interpreted vaguely and widely. . . . St. Thomas is most clear that such is not the case. The desire to see God is, for him, a "desire of nature" in man; better, it is "the desire of his nature," *naturae desiderium*: this expression, which he uses on several occasions, should be enough in itself to do away with any tendency to fancy interpretation. It therefore remains necessary to show how, even for a being animated with such a desire, there still is not and cannot be any question of such an end being "owed"—in the same sense in which the word rightly gives offence. It remains to show how it is always by grace even apart from the additional question of sin and its forgiveness that God "shows himself to him."[1] . . .

It is always within the real world, within a world whose supernatural finality is not hypothetical but a fact, and not by following any supposition that takes us out of the world, that we must seek an explanation of the gratuitousness of the supernatural in so far as the human mind can do so. But this is precisely what the modern hypothesis we are concerned with fails to do. I do not say that it is false, but I do say that it is insufficient. For it completely fails to show, as people seem to think and as by the logic of the theory it should, that I could have had another, more humble, wholly "natural" destiny. . . .

We do not find in him [Aquinas], any more than in the Fathers, that radical separation between abstract essence and the existing world which characterizes certain present-day scholastic speculation. . . . [W]hatever weight we attach to his argument, whatever its exact significance, how could anyone maintain that for him, in a "purely natural universe," the human soul would not have been directly created by God? St.

---

1. St. Thomas Aquinas, *Summa contra Gentiles*, III.52.

Thomas does not deal with a certain number of difficulties in regard to this matter which were only raised later on, and which we have to take into account nowadays; thus he does not treat in all its details the problem of gratuitousness: the philosophers or the heretics with whom he was arguing set him, as we have seen, a different task. It remains none the less true that, when he does deal with it, he never brings the finality itself into question. It seems likely, then, that had he ever had the problem put more immediately before him, he would have considered any solution dependent on the hypothesis of a "purely natural order," in other words the hypothesis of a different placed in a different world, to be verbal and irrelevant. No system entirely constructed on such a foundation-stone could legitimately base itself on him.

Sought along this path of a different finality, the solution to the problem of the gratuitousness of the supernatural could only really be found in the following way. It would have to be possible to note in the actual course of every real and personal existence—or, at least, if one envisages not so much individuals in themselves as the humanity of which they are a part and which unites them by the assignation of a single destiny, in the actual course of our race's concrete, historic existence—a definite moment when God intervenes either to assign an end which till then had been in doubt, or to change the end previously assigned to me. Either hypothesis would be absurd, if one considers it. In either case, one would be supposing a radical extrinsicism which must destroy either the idea of nature or that of finality, or possibly both. Neither the epic of the universe, nor the acting out of my personal destiny could include such a second start. Such a supposition is in any case—at least apparently and in principle—excluded by the axiom, which everyone admits, that the so-called state of "pure nature" can only be posited as a "futurable," as something which has never actually existed, even for a moment. However, it becomes impossible to escape from it once one has produced the theory that an end cannot be given freely for a definite being, existing here and now, unless there had first of all been a different end for him that was objectively, concretely realizable—in other words, once one has made "pure nature" in the modern sense the indispensable and sole guarantee of the gratuitousness of the supernatural. . . .

Either the idea of "pure nature" must be conceived as being actually in our world now, as its protagonists see it; in that case, if we are not to be led into absurdity, we must return to its earlier significance which never questioned the supernatural character of the last end, but only described "the structure proper to created spirit in our world." Or this idea of "pure nature" must be related to a different universe, since a purely natural order has never in fact existed, as the great majority of theologians would hold nowadays; in that case, being quite abstract, though there is nothing to criticize in it of itself, it does not appear wholly suitable for the service expected of it. However, whether one adopts or rejects it, if one succeeds in making clear—as at all costs we must—that the supernatural end can in no case be the object of any requirement or debt, even by a being who here and now has no other end, then there will no longer be any need to refer to this indirect consideration of an order that is purely natural even as to its finality. We have seen that it is not an adequate consideration. Perhaps we may now go so far as to admit that it is not a necessary one either. By trying, without seeking any fiction to take us beyond the limits of our world as God has made it, the only world we know, to show that the gift God offers of himself is and can only be totally free, and that one could never imagine any loftier or purer gratuitousness, I think we are embarking upon a really effective way, a way along which others may happily advance further. It seems to me, too, that this is the chief ways opened to us by tradition. If I succeed in this, without totally rejecting or obliging anyone else to reject every idea of "pure nature," then I shall have reinforced this all too fragile rampart of a fortress which defends for us all a truth older and loftier than all our reasonings and theories, a Truth which the Church's magisterium has recalled to us many times in the most explicit terms, and reiterated quite recently, without ever having allowed any one explanatory theory to become tied to it. And if there are those who feel that it is impossible to preserve that divine truth except by reference to the system of "pure nature," I would be the first to tell them that not merely have they every right to maintain it, but that they would be wrong to reject it.

IV: Modern and Postmodern

C. Catholic

76. Adrienne von Speyr (1902–1967) | *The Victory of Love*

The Swiss spiritual writer and medical doctor Adrienne von Speyr is one of the twentieth century's most significant, and indeed prolific, mystics. Her spiritual director was fellow Swiss theologian, Hans Urs von Balthasar, who directed her conversion to Roman Catholicism. The two formed a lifelong theological partnership—united by their shared interest in the mystical traditions, the relationship between spirituality and theology, and their commitment to lay ministry that combined contemplation and action. Over the course of her life, Speyr was flooded with vivid mystical visions (including apparitions of Mary and St. Ignatius). In fact, so regular were her mystical experiences that John Paul II said of Speyr that she led a "double life" in heaven and on earth. She regularly drew on these experiences in the sixty or so books she published over the course of her life, many of which took the form of biblical commentary.

The extract below is one such text. It is taken from her meditation on Romans 8, first published in 1953. The inspiration for this short text came from both a deep reading of Paul's writings and her own mystical experience of God.

It is not surprising that Speyr was attracted to Romans 8. The eighth chapter of Paul's Letter to the Romans has a long and fascinating reception history. It has attracted the attention of many of the Christian tradition's spiritual writers—stretching back at least to Origen. Curiously, it has tended to appeal to the fringes of what might be called the "institutional church": mystics, women, spiritual writers, even heretics.

The theological profundity of Speyr's short meditation is disproportionate to its size. Riffing on Romans 8, Speyr speaks of grace as the vehicle of our "incorporation" into the trinitarian life of the divine: it is through the gift of the Holy Spirit that we are conformed into the divine Sonship of Christ, and caught up in the love story of the trinitarian God. This grace, for Speyr, has no bound. It is given to all—irrespective of proximity to ecclesial "power." Perhaps that is why the kind of trinitarian logic Paul expounds, and Speyr develops in this text, has tended to be historically sidelined by mainline Christianity.

So profound was Speyr's experience of her spiritual incorporation into the divine Sonship that one Holy Week, after a particularly acute mystical vision, it is reported that she received the stigmata. Here incorporation into the Sonship of Christ was as much physical as it was spiritual. Whatever one makes of the remarkable mystical experiences Speyr had, her God-intoxicated life is an example to all of the power of grace. Like Speyr, let us be victorious in love, let us be adopted in the Sonship of Christ, and let us be caught up into the life of the trinitarian God of grace that knows no bounds. Let us, then, be "children of God."

The Victory of Love (1953)

It is the Spirit himself bearing witness with our spirit that we are children of God.

The Spirit of God is witness and testimony. By witnessing to our spirit he lifts it to a higher level and enables it to receive the testimony, to understand it. The Spirit confirms therefore that we are children of God; but he does not confirm it within a sphere of God to which we have no access, but to our spirit. He accepts therefore that our spirit exists and is capable of understanding his witness. For us this means that we know about this capacity, that we take part in this witness of which the highest content is: we are *children of God*. The mystery is revealed. We are no longer waiting in the place of slavery for unclear and uncertain things. We are children to whom the Father reveals himself, and our spirit receives the fullness of the message. And in this acceptance of the message a totally new light is thrown on this testimony that is the whole life and sacrifice of the Son. We do not make the mistake of putting ourselves in the place of the Son; we have not suddenly become gods, heavenly beings, unfit for the tasks of this earth. Such as we were we have been received into the new truth and teaching, into a place to which we were destined beforehand by the Father who wanted to make us his adopted children. If we are believers and our spirit hears the message of the Spirit, then we cannot complain of not knowing where our faith is directed, what we shall do with our hope or where our reward is. The whole plan of God is revealed before our eyes, and we can say a valid Yes to the Spirit who explains it to our spirit. This consent has quite a different form from the consent given by the Lord's Mother to the angel. For her it was made harder; she only knew the Son from the promise, and she carried him all alone. Our consent takes place within the fulfillment and in the community. Led by Paul we are allowed to cry out *Abba Father* together, in the certainty given by the Spirit that we call God by the right name, for we are truly his children.

C. CATHOLIC

7. If children, then heirs, heirs of God and fellow heirs with Christ, provided we suffer with him in order that we may also be glorified with him.

To be child is to be heir, that is the law of life and above all the law of the new teaching: in love. Within this childhood there is no exclusion. To be child of the Father means to be joined to the eternal Son with the right of the same things he has a right to. . . .

27. And he who searches the hearts of men knows what is the mind of the Spirit, because the Spirit intercedes for the saints according to the will of God.

Repeatedly and from ever-different angles Paul shows us how the Triune God works in man. This work is immediate, but alongside and in between the acts of God and their effects in man there is the contemplation of what takes place in Heaven. There is a structure in the acts of God that allows us to have insight into something of its manner of working, to divine what God does together with God. God the Father *searches the hearts of men.* He knows them, penetrates into their ultimate depth and sees everything from the beginning, at this moment and for all the future. His knowledge does not become clouded over. Even should someone believe that in his hidden solitude he could reserve a thought to himself, or plan something or keep a secret from God, God is far better informed than he is himself. He disentangles the whole web of thoughts. But this knowledge of the heart of man in no wise intrudes on his knowledge of the Holy Spirit. He knows *what is the mind of the Spirit,* what he has done and intends to do; he knows it not only at the very instant but in the eternal interrelation of his eternal thoughts. And God recognizes himself in it. He is at home in the thoughts of the Spirit. This at-homeness is based on God's unity of being, but does not prevent any of the three Persons from acting in a personal way.

The Son says: Not my will be done, but Yours. In this consent to the divine will he expresses his utter obedience, but also his knowledge of the Father's will. Similarly the Father knows the thoughts of the Spirit, and these thoughts are in accord with him. And when the Spirit intercedes for the saints, stands in for the believers and gives them in this representation something that brings them into accord with the Father, then this representation also corresponds to the Father's plan and will. There is no trace of contradiction or delay in submission or consent. What the Spirit demands and achieves is from the outset what the Father has known and desired. The believer knows himself held by the Spirit: on the one hand in himself, since the Spirit dwells in him and works in him as in his own house, on the other hand before the Father, since the Spirit puts him into his proper place before the Father and gives his faith the position the Father expects. This expectation expresses the faith and hope of man, and it also expresses the love of the Holy Spirit toward the Father's creatures, and finally the love of the Creator himself.

Love appears in this way not in a graduated form but made transparent for different levels and structures; for the Spirit is transparent before the Father, and the Son makes us transparent through his representation before the Father and enables us in this transparency given by him to understand the things of the Spirit. Were we expected to understand the life of the Son and his love and his sacrifice for us apart from the Spirit, we could not but humanize everything and it cannot take effect. For the Son lives and dies in obedience to the Father as much as in the unity of Father and Son, a unity revealed through love, giving to this love the true perspective and the proper foundation. Only now we are able to learn in a Christian way in our attempts at loving, learn from our teacher, the Spirit, who represents us before God, who even represents God before God; which has no other purpose than that of revealing to us the living interplay of the being and the love of the Triune God.

IV: Modern and Postmodern

C. Catholic

77. Gustavo Gutiérrez (1928–) | *The Power of the Poor in History*

The Peruvian theologian and Dominican priest Gustavo Gutiérrez is regarded as one of the founding fathers of a new way of doing theology that emerged out of the context of 1960s Latin America: it was known as liberation theology. Liberation theology takes as its point of dogmatic departure the particular context of the Latin American struggle against the social conditions of oppression and poverty. Gutiérrez was himself born into poverty and spent much of his ordained life living and working among the poor in Lima. For Gutiérrez, and other theologians of liberation, poverty is not simply a social question but a *theological* one. Read from the perspective of the poor, liberation theology finds in the Bible a God who is constantly on the side of the oppressed, who liberates his people from slavery, who even *becomes* poor in the person of Jesus Christ. Gutiérrez would go further by saying that the grace of God is seen most clearly on the faces of the poor, the oppressed, and the marginalized.

At the heart of liberation theology is not orthodoxy, as such, but *orthopraxis*. That is, it is concerned chiefly with action. Given God's "preferential option for the poor," right action involves both being in loving solidarity with the poor and working towards the liberation of the oppressed from unjust social, economic, and political conditions.

The vision of grace explored by Latin American liberation theology, some of which is captured in the extract below, was at the time deeply challenging to conventional ways of doing theology. So controversial were the views of some Latin American theologians of liberation that many were censured for sailing too close to the winds of Marxism. Others, like Oscar Romero, were even martyred for their prophetic action against the unjust structures of the status quo. Although rooted in a particular context, the message of liberation theology remains relevant to living out the Christian life today: the grace of God bends history toward justice, the grace of God implies an ethics of action for the "establishment of justice" in solidarity with the poor, and the grace of God stands on the side of the poor.

For liberation theology, the task of theology is not the reserve of the academic elite but "of the people." And because of this it is appropriate that our reading is taken from an essay addressed to lay people in Lima, the theologians from "below."

The Power of the Poor in History (1975)

It is not enough . . . to say that God reveals himself in history, and that therefore the faith of Israel fleshes out a historical framework. One must keep in mind that the God of the Bible is a God who not only governs history, but who orientates it in the direction of establishment of justice and right. He is more than a provident God. He is a God who takes sides with the poor and liberates them from slavery and oppression. . . . This is the meaning of Yahweh's interventions in history. The purpose of his activity is not to demonstrate his power, but to liberate, and make justice reign:

> Father of orphans, defender of widows,
>
> such is God in his holy dwelling;
>
> God gives the lonely a permanent home,
>
> makes prisoners happy by setting them free,
>
> but rebels must live in an arid land [Ps 68:5–6].

This is Yahweh. His might is at the service of justice. His power is expressed in the defense of the rights of the poor (see Ps 146:7–9). The real theophany, or revelation of God, is in the liberation of the person who is poor.

To know God is to do justice. . . . Knowledge of God is love of God. In the language of the Bible, "to know" is not something purely intellectual. To know means to love. Sin is the absence of the knowledge of Yahweh, and it is on this that the people will be judged: "Sons of Israel, listen to the word of Yahweh, for Yahweh indicts the inhabitants of the country" (Hos 4:1). To know God as liberator *is* to liberate, *is* to do justice. . . .

Christ the Liberator

The nub, the nucleus, of the biblical message, we have said, is in the relationship between God and the poor. Jesus Christ is precisely *God become poor*. This was the human life he took—a poor life. And this is the life in and by which we recognize him as Son of his Father.

He was poor indeed. He was born into a social milieu characterized by poverty. He chose to live with the poor. He addressed his gospel by preference to the poor. He lashed out with invective against the rich who oppressed the poor and despised them. And before the Father, he was poor in spirit.

Christ came to proclaim the kingdom of God to us. Matthew and Mark say so at the beginning of their gospels. Kingdom signifies globalization. Nothing escapes it. "Kingdom of God" means, God reigns—that is, that his love, his fatherhood, and a community of brothers and sisters, is going to reign among all human beings. This is the mystery hidden until this moment and now revealed (Rom 16:25). . . . This proclamation of the kingdom, this struggle for justice, leads Jesus to death. His life and his death give us to know that the only possible justice is definitive justice. The only justice is the one that goes to the very root of all injustice, all breach with love, all sin. The only justice is the one that assaults all the consequences and expressions of this cleavage in friendship. The only justice is the definitive justice that builds, starting right now, in our conflict-filled history, a kingdom in which God's love will be present and exploitation abolished. . . .

To believe in the God who reveals himself in history, and pitches his tent in its midst, means to live in this tent—in Christ Jesus—and to proclaim from there the liberating love of the Father. . . . The God who rescues his people in history, just as the Christ who is poor, can be proclaimed only with works, with deeds—in the practice of solidarity with the poor. This was the basic demand of the covenant. The fact is that Jesus Christ makes this demand even more imperative. "The man who lives by the truth comes out into the light," the gospel says (John 3:21). Truth is made. It is not automatic. Faith without works is dead, says St. James, in a text that bears reading in its entirety. . . .

Only from a point of departure at the level of practice, only from deed, can the proclamation by word be understood. In the deed our faith becomes truth, not only for others, but for ourselves as well. We become Christians by acting as Christians. Proclamation in word only means taking account of this fact and proclaiming it. Without the deed, proclamation of the word is something empty, something without substance. . . .

The history of humanity, as someone has said, has been "written with a white hand." History has been written from the viewpoint of the dominating sectors. We have a clear example of this in the history of Latin America and Peru. The perspective of history's vanquished is something else again. But history's winners have sought to wipe out their victims' memory of the struggles, so as to be able to snatch from them one of their sources of energy and will in history: a source of rebellion.

As it has been lived in history, Christianity has largely been, and still is, closely linked with one culture (Western), one ethnic strain (white), and one class (the dominant). Its history, too, has been written from a white, occidental, bourgeois bias.

We must recover the memory of the "scourged Christs of America," as Bartolomé de las Casas called the Indians of our continent. This memory never really died. It lives on in cultural and religious expressions, it lives on in resistance to ecclesiastical apparatus. It is a memory of the Christ who is present in every starving, thirsting, imprisoned, or humiliated human being, in the despised minorities, in the exploited classes (see Matt 25:31–45). It is the memory of a Christ who not only "freed us, he meant us to remain free" (Gal 5:1).

But *rereading* history means *remaking* history. It means repairing it from the bottom up. And so it will be a subversive history. History must be turned upside-down from the bottom, not from the top. What is criminal is not to be subversive, struggling against the capitalist system, but to continue being "superversive"—bolstering and supporting the prevailing domination. It is in this subversive history that we can have a new faith experience, a new spirituality—a new proclamation of the gospel. . . .

The gospel read from the viewpoint of the poor, the exploited classes, and their militant struggles for liberation, convokes a church of the people. It calls for a church to be gathered from among the poor, the marginalized. It calls for the kind of church that is indicated in Jesus' predilection for those whom the great ones of this world despise and humiliate (see Matt 22:1–10; Luke 14:16–24). In a word, it calls together a church that will be marked by the faithful response of the poor to the call of Jesus Christ. It will spring from the people, this church. And the people will snatch the gospel out of the hands of their dominators, never more to permit it to be utilized for the justification of a situation contrary to the will of the God who liberates. For this God is a God who "reincorporates himself," as Arguedas says—reincorporates himself into a history that bears the mark of the poor, into the popular struggles for liberation, into hope for the exploited.

This reincorporation of God will come about only when the poor of the earth effectuate a "social appropriation of the gospel"—when they dispossess those who consider it their private property. The gospel tells us that the sign of the arrival of the kingdom of God is that the poor have the gospel proclaimed to them. The poor are those who believe and hope in Christ. That is to say the poor are the Christians. Strictly speaking, the Christians are, or should be, the poor who receive the gospel—those in solidarity with the interests, aspirations, and combats of the oppressed and repressed of the world today.

Evangelization, the proclamation of the gospel, will be genuinely liberating when the poor themselves become its messengers. That is when we shall see the preaching of the gospel become a stumbling block and a scandal. For then we shall have a gospel that is no longer "presentable" in society. It will not sound nice and it will not smell good. The Lord who scarcely looks like a human at all (cf. the songs of the Servant of Yahweh in Isaiah) will speak to us then, and only at the sound of his voice will we recognize him as our liberator. That voice will convoke the *ek-klesia*, the assembly of those "called apart," in a new and different way.

Long has the church been built *from within*, in function of Christendom and its extension and preservation in the world—"ecclesiocentrism." A more recent perspective has led some to think of the church *from without*, from the world, from a world that does not believe, a world that often is hostile. This is the world in which the church was to be a sign of salvation according to Vatican Council II.

Today we understand even better. We are called to build the church *from below,* from the poor up, from the exploited classes, the marginalized ethnic groups, the despised cultures. This is what we call the project of a popular church, a church that, under the influence of the Spirit, arises from within the masses.

IV: Modern and Postmodern

C. Catholic

78. Janet Soskice (1957–) | *Trinity and "the Feminine Other"*

Janet Soskice is a Canadian-born Roman Catholic theologian. Based at the University of Cambridge, Soskice has written extensively on the nature of religious language, the doctrine of creation, the tradition of the names of God, the doctrine of the Trinity, and issues surrounding sexuality and gender. These themes converge in the extract below.

Part of Soskice's aim in the reading is to utilize the tools of French feminist theory to ask some critical questions of the versions of the doctrine of the Trinity in which the Holy Spirit is, she concludes, unhelpfully feminized. Although the feminization of the Spirit it often invoked as a tactic to disrupt the gender imbalance in the Trinity, if the Spirit occupies a subordinate position within the Godhead (as is often the case in Western theology), the genderization of the Spirit risks inadvertently perpetuating the subordination of women; or as Soskice's terms, rendering women the "feminine Other" to men. Another part of Soskice's aim is to raise a more fundamental question of the way the doctrine of the Trinity is used to shape the Christian life. For some, the inner life of persons of the Trinity (the way the Father relates to the Son, and the way both relate to the Holy Spirit) represents a kind of celestial blueprint on which the Christian life should be modelled. Because God is relational, so are we, and so too should be our societies and churches. Soskice's conclusion, however, is that the role of the Trinity is not so much to provide the "model" for human relations to imitate but to furnish a grammar that helps to speak more wisely of the nature of God.

The Christian life, following Soskice, means *more* than saying that to be fully human means to be relational—modeling and mimicking the relationality of God. It means that we are most fully human, most fully who we are created to be, when we are (by the grace of God) actually caught up in the divine relationality that lies at the very heart of the doctrine of God. In a word, the Christian life is about "participation." It is about participating in the life of the trinitarian God in whom we live and move and have our being: all this is made possible by grace.

C. CATHOLIC

Trinity and "the Feminine Other" (1994)

There would seem to have been, over the last three hundred years of Western Christianity, equal numbers of theologians who think either that the doctrine of the Trinity has outworn its usefulness and might now be scrapped, or that the doctrine is at the very centre of the Christian faith. If we start from the recognition that the doctrine was developed by Christians, not in order to reject their Jewish ancestry, but to demonstrate why they could claim to stand in continuity with it, we may see why. Trinitarian language, developed for particular purposes, can so often appear to suggest their opposite.... Trinitarian language may be introduced, historically, as a corrective to the tendency of idolatry, but how successful has it been? How frequently, as Ann Loades has reminded us, do we hear such phrases as "divine fatherhood does not have masculine characteristics but...."?[1] Christians are good at rejecting heresies they never found very attractive anyway, like tritheism, and less successful at rejecting those they quite like, such as various and related forms of subordinationism, monarchianism and deistic sexism, all in their way idolatrous.

Recent years have seen a number of feminist criticisms of classical formulations of the doctrine. These vary from simple rejection of what sounds like a three-man club, to more nuanced critiques of the way in which, despite best efforts, the Father always seems accorded a status superior to the other two persons, with the Holy Spirit as a distinct third. The Trinity appears still hierarchical, still male—maleness, indeed, seems enshrined in God's eternity.

One line of thought has been to emphasise the putatively female characteristics of the Spirit. We can readily uncover a tradition of regarding the Spirit as the maternal aspect of God—brooding, nurturing, bringing new members of the Church to life in baptism. There is, too, the early Syriac tradition of styling the Spirit as feminine, following the female gender of the noun in the Semitic languages, but these evocations have failed to convince feminist and other theologians of their enduring merit for women or, for that matter, for the Trinity. Consider the implications of these remarks of Yves Congar,

> The part played in our upbringing by the Holy Spirit is that of a mother—a mother who enables us to know our Father, God, and our brother, Jesus... He (the Spirit) teaches us how to practise the virtues and how to use the gifts of a son of God by grace. All this is part of a mother's function.[2]

Along with deifying one particular, and particularly Western, version of "a mother's function" (why is it not a mother's function to raise the crops so that her family may eat?) the Spirit by implication is ancillary to the other two persons who are the ones really to be known and loved.

---

1. In a paper given to a conference on "The Trinity," Trinity College, Dublin, May 1992.
2. Congar, *I Believe in the Holy Spirit* (London, 1983), vol. 3, 161.

Even less satisfactory, as Elizabeth Johnson notes, is the valiant effort by the process theologian, John Cobb, to align the Logos, as the masculine aspect of God, with order, novelty, demand, agency and transformation, while the feminine aspect of God, the kingdom or Spirit, is linked with receptivity, empathy, suffering and preservation.[3]

Feminists are surely right to reject what Sarah Coakley has called "mawkish and sentimentalised versions of the feminine" as both providing warrant for a particular stereotype of the feminine and at the same time feeding the unorthodox suggestion that there is sexual difference in the Trinity. Furthermore this kind of feminising rhetoric does nothing to counteract the genuine neglect of the Spirit in modern theology, in which the Spirit appears a sort of "edifying appendage" to the two real persons, those who have faces, the Father and the Son.[4] We must avoid, as Coakley says, subordinating "the Spirit to a Father who, as 'cause,' and 'source' of the other two persons, remains as a 'masculine' stereotype with the theological upper hand."[5] It is this covert monarchianism which is perhaps the main fear of feminist theologians: a patriarchal "father-god" who exhibits an exclusive and narcissistic love for the Son. Unfortunately the history of theology resounds with just such deficiencies.

God, we all know, is not male but God's "fatherhood," equally obviously, has been used to underwrite patterns of male dominance in marriage, family, state, and Church. So what do we do? One strategy ready to hand is to desexualize the language of the Trinity altogether and speak instead of Creator, Sustainer and Redeemer. But while this is acceptable and at times necessary as an alternative liturgical usage, it does not carry the relational content of Father, Son and Spirit. The Creator is not the Creator of the Sustainer, and so on. Creator, Sustainer and Redeemer are three names of what God is "for us" in the economy of salvation but say nothing of the eternal mutuality of the Three-In-One. They can also suggest, misleadingly, that it is only the First Person who creates, the Second who redeems and the Third who sustains when, for instance, creation is properly the action of all three persons. Taking a page from the French feminists, we need furthermore to ask whether neutering texts simply makes their sexual imagery less easy to spot and to recognise as imagery.

I am suspicious of attempts to purge offensive metaphors and "tidy up" the stories. They veil the historically placed nature of the biblical texts and are especially misleading if, by purging, we think we will achieve a theology that is "pure": scientific and free of fable. "Scientific" or ostensibly "value-free" fables are the most deceptive of all, since they conceal their own interpretive and cultural biases. . . .

---

3. Elizabeth A. Johnson, "The Incomprehensibility of God and the Image of God Male and Female," *Theological Studies* 45 (1984), 459.

4. Johnson, "The Incomprehensibility of God and the Image of God Male and Female," 457.

5. Sarah Coakley, "Femininity and the Holy Spirit," in M. Furlong (ed.), *Mirror to the Church* (London, 1988).

C. CATHOLIC

Let me then seek not just to comment on previous formulations of the doctrine but also to tell a Trinitarian tale which takes seriously the language of the economy, with all its gendered relational and procreational imagery.

We can start with the title "Father." In a suggestive article on "fatherhood," Paul Ricoeur notes that whereas God is called "father" 170 times by Jesus in the Synoptics, God is styled as "father" only 11 times in the entire Hebrew Bible, and never there invoked as "father" in prayer. Ricoeur also points out that "father" is a semantically dependent title—it is because there is a child that someone is called a father. It is, in short, in this technical sense, a relational term. So the advent of the child, in a sense "gives birth" to the father. . . .

The trinitarian narrative of the economy, in this telling, moves both ways—the Father begets the Son. The Spirit proceeds from the Father and the Son. Yet we can also say that the Son is raised in the Spirit. And the Father is Father in virtue of the Son—because it is the child who "makes" someone a father. . . . In this telling of the economy the father, too, "is born"—or better "becomes father"—with the Son, and in the Spirit.

This is a vision of a Trinity of complete mutuality, yet it is not one in which all three persons become the same, as three sides of an equilateral triangle. The First person, as Unoriginate Origin, begets the Son (and is thus named "Father" or we could say equally "Mother"), and from these two proceeds the Spirit. The Son, by being Son, is the one who makes God Father/Mother. The Son gives birth to the Church in the Spirit, represented figuratively in the high tradition of western religious art by the water and the blood flowing from Christ's pierced side on the Cross—clear birth imagery from which medieval artists did not shrink. The Spirit is the Lord, the Giver of Life, in whom the Son is raised in resurrected Life.

From the economic point of view, this story has an exitus-reditus structure: Father–Son–Spirit, Spirit–Son–Father, but at the immanent level it is a story of the perichoretic outpouring of love and birth between the Three who only *Are* in relation one to another. All three persons, figuratively, give birth—the First person as Unoriginate Origin begets Son and gives the Spirit, the Second as Son "makes" God the father and "gives birth" to the Church on the Cross, and the Holy Spirit, the Lord the Giver of Life, animates the Church in the world. The activity of all three can be styled in the procreative imagery of the human feminine and of the human masculine. . . .

We frequently read in the texts of modern theology that we need the doctrine of the Trinity in order to teach us how to be relational beings. This often sounds a kind of utilitarian apologetics—"the doctrine doesn't mean much anymore but at least its socially useful." But, we might ask, what does the Trinity tell us of human relational experiences? Personally I think something has gone seriously wrong if theologians can even ask that kind of question in the way they so often now do. I must emphasise, then, that the sense in which I discuss relation in the Trinity is here a formal one. To give a mundane example, a man becomes a father in a technical sense when he has a child. Even were he to have no idea of the child's existence and thus no "relationship" (in the vernacular sense) with it, he would nonetheless be related to this child as father....

The doctrine of the Trinity tells us nothing of how men and women should relate to one another as males and females. It does not show that all men should be like the "father" and all women model themselves on a feminised Spirit. In this sense the doctrine tells us nothing of sexual difference. But it does let us glimpse what it is, most truly, to be. "To be" most fully is "to-be-related" in difference. This tells us a great deal.

IV: Modern and Postmodern

D. Orthodox

79. Sergei Bulgakov (1871–1944) | *The Comforter*

Sergei Bulgakov was born in Russia to a poor provincial priest. In the footsteps of his father he entered seminary but left before finishing. Eventually he became a priest (1917), but only after a season of alienation from the church, during which he taught economics as a Marxist at the University of Moscow. He published books on economics and philosophy, but later rejected Marxism and found his way back to the church. After being expelled from Russia in 1923 by the Bolshevik government, he spent his remaining years in Prague and then Paris where he helped found a seminary for Russian emigrants (l'Institut de Théologie Orthodoxe Saint-Serge). He remained in Paris until his death, serving as the dean of the seminary and professor of dogmatic theology. In his later years Bulgakov was also active in ecumenical dialogues with the Anglican Church.

Earlier in the nineteenth century, one of the most significant figures in Russian philosophy and theology was Vladimir Soloviev (1853–1900). Bulgakov's association with his work made him a highly controversial figure and eventually led to charges of heresy. Soloviev fell outside Orthodox thought by presenting Sophia as a distinct divine person. Bulgakov tried to rework Soloviev's thought more in line with traditional Orthodox theology, but many were unconvinced. Meetings were held about Bulgakov, and apologies and counter-apologies were written (1935–1937). It was eventually decided that Bulgakov's teachings about Sophia did not rise to the level of heresy.

The following selection is taken from the final section of Bulgakov's *The Comforter*, the middle book of his trilogy *On Divine Humanity*, written during the years in which he was embroiled in controversy. The section is called "The Gifts of Pentecost." As Bulgakov explains, in ways entirely resonant with the Eastern Orthodox tradition, we are all spiritual beings with "the potential for divine life, which can become a reality by the power and action of the grace of the Holy Spirit." The Holy Spirit doesn't make us what we were never meant to be, but brings to fruition the "*proper nature* of the human spirit." In the final paragraphs, notice the reference to *sobornost*. The term refers to the distinctly Orthodox way of intertwining individuality and communality in the church ("supra-individual consciousness"[1]). To be sure, it is individuals who experience the Christian life, what Bulgakov calls the "direct subject," but individuals in Christ are no longer *merely* individuals. Because they are members of Christ's body by the common gift of the Spirit, "isolation in salvation and in the spiritual life is impossible."

The Comforter (1936)

The Lord describes the reception of the Spirit as a new birth: "That which is born of the flesh is flesh; and that which is born of the Spirit is spirit" (John 3:6). This new life appears in the old man, whence arises the antithesis and opposition of these two principles of life: according to the spirit and according to the flesh, the spiritual man and the natural man (Rom 8:1, 5, 9; Gal 5:16–17; 1 Pet 4:6). This new life is our life in Christ by the Holy Spirit. In the Pentecost, Christ's humanity becomes a reality by the Holy Spirit. The Dyad of the son and the Spirit, in Their inseparability and inconfusability, determine the life of the Church. Therefore, this life is simultaneously life in Christ ("yet not I, but Christ liveth in me" [Gal 2:20]) and life in the Holy Spirit ("ye are the temple of God, and . . . the Spirit of God dwelleth in you" [1 Cor 3:16]). There is neither separation nor opposition here: the reality of life in Christ is the body of Christ, animated by the Holy Spirit dwelling in it. This makes understandable the convergence, approaching identification, of the life in Christ and the life in the Holy Spirit, as can be seen in the following comparisons from the apostolic epistles: We are "justified in Christ" (Gal 2:17) and "by the Spirit of our God" (1 Cor 6:11); we are "sealed" (Eph 1:13; 4:30) and "circumcised" (Col 2:11) in both; we have joy (Phil 3:1; cf. Rom 14:17), faith (Gal 3:26; 1 Cor 1:9), love (Rom 8:39; Col 1:8), and fellowship (1 Cor 1:9; 2 Cor 13:14) in both. Likewise, sanctification is sometimes attributed to Christ (1 Cor 1:30; Eph 5:26; Heb 2:11; 10:29; 13:12) and sometimes to the Holy Spirit (Rom 15:16; 1 Cor 6:11; 2 Thess 2:14; 1 Pet 1:2); this indicates the united of this act which is accomplished dyadically by the Second and Third hypostases.

The being clothed in Christ, which is accomplished by the Holy Spirit, is at the same time adoption by God. The God-Man Himself in His human nature was adopted by the Father in the descent of the Holy Spirit, as was attested by the Father's voice calling from heaven: "This is my beloved Son" (Matt 3:17). Consequently, for the

---

1. Williams, "Eastern Orthodox Theology," 574.

God-Man too the Holy Spirit was the Spirit of adoption. And for us too He is the Spirit of adoption, by virtue of our union with Christ . . .[2]

The general idea expressed in this series of New Testament texts, which is far from exhaustive, is that the Holy Spirit, being communicated to man through the Church, produces in him a new, spiritual life, or, in the language of theology, bestows *grace* upon him. "Grace is a theological term, not a Biblical one; it serves to generalize various manifestations of the spiritual life (in the Bible, the word "grace" is used in the most diverse senses). The doctrine of grace occupies an important place in contemporary theology (in the different confessions).

Through the descent of the Holy Spirit, so-called *spiritual life* arises in the members of the Church. This is a wholly new fact, which depends entirely on the Pentecost and is impossible prior to it or outside it. . . . However diverse its manifestations or aspects, spiritual life contains a constant element: man receives something higher than himself, a supernatural principle. But this principle is assimilated by him, enters into his proper life, which thereby becomes natural and supernatural at the same time. . . .

Man is an incarnate spirit. On the one hand, he has a natural life, a pyscho-corporeal existence. On the other hand, he is a spirit and has his proper spiritual nature. Since it is a spark of Divinity that has received the personal principle and become a person, the spirit has *the potential for divine life, which can become a reality by the power and action of the grace of the Holy Spirit. In this action, divine life becomes, as it were, the proper nature of the human spirit*; and man lives this life in parallel with that of his natural essence. He lives bi-naturally, but unihypostatically. The kinship between the human and the angelic spirits is manifested here. Angels do not have their own natural world, and, being creaturely, they participate in the nature of Divinity and in divine life, while at the same time participating, in their own manner, in human life. Similarly, the co-angelic essence of the human spirit participates in divine life, while preserving its autonomy.

By its nature, the human spirit is neither closed nor impenetrable. It is created in the image of the Divine spirit, which, being one and trihypostatic, is thus "communal" and mutually transparent. The Father lives in the Son and in the Spirit; the Son lives by the life of the Father and of the Spirit; and the Spirit lives by the life of the Father and of the Son. Creaturely beings, too, are open to communal being, as race (human) or assembly (angelic). This mutual transparence of creaturely spirits, this capacity to receive "influences," is expressed not only in a certain commonality of life within the limits of the creaturely essence (which is a self-evidence fact), but also in the capacity to receive divine life, to be deified. Having in itself the image of God, i.e. an essential conformity with Divinity, the human spirit has the capacity to receive the Divine Spirit and to be livingly united with the latter . . . while preserving its proper natural life, although transforming it in conformity with the new powers entering into it.

2. Bulgakov proceeds by listing the following texts: Rom 8:15–17; Gal 4:6–7; Rom 8:23, 26; Eph 1:13; 2 Cor 3:3; Rom 6:22; Gal 5:17–23; 1 Cor 6:10; Rom 14:17.

But in order to be actualized such a possibility presupposes a certain state of readiness of the human spirit for communion with God; but this possibility is paralyzed by the fact that the spirit has been made heavy and worldly as a result of original sin. This possibility is restored by the Incarnation, by which Christ realized the norm of the relations between the spirit and nature in man, the equilibrium of the two principles. The principle of spiritual life thus appeared in the human race through its participation in the New Adam, Christ. This possibility is actualized by the Holy Spirit, Who makes man a participant in Christ's life. But this life in Christ is the communion with the Holy Spirit; and according to the form of this life, "Christians" become "spirit-bearing." This is accomplished as a new, spiritual birth in man, through baptism by water and the Spirit. This is a new life: the doors of the inner cell of the human spirit are opened for the entry of the Holy Spirit. This is an action of God in man, which is accomplished by God's will ("the Spirit bloweth where it listeth"), although, by God's will, it is connected, in the life of the Church, with sacrament, specifically with baptism. In the life of the God-Man as well, baptism signified the descent of the Holy Spirit, and that is what it signifies in every human life....

This new life in the Spirit is, of course, indescribable and inexhaustible: "the things of God knoweth no man, but the Spirit of God" (1 Cor 2:11); and we can find only a few indications of this life in the apostolic epistles. The life of grace in the Holy Spirit, uniting our life with Christ, is bestowed in the Church in specific ways such as sacraments, *sacramentalia*, and prayers, as well as by direct illumination. One should not consider these two paths to be opposed, however, for there is one active Spirit and the grace bestowed in the sacraments continues to operate beyond the limits of their immediate celebration. In the descent of the Holy Spirit were given not only the cloven tongues, reposing upon each of the apostles, but also their *unity*, or the fullness of the Church, which is the abiding Pentecost. In this sense, the Church is simultaneously the organization and the organism of spiritual life.

The churchly character of spiritual life leads to further questions concerning its reception. The direct subject of spiritual life is the individual human person. That is why when one speaks of salvation, i.e., the attainment of life full of grace, one usually means *personal* salvation, inasmuch as the feat of *ascesis*, as well as the acquisition of humanity, can be accomplished by separate individuals. If we go no further than this personal aspect of salvation, however, we risk considering the Church as a mere series of separate atoms. This will abolish the very concept of the Church as a unity, whereas the Church exists precisely as a *multi-unity*, akin to the natural multi-unity of the human race. But we know that the "catholic" nature (or sobornost[3]) of the personal consciousness is disclosed precisely in churchly love; and the gift of love, which is from the Holy Spirit, makes this sobornost of churchly life as a body composed of multiple members a self-evident reality. Likewise, the sacraments are be-

---

3. The "supra-individual consciousness" of the Orthodox Church (Williams, "Eastern Orthodox Theology," 574).

stowed from the entire Church and for the entire Church, although they are received as individual persons. The sacraments are essentially churchly, and they thus liberate man from the condition of his isolation. That is why the spiritual life of individual persons in the Church takes on a universal character in its power and significance. This connection cannot be fully understood at the present time, but isolation in salvation and in the spiritual life is impossible: "And whether one member suffer, all the members suffer with it; or one member be honoured, all the members rejoice with it" (1 Cor 12:26). The catholicity or integrity of life realized in each member is the fundamental quality of spiritual life.

IV: Modern and Postmodern

D. Orthodox

80. Vladimir Lossky (1903–1958) | *The Mystical Theology of the Orthodox Church*

Vladimir Lossky was born in St. Petersburg, the son of a famous Russian philosopher and university professor. Like Sergei Bulgakov (the previous selection), Lossky was among the Russian emigrants of his generation. Expelled after the Russian Revolution in 1917 he, spent the later years of his life teaching and writing in Paris. Unlike Bulgakov, however, Lossky's theological career was neither controversial nor innovative but sought a creative retrieval of classic Orthodox thought for the twentieth century. "His project," Rowan Williams explains, was "to uncover in patristic tradition the kind of central and normative strand that can allow Orthodoxy to offer a resolution to the tensions of Western Christianity."[1]

Lossky died in 1958, just days after completing the doctoral dissertation he had worked on for twenty years. Alexander Schmemann expresses the spirit of Lossky's personality and theology in the following remembrance. It is beautifully personal testimony.

> The great Russian Church historian V. V. Bolotov said once that a theologian ought to know only three itineraries: to the Church, to the classroom and to his own desk. Professor Lossky was the very type of such a theologian. Very humble in his personal life, indifferent to the vainglory of human titles, ranks and honors, he declined several offers of academic positions because he was concentrated on the "one thing necessary" and preferred his vocation of thinker and theologian to everything in this world . . . It was a pleasure to know him, to visit him in his small apartment of St. Louis Island in the very heart of Paris. Once there, one would find himself immediately discussing vital issues in a noble and high spirit, for such was Vladimir Lossky's approach to the Church, to theology, or to any aspect of life, never trivial, bitter or destructive, but always generous and deep . . . He knew that it is "more

---

1. Williams, "Eastern Orthodox Theology," 580.

blessed to give than to receive" and he gave much to the Church and to all those who wanted to receive from him. He must have joyfully entered into the joy of his Lord.[2]

Lossky did in fact interact with Bulgakov, being drawn into the controversy that swirled around Bulgakov's sophism. Lossky published a pamphlet against Bulgakov's theology in 1936 (*The Dispute About Sophia*), the same year Bulgakov's *The Comforter* was published (from which the last selection is taken).

Lossky's most well-known work is *The Mystical Theology of the Eastern Church*, from which the following selection is taken. Lossky first shows that in Eastern Christianity God's grace and free will are not conceived separately. They are, as he says, "two poles of one and the same reality." Eastern Christianity has long thought of God's gracious movement toward creatures and their graced responses in non-competitive ways like this (unlike much Western theology). Lossky then distinguishes this belief from Pelagianism, which makes God's grace a *reward* for human action. Eastern theology doesn't teach this, Lossky explains, because the "coincidence" of grace and human freedom is a mystery incomprehensible on purely rational grounds. The place in which the mystery of divine grace and human freedom comes to life is not in the realm of rational explanation but in the *heart* where action and contemplation are held together. Arising from the heart, the Christian life is an ascent toward God in which *contemplation* and *action* mutually assist each other, both brought to life by God's grace and both fully actions of the human person brought to life by God.

The Mystical Theology of the Eastern Church (1957)

The Way of Union

The deification or [*theosis*] of the creature will be realized in its fullness only in the age to come, after the resurrection of the dead. This deifying union has, nevertheless, to be fulfilled ever more and more even in this present life, through the transformation of our corruptible and depraved nature and by its adaptation to eternal life. If God has given us in the Church all the objective conditions, all the means that we need for the attainment of this end, we, on our side, must produce the necessary subjective conditions: for it is in this synergy, in this co-operation of man with God, that the union is fulfilled. This subjective aspect of our union with God constitutes the way of union which is the Christian life.

---

2. Schmemann, "In Memoriam—Vladimir Lossky," 47–48.

Early in the last century, St. Seraphim of Sarov sought, in the course of a conversation, to define the object of the Christian life. This definition, though it may at first sight appear over-simplified, sums up the whole spiritual tradition of the Orthodox Church. "Prayer, fasting, vigils, and all other Christian practices," he says, "although wholly good in themselves, certainly do not in themselves constitute the end of our Christian life: they are but the indispensable means for the attainment of that end." For the true end of the Christian life is the acquiring of the Holy Spirit. As for fasts, vigils, prayers, alms, and other good works done in the name of Christ—these are the means whereby we acquire the Holy Spirit. Note well that it is only those good works which are done in the name of Christ bring us the fruits of the Holy Spirit. Other actions, even good ones, not done in the name of Christ, can neither procure us a reward in this life or the age to come, nor win us the grace of God in this present life. That is why our Lord Jesus Christ has said: "he that gathereth not with me, scattereth" (Matt 7:30). In other words, there is for the Christian no such thing as an autonomous good: a work is good in so far as it furthers our union with God, in so far as it makes grace *ours*. The virtues are not the end but the means, or, rather, the symptoms, the outward manifestations of the Christian life, the sole end of which is the acquisition of grace.

The notion of merit is foreign to the Eastern tradition. The word is seldom encountered in the spiritual writings of the Eastern church, and has not the same meaning as in the West. The explanation is to be sought in the general attitude of Eastern theology towards grace and free will. In the East, this question has never had the urgency which it assumed in the West from the time of St. Augustine onwards. The Eastern tradition never separates these two elements: grace and human freedom are manifested simultaneously and cannot be conceived apart from the other. St. Gregory of Nyssa describes very clearly the reciprocal bond that makes of grace and free will two poles of one and the same reality: "As the grace of God cannot descend upon souls which flee from their salvation, so the power of human virtue is not of itself sufficient to raise to perfection souls which have no share in grace . . . the righteousness of works and the grace of the Spirit, coming together to the same place (προελθοῦσαι εἰς ταυτόν), fill the soul in which they are united with the life of the blessed."[3]

Thus, grace is not a reward for the merit of the human will, as Pelagianism would have it; but no more is it the cause of the "meritorious acts" of our free will. For it is not a question of merits but of a co-operation, of a synergy of the two wills, divine and human, a harmony in which grace bears ever more and more fruit, and is appropriated—"acquired"—by the human person. Grace is a presence of God within us which demands constant effort on our part; these efforts, however, in no way determine grace, nor does grace act upon our liberty as if it were external or foreign to it. This doctrine, faithful to the apophatic spirit of the Eastern tradition, expresses the mystery of the coincidence of grace and human freedom in good works, without recourse to positive and rational terms. The fundamental error of Pelagius was that of

---

3. "De Instituto Christiano," P.G. XLVI, 289 C.

transporting the mystery of grace on to a rational plane, by which process grace and liberty, realities of the spiritual order, are transformed into two mutually exclusive concepts which then have to be reconciled, as if they were two objects exterior to one another.... Eastern tradition has always asserted simultaneity in the synergy of divine grace and human freedom. As St. Macarius of Egypt says: "The will of man is an essential condition, for without it God does nothing."[4] In the nineteenth century, Bishop Theophanes, a great Russian ascetic writer, asserted that "the Holy Ghost, acting within us, accomplishes with us our salvation," but he says at the same time that "being assisted by grace, man accomplishes the work of his salvation."[5] Grace, which according to St. Macarius, permeates the human personality like the yeast in the making of bread, "becomes fixed in a man like a natural endowment, as though it were one substance with him."[6] It is this that St. Seraphim calls "the acquisition of grace"—the subjective aspect of union with God....

For the ascetic tradition of the Christian East, the heart (ἡ καρδία) is the center of the human being, the root or the "active" faculties, of the intellect and of the will, and the point from which the whole of the spiritual life proceeds, and upon it converges. Source of all intellectual and spiritual activity, the heart, according to St. Macarius of Egypt, is a "workshop of justice and injustice."[7] It is a vessel which contains all the vices, but where at the same time, "God, the angels, life and the Kingdom, light and the apostles, and the treasures of grace are to be found."[8] ... The spirit (νοῦς, πνεῦμα), the highest part of the human creature, is that contemplative faculty by which man is able to seek God. The most personal part of man, the principle of his conscience and of his freedom, the spirit (νοῦς) in the human nature corresponds most nearly to the person; it might be said that is the seat of the person, of the human hypostasis which contains in itself the whole of man's nature—spirit, soul and body. ... Without the heart, which is the center of all activity, the spirit is powerless. Without the spirit, the heart remains blind, destitute of direction. It is therefore necessary to attain to a harmonious relationship between the spirit and the heart, in order to develop and build up the personality in the life of grace—for the way of union is not a mere unconscious process, and it presupposes an unceasing vigilance of spirit and a constant effort of the will. "This world is an arena and a running place.... And this is a time of struggle," says St. Isaac the Syrian. In order to overcome in this struggle our attention must be constantly directed towards God ... When ardour slackens, resolution falters and grace remains inactive. The evangelical precept to watch, not to allow oneself to be weighed down by sleep, is a constant theme of Eastern asceticism,

---

4. "Spiritual Homilies, XXXVII, 10," *P.G.*, XXXIV, 757 A.
5. Mgr Theophanes, *Letters on the Spiritual Life*, pub. Mount Athas, pp. 19, 65, 67, 83 (in Russian).
6. "Spiritual Homilies, VIII, 2," *P.G.*, 528, D, 529 A.
7. "Hom. Spirit., XV, 32," *P.G.*, XXXIV, 597 B.
8. Ibid., XLIII, 7, 776 D.

which demands the full consciousness of the human person in all the degrees of its ascent towards perfect union.

This ascent is composed of two stages, or, more exactly, it is achieved simultaneously on two different but closely interrelated levels: that of action (πρᾶξις) and that of contemplation (θεωρία). The two are inseparable in Christian knowledge, which is the personal and conscious experience of spiritual realities— ἡ γνῶσις—"gnosis."[9] According to St. Maximus, contemplation without action, theory which is not applied in practice, differs in no way from imagination, from fantasy without any real substance—ἀνυπόστατος φαντασία; similarly, action, if it is not inspired by contemplation, is as sterile and rigid as a statue.[10] "The very life of the spirit being the work of the heart," says St. Isaac the Syrian, "it is purity of heart which gives integrity to the contemplation of the spirit."[11] Thus the active life consists in the purifying of the heart, and this activity is conscious, being directed by the spirit (νοῦς), the contemplative faculty which enters into and unites itself with the heart, co-ordinating and uniting the human being in grace.

---

9. It should be unnecessary to point out that this term, signifying that knowledge of the divine which the human person acquires by the Holy Spirit, has nothing in common with the speculations of the gnostics.

10. "Capita theological et oeconomica, Centuria IV, cap. 88," *P.G.*, XC, 1341–44.

11. Theotoki ed., XVII, pp. 87–88; Wensicki, XL, p. 202. Cf. Ibid., I, p. 20.

IV: Modern and Postmodern

D. Orthodox

81. John Zizioulas (1931–) | *Being as Communion*

The previous two Orthodox theologians, Bulgakov and Lossky, represent Russian voices of the Eastern church, but John Zizioulas is an important voice from the Greek-speaking church. Metropolitan John (as he is known) has been the archbishop (or "Metropolitan") of the Turkish city of Pergamon since 1986. Before taking holy orders, he taught theology at the Universities of Athens, Glasgow, Edinburgh, and King's College London. As a bishop, he has played a significant part in ecumenical dialogue in the later twentieth century, participating in the Joint International Commission for Theological Dialogue Between the Catholic Church and Orthodox Church, at one time serving as its co-chair.

Our selection is taken from Zizioulas's work *Being as Communion*, which centers on the relationship between human personhood and the church. Zizioulas offers a relational definition of the human person derived from the doctrine of the Trinity (indebted to the Cappadocian Fathers). According to Zizioulas, the source of all reality is God, who is Father, Son, and Spirit—not a substance, but a relational being. To be a creature of this God is to be "*essentially* relational."[1]

> To say that the Son belongs to God's substance implies that substance possesses almost by definition a relational character . . . If God's being is by nature relational, and if it can be signified by the word "substance" can we not then conclude almost inevitably that, given the ultimate character of God's being for all ontology, substance can be conceived only as communion? (*Being as Communion*, 84).

The Godhead is "intrinsically *communion* and *freedom*"—each person bound to the other in fellowship but each free as distinct divine persons.[2] God's creatures are therefore "plural" beings. "The identity of a particular person is not to be found somewhere deep inside him or her: he has no self, center, soul or other form of private exis-

---

1. Williams, "Eastern Orthodox Theology," 584.
2. Knight, "John Zizioulas on Eschatology and Persons," 91. Emphasis added.

tence before coming into relationship with others."[3] The Christian life is irreducibly communion, because it represents the fulfillment of one's ontology, their deepest being. In the church they are bound to God and others, free to be *in relation*.

Zizioualas's argument is complex, tightly wound, and it stretches across long swaths of the work, so keep two details in mind as you read the selection from *Being in Communion*. First, just prior to this he contrasted biological existence (simply existing as a living organism) with ecclesial existence (existing as a baptized member of the church). The latter is more fundamental than the former, he argues, because the Son of God establishes the church, marking the way back to himself and therefore back to real, authentic personhood in communion with God and others. Second, with the word *hypostasis* he means a unique center of being, or center of willing, acting, and selfhood.

Being as Communion (1997)

2. *The hypostasis of ecclesial existence* is constituted by the new birth of man, by baptism. Baptism as new birth is precisely an act constitutive of hypostasis. As the conception and birth of a man constitute his biological hypostasis, so baptism leads to a new mode of existence, to a regeneration (1 Pet 1:3, 23), and consequently to a new "hypostasis." What is the basis of this new hypostasis? How is man hypostasized by baptism and what does he become?

We have seen that the fundamental problem of the biological hypostasis of man lies in the fact that the ecstatic activity which leads to his birth is bound up with the "passion" of ontological necessity, in the fact that ontologically nature precedes the person and dictates its laws (by "instinct"), thus destroying freedom at its ontological base. This "passion" is closely connected with createdness, that is, with the fact that man as a person confronts, as we have already seen, the necessity of existence. Consequently it is impossible for created existence to escape ontological necessity in the constitution of the biological hypostasis: without "necessary" natural laws, that is, without ontological necessity, the biological hypostasis of man cannot exist.

Consequently, if, in order to avoid the consequences of the tragic aspect of man which we have discussed, the person as absolute ontological freedom needs a hypostatic constitution without ontological necessity, his hypostasis must inevitably be rooted, or constituted, in an ontological reality which does not suffer from createdness. This is the meaning of the phrase in Scripture about being born "anew" or "from

---

3. Ibid., 92.

above" (John 3:3, 7). It is precisely this possibility that patristic Christology strives to proclaim, to announce to man as the good news.

Christology, in the definitive form which the Fathers gave it, looks towards a single goal of purely existential significance, the goal of giving man the assurance that the quest for the person, not as a "mask" or as a "tragic figure," but as the authentic person, is not mythical or nostalgic but is a *historical reality*. Jesus Christ does not justify the title of Savior because he brings the world a beautiful revelation, a sublime teaching about the person, but because He realizes in history *the very reality of the person* and makes it the basis and "hypostasis" of the person for every man. Patristic theology therefore regarded the following points as the indispensable elements of Christology:

a) The identification of the person of Christ with the hypostasis of the Son of the Holy Trinity. The long dispute with Nestorianism was not an exercise of academic theology but a hard struggle with the existential question: how is it possible for Christ to be the Savior of man if His hypostasis is what I have called here the "hypostasis of biological existence"? If Christ as a person "subsists" not in freedom but according to the necessity of nature, then He too finally, that is, definitively, fails to escape the tragic aspect of the human person. The meaning of the virgin birth of Jesus is the negative expression of this existential concern of patristic theology. The positive expression of the same concern consists in the Chalcedonian doctrine that the person of Christ is one and is identified with the *hypostasis of the Son of the Trinity*.

b) The *hypostatic* union of the two natures—divine and human—in Christ. At this point it is important that a difference of emphasis should be stressed between the Greek and the Western Fathers which is parallel to that which was noted earlier in relation to the doctrine of the Holy Trinity. In the West, as is apparent in the *Tome* of Pope Leo I, the starting-point of Christology is found in the concept of the "natures" or "substances," whereas in the Greek Fathers, for example in Cyril of Alexandria, the starting-point of Christology is the hypostasis, the person. However much this might seem at first sight a mere detail, it is of the greatest significance. For it stresses not only, as we have seen, with regard to God but now also with regard to man that the basis of ontology is the person: just as God "is" what He is in His nature, "perfect God," only as person, so too man in Christ is "perfect man" only as hypostasis, as person, that is, as freedom and love. The perfect man is consequently only he who is authentically a person, that is, he who subsists, who possesses a "mode of existence" which is constituted as being, *in precisely the manner in which God also subsists as being*—in the language of human existence this is what a "hypostatic union" signifies.

Christology consequently is the proclamation to man that his nature can be "assumed" and hypostasized in a manner free from the ontological necessity of his biological hypostasis, which, as we have seen, leads to the tragedy of individualism and death. Thanks to Christ man can henceforth himself "subsist," can affirm his existence as personal not on the basis of the immutable laws of his nature, but on the basis of a relationship with God which is identified with what Christ in freedom and love possesses as Son of God with the Father. This adoption of man by God, the identification of his hypostasis with the hypostasis of the Son of God, is the essence of baptism.

I have called this hypostasis which baptism gives to man "ecclesial" because, in fact, if one should ask, "How do we see this new biological hypostasis of man realized in history?" the reply would be, "In the Church." In early patristic literature the image of the Church as mother is often employed. The spirit of this image is precisely that in the Church a birth is brought about; man is born as "hypostasis," as person. This new hypostasis of man has all the basic characteristics of what I have called authentic personhood, characteristics which distinguish the ecclesial hypostasis from the first hypostasis, the biological one.

IV: Modern and Postmodern

E. Anabaptist & Baptist

82. James McClendon (1924–2000) | *Doctrine: Systematic Theology, Vol. 2*

James William McClendon, Jr. was raised in the Baptist tradition, served for a short time as a Baptist minister, and then taught theology in schools ranging from Southern Baptist to Roman Catholic, from secular to Episcopalian. McClendon struggled to find his place within the Christian tradition and was unsure how to embody the Baptist upbringing that had formed his self-understanding of the Christian faith, but then he fell upon the work of the Mennonite theologian John Howard Yoder, *The Politics of Jesus*. McClendon described the effect:

> That book changed my life. Implicit in it I found all the old awareness of being part of a Christianity somehow unlike the standard-account sort I had worked so hard to learn and to teach, yet somehow like what I had known as a youth growing up Baptist. Night and day I read through the Politics, and by the time I had finished, I had undergone a second conversion, not as at my baptism merely to follow Jesus, but now to follow Jesus understood this way—Jesus interpreted by John Yoder's scornful passion to overcome standard-account thinking, Jesus who (among other things) rejected the Zealot option, Jesus who would not do harm even in the best of causes, even in his own . . . I was converted. I was—though I still have no love for the term itself—an "Anabaptist" Baptist.[1]

McClendon eventually settled down at Fuller, a Protestant Evangelical seminary, and began work on a three volume systematic theology. "I was determined," he later reflected, "to write every sentence in light of my new-gained radical convictions, but to write in such a way that standard-account people, those who shared my pre-Yoder standpoint, could make sense of it, and if not be convinced (for who can say when God will work a conversion), could at least recognize that this, too, was a distinct, responsible Christian heritage that could not be subsumed under the other sorts."[2] He spent nearly two decades completing it.

1. McClendon Jr., "The Radical Road One Baptist Took," para 12.
2. Ibid.

Our selection is from the second volume of McClendon's systematic theology, "Doctrine," in which he portrays the Christian life according to its essential *communal practices* (Yoder's influence is apparent). Notice how McClendon creatively and critically receives the Anabaptist practice of the ban by shifting its focus away from exclusion and *toward* communal discernment. Also notice how McClendon deals with the issue of "attainment" in the Christian life. While all Christians are disciples are some capable of higher levels of attainment than others? This was a divisive issue for sixteenth-century Reformers, particularly Anabaptists. McClendon's approach is dialectic and altogether in the tradition of the Radical Reformers. On one hand, he stresses the Christian life as a process of growth open to all disciples. Like the Reformers at the headwaters of his Baptist tradition, McClendon rejects different levels of discipleship. All follow the same path, common and ordained: "the heights are not for some disciples but for all . . . they wait up the trail every Christian sooner or later must climb." On the other hand, he leaves the possibility open of a "higher Christian life," and thus emphasizes the importance of *communal discernment*.

Doctrine: Systematic Theology, Vol. 2 (1994)

§3. Following Jesus: The Christian Journey

a. Guideposts for the journey.—Is it beginner Christians who are in best position to understand the newness of salvation? Theirs is the vivid discovery of new relations to enjoy, a new selfhood that is their own, a new path to follow. This same new light illuminates their failures, showing sin in its loneliness and gloom and disorder, and the road not taken as a way of death. Yet all of this becomes far more clear as Christian community builds and the journey proceeds. Followers find that the new relations, new selfhood, and new path are a full life adventure. So our present task is to show how the elements of salvation connect over time and space. This could not be accomplished merely by stringing together the several apostolic terms for the new in Christ-justification, sanctification, and the like. A doctrine of salvation must continue to attend to (and will likely employ) many of these terms as well as the syntactic shifts and novel narratives that signal the new in Christ, but it must relate all these to the full reality to which each bears partial witness.

We saw that the apostolic generation discovered the new in Christ when they found their own lives transformed. Where Jesus was known to be alive from the dead, everything was changed. End time was beginning, even if there was more to come. There was now a new world to experience, a new life together. This newness in the risen Christ Jesus and its availability to all people everywhere was the content of the apostolic message, Christian doctrine sprang from these beginnings,[3] and we sketched three historic forms of it, each related to a cluster of seminal terms in the Apostolic Writings. In all three versions the gospel was not merely formative but transformative. As we explore the community and continuity that define the new in Christ for us, it is vital to maintain this transformative understanding throughout. Rosemary Haughton was right: the forms of ongoing community (its structures of common life, its rules of admission and maintenance, its sacraments or salvific signs) must be birth canals of transformation as well as matrices of formation.[4] [. . .]

The guideline, or rather the series of guideposts I propose is an obvious one. A sequence of significant communal practices in the church marks the progress of the pilgrim on the Christian journey. Thus the church's *catechesis* (not to be confused with *catachresis!*), its primary *teaching* or preaching or instruction, is distinctly related to the journeyer's first stage of preparation. Second, the great initiatory sign of *baptism* in the church is specially related, at least in Scripture, to the disciple's conversion (Greek *metanoia*). Conversion is the aim of preparation and the onset of discipleship or following Jesus. Third, the repeated evangelical sign of *eucharist* or Lord's supper as a church practice guides the faithful following Jesus along the way to the cross. And fourth, the (less recognized, but vital) practice of *communal discernment* both acknowledges and directs the (also less recognized) progress I will dub Christian soaring (cf. Isa. 40:31). By this I intend that finding of the higher way some connect with special vocation, some with what Wesleyans called perfect love or entire sanctification, some with perfection in the Christian life. [. . .] Each is a discernible stage in many Christian lives, and each can be correlated with an element of the churches' practice-instructing, baptizing, communing, discerning. Christian life is calibrated by these, from the very beginning. At the same time the course of each Christian life displays limitless variation in detail and remains necessarily an adventure for each. [. . .]

iv. 'Soaring.'—Discernment has been supposed and implied throughout this entire account of the Christian journey. As the teaching church prepares her candidates, as the evangelizing church baptizes them, as the disciple church gathers at the Lord's table, informal and formal discernment has been at work, distinguishing those ready for the next leg of the Christian journey, identifying converts, admitting disciples to her shared tasks and to the memorial table of her Lord. Now something more must be said about discernment and about still another phase of the journey.

In the New Testament we meet the practice of *communal discernment*. With nominations, prayer, and the casting of lots a successor apostle is chosen (Acts 1:15–26). The Jerusalem church faces a question of tactics in the mission to the Gentiles, and after discussion sends a community letter (Acts 15). The Matthean community

---

3. Ernst Käsemann, *New Testament Questions of Today* (Philadelphia: Fortress), chapter 4.
4. Rosemary Haughton, *The Transformation of Man* (Springfield: Templegate, 1980); with what follows, cf. James Wm. McClendon, Jr. and James M. Smith, *Convictions* (Salem, MA: Trinity Press International, 1994).

is given guidance for dealing with a brother or sister who does wrong; congregational discernment is required (Matt. 18:15–20). What became of this shared discernment in the post-apostolic age and after? The answer seems to be that the practice continued, but at least in the West came more and more to deal with notorious sin in the church-immoral living, defection under persecution, or the like. At first these offenses were considered by the entire congregation, which heard the case and handed down judgment. In time (and in step with the developing Western doctrine of sin) the common task devolved upon bishops or presbyters alone, and the medieval sacrament of penance took shape: priests alone heard confession, assigned acts of penance, and granted God's forgiveness.

What seems wrong about this development or devolution is not that Christians judged fellow members—that practice stood on solid New Testament ground such as Matthew 18—but that the focus of discernment narrowed to cases of failure. To be sure, there were two exceptions to the negative focus on sin. As the idea of a separate Christian 'ministry' developed, communal discernment in a positive vein was called into play to select officeholder. In a controversy in fourth-century Milan over the election of a new bishop, the quarrelling congregation heard the voice of Ambrose, a public official still in preparation for baptism, and chose him bishop by acclamation. The choice was not altogether happy (Ambrose was a furious adversary to Jews as well as pagans), but the story portrays the common responsibility still being exercised at that time. Men were sought (by this time women had been disqualified) who were worthy to preside at the sacred rites, to preach the gospel, to exercise charity and further discernment. At its best, communal discernment sought the Spirit's leadership.

The other exception was the discernment of holy men and women (here women were not disqualified). The standard was set by martyrs, witnesses who had given their lives for the faith. In time, holiness of life was detected in living saints as well, and the holy ones were sought out by ordinary Christians who hoped to draw upon their wisdom and sanctity.[5] While the cult of saints verged upon idolatry, it correctly perceived one part of Christian discernment—the lifting up of specially luminous Christian lives as models and examples for all. The present work has continued this theme.[6]

Anabaptist Christians restored the task of discernment to the community, no longer leaving it to ordained clergy. Still they retained its medieval focus upon rooting out sin—the practice of the ban. In consequence baptist congregations found it difficult to exercise discipline without invoking exclusion. Whatever the virtues of the ban, it conveyed a message of exclusive rather than inclusive sociality. However, these

---

5. Peter Brown, *Augustine of Hippo* (Berkeley, CA: University of California Press, 1982).

6. McClendon, *Ethics: Systematic Theology, Vol. 1*, chapters Four, Seven, Ten; cf. McClendon, "Christian Identity in Ecumenical Perspective," *Journal of Ecumenical Studies* 27 (Summer) 1990, 115ff.; see also James, *Varieties of Religious Experience* (New York: Viking, 1987).

baptists also restored the entire community to the New Testament role of saints in common, including the sainthood of suffering martyrdom.[7]

Wherever discernment was preoccupied with fault, it gave less attention to model discipleship. Yet from time to time movements arose to suggest that though preparation and conversion and persevering discipleship were necessary, there was something more to be discerned, a further gift of the Spirit, a call to press on to perfection, a depth in the new in Christ that was not only possible in the present earthly life but indeed was God's intended destiny for every disciple. As noted, in Wesleyan teaching this 'more' was "perfect love"; in nineteenth-century holiness doctrine it was "entire sanctification" or "the second blessing." And in twentieth-century Pentecostal life, it was the new Pentecost, the fresh outpouring of the Spirit in which (ideally) all were touched by the renewal signs of tongues and miracles. Yet even Christian communities that made no allowance in theory for a further stage in Christian faith often hinted at it. They acknowledged special or extraordinary 'saints.' Or they spoke of those with unusual insight as 'mystics.' Or they acknowledged difference by urging ordination on some as if office in the church were provided for an honors class. Ordination may rightly be included here if we see it as partial recognition of distinctive vocations in the kingdom of God.

Is it possible, then, to summarize what these varied teachings and practices have in common—the conviction that beyond conversion and loyal following in Jesus' way there is a 'higher Christian life' (to use the Keswick Movement's term), a second blessing' (in holiness teaching)? Is it possible to grant this *and* to insist with John Wesley that the heights are not for some disciples but for all, that they wait up the trail every Christian sooner or later must climb? At least we must not discount this possibility, must not rule out in advance such attainment for each or for all. If we do accept this, we must accept soaring as an adventurous stage, in principle less predictable than any other aspect of the Christian life. Hence the 'sign' to which it best relates is the practice of communal discernment. Discernment not preoccupied with sin and fault and exclusion may find a better task in the church, the task of recognizing vocations, acknowledging and encouraging gifts, and helping the gifted, to see their role within the rule of God. To be sure, such discernment is required throughout the Christian journey—in enlisting genuine seekers—or the path of preparation, in discriminating real conversions, in discovering the shared way of the cross at a given time and place in kingdom life. Yet because of the great variety of unique blessings and distinctive attainments, communal discernment meets its highest demand at this stage.

> Those who look to the LORD
> > will win new strength,
> they will soar as on eagles' wings;
> they will run and not feel faint,
> > march on and not grow weary (Isa 40:31).

---

7. *Martyrs Mirror* (Scottdale, PA: Herald, 1979).

IV: Modern and Postmodern

E. Anabaptist & Baptist

83. John Howard Yoder (1927–1997) | *Body Politics* & *The Politics of Jesus*

John Howard Yoder was a theologian and ethicist in the Anabaptist tradition. He is most well-known for his defense of Christian pacifism, but his account of Christian practice has been more influential on theological ethics. Yoder championed a way of framing ethics and theology which emphasized the importance of action for comprehension. Here is the basic idea: we cannot know what our words mean if we do not know how to put them into practice. Living in obedience to Christ's teaching—actually doing it—is critical, fundamental really, to comprehending what one *believes* about Christ's teaching. "Nonviolence is not only an ethic about power, but also an epistemology about how to let truth speak for itself" wrote Yoder.[1]

The legacy of Yoder, however, is tragically tainted by decades of sexual abuse against women. In 2014, Anabaptist Mennonite Biblical Seminary (AMBS), where Yoder taught and had once been president, publically acknowledged his abuse of women: "As an AMBS Board, we lament the terrible abuse many women suffered from John Howard Yoder. We also lament that there has not been transparency about how the seminary's leadership responded at that time or any institutional public acknowledgement of regret for what went so horribly wrong."[2] Receiving the witness of Yoder is thus fraught for many. On one hand, Jesus Christ is the only sinless human, so we should not expect moral perfection from anyone in this life, ethicist or otherwise. On the other hand, many struggle to receive Yoder's witness of peace given his violence against women. Does his application of his own ethic invalidate the ethic he advanced? Regardless of how one receives the work of John Howard Yoder, his way of framing the dialectic of thought and life, doctrine and practice influenced many inside and outside the Mennonite tradition (perhaps most notably, Stanley Hauerwas).

---

1. Yoder, "'Patience' as Method in Moral Reasoning," 27–28.
2. Klassen, "AMBS service to acknowledge harm from Yoder actions," para 4. See also Goossen, "'Defanging the Beast.'"

E. ANABAPTIST & BAPTIST

The following two selections both center on Christian life in terms of one's inclusion in a church whose collective life witnesses to God's future for the world. That is, Yoder envisions Christian existence in terms of one's membership in a body of believers whose lives offer a collective witness of what the world will look like in God's future. In *Body Politics,* Yoder states the point in terms familiar to his tradition of Anabaptism. Anabaptists present a highly contrastive vision of the relation between the kingdoms of the world and the kingdom of God. Here Yoder develops the point of "contrast" in positive terms: the church must be "against" the world in order to present an image of God's future for the world. Thus, the "politics" of the church—*how the church manages itself as a social body*—will constitute her witness.

In the second selection, from Yoder's *The Politics of Jesus,* we see how he develops one of the practices that constitute the witness of the church: pacifism. Going back to Menno Simmons, from which *Menno*-nites take their name, Anabaptists have always championed pacifism. Yoder explains the theological roots of pacifism by anchoring the practice not in its effectiveness but in its *obedience* to the kind of power exhibited by the Lamb. According to Yoder, nonviolence is the practice by which Christian learn what it means to believe in the self-sacrificial power of the Christ's crucifixion.

Body Politics (1992)

The believing body is the image that the new world—which in the light of the ascension and Pentecost is on the way—casts ahead of itself. The believing body of Christ is the world on its way to renewal; the church is the part of the world that confesses the renewal to which all the world is called. The believing body is the instrument of that renewal in the world, to the (very modest) extent to which its message is faithful. It may be "instrument" as proclaimer, or as pilot project, or as pedestal.

For the people of God to be over against the world at those points where "the world" is defined by its rebellion against God and for us to be in, with, and for the world, as anticipation of the shape of redemption, are not alternative strategies. We are not free to choose between them, depending on whether our tastes are more "catholic" or more "baptist," or depending on whether we think the times are friendly just now or not. Each dimension of our stance is the prerequisite for the validity of the other. A church that is not "against the world" in fundamental ways has nothing worth saying to and for the world. Conversion and separation are not the way to become otherworldly; they are the only way to be present, relevantly and redemptively, in the midst of things.

Long ago, the French Reformed lay theologian Jacques Ellul wrote a book title *The Presence of the Kingdom,* arguing that, for the witnessing community, the very fact that we stand in the midst of the world is more basic for what God wants to see happen than are the particular projects Christians might undertake. A half-generation later, Ellul had to write *False Presence of the Kingdom*, objecting to the use that had been made of his slogan to justify too simply claiming this or that set of institutions or events as God's cause. It was not that Ellul changed his mind; it was rather that loving the world and refusing conformity to it, being present in its midst and being a foreign body, are not opposite ends of a scale, components which one is free to choose between or to mix as one pleases, but two sides of a coin, both always necessarily present.

The Politics of Jesus (1994)

One way to characterize thinking about social ethics in our time is to say that Christians in our age are obsessed with the meaning and direction of history. Social ethical concern is moved by a deep desire to make things move in the right direction. Whether a given action is right or not seems to be inseparable from the question of what effects it will cause. Thus part if not all of social concern has to do with looking for the right "handle" by which one can "get hold on" the course of history and move it in the right direction. [Right actions are "effective" in moving history in that direction] . . .

The key to the obedience of God's people is not their effectiveness but their patience (Rev 13:10). The triumph of the right is assured not by the might that comes to the aid of the right, which is of course the justification of the use of violence and other kinds of power in every human conflict. The triumph of the right, although it is assured, is sure because of the power of the resurrection and not because of any calculation of causes and effects, nor because of the inherently greater strength of the good guys. The relationship between the obedience of God's people and the triumph of God's cause is not a relationship of cause and effect but one of cross and resurrection.

We have observed this biblical "philosophy of history" first of all in the worship of the late New Testament church, since it is here that we find the most desperate encounter of the church's weakness (John was probably in exile, Paul in prison) with the power of the evil rulers of the present age. But this position is nothing more than a logical unfolding of the meaning of the work of Jesus Christ himself, whose choice of suffering servanthood rather than violent lordship, of love to the point of death rather than righteousness backed by power, was itself the fundamental direction of his life. Jesus was so faithful to the enemy-love of God that it cost him all his effectiveness; he gave up every handle on history.

Not only does the New Testament church claim knowledge about the meaning of history or the meaning of meekness in history; it relates this very specifically to the coming and the ministry of the man Jesus. If we had only the book of Revelation we would not necessarily know what is meant by this Lamb in whom all sovereignty is said to reside. What therefore matters ultimately is how this Lamb relates to the rest of the human history of the people who praise him. The answer lies of course in the person of Jesus Christ, of whom this same early church said in another context that "the Word became flesh and dwelt among us."

Thus early Christian confession means to things for our present concern. Speaking negatively, it means that the business of ethical thinking has been taken away from the speculation of independent minds each mediating on the meaning of things and has been pegged to a particular set of answers given in a particular time and place. Ethics as well as "theology" (in the sense in which in the past they have been distinguished) must, if it is to be our business as Christians to think about them, be rooted in revelation, not alone in speculation, nor in self-interpreting "situation."

But still more important is the other side, the positive side of this confession. This will of God is affirmatively, concretely knowable in the person and ministry of Jesus. Jesus is not to be looked at merely as the last and greatest in the long in of rabbis teaching pious people how to behave; he is to be looked at as a mover of history and as the standard by which Christians must learn how they are to look at the moving of history. . . .

Accepting Powerlessness

We thus do not adequately understand what the church was praising in the work of Christ, and what Paul was asking his readers to be guided by, if we think of the cross as a peculiarly efficacious technique (probably effective only in certain circumstances) for getting one's ways. The key to the ultimate relevance and to the triumph of the good is not any calculation at all, paradoxical or otherwise, of efficacy, but rather simple obedience. Obedience means not keeping verbally enshrined rules but reflecting the character of the love of God. The cross is not a recipe for resurrection. Suffering is not a tool to make people come around, nor a good in itself. But the kind of faithfulness that is willing to accept evident defeat rather than complicity with evil is, by virtue of its conformity with what happens to God when he works among us, aligned with the ultimate triumph of the Lamb. . . .

If what we have said about the honor due the Lamb makes any sense, then what is usually called "Christian pacifism" is most adequately understood not on the level of means alone, as if the pacifist were making the claim that he can achieve what war promises to achieve, but do it just as well or even better without violence. . . . That Christian pacifism which has a theological basis in the character of God and the work of Jesus Christ is one in which the calculating link between our obedience and ultimate efficacy has been broken, since the triumph of God comes through resurrection and not through effective sovereignty or assured survival.

IV: Modern and Postmodern

E. Anabaptist & Baptist

84. Thomas Finger (1947–) | *A Contemporary Anabaptist Theology*

Anabaptists have never been known for producing the kind of theology one readily finds among the heirs of Martin Luther and John Calvin. The comprehensiveness of Calvin and the range of Luther is simply not found among the Anabaptists of the sixteenth century or those who followed. The practical outworking of faith has always been the focus, rather than working out the theological underpinnings of faith through systematic or dogmatic treatises. "For traditional Mennonite understandings of Christian faith, what was most important for humans was not the creeds that we confess but how we live our lives in the midst of our neighbors and our enemies," Gordon Kaufman writes.[1] The practices and worship of Anabaptists have always been, of course, *theological*, but as Thomas Finger describes it, the theology guiding historic Anabaptism has largely been "implicit." Making the largely implicit theology of Anabaptists *explicit* was the goal of his highly significant systematic theology, *A Contemporary Anabaptist Theology* (significant because nothing of this scope has been attempted in doctrinal theology among Anabaptists).

Thomas Finger has been one of the most prolific and widely respected theologians in the Mennonite tradition of his generation. Finger was not Mennonite until adulthood, and then served as a pastor, then later as professor of systematic and spiritual theology at Eastern Mennonite Seminary. He also represented Mennonites in various ecumenical endeavors and was an observer to the World Council of Churches. His ecumenism is readily apparent throughout *A Contemporary Anabaptist Theology*, but in a characteristically Anabaptist "key." Following the style of sixteenth-century Anabaptists, Scripture is the final authority for every theological formulation. The approach doesn't prevent Finger, however, from substantively engaging other Christian traditions (as some might argue Anabaptists did not do well in the sixteenth century). This is especially apparent when he addresses the Christian life.

---

1. Kaufman, *In the Beginning . . . Creativity*, 126.

"Christomorphic divinization" is Finger's term for the Christian life, and he develops the term through a creative reception of traditional Anabaptist sources in conversation with Eastern Orthodoxy. In the first part of our selection, Finger draws from the Eastern church's long-held conception of the Christian life as "divinization" (*theosis*) in order to sharpen traditional Anabaptist sources. Early Anabaptists predominantly frame the Christian life as "new birth," and Finger believes this resonates with Orthodox divinization. Both emphasize the "renewal of our thoroughly human being by the divine Being's direct action or touch." The second part of our selection is drawn from the final pages of Finger's systematic theology in which he criticizes historic Anabaptism for a too negative view of physical matter. Such a view is untenable in light of the Spirit's work of new creation.

A Contemporary Anabaptist Theology (2004)

Part II – The Coming of the New Creation

Chapter 5 – The Personal Dimension . . .

Divinization and the broader term "ontological transformation," by which I designate Swiss Anabaptist soteriology, can appear to mean transformation *into* God rather than *by* God while remaining fully human. Marpeck and Dirk explicitly rejected this understanding.[2] Other Christian theologies have denied it by defining divinization as becoming by grace what God is by nature. This distinguishes God from creatures by making divine action, and divine being insofar as it initiates that action, prior. Yet if we become all that God is, we will apparently be omnipotent, omniscient and omnipresent (for starters). This is hard to square with truly remaining creatures. Such expectations can encourage unrealistic behavior, as displayed by some Anabaptists (notably Hoffman and the Münsterites).

The above definition appears in Eastern Orthodoxy.[3] This tradition, however, also insists that God's essence will remain forever transcendent, beyond our being and knowledge.[4] Gregory Palamas (1296–1359) elucidated this by differentiating God's essence from God's energies, which act directly on us. This strikingly recalls Menno and Dirk's distinction between the eternal Word's birth "from *[van]*" God, which conveys

---

2. Marpeck, *Writings of Pilgrim Marpeck*, p. 531; Philips, *Writings of Dirk Philips*, p. 145.

3. E.g., Maximus the Confessor could say that "All that God is, except for an identity in ousia, one becomes when one is deified by grace" (quoted in Pelikan, *Spirit of Eastern Christendom*, p. 267).

4. Catholic theology, in contrast, traditionally understands eternal life as the beatific vision, or beholding God's essence (Aquinas, *Summa Theologica* pt. 3, sup. Q. 96) and that God is presently in all creatures "by essence" (pt. I, Q. 8.a.3).

God's essence, and our new birth "out of *[uit]*" God, which does not. In Orthodox and most historic Anabaptist theologies, humans will never become or know God's essence, yet they are transformed by the energies' direct operation on them.[5]

For example, the divine righteousness that renews us (Rom 5—6) is not some force created by God, however sublime. It is God's very own action on, in and through us. This righteousness is not simply judicial, ethical or social; it also draws us into direct communion with God, with its unimaginable closeness and transformative potential. Divine energies are not impersonal forces but God's own direct, personal action.

Though Orthodoxy has sometimes included toward spiritualism, it has often stressed christomorphism: "participation in Christ's death and resurrection . . . extends dynamically to cover all the places and forms of human existence. The crucified body of Christ . . . teaches [us] how to share in the virtues and sufferings of hum who was crucified; it shows [us] the way of love, humility, obedience, mortification of the passions, and, in general, of life according to God's will.[6] The first passion to be crucified is avarice, or grasping after earthly possessions, much as among South German-Austrian Anabaptists. The emerging "deified humanity . . . does not in any way lose its human characteristics . . . [T]hese characteristics become even more real and authentic by contact with the divine model [Christ] according to which they were created."[7]

In sum, Orthodoxy's concept of the divine energies can help Anabaptist theology characterize divinization and ontological transformation as not becoming a different, divine being, but as renewal of our thoroughly human being by the divine Being's direct action or touch. Christomorphism can help Anabaptists insist that this occurs through earthly following of and increasing conformity to Jesus and his way.

Biblical Considerations. Is something like this historic Anabaptist notion, now sharpened by Orthodoxy, found in Scripture? Precise theological language of divinization appears only in 2 Peter 1:4, which Anabaptists often cited: we are becoming "participants in the divine nature." But something quite similar is conveyed by the Anabaptists' foremost biblical image, the new birth: we are born from the Word of truth (Jas 1:18), from imperishable seed through the living Word (1 Pet 1:23), through Jesus' resurrection (1 Pet 1:3-4), "from above . . . of water and Spirit" (John 3:3, 5). Birth seems to indicate impartation of something of divine reality itself.

The Bible also attributes such a direct transformation to the Holy Spirit's work in and among us. This can operate below conscious levels (Rom 8:26-27; cf. Gal 4:6; 1 Cor 2:9-11). God's Spirit makes our bodies, personal and corporate, God's own temple (1

---

5. For Palamas, direct experience of God was of God's own, uncreated grace. His opponent, Barlaam, insisted that this must be indirect or through created channels . . .

6. Georgios Mantzaridis, *The Deification of Man* (Crestwood, NY: St. Vladimir's Seminary Press, 1984), pp. 64-65, describing Palamas' view. . . .

7. Meyendorff, *Byzantine Theology,* p. 164. . . .

Cor 3:16–17; 6:18, 19; cf. 1 Cor 12:13; Eph 2:18, 22). The Spirit liberates us and transforms us into the divine glory (2 Cor 3:17–18; Rom 8:12–22, 1 Pet 4:13–14).

Paul often spoke of Christ in a similar way: as being in us (Col 1:27; Gal 2:20; 4:19) and of our being in Christ.[8] This "in" was no static position but dynamic inward participation in Jesus' crucifixion and resurrection, expressed outwardly in a life like his.[9] Paul could beautifully express this indwelling as trinitarian (Eph 1:7–12, 17–23; 3:14–21). It involved "a mystical sense of the divine presence of Christ"; yet not only within individuals, for being in or with Christ "cannot be fully enacted as a 'with others' and 'with creation.'"[10]

The Johannine writings expressed the same realities. Christians "abide" in Christ (1 John 2:6; 3:6; 4:15), as branches in a vine (John 15) and in his teaching, in which we have both Father and Son (1 John 2:25; 2 John 9, cf. 1 John 4:14). We abide in the Son (1 John 5:30) and in the Son and Spirit (1 John 2:27; 3:24). Conversely, the Son is in us (1 John 5:9–12) as living water (John 4:13–14; 7:37–38) and living bread (John 6:35, 50–58). This indwelling prompts us to act with and for others as Jesus did for us (John 15:12–13; 1 John 3:16–17; 4:9–11; 5:1–3). We are also "born" of the Spirit (John 3:3–8), of the Son (1 John 2:29) and of God (1 John 3:9; 4:7, 12; 5:1, 18). Moreover, the Son and Father dwell in each other (John 14:10–11), and Christians dwell in both (John 14:20–23; 17:22–23), so that salvation involves participation in the trinitarian dynamic (John 14:16–17; 15:26; 16:13–16).

For various New Testament writers, then, salvation involved God's direct, personal transforming action within and among individuals. This was often depicted christomorphically: as participating inwardly and living outwardly in accord with Jesus' death and resurrection. Yet few texts can be stretched to suggest that Christians actually become divine—in essence. The process they portray, however, can aptly be called "transformation by divine energies—of our thoroughly human existence through concrete, earthly activities. . . .

Part III – The Convictional Framework

Chapter 10 – The Last Things . . .

Since the new creation arrives through God's Spirit, and since it reshapes the physical world, every theological locus is informed by the Spirit's transformation of matter-energy. Historic Anabaptists, however, often overplayed Spirit and down-graded matter. I attribute this largely to the (conceptual) ontological barrier that prevented the two from interacting. I find true Anabaptist convictions better expressed in their

---

8. Esp. 1 Cor 1:30; 2 Cor 5:17; Eph 2:5–6, 21–22; Col 2:9–13; 2 Tim 2:11–12.

9. Esp. 2 Cor 4:10–11; Rom 6:3–13; 8:10–11, 16–17; Phil 3:8–11; Col 2:6–7, 20. . . .

10. James D. G. Dunn, *The Theology of Paul the Apostle* (Grand Rapids: Eerdmans, 2006), pp. 401, 404.

practices, which contradicted this assumption. Spirit-matter intertwining is particularly evident in the inseparability of the new creation's three dimensions: personal, communal and missional. . . .

Mission calls for personal conversion, and community life requires each member's participation. Personal salvation, initiated by mission and mediated through communal involvement, is thoroughly transformation by divine energies—divinization. This spiritual process revitalizes the body and often works gradually. Some historic Anabaptists, though, presupposing an ontological barrier, overlooked this, etherializing salvation and arousing unrealistic expectations. But divinization is christomorphic: patterned in his life, death and resurrection. So understood, it can be called discipleship. Divinization is transformation by, but not into, God; an ontological transformation by, but not into, divine being. While highly spiritual, it takes distinct personal, physical forms.

IV: Modern and Postmodern

F. Anglican

85. Michael Ramsey (1904–1988) | *The Glory of God and the Transfiguration of Christ*

Michael Ramsey was one of the great Anglicans theologians of the twentieth century. Born and educated in Cambridge, he held the most prominent ecclesial offices of the land as Bishop of Durham, Archbishop of York and then Canterbury. Unusually, Ramsey also occupied two of the most prestigious professorial positions of the time: the Van Mildert Professor of Divinity at Durham University and the Regius Professor of Divinity at the University of Cambridge.

An Anglo-Catholic ecclesially, theologically Ramsey was broad and interestingly eclectic. He read widely and was influenced by a number of close theological acquaintants. At Cambridge he was influenced by Edwyn Hoskyns (who translated the 1922 edition of Barth's Romans commentary) and in Oxford he came into contact with Austin Farrer (through whom Ramsey was exposed to insights from Orthodox Christianity). That Eastern Orthodox influence can be clearly felt in the following extract, which is the conclusion from *The Glory of God and the Transfiguration of Christ*. Reputed to be his most prized publishing accomplishment, in this book Ramsey explores the theme of the transfiguration of Christ, which although is deeply biblical is generally associated more with the Eastern than the Western theological imagination.

Despite its publication date (1949), this book was written during the Second World War. In fact, Ramsey considers this book as forming part of his theological response to the tragedy of war. "But from Calvary and Easter there comes a Christian hope of immense range: the hope of the transformation not only of humanity of the cosmos too. The bringing of human beings to glory will be the prelude to the beginning of a renewed creation." The transfiguration, in other words, is about the hope that the bright light of God's grace will shine through and transform even the bleakest times of human history. The gospel is "the Gospel of transfiguration."

Published as an appendix to the book, Ramsey included a series of Collects (short prayers) relating to the theme of the transfiguration. The close relationship between theology and the liturgy was as important to Ramsey as it was to the Eastern Orthodox tradition and indeed his Anglican forbears. In the reading below, two of those Collects (one from the American Prayer Book and the other from the Scottish Prayer Book) have been brought forward so that they stand at the beginning of the reading. It is through the lens of these prayers that we read his theological writings on the transfiguration, and it is through these prayers that the good news of the grace of God that transfigures all things into the glory of God works in us and through us.

The Glory of God and the Transfiguration of Christ (1949)

It may be of interest to give the text of some collects which present to English Churchmen the many-sided doctrine which the Transfiguration embodies. The American Prayer Book has this:

> O God, who on the mount didst reveal to chosen witnesses thine only-begotten Son wonderfully transfigured in raiment white and glistering, mercifully grant that we being delivered from the disquietude of this world may be permitted to behold the King in His Beauty.

The Scottish Prayer Book has this:

> Almighty and everlasting God, whose blessed Son revealed himself to his chosen apostles when he was transfigured on the holy mount, and amidst the excellent glory spake with Moses and Elijah of his decease which he should accomplish at Jerusalem: grant to us thy servants that, beholding the brightness of thy countenance, we may be strengthened to bear the Cross. . . .

The transfiguration does not belong to the central core of the Gospel. The apostolic *Kerygma* did not, so far as we know, include it; and it would be hard for Christians to claim that the salvation of mankind could not be wrought without it. But it stands as a gateway to the saving events of the Gospel, and is as a mirror in which the Christian mystery is seen in its unity. Here we perceive that the living and the dead are one in Christ, that the old covenant and the new are inseparable, that the Cross and the glory are of one, that the age to come is already here, that our human nature has a destiny of glory, that in Christ the final word is uttered and in Him alone the Father is well pleased. Here the diverse elements in the theology of the New Testament meet.

Forgetfulness of the truths for which the Transfiguration stands has often led to distortions. The severance of the New Testament from the Old, the cleavage between

F. ANGLICAN

God the Redeemer and God the Creator are obvious illustrations. It is possible, alike in Christology and in sacramental teaching and in the idea of the Christian life, to regard the supernatural as replacing the natural in such a way as to "overthrow the nature of a sacrament." It is possible to regard the redemptive act of God in Christ in terms so transcendental that nature and history are not seen in real relation to it, or to identify the divine act with nature and history in such a way that the otherworldly tension of the Gospel is forgotten. Against these distortions the Transfiguration casts its light in protest....

"The Transfiguration," wrote F. D. Maurice, "has lived on through ages, and shed its light upon all ages.... In the light of that countenance which was altered, of that raiment which was white and glistering, all human countenances have acquired a brightness, all common things have been transfigured."[1] So great is the impact of theology upon language that the word "transfigure," drawn from a Biblical story to which scant attention has often been paid, has entered into the practical vocabulary of the Christian life.

1. To the Christian suffering is transfigured. "Our tribulation without ceasing to be tribulation is transformed. We must suffer, as we suffered before, but our suffering is no longer a passive perplexity ... but is transformed into a pain which is fruitful, creative, full of power and promise.... The road which is impassable has been made known to us in the crucified and risen Lord."[2]

2. To the Christian knowledge is transfigured. The knowledge of the world and its forces may be used for the service of man's pride and man's destruction, or else for the unfolding of God's truth and the enlarging of God's worship. "It is not too much to say," wrote Dr. Hort, "that the Gospel itself can never be fully known till nature as well as man is fully known; and that the manifestation of nature as well as man in Christ is part of His manifestation of God. As the Gospel is the perfect introduction to all truth, so on the other hand it is in itself known only in proportion as it is used for the enlightenment of departments of truth which seem at first sight to lie beyond its boundaries.... The earth as well as the heaven is full of God's glory, and His visible glory is but the garment of His truth, so that every addition to truth becomes a fresh opportunity for adoration."[3]

3. To the Christian the world is transfigured. Liberated from its dominance he discovers it afresh as the scene both of divine judgment and of divine renewal within the new creation of Christ. The measure in which he accepts the judgment is the measure in which he discerns, in the face of every calamity, the divine renewal in the raising of the dead.

---

1. F. D. Maurice, *The Gospel of the Kingdom of Heaven* (London: Macmillan and Co., 1879), 157.
2. Karl Barth, *The Epistle to the Romans* (London: Oxford University Press, 1933), 156.
3. F. J. A. Hort, *The Way, The Truth, The Life* (London: MacMillian and Co., 1908), 83–84.

The transfiguring of pain, of knowledge and of the world is attested in centuries of the experience of Christians. It comes neither by an acceptance of things as they are nor by a flight from them, but by that uniquely Christian attitude which the story of the Transfiguration represents. It is an attitude which is rooted in detachment—for pain is hateful, knowledge is corrupted and the world lies in the evil one, but which so practises detachment as to return and perceive the divine sovereignty in the very things from which the detachment has had to be. Thus the Christian life is a rhythm of going and coming; and the gospel narrative of the ascent of Hermon, the metamorphosis and the descent to a faithless and perverse generation is a symbol of the mission of the Church in its relation to the world. . . .

Our contemporary distresses have not made the message of Mount Hermon obsolete. Analysing the possibilities open to those who are aware that they live in a "declining civilization" Dr. Toynbee distinguishes four principles: archaism, futurism, detachment, transfiguration. *Archaism* is the yearning for a past golden age; *futurism* is a phantasy of a new age utterly unrelated to that which now exists, and the quest of it is often pursued by violent means; *detachment* (for which "escapism" would be a better word, since Christians know detachment in a good sense) is an escape into contemplation; but *transfiguration* is a faith where by "we bring the total situation, as we ourselves participate in it, into a larger context which gives it a new meaning."[4] Of such a faith, so the contention of this book has been, the Biblical doctrine of the glory provides the pattern and the event of the Transfiguration provides the symbol. Peter on Mount Hermon may have longed to *return* to the happiness of his discipleship before the Passion was announced, or to *escape* from the conflict into a heavenly rest, or to *advance* at once into the peace of the last things. But the Transfiguration meant the taking of the whole conflict of the Lord's mission, just as it was, into the glory which gave meaning to it all.

Confronted as he is with a universe more than ever terrible in the blindness of its processes and the destructiveness of its potentialities mankind must be led to the Christian faith not as a panacea of progress nor as an other-worldly solution unrelated to history, but as a Gospel of Transfiguration. Such a Gospel both transcends the world and speaks to the immediate here-and-now. He who is transfigured is the Son of Man; and, as He discloses on mount Hermon another world, He reveals that no part of created things and no moment of created time lies outside the power of the Spirit, who is Lord, to change from glory into glory.

---

4. The phrase is C. H. Dodd's.

IV: Modern and Postmodern

F. Anglican

86. Sarah Coakley (1951–) | *"Deepening 'Practices'"*

Part of Sarah Coakley's way of doing systematic theology, which she has come to style *théologie totale*, involves engaging with a diverse set of disciplines (including doctrinal theology, patristics, philosophy of religion, philosophy of science, feminist theology, gender theory, political theory, the arts, and spirituality) and attending to areas of the Christian tradition that have been marginalized by mainstream theological thinking. It is an enticing and exciting renewal of the systematic task. The fruit of Coakley's lifelong work is appearing as a four-volume systematic theology—the first volume of which is entitled *God, Sexuality, and the Self: An Essay on the Trinity* and embodies the *théologie totale* methodology. The overall aim of Coakley's systematic theology is to be more systematic (by broadening the sometimes monochrome canons of literature) and being more resistant to the systematization of theology that domesticates "God" into a controllable system (she does this by rooting her theology in the "dazzling darkness" of prayer). Conceived in prayer, Coakley's work can be seen to be recovering an ancient way of doing theology in which theology and spirituality are one and the same. It is in prayer, that the grace of God, by the work of the Holy Spirit, borrows deeply in human desire, christically transforms it from within, and incorporates it into desire of the trinitarian divine.

An important strand of Coakley's systematic theology has been to reconnect doctrine with practice. For Coakley, as we'll read below in an extract that is part of a broader engagement with aesthetic and mystical sources (including Benedict, Evagrius of Pontius, and Carmelite spirituality), "practices" of the Christian life take on specific meaning. Understood within a context of grace, practices are no longer to be thought of as "self-propelled" human actions but as "grace-propelled." By this Coakley means that the practices of the Christian life, at their deepest level, are best understood in terms of God's graced practice "in" us.

SECTION IV. MODERN AND POSTMODERN

"Deepening 'Practices'" (2001)

[T]he ostensibly bland term "practice" must give place to an overt theology of grace. And once this is realized, the question inevitably arises, retroactively, whether grace was not propelling the engagement in practices all along—a view readily asserted by the "orthodox" believer, of course (especially the Reformed one), but often far from manifest to the observer (or even initially, perhaps, to the believer herself). In short, there is a subtle sliding scale here: one starts from practices one might be tempted to regard as entirely self-propelled; but they are joined over time by practices that involve deeper and more demanding levels of response to divine grace and that uncover by degrees the implications of our fundamental reliance on that grace as initiated in baptism. In short, Christian practices do not happen on a flat plane. . . .

If we return for a moment to a much-quoted definition of "practice" enunciated by Alasdair MacIntyre in *After Virtue*, we shall be able to make this point about the paradox of grace and "practice" a little more explicit. MacIntyre defines "practice" specifically in terms of "socially established" *human* projects: it is "cooperative *human* activity" resulting in an extension of "*human* powers to achieve excellence" and "*human* conceptions of the ends and goods involved" (emphasis mine).[1] If we were to go straight from this definition to an examination of distinctive Christian practices, we would run the risk of embracing an implicitly Pelagian understanding of the undertakings involved, or at least an account that sidelines a theology of divine interaction or cooperative grace. In order to offset this tendency, we shall here chart the progression from a level of practice that actively (and even aggressively) demarcates itself from non-Christian alternatives, through to the apparently passive practice of contemplation, in which an ostensibly time-wasting attentiveness is claimed to be the unimpeded receptacle of infused grace . . . . The stereotypical gender evocations of these two poles should also not escape our notice: the unexpected power of the apparent "powerlessness" of contemplation is one that female writers in the contemplative tradition have drawn attention to, often with profoundly subversive effects; yet there is still the danger of trivializing their undertakings as mere feminine submissiveness. . . .

"[P]ractice" may have a variety of meanings in the Christian context, and those meanings are significantly affected by the depth of response involved in the believer. The contemplation of the Carmelites may be termed a practice, but strictly speaking it is done by God in the believer—from the human side, the purest act of willed "passivity." Still, the contemplative believer does not then give up practices of more mundane sorts that have formed and shaped her in the earlier stages of ascent; ostensibly trivial decisions about modest dress or habits of hospitality to the poor continue to be taken for granted, yet they get taken up and further transfigured. Just as a concert pianist never ceases from the mundane, and often tedious, practices of scales, so contemplation, as Teresa shows with such genius, is thrust back into the repetitive hurly-burly of

---

1. Alasdair MacIntyre, *After Virtue* (Notre Dame: University of Notre Dame Press, 1981), 175.

the kitchen or the marketplace. Even the hermit, as the literature of the Desert Fathers so memorably reminds us, goes back to basics of daily life as he is reminded of the frailty of his endeavors.

Are then the traditions of contemplative ascent sketched here compatible with the Reformed reading of justification and sanctification? Here we have to face some hard questions . . . . Luther and Calvin of course both held Pauline-inspired views about the incorporation of the believer into the "body of Christ": christologically, they were in line with pre-Reformation tradition. But whereas Calvin was to work out his ecclesiology in terms of the paradoxical relation of the two narratives of justification and sanctification . . . , the material we have here charted was, in its Western medieval forms, undergirded by theories of grace that distinguished different levels and types of grace's effects. The danger of spiritual elitism in those theories that caused nervousness (if not outright rebuke) in the Reformers is hard to deny altogether . . . . And the significant differences in emphasis, at least, between pre-Reformation and Reformed theories of justification are not ones that can be simply waved away, as the recent Concordat between Rome and the Lutherans amply shows. It is not my purpose here to claim that these historic points of division can be erased by an irenic smudging of them with the category of "practice," for that would be a mere sleight of hand. If the argument has been successful, however, a theology of "deepening practices" may take from the insights of classic ascetical and mystical theology a message about the relation of practice and belief not obviously incompatible with the central instincts of the Reformers, although certainly questioning some of their rhetorical disjunctions. This position has been forwarded on the assumption (I trust sufficiently supported) that the monastic circles that spawned these traditions are not the sole preserve of their application; lay theologies of belief and practice are equally open to the transformative undertakings this literature proposes for body and soul, not least the vocation of a contemplative life. . . .

I have here suggested a spectrum of interactive forms of beliefs and practices through which, over a lifetime of faithful observation of both public acts of worship and charity on the one hand, and private devotions on the other, one might hope ultimately to come to "know" God in God's intimate life—to breathe his very Spirit, as John of the Cross puts it. I have proceeded on the assumption that this is the vocation to which we are all called, and I have attempted to give clarity to an admittedly complex and messy entanglement of beliefs and practices by suggesting a three-stage heuristic schema of the relation of belief to practice. At the first stage, when the neophyte sets out to delineate the differences between Christian and secular life, it is the public, given beliefs of the creeds that logically precede and substantially inform the initial practices of Christian life, and certain "pagan" practices are foresworn. . . . But a devout life cannot stop with such externals, however meritorious; it engages in a whole web of interactive everyday Christian practices, such as Benedict prescribes, in which the logical relation of practices to beliefs becomes one of mutual interaction.

More or less subliminally, and with a loosening of previous moral judging, the inner meanings of beliefs start to make their impact: Christ ceases to be merely an external model to be imitated, but is recognized in the poor, the stranger at the gate; creeds cease to be merely tools of judgment, but rather rules of life into which to enter and flourish; beliefs cease to be merely charters of orthodoxy dictating right practice, but rather practices start to infuse beliefs with richer meaning. Finally, the practices of prayer that have all along sustained this process may be purified and simplified, if the contemplatives are to be believed, into silent responsiveness, into an empty waiting on God that precedes union in its full sense. This practice of contemplation is, strictly speaking, God's practice in humans—a more unimpeded or conscious form of that distinctive human receptivity to grace that has sustained the process all along and that is itself a divine gift. But it does not obliterate or invalidate all the other practices; rather, it sets them all in a new light, reversing more obviously now the logical relation of beliefs and practices as this practice finally discloses the incorporative telos and meaning of "beliefs." In particular, the Trinity is no longer seen as an obscure though authoritative ecclesial doctrine of God's nature, but rather a life into which we enter and, in unbreakable union with Christ, breathe the very Spirit of God.

IV: Modern and Postmodern

F. Anglican

87. John Milbank (1952–) | *Being Reconciled: Ontology and Pardon*

Grace is God's gift. That much we know. But what does it actually mean to speak of the "gift" of grace? This has been one of the defining questions that has shaped the theological career of the British theologian John Milbank.

One of the founders of the Radical Orthodox movement, Milbank is a famed polemicist. In terms of "gift," he is particularly critical of those theories of grace that imply that the receiving of grace is in any way a passive event as if grace is simply imputed to the receiver with no expectation for "exchange." Transposing (not without modification) the French anthropologist Marcel Mauss's landmark theory of "gift-giving" to a theological, that is, trinitarian key, Milbank seeks to overcome this "unilateral" account of grace with one that is fully and genuinely "reciprocal"—in other words, one that is based on "*active* reception." Although the gift of grace is always in "excess," far exceeding either the expectations of the recipient or the obligation of the giver, one of the key things for Milbank is that the giving of the gift implies relationship. Milbank's theory of the gift of grace is another way, then, of speaking of the Christian doctrine of participation. In addition to classical, premodern resources concerning participation from which Milbank readily draws (in particular, Plato, Augustine, and Aquinas), his Anglicanism is also quietly plentiful in resourcing a rich theology of participation (in particular, Richard Hooker, Lancelot Andrewes, the Wesleys, Edward Bouverie Pusey, and the early John Henry Newman).

On one level, reading Milbank could give the impression that his concerns are highly abstract and insufficiently worked out in connection with the actual living of the Christian life. But on another level, Milbank can be read as proclaiming a simple message about what the Christian life, when all is said and done, is really about. It is about the living out of the inherent connection between grace and gratitude. It is strictly impossible, for Milbank, to be able to receive the gift of grace without becoming a giver of unobligated gratitude and a sharer of that gift to others. This key insight—coupled with Milbank's refusal to speak of the gift in the past tense (as simply "given") and his insistence that at the heart of an ontology of gift is the peace that comes only from being for*given*—must surely lie somewhere close to the heart of any theological account of Christian life.

Being Reconciled: Ontology and Pardon (2003)

Why "gift" exactly? The primary reason is that gift is a kind of transcendental category in relation to all the topoi of theology, in a similar fashion to "word." Creation and grace are gifts; Incarnation is the supreme gift; the Fall, evil and violence are the refusal of gift; atonement is the renewed and hyperbolic gift that is forgiveness; the supreme name of the Holy Spirit is *donum* (according to Augustine); the Church is the community that is given to humanity and is constituted through the harmonious blending of diverse gifts (according to the apostle Paul). . . .

For theology there are no "givens," only "gifts." Normally, in our secular society, one can say "Oh, there's a box," an inert "given," and then maybe in addition one can say, "yes, it was a gift." But in Creation there are only givens in so far as they are also gifts: if one sees only objects, then one misapprehends and fails to recognize true natures. Here something can only be at all as a gift, and furthermore never ceases to be constantly given; in this case the act of giving is never something that reverts to the past tense.

It is just *because* things as created can only be as gifts, just because their being is freely derived, that one has to speak of Creation in terms of participation and of analogical likeness of the gift to the giver—since if his mark is not upon the gift, how else shall we know that it is a gift? Those who imagine that participation is for Christian theology some sort of alien Hellenistic theme (besides the fact that they can never have read the Bible with any attention) fail to see just this, as they equally fail to see that for Greek philosophy there was an uncreated material residue that was not created, and so not a gift, and which therefore *limited* the sway of *methexis*. . . . Gift is an exchange as well as an offering without return, since it is asymmetrical reciprocity and non-identical repetition. Because gift is gift-exchange, participation of the created gifts in the divine giver is also participation in a Trinitarian God. . . .

It seems that while the Incarnation is ontologically in excess of our being forgiven, this circumstance alone is precisely what ensures that we *are* forgiven. To receive forgiveness is not only to continue to receive the gift through and despite Kierkegaard's "jolt"; it is also to receive the intensified gift of identity with the giver, an identity of shared *character*, idiom, ethos or *tropos* which still respects independence of will—although the wills unite in a shared intention. In this way, we need to add Maximus's Christological insights to Augustine's insights on time in order fully to grasp forgiveness. Where people differ, struggle and quarrel, then finally the only solution is to become one flesh, to forge one shared identity, one harmony, one tone, one flavour, which does not mean that asymmetrical contributions to this are denied (though in the case of the divine-human union, there is, of course, really no intrinsic human contribution to the shared *persona*). It may be unpopular to say this, but reconciliation is the absoluteness of shared taste, the freedom of the dance in joint measure which is the gift of lovers to an audience—their transmitted bond which binds a community to them, just as the bond of the Holy Spirit forges the hypostatic union.

Forgiveness, therefore, perfects gift-exchange as *fusion*. If gift-exchange retains free gift as non-identical repetition and asymmetrical reciprocity, then forgiveness exceeds this to the measure that in perfected exchange every surprise is anticipated by the other, since the surprise she offers is also the surprise he arrives at in that very instance, as requiring a perfectly *improvised* and yet absolutely consensual dance. But since . . . forgiveness is only inaugurated by the sovereign victim, this perfection of exchange as fusion is first granted to us in the idiomatic characterizing of victim as sovereign, sovereign as victim. It is their relation, their dance, that first and alone reconciles.

All this seems to point to a further inescapable mystery. To receive forgiveness, we have discovered, can only mean to receive the God-Man, and to receive him as an outcome which infinitely exceeds the forgiveness he proffers, although this exceeding *is* after all forgiveness, since forgiveness is unshakable finality. . . .

Where life is realized and enjoyed as passage, there wealth lies in glorious expenditure, and personal freedom in acts of generosity which bond us to others. This passage is, as we have seen, a passage of gift, which as Pickstock says,[1] cannot begin or cease to be gift, if it is ever to be given at all, since a thing given is regarded as always having had this fundamental destiny, if we are not to devalue the recipient; while a gift must go on giving itself, if it is not to lapse into mere possession, in forgetfulness of the donor. In consequence life celebrated as passing gift is life thankfully received from the outset, and also life shared without restraint. Doxology and charity are here inseparable, but also consummated in the shared festival, for to obliterate oneself as recipient is to blaspheme the transcendent giver; while to refuse the return gift of gratitude from the one to whom one gives is to celebrate's one will to give (in Kantian, Levinasian or Derridean mode) instead of the miraculous and unpredictable arrival of achieved affinity and surprising reciprocity. Hence Pickstock restores to our gaze the full dimensions of charity as also celebration, kinship, fraternity, *eros* and ritual. From this perspective charity ceases to be an anxious duty, just as bereavement ceases to be an unmediated private loss; instead to give has its seasons, and loss its place in a general economy, although neither in an exhaustively prescribed fashion.

---

1. Milbank is here referring to Catherine Pickstock, the Cambridge theologian and (with Graham Ward) co-architect of Radical Orthodoxy.

IV: Modern and Postmodern

F. Anglican

88. Kathryn Tanner (1957–) | *The Economy of Grace*

In the extract below, Kathryn Tanner seeks to describe an alternative vision of society to what has become the status quo: global capitalism. Tanner's theological vision for a new way of organizing and imagining society is rooted in what she calls the "economy of grace." The economy of grace, which is itself grounded in the doctrine of the Trinity, celebrates the grace-drenched themes of abundance, unconditional giving, universal giving, and "noncompetitive" relations.

In an earlier and much celebrated book, *God and Creation* (1988), Tanner developed what she called a "noncompetitive" understanding of the God-world relationship. What she meant by this is that when God and the world relate they do so without competing for the same kind of space (which is akin to a "scarcity" model of economic relations). Much like how two musical notes can occupy the same "space" without competition or confusion, so too can God and the world. The divine "sovereignty" does not, then, cancel out human "freedom" in the sense that the more God's grace is sovereign the less we are free. This "noncompetitive" understanding of the God-world relation provides a model on which to base her vision for the economy of grace: a theological economy is based not on the pursuit of my happiness at the cost of your happiness nor on the concept of "dog-eat-dog" rivalry but on the pursuit of mutual benefit and the free sharing of possessions and property.

The economy of grace is full of profound implications for the reordering of unjust paradigms of power and the imagining of a radically different (genuinely theological) economic system based on the free "gift" of God's grace. But more than this, Tanner describes how the grace of God touches every aspect of life and society, including and especially reconfiguring our understandings of economics.

F. ANGLICAN

The Economy of Grace (2005)

If human relations are structured in a way that reflects the character of God's own giving, they should be marked by unconditional giving—that is, giving that is not obligated by the prior performance of the recipients and that is not constitutional upon a return being made by them. This principal marks all these relations off from *do ut des* giving, or "I give so that you will give," the alternative principal of conditional giving that covers barter commodity exchange, and debtor-creditor relations of all sorts.

God does not give gifts to us because of what we have done to deserve them. They are not payments for services rendered. They are not owed by the fulfillment of some prior condition. This is shown, first of all, by God's gift of creation, by the way God gives in creating the world and everything in it. God's creating of the world cannot be a response to anything creatures have done, since God makes a total gift here; God brings into existence the whole of what is from the bottom up, without its existing in any respect before God acts to create it. Prior to God's creating the world, there is nothing, then, to the world to obligate God's creating of it. This same character of giving is evident, second, in the way God sets up covenant relations with Israel unilaterally, from sheer beneficence and not because of this particular people's special merits. One sees this form of giving, finally, in the way the gifts of salvation are offered to human beings in Christ. They seem to be given to us simply because our need, our sufferings and incapacities, not because of our righteousness and bountiful living in communities where justice and peace reign, not because of our good use of gifts already given. Christ is the way God comes, not to the righteous and the already blessed, who fully expect their privileges of moral standing and good fortune to bring with them all the further goods of life, but to sinners in the midst of their sin, to the poor crushed by burdens of pain and injustice, to all who seem to be owed nothing.

God's giving is not conditioned upon a proper return being made by us for it. God continues to give for our benefit whatever our response might be. And this is a good thing, too, since mired in sin as we are, no one but the God-man Christ ever makes a proper return to God. God simply never stops giving even when we fail to make an entirely proper return. God maintains a gift-giving relation with us, however fragile the exhibition of those gifts in our lives or corrupt our performance in response to their being given. As God's creatures, a continuing relationship with God is the condition of our continuing to live, move, and breathe; if we continue to have the time and space of this created existence, despite our failings, God must be maintaining this gift-giving relationship with us from God's side.

God still gives and is willing to give more; that seems to be God's only reaction to failed response. The human race falls, but God establishes a covenant with Israel—a gift far greater than the goods of mere creation—and maintains a steadfast faithfulness to it, keeps the covenant in force from God's side, even when the human partners to it do not always manage to live up to it. In Christ God gives the greatest gift of God's own life even to the worst sinners, indeed especially to them, just to ease their burden of sin. And when the gifts of salvation fail to make their mark on Christians, God has only other gifts to offer: at the communion rail we can come to feed on Christ when we falter. . . .

God's purpose in giving is to benefit creatures, and therefore the proper return for God's giving is not so much directed back to God as directed to those creatures. A proper return here is one in which God's gifts both do the creatures who receive them good and are used for the good of others. A proper return displays what the gifts of God are good for: furthering the creatures' own good. A proper return in this way just demonstrates or puts into effect God's intent in giving them: creatures become the ministers of divine benefit, givers as God is in this sense, with the same goal of benefiting the recipients of God's gifts. . . .

The reasonableness of such hopes gains support when the economic logic of a community dedicated to addressing the needs of all is further specified by a principle of noncompetitive relations that God's gift-giving abides by. So specified, unconditional giving in human relations to meet the needs of all takes on the shape of a community of mutual fulfillment.

Without this understanding of noncompetitive relations, the economy of grace might seem to require the superhuman, heroic efforts of isolated individuals. It might seem to require saints, with an utterly generous, unself-concerned love for others supremely uncommon in a world of sin and deprivation. Where giving back is not demanded from others and one gives regardless, what is to prevent one's own life from going down the drain? Mustn't that sort of awful outcome be the constant fear against which one battles? How can one expect people to give to others unconditionally in a dog-eat-dog world where every advantage offered to another is liable to be turned against them? Even where common possession rights are the norm, what is to stop a constant tug of war over possessions from breaking out in a world of scarce resources? Even when one recognizes that what one holds is a gift from another, how can one help clasping it to oneself in a possessive and defensive way against others, whose enjoyment of it will lessen yours? A very unrealistic demand will have to be placed on individuals to resist all this; the whole weight of the economy of grace will fall on the dispositions and attitudes of hapless individuals, unless that economy is structured in fundamentally noncompetitive ways. Noncompetitive relations are necessary to set up a social structure that encourages unconditional giving to others. In an economy organized noncompetitively the only sensible thing to do is to give unconditionally to others without regard for a return; that sort of giving now pays, rewards for it having simply been built into the way the system works.

Noncompetitive relations mean the following more specifically: First, there is no competition in property or possession. Something can be my property at the same time as it is another's; my having something in my possession need not lessen the degree to which it is in another's. Second, there is no competition between having oneself and giving to others. Giving is not to come at one's own expense; it is not self-sacrificial, in short. And my having is not at any one else's expense; to the contrary, it enables my giving to them for their good. These noncompetitive relations between having and giving develop the implications of noncompetitive forms of property and possession. . . .

Rather than being in competition with our benefiting others, having becomes in this way the very condition of our giving to others. Having does not stand in the way of and is not incompatible with giving to others; having need not, therefore, come at the expense of others. As elsewhere in a theological economy, we are to give to others not out of our poverty but out of our own fullness. Jesus entered into our poverty for the sake of the poor, but he did so as someone rich with the Father's own love. We do not give of our poverty but of what we have already received for our good so as to work for the good of others in response to their need. It is not as the poor that we are to give to others but as those rich, to whatever extent we are, giving to those poor in what we have, in solidarity with them. Efforts to realize one's own perfection, therefore, need not be at odds with concern for the needs of others. Self-concern is not at odds with that, just to the extent one's own perfections are what enable gift giving to others. . . .

Making what one has the root and impulse of giving to others is simply the summary story of God and the world on my telling of it. The triune God is a God that communicates the goodness of the dynamic go-round of God's own life outward in love for what is not God. The whole point of God's dealings with us as creator, covenant partner, and redeemer in Christ is to bring the good of God's very life into our own. Our lives participate in that divine mission and thereby realize the shape of God's own economy by giving that follows the same principle: self-sharing for the good of others.

IV: Modern and Postmodern

G. Evangelical

89. J. Gresham Machen (1881–1937) | *Christianity and Culture*

The Christian life is always local—lived in particular times and places—and thus unavoidably related to one's culture. For evangelicals at the turn of the twentieth century, the relation between Christianity and culture was vexing. They sought to retain vital, living faith while Western culture was altogether rejecting Christianity or, as many evangelicals feared, adapting it to culture in such a way that the gospel was lost. J. Gresham Machen was caught in the middle of that debate, and he argued for Christians to *engage* their culture rather than avoid it or seek to destroy it.

Machen was raised in a wealthy, aristocratic family in the American South. He attended a private school of boys, then John Hopkins University where he majored in Classics. Princeton Seminary was next, and then he left for Germany to study New Testament with the best German scholars of his day. His time in Europe shook him, for he encountered modern Protestant liberalism firsthand, and it was *not* what he expected. The following lengthy—and very revealing—quote is drawn from several of Machen's letters to his parents and brother, written while he was studying overseas.

> The first time that I heard [Wilhelm] Herrmann may almost be described as an epoch in my life . . . I have been thrown all into confusion by what he says—so much deeper is his devotion to Christ than anything I have known in myself during the past few years. . . . Herrmann affirms very little of that which I have been accustomed to regard as essential to Christianity; yet there is no doubt in my mind but that he is a Christian, and a Christian of a peculiarly earnest type. He is a Christian not because he follows Christ as a moral teacher; but because his trust in Christ is (practically, if anything even more truly than theoretically) unbounded . . . In New England those who do not believe in the bodily Resurrection of Jesus are, generally speaking, religiously dead; in Germany, Herrmann has taught me that is by no means the case. He believes that Jesus is the one thing in all the world that inspires absolute confidence, and an absolute, joyful subjection; that through Jesus we come into communion with the living God and are made free from the world. It is the faith that is a real

experience, a real revelation of God that saves us, not the faith that consists in accepting as true a lot of dogmas on the basis merely of what others have said. Perhaps he is something like the devout mystics of the middle ages—they were one-sided enough, but they raised a mighty protest against the coldness and deadness of the church and were forerunners of the Reformation.[1]

Had Machen expected modern, Protestant liberalism to be dead religion, Hermann's living faith rattled him. Rejecting modern scholarship and theology for the sake of vibrant piety, as some Evangelicals were doing, was not an option for Machen.

Machen returned to America not convinced of liberalism but committed to engaging it head on. For Machen, the Christian life includes a vital, living faith that neither runs from nor acquiesces to culture, but seeks to "consecrate" it for the sake of proclaiming the saving gospel of Jesus the Messiah. The following selection is drawn from an address to seminary students at Princeton University.

Christianity and Culture (1913)

One of the greatest of the problems that have agitated the Church is the problem of the relation between knowledge and piety, between culture and Christianity. This problem has appeared first of all in the presence of two tendencies in the Church—the scientific or academic tendency, and what may be called the practical tendency. Some men have devoted themselves chiefly to the task of forming right conceptions as to Christianity and its foundations. To them no fact, however trivial, has appeared worthy of neglect; by them truth has been cherished for its own sake, without immediate reference to practical consequences. Some, on the other hand, have emphasized the essential simplicity of the gospel. The world is lying in misery, we ourselves are sinners, men are perishing in sin every day. The gospel is the sole means of escape; let us preach it to the world while yet we may. So desperate is the need that we have no time to engage in vain babblings or old wives' fables. While we are discussing the exact location of the churches of Galatia, men are perishing under the curse of the law; while we are settling the date of Jesus' birth, the world is doing without its Christmas message.

The representatives of both of these tendencies regard themselves as Christians, but too often there is little brotherly feeling between them. The Christian of academic tastes accuses his brother of undue emotionalism, of shallow argumentation, of cheap methods of work. On the other hand, your practical man is ever loud in his denunciation of academic indifference to the dire needs of humanity. The scholar is represented either as a dangerous disseminator of doubt, or else as a man whose faith is a faith

---

1. Stonehouse, *J. Gresham Machen*, 106–8.

without works. A man who investigates human sin and the grace of God by the aid solely of dusty volumes, carefully secluded in a warm and comfortable study, without a thought of the men who are perishing in misery every day!

But if the problem appears thus in the presence of different tendencies in the Church, it becomes yet far more insistent within the consciousness of the individual. If we are thoughtful, we must see that the desire to know and the desire to be saved are widely different. The scholar must apparently assume the attitude of an impartial observer—an attitude which seems absolutely impossible to the pious Christian laying hold upon Jesus as the only Savior from the load of sin. If these two activities—on the one hand the acquisition of knowledge, and on the other the exercise and inculcation of simple faith—are both to be given a place in our lives, the question of their proper relationship cannot be ignored.

The problem is made for us the more difficult of solution because we are unprepared for it. Our whole system of school and college education is so constituted as to keep religion and culture as far apart as possible and ignore the question of the relationship between them. On five or six days in the week, we were engaged in the acquisition of knowledge. From this activity the study of religion was banished. We studied natural science without considering its bearing or lack of bearing upon natural theology or upon revelation. We studied Greek without opening the New Testament. We studied history with careful avoidance of that greatest of historical movements which was ushered in by the preaching of Jesus. In philosophy, the vital importance of the study for religion could not entirely be concealed, but it was kept as far as possible in the background. On Sundays, on the other hand, we had religious instruction that called for little exercise of the intellect.

Careful preparation for Sunday-school lessons as for lessons in mathematics or Latin was unknown. Religion seemed to be something that had to do only with the emotions and the will, leaving the intellect to secular studies. What wonder that after such training we came to regard religion and culture as belonging to two entirely separate compartments of the soul, and their union as involving the destruction of both?

Upon entering the Seminary, we are suddenly introduced to an entirely different procedure. Religion is suddenly removed from its seclusion; the same methods of study are applied to it as were formerly reserved for natural science and for history. We study the Bible no longer solely with the desire of moral and spiritual improvement, but also in order to know. Perhaps the first impression is one of infinite loss. The scientific spirit seems to be replacing simple faith, the mere apprehension of dead facts to be replacing the practice of principles. The difficulty is perhaps not so much that we are brought face to face with new doubts as to the truth of Christianity. Rather is it the conflict of method, of spirit that troubles us. The scientific spirit seems to be in-compatible with the old spirit of simple faith. In short, almost entirely unprepared, we are brought face to face with the problem of the relationship between knowledge and piety, or, otherwise expressed, between culture and Christianity....

G. EVANGELICAL

[Rather than subordinate Christianity to culture or seek to destroy culture] A third solution, fortunately, is possible—namely consecration. Instead of destroying the arts and sciences or being indifferent to them, let us cultivate them with all the enthusiasm of the veriest humanist, but at the same time consecrate them to the service of our God. Instead of stifling the pleasures afforded by the acquisition of knowledge or by the appreciation of what is beautiful, let us accept these pleasures as the gifts of a heavenly Father. Instead of obliterating the distinction between the Kingdom and the world, or on the other hand withdrawing from the world into a sort of modernized intellectual monasticism, let us go forth joyfully, enthusiastically to make the world subject to God.

Certain obvious advantages are connected with such a solution of the problem. In the first place, a logical advantage. A man can believe only what he holds to be true. We are Christians because we hold Christianity to be true. But other men hold Christianity to be false. Who is right? That question can be settled only by an examination and comparison of the reasons adduced on both sides. It is true, one of the grounds for our belief is an inward experience that we cannot share—the great experience begun by conviction of sin and conversion and continued by communion with God—an experience which other men do not possess, and upon which, therefore, we cannot directly base an argument. But if our position is correct, we ought at least to be able to show the other man that his reasons may be inconclusive. And that involves careful study of both sides of the question. Furthermore, the field of Christianity is the world. The Christian cannot be satisfied so long as any human activity is either opposed to Christianity or out of all connection with Christianity. Christianity must pervade not merely all nations, but also all of human thought. The Christian, therefore, cannot be indifferent to any branch of earnest human endeavor. It must all be brought into some relation to the gospel. It must be studied either in order to be demonstrated as false, or else in order to be made useful in advancing the Kingdom of God. The Kingdom must be advanced not merely extensively, but also intensively. The Church must seek to conquer not merely every man for Christ, but also the whole of man. We are accustomed to encourage ourselves in our discouragements by the thought of the time when every knee shall bow and every tongue confess that Jesus is Lord. No less inspiring is the other aspect of that same great consummation. That will also be a time when doubts have disappeared, when every contradiction has been removed, when all of science converges to one great conviction, when all of art is devoted to one great end, when all of human thinking is permeated by the refining, ennobling influence of Jesus, when every thought has been brought into subjection to the obedience of Christ. . . .

Christianity is the proclamation of an historical fact—that Jesus Christ rose from the dead. Modern thought has no place for that proclamation. It prevents men even from listening to the message. Yet the culture of today cannot simply be rejected as a whole. It is not like the pagan culture of the first century. It is not wholly non-Christian.

Much of it has been derived directly from the Bible. There are significant movements in it, going to waste, which might well be used for the defense of the gospel. The situation is complex. Easy wholesale measures are not in place. Discrimination, investigation is necessary. Some of modern thought must be refuted. The rest must be made subservient. But nothing in it can be ignored. He that is not with us is against us. Modern culture is a mighty force. It is either subservient to the gospel or else it is the deadliest enemy of the gospel. For making it subservient, religious emotion is not enough, intellectual labor is also necessary. And that labor is being neglected. The Church has turned to easier tasks. And now she is reaping the fruits of her indolence. Now she must battle for her life. . . .

The Church is puzzled by the world's indifference. She is trying to overcome it by adapting her message to the fashions of the day. But if, instead, before the conflict, she would descend into the secret place of meditation, if by the clear light of the gospel she would seek an answer not merely to the questions of the hour but, first of all, to the eternal problems of the spiritual world, then perhaps, by God's grace, through His good Spirit, in His good time, she might issue forth once more with power, and an age of doubt might be followed by the dawn of an era of faith.

IV: Modern and Postmodern

G. Evangelical

90. John Stott (1921–2011) | *Basic Christianity*

The historian David Bebbington describes modern evangelicalism in terms of four distinctives or marks: conversionism, activism, biblicism, and crucicentrism.[1] In this sense modern evangelicalism is a set of *emphases* rather than a distinct theological tradition. Thus people across the range of classic Christian traditions identify themselves as evangelicals; they identify with the marks despite what might otherwise divide them, such as doctrinal, liturgical, or political differences. John R. W. Stott exemplified the marks of modern evangelicalism in Great Britain.

Born in 1921 and confirmed in the Anglican Church in 1936, Stott was ordained for ministry at twenty-four. He began his ministry as assistant curate of All Souls Church, the church where he was raised, and was appointed rector just five years later. Stott's influence as an evangelical was widespread in London and around the world. At the International Congress on World Evangelization he was the chair of the drafting committee for the Lausanne Covenant in 1974 and the Manilla Manifesto in 1989, two influential documents on evangelism. As an Anglican, Stott sought to promote the marks of evangelicalism in his tradition. He founded the Evangelical Fellowship in the Anglican Communion, which promotes the evangelical heritage of the Anglican Church around the world. He also served as chair of the Church of England Evangelical Council for two decades and served four terms as president of the Universities and Colleges Christian Fellowship.

Stott's long commitment to university ministry is glimpsed in our selection from *Basic Christianity*. The writing is plain and direct, without being pedestrian. A discussion leader in a dorm could easily distribute it to those without close exposure to Christianity, which is the audience for which Stott wrote it. The emphases of modern evangelicalism are clear throughout, particularly the centrality of the Bible (biblicism) and the cross (crucicentrism) and the important of personal, felt experience of faith

---

1. Bebbington, *Evangelicalism in Modern Britain*. "Bebbington's Rule," as it came to be known, is not without its detractors. See Haykin and Stewart, eds., *The Advent of Evangelicalism*.

(conversionism). Even as Stott recollects his childhood faith one detects the spirit of modern evangelicalism that *Basic Christianity* exudes:

> As a typical adolescent, I was aware of two things about myself, though doubtless I could not have articulated them in these terms then. First, if there was a God, I was estranged from him. I tried to find him, but he seemed to be enveloped in a fog I could not penetrate. Secondly, I was defeated. I knew the kind of person I was, and also the kind of person I longed to be. Between the ideal and the reality there was a great gulf fixed. I had high ideals but a weak will. . . . [W]hat brought me to Christ was this sense of defeat and of estrangement, and the astonishing news that the historic Christ offered to meet the very needs of which I was conscious.[2]

For Stott, simply put, the Christian life is about the transformation of our lives into the likeness of Christ: "Every son of God longs to become more and more conformed in his character and behavior to the Son of God himself."[3] Such transformation includes a series of responsibilities or "duties," which Stott unpacks in this selection.

Basic Christianity (1958)

To be a child of God is a wonderful privilege. It involves obligations also. Peter implied this when he wrote: "Like newborn babes, long for the pure spiritual milk, that by it you may grow up to salvation" (1 Pet 2:2).

The great privilege of the child of God is relationship; his great responsibility is growth. Everybody loves children, but nobody in his right mind wants them stay in the nursery. The tragedy, however, is that many Christians, born again in Christ, never grow up. Others even suffer from spiritual infantile regression. Our heavenly Father's purpose, on the other hand, is that "babes in Christ" should become "mature in Christ." Our birth must be followed by growth. The crisis of justification (our acceptance before God) must lead to the process of sanctification (our growth in holiness, what Peter terms "growing up to salvation").

There are two main spheres in which the Christian is meant to grow. The first is in understanding and the second in holiness. When we begin the Christian life, we probably understand very little, and we have only just come to know God. Now we must increase in the knowledge of God and of our Lord and Savior, Jesus Christ. This knowledge is partly intellectual and partly personal. In connection with the former,

---

2. Dudley-Smith, *John Stott*, 89.
3. Ibid., 136.

I would urge you not only to study the Bible but to read good Christian books. To neglect to grow in your understanding is to court disaster.

We must also grow in holiness of life. The New Testament writers speak of the development of our faith in God, our love for our fellow men and our likeness to Christ. Every son of God longs to become more and more conformed in his character and behavior to the Son of God himself. The Christian life is a life of righteousness. We must seek to obey God's commandments and do God's will. The Holy Spirit has been given us partly for this purpose. He has made our bodies his temple. He dwells within us. And as we submit to his authority and follow his leading, he will subdue our evil desires and cause his fruit to appear in our lives, which is "love, joy, patience, kindness, goodness, faithfulness, gentleness, self-control" (Gal 5:16, 22, 23).

But how shall we grow? There are three main secrets of spiritual development. They are also the chief responsibilities of the child of God.

Our duty to God

Our relationship to our heavenly Father, though secure, is not static. He wants his children to grow up to know him more and more intimately. Generations of Christians have discovered that the principal way to do so is to wait upon him every day in a time of Bible reading and prayer. This is an indispensable necessity for the Christian who wants to make progress. We are all busy nowadays, but we must somehow rearrange our priorities in order to make time for it. It will mean rigorous self-discipline, but granted this, together with a legible Bible and an alarm clock that works, we are well on the road to victory. . . .

Our duty to the church

The Christian life is not just a private affair of your own. If we are born again into God's family, not only has he become our Father but every other believer in the world, whatever his nation or denomination, has become our brother or sister in Christ. One of the commonest names for Christians in the New Testament is "brethren." This is a glorious truth. But it is no good supposing that membership of the universal church of Christ is enough; we must belong to some local branch of it. Nor is it sufficient to be a member of a Christian Union in a college or elsewhere (although I hope you will become active in yours). Every Christian's place is in a local church, sharing in its worship, fellowship and witness. . . .

Our duty to the world

The Christian life is a family affair, in which the children enjoy fellowship with their Father and with each other. But let it not for one moment be thought that this exhausts the Christian's responsibilities. Christians are not a self-regarding coterie of smug and selfish prigs, who are interested only in themselves. On the contrary, every Christian should be deeply concerned about all his fellow men. And it is part of his Christian vocation to serve them in whatever way he can.

The Christian church has a noble record of philanthropic work for the needy and neglected people of the world—the poor and hungry, the sick, the victims of oppression and discrimination, slaves, prisoners, orphans, refugees and drop-outs. Still today all over the world the followers of Christ are seeking in his name to alleviate suffering and distress. Yet an enormous amount of work is waiting to be done. And sometimes, it must be confessed with shame, others who make no Christian profession seem to show more compassion than we who claim to know Christ.

There is another and particular responsibility which Christians have towards "the world," as the Bible describes those outside Christ and his church: evangelism. To "evangelize" means literally to spread the good news of Jesus Christ. There are still millions of people who are ignorant of him and his salvation, not only in Asia, Africa and Latin America, but in the secularized Western world as well. For centuries the church seems to have been half asleep. Is this the generation in which Christians will wake up and win the world for Christ? Perhaps he has a special task for you to do as an ordained minister of the gospel or as a missionary. If you are a student already launched on your course, it would be quite wrong for you to do anything rash or hasty. But seek to discover God's will for your life, and be surrendered to it.

Although every Christian is not called to be a minister or a missionary, God does intend every Christian to be a witness to Jesus Christ. In his own home, among his friends in his college or at his place of business, it is his solemn responsibility to live a consistent, loving, humble, honest, Christ-like life, and to seek to win other people for him. He will be discreet and courteous, but determined.

The way to begin is by prayer. Ask God to give you a special concern for one or two of your friends. It is usually wise to keep to people of your own sex and about your own age. Then pray regularly and definitely for their conversion; foster your friendship with them for its own sake; take trouble to spend time with them; and really love them for themselves. Soon an opportunity will come to take them to some service or meeting where they will hear the gospel explained; or to give them some Christian literature to read; or to tell them simply what Jesus Christ has come to mean to you and how you found him. I need hardly add that our most eloquent testimony will be without effect if we are contradicting it by our conduct; while little is more influential for Christ than a life which he is obviously transforming.

IV: Modern and Postmodern

G. Evangelical

91. J. I. Packer (1926–) | *Rediscovering Holiness*

Modern evangelicalism prioritizes the experience of living faith: the active and conscious sense of one's relation to God in Christ. John Wesley (eighteenth century) stands near the headwaters of the movement, and surely his conversion experience has something to do with it—his "heart strangely warmed." To be sure, what evangelicals value is different from and more than mere *emotionalism*. It is the felt experience of *communion* with God they prize and seek, and in this respect one sees the tight connections between modern Evangelical conceptions of the Christian life with a great many similar conceptions throughout the Christian tradition. As those connections relate to holiness, J.I. Packer draws upon many of them in this selection from his book *Rediscovering Holiness*.

J. I. Packer is a British-born Canadian theologian in the Calvinist Anglican tradition. Educated at Oxford University and ordained in the Church of England in 1953, he taught in England for some time before moving to Regent College, Vancouver, in 1979. Packer taught theology at Regent until in retirement in 2016 due to blindness caused by macular degeneration (he was eighty-nine years old). Throughout his long career Packer has been as a leader in the evangelical movement in Britain and North America, and through his publications his influence has been global. He was a remarkably prolific scholar with more than 300 publications, though he is most widely known for his book *Knowing God,* which has sold over one million copies just in North America. Packer was ordained Anglican, and he retained a strong connection to the Church of England throughout this life. Packer left the Anglican Church of Canada in 2008 when their diocese authorized marriages for same-sex couples, and realigned with the more conservative Province of the Southern Cone. Since the inception of the Anglican Church of North America in 2009, Packer has been the ACNA's theologian emeritus and was the general editor for their catechism, *To Be A Christian.*

The Puritans have been particularly influential for Packer, but it is entirely misleading to think of him as a Puritan theologian. Packer is a student of the Christian tradition of spirituality and conversant with the long story of Christian reflection and practice on the Christian life. In our selection from *Rediscovering Holiness*, Packer reflects on the Christian life in terms of desire and holiness, themes that reappear time and again throughout this anthology. As he traces the relation between desire and holiness—from Origen to Augustine, and from St. Gregory all the way forward to Wesley and the Puritans—he emphasizes the dark night of the soul: "God brings on dryness, with resultant restlessness of heart, in order to induce a new depth of humble, hopeful openness to himself, which he then crowns with a liberating and animating reassurance of his love—one that goes beyond anything that was sensed before."

Through the lens of the dark night, many times the felt distance of God is by the hand of God; not accidental but providentially ordered to draw us closer to himself. It is, in fact, how Packer views the blindness that brought an end to his writing and preaching ministry. "The author of Ecclesiastes has taught me that it is folly to suppose that you can plan life and master it, and you will get hurt if you try," he said. "You must acknowledge the sovereignty of God and leave the wisdom to him . . . Some good, something for his glory, is going to come out of it."[1] Hold this in mind when reading the selection.

Rediscovering Holiness (1992)

As the landscape of holiness unfolds before us, the practical question becomes sharper and more pressing: just what, then, are we to do? We know ourselves to be justified through faith in Christ, adopted into God's royal family, united to Christ, regenerated, sealed, and indwelt by the Holy Spirit. We know that God is at work in us sanctifying us, changing us into Christ's likeness from one degree of glory (divine self-display in us) to another, and energizing us for works of love and obedience. We know that we are called to cooperate with what our God is doing in our lives. What from one standpoint is our cooperation with the process is from another standpoint a part of the process itself.

What form, then, should our cooperation be taking? How are we to "work out" our salvation (express, exhibit, and advance it) with appropriate "fear and trembling" (awe and reverence in God's presence—not panic and alarm in our hearts!)? What is the relevance of the reminder that "it is God who works in you to will and to act according to his good purpose" (Phil 2:13)? "Be holy," says God, and that, as we have seen, is a summons to obedience—consecration to God's service, with conformity to his standards. But what does this mean, in practical terms? Just what are we to do? . . .

---

1. Quoted by Mesa, "J. I. Packer, 89, On Losing Sight but Seeing Christ," para 11.

G. EVANGELICAL

Holiness as the Redirecting of Desire

Desire is the "I-want" state of consciousness. In this line of teaching (which goes back at least to Origen in the third century, Augustine in the fifth, and Gregory the Great in the sixth), holiness is viewed first and foremost as the detaching of desire from created things in order to attach it through Christ to the Creator, for expression and satisfaction in and through God-centered prayer. Important as the outward life of justice, integrity, and neighbor-love is, the inner life of pure-hearted prayer is held (surely rightly) to be far more important. God calls on his children to give him their hearts. Finding their fullness of life here and now in the relationship of knowing, loving, and enjoying him will be a foretaste of their life in heaven. Prayer is thus the top priority in the life of holiness. Indeed, only insofar as prayer is the breath, heartbeat, and energy source of one's inner being can one be said to be living a life of holiness at all.

Achieving and maintaining steady, God-centered prayerfulness is a struggle. Christians find themselves in constant conflict with the devil and his hosts, who by God's permission tempt us to sin and distract us from obedience in order to obstruct and destroy holiness in our inner life. Honest prayer comes only from honest hearts, hearts that are set against sin and that practice regular self-search lest they be self-deceived. So the essence of Satan's strategy is to prevent us being honest in heart (he does not mind our behavior being blameless in human eyes as long as our hearts are crooked before God; proud self-absorption and self-indulgence in our fantasies and motivations are all he needs to get his effect). God allows us to be thus infiltrated and assaulted partly, at least, so that we may be toughened, matured, and anchored in him more deeply through the experience of fighting back in his strength. This is spiritual warfare, in the true meaning of that phrase (see Eph 6:10–20).

Desiring God. The teaching under review assumes that desiring and contemplating our Savior-God in the reciprocity of love is life's highest and noblest activity. In developing that thought, it makes two further affirmations: first, Christians often forfeit enjoyment of this relationship through their own negligence and preoccupation with other things; second, God sometimes withholds the sense of his presence and love which he gives at other times, in order to teach us lessons about patience and pure-heartedness that we would not otherwise learn. A variety of presentations have been developed to articulate these truths. We glance now at some of these.

The importance of distancing oneself from what has held one's heart has often been expressed in terms of withdrawing into the "desert" of solitude, where desire is purified. The same point has been made in the West by directing Christians to strip off (renounce, leave behind) all the distracting things that overlay the "cone" or "apex" of their souls, and in the East by requiring *apatheia* (not inner impassivity, but the self-mastery that redirects passion into the pursuit of God). Paths of thought and prayer for detaching desire from the magnetic pulls of this world in order to attach it more firmly to God in Christ have been mapped by Augustine, Bernard, and Thomas à

Kempis; Roman Catholics like Ignatius Loyola and Francis de Sales; and Puritans such as Richard Sibbes, Richard Baxter, Thomas Goodwin, and John Owen, with many others before and since.

The relationship between, on the one hand, verbal meditation and petition and on the other, post-verbal and non-verbal contemplation and self-offering to the Lord whom one knows, trusts, and loves, has been explored by teachers of the "spiritual marriage." They have developed the analogy of love-language and love-communion between the sexes and applied it to one's relationship with God. In the same connection, Cistercians, Franciscans, and others have highlighted the links between loving contemplation of God and compassionate action among men and women, while Jonathan Edwards' *Treatise on Religious Affections* sets up tests that show whether strong driving feelings in a devotional context are authentically spiritual (stemming from the Holy Spirit's work in the heart) or not. All of this instruction seeks, one way or another, to mark out the path to *that enjoyment of God which is life's supreme value and glory.*

Unfulfilled Desire. On God's use of the discipline of dryness and temporarily unfulfilled desire for himself as a means of strengthening the inner life of his servants, other classic presentations have been made. Teresa of Avila and John of the Cross described different stages or phases in the life of prayer, including the "dark night of the soul" that may precede the joy of realized union with God. Puritan teaching on "spiritual desertion" was substantially the same as that of the two Spanish mystics just cited. John Wesley formulated a two-level account of the inner life whereby, through seeking and agonizing for the post-conversion blessing of "perfect love," the Christian's heart is totally purged of sin and imbued with an all-consuming passion of love God and fellow human beings.

The variations on this "second blessing" theme (concepts of entire sanctification, the clean heart, Spirit-baptism, Spirit filling, and eradication of sin) have been vastly influential in popular Protestantism, and more recently in the global charismatic movement. One does not have to give full endorsement to any of these formulations to recognize the recurring pattern: God brings on dryness, with resultant restlessness of heart, in order to induce a new depth of humble, hopeful openness to himself, which he then crowns with a liberating and animating reassurance of his love—one that goes beyond anything that was sensed before. As Christ's humiliation and grief on the cross preceded his exaltation to the joy of his throne, so over and over again humbling experiences of impotence and frustration precede inward renewing, with a sense of triumph and glory, in the believer's heart. Thus, with wisdom adapted to each Christian's temperament, circumstances, and needs, our heavenly Father draws and binds his children closer to himself. Consider the words of Paul and the psalmist on this theme:

> Whatever was to my profit I now consider loss for the sake of Christ.... I consider everything a loss compared to the surpassing greatness of knowing Christ Jesus my Lord, for whose sake I have lost all things. I consider them rubbish, that I may gain Christ and be found in him.... I want to know Christ. (Phil 3:7–10)

> Earth has nothing I desire besides you.... God is the strength of my heart and my portion for ever (Ps 73:25–26).

These statements are classic transcripts of genuinely holy hearts. The redirecting of desire so that it focuses on fellowship with the Father and the Son, and the strengthening of desire so redirected, is the real essence of holiness. All mature forms of Christian holiness teaching down the centuries have started here, seeing this as the true foundation to everything else in the Christian life, and insisting that the only truly holy people are those with a passion for God. We today have to start here too.

IV: Modern and Postmodern

G. Evangelical

92. Donald Bloesch (1928–2010) | *The Crisis of Piety*

Donald Bloesch was an American theologian who worked at the hinge between the Reformed theology he found in Karl Barth and the Pietism of his own faith background. Bloesch's father and grandfather were ministers in the Evangelical Synod, a German church with roots in Lutheran and Reformed Pietism ("Pietism" was a movement in the Lutheran and Reformed traditions that emphasized biblical authority and rigorous pursuit of spiritual growth). Bloesch was ordained in the Evangelical and Reformed Church, which later joined the United Church of Christ, and for a short time he pastored a church in Illinois while pursuing doctoral studies at the University of Chicago. Bloesch later visited the Universities of Oxford, Basil, and Tubingen where he studied with Karl Barth and Hans Kung. Beginning in 1957 Bloesch taught for thirty-five years at the University of Dubuque Theological Seminary. He authored forty books, including a seven-volume systematic theology, *Christian Foundations*.

Bloesch's pietistic upbringing emphasized the *subjective* experience of faith and rigorous pursuit of holiness, which he sought to wed with the *objective* revelation of Jesus Christ, found in historic orthodoxy and particularly emphasized by Karl Barth. "The focus on personal piety must never supplant the more basic focus on the life, death, and resurrection of Jesus Christ," he wrote in the foreword to *The Crisis of Piety*, from which our selection in taken. Thus, while the pietistic elements of evangelicalism do well to emphasize the felt experience of faith (conversionism), Pietism can unwittingly de-emphasize the ground of Christian belief in the objective revelation of Christ.

> The bane of classical Pietism was that it sought to cultivate the Christian life without a corresponding emphasis on the decision of God for humanity in Jesus Christ. Morality and Christian character became more important than the incarnation and substitutionary atonement of Christ in biblical history. Pietism invariably fades into latitudinarianism [i.e., showing no preference among creeds] and liberalism unless it is informed by the wisdom of

orthodoxy. Orthodoxy, on the other hand, becomes barren and deadening unless it is nurtured by an abiding seriousness concerning personal salvation and the life of discipleship. What is called for is a live orthodoxy, which is none other than a biblically grounded and theologically robust Pietism.[1]

Bloesch's appeals for "live orthodoxy" is a simultaneous effort to pull pietistic evangelicalism back to its creedal heritage in the catholic tradition of faith, and to push Protestant liberalism toward the living faith emphasized by Pietism. Raised by Pietists and educated by liberals, Bloesch was intimately acquainted with the challenge of portraying the Christian life as a *dynamic unity* of loving God (personal faith) and loving neighbors (faith at work) rooted in the work of the Word and the Spirit.

In our selection, Bloesch portrays the Christian as neither *secluded from the world*, a recurring challenge among pietistic Evangelicals, or *unrecognizable from the world*, a frequent charge against Protestant liberals. "Piety apart from mercy is piosity; mercy apart from piety is do-goodism," he writes. According to Bloesch, "holiness in the world" is the vigorous pursuit of holiness that follows the way of the cross *toward* one's neighbor.

The Crisis of Piety (1988)

Piety in the Christian context essentially means heartfelt devotion and consecration to the God who has revealed himself in Jesus Christ.[2] It signifies the organizing pattern or style of Christian life, the way by which we seek to give concrete or practical expression to our faith. It involves a commitment that is total, one that affects every area of human life. There can be various types of piety insofar as certain elements of the gospel become the focal point of attention. Yet a piety that is grounded in Scripture will always be characterized by inward zeal or consecration, godly fear, and total dedication. Scriptural piety will be directed to the holy God incarnate in Jesus Christ. A piety that is directed solely to Jesus and not to Jesus Christ, the God-man, can only be regarded as a pseudo-piety. In Calvin's judgment: "True piety consists . . . in a pure and true zeal which loves God altogether as Father, and reveres him truly as Lord, embraces his justice and dreads to offend him more than to die."[3] Here it can be seen that piety is essentially a synthesis of the love and fear of God.

1. Bloesch, *The Crisis of Piety,* xi–xii.

2. The word "pious," which is related to the Latin *pius,* originally meant "careful of the duties owed by created beings to God." See *The Oxford Universal Dictionary.*

3. John Calvin, *Instruction in Faith* (Philadelphia: Westminster, 1959), p. 19. This is the definition he gives in his *Institutes*: "I call 'piety' that reverence joined with love of God which the knowledge of his benefits induces." *Institutes of the Christian Religion,* ed. John T. McNeill; trans. Ford L. Battles,

In the theology of the Reformation, piety was sharply distinguished from moralism, which signifies seeking to make oneself worthy in the sight of God. True piety presupposes a heartfelt conviction of one's own unworthiness before God and a sincere trust and confidence in his mercy. Piety is grounded in and sustained by faith; it might even be considered the working out of faith to its fulfillment. It entails renouncing and denying the self and cleaving to Christ in repentance and devotion. But in the thought of the Reformers (particularly Calvin), piety also has another aspect—the pursuit of Christian holiness, a seeking after the perfection to which Christ calls us. In their view we cannot earn our salvation, but we should seek to uphold and confirm it in our lives. In this sense piety consists in the bearing of the cross after the example of Christ, an *imitatio Christi*. It was this aspect of piety that was especially pronounced in the later movements of Pietism and Puritanism. . . .

A theology of devotion or Christian life must be grounded in the doctrine of justification of the ungodly if we are to avoid the perils of works-righteousness. Christ has justified us while we are still sinners—this is a truth propounded by Paul and reaffirmed by the Protestant Reformers. At the same time Christ also sanctifies us by his Spirit, and this is a truth we can learn from Pietism and Evangelicalism. We are not regenerated all at once at our baptism and conversion, but our regeneration has certainly commenced, and throughout our lives we can make real progress toward evangelical perfection if we abide in Christ.

The order of salvation (*ordo salutis*) will play a major role in any theology that seeks to take the Christian commitment with the utmost seriousness. It is fashionable in contemporary theological circles to speak only of various facets of the one great event of our salvation rather than of an order of salvation. Yet this kind of thinking fails to do justice to the biblical testimony that salvation has a definite beginning and that it progresses through a series of stages toward a final culmination.

I affirm that the Christian life plays a decisive role in the divine plan of salvation, although it is not its basis or source. Rather the Christian life is the arena in which our salvation is fought for and continually recovered. A life of devotion is not the foundation of salvation, but it is a vital element in our salvation. We are not justified by a Christian life, but we are sanctified through a Christian life.

A theology of Christian devotion will be oriented about the costliness of grace. Just as the grace of God cost the life of his own Son, so it must also cost us our comfort and security in this world. God's grace is free, but it is not cheap, as both Kierkegaard and Bonhoeffer recognized. This grace is given to us while we are still sinners, but it demands from us that we strive against sin and seek holiness in all manner of living (1 Pet 1:15). In order to retain the grace of Christ we must take up our cross and follow him. Salvation is neither instant nor automatic. It involves a life of struggle and perseverance under the cross.

(Philadelphia: Westminster Press, 1960), I, 2, I, p. 41.

G. EVANGELICAL

The new secular theology speaks of "servanthood" and "holy worldliness." The old orthodoxy placed the accent upon churchliness. I am calling for an emphasis on godliness or holy fear. There is much talk today of the need for becoming authentically human, yet, as John Chrysostom so poignantly stated, "To be a man is to fear God." The strategy that I favor is not withdrawal from the world into permanent seclusion but rather a hidden life of devotion held together with outgoing service to the outcasts and unfortunates in our midst. My motto is separation *and* identification. We are to be *in* the world but not *of* it (cf. John 17:11, 14).

Yet I contend that devotion to God takes priority over charity to our neighbor. We are called to love both God and neighbor but to adore only God. Although Jesus had a strong healing ministry, he nevertheless withdrew to the wilderness for prayer even while crowds were seeking him to be healed of their infirmities (Luke 5:15, 16). John Wesley distinguished between works of piety, which fulfill our duties to God and the church, and works of mercy, which discharge or obligations to our fellowman. In Wesley's theology the works of piety come first, although the two must always go together. Piety apart from mercy is piosity; mercy apart from piety is do-goodism.

The distinction inherited from Catholic mysticism and Protestant Pietism between the God-life and the good life (in the material sense) is now under criticism in various quarters. The Christian faith, secular theologians rightly contend, certainly supports the human quest for social justice and personal well-being in the world. Yet what must also be recognized is that there will always be a tension between the God-life and the good life. The Christian faith teaches self-denial before it speaks about self-fulfillment (Matt 16:24, 25). Christians can hold the good things of life only as stewards (1 Cor 7:25–31), and they must always be prepared to forsake these things out of loyalty to their Lord. Indeed it is precisely this readiness to forsake one's life for the kingdom that is the hallmark of discipleship.

A theology of the Christian life must at the same time be a theology of the Word of God. Indeed a life of faith and piety springs from the preaching and hearing of the gospel. In the last analysis no life however saintly can bring people the assurance of forgiveness they so desperately need. It is only when we are confronted with the message of salvation through the shedding of blood of Jesus Christ that we are awakened to heartfelt faith and consecration. Life and word are organically related, and yet it is the Word of God that brings us the power to live a life of devotion and consecration.

This is not to deny, however, that works of piety and mercy can also be potent means of grace. To be sure they must be accompanied by the Word, and they must spring from the Word. Yet the Word of God does not take permanent root within us until we obey as well as believe. Faith apart from works is dead, and this means that our preaching is not effectual apart from a life of obedience under the cross. A theology of proclamation must be supplemented by a theology of devotion if Protestantism is to maintain itself in a secular age.

SECTION IV. MODERN AND POSTMODERN

What is here proposed is a holiness in the world, a piety that is to be lived out in the midst of human suffering and dereliction. Such a holiness should be sharply distinguished from the other-worldliness of modern secularism and the ethereal other-worldliness of a certain kind of mysticism. Holiness is a gift from God, but it is also a goal that we are called to strive for in this world, in this life. We are summoned neither to separation nor solidarity with the world but rather to combat with the evil forces of the world, and this means that the way of holiness is also the way of the cross.

IV: Modern and Postmodern

H. Contextual

93. Anne Carr (1934–2008) | *Transforming Grace: Christian Tradition and Women's Experience*

Alongside groundbreaking texts such as Rosemary Radford Ruether's *Sexism and God-Talk* (1983) and Elisabeth Schüssler Fiorenza's *In Memory of Her* (1983), Anne Carr's *Transforming Grace* (1988) helped to pioneer the field of Christian feminist theology in the late twentieth century. The first woman to hold a permanent faculty position at the University of Chicago's Divinity School, Carr was critical of Christianity's historical tendency to sideline and silence the voices and experiences of women. While patriarchy was, for some, too deeply entrenched in Christianity to make staying in church possible, Carr argues in *Transforming Grace* that Christianity can be integrated positively with the project of feminist thinking. In order for this to happen Christianity needs to be transformed (by grace) from within. Importantly, for Carr, this transformation enables Christianity to live more fully up to its namesake: it allows Christianity to be *more* Christian.

This transformation from within involves a three step-process: *critiquing the past* (calling out Scripture and the writings of the church that denigrate women); *recovering the "lost history" of women* (for example, the unnamed women in the Gospel narratives, the unsung history of women leadership); and finally *revising Christian categories* (for example, masculinist language for God, the maleness of Christ, the male dominance of church hierarchy, Christian doctrine described from "male experience"). The extract below provides an example of Carr in this third, revisionist, mode. Here we find Carr reconstructing the traditional doctrine of grace as "the gift of self-sacrificial love" in terms of the liberating metaphor of "friendship." We experience God, Carr says, through grace as a friend. Indeed, grace comes in all sorts of shapes and sizes. For some it rightly involves the kind of self-sacrificial love of which traditional doctrines speak; for others "grace takes on a wholly different character as the gift of claiming responsibility for one's life."

Carr writes in the introduction to *Transforming Grace* that "it is important to note that all theology bears the imprint of its own time and place." Although Christian theology has moved on since the late 1980s, as has the now flourishing field of feminist theology, this book serves as an important reminder of the church's ongoing task to "honour and celebrate the dignity and full personhood" of the marginalized, the oppressed, and the silenced.

Transforming Grace: Christian Tradition and Women's Experience (1988)

An important example of such theological reconstruction begins with criticism of traditional Christian doctrines of sin and grace as cast exclusively in terms of male experience. Christian writers have been inclined to speak of sin as pride, self-assertion, and rebellion against God and of grace as the gift of self-sacrificial love. But in fact such categories relate more to the experience of men, in cultures that encourage them toward roles of domination and power. Women's temptation or "sin," conversely, relates to *lack* of self-assertion in relation to cultural and familial expectations, failure to assume responsibility and make choices for themselves, failure to discover their own personhood and uniqueness rather than finding their whole meaning in the too-easy sacrifice of self for others. Reinterpreted by feminist theologians, grace takes on a wholly different character as the gift of claiming responsibility for one's life, as love of self as well as love of others, as the assumption of healthy power over one's life and circumstances. From this brief example it is apparent that feminist theology seeks to correlate the central and liberating themes of biblical and Christian tradition with the experience of women in the contemporary situation. . . .

Christian feminists can appropriate contemporary theological language for God as the ground and dynamic power of Being, the infinite and incomprehensible horizon of Holy Mystery, the absolutely, related Thou, language that serves to underscore the final transcendence and absolute immanence of God beyond all human understanding. Women can appropriate these theological concepts as they affirm that God can be known, as the term of human questioning at least and with paradoxical clarity, in the event of Jesus Christ and thus can be inadequately but truthfully named in human images, symbols, and concepts. Nevertheless, feminist theology's particular critique of male images for God and of God's attributes bears its specific contribution to the wider contemporary theological discussion. In particular, it focuses on the meaning of power and authority in our human understanding of the reality of God. Many traditional theological and popular concepts of God are rooted in naive and crude perceptions of God as the epitome and ultimate personification of masculine stereotypes of power as domination.[1] The theological tradition and (more often) popular Christian usage have spoken, perhaps too simply, of God's omnipotence, omniscience, aseity (absolute independence), immutability, impassivity. Though not alone in its criticism of these traditional notions, feminist thought challenges them in a dramatic way. If such concepts of God are derived from the patriarchal male image as an androcentric, and so distorted, aspect of the whole human and Christian experience, important correctives and reorientations emerge when the other half, indeed the majority of human experience, is taken into account in the analogical symbolization of God as the transcendent referent and horizon of the whole of human experience. . . .

As feminist theology suggests new images of God as mother, sister, and friend, its goal is to find language that can freshly evoke, for our time with its particular struggles, the inclusive, compassionate, and passionate love of God for all creation that is proclaimed in the message and the life, death, and resurrection of Jesus. It is a search for a more adequate understanding of God that addresses the experience of women who have been marginalized in the church, excluded from recognition and participation for centuries. Such concrete images of God issue in new models or concepts that have been recently suggested by a variety of voices in the theological community, concepts that are nonhierarchical and that fit the experience of women today. These new concepts must still be interpreted in strictly metaphorical and analogical ways. But in their evocation of the disclosive truth of the Christian message about God, their broad incorporation into the church's preaching and teaching might well reorient the Christian imagination today and in the future.

The liberating God is a concept familiar from the Latin American and black theologians and movements for emancipation. Like the women's movement, these movements include both secular and religious components and their theologians insist that the religious or Christian meaning of liberation encompasses the *whole* of human life, including the secular. Rooted in the biblical themes of the exodus from slavery to freedom and of the liberating action of God in human history for those held in bondage, the concept of the liberating God is particularly evocative for all who search for new freedom today, including Christian women.[2] On one level, the image of God as liberator is an image modeled after important human liberator figures in history. On another level, the idea of a liberating God moves into the realm of concept as it affirms a specific attribute of God and the specific character of God's power. In the Latin American context, Christian freedom is interpreted as the possibility of becoming persons, subjects, responsible agents in history.[3] And the action of the liberating God is seen as

1. See Edward Farley, "God as Dominator and Image-Giver: Divine Sovereignty and the New Anthropology," *Journal of Ecumenical Studies* 6.3 (Summer 1969), pp. 354-75.

2. Elisabeth Schüssler Fiorenza, "Feminist Theology as a Critical Liberation Theology," *Theological Studies* 36 (1975), pp. 605-26.

3. See Gustavo Gutiérrez, "Faith as Freedom: Solidarity with the Alienated and Confidence in the Future," in Francis A. Eigo, ed., *Living with Change, Experience, Faith* (Villanova, PA: Villanova University, 1976), p. 37; Juan Segundo, *Grace and the Human Condition* (Maryknoll, NY: Orbis Books,

that which empowers human persons to become genuine subjects in the context of human solidarity and collaborative human action in relation to God. To speak of God as liberating is to evoke the God who does not will human suffering but justice, the God who is on the side of the poor, and who favors and graces the oppressed, the marginal, the outcasts of society, those who hunger and thirst for justice.[4]

Knowledge of God's active empowerment of people who are powerless drives out fear, gives human communities—and the Christian community of women—new faith, courage, and ability to take risks in speaking and acting for the cause of those who have little or no power because of their class, race, or sex. The understanding of God as liberator is liberating in itself in its suggestion that in the cause of justice one is not acting alone, but with others and with the Other with whom all things are possible. The suggestion of the power of God as liberating precisely in the human power of the oppressed makes it clear that God's power, in some mysterious way, waits upon and works through human power, works through human freedom, agency, and responsibility. To speak of God as liberating is, of course, to speak metaphorically and analogously. But it gives primacy of place to a biblical reading of human life and history in relation to God, rather than a metaphysical, rationalist, or simply naturalistic point of view.

If the retrieval of the biblical idea of the liberating God is perhaps the most important new concept of God in our time, its closer analysis, which shows that God's power is resident in human power, leads to a very traditional Christian theme in the idea of *the incarnational God.* While the theological tradition focused its attention on the meaning of Jesus as the incarnation of God, the contemporary feminist context suggests some further ramifications of this theological affirmation. For women, the central theme of incarnation suggests that in Christian perspective, there can be no fundamental split, no ultimate dualism in the world. The richly symbolic idea of God's incarnation in Christ, which means the enfleshment or embodiment of God and the consequent sacramentality of all creation, especially human creation, indicates that God and creation or the world are not in competition but are irrevocably united, joined, made one in God's self-gift to humankind and so to the world. The symbol of God's embodiment also suggests that there is no fundamental matter/spirit, body/mind, female/male dichotomy in which one member of each air is inferior to the other. Nor is there, in incarnational understanding, a hierarchical dualism between humankind and the world of nature. The relationship of the divine and human and of God and creation in the incarnation is rather a relationship of irrevocable union, reverence, and compassionate love.

Yet, within the irrevocable union of incarnation and the sacramentality it entails, there is diversity: divine and human, grace and nature, spirit and matter. How does

---

1973), pp. 14–57.

4. Johann Baptist Metz, *Faith in History and Society: Toward a Practical Fundamental Theology*, trans. David Smith (New York: Seabury Press, 1980), pp. 60–77.

one think of the transcendence, the over of God if that transcendence and power are only and always mediated through Christ, through the sacraments of the human, the natural, the material? The notion of the self-limitation of God[5] has been proposed to indicate the superabundance of God's compassionate love for that which is other than God in creation, incarnation, and grace. God is self-limited in a way that allows creatures, especially humans, their own autonomy. As one follows the clue of incarnation, the important principle in Karl Rahner's thought about the inversion of the proportion between autonomy and dependence takes on clear meaning: the more autonomy creatures possess, the more dependent they are (precisely through union) on God.[6] We usually think in human terms that autonomy means independence. In the Christian incarnational scheme, the opposite is true. God is the self-limiting creator of human autonomy. God wills human freedom in creation and grace and so is the God who desires the equality of friendship with humankind.

The image of God as friend has sometimes met with the objection that the metaphor is not appropriate because there is no real equality between God and human beings. On a philosophical or metaphysical level this is true: God infinitely transcends the reach of the human. But in Christian, New Testament terms, in the parables of Jesus and the parable of the Christ event, the compassionate love of God is revealed in the image of friendship: "I call you friends" (John 15:15). The image is disturbing precisely because it shows us the love of God as desiring and giving humankind the equality of friendship.[7] A biblical interpretation of God from the perspective of the experience women shows that this favored metaphor is firmly grounded in the incarnational tradition as a disclosure of the character of God who desires relationship, even the relationship of equality that is friendship.

---

5. Langdon Gilkey, *Reaping the Whirlwind: A Christian Interpretation of History* (New York: Seabury Press, 1976), pp. 248–49, 271–81.

6. Karl Rahner, "On the Theology of the Incarnation," *Theological Investigations*, trans. Kevin Smith (Baltimore: Helicon Press, 1966), IV: 177.

7. Thomas Aquinas deals with this precise problem in his discussion of the theological virtue of charity in the *Summa Theologiae* II-II, q. 23, art. 1, where he argues against Aristotle and cites John's Gospel as his authority.

IV: Modern and Postmodern

H. Contextual

94. Delores S. Williams (1929–) | *Sisters in the Wilderness: The Challenge of Womanist God-Talk*

Delores S. Williams is one of the founding voices in womanist theology. Womanist theology began from a concern to speak of God from the experience of African-American women who face multiple oppressions due to intersecting inequalities relating to gender, ethnicity, and class. Williams's now-classic *Sisters in the Wilderness* draws from her own experience as an African-American woman in dialogue with the stories of black women from the history of slavery and the overlooked presence of African women in the biblical narrative. One such overlooked biblical figure is Hagar. Williams reads the familiar passages from Genesis not from the perspective of Abraham and Sarah (the slave owners) as is customary, but from Hagar, an enslaved Egyptian woman. There she finds "striking similarities" between Hagar and the living reality of many African-American women. In particular, African-American women, like Hagar, have often been required to take on domestic roles—to be "surrogates"—in homes and families that are not their own.

Hagar also models a way of doing theology. Speaking out of her context, Hagar, we read in Genesis, "named the Lord who spoke to her, 'You are El-roi,' she said" (Gen 16:13). Likewise, womanist theology follows Hagar's example by seeking to name God differently and challenging us to think more expansively about the language we use to speak of God. Hagar also provides Williams with a critique of the "classical" doctrines of the atonement, which in various ways center on the redemptive significance of the cross. Williams refuses to see the grace of God in any form of violence, including the suffering of Christ. God's saving work is revealed in Jesus' ministry of justice and life of resistance, rather than his suffering on the cross.

One further feature of Williams's *Sisters in the Wilderness*, as it relates to the theme of grace, is that the Christian life is not only about the liberation from the multiple oppressions many in the world continue to face but also about *survival*. In the ordinary, everyday miracles of survival the grace of God is found. And survival in this context is not about passively waiting around for God to act. It is about participating actively in our survival, finding a way forward with God's help and by God's grace to a better future.

Sisters in the Wilderness: The Challenge of Womanist God-Talk (1993)

As I encountered Hagar again and again in African-American sources, I reread her story in the Hebrew testament and Paul's reference to her in the Christian testament. I slowly realized there were striking similarities between Hagar's story and the story of African-American women. Hagar's heritage was African as was black women's. Hagar was a slave. Black American women had emerged from a slave heritage and still lived in light of it. Hagar was brutalized by her slave owner, the Hebrew woman Sarah. The slave narratives of African-American women and some of the narratives of contemporary day-workers tell of the brutal or cruel treatment black women have received from the wives of slave masters and from contemporary white female employers. Hagar had no control over her body. It belonged to her slave owner, whose husband, Abraham, ravished Hagar. A child Ishmael was born; mother and child were eventually cast out of Abraham's and Sarah's home without resources for survival. The bodies of African-American slave women were owned by their masters. Time after time they were raped by their owners and bore children whom the masters seldom claimed—children who were slaves—children and their mothers whom slave-master fathers often cast out by selling them to other slave holders. Hagar resisted the brutalities of slavery by running away. Black women have a long resistance history that includes running away from slavery in the antebellum era. Like Hagar and her child Ishmael, African-American female slaves and their children, after slavery, were expelled from the homes of many slave holders and given no resources for survival. Hagar, like many women throughout African-American women's history, was a single parent. But she had serious personal and salvific encounters with God—encounters which aided Hagar in the survival struggle of herself and her son. Over and over again, black women in the churches have testified about their serious personal and salvific encounters with God, encounters that helped them and their families survive....

[I]t seemed to me that God's response to Hagar (and her child's) situation was survival and involvement in their development of an appropriate quality of life, that is, appropriate to their situation and their heritage. Because they would finally live in the wilderness without the protection of a larger social unit, it was perhaps to the advantage that Ishmael be skillful with the bow. He could protect himself and his mother. The fact that Hagar took a wife for Ishmael "from the land of Egypt" suggests that Hagar wanted to perpetuate her own cultural heritage, which was Egyptian, and not that of her oppressors Abraham and Sarah.

Even today, most of Hagar's situation is congruent with many African-American women's predicament of poverty, sexual and economic exploitation, surrogacy, domestic violence, homelessness, rape, motherhood, single parenting, ethnicity and meetings with God. Many black women have testified that "God helped them make a way out of no way." They believe God is involved not only in their survival struggle, but that God also supports their struggle for quality of life, which "making a way" suggests. . . .

Surrogacy

Because she was a slave, Hagar had no control over her body or her labor. Her body, like her labor, could be exploited in any way her owners desired. Her reproduction capacities belonged to her slave holders, Abraham and Sarah. Thus surrogacy became a major theme in Hagar's story of exploitation. But whereas Hagar's experience with surrogacy was primarily biological, African-American women's experience with surrogacy has been primarily associated with social-role exploitation. . . .

Poverty among African-Americans often pressured some black women into certain surrogacy roles. For poor black women voluntary surrogacy could mean that, as domestics employed by white families, these women could still perform nurturing tasks for white children. In the black community black women could be pressured by social circumstances to step into the role of head of household in lieu of absent male energy and pressure.

Today the growing surrogacy industry in North America and the escalating poverty among black people can pressure poor black women to become heavily involved in this industry at the level of reproduction. Though legislation has been passed that makes surrogacy contracts non-binding for surrogate mothers, poverty can influence black women to honor such contracts. However, the point here is that since emancipation, black women have been able to exercise choice with regard to surrogacy roles, even though economics and other social forces exert undue influence upon the choices of black women make.

Doctrine: Surrogacy and Redemption

One of the results of focusing upon African-American women's historic experience with surrogacy is that it raises serious questions about the way many Christians, including black women, have been taught to image redemption. More often than not the theology in mainline Protestant churches (including African-American ones) teaches believers that sinful humankind has been redeemed because Jesus died on the cross in place of humans, thereby taking human sin upon himself.

In this sense Jesus represents the surrogate figure; he stands in the place of someone else: sinful humankind. Surrogacy, attached to this divine personage, thus takes on an aura of the sacred. It is therefore fitting and proper for black women to ask whether the image of a surrogate-God has salvific power for black women or whether this image supports and reinforces the exploitation that has accompanied their experience with surrogacy. If black women accept this idea of redemption, can they not also passively accept the exploitation that surrogacy brings?

I recognize that reflection upon these questions causes many complex theological issues to surface. For instance, there is the issue of the part God the Father played in determining the surrogate role filled by Jesus, the Son. For black women, there is also the question of whether Jesus on the cross represents coerced surrogacy (willed by the Father) or voluntary surrogacy (chosen by the Son) or both. At any rate, a major theological problem here is the place of the cross in any theology significantly informed by African-American women's experience with surrogacy. Even if one buys into the notion of the cross as the meeting place of the will of God to give up the Son (coerced surrogacy?) and the will of the Son to give up himself (voluntary surrogacy?) so that "the spirit of abandonment and self-giving love" proceeds from the cross "to raise up abandoned men," African-American women are still left with the question: Can there be salvific power for black women in Christian images of oppression (for example, Jesus on the cross) meant to teach something about redemption? . . .

While . . . ransom, satisfaction, substitution and moral theories of atonement may not be serviceable for providing an acceptable response to African-American women's question about redemption and surrogacy, they do illustrate a serviceable practice for theologians attempting today to respond to this question. That practice . . . is to use the language and socio-political thought of the time to render Christian ideas and principles understandable. So the womanist theologian uses the sociopolitical thought and action of the African-American woman's world to show black women their salvation does not depend upon any form of surrogacy made sacred by traditional and orthodox understandings of Jesus' life and death. Rather their salvation is assured by Jesus' life of resistance and by the survival strategies he used to help people survive the death of identity caused by their exchange of inherited cultural meanings for a new identify shaped by the gospel ethic and world view. This death of identity was also experienced by African women and men brought to America and enslaved. They too relied upon Jesus to help them survive the forging of a new identity. This kind of account of Jesus' salvific value—made compatible and understandable by use of African-American women's socio-political patterns—frees redemption from the cross and frees the cross from the "sacred aura" put around it by existing patriarchal responses to the question of what Jesus' death represents. . . .

What this allows the womanist theologian to show black women is that God did not intend the surrogacy roles they have been forced to perform. God did not intend the defilement of their bodies as white men put them in the place of white women to provide sexual pleasure for white men during the slavocracy. This was rape. Rape is defilement, and defilement means wanton desecration. Worse, deeper and more wounding than alienation, the sin of defilement is the one of which today's technological world is most guilty. Nature (the land, the seas, the animals in the seas) are every day defiled by humans. Cultures and people (Native Americans, Africans, Jews) have been defiled and destroyed by the onslaught of Western, Christian, patriarchal imperialism in some of its ugliest forms. The oceans are defiled by oil spills, and industrial waste destroys marine life. The rain forest is being defiled. The cross is a reminder of how humans have tried throughout history to destroy visions of righting relationships that involve transformation of tradition and transformation of social relations and arrangements sanctioned by the status quo.

The resurrection of Jesus and the kingdom of God theme in Jesus' *ministerial* vision provide black women with the knowledge that God has, through Jesus, shown humankind how to live peacefully, productively and abundantly in relationship. Jesus showed humankind a vision of righting relations between body, mind and spirit *through an ethical ministry of words* (such as the beatitudes, the parables, the moral directions and reprimands); *though a healing ministry of touch and being touched* (for example, healing the leper through touch; being touched by the woman with an issue of blood); *through a militant ministry of expelling evil forces* (such as exorcising the demoniacs, whipping the moneychangers out of the temple); *through a ministry grounded in the power of faith* (in the work of healing); *through a ministry of prayer* (he often withdrew from the crowd to pray); *through a ministry of compassion and love.*

Humankind is, then, redeemed through Jesus' *ministerial* vision of life and not through death. There is nothing divine in the blood of the cross. God does not intend black women's surrogacy experience. Neither can Christian faith affirm such an idea. Jesus did not come to be a surrogate. Jesus came for life, to show humans a perfect vision of ministerial relation that humans had very little knowledge of. As Christians, black women cannot forget the cross, but neither can they glorify it. To do so is to glorify suffering and to render their exploitation sacred. To do so is to glorify the sin of defilement.

IV: Modern and Postmodern

H. Contextual

95. François Kabasélé (1947–) | *Christ as Ancestor and Elder Brother*

To a certain extent, this essay by the African theologian François Kabasélé is about responding to Bonhoeffer's famous question, "Who is Jesus Christ for you today?," from the particular context of African theology. Kabasélé embarks on a quest for the true face of Jesus Christ in Africa, that is one free from the colonial Christ that had been imposed on Africa. What Kabasélé and others saw in the faces of Jesus in Africa was a Christology that drew less on the historical formulas and creeds and more on the vibrant language of African religious and spiritual culture. They saw Christ as the ancestor, elder brother, chief, healer, warrior, friend, brother, liberator, and black messiah. Africans no longer had to choose between Christianity and their African-ness: Christ met them, as Christ meets us all, precisely in their context.

While some of these christological titles are drawn from the biblical portrayals of Jesus Christ (healer, for example), others are more explicitly rooted in the particular context of African spirituality. Christ as "ancestor" fits into the latter of these approaches. Notice, then, that Kabasélé begins his essay with a careful description of what the "Ancestor" represents for a Muntu, and then applies that rich conceptuality onto his discussion of Christ. More specifically there four distinguishing marks of the Ancestor (life, presence, the eldest, and the mediator), each of which Kabasélé explores christologically. The extract below focuses on the third of these four marks.

This is not so much a text that describes a particular account of grace, and its internal logic, as it is an example of grace itself: that grace both interrupts history from above but also emerges from below. For Kabasélé, it is in the face of the poor and the oppressed that the face of Jesus is seen. This text also us to think expansively and contextually about Jesus Christ and Christ's grace. But more than this, Kabasélé reminds us that as we follow the example of Christ at its heart the grace of God is about liberation.

SECTION IV. MODERN AND POSTMODERN

Christ as Ancestor and Elder Brother (1986)

The Bantu Ancestor

It was to Ancestors that God first communicated the divine "vital force." Thus, they constitute the highest link, after God, in the chain of beings. But they still remain human beings. In their death passage they have become more powerful than other human beings—in their capacity to exert influence, to increase or to diminish the vital force of earthly beings. In their present state, they behold both God and God's subject. Not just anyone accedes to the rank of Ancestor. It is not enough to die; one must have "lived well"—that is, have led a virtuous life.

They must have observed the laws—have incurred the guilt neither of theft nor of a dissolute life. They must not have been wrathful persons or quarrelsome ones, or have dabbled in sorcery. They must have been a leaven of unity and communion among human beings. . . .

Recourse to them is made not only to ask some favour, such as a cure or the satisfaction of some need, but also, simply in order to remember them—as a memorial to perpetuate a memory, a history of deeds and words, an experience of the victory of life over death. Recourse to the Ancestors, whatever its motive or occasion, is always a source of blessing. Thus, all important events in the life of the Muntu become either an epiphany of the activity of the Ancestors or an occasion of renewing contact with them, like closing ranks before battle. For the more "devout" among the Bantu, all acts of daily life must be steeped once more in this presence of the Ancestors. Before taking a drink or tasting a plate, the devote Muntu will pour a drop on the ground, in token of deference to and participation in the life of the Ancestors. If such a one happens to sneeze, he or she will speak the name of an Ancestor, as if asking for a blessing. When surprised, the devout Muntu will utter an Ancestor's name, as if to say, "Be surprised with me!"

Application to Christ

The figure of the Ancestor is quite complex. Indeed, the various aspects so converge that any attempt to dissociate them will deform this noble figure. But circumstances oblige us to do so. We shall list various elements of the ancestral figure under certain major headings, and then, in light of these aspects, sketch the main lines of the application of this Bantu figure to Jesus Christ.

The Eldest

Christ is the Ancestor in the sense of Elder Brother. . . . The Bantu notion of eldest child, eldest sibling, focuses on the notion of anteriority. The Ancestors, these elder siblings, are closer to the courses and foundations. They came first. The prime analogy here is God. The very name of God in the Lubu language is revealing: *Mvidi-Mukulu* —literally, *Mvidi*-Eldest.

The literary translation of *Mvidi-Mukulu* as "Spirit-Elder" neglects the material aspects of the notion of *Mvidi*. The word *Mvidi* denotes a category of trees that multiply through their seeds, their roots, and their branches. Their bark secretes a white, viscous latex. In the dry season, these trees survive. When a Luba had experienced joyous events (abundant wealth, brilliant victories in combat, numerous, beautiful offspring), he planted a *Mvidi* before his home as a symbol of this happiness, and as a "memorial" (in the Deuteronomic sense) of what he had experienced. Henceforth the family communion meals would be held at the foot of this tree. And it would be whitewashed—white being the color of the Beyond, the color of Ancestors.

The reason why God is called by the name of this tree, it seems to me, is to mark that God is the source of life, an overflowing life, a life ever constant and stable, and so on. But here it is the addition of the qualifying name "Eldest" that is of interest for our present concern. The combination, "*Mvidi*-Eldest" marks God's anteriority to all life, all being.

Christ, God's only Son, likewise receives the attribute "Eldest." Among the Bantu, the children of the elder brother will always be "elder" vis-à-vis those of the younger. Even if the latter are chronologically older, the line issuing from the elder will always be "upstream." The other lines will owe it a corresponding difference and respect. The children of the eldest line will have the last word in clan reunions, as well as the initiative in convoking these reunions. They will have the right to ritual presents from those of the younger—after all, according to a Luba proverb, "it is never the earth that gives its gift to the rain, but the rain that gives its gift to the earth." Among the patrilinear people of Kasia (a region of Zarie), the respect due to an elder brother requires a father who gives his first and second daughters in marriage not to receive their dowry for himself, but to make an entire gift of it to his elder brother or to the latter's sons. It is the same with a younger brother's first wages: they are handed over entirely to the eldest.

In this perspective, Christ is the Elder Brother par excellence: it is to him alone that offering must be made. Or again: once we know Christ, all of our offerings must henceforth be made through him. It is the eldest brother who makes an offering to the Ancestors and to the Supreme Being on behalf of all the rest. . . .

Certain Christian communion hymns attribute to Christ the title "Eldest Brother of the anointed ones" (*Maluba-Mukulu*), in the sense that he is the model according to which the others will be anointed. The Bantu eldest brother represents an example to follow, except in the case of where he does not conduct himself as an "eldest brother." It is not enough to have seen the light of day before the others in order to have the above-mentioned prerogatives. Here, as in all social groups, there are individuals who fail to live up to the expectations of the community in performing the role with which they have been entrusted. We call them the "melancholy-eldest," as they have disappointed the expectations of their families. . . .

Christ is a true "elder one," as he has disappointed neither our expectations nor those of his Father. His Father has restored and crowned him (in the resurrection). As for ourselves, Jesus has been our example: "I have given you an example, that as I have done to you, you also may do" (John 13:15): the eldest sibling discharges an exemplary function for the younger or for the age group that follows. For the living, it is the Ancestors who have "founded" them, who have laid the foundations of societies, thereby permitting life to "rise" and be maintained. Accordingly, we must follow them if we would preserve our lives. Their will is sovereign.

In virtue of his function of exemplary, the eldest child is charged with responsibility for the acts of the younger. For the Bantu, Christ has shown himself to be our eldest brother in taking responsibility for our wrongs, in performing expiation for us (Isa 53:4–5, Heb 8—10).

IV: Modern and Postmodern

H. Contextual

96. Andrew Sung Park (1951–) | *The Wounded Heart of God: The Asian Concept of Han and the Christian Doctrine of Sin*

Andrew Sung Park's *The Wounded Heart of God* is rooted in the particularities of the Korean context (where Sung Park was born, though the book was published whilst Sung Park was based at the United Theological Seminary, Ohio). The extract below explores the Korean concept of "han" in relation to the Christian understandings of sin. Although han is far reaching and refuses too neat a systematic shape—it is "essentially untranslatable," Sung Park writes—it is perhaps best described as the "scar" that leaves the heart (of a nation, a society, or a person) wounded. Whereas classical accounts of sin are generally concerned with the state of the sinner and their forgiveness, Sung Park is more concerned with the "other side of sin," that is with the *victims* of sin—those who bear the wounds of sin inflicted by unjust structures of violence. Throughout the book, he attends to the stories of those who have been oppressed by individuals and systems—the ones who have been harmed by han firsthand. One other important aspect of Sung Park's work worth mentioning is his exploration of the "divine han." He argues in a way not dissimilar to Moltmann's *The Crucified God* that God's heart, like ours, is "wounded" by sin. The structures of sin, our sinful actions, cause God pain and hurt.

They say of Augustine that although he spent a lot of time thinking about sin, he is remembered in the Christian tradition as the doctor of grace. Similarly, as much as this is a book about sin, it is also very much about grace. If sin is about the wound, grace is about "healing": the grace of God that heals the wounds that cause pain. But Sung Park is also concerned with "the other side of grace." It is not enough simply to rest on the laurels of God's healing grace. The Christian life is about seeking out healing and pursuing an "alternative [han-less] vision of society." The challenge set before us by Sung Park is to recognize our "complicity in the suffering of others" so that in turn we might engage in what he calls "compassionate confrontation" against the systems of oppression—capitalist economies, social patriarchy, racial discrimination—that continue to wound the lives of others and pain the heart of God.

The Wounded Heart of God: The Asian Concept of Han and the Christian Doctrine of Sin (1993)

Throughout history, the church has been concerned with the sin of people, but has largely overlooked an important factor in human evil: the pain of the *victims* of sin. The victims of various types of wrongdoing express the ineffable experience of deep bitterness and helplessness. Such an experience of pain is called *han* in the Far East. Han can be defined as the critical wound of the heart generated by unjust psychosomatic repression, as well as by social, political, economic, and cultural oppression. It is entrenched into the hearts of the victims of sin and violence, and is expressed through the diverse reactions as sadness, helplessness, hopelessness, resentment, hatred and the will to revenge. Han reverberates in the souls of survivors of the Holocaust, Palestinians in the occupied territories, victims of racial discrimination, battered wives, children involved in divorces, the victims of child molestation, laid-off workers, the unemployed, and exploited workers.

Sin and han must be treated together, if we are to grasp a more comprehensive picture of the problems of the world than delineated by the doctrine of sin alone. In brief, the traditional doctrine of sin has been one-sided, seeing the world from the perspective of the sinner only, failing to take into account of the victims of sin and injustice. . . .

The various structures of han have their roots in the diverse structures of sin. In general, individual han results from personal sin, and collective han derives from collective sin, but they are entangled in cause-effect relationships. Collective sin, however, generates a great deal of personal han as well as collective han.

In the course of history, sin has produced more sin, which has created corporate expressions of evil at the socio-economic, political, and cultural dimensions of life. The diverse modes of sin as the vortex of evil have produced sin and han in the world. There have been many structural bastions of sin throughout the years; whilst some of them have been destroyed by the forces of history or have disintegrated by themselves, the rest still remain. A few can be named: neo-colonialism, totalitarianism, hierarchical social structures, provincialism, racism, sexism, handicappism, ageism, religious exclusivism, and militarism. . . .

Sin hurts God and one's fellow human beings. Every sin which is committed against others wounds God, for God created and has loved those against whom we have sinned. As Anselm asserted, God is not passible, yet God suffers with human beings. God suffers not because sin is all powerful, but because God's love for humanity is too ardent to be apathetic toward suffering humanity. No power in the universe can make God vulnerable, but a victim's suffering breaks the heart of God. For Moltmann, God's suffering in Christ on the cross is due to God's love for the Son. To me, God suffers for the Son on the cross not only out of God's love for the Son, but also God's love for humanity. God's love for humans suffers on the cross. The cross represents God's full participation in the suffering of victims. That is, Jesus' death was the example of an innocent victim's suffering in which God was *fully* present. Yet every victim's suffering also involves God's presence. . . .

Awakening

The han-ridden need two kinds of awakening: one to the reality of their own han and the other to the causes of han. It is common that people do not acknowledge the pain of han in themselves; even if they are aware of it, they deny its pain until its severity will allow them to deny it no longer. Han quite often operates at an unconscious level, and as such is invisible and unrecognizable. People need to recognize their han, or the deep pain of suffering. At this point, the dissolution of han begins.

The next step for the han-ridden is to awaken to the matrixes which engender han in the world. They need to identify han-causing vortices at a personal level as well as at the collective level. The personal level of han is generally derived from family relations, personal traumas, and job-related issues. They are in general interconnected with the collective level of han. Various collective han-generating centers exist—e.g., militarism, political tyranny, economic exploitation, and social discriminations. As we have already seen, the capitalist global economy, patriarchy, and racial and cultural discrimination are the primary centers of collective han, from which many others emerge. . . .

Engagement: compassionate confrontation

This last step for the resolution of han is *compassionate confrontation*. Confrontation without understanding will cause unnecessary, hostile conflict. Compassion without confrontation will result in ineffective transformation. Confrontation with the heart of compassion for the oppressors will genuinely change their heart through creative tension.

Understanding and envisagement empower the people of han to take action in dismantling han-causing elements in the world. The disentanglement of conscious han is different from that of unconscious han. While conscious han is resolved in an effort to transform the world of han, unconscious han is dissolved in an attempt to transcend the irreversible world of han. Engagement in resolving conscious han signifies the transformation of the reality of han-causing people and evil. Confrontation is the will to action, the determination to face this reality rather than escape from it. Engagement in resolving unconscious han means transcending the painful event of whatever caused han. The han that lies beyond the reach of our conscious efforts can only be transcended. This indicates that there is an unresolvable dimension of han. The transcendence of unconscious han transpires as a gift when the person of han is engaged in a task of converting han-causing people and removing han-causing evil.

Transformation: Conscious Han

Understanding and envisagement will enable han-ful persons to have the hearts of compassionate confrontation. This confrontation is the courage to call offenders to repentance. If offenders are willing to change their ways, they and their victims can work together toward an alternative vision of society. In this case, the han of the victims will be dissolved in the midst of transforming han-causing elements. At a personal level, a vision may be reunion, restoration of broken relationships, and reconciliation between victims and their offenders. At a collective level, a vision can be a new world order which may inspire victims and offenders alike to change the capitalist global economy, patriarchy, hierarchy, and racism into a hanless society—the global community of political and economic democracy, equity, respect, and affection.

In the course of participation in the transformation of the root causes of han, victims experience the dissolution of han, using up han as fuel. Han is the thick energy that is continually collapsing inward. If it is wrongly handled, it will explode and destroy others as well as the han-ful person. If it is rightly unraveled, then it can be used as the positive dynamic energy which empowers victims to reconstruct the reality of the world which inflicted pain upon them. . . .

The compassionate confrontational act is similar to Paulo Freire's definition of praxis, in which reflection and action transform reality. This compassionate confrontation, however, includes all the considerate movements and efforts toward the transformation of the world pain of han, whether they are words, deeds, thoughts, or commitments. In other words, this act does not mean to do something physically, but encompasses all the compassionate striving of various people for the transformation and the transcendence of han-inducing situations and han-causing persons. Such endeavors as writers' writings, teachers' teaching, activists' activities, and artists' works of art with the heart of care and compassion are transformative acts. The compassionate confrontational act involves preparatory toil for practice and practice for the meaningful transformation of the world's han. In the midst of participating in a compassionate confrontational act, the people of han can transform the world of han as well as their own han.

Bibliography

Adams, Nicholas. "Confessing the Faith: Reasoning in Tradition." In *The Blackwell Companion to Christian Ethics*, 2d ed., edited by Stanley Hauerwas and Samuel Wells, 209–21. London: Blackwell, 2011.

Aelred of Rievaulx. *Spiritual Friendship*. Translated by M. Eugenia Laker. Notre Dame, IN: Ave Maria, 2008.

Allen, Paul. *Theological Method: A Guide for the Perplexed*. London: T&T Clark, 2012.

Anderson, William, ed. *A Journey Through Christian Theology*. 2d ed. Minneapolis: Fortress, 2010.

Augsburg Confession. http://bookofconcord.org/augsburgconfession.php.

Athanasius. *On the Incarnation*. Translated by Penelope Lawson. St. Vladimir's Seminary Press, 1977. https://www.ccel.org/ccel/athanasius/incarnation.txt.

———. *Against the Arians* and *To Adelphius, Bishop and Confessor: Against the Arians*. In *Nicene and Post-Nicene Fathers*, Second Series, Vol. 4. Translated by Edwin Hamilton Gifford. Edited by Philip Schaff and Henry Wace. Buffalo, NY: Christian Literature Publishing Co., 1894. https://www.ccel.org/ccel/schaff/npnf207.txt.

Augustine of Hippo. *Enchiridion (The Handbook on Faith, Hope and Love)*. In *Nicene and Post-Nicene Fathers, First Series*, Vol. 3, translated by J.F. Shaw, edited by Philip Schaff. Buffalo: Christian Literature, 1887. https://www.newadvent.org/fathers/1302.htm

———. *Sermon 22.8–10 (John 5:26)*. In *Nicene and Post-Nicene Fathers, First Series*, Vol. 7, translated by John Gibb, edited by Philip Schaff. Buffalo: Christian Literature, 1888. https://www.ccel.org/ccel/schaff/npnf107.txt.

Ayres, Lewis. *Nicaea and its Legacy: An Approach to Fourth-Century Trinitarian Theology*. Oxford: Oxford University Press, 2006.

Balthasar, Hans Urs von. *Love Alone is Credible*. Translated by D. C. Schindler. San Francisco: Ignatius, 2004.

Barnes, Timothy. *Athanasius and Constantius: Theology and Politics in the Constantinian Empire*. Cambridge, MA: Harvard University Press, 1993.

Barth, Karl. *Evangelical Theology: An Introduction*. Grand Rapids: Eerdmans, 1992.

Bebbington, David. *Evangelicalism in Modern Britain: A History from the 1730s to the 1980s*. London: Routledge, 1989.

Bede. *Bede's Ecclesiastical History of England*. Translated by A. M. Sellar. London: George Bell and Sons, 1907. http://www.sacred-texts.com/chr/bede/hist049.htm.

Benedict XVI. *The Fathers of the Church: From Clement of Rome to Augustine of Hippo*. Edited by Joseph T. Leinhard. Grand Rapids: Eerdmans, 2009.

Berardino, Angelo Di. *Encyclopedia of Ancient Christianity*. 3 vols. Translated by Joseph T. Papa, et al. Downers Grove, IL: IVP Academic, 2014.

Bloesch, Donald. *The Crisis of Piety: Essay Toward a Theology of the Christian Life*. Colorado Springs: Helmers and Howard, 1968/1988.

Bonhoeffer, Dietrich. *Letters and Papers from Prison*. Edited by Victoria J. Barnett and Barbara Wojhoski. Minneapolis: Fortress, 2009.

Book of Concord. http://bookofconcord.org/sd-righteousness.php.

Bonaventure. *The Journey of the Mind to God*. Translated by Philotheus Boehner, edited by Stephen F. Brown. Indianapolis: Hackett, 1956. http://www.ecatholic2000.com/bonaventure/road4.shtml.

Bouyer, Louis. *The Meaning of Monastic Life*. New York: P. J. Kennedy and Sons, 1955.

Brock, Sabastian. *Hymns on Paradise*. Crestwood, NY: St. Vladimir's Seminary Press, 1990.

Buschart, W. David, and Kent Eilers. *Theology as Retrieval: Receiving the Past, Renewing the Church*. Downers Grove, IL: IVP Academic, 2015.

Cabasilas, Nicholas. *The Life in Christ*. Translated by Carmino J. deCatanzaro. Crestwood, NY: St. Vladimir's Seminary Press, 1974.

Calvin, John. *Golden Booklet of the True Christian Life*. Translated by Henry J. Van Andel. Grand Rapids: Baker, 2004.

Camplani, Alberto. "Athanasius of Alexandria." Translated by Joseph T. Papa, et. al. In *Encyclopedia of Ancient Christianity*, vol. 1, edited by Angelo Di Berardino, 274–84. Downers Grove, IL: IVP Academic, 2014.

Catherine of Siena. *The Dialogue of the Seraphic Virgin Catherine of Siena*. Translated by Algar Thorold, edited by Kegan Paul. London: Paul, Trench, and Trubner, 1907.

Clement of Rome. *First Letter of Clement*. Translated by Alexander Roberts and James Donaldson. In *Ante-Nicene Fathers*, vol. 1. Edited by Alexander Roberts, James Donaldson, and A. Cleveland Coxe. Buffalo, NY: Christian Literature Publishing Co., 1885. https://www.ccel.org/ccel/schaff/anf01.

Clifford, Cornelius. "St. Athanasius." In *The Catholic Encyclopedia*. Vol. 2. New York: Robert Appleton Company, 1907. http://www.newadvent.org/cathen/02035a.htm.

Cohick, Lynn H., and Amy Brown Hughes. *Christian Women in the Patristic World: Their Influence, Authority, and Legacy in the Second through Fifth Centuries*. Grand Rapids: Baker Academic, 2017.

Cranmer, Thomas. *Formularies of Faith put forward by authority during the reign of Henry VIII*. Oxford: Clarendon Press, 1825.

Cyril of Alexandria. *Commentary on the Gospel of St. Luke by Saint Cyril of Alexandria*. Translated by R. Payne Smith. Oxford: Oxford University Press, 1859. http://tertullian.org/fathers/cyril_on_luke_13_sermons_135_145.htm.

Cyril of Jerusalem. *Catechetical Lectures*. In *Nicene and Post-Nicene Fathers*, Second Series, Vol. 7. Translated by Edwin Hamilton Gifford. Edited by Philip Schaff and Henry Wace. Buffalo, NY: Christian Literature Publishing Co., 1894. https://www.ccel.org/ccel/schaff/npnf207.txt.

Dalferth, Ingolf. *Crucified and Resurrected: Restructuring the Grammar of Christology*. Translated by Jo Bennett. Grand Rapids: Eerdmans, 2016.

de Sales, Francis. *Introduction to the Devout Life*. In *Library of Spiritual Works for English Catholics*. London: Rivingtons, 1875. http://www.ccel.org/ccel/desales/devout_life.txt.

Del Colle, Ralph. "Penance." In *The Cambridge Dictionary of Theology*, edited by Ian A. MacFarland et. al., 378–79. Cambridge: Cambridge University Press, 2011.

Dudley-Smith, Timothy. *John Stott: The Making of a Leader*. Vol. 1. Downers Grove, IL: InterVarsity, 1999.

Eckhart, Meister. "Homily on the Birth of Jesus" and "Treatise on Detachment." In *The Best of Meister Eckhart*, edited and translated by Halcyon Backhouse, 18–19, 88–89, 96. New York: Crossroad, 1993.

———. *Meister Eckhart: The Essential Sermons, Commentaries, Treatises and Defense*. Translated by E. Colledge and B. McGinn. Ramsey, NJ: Paulist, 1981.

———. "Treatise on the Birth of the Eternal Word in the Soul." In *Meister Eckhart*, vol. 1, translated by C. de B. Evans, 336–37. London: John M. Watkins, 1931.

Edwards, Jonathan. *Discourse on the Trinity*. In *Writings on the Trinity, Grace, and Freedom, Works of Jonathan Edwards*, vol. 21, edited by Sang Hyun Lee, 109–45. New Haven, CT: Yale University Press, 2002.

———. *Treatise on Grace*. In *Writings on the Trinity, Grace, and Freedom, Works of Jonathan Edwards*, vol. 21, edited by Sang Hyun Lee, 149–98. New Haven, CT: Yale University Press, 2002.

Eilers, Kent. "The Beauty and Strangeness of Being: Imagining God in Marilynne Robinson's *Lila*." *Crux* 52 (2016) 60–68.

———. "Hermeneutical Empathy: Reading Global Texts in Local Classrooms." *Teaching Theology and Religion* 17/2 (April 2014) 165–66.

Eilers, Kent, and David Buschart. "An Overtaking of Depth: Theology as Retrieval." *American Theological Inquiry* 8/1 (2015) 1–20.

Eilers, Kent, and Kyle Strobel. "The Christian Life in Dogmatic Key." In *Sanctified by Grace: A Theology of the Christian Life*, edited by Kent Eilers and Kyle Strobel, 1–18. London: T&T Clark, 2014.

Eliot, T. S. *For Lancelot Andrewes: Essays on Style and Order*. London: Faber, 1928.

Eusebius of Caesarea. *Church History*. In *Nicene and Post-Nicene Fathers, Second Series, Vol. 1*, translated by Arthur Cushman McGiffert, edited by Philip Schaff and Henry Wace. Buffalo: Christian Literature, 1890. https://www.newadvent.org/fathers/250105.htm.

Fairbairn, Donald. "Introduction." In *Fulgentius of Ruspe and the Scythian Monks: Correspondence on Christology and Grace*, The Fathers of the Church, 126, translated by Rob Roy McGregor and Donald Fairbairn, 3–22. Washington DC: Catholic University Press of America, 2013.

———. *Grace and Christology in the Early Church*. Oxford: Oxford University Press, 2003.

Firpo, Massimo. *Juan de Valdes and the Italian Reformation*. Surrey: Ashgate, 2015.

Ford, David F. *The Shape of Living: Spiritual Directions for Everyday Life*. Norwich: Canterbury, 2012.

Ford, David F., and Rachel Muers, eds. *The Modern Theologians: An Introduction to Christian Theology Since 1918*. Oxford: Blackwell, 2005.

Francis of Assisi. *The Little Flowers of St Francis of Assisi*. Translated and edited by Dom Roger Huddleston. London: Burns & Oates, 1953. https://www.ccel.org/ccel/ugolino/flowers.txt.

Fry, Timothy, ed. *RB 1980: The Rule of St. Benedict in Latin and English with Notes*. Collegeville, MN: Liturgical, 1981.

Gloubokowsky, Nicholas N. "Grace in the Greek Fathers (To St. John of Damascus) and Inter-Church Union." In *The Doctrine of God*, edited by W. T. Whitley, 61–105. London: Student Christian Movement, 1932.

Goossen, Rachel Waltner. "'Defanging the Beast': Mennonite Responses to John Howard Yoder's Sexual Abuse." *Mennonite Quarterly Review* 89 (January). https://themennonite.org/feature/failure-bind-loose-responses-john-howard-yoders-sexual-abuse/.

González, Justo. *A History of Christian Thought, Vol. 2: From Augustine to the Eve of the Reformation*. Rev. ed. Nashville: Abingdon, 1987.

Green, Bradley G. *Shapers of Christian Orthodoxy: Engaging with Early and Medieval Theologians*. Downers Grove, IL: IVP Academic, 2010.

Gregory of Nyssa. *The Great Catechism*. In *Nicene and Post-Nicene Fathers,* Second Series, Vol. 5. Translated by William Moore and Henry Austin Wilson. Edited by Philip Schaff and Henry Wace. Buffalo, NY: Christian Literature Publishing Co., 1893. http://www.ccel.org/ccel/schaff/npnf205.txt.

Griffiths, Paul. *Religious Reading: The Place of Reading in the Practice of Religion*. Oxford: Oxford University Press, 1999.

Gritsch, Eric W. "Vocation." In *The Oxford Encyclopedia of the Reformation*, edited by Hans J. Hillerbrand, 245–46. Oxford: Oxford University Press, 1996.

Haykin, Michael A. G., and Kenneth J. Stewart, eds. *The Advent of Evangelicalism: Exploring Historical Continuities*. Nashville: B&H Academic, 2008.

Herbert, George. "Grace." In *The Temple*. Cambridge: Thomas Buck and Roger Daniel, 1633. https://www.ccel.org/h/herbert/temple/Grace.html.

———. "A Priest to the Temple, or, The Country Parson, His Character, and Rule of Holy Life." London: T. Garthwait, 1652. https://www.ccel.org/ccel/herbert/temple2.xxxvi.html.

Higton, Mike, and Rachel Muers. *Modern Theology: A Critical Introduction*. London: Routledge, 2013.

Hilary of Poitiers. *On the Trinity*. In *Nicene and Post-Nicene Fathers*, series II, vol. 9. Translated by E. W. Watson and L. Pullan. Edited by Philip Schaff and Henry Wace. Grand Rapids: Eerdmans, 1963.

Hillerbrand, Hans. *The Oxford Encyclopedia of the Reformation*. 4 vols. Oxford: Oxford University Press, 1996.

Holcomb, Justin S., ed. *Theologies of Scripture: A Comparative Introduction*. New York: New York University Press, 2006.

Ignatius of Antioch. *Letter to the Romans*. In *Ante-Nicene Fathers,* Vol. 1. Translated by Alexander Roberts and James Donaldson. Edited by Alexander Roberts, James Donaldson, and A. Cleveland Coxe. Buffalo, NY: Christian Literature Publishing Co., 1885. http://www.ccel.org/ccel/schaff/anf01.txt.

Irenaeus. *Against Heresies*. From *Ante-Nicene Fathers, Vol. 1.* Translated by Alexander Roberts and James Donaldson. Edited by Alexander Roberts, James Donaldson, and A. Cleveland Coxe. Buffalo, NY: Christian Literature Publishing Co., 1885. http://www.ccel.org/ccel/schaff/anf01.txt.

Isaacs, Julienne. "Marilynne Robinson reflects on grace, the value of life." In *Anglican Journal*. http://www.anglicanjournal.com/articles.marylinne-robinson.reflects-on-grace-the-value-of-life.

John Chrysostom. *Homilies on Hebrews*. In *Nicene and Post Nicene Fathers*, First Series, Vol. 14. Edited by Philip Schaff. Translated by Frederic Gardiner. Buffalo, NY: Christian Literature Publishing Co., 1889. https://www.ccel.org/ccel/schaff/npnf114.txt.

John of the Cross. *En una noche oscura*. In *St John of the Cross Poems*, translated by Roy Campbell, 26–29. Harmondsworth: Penguin, 1960.

John of Damascus. *On the Orthodox Faith*. In *Nicene and Post Nicene Fathers, 2nd series*, Volume 9. New York, Charles Scribner and Sons, 1899. https://www.ccel.org/ccel/schaff/npnf209.iii.iv.i.i.html.

———. *Against those who Decry Images*. In *On Holy Images*, translated by Mary H. Allies. London: Thomas Baker, 1898. http://sourcebooks.fordham.edu/basis/johndamascus-images.asp.

Jones, Gareth, ed. *The Blackwell Companion to Modern Theology*. Oxford: Blackwell, 2004.

Jerome. *Letter 52: To Nepotian*. In *Nicene and Post-Nicene Fathers*, Second Series, Vol. 6. Edited by Philip Schaff and Henry Wace. Translated by W. H. Fremantle, G. Lewis, and W.G. Martley. Buffalo, NY: Christian Literature Publishing Co., 1893. http://www.ccel.org/ccel/schaff/npnf206.txt.

Kapic, Kelly M., and Bruce L. McCormack, eds. *Mapping Modern Theology: A Thematic and Historical Introduction*. Grand Rapids: Baker Academic, 2012.

Kaufman, Gordon. *In the Beginning . . . Creativity*. Minneapolis: Fortress, 2004.

Kelly, John Norman Davidson (J. N. D.). *Early Christian Doctrines*. New York: HarperOne, 1978.

Kelsey, David H. *Proving Doctrine: The Uses of Scripture in Modern Theology*. Salem, MA: Trinity Press International, 1999.

Kempis, Thomas á. *The Imitation of Christ*. Translated by Ronald Knox and Michael Oakley. London: Burns and Oates, 1959.

Klassen, Mary E. "AMBS service to acknowledge harm from Yoder actions." https://themennonite.org/daily-news/ambs-service-acknowledge-harm-from-yoder-actions/.

Knight, Douglas. "John Zizioulas on Eschatology and Persons." In *Phenomenology and Eschatology: Not Yet in the Now*, edited by Neal DeRoo and John Panteliemon Manoussakis, 91–100. Abingdon: Routledge, 2009.

Kolb, Richard. "In Memoriam." http://concordiatheology.org/2015/01/tuomo-mannermaa-father-of-finnish-interpretation-of-luther-dies/.

Kolb, Robert, et al., eds. *The Oxford Handbook of Martin Luther's Theology*. Oxford: Oxford University Press, 2014.

Krahn, Cornelius, and Cornelius J. Dyck. "Menno Simons (1496–1561)." In *Global Anabaptist Mennonite Encyclopedia Online* (1990). http://gameo.org/index.php?title=Menno_Simons_(1496-1561)&oldid=145845.

Küng, Hans. *Justification: The Doctrine of Karl Barth and a Catholic Reflection*. Louisville: Westminster John Knox, (1964) 2004.

Lehner, Ulrich, et al., eds. *The Oxford Handbook of Early Modern Theology, 1600–1800*. Oxford: Oxford University Press, 2016.

Leithart, Peter J. *Athanasius*. Foundations of Theological Exegesis and Christian Spirituality. Grand Rapids: Baker Academic, 2011.

Leppin, Volker. "Luther's Transformation of Medieval Thought." In *The Oxford Handbook of Martin Luther's Theology*, edited by Robert Kolb, Irene Dingel, and L'ubomír Batka, 115–24. Oxford: Oxford University Press, 2016.

Letter to Diognetus. In *Early Christian Fathers, Library of Christian Classics Series.* Edited and translated by Cyril C. Richardson. Philadelphia: Westminster, 1953. https://www.ccel.org/ccel/richardson/fathers.txt.

Lubac, Henri de. *A Brief Catechism on Nature and Grace.* Translated by Richard Arnandez. San Francisco: Ignatius, 1984.

Luther, Martin. *The Freedom of a Christian.* From *First Principles of the Reformation or The 95 Theses and the Three Primary Works of Dr. Martin Luther,* edited by Henry Wace and C. A. Buchheim, 104–5, 109–13, 125–27, 131–32. London: John Murray, 1883. https://legacy.fordham.edu/halsall/mod/luther-freedomchristian.asp.

———. *Lectures on Galatians* (1535). *Luther's Works,* vol. 26, edited by Jaroslav Pelikan and Helmut T. Lehmann. Philadelphia: Muehlenberg and Fortress; St. Louis: Concordia, 1963.

Machen, J. Gresham. "Christianity and Culture." In *The Princeton Theological Review*, vol. 11, (1913) 1–3, 5–6, 12–13, 14–15. Originally delivered as an address on September 20, 1912 at the opening of the one hundred and first session of Princeton Theological Seminary: "The Scientific Preparation of the Minister." http://scdc.library.ptsem.edu/mets/mets.aspx?src=BR1913111&div=1.

Malingrey, A. M., and S. Zincone. "John Chrysostom." In *Encyclopedia of Ancient Christianity*, vol. 2, translated by Joseph T. Papa et. al., edited by Angelo Di Berardino, 429–33. Downers Grove, IL: IVP Academic, 2014.

Mannermaa, Tuomo. *Christ Present in Faith: Luther's View of Justification.* Translated by Kirsi Stjerna. Minneapolis: Fortress, 2005.

Marpeck, Pilgram. *The Writings of Pilgram Marpeck.* Translated and edited by William Klassen and Walter Klassen. Scottdale, PA: Herald, 1978.

Maxwell, David R. "Christology and Grace in the Sixth-Century Latin West: The Theopaschite Controversy." PhD diss., University of Notre Dame, 2003.

McClendon, James Wm., Jr. "The Radical Road One Baptist Took." In *Mennonite Quarterly Review* 74/4 (October 2000). https://www.goshen.edu/mqr/2000/12/october-2000-mcclendon/.

McGrath, Alistair E. *Reformation Thought: An Introduction.* 2d ed. Oxford: Blackwell, 1993.

Mees, M. "Clement of Alexandria." In *Encyclopedia of Ancient Christianity,* vol. 1, translated by Joseph T. Papa et al., edited by Angelo Di Berardino, 546–49. Downers Grove, IL: IVP Academic, 2014.

Mesa, Ivan. "J. I. Packer, 89, On Losing Sight But Seeing Christ." *Gospel Coalition.* January 14, 2016. https://www.thegospelcoalition.org/article/j-i-packer-89-on-losing-sight-but-seeing-christ/.

Neufeld, Josiah. "Marilynne Robinson's grace abolishes boundaries." In *Geez Magazine.* http://geezmagazine.org/blogs/entry/marilynne-robinsons-grace-abolishes-boundaries.

Nörregaard, J. "Grace in Saint Augustine." In *The Doctrine of God,* edited by W. T. Whitley, 114–32. London: Student Christian Movement, 1932.

Oaks, Edward T. *A Theology of Grace in Six Controversies.* Grand Rapids: Eerdmans, 2016.

Ocker, Christopher. "Explaining Evil and Grace." In *The Oxford Handbook of the Protestant Reformations,* edited by Ulinka Rublank, 23–46. Oxford: Oxford University Press, 2017.

Oden, Thomas C. *The Transforming Power of Grace.* Nashville: Abingdon, 1993.

Origen. *On First Principles.* In *Ante-Nicene Fathers, Vol. 4.* Translated by Alexander Roberts and James Donaldson. Edited by Alexander Roberts, James Donaldson, and A. Cleveland

Coxe. Buffalo, NY: Christian Literature Publishing Co., 1885. http://www.ccel.org/ccel/schaff/anf04.txt.

Osiek, Carolyn. *Shepherd of Hermas*. Hermeneia. Minneapolis: Fortress, 1999.

Packer, J. I. *A Quest for Godliness*. Wheaton, IL: Crossway, 1990.

Pannenberg, Wolfhart. "God's Presence in History." *The Christian Century* 8, March 11 (1981) 160–63.

———. *Systematic Theology*, vol. 3. Translated by G. Bromiley. Grand Rapids: Eerdmans, 1998.

Peters, Greg. *The Story of Monasticism: Retrieving an Ancient Tradition for Contemporary Spirituality*. Grand Rapids: Baker Academic, 2015.

Polycarp. *Letter to the Philippians* and *The Encyclical Epistle of the Church at Smyrna Concerning the Martyrdom of the Holy Polycarp*. From *Ante-Nicene Fathers, Vol. 1*. Translated by Alexander Roberts and James Donaldson. Edited by Alexander Roberts, James Donaldson, and A. Cleveland Coxe. Buffalo, NY: Christian Literature Publishing Co., 1885. http://www.ccel.org/ccel/schaff/anf01.txt.

Robinson, Marilynne. *The Death of Adam: Essays on Modern Thought*. New York: Houghton Mifflin, 1998.

———. *When I Was a Child I Read Books*. New York: Farrar, Straus and Giroux, 2012.

Rublack, Ulinka. *The Oxford Handbook of the Protestant Reformations*. Oxford: Oxford University Press, 2017.

Rufinus of Aquileia. *Church History*. In *The Church History of Rufinus of Aquileia: Books 10 and 11*. Translated by Philip R. Amidon. Oxford: Oxford University Press, 1997.

Rutledge, Fleming. *The Undoing of Death: Sermons for Holy Week and Easter*. Grand Rapids: Eerdmans, 2002.

Ryan, John K. "Translator's Introduction." In *Introduction to the Devout Life*, 1–20. New York: Random House/Image Classics, 1972.

Shelton, W. Brian. "Irenaeus." In *Shapers of Christian Orthodoxy*, edited by Bradley G. Green, 15–63. Downers Grove, IL: IVP Academic, 2010.

Shepherd of Hermas. From *Ante-Nicene Fathers, Vol. 1*. Translated by Alexander Roberts and James Donaldson. Edited by Alexander Roberts, James Donaldson, and A. Cleveland Coxe. Buffalo, NY: Christian Literature Publishing Co., 1885. http://www.ccel.org/ccel/lightfoot/fathers.

Sibbes, Richard. "The Bruised Reed and Smoking Flax." In *Works of Richard Sibbes*, vol. 1, edited by Alexander B. Grosart, 33–101. Edinburgh: Banner of Truth Trust, 1979. Modernized by William H. Gross. http://www.onthewing.org/Classics.html.

Sigurdson, Ola. *Heavenly Bodies: Incarnation, the Gaze, and Embodiment in Christian Theology*. Translated by Carl Olsen. Grand Rapids: Eerdmans, 2016.

Schmemann, Alexander. "In Memoriam—Vladimir Lossky." *St. Vladimir's Seminary Quarterly* 2/2 (Spring 1958) 47–48.

Scotus, Duns. *Duns Scotus: Philosophical Writings*. Edited and translated by Allan Wolter, OFM. Edinburgh: Thomas Nelson and Sons, 1962.

Southall, David. "Pilgrim Marpeck: An Ecumenical Anabaptist?" *Anabaptism Today*, Issue 24 (Summer 2000). http://www.anabaptistnetwork.com/article/pilgram-marpeck-an-ecumenical-anabaptist/

Stjema, Kirsi. *Women and the Reformation*. Oxford: Blackwell, 2008.

Stonehouse, Ned B. *J. Gresham Machen: A Biographical Memoir*. Edinburgh: The Banner of Truth Trust, 1987.

Tanner, Kathryn. *Jesus, Humanity, and the Trinity: A Brief Systematic Theology*. Minneapolis: Fortress, 2001.

Taylor, Charles. *A Secular Age*. Cambridge, MA: Belknap Press of Harvard University Press, 2007.

Thurston, Herbert. "The Venerable Bede." In *The Catholic Encyclopedia*. Vol. 2. New York: Robert Appleton Company, 1907. http://www.newadvent.org/cathen/02384a.htm.

Torrance, Thomas F. *The Doctrine of Grace in the Apostolic Fathers*. Eugene, OR: Wipf and Stock, 1996.

Voolstra, Sjouke. *Menno Simons: His Image and Message*. North Newton, KS: Bethel College, 1997.

Wainwright, Geoffrey. *Doxology: The Praise of God in Worship, Doctrine, and Life*. Oxford: Oxford University Press, 1984.

Watson, E. W. "Grace in the Latin Fathers to St. Augustine." In *The Doctrine of God*, edited by W. T. Whitley, 106–13. London: Student Christian Movement, 1932.

Webster, John. *God Without Measure: Working Papers in Christian Theology*. Vol. 1. London: Bloomsbury T&T Clark, 2016.

———. "Theologies of Retrieval." In *The Oxford Handbook of Systematic Theology*, edited by John Webster et al., 583–99. Oxford: Oxford University Press, 2007.

Weinandy, Thomas G. *Athanasius: A Theological Introduction*. Burlington, VT: Ashgate, 2007.

Wesley, John. *A Christian Library, Volume 2: Acts and Monuments of the Christian Martyrs, Part I*. Wesley Center Online. http://wesley.nnu.edu/john-wesley/christian-library/a-christian-library-volume-2/volume-2-acts-and-monuments-of-the-christian-martyrs-part-i/.

Whitley, W. T., ed. *The Doctrine of Grace*. London: Student Christian Movement, 1932.

Williams, A. N. *The Architecture of Theology: Structure, System, and Ratio*. Oxford: Oxford University Press, 2011.

Williams, Rowan. "Eastern Orthodox Theology." In *The Modern Theologians: An Introduction to Christian Theology*, edited by David F. Ford and Rachel Muers, 572–88. Oxford: Blackwell, 2005.

Winner, Lauren. "Foreword." In *Vintage Saints and Sinners: 25 Christians Who Transformed My Faith*, by Karen Wright Marsh, 1–4. Downers Grove, IL: InterVarsity, 2017.

Wyman, Christian. *My Bright Abyss: Meditation of a Modern Believer*. New York: Farrar, Straus, and Giroux, 2013.

Yoder, John Howard. "'Patience' as Method in Moral Reasoning: Is an Ethic of Discipleship 'Absolute'?" In *The Wisdom of the Cross: Essays in Honor of John Howard Yoder*, edited by Stanley Hauerwas et al., 24–42 Grand Rapids, MI: Eerdmans, 1999.

Young, Frances. "*Paideia* and the Myth of Static Dogma." In *The Making and Remaking of Christian Doctrine: Essays in Honour of Maurice Wiles*, edited by Sarah Coakley and David Pailin, 265–83. Oxford: Clarendon, 1993.

Subject Index

Page numbers in *italics* indicate illustrations.

Abelard. *See* Peter Abelard
Abraham (biblical patriarch), 458, 459–60
Acacius (desert father), 65
Adam and Eve, xxxi, 6, 68, 126, 127, 188, 190, 277, 289, 311, 370, 371, 394
adoption, Christian life as, xxix–xxx, xxxi, 346–49
Advaita Hinduism, 5
Aethelfrith (king of Northumbria), 155, 156
affirmative or *kataphatic* theology, 115
African American womanist theology, 458–62
African theology, 463–66
After Virtue (Alasdair MacIntyre, 1981), 424
Against Apollinarius (Gregory of Nazianzus, late 4th century), 67
Against Heresies (Irenaeus of Lyons, 190), 27, 28–29
Against those who decry images (John of Damascus, c. 710-720), 121, 124–25
Agathon (desert father), 64
Agrippa (in New Testament), 316
Alcaraz, Pedro Ruiz de, 291
Alexander of Hales, 179
Alphabetical Collection, 63–66
alumbrado movement, 291
Alvarez, Catalina, 300
Ambigua (Maximus the Confessor), 141n5
Ambrose of Milan, 158
Anabaptists/Baptists. *See also specific Anabaptists and Baptists*
    Bonhoeffer on, 341
    in modern/postmodern period, 405–18
    Münsterites, 281, 415
    persecution, experience of, xxxviii, 271, 276, 279–85, 286
    in Reformation/Post-Reformation period, 271–90
Anastasis icon (Descent into Hell), *xxx*, xxx–xxxi
ancestor/elder brother, Christ as, 463–66
anchorites and anchoresses, 170, 187
Anderson, William, 93
Andrewes, Lancelot, 314–18, 427
Andronikos II Palaiologos (emperor), 138
Angel of Repentance, in *Shepherd of Hermas*, 11–14
Anglicanism. *See also specific Anglicans*
    Articles of Religion, 309
    Book of Common Prayer, 309
    Eastern Orthodoxy influencing, 391, 419, 420, 424
    Evangelicalism and, 439
    in modern/postmodern period, 419–33
    Radical Orthodox movement, 427, 429n1
    in Reformation/Post-Reformation period, 209–327, 258
    Scottish and American Prayer Books, 420
Another Prayer for a Safe Journey (Gregory of Nazianzus, late 4th century), 69
Anselm of Canterbury (saint), 151, 204–7, 468
An Answer in Verse (Argula von Grumbach, 1524), 247, 249–52
Antony (desert father), 63, 64
Apollonarius of Laodicea and Apollinarians, 67, 75
apophatic or negative theology, 110, 115–16, 191–93, 202
Apostolic Fathers, 7
Apostrophe to Sarah Pierpoint (Jonathan Edwards, 1723), 267, 270
Aquinas. *See* Thomas Aquinas
Arguedas, José María, 384

SUBJECT INDEX

Aristotle and Aristotelianism, 201, 202, 208, 215, 221, 273, 427, 457n7
Arius and Arianism, 5, 40, 41, 46–50, 70, 75
Armenian Hymns: 49 (Ephrem the Syrian, 4th century), 56–58
Arndt, John, 243–45
Arsenios, 134
Arsenius (desert father), 63–64
The Ascent of Mount Carmel (John of the Cross, c. 1578-1579), 302–3
ascetic life. *See* monasticism and ascetic life
The Ascetic Life (Maximus the Confessor, c. 630), 118–20
Asian concept of han, 467–70
askesis, xxii
Assumption of Mary (translation of body to heaven), 121
Athanasius of Alexandria (saint), 40–41
    To Adelphius, Bishop and Confessor: Against the Arians (370-371), 49–50
    Four Discourses Against the Arians (360-265), 46–49
    On the Incarnation (c. 318/328), 41–45, 51
    on *Shepherd of Hermas*, 11
    on *theosis*, 5, 46, 49–50, 51
atonement. *See also* repentance/reconciliation; salvation/redemption
    in medieval thought, 190, 204, 208
    in modern/postmodern period, 428, 448, 458, 460–62
    in Reformation/post-Reformation period, 265, 325
    surrogacy of Christ, 458, 460–62
Augsburg, Diet of (1530), 239, 271
Augsburg Confession (1530), 239, 240–41
Augustine of Hippo (saint), 85–86
    Confessions (379-400), 85, 86–88, 162, 296
    grace, doctrine of, 4–5, 232, 347, 467
    on immortality of the soul, 221
    Marpeck compared, 287
    medieval West, influence in, 151, 152, 186, 191, 202, 211–14, 215, 216, 221, 223
    modern/postmodern writers citing, 347, 348, 398, 428, 444, 445
    On the Agreement of the Evangelists, 216
    Origen compared, 35
    Pelagians and, 110
    Shepherd of Hermas quoted by, 11
    Speculum de scriptum sacra, xxiii
    On the Trinity, 212–14, 221, 223

Balthasar, Hans Urs von, xxxiv–xxxv, 377
baptism
    chrism, 59–61
    of Christ, 128
    infant baptism, 271
    in late Patristic/Eastern medieval church, 121, 136
    in modern/postmodern period, 348, 407
    in Patristics/early church, 11, 12, 59–61, 76–78, 82
    re-baptism, 271
    in Reformation/Post-Reformation period, 247–48, 276, 278, 317
    triple immersion, 121
Baptists. *See* Anabaptists/Baptists
Barlaam of Calabria, 138, 139
Barmen Declaration (1934), 339
Barth, Karl, xxxvi, 345, 356, 360–63, 419, 422n2
Basic Christianity (John R. W. Stott, 1958), 439–42
Basil of Caesarea/Basil the Great (saint), 70–74, 75, 141, 142, 151, 314
beatific vision, 221, 415n4
Bebbington, David, 439
Bede (venerable), 151, 152, 154–57, 194
Being as Communion (John Zizioulas, 1997), 401–4
Being Reconciled: Ontology and Pardon (John Milbank, 2003), 428–29
belief/faith, xxix. *See also* justification by faith alone
    in late Patristic/Eastern medieval church, 119
    light of, Catherine of Siena on, 225–27
    in Patristics/early church, 94
    in Reformation/Post-Reformation period, 235–37, 241–42, 244, 272, 302
Benedict XVI (pope), 171
Benedict Biscop (saint), 154
Benedict of Nursia (saint), 98–101, 151, 152, 202
Bernard of Clairvaux (saint), 151, 166–67, 201
    Cloud of Unknowing and, 191
    de Consideratione, 166
    Hildegard of Bingen and, 170
    Homilies on the Song of Songs (begun 1135; unfinished), 166, 167–69
    Hug of St. Victor and, 158
    J. I. Packer citing, 446
    Peter Abelard and, 166–67, 208
    William of St. Thierry and, 162
Bible. *See* Scripture
Bloesch, Donald, 448–52
body and soul, 15, 16–17, 63. *See also* eternal life; immortality of the soul; resurrection
Body Politics (John Howard Yoder, 1992), 411–12
Bolotov, V. V., 396
Bonaventure (saint), 179–82, 202, 273

Bonhoeffer, Dietrich, xxix, 331, 339–44, 463
Boniface VIII (pope), 220
The Book of Her Life (Teresa of Ávila, 1554-1565), 296–99
Book of Pastoral Rule (Gregory the Great, 590), 102–5
Borgia, Francis, 295
Bouyer, Louis, 62
Braudel, Fernand, xxi
Brethren of the Common Life, 194
bridegroom, Christ as. *See* marriage and spousal mysticism
The Bruised Reed and the Smoking Flax (Richard Sibbes, 1630), 258–61
Buddhism, 5
Bulgakov, Sergei, 391–95, 396, 397
Bunyan, John, 11

Cain and Abel (biblical figures), 370
The Calling of St. Matthew (painting; Caravaggio), xxxii, xxxii–xxxiii
Calvin, John, 231, 232, 253–54, 305
    Anabaptist theology compared, 414
    Golden Booklet of the True Christian Life (1539), 253–57
    The Institutes of the Christian Religion, 253, 368n5, 369, 449n3
    modern/postmodern authors citing, 368, 369, 425, 449, 450
Calvinism. *See* Reformed church
Cana, wedding feast at, 52–53
Canticle of the Creatures (Francis of Assisi), 176
Cappadocian Fathers, 75, 138, 191, 401. *See also* Basil of Caesarea; Gregory of Nazianzus; Gregory of Nyssa
Caravaggio, *The Calling of St. Matthew* (painting), xxxii, xxxii–xxxiii
Carmelites, 295, 424
Carr, Anne, 453–57
Carthusians, 191
Cassian, 151
Catechetical Lecture 21, On the Mysteries: Chrism (Cyril of Jerusalem, c. 348-350), 59, 60–61
Catherine of Aragon, 309, 310
Catherine of Siena, 202, 224–27, 287
Catholicism. *See* Roman Catholicism
The Celestial Hierarchy (Pseudo-Dionysius the Areopagite), 112, 158
Celsus, 35
Chalcedon, Council of (451), 3, 70n2, 75, 109
charity. *See* love

Charity and Its Fruits (Jonathan Edwards, 1738), 267–69
Charles V (emperor), 239, 276
Charmoisy, Marie de, 305
children of God/sonship, 94–97, 163–64, 263–64, 378–80, 389, 440
chrism, Cyril of Jerusalem on, 59–61
Christ as Ancestor and Elder Brother (François Kabasélé, 1986), 463–66
Christ Present in Faith (Tuomo Mannermaa, 1989), 350–55
Christ the Educator (Clement of Alexandria, early 3rd century), 30–34
The Christian Alphabet (Juan de Valdes, c. 1535), 233, 292–94
The Christian Doctrine of Justification and Reconciliation (Albrecht Ritschl, 1870-1874), 334–38
The Christian Faith (Friedrich Schleiermacher, 1830-1831), 356–59
Christian Foundations (Donald Bloesch), 448
A Christian Library (John Wesley), xxiii, xxxix
The Christian Life (Karl Barth, 1976), 360–63
Christian life of grace, xxiii–xxiv, xxvii–xxxix. *See also* medieval church; modern/postmodern period; Patristics/early church; Reformation/Post-Reformation
    communal perspective on, xxxviii–xxxix
    definition of grace, xxxiii
    disposition of reader and, xxxix
    as evidence of divinity and power of Christ, 41
    grammar of, xxxiii–xxxv
    historical perspective on, xxxvii–xxxviii
    imperatives and indicatives of, 8
    as life with God, xxviii, xxxvi, 7–8
    as proximity and pilgrimage, xxix–xxxiii
    scriptural antecedents of, xxvii–xxix
    theological retrieval of, xxiv
    as voyage or journey, xxi–xxii, 67–68, 69, 179–82, 406–9
Christianity and Culture (J. Gresham Machen, 1913), 434–38
Christology. *See also* Incarnation
    in African theology, 463–66
    bridegroom, Christ as (*See* marriage and spousal mysticism)
    communicatio idiomatum, 354–55
    communion with the Son, 264, 265
    at Council of Nicaea (325), 3, 41, 46, 59
    divinity of Christ, 40–50, 53
    educator, Christ as, 30–34
    humanity of Christ, 19, 27–28, 53
    imitation of Christ and, 23–24

Christology (continued)
  in late Patristic/Eastern medieval church, 109, 110, 115, 117, 118, 120
  Letter to Diognetus on, 17–18
  in liberation theology, 382–85
  in modern/postmodern period, 354–55, 382–85, 394, 403–4, 463–66
  monophysites, 70
  New Adam, Christ as, 394
  in Patristics/early church, 3, 17–18, 19, 23–24, 27–28, 30–33, 40–50, 53, 59, 68–69, 70n2, 75, 93, 94–95
  physician, Christ as, 274
  in Reformation/Post-Reformation period, xxxvii, 264, 265
  sonship of Christ, 94–95
  soteriology, relationship to, 93, 118, 120
  theological perspective on Christian life of grace and, *xxxvii*
Christomorphic divinization, 415
Chronicle of Symeon the Logothete (10th century), on Kassia the Melodist, 126, 127
church
  Clement of Rome on, 10
  theological perspective on Christian life of grace and, *xxxvii*
  as tower under construction, in *Shepherd of Hermas*, 12, 14
Church Dogmatics (Karl Barth), 360
Church History (Rufinus of Aquileia), 41n1
Cistercian monasticism and spirituality, 151, 153, 166, 446
Clare (saint), 175, 182n3
Clement of Alexandria (saint), 30–34, 35, 112
Clement of Rome (saint), 7–10
clergy and clerical life
  Gregory I the Great's *Book of Pastoral Rule*, 102–5
  Jerome on, 90–92
  in Reformation/Post-Reformation period, 273, 320, 321–22
The Cloud of Unknowing (late 14th century), 191–93
Cluniac monastic reforms, 151, 153
Coakley, Sarah, 388, 423–26
Cobb, John, 388
Collect for the First Sunday in Lent (Thomas Cranmer, 1662), 309, 310
The Comforter (Sergei Bulgakov, 1936), 391–95
Commentary on Romans (Origen, early 3rd century), 36–38
Commentary on the Celestial Hierarchy (Hugh of St. Victor), 158

Commentary on the Divine Liturgy (Nicholas Kabasilas), 143
Commentary on the Epistle to the Romans (Peter Abelard), 208
Commentary on the Gospel of John (Cyril of Alexandria, c. 425), 94–97
Commentary on the Gospel of Luke (Cyril of Alexandria, before 451), 97
communicatio idiomatum, 354–55
Communion. *See* Eucharist
communion with God. *See* union/communion with God
Communion with God (John Owen, 1657), 263–65
community/communal context, xxxviii–xxxix. *See also* monasticism and ascetic life
  Devotio Moderna and Brethren of the Common Life, 194
  discernment, communal, 406–9
  hierarchical complementarity in medieval world, 306
  in modern/postmodern period, 340, 342–44, 365, 392, 394–95, 406–9, 411–12, 441
  of Patristics/early church, 4
  of Reformation/Post-Reformation, 232
conciliar movement, 231
Confessions (Augustine, 379-400), 85, 86–88, 162, 296
Congar, Yves, 387
congregationalism, 258
Constans II (emperor), 117
Constantine I (emperor), 3, 102
Constantinople
  fall to Turks (1453), 202
  Latin sacking of (1204), 202
Constantinople, Council of (381), 59
Constantinople, Council of (553), 36
contemplation
  of Francis of Assisi, 176–78
  practice opposed to, 424–26
  theoria in Eastern Christianity, 110
  Thomas Aquinas on, 216–18
A Contemporary Anabaptist Theology (Thomas Finger, 2004), 414–18
Contra Celsum (Origen), 35
conversion experiences
  modern/postmodern, 366, 377, 405, 407, 409, 411, 418, 437, 439–40, 442, 443, 446, 448, 450, 470
  Patristics/early church, 3, 30, 37, 38, 42, 85–86, 102
  Reformation/Post-Reformation, 253, 259, 268, 295, 323
  Vikings, 153

Corinthian church, Clement of Rome's *First Letter* to (c. 96), 7–10
Cornelius (in New Testament), 316
Councils
    Chalcedon (451), 3, 70n2, 75, 109
    Constantinople (381), 59
    Constantinople (553), 36
    Lateran (649), 117
    Lyons II (1274), 179
    Nicaea I (325), 3, 41, 46, 59, 93
    Sens (1141), 166, 208
    Trent (1545-1563), 233, 295, 348
    Vatican II (1963-1965), 372, 373, 385
Counter Reformation. *See* Reformation/Post-Reformation
The Country Parson (George Herbert, 1652), 319, 320, 321–22
Cranmer, Thomas, 231, 309–13
Crescens and his sister (in Polycarp's *Letter to the Philippians*), 25–26
The Crisis of Piety (Donald Bloesch, 1988), 448–52
cross
    Calvin on, 254, 255–57
    Evangelicalism, crucicentrism in, 439, 452
The Crucified God (Jürgen Moltmann), 467
Crusades, 166, 202
culture and Christianity, relationship between, 434–38
Cur Deus Homo (Anselm of Canterbury), 204
Cydones, 143
Cyril of Alexandria (saint), 93–97, 403
Cyril of Jerusalem (saint), 59–61

Dante Alighieri, 176
dark night of the soul
    J. I. Packer on, 444, 446–47
    En una noche oscura (John of the Cross, c. 1577-1579), 300, 301–2
David (biblical king), 144, 274, 307, 370
de Consideratione (Bernard of Clairvaux), 166
de Lubac, Henri, 372–76
de Sales, Francis (saint), 231, 232, 305–8, 446
de Valdes, Juan, 231, 233, 291–94
deCatanzaro, Carmino J., 143–44
Decius (emperor), 35
"Deepening '*Practices*'" (Sarah Coakley, 2001), 424–26
deification. *See theosis*
Del Colle, Ralph, 287n4
desert fathers and mothers, sayings of (4th to 6th centuries), 62–66, 191, 425
desire and holiness, 443–47

detachment, Meister Eckhart on, 186
Devotio Moderna, 194, 231
devotion/piety, 305–8, 448–52
The Dialogue of Divine Providence (Catherine of Siena, 1378), 225–27
Dialogue on Christian Doctrine (Juan de Valdes, 1529), 291
Diocletian (emperor), 40
Diognetus, Letter to (late 2nd century), 15–18
Dionysius the Areopagite (convert of Paul), 112, 222. *See also* Pseudo-Dionysius the Areopagite
discernment, communal, 406–9
Discipleship (Dietrich Bonhoeffer, 1937), 340–42
The Dispute About Sophia (Vladimir Lossky, 1936), 397–400
divinization. *See theosis*
Docetism, 24
Doctors of the Church
    Bonaventure, 179
    Catherine of Siena, 224
    Ephrem the Syrian, 152
    Hildegard of Bingen, 171
    John Duns Scotus, 202
    John of the Cross, 300
    Teresa of Ávila, 296
    Thomas Aquinas, 215
Doctrine: Systematic Theology, Vol. 2 (James McClendon, 1994), 406–9
Dominicans, 183, 202, 215, 224
Donatism, 130
dryness, spiritual. *See* dark night of the soul
Duns Scotus. *See* John Duns Scotus
Durandus of St. Pourçain, 202
Dyophysites, 112, 115–16n14, 117
Dyothelites, 117

early Christianity. *See* Patristics/early church
Easter *Exultet*, 6, 188
Eastern Christianity. *See also specific authors, selections, and topics*
    Anabaptist adaptation from, 415–18
    Anglicanism influenced by, 391, 419, 420, 424
    Finnish Lutheran/Russian Orthodox ecumenical dialogue, 350–52
    late Patristic/Eastern medieval church, 109–11
    in modern/postmodern period, 350–52, 391–404
    schism with Western church, 202
Ecclesiastical Hierarchy (Pseudo-Dionysius the Areopagite), 112

Ecclesiastical History (Eusebius of Caesarea), 27n1
Ecclesiastical History of the English People (Bede, finished c. 731), 154–57
Eck, John, 271
Eckhart, Johannes "Meister," 183–86, 220
economic/social concerns
    han, Asian concept of, 468
    in liberation theology, 381–85, 455–56
    Pietism and, 451
    poverty, as theological issue, 34, 90–92, 166, 175, 381–85
    social gospel movement, 335, 364
    Tanner's "economy of grace," 430–33
The Economy of Grace (Kathryn Tanner, 2005), 430–33
ecumenism, 339, 350–52, 391, 401, 414
educator, Clement of Alexandria on Christ as, 30–34
Edwards, Jonathan, 266–70, 446
Edwin (king of Northumbria), 155–57
Eighteen Theses Concerning the Christian Life (Balthasar Hubmaier, 1524), 271–73
elder brother/ancestor, Christ as, 463–66
Eliot, T. S., 314
Elizabeth (saint and cousin of Mary), 311–13
Ellul, Jacques, 411–12
Emden, Maynaart von, 281
Enlightenment, 334, 356
Ephrem the Syrian (saint), 51–58, 152
Epiphanius, 121
Episcopalians. *See* Anglicanism
Erasmus, Desiderius, 36, 231, 277
eschatology, *xxxvii*, 14, 66, 179, 281
eternal life
    on Anastasis icon, xxxi
    in medieval church, 146, 185, 213, 223
    in modern/postmodern period, 344, 349, 397, 415n4
    in Patristics/early church, 22, 26, 29, 31, 48, 100, 101
    in Reformation/post-Reformation period, 223, 235, 241, 242, 244, 245, 274, 278
Eucharist
    grace, as means of, 326
    in late Patristic/Eastern medieval church, 121, 135, 145–46
    in modern/postmodern period, 407
    in Patristics/early church, 19, 56–58, 60, 65, 76
    in Reformation/Post-Reformation period, 272, 275, 276, 278, 317, 326–27
    transubstantiation, 276

    in Western medieval scholasticism, 216, 218–19
Eugene III (pope), 166, 170, 172
Eunomius and Eunomianism, 75
Eusebius of Caesarea, 27n1
Eustochium, Letter to (Jerome), 89–90, 92
Eutychians, 28
Evagrian tradition, 130, 151
Evagrius (desert father), 64
Evagrius of Pontus, 162, 423
evangelical repentance, 287n4
Evangelicalism, 434–52. *See also specific Evangelicals*
existence of God, arguments for, 204
exorcism, 170
Exposition of the Epistle to the Romans (William of St. Thierry), 162
Exultet (Easter liturgy), 6, 188

False Presence of the Kingdom (Jacques Ellul), 412
Farrer, Austin, 419
fasting, 24, 139, 306, 309, 398
Father whose everlasting love (Charles Wesley, 1741), 324–25
Felix (in New Testament), 316
feminist theology, 386–90, 423, 453–57. *See also* Carr, Anne; Coakley, Sarah; Soskice, Janet
Fifth Commandment (Honor Thy Father and Mother), 369, 370–71
Filioque controversy, 121, 314
Finger, Thomas, 414–18
Finnish Lutheran/Russian Orthodox ecumenical dialogue, 350–52
Fiorenza, Elisabeth Schüssler, 453, 455n2
Fioretti (Francis of Assisi, early 14th century), 175–78
First Council of Nicaea (325), 3, 41, 46, 59, 93
First Letter of Clement (Clement of Rome, c. 96), 7–10
First World War, 360, 372
Five Fruits of Repentance (Pilgram Marpeck, 1550), 286–90
forgiveness. *See* atonement; repentance/reconciliation; salvation/redemption
Formula of Concord (1578), 240, 241–42, 347, 352, 353
Fountain of Wisdom (John of Damascus), 121
Four Books of Sentences (Peter Lombard, 1150-1152), 211–14, 220
Four Discourses Against the Arians (Athanasius of Alexandria, 360-265), 46–49
Fourth Crusade, 202

Francis of Assisi (saint), 175–78, 179, 180, 181, 182, 202
Franciscans, 176, 202, 446
freedom
    in medieval church, 110, 144, 162, 184, 201, 204, 205
    in modern/postmodern period, 332, 336, 361, 362, 367, 397–403, 429, 430, 455–57
    in Patristics/early church, 6, 34, 38, 65, 77, 96
    in Reformation/Post-Reformation period, 235–37, 277, 286
Freire, Paulo, 470
friendship, 453, 457

Gabriel, 311
gender. *See also* women
    contemplation versus practice and, 424
    in feminist theology, 386–90, 423, 453–57
    feminization of Holy Spirit, 386–90
    theological reflection, gendered nature of, 365, 454
    in womanist theology, 458–62
Ghibellines and Guelphs, 224
gift, theology of, 319, 352–54, 427–29, 431–32
Gilead (Marilyn Robinson, 2004), 369–71
The Glory of God and the Transfiguration of Christ (Michael Ramsey, 1949), 419–22
gnophos, 113n2
Gnosticism, 27, 30–31, 400n9
God, Sexuality, and the Self: An Essay on the Trinity (Coakley), 423
God and Creation (Kathryn Tanner, 1988), 430
God the Father
    as *arche* of Trinity, 115n13, 140n3, 180n1
    communion with, 263–64, 265
    as gender issue, 389
Golden Booklet of the True Christian Life (John Calvin, 1539), 253–57
"Golden Canon," third ode of (John of Damascus), 122
Golden Epistle (William of St. Thierry), 162, 191
Gonsalvus, 220
Gonzaga, Giulia, 292
González, Justo, 85
Gonzalo de Yepes, 300
good works
    late Patristic/Eastern medieval church on, 146
    as love, 146
    in modern/postmodern period, 451
    Patristics/early church on, 25, 64, 99
    in Reformation/Post-Reformation period, 236–38, 272, 293–94

vices appearing as virtues, 103
goodness
    Anselm of Canterbury on, 205–7
    Julian of Norwich on, 187–90
Goodwin, Thomas, 446
Gospel of Bartholomew, 114
grace. *See also* Christian life of grace
    in African theology, 463
    cheap versus costly, 341–42
    doctrines of, xxxvn11
    as friendship, 453
    gift, theology of, 319, 352–54, 427–29, 431–32
    gratitude and, 427
    in late Patristic/Eastern medieval church, 136
    in liberation theology, 381
    means of, 325–27
    in medieval period, 182, 232, 233, 347
    in modern/postmodern period, 332, 336–37, 340–42, 347, 356, 357, 360–67, 372–76, 377, 381, 386, 393, 397–400, 424, 427–33, 453–57, 458–60, 463, 467–68
    nature and grace (supernatural), relationship between, 372–76
    orthopraxis and, 424
    in Patristics/early church, 4–5, 28, 52, 99
    preventing grace, 324
    in Reformation/Post-Reformation period, 232–33, 258–61, 266, 286, 310–13, 319–21, 323–27
    survival and, 458–60
Grace (George Herbert, 1633), 320–21
gratitude and grace, 427
Great Awakening (eighteenth century), 266
Great Catechism (Gregory of Nyssa, c. 385), 75–80
Greek Orthodoxy. *See* Zizioulas, John
Greek philosophy, contextualization of Christian faith through, 30–34, 36
Gregory I the Great (saint and pope), 102–3
    Book of Pastoral Rule (590), 102–5
    medieval Western thought, influence on, 151, 158, 191, 223
    Moralia in Job, 223
    J. I. Packer citing, 444, 445
    on seven deadly sins, 208
Gregory XI (pope), 224
Gregory of Nazianzus (saint), 5, 41, 67–69, 122, 141
Gregory of Nyssa (saint), 75–80, 114n8, 158, 162, 191, 398
Gregory Palamas, 111, 134, 138–42, 143, 415, 416nn5–6
Gregory of Sinai, 134–37

Groote, Gerard, 194
Grumbach, Argula von, 246–52
Guelphs and Ghibellines, 224
Guigo the Carthusian, 152–53
Gutiérrez, Gustavo, 381–85

Hagar (biblical figure), 458–62
han, Asian concept of, 467–70
Harnack, Adolph von, 334
Hauerwas, Stanley, 410
Haughton, Rosemary, 407
heart of Christ, 144, 162, 164–65
Heloise of Argenteuil, 208
Hemerken, Thomas. *See* Thomas à Kempis
Henry I (king of England), 204
Henry VIII (king of England), 309, 310
Henry of Cologne, 183
Heraclius (emperor), 117
Herbert, George, 319–22
Hermann, Wilhelm, 434–35
Hermas, in *Shepherd of Hermas*, 11–14
hesychasm, 111, 134, 138
Hexapla (Origen), 35
hierarchical complementarity, 306
Hilary of Poitiers, xxxvi–xxxvii
Hildegard of Bingen (saint), 170–74
Hilton, Walter, 191
Hincmar of Reims, 151
historical context, xxxvii–xxxviii
  of Patristics/early church, 3–4
  of Reformation/Post-Reformation, 231–32
Hitler, Adolf, 339, 360
Hoffman, Melchior, 416
holiness
  desire and, 443–47
  in modern/postmodern period, 357–58, 364, 408, 441, 443–47, 449, 451–52
  in Reformation/Post-Reformation period, 254–55, 286, 320, 323
Holy Spirit. *See* Pneumatology
The Holy Spirit (Lancelot Andrewes, 1612), 314–17
Home (Marilyn Robinson), 369
Homilies on the Song of Songs (Bernard of Clairvaux, begun 1135; unfinished), 166, 167–69
Homily 16 (Origen), 35
Homily on the Birth of Jesus (Meister Eckhart, c. 1310s), 185–86
Homily on Hebrews 7 (John Chrysostom, 398–403), 81–84
Hooker, Richard, 427

hope
  in medieval church, 118, 119, 122, 133, 135, 139, 155, 168, 181, 206–7, 213–14, 223, 226
  in modern/postmodern period, 349, 367, 378, 379, 384, 408, 419, 425, 432, 444, 446
  in Patristics/early church, 8, 11, 20, 24, 34, 87, 88, 101, 105
  in Reformation/Post-Reformation period, 235, 247, 256–57, 261, 278, 285, 288, 289, 290, 315, 316, 317, 325
Hort, F. J. A., 421
Hoskyns, Edwyn, 419
Housekeeping (Marilyn Robinson), 369
Hubmaier, Balthasar, 231, 271–75
Hugh of St. Victor, 158–61, 162, 180, 211
humility, 64, 255–56
Hutterites, 286
Hymn for the Theophany (Kassia the Melodist, c. 850s), 127, 128
hymnody. *See* poetry and hymnody
Hymns 17, 21, and 25 (Symeon the New Theologian, c.1010-1020), 132–33
Hymns on Faith: 14 (Ephrem the Syrian, 4th century), 52–53
hypostasis/hypostatic union, 6n8, 70, 140–41n4, 392–93, 399, 402–4, 429

Ignatius Loyola, 446
Ignatius of Antioch (saint), 19–22, 25
image of God *(imago Dei)*, humanity in, xxxv, 60, 164, 169n1, 181
images and iconoclasm
  late Patristic/Eastern medieval church, iconoclastic controversy in, 109, 121
  in Reformation/Post-Reformation period, 273
imitation of Christ
  as concept, xxxi
  in modern/postmodern period, 334–35, 415–18, 450
  Patristics/early church on, 9–10, 19, 23–24, 31, 81–84
  in Reformation/Post-Reformation period, 243, 244
  Thomas à Kempis on, 194–97
The Imitation of Christ (Thomas à Kempis, 1418-1427), 194–97
immortality of the soul. *See also* eternal life; resurrection
  in medieval church, 122, 220–23, 245
  in Patristics/early church, 17, 29, 43, 44, 48

improvisation and theology of grace in modern/postmodern period, 332
In Memory of Her (Elisabeth Schüssler Fiorenza, 1983), 453
In Praise of the Bridegroom (Hugh of St. Victor, early 1130s), 158–61
Incarnation
    in feminist theology, 456–57
    imitation of Christ and, 23–24
    in late Patristic/Eastern medieval church, 109, 110
    life of Moses and significance of, xxvii–xxviii
    in modern/postmodern period, 394, 428, 456–57
    Nicene Creed on, 93
    in Patristics/early church, 19, 23–24, 28, 40, 41–45, 51, 93
    in Reformation/Post-Reformation period, 254, 263, 277, 314
Innocent II (pope), 208
Innocent III (pope), 176
The Institutes of the Christian Religion (John Calvin), 253, 368n5, 369, 449n3
The Institution of a Christian Man (Thomas Cranmer, 1537), 309–13
The Interior Castle (Teresa of Ávila), 295–96
Introduction to the Devout Life (Francis de Sales, 1609), 305, 306–8
Invocation of the Holy Spirit (Symeon the New Theologian, c. 1010-1020), 131–32
Irenaeus of Lyons (saint), 7, 11, 23, 27–29
Isaac (desert father), 65
Isaac the Syrian/Isaac of Nineveh (saint and bishop), 139, 399
Ischyrius (desert father), 66
Ishmael (biblical figure), 459–60
Isidore (desert father), 65–66
Islam
    conquest of Jerusalem (637), 63
    fall of Constantinople (1453), 202
    Al Khalil (sultan) and St. Francis, 175
    late Patristic/medieval Eastern church and, 109, 111, 121, 134

Jacob, 370
James (apostle), 316
James I and VI (king of England and Scotland), 315
Jansz, Anna, 232, 281–85
Jansz, Isaiah, 282, 283n1
Jeremiah, 274
Jerome (saint), 11, 23, 89–92
Jesus. *See* Christology; Incarnation

Jesus Prayer, 134
Joachim of Fiore, 179
Job (biblical figure), 274, 316
John (apostle), 274
John (desert father), 65
John VI Kantakouzenos (emperor), 143
John XXII (pope), 183
John the Baptist (saint), xxix, 127, 128, 311
John of Beverley (saint), 154
John Cassian, 151
John Chrysostom (saint), 81–84, 135, 451
John Climacus (saint), 134
John of the Cross (saint), 191, 231, 300–304, 425, 446
John of Damascus/John Damascene (saint), 110, 121–24, 222
John Duns Scotus (blessed), 202, 220–23, 273
John Paul II (pope), 373, 377
John Scotus Eriugena, 151, 158, 162
Johnson, Elizabeth, 388
Joseph (desert father), 64, 65
journey, Christian life envisioned as, xxi–xxii, 67–68, 69, 179–82, 406–9
The Journey of the Mind Into God (Bonaventure, 1259), 179, 180–82
Julian of Norwich (saint), 187–90
justification by faith alone, 232–33
    in modern/postmodern period, 334–38, 340, 341, 346, 347–49, 350–55
    in Reformation/Post-Reformation period, 234–38, 240–41, 272
Justin Martyr (saint), 126, 216
Jutta von Sponheim (blessed), 170

Kabasélé, François, 463–66
Kabasilas, Neilos, 143
Kabasilas, Nicholas (saint), 143–47
Kassia the Melodist, 109, 126–29
kataphatic or affirmative theology, 115
Kaufman, Gordon, 414
Keswick Movement, 409
Al Khalil (sultan) and St. Francis, 175
Kierkegaard, Søren, 243, 428
King, Martin Luther, Jr., 364
Knights Templar, 166
Knowing God (J. I. Packer), 443
Knox, Ronald, 194
Kolb, Robert, 350, 351
Korean concept of han, 467–70
Küng, Hans, xxxviii–xxxix

Ladder of Monks (Guigo the Carthusian), 152–53

SUBJECT INDEX

Lanfranc of Bec, 204
las Casas, Bartolomé de, 383
Lateran Council (649), 117
Lausanne Covenant (1974), 439
lectio divina, 152, 154, 162, 166, 204
Leithart, Peter, 41
Leo I the Great (pope), 141, 403
Leo (Franciscan brother), 176, 178, 182n3
Leo the Isaurian (emperor), 121
Letter to Diognetus (late 2nd century), 15–18
Letter to Eustochium (Jerome), 89–90, 92
Letter to Nepotian (Jerome, 394), 90–92
Letter to Rusticus (Jerome), 89
Letter to the Philippians (Polycarp, 2nd century), 23–26
Letter to the Presbyter George (Maximus the Confessor), 110–11
Letter to the Romans (Ignatius of Antioch, early 2nd century), 19–22
Letters (Pseudo-Dionysius the Areopagite), 112
liberalism/liberal theology, 334, 360, 434, 435, 448–49
liberation theology, 381–85, 455–56
Licinus (emperor), 3
Life of Francis (Bonaventure), 179
life of grace. *See* Christian life of grace
Life of Hildegard (Theoderic of Echternach, 1181-1187), 171–73
Life of Kassia the Melodist, in Symeon the Logothete, *Chronicle* (10th century), 127
Life of Moses (Gregory of Nyssa), 114n8, 191
Life of Paul the First Hermit, 63
Life Together (Dietrich Bonhoeffer, 1939), 340, 342–44
light of faith, Catherine of Siena on, 225–27
Lila (Marilyn Robinson), 369
liturgy and worship
   in Anglicanism, 309
   in late Patristic/Eastern medieval church, 109–10, 113–14, 143–44
   in Patristics/early church, 52–56
   in Western medieval thought, 201
logos, as Gnostic concept, 31
Logos, Christ as, 3, 5, 6n8, 31, 46, 109, 134, 140n4, 347, 353, 388
Lombard. *See* Peter Lombard
Longinus (desert father), 65
la longue durée, xxi
Lord's Prayer, 309, 360, 362
Lord's Supper. *See* Eucharist
Lossky, Vladimir, 396–400
Lothair II (emperor), 170

love
   detachment compared, by Meister Eckhart, 186
   as first commandment, 71–73
   grace, as origin of, xxxiv–xxxv
   Holy Spirit as, 211–14, 267
   in late Patristic/Eastern medieval church, 120, 145, 146–47
   in modern/postmodern period, 336, 344, 345–46, 366–67, 368–69, 380, 382, 446
   in Patristics/early church, 6, 71–73
   in Reformation/Post-Reformation period, 237–38, 245, 267–70, 293–94, 307
   as relational, 6, 345–46, 386, 389–90, 457
   self-love, 293–94, 366–67
   in Western medieval church, 163, 188–90, 192, 193, 211–14
Lubac, Henri de, 372–76
Luther, Martin, 231, 234–35, 239
   Anabaptist theology compared, 414
   Bonhoeffer citing, 341
   Calvin and, 253
   Church Postil (1544), 353–54
   Coakley on, 425
   Cranmer drawing on, 310
   The Freedom of a Christian (1520), 235–38
   Mannermaa and, 350, 352–54
   on Origen, 36
   Pannenberg influenced by, 345, 346, 348
   Ritschl compared, 334
   von Grumbach and, 246, 247
Lutheran Defense, Augsburg Confession (Philip Melanchthon, 1530), 240–41
Lutherans. *See also specific Lutherans*
   Finnish Lutheran/Russian Orthodox ecumenical dialogue, 350–52
   in modern/postmodern period, 334–55
   Reformation/Post-Reformation, 234–52
Lyons, Second Council of (1274), 179

Macarius of Egypt (saint), 5, 65, 66, 399
Machen, J. Gresham, 434–38
MacIntyre, Alasdair, 424
Macrina, 75
Manichaeism, 85
Manifesto of the Intellectuals, 360
Manilla Manifesto (1989), 439
Mannermaa, Tuomo, 350–55
Mantzaridis, Georgios, 416n6
Marpeck, Pilgram, 286–90, 415
marriage and spousal mysticism
   Catherine of Siena and, 224
   Kassia the Melodist and, 126, 127

in modern/postmodern period, 348, 446
in Patristic thought, 158
in Reformation/Post-Reformation period, 273, 300
same-sex marriage, 443
in Western medieval thought, 153, 158–61, 166–69, 196, 211
Martin I (pope), 117–18
martyrdom. *See* persecution and martyrdom
Martyrdom of Polycarp (c. 155), 23, 26
Martyr's Song (Anna Jansz, 1539), 282–85
Mary
    Assumption (translation of body to heaven), 121
    Bernard of Clairvaux on "Our Lady," 166
    Cranmer's "Ave Maria" from *The Institution of a Christian Man*, 309–13
    in late Patristic/Eastern medieval church, 121, 126, 127
    Nativity of Jesus and, 184
    as New Eve, 126, 127
    in Patristics/early church, 65, 93
    as *Theotokos*, 93
    in Western medieval thought, 166, 184, 187, 192
Mary I (queen of England), 310
Matthew (apostle), calling of, xxxii–xxxiii
Maurice, F. D., 421
Mauss, Marcel, 427
Maximus the Confessor (saint), 110, 117–18
    Ambigua, 141n5
    The Ascetic Life (c. 630), 118–20
    Gregory Palamas and, 141
    Letter to the Presbyter George, 110–11
    modern/postmodern authors citing, 400, 415n3, 428
    Pseudo-Dionysius influencing, 112
McClendon, James, 405–9
medieval church (6th-15th centuries). *See also specific authors, selections, and topics*
    Christian vocation in, 233
    grace, doctrine of, 182, 232, 233
    late Patristic/Eastern medieval church, 109–11
    scholasticism, 158, 201–3, 240, 243, 273
    Western mystical and monastic works, 151–53
Meditative Orations (William of St. Thierry, c. 1135), 162–65
Melanchthon, Philip, 239, 240–41, 347
Mennonites, 276, 405, 410, 414
Methodism, 323–24
Milan, Edict of (313), 3
Milbank, John, 427–29

Millenarian sects, 179. *See also* eschatology
modern/postmodern period (19th century to present), 331–33. *See also specific authors, selections, and topics*
    Anabaptists/Baptists in, 405–18
    Anglicans in, 419–33
    Evangelicals in, 434–52
    Lutherans in, 334–55
    Orthodox in, 350–52, 391–404
    Reformed church in, 356–71
    Roman Catholicism in, 348, 372–90, 415n4
    theologically contextual writings in, 332–33, 453–70
Moltmann, Jürgen, 467, 469
monasticism and ascetic life. *See also* community; *specific orders*
    anchorites and anchoresses, 170, 187
    Basil of Caesarea, *Rule of St. Basil (Small Asketikon)*, 70–74
    Benedict of Nursia, *Rule* of, 98–101, 151, 152, 202
    Brethren of the Common Life and Devotio Moderna, 194
    cenobitic or common life, 70–71, 98
    contemplation and praxis in, 424–25
    desert fathers and mothers, sayings of, 62–66, 191, 425
    eremitic or desert life, 62–66, 81, 98
    Jerome on, 89
    in late Patristic/Eastern medieval church, 109, 118–20
    Luther on, 234
    Maximus the Confessor, *The Ascetic Life*, 118–20
    persecution and martyrdom, relationship to, 4, 62
    reforms in, 231
    sayings of desert fathers and mothers, 62–66, 191
    Western medieval church and, 152, 170, 187
    world, Christian withdrawal from, 4, 62
Monica (saint), 85
monism, philosophical, 5
monoenergism, 117
Monophysites, 70, 112, 115–16n14
Monothelitism, 117–18
Monte La Verna, 176, 177, 179, 180
Moralia in Job (Gregory the Great), 223
mortal sin, 146
mortification (death to sin), 76–80
Moses (biblical figure)
    incarnation and, xxxvii
    in late Patristic/Eastern medieval church, 114, 119, 135, 141

Moses *(continued)*
    in modern/postmodern period, 420
    in Patristics/early church, 29, 48, 61, 96
    in Reformation/Post-Reformation period, 241, 245, 273, 278
    in Western medieval church, 177, 191
Moses (desert father), 65–66
Münsterites, 281, 415
Muratorian Fragment, 11
mystagogy, 114
The Mystery of the Supernatural (Henri de Lubac, 1965), 373–76
Mystical Theology (Pseudo-Dionysius the Areopagite, 520s), 112–16, 182
The Mystical Theology of the Eastern Church (Vladimir Lossky, 1957), 397–400
mysticism. *See also* marriage and spousal mysticism; union/communion with God
    alumbrado movement, 291
    hesychasm, 111, 134, 138
    in late Patristic/Eastern medieval church, 111, 112–16, 138–42
    in modern/postmodern period, 345–46, 348, 377–78, 397–400, 451, 452
    in Reformation/Post-Reformation period, 291, 295–96, 300
    in Western medieval church, 152, 153, 158, 166, 172, 176–78, 179, 182, 183, 191, 201–2, 215, 224–27

Nativity of Jesus, 184–86
The Nature and Destiny of Man (Reinhold Niebuhr, 1943), 364, 365–67
nature and grace (supernatural), relationship between, 372–76
Nazis and Nazism, 339–40, 345, 360, 372
negative or apophatic theology, 110, 115–16, 191–93, 202
Neilos Kabasilas, 143
neo-nicene movement, 70
Neoplatonism, 85, 183
Nepotian, Letter to (Jerome, 394), 90–92
Nestorius and Nestorians, 93, 403
The New Birth (Menno Simons, 1537), 276–79
Newman, John Henry, 427
Nicaea, First Council of (325), 3, 41, 46, 59, 93
Nicene Creed, 93, 314
Nicene-Constantinopolitan Creed, 216
Nicholas Kabasilas (saint), 143–47
Nicholas of Cusa, 183
Nicomachaean Ethics (Aristotle), 221
Niebuhr, Reinhold, 339, 364–67
Nietzsche, Friedrich, 331, 345

Nisibene Hymns: 50 (Ephrem the Syrian, 4th century), 53–56
nous/noos (mind/reason/intellect)
    in late Patristic/Eastern medieval church, 118, 133, 138, 139
    in Western medieval thought, 179, 202
Novatians, 93

O Lord, she who in many sins (Kassia the Melodist, c. 850s), 127, 129
Obama, Barack, 364
obedience, as Christian virtue, 99, 101, 124, 164, 257, 411, 412, 413
oblates, 170
Odo of Lucca, 211
omnipotence of God, 8, 124, 185, 415, 455
On the Agreement of the Evangelists (Augustine), 216
On Commandments and Doctrines (Gregory of Sinai, c. 1310-1320), 135
On Divine Humanity (Sergei Bulgakov), 391
On the Divine Names (Pseudo-Dionysius the Areopagite), 112, 116
On First Principles (Origen, early 3rd century), 36, 38–39
On the Holy Spirit (Basil of Caesarea), 314
On the Incarnation (Athanasius of Alexandria, c. 318/328), 41–45, 51
On the Life in Christ (Nicholas Kabasilas, c. 1370s), 143, 144–47
On the Orthodox Faith (John of Damascus, c. 730s), 121, 122–24, 222
On Providence (Gregory of Nazianzus, late 4th century), 69
On the Signs of Grace and Delusion (Gregory of Sinai, c. 1310-1320), 136–37
On the Soul (Gregory of Nazianzus, late 4th century), 67–68
On the Trinity (Augustine), 212–14, 221, 223
On the Trinity (Hilary of Poitiers), xxxvi–xxxvii
On the Two Covenants and the Appearing of Christ (Gregory of Nazianzus, late 4th century), 68–69
ontological argument for existence of God, 204
Ordinatio (John Duns Scotus, 1298-1299/1303-1308), 220–23
Origen, 11, 35–38, 112, 158, 162, 377, 444, 445
Orthodox churches. *See* Eastern Christianity
orthodoxy, pursuit of
    in late Patristic/Eastern medieval church, 121, 122–24
    in Patristics/early church, 4, 27–29, 35–36
    in Western medieval church, 183

orthopraxis, 381, 410, 414, 423–26
Owen, John, 262–65, 446

pacifism, 276, 410, 411, 412–13
Packer, J. I., 262, 443–47
paideia, 32
Panarion (Epiphanius), 121
Pannenberg, Wolfhart, 345–49
pantheism, 5, 183, 215
Paphnutius (desert father), 63
Paradiso (Dante), 176
parents, honoring, 369, 370–71
Paschasius Radbertus, 151
pastoral responsibilities. *See* clergy and clerical life
patience/impatience
    in medieval church, 120, 130, 177, 213
    in modern/postmodern period, 412, 441, 445
    in Patristics/early church, 13, 24–25, 29, 99, 100, 101, 103–4
    in Reformation/Post-Reformation period, 244, 256, 257, 261, 279, 288, 296, 305, 308
Patristics/early church (1st-7th centuries), xxxvii, xxxviii, 3–6. *See also specific authors, selections, and topics*
    late Patristic/Eastern medieval church, 109–11
    Nicaea, First Council of (325), 3, 41, 46, 59, 93
    Reformation/Post-Reformation engagement with patristic texts, 310, 314
Paul the First Hermit, *Life* of, 63
Paul VI (pope), 224
Paulinus of York (saint), 155, 156–57
Pelagius and Pelagianism, 110, 397, 398–99, 424
penance/penitence. *See* repentance/reconciliation
Pentecost Hymn (Peter Abelard, 1129), 209–10
perfection, Christian, 292–94, 305, 306
Perkins, William, 258
persecution and martyrdom
    early Christian experience of, xxxviii, 3, 16, 19–21, 23, 24, 26, 35, 40, 281
    in late Patristic/Eastern medieval church, 117–18
    in modern/postmodern period, 339–40, 412
    monasticism, foundations of, 4, 62
    in Reformation/Post-Reformation period, xxxviii, 232, 246–47, 248–49, 271, 275, 279–85, 286, 291, 308, 310
Peter (apostle), xxi, xxxiii, 7, 316, 422
Peter Abelard, 162, 166–67, 208–10, 215
Peter Lombard, 211–14, 220

Philip IV (king of France), 220
Philippi, *Letter* of Polycarp to church at, 23–26
Philips, Dirk, 415
Philokalia, 134
philosophical monism, 5
Pickstock, Catherine, 429
Pierpoint, Sarah, 267, 270
Pietism, 243, 448–49, 450, 451
piety/devotion, 305–8, 448–52
pilgrimage and proximity, Christian life as, xxix–xxxiii. *See also* union/communion with God
    in Patristics/early church, 9, 11–12, 15
    Shepherd of Hermas on, 11–12
    voyage or journey, Christian life envisioned as, xxi–xxii, 67–68, 69, 179–82, 406–9
Pilgrim's Progress (John Bunyan), 11
Pius XI (pope), 300
Pius XII (pope), 166
Plato and Platonism, 30, 201, 215, 427
Pneumatology
    communion with the Spirit, 264–65
    feminization of Holy Spirit, 386–90
    Filioque controversy, 121, 314
    in late Patristic/Eastern medieval church, 121, 131–33, 136–37
    love, Holy Spirit as, 211–14
    in modern/postmodern period, 365–66, 391–95, 398
    of Origen, 36, 37, 38–39
    in Reformation/Post-Reformation period, 244, 264–65, 266, 314–17
    seven gifts of the Holy Spirit, 208, 209–10
    theological perspective on Christian life of grace and, *xxxvii*
    in Western medieval church, 163–64, 209–10
Poemen (desert father), 65
poetry and hymnody. *See also* Ephrem the Syrian; Gregory of Nazianzus; John of the Cross
    Andrewes's *Point of Meditation Before Prayer*, 317–18
    of George Herbert, 319–21
    Anna Jansz, *Martyr's Song*, 282–85
    of John Damascene, 122
    in Methodism, 324
    Peter Abelard, *Pentecost Hymn*, 209–10
    of Teresa of Ávila, 296
    von Grumbach's *An Answer in Verse*, 247, 249–50
    Charles Wesley, *Father whose everlasting love* (1741), 324–25
Point of Meditation Before Prayer (Lancelot Andrewes, 1675), 315, 317–18

The Politics of Jesus (John Howard Yoder, 1994), 405, 412–13
Polycarp (saint), 23–26, 27
postmodernism. *See* modern/postmodern period
Post-Reformation. *See* Reformation/Post-Reformation
poverty, as theological issue, 34, 90–92, 166, 175, 381–85
The Power of the Poor in History (Gustavo Gutiérrez, 1975), 382–85
practice. *See* orthopraxis
prayer
    Cranmer's "Ave Maria" from *The Institution of a Christian Man*, 309–13
    grace, as means of, 325–26
    in late Patristic/Eastern medieval church, 118, 121, 135, 139
    Lord's Prayer, 309, 360, 362
    in modern/postmodern period, 360, 362, 420, 423, 442, 445
    in Patristics/early church, 24, 63, 64, 65, 66
    in Reformation/Post-Reformation period, 245, 295, 297, 313, 315, 317–18, 325–26
    systematic theology and, 423
    on Transfiguration, 420
    in Western medieval church, 152–53, 154, 177, 186
Prayer of a Soul Taken with Love (John of the Cross, c. after 1578), 304
"preferential option for the poor," 381
The Presence of the Kingdom (Jacques Ellul), 411–12
preventing grace, 324
Primitive Methodists, 323
Prodigal Son, 371
prophecy/visions
    of Francis of Assisi, 175–80
    of Hildegard of Bingen, 170, 171–72
    Irenaeus of Lyons on, 28
    John of the Cross on, 302–3
    of Julian of Norwich, 187–90
    of Adrienne von Speyr, 377–78
    of Teresa of Ávila, 296
Proslogion (Anselm of Canterbury, 1077-1078), 204–7
Protestantism, 231–33, 253, 291. *See also specific denominations*
proximity and pilgrimage. *See* pilgrimage and proximity, Christian life as
Pseudo-Dionysius the Areopagite, 110, 112–13
    The Celestial Hierarchy, 112, 158
    On the Divine Names, 112, 116
    Eastern medieval church fathers influenced by, 130, 140
    Ecclesiastical Hierarchy, 112
    John of the Cross influenced by, 300
    John Scotus Eriugena translating, 158, 162
    Letters, 112
    Mystical Theology (520s), 112–16, 182
    Symbolic Theology, 116
    Theological Outlines, 115–16
    Western medieval thought influenced by, 151, 158, 162, 180, 182, 191, 215
Pseudo-Macarius, 110, 130
purgatory, 225, 273
Puritans and Puritanism, 258–59, 262–63, 266, 443–44, 446, 450
Pusey, Edward Bouverie, 427
Pyrrhus of Constantinople, 117

Quodlibetal Questions (John Duns Scotus), 220

Radical Orthodox movement, 427, 429n1
Ramsey, Michael, 419–22
Rauschenbusch, Walter, 335
reconciliation. *See* repentance/reconciliation
redemption. *See* salvation/redemption
Rediscovering Holiness (J. I. Packer, 1992), 443–47
Reformation/Post-Reformation (16th-18th centuries), xxxvii, 231–33. *See also specific authors, selections, and topics*
    Anabaptist thought in, 271–90
    Lutheran thought in, 234–52
    Reformed church in, 253–70
    Roman Catholic thought in, 231–33, 239, 291–308
Reformed church. *See also specific members*
    in modern/postmodern period, 356–71
    in Reformation/Post-Reformation period, 253–70
regula fidei (rule of faith), 46, 47, 48
Reinhard of Blankenburg, 158
relational, God's love as, 6, 345–46, 386, 389–90, 457
repentance/reconciliation
    Christian life of grace and, xxix
    evangelical, 287n4
    in late Patristic/Eastern medieval church, 119–20
    in modern/postmodern period, 334–38, 341, 427–29
    mortification (death to sin), 76–80
    in Patristics/early church, 12–14, 36–38, 61, 65, 76–80
    in Reformation/Post-Reformation period, 273–75, 276–79, 286–90

in Western medieval church, 189–90
ressourcement movement, 372
resurrection
    Christian life of grace in burial and resurrection with Jesus, xxx–xxxi
    in medieval Western scholasticism, 220–23
    in Patristics/early church, 8, 42–44
    in Reformation/Post-Reformation period, 261
Revelations of Divine Love (Julian of Norwich, c. 1390s), 187, 188–90
Richard of St. Victor, 158, 191
Ritschl, Albrecht, 334–38
Robinson, Marilyn, 368–71
Roman Catholicism. *See also* Councils; Doctors of the Church; *specific Roman Catholics*
    in modern/postmodern period, 348, 372–90, 415n4
    pre-Reformation reforms in, 231
    in Reformation/Post-Reformation period, 231–33, 239, 291–308
Romans, letter of Ignatius of Antioch to (early 2nd century), 19–22
Romanus the Melodist, 110
Roscelin of Compiegne, 208
Ruether, Rosemary Radford, 453
Rufinus of Aquileia, 41n1
Rufus (in Polycarp's *Letter to the Philippians*), 25
Rule of St. Basil (*Small Asketikon;* Basil of Caesarea, c. 366-378), 70–74
Rule of St. Benedict (c. 529), 98–101, 151, 152, 202
Russian Orthodoxy
    Bulgakov, Sergei, 391–95, 396, 397
    Finnish Lutheran ecumenical dialogue with, 350–52
    Lossky, Vladimir, 396–400
Rusticus, Letter to (Jerome), 89
Rutledge, Fleming, xxxi
Ruysbroeck, John, 183
Ryan, John, 305

sacraments, Peter Lombard on, 211. *See also* baptism; Eucharist; marriage and spousal mysticism
saints, mediation of, 273, 313
Saiving, Valarie, 364
Sales, Francis de (saint), 231, 232, 305–8, 446
salvation/redemption. *See also* atonement; repentance/reconciliation; *theosis*
    Christology, relationship to, 93, 118, 120
    educator, Christ as, 31–34
    grace as accomplishment of, xxxiii–xxxiv
    in late Patristic/Eastern medieval church, 109, 110, 119–20, 122–24
    in Patristics/early church, 5–6, 17–18, 28–29, 31–34, 37, 93
    in Reformation/Post-Reformation period, 277–79, 303
    sonship of God and, 94–97
    surrogacy and, 458, 460–62
    theological perspective on Christian life of grace and, *xxxvii*
    in Delores S. Williams's womanist theology, 458, 460–62
same-sex marriage, 443
sanctification
    Holy Spirit, as work of, xxxvii
    in modern/postmodern period, 350, 356–59, 392, 406, 407, 409, 425, 440, 446
    in Patristics/early church, 37–39, 58
    in Reformation/Post-Reformation period, 233, 243, 260
Sarah (biblical matriarch), 458, 459–60
Sarah (desert mother), 64–65
Satan
    in late Patristics/Eastern medieval church, 122
    Patristics/early church on, 24, 65
    in Reformation/Post-Reformation period, 248, 259, 311, 312
    in Western medieval thought, 197
Sayings of Light and Love (John of the Cross, after 1578), 303–4
Schleiermacher, Friedrich, 334, 337, 356–59
Schmemann, Alexander, 396–97
scholasticism, 158, 201–3, 240, 243, 273
Scivias (Hildegard of Bingen, 1142-1151), 171, 173–74
Scripture
    canon, formation of, 11
    Christian life of grace. scriptural antecedents of, xxvii–xxix
    grace, as means of, 326
    Jerome's Vulgate (Latin translation of Bible), 89
    King James Version, 314
    lectio divina, 152, 154, 162, 166, 204
    in modern/postmodern period, 416–17, 439
    Origen's *Hexapla*, 35
    Polycarp on knowledge of, 25
    in Reformation/Post-Reformation period, 272, 273, 286, 310, 326
    Septuagint, 8n2, 113n2
    Western medieval church and, 152
Second Council of Lyons (1274), 179
Second Crusade, 166

Second Vatican Council (1963-1965), 372, 373, 385
Second World War, 419. *See also* Nazis and Nazism
Seehofer, Arsacius, 246–47, 248
Sens, Council of (1141), 166, 208
Sentences (Peter Lombard, 1150-1152), 211–14, 220
Septuagint, 8n2, 113n2
Seraphim of Sarov (saint), 398, 399
Sermon 16: The Means of Grace (John Wesley, 1746), 325–27
seven deadly sins/seven demons of wickedness, 208, 209
seven gifts of the Holy Spirit, 208
Severus (emperor), 35
Sexism and God-Talk (Rosemary Radford Ruether, 1983), 453
sex/sexuality. *See also* gender; marriage and spousal mysticism; women
    desire and holiness, 443–47
    Patristics/early church on, 64–66, 85, 86–88
    same-sex marriage, 443
shepherd, Jesus as, 32
Shepherd of Hermas (1st or 2nd century), 11–14
Sibbes, Richard, 258–61, 446
Sigewize, 170
Simons, Menno, 232, 276–80, 411, 415
sin. *See also* repentance/reconciliation
    derived from abortive efforts to fulfill true meaning of life, 365, 366
    han, Asian concept of, 467–70
    mortal sin, 146
    mortification (death to sin), 76–80
    nothingness of, 189
Sisters in the Wilderness (Delores S. Williams, 1993), 458–62
skoteinos, 113n2
social gospel movement, 335, 364
social/economic concerns. *See* economic/social concerns
soldiers of Christ, images of
    in Patristics/early church, 10, 21, 36–37, 61, 83–84, 90–91
    in Western medieval thought, 197
Soloviev, Vladimir, 391
Sonderegger, Katherine, xxi–xxii
sonship/children of God, 94–97, 163–64, 263–64, 378–80, 389, 440
Sophia, as divine personage, 391, 397
Sophronius of Jerusalem, 63, 117
Soskice, Janet, 386–90
soteriology. *See* salvation/redemption
soul and body, 15, 16–17, 63. *See also* eternal life; immortality of the soul; resurrection

Spanish Inquisition, 291
Speculum de scriptum sacra (Augustine), xxiii
Speyer, Diet of (1529), 231
Speyr, Adrienne von, 377–80
The Spiritual Alphabet (Juan de Valdes), 291–92
spiritual dryness. *See* dark night of the soul
spiritual fathers/confessors/guides, 109, 126, 130–31, 152, 296
Spiritual Meadow, 62–63
Spiritualists (Anabaptist), 286
spousal mysticism. *See* marriage and spousal mysticism
Stephen of Nicomedia, 130
Stephen protomartyr, 141
stigmata
    of Francis of Assisi, 176, 178, 181
    of Adrienne von Speyr, 378
Stjema, Kirsi, 246
Stoicism, 30–31
Stott, John R. W., 439–42
substance
    in late Patristic/Eastern medieval church, 115, 133, 135, 138, 140n3
    in modern/postmodern period, 353, 383, 399, 400, 401, 403
    in Patristics/early church, 37, 41, 42, 70, 95, 97
    in Reformation/Post-Reformation period, 262
    in Western medieval church, 169, 189, 216, 217, 218, 222
Summa of the Entire Christian Life (Balthasar Hubmaier, 1525), 273–75
Sung Park, Andrew, 467–70
supernatural and natural, relationship between, 372–76
Surnaturel (Henri de Lubac, 1946), 373
surrogacy and salvation/redemption, 458, 460–62
Suso, Henry, 183
Sutton, Oliver, 220
Symbolic Theology (Pseudo-Dionysius the Areopagite), 116
Symeon the Logothete, *Chronicle* (10th century), 127
Symeon the New Theologian (saint), 110, 130–33
Symeon the Pious, 133
Syncletica (desert mother), 65
synergeia (co-working) of believer with God, 110
systematic theology, xxxvi, 346–49, 406–9, 423, 448
Systematic Theology (Wolfhart Pannenberg, 1993), 346–49

Taboric Light, 138, 139
Tanner, Kathryn, xxxi, 430–33
Tauler, Johannes, 183
Taylor, Charles, 306
teleiosis (perfection), 110
Témoignage chrétien (Christian Testimony; anti-Nazi periodical), 372
The Temple (George Herbert), 319
Ten Commandments, 369–70
Teresa of Ávila (saint), 231, 295–96, 300, 446
Tertullian, 11
Theoderic of Echternach, 171–73
Theodore the Studite (saint), 109, 126
Theologia (Peter Abelard), 208
Theological Outlines (Pseudo-Dionysius the Areopagite), 115–16
théologie totale, 423
theology/theological context, xxxv–xxxvii, *xxxvii*
    affirmative or *kataphatic* theology, 115
    African American womanist theology, 458–62
    African theology, 463–66
    Anabaptist, 414–18
    Arndt's *True Christianity* as exposition of, 243, 244–45
    feminist theology, 386–90, 423, 453–57
    gendered nature of, 365, 454
    grammar, theology as, xxvn10
    liberation theology, 381–85, 455–56
    in modern/postmodern period, 332–33, 453–70
    negative or apophatic theology, 110, 115–16, 191–93, 202
    normed, theology as, xxviii
    of Patristics/early church, 5–6
    poverty, as theological issue, 34, 90–92, 166, 175, 381–85
    of Reformation/Post-Reformation period, 232–33
    systematic theology, xxxvi, 346–49, 406–9, 423, 448
Theophanes the Recluse, 126
Theophilos (emperor), 126
Theophilus of Alexandria, 93
theoria. *See* contemplation
theosis (divinization or deification)
    Anglican theology of, 314
    Christomorphic divinization, Anabaptist, 415–18
    in late Patristic/Eastern medieval church, 110, 141–42
    in modern/postmodern period, 350–55, 397, 415–18
    in Patristics/early church, 5, 46, 49–50, 51, 94
    Thomas Aquinas on, 216

Theotokos, Mary as, 93
Thomas (apostle), 40
Thomas Aquinas (saint), 201–2, 215–16
    Bonaventure and, 179
    Calvin compared, 253
    Commentary on John (1260-1272), 215–18
    Finger citing, 415n4
    Homily on the Eucharist (1264), 216, 218–19
    Hubmaier on, 273
    modern/postmodern authors citing, 372, 374–75, 427, 457n7
    Summa Contra Gentiles, 215, 374n1
    Summa Theologiae, 215, 415n4, 457n7
Thomas Beckett (saint), 204
Thomas à Kempis, 194–97, 445–46
Timothy (in New Testament), xxiv
To Adelphius, Bishop and Confessor: Against the Arians (Athanasius of Alexandria, 370-371), 49–50
To the Council of Ingolstadt (Argula von Grumbach, 1523), 246–49
Tome of Leo, 403
Torrance, Thomas F., xxxivn7
Toynbee, Arnold, 422
Trajan (emperor), 19
transcendence of God, 51, 53–56
Transfiguration of Christ, 134, 419–22
Transforming Grace (Anne Carr, 1988), 453–57
Treatise on the Birth of the Eternal Word (Meister Eckhart, 1310s), 184–85
Treatise on Detachment (Meister Eckhart, c. 1320s), 186
Treatise on Religious Affections (Jonathan Edwards), 446
Trent, Council of (1545-1563), 233, 295, 348
Triads (Gregory Palamas, late 1330s), 139–42
Trinity
    gender and, 386–90
    God the Father as *arche* of, 115n13, 140n3, 180n1
    grace and, xxxiv
    in late Patristic/Eastern medieval church, 113, 115
    in modern/postmodern period, 345–46, 377, 379–80, 386–90, 401–4
    in Patristics/early church, 28, 29, 36, 38–39, 70, 75–76, 94–95
    in Reformation/Post-Reformation period, 263–65, 266–67, 268–69, 312
    relationality of God's love in, 6, 345–46, 386, 389–90
    sonship of Christ, 94–95
    in Western medieval church, 153, 163–64, 173–74, 179, 182

Trinity and "the Feminine Other" (Janet Soskice, 1994), 386–90
The True Christian Faith (Menno Simons, 1556), 279–80
True Christianity (John Arndt, 1610), 243, 244–45

union/communion with God. *See also* mysticism
   as divine indwelling, 352
   in modern/postmodern period, 352–55, 401–4, 443–47
   in Reformation/Post-Reformation period, 237, 245, 263–65, 298
   in Western medieval church, 179, 180–82
Urban VI (pope), 224

Valdes, Juan de, 231, 233, 291–94
Valdesian Circle, 291
Valentinus and Valentinians, 27, 48
Vatican II (1963-1965), 372, 373, 385
Venerable Bede, 151, 152, 154–57, 194
Victorine monasticism and spirituality, 153, 158, 202
The Victory of Love (Adrienne von Speyr, 1953), 377–80
Vikings, conversion of, 143
Virgin Mary. *See* Mary
visions. *See* prophecy/visions
vocation, Christian, 233
von Balthasar, Hans Urs, xxxiv–xxxv, 377
von Emden, Maynaart, 281
von Grumbach, Argula, 246–52. *See* Grumbach, Argula von
von Harnack, Adolph, 334
von Speyr, Adrienne, 377–80
Voolstra, Sjouke, 277
voyage, Christian life envisioned as, xxi–xxii, 67–68, 69, 179–82, 406–9

Walton, Izaak, 258
Webster, John, xxxiv
Wesley, Charles, 324–25, 427
Wesley, John, xxiii, xxxix, 243, 323–27, 409, 427, 443–44, 446
Wesleyan Methodists, 323, 407
Western church. *See also* modern/postmodern period; Reformation/Post-Reformation; *specific authors, selections, and topics*
   medieval mystical and monastic works, 151–53
   schism with Eastern Christianity, 202
   scholasticism, 158, 201–3, 240, 243, 273
Wilhelm II (kaiser of Germany), 360
William II (king of England), 204
William of Occam, 273
William of St. Thierry, 162–65
Williams, Delores S., 458–62
Williams, Rowan, 396
womanist theology, 458–62
women. *See also* feminist theology; gender; *specific women*
   absence from theology of early Christianity, 3n1
   in late Patristic/Eastern medieval church, 109
   misogynistic responses to, 246–47
   von Grumbach's defense of spirituality of, 251
   Yoder's sexual abuse of, 410
world, Christian relationship to. *See also* economic/social concerns
   culture and Christianity, relationship between, 434–38
   in late Patristic/Eastern medieval church, 120
   in liberation theology, 381–85
   in modern/postmodern period, 368, 369, 381–85, 411–12, 430, 434–38, 441–42, 449, 451, 452
   monasticism, introduction of, 4, 62
   in Patristics/early church, 3–4, 15, 16–17, 22, 73–74
   persecution and martyrdom shaping, 3
   in Reformation/Post-Reformation period, 305–8
   sacralized emperor, in late Patristic/Eastern medieval church, 109
   in Western medieval thought, 195–96
World War I, 360, 372
World War II, 419. *See also* Nazis and Nazism
worship. *See* liturgy and worship
The Wounded Heart of God (Andrew Sung Park, 1993), 467–70

Yoder, John Howard, 405, 406, 410–13

Zebedee, sons of (in New Testament), xxi
Zelanti faction, 179
Zizioulas, John, 401–4
Zosimus, 25
Zwingli, Ulrich, 271, 272, 310

Scripture Index

Old Testament

Genesis

1:1	5
1:2	58
1:25	205
1:26	169n1, 172
1:27	164, 181, 189, 226
3:8	129
3:24	57
6:3	136
6:16	165
16:13	458
28:12	181
32:28	182
39:15	53

Exodus

2:22	168
3:2	226
12:8	288
12:11	181
12:13	146
12:23	58
16:35	57
17:6	57
19 and 20	114n8
19:14	53
20:21	114
24:17	182
25:20	181
25:30	165
25:40	135
32:1ff	53
32:19	53
32:20	182
33:11	132
33:14	xxvii
33:18	xxvii
33:20	xxvii, 28
34:9	141

Leviticus

19:2	255
19:18	369
26:12	96

Numbers

13:32	307
14:14	53
18:24	90
28:27 Sept	9

Deuteronomy

5:24	29
8:3	302
10:14	163
32:8, 9 Sept	9
32:15	257
32:22	119

Joshua

5:2-12	57, 58

Judges

13:17-18	140
15:15-19	57

1 Samuel

3:18	326

2 Samuel

2:29	160

1 Kings

1:39	61
1:46	181
17:6	54
19:3	196

2 Kings

13:21	55

1 Chronicles

29:15	196

2 Chronicles

31:14 Sept	9

Job

7:15	182
11:2, 3 Sept	9
38:16	226
40:5	64

Psalms

2:7, 8 Sept	10
3:6	248n4
4:2, 3	79
7:11	79
8:1	218
101:2	227
11:4	163
12:4	74
14[15]:1	100
14[15]:2-3	100
14[15]:4	100
14:1-3 Sept	8
15:1-2	255
16:8	303
16:15	206
18:9	123, 129
18:11	114
19:13	168
20:6-7	256
24:3-4	255
27:1	197
27:3	197
27:13	165
33[34]:12	100
33[34]:13	100
33[34]:14-15	100
34:5	181
35:3	196
35:9	157, 206
36:1	119
36:6	226
36:8	206
36:9	5–6, 120, 128, 181, 225, 226
36:39	206
38:4	119
40:21	197
42:1	65, 226
42:7	226
45:6	217
45:6, 7	60
45:13	195
49:2	168
50:13	218
50:14-15	120
51:12 Sept	146
51:14	168
68	287n5
68:3	168
68:5-6	382
68:11 Sept	136
70:5	213
73:25-26	447
75:2	180
77:17	129
77:19	167
78:25	227
82:6	95
83:18	185
85:1	164
85:8	196
85:12	164
89:1	327
89:9	217
94[95]:8	99
94:8	99
95:6-7	119
98:2	164
103:1	168
103:12	79
104:15	146
105:15	60

106:1	167	2:2	61
107:16	xxxi	5:7	61
108:22	168	6:	51
109:7	287n5	6:1	216
110:1 Sept	10	6:2	179
110:3	95	9:6, 7	260
112:15	79	11:1-2 Sept and Vulgate	208
113:9[115:1]	100	25:6	61
119:6-7	180	30:9b-10a	249
119:16	144	30:17	248n4
122:6	180	30:18b	247
123:7	303–4	31:9	182
132:1	74	35:10	131, 255
132:1-2	74	40:4	168
132:4-5	245	40:26	216
136[137]:9	100	40:31	407, 409
138:21	105	43:5	248n4
139:7-10 Sept	8	51:12	248n4
139:15 Sept	10	53:4	146
145:16	79	53:4-5	466
145:18	120	54:13	136
146:7-9	382	55:1	259
150:2	168	58:6-10	120
		58:9	100
		61:1	60
		63:7	159
		64:4	79
		66:1	131

Proverbs

3:5	196
3:34 Sept	9
7:22	47
22:24	73
27:2 Sept	10

Jeremiah

1:5	48
1:10	167
2:19, 21	119
9:1	129
10:22	249n5
13:16	119
20:11	197
23:36b, 40	249n5
46:22	196

Ecclesiastes

1:2	195
1:8	195
4:10	73
7:25	168

Song of Solomon 158, 300

2:5	72
4:6b-8	159
4:9	167
4:16	298
5:6	168
7:10	169

Ezekiel

22:15	128
33:11	100
37:27	97

Daniel

9:23	181
10:5	131
13:52 Sept	128

Isaiah

1:2	96
1:4	61, 94
1:16	78

Hosea

2:14-20	158
2:19, 20	237
4:1	382
11:9	xxxiv
12:10	29

Joel

1:30	250
2	250
2:12	119
2:13	79
2:28	248
2:28-31	250

Amos

9:6	129

Micah

7:19	226

Habakkuk

2:3	304

Malachi

1:6	264
3:1	128
4:2	55

Deuterocanonical Books

Baruch

3:11	168

Sirach (Ecclesiasticus)

3:27	167
24:23	55
24:31	128
40:11	129

Tobit

4:10	25
12:9	25

Wisdom

2:24	122
5:16	206
7:22	213
8:1	213
9:17	206
11:22	8
12:12	8

New Testament

Matthew 383

3:14	128
3:17	255, 392
4:10	197
5:7	120
5:8	28, 133
5:9	347
5:11	249, 281
5:44-45	346
6:4	63, 304
6:13	24
6:14	120
6:38	54
7 and 13	249
7:2	120
7:3-5	92
7:7-8	326
7:23	244
7:24-25	100
7:30	398
9:9	xxxiii
10	249, 250, 252
10:28	250
10:32	248
10:32-33	248
10:34-37	185
10:37	248
10:38	xxix
11:15	61
11:28	259
11:30	168
12:20	258
13:24-30	132
13:25	290
13:37	298
13:43	205
16:6	249
16:24	73, 255
16:24, 25	451
17	134

17:5	255, 303	10:15	347
17:8	303	10:18	205
17:23	159	12:28-31	71
18	408	12:30-31	293
18:7	189	12:42	304
18:15-20	408	13	281
18:15ff	275	14:3-9	127
19:17	72, 205	14:8	129
19:26	119	14:38	24
22:1-10	384	15:13	53
22:22	287n5		
22:30	205	## Luke	
22:36-39	71		
22:37	206	1:17	128
22:39	72	1:36	128
22:40	71	1:49	131
23:4	249n5	1:79	128, 180
24	281	2:19, 51	187
24:9	279	4:8	195
24:35	8	5:15, 16	451
24:43	290	6:35	347
25	252	6:36	346
25:11	163	6:37	120
25:18-25	74	6:45	144
25:21	206, 207	7:36-50	127
25:29	136	7:37	129
25:31-33	213	7:38	129, 132
25:31-45	384	9:	134
25:35	72	9:23	xxix
25:35-36	73	10:42	186, 205
25:40	72	11:4	346
26:26	145	11:24-26	289
26:38	168	11:26	287
26:41	24	12:49	182, 227
27:33-34	124	12:49-50	182
27:45	53	14	252
28:18	265	14:8	79
28:18-20	xxxiii	14:16-24	384
28:19	6, 264	14:16ff	287n5
28:19-20	xxix	15:17	161, 259
		15:20	132
## Mark	383	15:25	132
		17:21	195
1:15	xxix, 273	18:17	347
2:19	158	18:19	205
3:27	132	18:27	28
3:29	160	19:12	xxvii
4:39	197	21	281
7:21	132	21:12, 17	281
8:3	226	22:17-22	97
8:34	xxvii	22:19	218
9:	134	23:34	249
9:35	74	23:39f	289
10	252	23:43	182

501

Luke (continued)

23:55-24:1	129
24:29	132

John

1:1	123, 172, 217
1:4	196
1:9	131, 226
1:11	217
1:12	79, 94, 120, 236
1:12-13	349
1:13	95, 145
1:14	xxvii, xxviii, 123, 165
1:16	265
1:18	xxviii, 123, 218
1:27	131
1:38	163
1:51	238
2:4	126
2:6	52
2:11ff	52
2:20-28	60
2:51	181
3:3, 5	416
3:3, 7	403
3:3-8	4, 417
3:6	136, 392
3:8	167
3:16	xxxiv, 23, 264
3:16-17	xxxi
3:21	383
3:31	77
3:34	214
4:	235
4:13-14	417
4:14	131
5:21	265
5:25-27	265
5:26	xxxiv, 97
5:39	326
6:32	146
6:35, 50-58	417
6:45	136
6:54	132
6:55	218
6:63	146
7:	250
7:37-38	417
7:37-39	250
8:12	195, 226
8:24	264
9:22	248
9:36	264
10:7	181
10:9	163
11:25	131, 147
12:1-8	127
12:35	100
12:41	216
12:50	146
13:1	182, 219
13:5	74
13:15	466
13:35	72
14:1	264
14:3	xxxii
14:6	181
14:10	163
14:10-11	417
14:14	218
14:15	72
14:16	165
14:16-17	417
14:17	131
14:20	163
14:20-23	417
14:23	97, 196
14:26	164, 265
14:27	105, 180
14:30	197
15	417
15:4	196
15:4, 10-11	xxix
15:12	72
15:12-13	417
15:15	457
15:26	265, 417
16:7	265
16:13-16	417
16:22	219
16:24	206, 207
16:33	196
17:11, 14	451
17:21-23	269
17:22	140
17:22-23	417
17:23	163
17:24	140
19:7	248
19:25-27	126
19:28-29	124
19:30	303
19:34	57, 164
20:16	159
20:27	164
20:28	40, 180

Acts

1:15-26	407
2:44	74
3:6	89
3:15	120
4:32	144
6:17	141
8:2	213
10:38	60
13:22	144
14:22	255
15	407
17:18	222
17:25	131
17:28	167
17:31	223
20:35	92
26:23	223

Romans

1:	370
1:25	207
2:4	100
2:21	322
3 and 4	240
3:5	131
3:8	82
3:28	242
4:5	242
5:1	349
5:3-4	257
5:5	213, 266
5-6	416
5:14	48, 126
5:18	242
5:19	242
6:	xxx, 36
6:3-13	417n9
6:12-14	36
6:19	37
6:22	393n2
7:18	167
8:	377
8:1	xxviii, 234
8:1, 5, 9	392
8:3	50
8:5, 12	119
8:6	146
8:8	236
8:9	133, 195
8:10-11, 16-17	417n9
8:11	265
8:12-22	417
8:13	159
8:14	244, 346
8:15	96
8:15-17	xxix, 393n2
8:17	349
8:23	xxxi
8:23, 26	393n2
8:26-27	416
8:28-30	4
8:29	255
8:32	164
8:39	392
9:5	132
11:10	77
11:16	61
11:17	55
11:22	288
11:24	94
11:33	167
11:34	326
12:5	73
12:6	74
12:15	74
12:17	120
13:11	99
13:13-14	85
14:7, 8	237
14:17	195, 392, 393n2
15:16	392
16:25	383

1 Corinthians

1:9	392
1:30	417n8
2:	251
2:9	79, 139, 205, 206
2:9-11	416
2:9-13	251
2:10	182
2:11	394
3:	251
3:3	105
3:7	xxxiii
3:16	55, 96, 392
3:16-17	416–17
4:19	236
6:10	393n2
6:11	392
6:17	131, 169
6:18, 19	417
6:19	139
7:25-31	451

1 Corinthians (continued)

7:29	92
9:13	90
9:24	186
10:2	96
10:11	92
11:1	xxxi
11:24	218
11:26	219
12:4-7	29
12:6	38, 135
12:8	74
12:11	213
12:12	10
12:13	417
12:26	395
13	267
13:1-3	213, 267
13:4	73, 104
13:7	63
13:8, 10	147
15:10	100
15:19	223
15:20	223
15:22, 45	126
15:28	245
15:33	91
15:44	206
15:47	77
15:49	95

2 Corinthians

2:15	61
3:3	136, 393n2
3:17-18	417
3:18	61, 226, 261
4:6	xxxiv, 141
4:8-11	248n4
4:10	37
4:10-11	417n9
4:18	21
5:4	221
5:17	xxx, 417n8
6:6	266
6:16	96, 139
6:17	73
10:17	100
11:1	167
12:1	167
12:2	180
12:4	141
13:5	136

Galatians

1:1	25
1:8	303
2:17	392
2:19	180
2:20	238, 392, 417
3:19	96
3:24-26	349
3:26	392
3:26-27	349
3:27	60
4:5	xxix
4:6	416
4:6-7	393n2
4:7	349
4:19	417
5:1	384
5:16	195
5:16, 22, 23	441
5:16-17	392
5:17	36, 37, 119
5:17-23	393n2
5:22	105
6:3	79
6:17	176

Ephesians

1:5	xxix, 60
1:7-12, 17-23	417
1:13	168, 392, 393n2
1:18	180
1:19-20	261
2:1-10	xxxiv
2:3	163
2:5-6, 21-22	417n8
2:6	261
2:8	244
2:14	343
2:18, 22	417
2:19	xxix
2:19-22	15
3:8	164
3:9	131, 181
3:14-21	417
4:3	248
4:3-4	105
4:4-16	247
4:6	xxvii, 133
4:10	131, 163, 288
4:15	247
4:22	128
4:23	168, 244, 268

4:24	349
4:26	25
4:30	392
4:31	104
5:	23
5:1	xxxi, 169
5:26	392
5:33	158
6:10-20	445
6:12	120
6:14, 11	61
6:24	264

Philippians

1:4	xxxi
1:23	78
2:	23
2:1	266
2:1-11	xxxi
2:5	120, 346
2:6	123
2:6, 7	50
2:7	129, 145
2:8	124
2:8-11	265
2:10, 11	49
2:12, 13	336
2:12-13	5
2:13	444
3:1	392
3:7-10	447
3:8	19
3:8-11	417n9
3:9	132
3:10	255
3:20	15, 120
3:21	60
4:3	7
4:7	180
4:13	59, 61

Colossians

1:8	266, 392
1:9	265
1:24	19
1:27	417
2:6-7, 20	417n9
2:9	128
2:9-13	417n8
2:9-15	xxx
2:11	392
2:15	xxxi
2:19	165
3:3	xxvii, xxx
3:5	37
3:9-10	349
3:15	189

1 Thessalonians

2:12	100
3:2	110
4:9, 10	344
5:17	63, 118
5:18	159

2 Thessalonians

2:14	392

1 Timothy

1:18	8
2:5	181
3:2	92
3:16	113
6:8	90
6:12	362
6:16	141, 218
6:20	23

2 Timothy

1:12	132
2:3-4	8
2:11-12	417n8
3:6	168

Titus

1:2	8
3:4	164
3:6	132
3:7	349

Hebrews

1:1-2	303
1:3, 4	9
1:5	10
2:10	76
2:11	392
2:14	xxxi, 28
3:6	139
3:14	60
4:12	167

Hebrews (continued)

5:8	255
6:6	289
6:18	8
7:28	82
8:10	97
8-10	466
9:	110
9:10	96
10:1	96
10:26	289
10:29	392
11:1	135
12:2	76
12:14	105
12:29	65, 128, 182, 226
13:8	217
13:12	392
13:14	196
13:21	336

James 383

1:17	180
1:18	265, 416
2:	12
2:17, 26	119
4:6	9

1 Peter

1:1-3	15
1:1-4	xxxii
1:2	392
1:3, 23	402
1:3-4	349, 416
1:12	25
1:15	450
1:16	255
1:18ff	241
1:23	159, 416
1:25	248
2:2	440
2:9	94
2:9-17	15
2:22	24
2:24	24
4:1	48
4:6	392
4:7	24
4:11	327
4:13-14	417
5:4	131
5:5	9
5:7	196
5:8	132

2 Peter

1	353
1:3-5	5
1:4	xxx, 46, 49, 50, 94, 96, 132, 218, 266, 351n4, 416

1 John 24

1:1-4	xxvii
2	59
2:1-2	120
2:5	336
2:6	417
2:15	264
2:20	61
2:25	417
2:27	417
2:29	417
3:1	164
3:2	164
3:6	417
3:9	164, 417
3:16-17	417
3:24	417
4:3	24
4:7	212
4:7, 12	417
4:8	6, 212
4:8, 16	213
4:9-11	417
4:12	336
4:13	97, 213
4:14	417
4:15	417
4:16	133, 147, 212
5:1, 18	417
5:1-3	417
5:7	263
5:9	263
5:9-12	417
5:10	263
5:13	264
5:16	146
5:20	131
5:30	417

2 John

9	417

Jude

24	132

Revelation

1:18	xxxi
2:7	100
2:17	181, 182, 195
3:20	145, 184
4:1	163
13:10	412
18:2	119
22:1	131
22:14	181

Apocrypha (New Testament)

Gospel of Bartholomew

	114n7

Early Christian Writings

Abelard, Peter (Pierre le Pallet)

Commentary on the Epistle to the Romans

	208

Pentecost Hymn

	209–10

Theologia

	208

Anselm of Canterbury

Cur Deus Homo

	204

Proslogion

	204, 205–7

Athanasius

	5

To Adelphius, Bishop and Confessor: against the Arians

	49–50

Four Discourses Against the Arians

I.11	46–47
II.21	47–48
III.26.33	46, 48–49

On the Incarnation

	51
54:3	41
54.3	46n6
Chapter 5	42–45

Augustine of Hippo

On the Agreement of the Evangelists

	216

Confessions

	85, 162, 296
Bk 8, ch. 12	85
Bk 10	86–88
Bk 10, ch. 22	86
Bk I	223

de moribus Ecclesiae catholicae

I.II.18	214

De spiritu et litera

	232, 232n3

De Trinitate

Bk 15, c17, n31	212
Bk 15, cc 17-18, nn 31-32	213
Bk XIII, c. ix	223
Bk xiii, ch. 10	221
xiii, ch. 8	221

Enchiridion, ch. 14.53: "Mysteries of Christ's Mediatorial Work and Justification"

	86n3

Sermo

120, 2, PL 38, 677	152

Tractates on John, Sermon 22.8-10 (John 5:26)

	86n3

On the Trinity

Bk 8	212
Bk 15	212

Averroes

de Anima

Bk iii	222

Basil of Caesarea

Asketikon — 70

"Rule of Basil" — 70

Rule of Benedict — 70

The Rule of St. Basil
(Questions 2 and 3) — 71
    Question 2 — 71–73
    Question 3 — 73–74

small *Asketikon* — 71

Basil the Great

On the Holy Spirit — 314

Letter 2.4 — 142, 142n6

Benedict of Nursia

Rule — 98, 99–101

Bernard of Clairvaux

de Consideratione — 166

Homilies on the Song of Songs — 166, 167–69

Rule of the Knights Templar — 166

Bonaventure (Giovanni Fidanza)

Itinerarium mentis in Deum ("The Journey of the Mind into God") — 179
Prologue and final chapter — 180–82

The Journey of the Mind Into God
chapter 7 — 181–82
Prologue — 180–81

Life of Francis — 179

Catherine of Siena (Caterina di Benincasa)

The Dialogue (Dialogue of Divine Providence)
chapter 167 — 225–27

Chrysostom, John

Homily on Hebrews 7 — 81, 82–84

Clement of Alexandria

Christ the Educator — 30
Book 1, Chapter 1 — 31–32
Book 1, Chapter 7 — 32–33
Book 1, Chapter 12 — 33–34

Clement of Rome

First Letter of Clement — 7
chapters 27-30 — 8–9
chapters 36-38 — 9–10

The Cloud of Unknowing — 191, 192–93

Council of Trent

Tridentine decree — 348

Cyril of Alexandria

Commentary on the Gospel of John — 94–97

Commentary on the Gospel of Luke — 97

Cyril of Jerusalem

Catechetical Lectures — 59, 60–61
Lecture 19 — 59
Lecture 21. On the Mysteries. III: On Chrism — 60–61

Desert Fathers and Mothers

Sayings and Lives
The Alphabetical Collection — 63–66
History of the Monks of Egypt — 63
Life of Paul the First Hermit — 63

Spiritual Meadow 62
Easter *Exsultet* 6

Eckhart, Johannes "Meister" (Eckhart von Hochheim)

Homily on the Birth of Jesus
185–86

Treatise on Detachment
186

Treatise on the Birth of the Eternal Word
184–85

Ephrem

Armenian Hymns
49   56–58

Hymns on Faith
14   52–53
17   51

Nisibene Humns
50   53–56

Epiphanius

Panarion   121

Eusebius

Ecclesiastical History
5.20.5-6   27n1

Formula of Concord
SD 3:11ff   348

Francis of Assisi

Fioretti   176–78

Gregory

Moralia in Job
xiv. cap.xl, PL 32 col. 1077   223

Gregory of Nazianzus

Another Prayer for a Safe Journey
69

Against Apollinarius   67

Oration, 21,6   41, 41n2

Oration 35   5

On Providence   69

On the Soul   67–68

On the Two Covenants and the Appearing of Christ
68–69

Gregory of Nyssa

"De Instituto Christiano," P.G. XLVI, 289 C
398, 398n3

The Great Catechism   75
Chapter 35 (Baptism)   76–78
Chapter 40 (Mortification of Vice)   78–80

Life of Moses   114n8, 191

Gregory of Sinai

On Commandments and Doctrines
135

On the Signs of Grace and Delusion
136–37

Gregory Palamas

Triads   139–42

Gregory the Great

The Book of Pastoral Rule   102
Part II, section symbol 9   103
Part III, section symbol 9   103–4
Part III, section symbol 22   104–5

Guigo the Carthusian

Ladder of Monks   152–53

Hildegard of Bingen

Life of Hildegard
171–73

Scivias
("Know the ways of the Lord")
11n1, 171, 173–74

Hillary of Poitiers

On the Trinity
2.6   xxxvi–xxxvii, xxxviin17

Hugh of St. Victor

Commentary on the Celestial Hierarchy
158

In Praise of the Bridegroom
158, 159–61

Ignatius of Antioch

Eph 14   19

The Epistle to the Romans
20–22
IV   20

Letter to the Smyrnaeans
6   19

Irenaeus

Against Heresies   28
3, 3, 3   7, 7n1
3.3.4   27
Book 4, Chapter 20, sections 5-6   28–29

Isaac the Syrian

Homily 72   139n2
Theotoki ed., XVII, pp. 87-88; Wensicki,
XL, p. 202 and 1, p. 20   400, 400n11

Jerome

Letter 52: To Nepotian
90–92

Letter to Eustochium
90

"Letter to Paulinus"
89

Letter to Rusticus
89

John Damascene

de fide orthodoxa, iv, ch. 26
222

John of Damascus

Fountain of Wisdom, "An Exposition of the Orthodox Faith," book 3
121, 122–24

"Golden Canon" hymn, third ode
122

Against Those who Decry Images
121

Against those who decry images
124–25

Julian of Norwich

Revelations of Divine Love
187, 188–90

Kabasilas, Nicholas

Commentary on the Divine Liturgy
143

On the Life in Christ
143, 144–47

Kassia the Melodist

Chronicle of Symeon the Logothete
127

Hymn for the Theophany
128

O Lord, she who in many sins
127, 129

Pope Leo I

Tome	403
Letter to Diognetus	15
section V	16
section VI	16–17
section VII	15, 17
section VIII	18

Lombard, Peter

Four Books of Sentences	211, 215
Bk I, Distinction 17: On Charity	212–14
books 1 and 2	220

Macarius of Egypt

Homily, 15:20	5
"Spiritual Homilies, VIII, 2," P.G., 528 D, 529A	399, 399n6
"Spiritual Homilies, XV, 32"	
P.G., XLIII, 7, 776 D.	399n7
P.G., XXXIV, 597 B.	399, 399n7
"Spiritual Homilies, XXXVII, 10," P. G., XXXIV, 757 A.	399, 399n4

Maximus the Confessor

	415n3
Ambigua	141n5
The Ascetic Life	120n1
"Capita theological et oeconomica, Centuria IV, cap. 88," P.G., XC, 1341-44	400, 400n10
Letter to the Presbyter George	110–11

Muratorian Fragment 11

Origen

Commentary on Romans, Book 6	36–38
Contra Celsum	35
On First Principles	36
I.3.8	38–39
Hexapla	35
Homily 16	35

Patrologia Graeca

xci 1000-1300	141n5

the Philokalia 134

Polycarp

The Encyclical Epistle of the Church at Smyrna Concerning the Martyrdom of the Holy Polycarp, chapter XIV	26
Letter to the Philippians	23
chapter 7	24
chapter 8	24
chapter 9	25
chapter 10	25
chapter 12	25–26
Martyrdom of Polycarp	
ch. 11	23
ch. 13	23

Pseudo-Dionysius the Areopagite

The Ascetic Life (Liber Asceticus)	118–20
The Celestial Hierarchy	112
Corpus Areopagiticum	112
De Mystica Theologia, I.1	182
The Divine Names	112
On the Divine Names	116
Ecclesiastical Hierarchy	112
Letters (10)	112
Mystical Theology	112
I–IV	113–16, 116n16

Symbolic Theology 116

Theological Outlines
115, 115n11, 116

Rufinus of Aquileia

Church History, 10.15
41n1

Rule of Benedict

19:7	202
48:1	152

Scotus, John Duns

Ordinatio 220
IV.43.q.2: On the Immortality of the Soul and the Resurrection 221–23

Quodibetal Questions 220

Shepherd of Hermas 11

Book III.6.I	12
Book III.7	12–13
Book III.9.31-33	13–14
Book III.10.4	14

Symeon the New Theologian

Hymn 17	132–33
Hymn 21	133
Hymn 25	133
Invocation of the Holy Spirit	131–32

Theodoric of Echternach

Life of Hildegard 171–73

Theophanes

Letters on the Spiritual Life, pub. Mount Athas, pp. 19, 65, 67, 83 (in Russian)
399, 399n5

Thomas à Kempis

The Imitation of Christ
194, 195–97

8   194n1

Thomas Aquinas

Commentary on John
216–18

Commentary on the Gospel of John
215

Homily on the Eucharist
216, 218–19

Summa contra Gentiles
215
III.52   374, 374n1

Summa Theologiae   215
II-II, q. 23, art. 1	457n7
pt. 3, sup Q. 96	415n4
pt. I, Q. 8.a.3	415n4

Venerable Bede

Ecclesiastical History of the English People
book 2, chapters 12 and 13	155–57
book 5, chapter 24	154–55

William of St. Thierry

Eposition of the Epistle to the Romans
162

Golden Epistle   162, 191

Meditative Orations
162, 163–65

Reformation Period Writings

Andrewes, Lancelot

The Holy Spirit   315–17

Points of Meditation Before Prayer
315, 317–18

Private Prayers   315

Arndt, Johann
 True Christianity   243, 244–45

Augsburg Confession   239
 Article 4   240–41

Calvin, John
 Commentary on the Psalms   253
 The Golden Booklet of the True Christian Life   253, 254–57
 Institutes, 1.14.20; 1.58; 2.6.1   368n5
 The Institutes of the Christian Religion   253
 Instructions in Faith, p. 19   449, 449n3

Cranmer, Thomas
 Articles of Religion   309
 "The Ave Maria" from *The Institution of a Christian Man*   310–13
 Book of Common Prayer   309
 Collect for the First Sunday in Lent   310
 The Institution of a Christian Man   309–13

Edwards, Jonathan
 Apostrophe to Sarah Pierpoint   267, 270
 Charity and Its Fruits: Sermon One —Love the Sum of All Virtue   267–69
 Discourse on the Trinity, Works of Jonathan Edwards, Vol 21, 124   266n1
 Treatise on Grace, Works of Jonathan Edwards, Vol 21, 185   266n2
 Treatise on Religious Affections   446

Formula of Concord (FC)   240, 352, 353
 III. The Righteousness of Faith   241–42

Francis de Sales
 Introduction to the Devout Life   305–8

Herbert, George
 The Country Parson   319, 320
 Grace   320–21
 The Parson's Library from *The Country Parson*   321–22
 The Temple   319

Hubmaier, Balthasar
 Eighteen Theses Concerning the Christian Life   271, 272–73
 Summa of the Entire Christian Life   272, 273–75

Jansz, Anna
 Martyr's Song (Ausbund, the 18th Hymn)   282–85

John of the Cross
 The Ascent of Mount Carmel   302–3
 En una noche oscura (Dark Night of the Soul)   300, 301–2

SCRIPTURE INDEX

"Night of the Spirit"   300

Prayer of a Soul Taken with Love   304

Sayings of Light and Love   303–4

Luther, Martin

Augsburg Confession   239

Article 4   232

Church Postil   353

Crucigers Sommerpostille, WA 21:458, 11-12   354n7

The Freedom of a Christian   235–38

Lectures on Galatians   350, 353

Luther's Works 26:100   353n6

Luther's Works 26:282   353n5

Luther's Works 44:128   233n4

Predict, WA 17/1:438, 14-28   354n8

Marpeck, Pilgram

Five Fruits of Repentance   286, 287–90

Writings of Pilgrim Marpeck
p. 315   286n3
p. 531   415n2

Melanchthon, Philip

Augsburg Confession   239

Owen, John

Communion with God   263–65

Philips, Dirk

Writings of Dirk Philips
p. 145   415n2

Sibbes, Richard

The Bruised Reed and the Smoking Flax   258–61

Simons, Menno

The New Birth   276, 277–79

The True Christian Faith   277, 279–80

Teresa of Avila

The Book of her Life   296–99

The Interior Castle   295–96

Valdes, Juan de

The Christian Alphabet   233, 292–94

Dialogue on Christian Doctrine   291

The Spiritual Alphabet   291–92

von Grumbach, Argula

An Answer in Verse   249–52

To the Council of Ingolstadt   247–49

Wesley, Charles

Father, whose everlasting love (hymn)
      324–25

Wesley, John

A Christian Library
vol. 2, part 1, para. 5   xxxix, xxxixn20
Sermon 16: The Means of Grace
      325–27

Greek-Roman Literature

Aristotle

Nicomachaean Ethics
Bk I [ch. 7]   221
Bk X [ch. 7-8]   221

www.ingramcontent.com/pod-product-compliance
Lightning Source LLC
Chambersburg PA
CBHW060415300426
44111CB00018B/2862